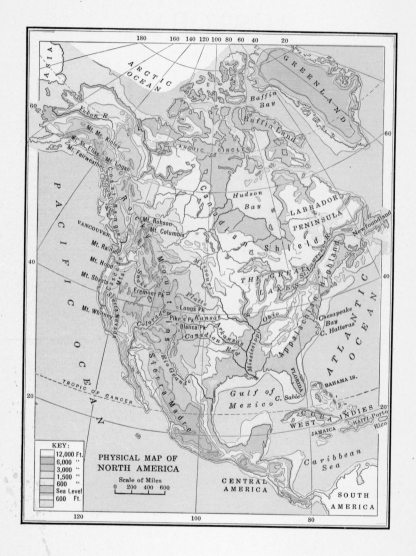

PHYSICAL MAP OF
NORTH AMERICA

SOCIAL AND ECONOMIC
HISTORY
OF THE
UNITED STATES

I

From Handicraft to Factory

1500–1820

By HARRY J. CARMAN, Ph.D.

ASSOCIATE PROFESSOR OF HISTORY
COLUMBIA UNIVERSITY

D. C. HEATH AND COMPANY

BOSTON   NEW YORK   CHICAGO   ATLANTA

DALLAS   SAN FRANCISCO   LONDON

PRINTED IN THE UNITED STATES OF AMERICA

TO
FOUR GENERATIONS OF STUDENTS
IN
COLUMBIA COLLEGE

PREFACE

A LITTLE over a generation ago the English historian E. A. Freeman boldly asserted that history was "past politics." That this conception of history was generally accepted during the nineteenth century, and that it even yet finds considerable vogue both in Europe and America must be evident to any one who examines the writings of many eminent historians on both sides of the Atlantic. Up to the last decade the vast majority of our history texts, both school and college, were little more than superficial compilations of political and episodical happenings. Indeed, it was against the writing and teaching of just this sort of history that the distinguished philosopher-historian James Harvey Robinson raised his voice nearly a quarter of a century ago. In his thought-provoking volume *The New History* he decried the fact that the content of so much of our historical writing was composed almost entirely of surface events and of the irrelevant and the melodramatic — of laws, of accounts of presidential administrations, dynasties, military exploits, romantic marriages, court scandals, diplomatic intrigues, assassinations, and reigns of terror — and that little or no space was given to the social, economic, spiritual, scientific, and intellectual aspects of human development. The time had come, he declared, for a broader understanding and a larger synthesis.

In America Professor Robinson was not alone in his crusade for a more comprehensive and a more synthetic treatment of the subject. In the field of American history J. B. McMaster, F. J. Turner, E. B. Greene, J. F. Jameson, C. M. Andrews, C. A. Beard, and others were already stressing the importance of getting away from the narrow political-nationalistic path followed by George Bancroft, Palfrey, Hildreth and others of the so-called older school of historians.

Largely as a result of their efforts, the last twenty years have witnessed four significant tendencies in American historiography:

v

(1) An increasing emphasis on the "new history"; (2) more general acceptance of the idea that American history in many respects cannot be isolated from world history; (3) a constant multiplying of monographs dealing with various phases of the social, economic, and cultural development of the people of the United States; and (4) the continued attempt to produce a better synthetic picture of American life.

The pages which follow are in large measure the fruit of these tendencies. They represent, in other words, an effort to give the college student as well as the general reader what seems to me to be the more salient features of American civilization. If in these volumes political history bulks less than in the great majority of treatises which deal with the story of American development, it is only because it has been forced to yield space to those social and economic factors which in my opinion constitute the warp and woof of our political life. Naturally it has been impossible, because of space limits, to include every topic or to survey adequately those selected.

The chapter bibliographies are in no sense exhaustive, nor are they intended to be. They are, as designated, merely suggested readings and may be supplemented by the numerous bibliographical aids now available. Particularly helpful in this respect are the bibliographical chapters in the volumes of *A History of American Life*, edited by Professors A. M. Schlesinger and D. R. Fox.

My indebtedness to those scholars and publicists upon whom I have drawn heavily for inspiration and material is too great to be adequately acknowledged here. I am also under special obligation to a number of my colleagues and friends who in one way or another have rendered valuable assistance. These include Professor Benjamin B. Kendrick of the North Carolina College for Women, at whose suggestion the work was undertaken, Professor R. F. Nichols of the University of Pennsylvania, Professor D. M. Fisk of Temple University, Dean W. E. Weld of Rochester University, and the members, past and present, of the Contemporary Civilization staff of Columbia College, especially T. C. Blaisdell, J. B. Brebner, J. J. Coss, L. W. Cramer, A. P. Evans, H. L. Friess, H. B. Howe, W. C. Langsam, J. D.

McGoldrick, Samuel McKee, Jr., D. C. Miner, I. W. Raymond, H. W. Schneider, R. E. Stryker, Horace Taylor, R. G. Tugwell, and J. H. Wuorinen. And to my wife, Cathryne Barrett Carman, who helped prepare the manuscript for the press and rendered valuable assistance in proofreading, I am deeply indebted. My greatest obligation, however, is to my colleagues, Mr. Samuel McKee, Jr., who read the manuscript, and to Professor John Allen Krout, who read the proof in its entirety. I have been aided in no small measure by their acute scholarship and sane judgment. For all errors of omission or commission, however, I alone am responsible.

HARRY J. CARMAN

COLUMBIA UNIVERSITY
NEW YORK CITY
APRIL, 1930.

CONTENTS

MAPS AND CHARTS

Supplementing this economic revival were the Crusades, those semi-economic, semi-religious, semi-military pilgrimages of the late eleventh and succeeding centuries which *b.* The brought together men from every part of Christian Crusades Europe. While the details of these movements need not concern us, their results are of prime importance. In the first place, they helped to break the barriers of isolation and to stimulate inter-communication of all kinds. Euro- 1. Broke peans saw new scenes and new ways of doing things. barriers of They became acquainted with each other; common isolation needs and desires came into existence, and common feelings and ideals were fostered. Nor should we overlook the fact that the many quarrels between the leaders stimulated the growth of nationalism.

Even more significant, the crusaders came into contact with the richer culture of the East. With the decline of the Roman Empire, Bagdad, the seat of the Arabian Caliphate, 2. Brought and later the Moslemized lands of Spain and Sicily, Western became the real centers of intellectual interest. Europeans into contact Not only did Bagdad inherit the Hellenistic culture with culture brought there by pagan scholars from Constanti- of East nople and by the Nestorian Christians, but it engaged in all sorts of intellectual endeavor. Its "House of Science," a learned academy manned with a corps of translators and learned men, was a veritable center of research, where savants devoted themselves to the study of astronomy, mathematics, chemistry, and medicine. Here the philosophical and scientific works of Aristotle and other Greeks were translated into Arabic. Similar institutions were founded at Cairo, Damascus, Cordova, Toledo, and Palermo. When, therefore, the crusaders invaded the Moslem world they came into intimate contact with peoples whose civilization was in many respects superior to their own. Not only did they perceive that the Moslem's food, raiment, art, and customs were different from those of Western Europe, but they soon learned that his conception of the world and of life did not correspond with their own. As a consequence their intellectual horizon was broadened, and the point of view of medieval Europe was altered. Moreover, returning crusaders bearing tales of

what they had seen and experienced aroused in others a burning
desire to know more about the non-European world, its products,
its peoples, and its culture.

But probably the greatest influence of the Crusades was on
commerce. Contrary to a prevailing notion, trade between
the East and the West, which reached immense
proportions under the Romans, did not completely
disappear with the barbarian invasions of the
Roman Empire. The church, for instance, continued to depend
upon the East for its ornaments and ritualistic vestments.
Europeans of wealth, moreover, showed no more inclination
than did their Roman predecessors to deny themselves those
articles of luxury — spices, fragrant woods, dyes, frankincense,
jewels, silks, rich tapestries — which only the gorgeous East
could supply. Consequently a remnant of the old Mediterranean trade continued. Indeed, during the most troublous
times Italian merchants, particularly the Venetians, dared to
send their galleys to the eastern shores of this inland sea, thus
laying the foundations for their later commercial supremacy
and empire. This commerce between Orient and Occident,
the Crusades affected in several ways. (1) In the first place,
the constant demand for men and supplies led to an increase
in the number and size of ships, and improvements in the art
of navigation. (2) As the West became better acquainted
with such commodities as muslin (cloth of Mosul), damask
(cloth of Damascus), rice, sugar, lemons, apricots (sometimes
called Damascus plums), and garlic, commerce in these and
other Eastern articles multiplied. (3) Commercial relations
were formed with new peoples, and new markets for Western
European products were established in the Greco-Arabian
world and in other regions hitherto unpenetrated. (4) European
cities, whose revival antedated the Crusades, increased in
size and number. (5) The development of capitalism was
fostered. In Italy, where a large number of Oriental industries
were introduced, the merchant and banker class grew more
powerful. (6) New commercial routes were either discovered
or opened up, geographical knowledge was increased, and
exploration and the use of advanced forms of commercial tech-

3. Increased commerce with the East

nique stimulated. (7) Finally, the Crusades enabled Christendom to recover naval control of the Mediterranean, lost since the ninth century.

Scarcely less important than the Crusades in broadening the mind of Europeans, adding to geographical knowledge, and giving new impetus to commerce and expansion, *c.* Work of were the remarkable journeys and explorations of missionaries the famous thirteenth and fourteenth century and travelers European missionaries and travelers. Prior to the middle of the thirteenth century Europeans knew little more about the world than Ptolemy had known in the second century. The crusaders, it is true, brought home information about the restricted area bordering the eastern Mediterranean, but they had little definite knowledge about the spice islands Europe's ig- or the lands whence came precious stones or other norance of luxurious articles of commerce. And the accounts rest of world of Eastern lands as written by travelers of the eleventh, twelfth, and early thirteenth centuries were neither widely known nor very informing. For Western Europe the greater part of Asia, not to mention Africa, was as yet "a half mythical land of alien races, of curious customs and infidel faiths, a land of interminable distances, rich and populous doubtless; certainly dangerous and inaccessible."

But this traditional notion of Asia was gradually supplemented with more exact knowledge. Beginning about the end of the first quarter of the thirteenth century an Christian mo- increasing number of Europeans motivated by tives for pene- missionary zeal, curiosity, trade ambitions, desire trating Asia for wealth, or mere love of adventure began to penetrate the unexplored lands to the East. Even before 1200 it was becoming apparent that Christian Europe could not retain the Holy Land by military force, and if it was to be held at all the Mohammedans would have to be converted to Christianity. No one was more strongly of this opinion than St. Francis of Assisi. Accordingly, in 1219 he embarked for Egypt for the purpose of converting Syria and the Holy Land. During the next thirty years the Franciscans acquired a store of accurate information about the lands and peoples of the Near East.

By the middle of the thirteenth century the great Tartar or Mongol Empire, the foundations of which had been laid earlier in the century by Ghenghiz Khan, had extended its sway over the greater part of Asia and Eastern Europe. Frightened lest the Mongol overrun Central and Western Europe, Pope Innocent IV and St. Louis of France conceived the idea of saving Europe by converting the Mongol to Christianity or by making an alliance with him against the Moslems.

It is unnecessary for us to detail the journeys of even the more renowned of that host of Christian missionaries, adventur-

Asiatic journeys and their results ers and traders — of John of Pian-Carpine, William of Ruysbroeck, John de Corvino, Jordanus de Severac, Ordoric of Pordenone, Giovannini de Marignolli, Pegalotti, Schiltberger and, most important of all, the two Venetian merchants, Nicolo and Matteo Polo, and the former's famous son Marco, the historiographer of their wide and varied wanderings. By the end of the thirteenth century they had visited practically every corner of Asia and had given Europe a veritable wealth of information about Tartary, China, Japan, Persia and India, not to mention many intervening lands. In the cloisters of lonely monasteries and on the quays of busy seaports, priests and merchants alike related the wonders of these Far Eastern lands, of their populous cities with walls of silver, of palaces roofed with gold, of rivers and lakes composed of pearls and other precious stones. We can well imagine how such wondrous tales of strange peoples, of marvelous riches, of unexploited wealth, stirred the rising curiosity of Europeans.

Of the accounts written by many of these travelers none is so interesting to our generation as *The Book of Ser Marco Polo, the*

The Book of Ser Marco Polo *Venetian, Concerning the Kingdom and Marvels of the East,* dictated by the author while a prisoner of war in Genoa. With its picturesque though astonishingly accurate description of Cathay and of the civilization of the Great Khan, its vivid though exaggerated account of Cipangu or Japan, which Marco Polo never actually visited, and its vague and extravagant statements about the "twelve thousand seven hundred islands" of the Pacific and Indian

Ocean archipelagoes, this fascinating story fired the imagination of its western readers. More than anything else, perhaps, it aroused in them an eager desire to exploit this vast eastern continent with its teeming wealth. Here indeed was a golden opportunity for princes in search of new lands to conquer, for merchants dreaming of profits, and for missionaries intent on saving souls. Even today the work is regarded as the greatest individual contribution to the geographical knowledge of the Middle Ages, and many eminent historians are of the opinion that Columbus, despite his lack of faith in Marco Polo, was profoundly influenced by it.

Nor was Africa entirely neglected by the traders and explorers of medieval Europe. As early as the eleventh century Genoese, Pisan, and Aragonese vessels were carrying on a thriving trade with Tripoli, Ceuta, and other North African ports. From these port towns enormously long trade routes stretched southward *Interest of medieval Europe in Africa* across the Sahara to the vast negro empire of the Hausa peoples, cattle raisers and goat herders and manufacturers of highly prized colored textiles. Before the middle of the fifteenth century this central African region had been visited by Anselme Disalguier and Antonio Malfante, two French trader-adventurers. Unfortunately neither was as adept in describing the country as the Asiatic travelers, and their explorations, therefore, apparently had little influence upon the cartography of the time. The Franciscan missionaries might have done better, but the fanaticism of the North African Mohammedans made it impossible for the Franciscans even to reach Lake Chad and the Niger River region.

While Europeans, thanks to the travelers, were thus gaining a more exact knowledge of the Old World and its possibilities, other influences were operating in the direction of further discovery and expansion. In the first place, the *d. Other factors influencing expansion* theory entertained first by the Egyptians and later by the Greeks and Romans that the earth was round came to be generally accepted by every scientifically-minded man in the Middle Ages. Not one of that galaxy of famous mathematicians — Albertus Magnus, Leonard of Pisa, Jordan of Saxony,

Conrad of Megenburg, Nicholas of Cusa, George Peuerbach, Johannes Müller of Königsberg (Regiomontanus), Albertus Brudzewski, and Copernicus — doubted that the earth was a sphere. Those acquainted with the reports of Marco Polo and his contemporaries knew that the eastern shore of Asia was not fringed by impenetrable marshes, as currently supposed, **1. Sphericity** but that it was accessible to sea-going vessels. **of the earth** Mohammedan travelers and geographers such as Ibn-Khordabeh and Ibn-Haukel, and above all the great Arabian geographer, Idrisi, who had seen ships on the Indian and Pacific Oceans, undoubtedly believed that the "Golden East" could be reached by sailing around Africa. Indeed, before Marco Polo returned from China two daring Genoese seamen, Tedisio Dorio and Vivaldi made the attempt "to go by sea to the ports of India to trade there." But their galleys, which passed through the Strait of Gibraltar and headed southward, never returned. Columbus and his great inspirer, Martin Alonzo Pinzon, as well as other navigators and pilots, accepted the theory that the earth was spherical. "I have always read that the world, comprising the land and the water," said Columbus, "is spherical, as is testified by the investigations of Ptolemy and others, who have proved it by the eclipses of the moon and other observations made from east to west, as well as by the elevation of the pole from north to south."

From about 1300 on, marked improvement was made in the art of cartography. Instead of basing their work on mere half **2. Maps and** mythical data gathered in part from biblical and *portolani* literary lore, many map makers began to give heed to exact measurements and outlines. In this connection the Europeans were deeply indebted to the Arabic cartographers who were sticklers for accuracy. The first notable advance was made in the construction of sailing charts or *portolani*, of which some five hundred have come down to us from the fourteenth and fifteenth centuries. By far the greater majority were drawn by Italians; all of them picture with considerable accuracy the coasts of Europe, Northern Africa, and Western Asia, and we may be fairly certain that every navigator had in his possession one or more of them. In addition to these

charts the mariner of the fifteenth century had access to world
maps based on the Italian *portolani* and constructed by learned
geographers and cartographers. Both maps and *portolani*
were revised or redrawn as new lands or waters were discovered.

Such discoveries were greatly facilitated by the use of the
compass and the astrolabe — a Moslem invention, the forerunner of the quadrant — which are known to have 3. Instruments
been in use during the latter part of the fourteenth for determin-
century. By means of these two instruments the ing location
sailor could determine both direction and location north or
south (latitude). The chronometer and longitude tables —
the latter largely the work of the mathematician Regiomontanus
— were in use before the end of the fifteenth century. With
these instruments, larger ships, and improved navigating charts
the mariner was no longer obliged to hug the shores for fear of
being lost. Unless he chanced to be prey to the superstitions
current in his time he was now more than ever before free to
sail the uncharted seas in quest of new lands, new peoples,
new trade routes, new sources of wealth.

And bold mariners there were who dared sail such seas. As
early as the eighth century adventurous Vikings bent on trade
and plunder began to pilot their vessels out of Early maritime
the Baltic and North Seas. In the next century activity
they colonized Iceland and before the year 1000 had touched
the coast of Labrador. In 1341 the forgotten Canaries, identified by the Italian, Lancelot Malocello, in 1270, were rediscovered by the Portuguese. Before the end of the fourteenth
century both the Madeira Islands and the Azores were visited
by Europeans.

Significant as these achievements were, they were dimmed by
the discoveries and explorations made under the auspices of
Prince Henry of Portugal during the next century. Prince Henry
Motivated by lively interest in trade, by a burning of Portugal
desire to spread Christianity, and above all by a (1394–1460)
keen curiosity for knowledge of the unknown world, this remarkable man, himself an accomplished cartographer and
expert seaman, devoted the best energies of his life to geographical discovery. It was while engaged in a campaign against the

hated Moors, first in 1415 and again in 1418, that he learned
of the caravan routes extending from Tripoli, Ceuta, and the
other Mediterranean towns southward across the Sahara and
the Soudan. Over these routes, Moorish prisoners informed
him, came gold, wines, textiles, and slaves from the Senegal
and Gambia river regions and from the gold and ivory coasts on
the Gulf of Guinea. News of this rich trade "inspired him to
seek those lands by way of the sea."

Thus determined, Prince Henry returned to Sagres where
he established a great maritime school. Unparalleled for its
equipment and scientific methods, and backed by
the resources of the state, it attracted the leading
navigators of Europe. Year after year increasing
numbers of caravels sailed southward from the
neighboring port of Lagos. In 1418 Porto Santo was discovered;
in 1441 Cape Blanco was rounded, and in 1443 Gil Eannes,
more daring than his predecessors, passed the dreaded Cape
Bayador; two years later Cape Verde was discovered. When ad-
versities — scurvy, tropical diseases, and fear growing out of the
ignorance and credulity of the age — seized both captains and
sailors, Prince Henry's enthusiasm never flagged. Finally intrepid mariners like Nuno Tristam, Denis Diaz, and the Venetian Cadamosto pushed southward as far as Sierra Leone.
When Prince Henry died in 1460 Portuguese mariners were
therefore familiar with two thousand miles of the West African
coast instead of six hundred miles as at the beginning of the
fifteenth century.

His contribu-
tion to
Old World
expansion

The enterprise so long and nobly fostered by Prince Henry
did not cease with his death. Already Portugal had opened up a
rich traffic in slaves and gold. Murmurings against
Prince Henry gave way to exultation and his work
was carried on. By 1484 the mouth of the Niger had been
passed and that of the Congo discovered. During the next
three years Portuguese mariners surveyed the coast of Angola,
in the process of which they found the mouth of the Orange
River. Meanwhile the search for the Gold Coast, which had
now been found, was replaced by a more ambitious undertaking,
namely, the long-dreamed-of passageway to India and the

Prince Henry's
work continued

PRINCE HENRY THE NAVIGATOR

From a 17th-century English print symbolic of the spirit of expansion

VENICE IN THE MIDDLE AGES

East. Four important factors made not only the Portuguese but the other peoples of Western Europe doubly eager to attain this much-sought-for goal.

2. COMMERCIAL RIVALRY AND A NEW ROUTE TO THE INDIES

The first of these factors was the emergence of modern capitalism and its transforming influence on the economic life of Western Europe. During and following the Crusades a class of wealthy merchants and bankers developed along the routes of trade, particularly in Genoa, Venice, Florence, Augsburg, Nuremberg, and other Italian and South German towns. At first, accumulating capital in a small way from trade, they gradually built up business structures very different from those that existed in the older agricultural society of the Middle Ages. These business structures, some of which were badly organized, emphasized the substitution of money for barter, the loaning of money at interest to state and church despite the church's prejudice against private profit and usury, the development of an elaborate banking technique — including exact bookkeeping, bills of exchange, stock companies, investment in commercial and industrial enterprises, and speculative trading. Powerful Florentine houses of the Bardi and Peruzzi, for example, financed Edward III of England, the Medici, and the papacy. Rich German bankers like the Fuggers, Welsers, and others invested extensively in such enterprises as mining, manufacturing, sheep-raising, and wheat growing. Like the capitalist of the present day, these merchants and bankers were staunch supporters of any movement that promised new markets and new fields for investment and financial exploitation, and they were, therefore, supporters of overseas trade and exploration.

Modern capitalism and its relation to expansion

Closely interwoven with the development of capitalism and the desire of the rising middle class to increase its profits, was the commercial-financial situation existing between Europe and Asia. Commerce between the two continents, stimulated as we have seen by the Crusades and the accounts of travelers, developed rapidly from the thirteenth to

The growth of commerce

the fifteenth century. From the markets of the Orient there came an ever-increasing volume of expensive luxuries — precious stones, fabrics of cotton and silk, rugs, glassware of all sorts, perfumes, dyes, woods, gums, ivory, medicaments and, most important of all, spices. These furnished the rich of Europe, her lords and kings, her bishops and abbots, and her wealthier merchants and their families, with articles of personal adornment, with food and with furnishings for their palaces and manor houses, their churches and cathedrals and guild halls. In return for these goods Europe sent to the East woolen fabrics, wines, coral, metals, furs, sulphur, slaves, oil, honey, amber, and grain.

These exports, however, were insufficient to pay for the imports. We shall note in Chapter IV that the colonial merchants **The adverse** were drained of their specie to settle their balance **trade balance** with the merchants of Great Britain. In much **and drain of** **precious metals** the same way the balance of trade in favor of the **from Europe** East drained the European merchants of their gold and silver. Unblessed with adequate mines of her own, Europe in the days of the Roman Empire and again during the Crusades had gained a sufficient gold supply by exploiting and plundering Syria and Asia Minor. With the end of successful crusading and the overthrow of the Kingdom of Jerusalem in 1291 this source was cut off, and for a hundred and fifty years or more the gold and silver coin and bullion of Europe flowed eastward in much the same way as it had for centuries passed from the agricultural regions of Northern Europe to the commercial centers of the Mediterranean. The money stringency which resulted was marked by specie appreciation, falling prices, debasement of the coinage, forced loans, bankruptcies, attempts to prevent the export of gold and silver, and the retardation of many European industrial enterprises.

This almost intolerable economic situation was in part the result of the method of transferring goods from producer to **The medieval** consumer. For centuries the products of the East **trade routes** had reached Europe by way of three main routes. The southernmost of these was in large measure a water route. Goods from China and Japan, and drugs, perfumes, gum, and spices from the Malay archipelago were brought in Chinese,

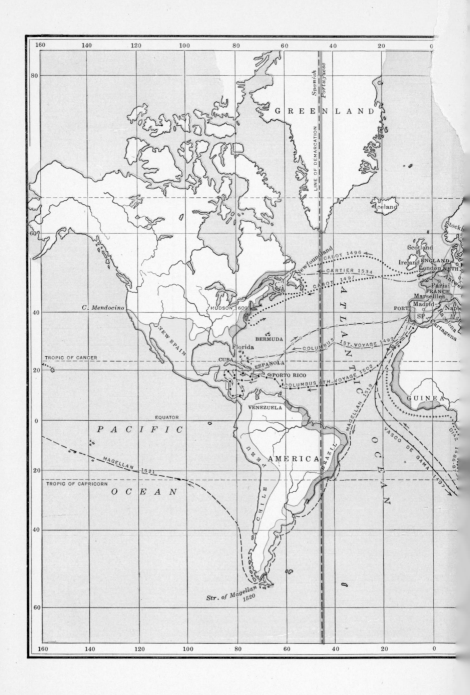

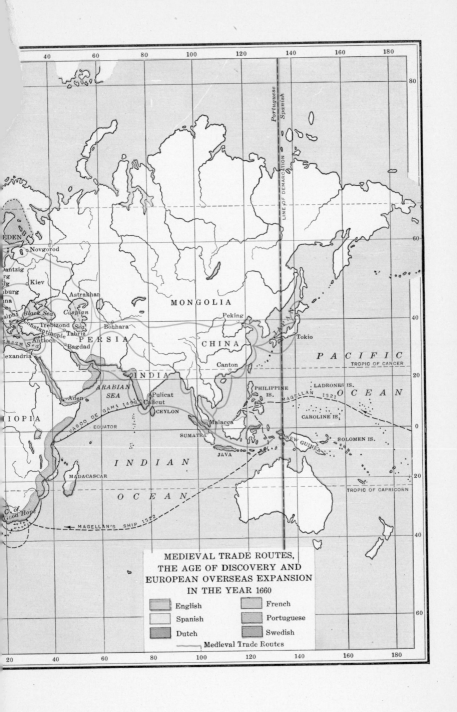

MEDIEVAL TRADE ROUTES,
THE AGE OF DISCOVERY AND
EUROPEAN OVERSEAS EXPANSION
IN THE YEAR 1660

English   French
Spanish   Portuguese
Dutch   Swedish
Medieval Trade Routes

Japanese, and Malay junks to Malacca, and thence by Indian or Arabian merchants to Pulicat or ports on the Malabar coast of India. Here other traders came with products from Ceylon and other Eastern lands. From these ports the shipper sailed directly across the Arabian Sea to the Strait of Babel-man-deb, up the Red Sea to Bernice. From this point the goods were carried by caravan to the Nile, whence they were floated to Cairo or Alexandria, there to be picked up by masters of Venetian ships. The middle route extended from the Indian ports northwestward through the Persian Gulf and up the Tigris River to Bagdad, thence to the Syrian cities of Antioch, Laodicea, Damascus, and Jaffa, and occasionally to Cairo and Alexandria. The northern or overland route ran from the inland provinces of India and China across Turkestan to Bokhara. From here the route branched out. Some caravans went south of the Caspian Sea to Trebizond and thence to the cities of Syria or Asia Minor. Others went north of the Caspian to Astrakhan at the mouth of the Volga, or on through Russia to Novgorod and the Baltic. Each of these routes had many ramifications and divergencies, and transportation over any one of them was at best a slow process.

Of vastly more consequence than the element of time, however, was that of danger and expense. Journeying over bleak mountains, hot deserts, and sparse plateaus, Transportation through all kinds of weather, the merchant was over these routes insecure and expensive ever subject to onslaught and robbery by highwaymen and numerous ungoverned tribes who made their living by plundering. To princes and officials, high and low, in the more civilized states through which the routes might pass, he was forced to pay tribute, sometimes even to the point of confiscation. Nor did the merchant who elected to send his goods by sea often fare much better, for pirates and storms vied with each other in their destructiveness, and port dues were usually more excessive and unreasonable than were tributes in the inland towns. All such losses and taxes were passed on to the consumer. Added to these was the cost of transhipment and the middlemen's profit, for no merchant brought goods all the way from India to Europe. A pound of pepper or a piece of fabric, for instance, might change hands a dozen times before it reached a Mediterranean port, and we may rest assured that each seller made a handsome profit. Thus the commodities that were purchased for a mere trifle in the markets of the East sold for exorbitant prices in the West.

While Italian statesmen, geographers, and merchants blamed the non-Christian middleman for the high cost of Oriental goods and preached a new crusade against him, he alone was not responsible for high prices, for as soon as the products of the East reached the Levantine cities scattered along the shores of the Black Sea and the eastern Mediterranean, they were monopolized for the most part by Italian merchants, especially Venetians. For centuries these keen Italian traders, who frequently formed a not inconsiderable part of the population of many of the near-eastern cities, handled the bulk of the commerce between Europe and Asia. Indeed, so powerful were they that in many cities of the Levant they established permanent quarters or *fondachi*, which included warehouses, offices, and often a market place. To the wharves of these cities came Venetian galleys laden with European produce for Oriental consumers; homeward bound they carried cargoes of coveted products from the East. Such goods as were not consumed in the Italian cities were sold to foreigners. Through the passes of the Alps came the traders and merchants of South Germany and the "back country" of Northern Europe for wares which they in turn disposed of in their home cities like Augsburg, Ulm, and Nuremberg, or sent to the French fairs or to the merchants of the Hanse towns of North Germany and the Netherlands. With England and Flanders the Venetians traded directly, and year after year until 1560 their merchant fleets passed through the Strait of Gibraltar on the way to these northern countries.

Thus Venice to a great extent became by the opening of the fifteenth century the commercial-financial-maritime center of Europe, completely overshadowing her Mediterranean rivals — Pisa, Genoa, Marseilles, and Barcelona. With a population of 190,000, she had an army of 40,000 men, a commercial fleet of 3,000 ships, and an

Land Routes......
Hanse Water Routes......
Principal Hanseatic Cities
are underlined

TRADE ROUTES BETWEEN NORTHERN AND SOUTHERN
EUROPE IN THE 13TH AND 14TH CENTURIES

annual revenue in excess of $2,500,000. Not only was she the distributing point for the wares of the East, but to her markets and warehouses came the products of Europe for re-export. Above all, her merchants and princes, because of their almost exclusive monopoly of the Levant trade, grew rich — some of them fabulously so — to the envy of the merchants and rulers of those rising nations on the Atlantic who, under the existing order of things, were deprived of the major profits of the Oriental trade. Their jealousy of Venice constitutes the third factor that motivated the Portuguese and their western neighbors to seek a new route to the East.

Finally, the rise of the national state itself lent support to the undertaking. In the early stages of their evolution the kings of these new national states — Portugal, Spain, France, Sweden, Denmark, and England — were only nominal rulers, real authority resting in the hands of powerful feudal lords, each of whom was practically sovereign over one or more of the many geographical fragments into which the country was divided. Upon these lords the monarch was virtually dependent for funds, military forces, and the administration of the law. Every effort on his part to limit their authority or to change the existing order they vigorously resisted. The monarch soon realized, however, that in the rising middle class he had a powerful ally, for the merchant hated and sought escape from the feudal system with its hierarchies, private wars, robber barons, arbitrary exactions, and varying customs duties, its hundred systems of coinage, and its multitudinous local courts from which there was often no appeal. Like the business man of today, he wanted order, uniformity, and above all security; and he soon came to appreciate that the realization of these objects hinged on the establishment of a strong central government. He realized too that it would in all probability mean better roads and bridges, wider markets, and increased protection for his interests. The merchant class, therefore, rallied to the support of the monarch in his relentless struggle against the feudal lords for supremacy. Its wealth, in the form of taxes, enabled him to raise a paid standing army and to hire loyal officers. From this

Importance of commerce to rising national states

class also he recruited those professional lawyers, skilled in the study of Roman law, who exalted the right of the sovereign to exact obedience, and who furnished him with highly perfected legal systems. In other words, the success of the monarch in his effort to unify his country geographically and to exercise his royal prerogatives throughout the length and breadth of his land depended in large measure on the prosperity of the middle or bourgeois class. For him their wealth spelled power and prestige and it was this fact that in large measure enlisted the rulers of those rising national states on the Atlantic seaboard in maritime exploration and discovery.

These four interrelated basic factors — the development of capitalism, an adverse balance of trade, Italian commercial monopoly, and the monetary needs and ambitions New route to of the monarchs and their subjects of the rising India discovered national states of Western Europe — together with the spirit of adventure and intellectual curiosity, were the forces which encouraged the mariners to persist in their search for an all-water route to the East. By 1471 Portuguese explorers, as we have noted, had crossed the equator. In 1488, Bartholemew Diaz, the third member of his family to carry the Portuguese flag along the shores of the "Dark Continent," rounded the Cape of Good Hope and turned northward into the Indian Ocean only to be forced back by threats of his mutinous crew. Nevertheless, the long-sought passageway had at last been found, and ten years later when Vasco da Gama anchored his fleet at Calicut on the southwest coast of India, and shortly after Albuquerque carried the flag of Portugal to the Spice Islands in the heart of the East Indies, the Portuguese triumph was complete.

Meanwhile Columbus, lover of the sea, expert sailor, skilled maker of charts, and firm believer that the Indies might be reached by sailing directly westward, had made Columbus and his great voyage and discovered America. The the discovery story of his achievement is too well known to require of America repetition here. Indeed, we may even venture to suggest that many historians have given it more space than it deserves. Had Columbus never lived, America would have been found in all probability at about the time it was discovered. In authorizing him to "discover and acquire certain islands and mainland in the ocean," Ferdinand and Isabella and their intimate advisers were influenced by much the same motives that induced their rivals, the Portuguese, to seek an all-sea route to the East.

Until recently it has been customary to attribute both the Portuguese explorations and the discoveries by Columbus to conquests which the Ottoman Turks made during the fifteenth century. These infidel people, so the old accounts ran, having conquered Syria and Asia Minor, cut off the old trade routes to the East and made it absolutely necessary to find new commercial arteries to the Orient. Research, however, has rendered this theory untenable. In the first place, not all the trade routes had been blocked by the Turks when Vasco da Gama made his memorable voyage to India and thus completed the work begun a half century before. In fact, a new route to the East had been thought of long before the advent of the Turks. Moreover, Professor Lybyer, an American scholar, has demonstrated pretty conclusively that Constantinople, largely due to basic changes in European economic organization, was on the decline long before its capture by the Turks; that the Turks did not deliberately interfere with trade; that under their régime commerce was little or no more hazardous than it had been under their predecessors; and that, next to the Italians, the Turks themselves were the heaviest losers by the change.

Ottoman Turks not responsible for overseas expansion

The exploits of Columbus and Vasco da Gama were soon equaled and even excelled by other men of skill and daring. In 1497 John Cabot, a Genoese, sailing under the English flag, anchored off the Canadian coast. In 1500 Cabral, in attempting to follow the da Gama route to India, was driven out of his course and discovered Brazil, which he claimed for the king of Portugal. During the same year Hojeda and Pinzon sailed along the greater part of the northern coast of South America, while in 1501 Americus Vespucci, the Florentine for whom America was named, followed a long stretch of the eastern coast of the same continent. About a

Other discoveries

decade later Balboa discovered the Pacific, and in 1522 the
Victoria — sole survivor of Magellan's fleet of five ships —
reached Spain, having sailed around the globe.

3. The Iberian States Attempt to Monopolize the Fruits of Discovery

The new water route enabled the Portuguese to secure
temporarily the Italian monopoly, for it was vastly cheaper to
ship eastern goods around Africa than over the old **Portugal falls**
trade routes. The distance, to be sure, was very **heir to the Ital-**
much greater, but larger cargoes could be brought **ian monopoly**
and both the necessity for transhipment and middlemen's
profits were eliminated. So panic-stricken were the Venetian
merchants when they learned that Vasco da Gama had returned
to Lisbon in 1499 with a cargo of spices worth sixty times the
cost of his expedition, that they reduced the price of these
particular products fifty per cent. In desperation they sought
to minimize the growing commerce of their new competitors
by encouraging the Arabs to hamper Portuguese activities in
India in every way possible. They even discussed opening
up a shorter water route by means of a canal across the Isthmus
of Suez. But all such schemes came to naught. The day of
Venetian supremacy was over; the commercial center of
Europe had passed from the Mediterranean to the Atlantic
seaboard.

Spain and Portugal were also the first of the European states
to benefit in a territorial way from the new discoveries. To tell
again in detail the familiar story of Portuguese **The Portu-**
and Spanish discovery, exploration, and coloniza- **guese Empire**
tion lies outside the province of this book. In the century
between the voyages of Diaz, Columbus, and da Gama on the
one hand, and the planting of the first French, Dutch, and
English colonies on the other, they accomplished much. Not
only did the Portuguese begin the colonization of Brazil, but
they also established a vast trading empire in India and the
East Indies with Goa as its center. They moreover controlled
most of the slave-trading stations along the coast of Africa, and
were thus enabled to add considerable sums to the enormous

profits accruing from the Oriental trade. Finally their commercial ventures in the East rendered the entire Indian Ocean
and Western Pacific regions tolerably well known to Europeans.
But Portugal was too frail to support such a pretentious and
far-flung empire. Possessing small population and resources,
honeycombed with graft and corruption, without experience in
colonial administration, and without adequate means for distributing her Eastern merchandise or protecting her monopoly,
it was only a question of time when she would be compelled
to relinquish what she had so long worked for. Her dreams and
ambitions were cut short in 1581 when the Spanish monarch,
Philip II, became the ruler of both Portugal and Spain, gobbled
up the Portuguese possessions, and closed the port of Lisbon to
the French, English, and Dutch, with whom he was at war.

The Spanish were no less active than the Portuguese. Setting
out to conquer, enslave, rule, and exploit, they laid claim
The Spanish   by the end of the sixteenth century not only to their
Empire   holdings in the eastern hemisphere but to all the
coastal regions and portions of the interior of South America,
and to the West Indies, Central America, and Mexico. Daring
adventurers like Ponce de Leon, De Vaca, De Soto, Narvaez,
and Coronado, in search of a fountain of perpetual youth,
treasure, slaves, a shorter passage to the South Sea, or conversion of the natives, headed expeditions which explored a great
deal of the interior of the southern half of the present United
States. Comparatively few permanent settlements were made
in this region, however, during the sixteenth and seventeenth
centuries, and it was never an important part of the Spanish
colonial empire. Up to 1630 the little town of Santa Fé, where
lived two hundred and fifty Spaniards and twice as many half-
breeds and Indian dependents, was the only Spanish settlement
in New Mexico. Twenty-five neighboring missions served
ninety pueblos claiming 90,000 resentful converts. Fifty years
later the Spanish population of New Mexico numbered approximately 2,500, nearly all of whom were living in the upper
Rio Grande valley. Plans to occupy eastern Texas and the
mouth of the Mississippi were abandoned near the close of
the seventeenth century. In Florida, St. Augustine was the

only important town founded by the Spanish; it had a population of about 5,000 when the English took possession in 1763.

Incidentally the Spaniards did much to further the economic advancement of their new territories. Numerous plants and seeds, for example, were introduced. These included wheat, barley, rice, rye, beans, lentils, almonds, mulberries, cherries, walnuts, chestnuts, tulip trees, alfalfa, quinces, apricots, and other pitted fruits; oranges, lemons, rosemary, sugar cane, and a multitude of old-

Spain's contribution to the New World

WORLD PRODUCTION OF GOLD AND SILVER, 1493–1760 [1]

Period	Total Gold Production	Total Silver Production
1493–1520	$107,931,000	$54,703,000
1521–1560	204,697,000	297,226,000
1561–1600	189,012,000	597,244,000
1601–1640	223,572,000	678,800,000
1641–1680	239,655,000	584,691,000
1681–1720	313,491,000	579,869,000
1721–1760	580,727,000	801,712,000
Totals	$1,859,085,000	$3,594,245,000

fashioned flowers. Horses and mules were also brought in, probably from Andalusia. Father Cobo in his *Historia del Nuevo Mundo* asserted that America received in plants and animals as much wealth as she returned in gold and silver. In 1600 the Spanish population of the New World, approximately 200,000, owned 40,000 negro slaves and drew some form of tribute from nearly 5,000,000 Indians. Grain, sugar, and cattle were raised in considerable quantities and either consumed in the colonies or shipped to Spain.

But it was as a source of precious metals that the Spanish Empire was important. From the middle of the fourteenth century adverse trade balances, as we have already noted, tended to drain Europe of its gold and silver. By the opening of the sixteenth century the mines of Europe were probably not producing more than $500,000 to $750,000 worth of precious metals annually; approximately the same amount was obtained from the west coast of Africa.

Influx of precious metals into Europe

[1] From Knight, Barnes and Flügel, *Economic History of Europe*, p. 310.

The amount of coinage in circulation in Europe at this time was, approximately, $170,000,000 to $200,000,000. By the middle of the sixteenth century, however, tons of gold and silver, especially the latter, were pouring into Europe from Spanish America. In fact, so great was the importation that it is estimated that from 1500 to 1600 the amount of gold was doubled, and that of silver increased ten-fold.

Not all of this treasure, as we shall subsequently see, flowed into the coffers of the Spanish monarch or into the pockets of the Spanish merchant class. But irrespective of this fact, the very importation of such enormous amounts of precious metals profoundly influenced the history of the Old World and the New. In the first place, no sooner did the influx begin than the European stock of money began to increase. It is estimated that at the end of the sixteenth century there were twelve times as many gold and silver coins in circulation as at the beginning of the century. Indeed, so plentiful did money become that its purchasing power depreciated; commodity prices soared to the detriment of persons with relatively fixed incomes, especially wage-earners. On the other hand, the great supply of gold and silver furnished Europe with adequate capital. Kings and princes were now able to spend greater sums than ever before for dynastic and national purposes; shipowners could build larger vessels to carry the increasing commerce; and manufacturers had sufficient means to reconstruct their business on a larger scale. Nor should we fail to note that an increased commerce and currency facilitated the growth of those banking and credit institutions which were developing north of the Alps during the sixteenth century.

The colonial policy of Spain and Portugal was exclusive. By the papal line of demarcation of 1493, supplemented the following year by the convention of Tordesillas, the two countries agreed to divide all newly discovered lands between them, Spain obtaining all west of an imaginary line 370 leagues west of Cape Verde Islands, and Portugal all east of it. Within the territory thus partitioned, each country attempted to monoplize the trade and the wealth. All trade, for instance, with the Spanish colonies was supposed to be carried on by Spaniards in Spanish vessels from specified Spanish ports to specified colonial ports. The same was true with regard to Portugal and her colonies. Such a policy, it was reasoned, would enable the home merchants to market their goods in the colonies in return for raw materials or gold and silver. At the same time shipowners would benefit and the government would obtain large sums in export and import taxes as well as a share of the products of the mines, called a royalty.

This policy, designed to benefit both government and business, failed for a number of reasons. First of all, the policy itself was too restrictive, for in designating the character of the cargo, the time and place of sailing, and the destination of the goods shipped, the government left the merchant no leeway. There was absolutely no flexibility, every detail being fixed by the *Casa de Contractacion*, as the bureaucratic Spanish trade organization was known. Official red tape smothered the merchant's initiative and hampered him at every turn, and he could achieve little in competition with the relatively free and daring Dutch or English trader.

Reasons for failure of Iberian commercial policy

1. Its restrictive character

Even more burdensome were the heavy and often unjust taxes and the method of their collection. When Philip II came to the throne of Spain in 1556 the country, though possessing a vast overseas domain, a navy rated second to none, and The Netherlands, the richest part of Northern Europe, was in financial straits. The wars of Charles V with the Turks, the French, and the Protestants, had been a severe drain in both men and money. The upkeep of the navy was expensive. Heavy sums, bearing from fifteen to thirty per cent interest, were owing to Flemish, Italian, and German bankers. To relieve the situation, property taxes underwent a thirty per cent increase, which all but ruined the already hard-pressed Spanish farmer. The *alcabala* or sales tax placed a ten per cent tax on every ware each time it was bought and sold until it frequently ate up the profits of the trade and forced the merchant out of business. Sometimes taxes exceeded earnings,

2. Excessive tax burdens

and many manufacturers, rather than pay forty to sixty per cent of the value of their goods to the government, closed the doors of their establishments. As if this were not enough, exorbitant customs duties were levied not only on the frontiers but in the interior, paralyzing trade and discouraging home manufacture. In addition, there were stamp taxes and confiscatory fees for offenses against religion. Revenue was even obtained by selling legitimacy to people born out of wedlock and by "alms for the King," a system which in reality amounted to forced gifts. Tens of thousands were reduced to vagabondage, while other thousands, to escape starvation, went into religious orders.

No less ruinous was the disastrous religious and administrative policy of Philip II who, like his father, aspired to the mastery of Europe. A devout Catholic and a true defender of the faith, Philip resolved to stamp out all heresy, particularly Protestantism, which was spreading rapidly in Germany, Switzerland, France, England, Scotland, The Netherlands, and Scandinavia. He first attempted to set his own house in order by completing the expulsion of the Jews, who formed the backbone of the trading and financial class, and who had been ordered to leave as early as 1492, and by getting rid of the non-Christian Moors, who were the leaders in agriculture and industry. Under the leadership of these two peoples the trade and manufacture of Spain had expanded enormously. Woolen manufacture, for example, supported a third of the population, and silk manufacture was increasing rapidly. With the loss of these industrious peoples Spain was unable to support herself agriculturally or to produce manufactured goods in sufficient quantities to supply the domestic needs of the country and the requirements of the colonies. After their departure, the city of Bruges, for example, produced more woolen cloth than all Spain. As a consequence Spain was compelled to export large sums of gold and silver to Germany, The Netherlands, France, and England, in payment for manufactured commodities. Ninety-five per cent of the cargoes exported to the colonies in 1560 was of foreign manufacture.

3. Philip and the expulsion of Moors and Jews

When these imported goods were re-exported to the colonies the Spanish merchant, in order to cover the heavy cost of taxes and freight and to make a profit, was virtually **4. Colonial** forced to charge excessively high prices. Fre- **dissatisfaction** quently the colonists refused to buy, and the mer- **and contra-** chant had either to reship his cargo or sell at a **band trade** sacrifice. Often he faced foreign competition, for almost from the first the inhabitants of New Spain engaged in contraband trade with merchants and buccaneers from other countries. Such a trade was carried on by various methods of smuggling and was often facilitated by the wholesale bribery of short-sighted, grasping colonial officials.

Lastly, Philip's religious zeal and his unwise administration cost him the loss of his richest province, The Netherlands. In-censed by his harsh measures against the Protes- **5. Loss of The** tants, exasperated by heavy taxes, and chafing under **Netherlands** his ruinous edicts respecting industry and commerce, The Nether-lands rose in revolt in 1566, and after a bloody struggle the north-ern, or Dutch, provinces succeeded in securing their independence. As a result the looms which might have supplied the goods for Spain's overseas colonies were either destroyed or deserted, their former operators migrating to England. The commercial mart, Amsterdam, was permanently lost to the Empire, and a great financial center, Antwerp, was for the time being ruined. It was a blow from which Spain was destined never fully to recover. Incidentally, the loss of The Netherlands marked the first step in that long-drawn-out process which ultimately culminated in the almost complete destruction of the Spanish Empire.

4. Iberian Supremacy Challenged: the Establish-ment of Rival Empires beyond the Sea

Prior to the middle of the sixteenth century no nation seems to have seriously thought of challenging the title of either the Portuguese or the Spanish to their far-flung empires. **Spain unable** In 1496, the Italian, John Cabot, it is true, re- **to maintain** ceived a patent from King Henry VII of England **exclusive** authorizing him to discover "new and unknown **monopoly** lands"; but eighty years elapsed before England made any

attempt to colonize, and aside from affording her a legal basis
for her later claims to the North American continent and opening up the Newfoundland fisheries, the Cabot voyages were relatively unimportant.   Nor were French activities in the New
World during the first half of the sixteenth century of much
greater significance, for the explorations of Verrazano in 1524
and Jacques Cartier in 1534–35 merely enabled France to stake
out a claim in America.

With the spread of Protestantism, however, and the determination of Philip II to extirpate this "accursed heresy" and at the
same time to maintain a monopoly of the world's
mineral wealth, the situation changed.   Protestant
countries, whose growing commercial and capitalist
classes had long fretted under the restraints imposed by the papal bulls, no longer felt bound to respect the
claims of the Iberian states.   Already the thrifty Dutch, economically, politically, and religiously oppressed by Spanish rule
and now on the verge of revolt, were reaping by far the larger
portion of the profits of the Portuguese trade with the East.
English buccaneers and freebooters — Hawkins, Drake, and
others — waged an unrelenting offensive against the Spanish
monopoly, raiding and plundering the coast towns of Spanish
America and capturing Spanish treasure ships on the high seas.
Even the port towns of Spain did not escape molestation.   To
prey upon Spanish commerce became, in fact, an eminently
respectable business.

Against such activities Spain protested in vain, for her rivals
came more and more to realize that Philip's power and, in turn,
the success of his policies, rested in large measure
upon the wealth which he obtained from the New
World.   This opinion was admirably expressed by
Richard Hakluyt, the younger, Anglican clergyman
and leading geographer of Elizabethan England, when he wrote,
"if you touche him [Philip] in the Indies you touch the apple
of his eye; for take away his treasure which is *nervus belli*, and
which he hath almoste oute of his West Indies, his olde bands
of soldiers will soon be dissolved, his purposes defeated, his
power and strength diminished, his pride abated and his tyranie

**Protestant
countries dis-
like Iberian
monopoly**

**Treasure of
New World
and Philip's
power**

utterly suppressed." Equally to the point was the statement of Francis Bacon that "money is the principal part of the greatness of Spain; for by that they maintain their veteran army. But in this part, of all others, is most to be considered the ticklish and brittle state of the greatness of Spain. Their greatness consisteth in their treasure, their treasure, in the Indies, and their Indies (if it be well weighed) are indeed but an accession to such as are masters of the sea."

Queen Elizabeth, who came to the English throne in 1558, and her bourgeois subjects fully understood this situation. Philip, in his desire to restore England to the Catholic fold, first tried to win Elizabeth's hand in marriage, but failing in this he took the attitude that she had no right to the throne and engineered several conspiracies designed to supplant her with her Catholic rival, Mary, Queen of Scots. His efforts in this direction, together with the popularity of Elizabeth, helped to weld the English people together and to make them bitter in their growing enmity toward Spain. Elizabeth, on her side, lost no opportunity to weaken those who would destroy her. To this end she assisted the Huguenots or French Protestants, secretly and then openly; she intervened in favor of the Dutch who revolted against Spain in 1566; she connived with the English sea-dogs in their warfare on the Spanish monopoly. Disappointed and angry, Philip finally resolved to subjugate England and humble its haughty queen by means of his "Invincible Armada." Its decisive defeat in 1588, so momentous in the history of Holland, England, and America, marked the end of Spanish maritime supremacy, the beginning of England's control of the seas, and the emergence of the English and the Dutch as the commercial leaders of the seventeenth- and eighteenth-century world. The defeat of the Armada cleared the way for a carnival of conquest by Spain's enterprising rivals. Within three years, eight hundred Spanish ships were taken. In 1596 the Englishman, Sir Thomas Howard, captured and plundered the city of Cadiz. But even more important, the destruction of the Spanish fleet paved the way for the establishment of rival empires beyond the sea.

The first empire in point of time was that of Holland or The

Defeat of Armada and breakdown of Spanish maritime supremacy

Netherlands. Beginning their maritime career as fishermen, the
Dutch long before they revolted from Spain had built up a
The Dutch   profitable carrying trade, bringing cloth, tar, timber,
Empire   and grain from the Baltic and North Seas to Spain
and France in exchange for wines and liquors and other products
of Southwestern Europe and the East Indies. The revolt of
The Netherlands and the union of Spain and Portugal not only
augmented this trade, but gave the Dutch a golden opportunity
to secure colonial possessions. In 1595, the year following their
exclusion from the port of Lisbon, they made their first voyage
to India. Direct trade with the Spice Islands increased annually, and by 1602 no less than sixty-five Dutch merchantmen
had made the return voyage from India. Scarcely less significant was their capture of 545 Spanish and Portuguese ships in
the thirteen years from 1602 to 1615. In 1602 the Dutch East
India Company was chartered and in a few years not only established new trading posts along the African and Asiatic coast, but
succeeded in ousting the Portuguese from the rich islands of
the Malay Archipelago and in monopolizing the bulk of their
commerce. Under the auspices of the Dutch West India
Company, trading posts were also established in the Americas
in spite of the fear that such action might result in new difficulties with Spain. The most important of these included
settlements along the coast of Brazil, in Guiana, in the Antilles,
and at the mouth of the Hudson. But the Dutch, though
shrewd and energetic, were unable to maintain their empire
intact; in 1654 they lost their last stronghold in Brazil, and
ten years later New Netherlands, their most important American
colony, passed into the hands of the more prosperous English.
Throughout the seventeenth century, however, they practically
monopolized the carrying trade between Asia and Europe, and
in addition increased their Baltic and Mediterranean commerce.

France was somewhat more tardy in building up an overseas
empire than were her continental neighbors, Portugal, Spain,
The French   and Holland. During the disastrous religious wars
tardy in estab- which continued intermittently from 1562 to 1596
lishing colonies French commerce and industry were almost ruined.
French merchant vessels, for example, practically disappeared

THE SPANISH ARMADA

One of a series of ten engravings of the House of Lords' tapestry (now destroyed) commemorating the English victory

+ Fort nieuw Amsterdam op de Manhatans

NEW AMSTERDAM ABOUT 1630

From Hartzer's *Beschrijvingh van Virginia*

from the Atlantic, and with the exception of one or two attempts on the part of the Huguenots to make settlements in the New World, nothing was done to follow up the work of the Florentine, Verrazano, sent out by Francis I in 1524, or that of Cartier, who made his first voyage to America in 1534.

As soon as civil strife ceased, however, trade, both domestic and foreign, began to revive and French business men to manifest a renewed interest in overseas expansion. The French Henry IV and his great Huguenot minister, the Empire Duke of Sully, attempted to stimulate this interest by subsidizing a merchant marine, starting a navy, and encouraging the formation of powerful mercantile companies.   In 1603 Champlain, in the employ of one of these companies, sailed up the St. Lawrence to the rapids above Montreal and explored the Acadian coast as far as the Bay of Fundy.   Five years later, under the patronage of Henry IV, he laid the foundations of Quebec, destined to be the capital of New France and the center of French endeavor in America.   Under Richelieu, who virtually ruled France from 1624 to 1642, and Colbert, famous minister of Louis XIV, the French Empire in America was expanded to include all eastern Canada, the great central valley of North America, French Guiana, Haiti, and over a dozen of the Antilles, including Guadeloupe and Martinique.   In the Old World the French established trading posts on the African coast, laid claim to Madagascar, and gained a strong foothold in India, where they had thriving commercial centers at Surat, Chandernagore, and Pondicherry.

Two other continental states, Sweden and Denmark, also made settlements in America.   During the seventeenth century Sweden rose to the position of a first-class power Sweden and and, like her neighbors, desired to extend her Denmark commerce.   In 1638, after several futile attempts, a Swedish company established a trading post on the Delaware.   The venture, however, proved unsuccessful, and in 1655 New Sweden surrendered to the Dutch.   Outside of Greenland and Iceland, the Virgin Isles represented Denmark's only other important colonial possession.

As an empire builder, England, in comparison with her rivals, enjoyed certain distinct advantages. Ranking foremost among these was her insularity. The very presence of the English

England enjoys advantages as an empire builder

Channel protected her against the ravages of ambitious and warlike neighbors. In fact, no foreign invader seriously menaced English soil after 1066. Unlike France and Spain, she was not forced to maintain powerful armies to safeguard her boundaries against dangerous enemies. She, therefore, had no military caste to contend with. Even her old feudal aristocracy, which might well have formed the nucleus of such a caste, was decimated and weakened by the Wars of the Roses. On the other hand, her

1. Her insularity

insularity virtually compelled her to build a navy that was second to none. As sovereign of the seas she was able not only to protect the homeland but to seize and colonize distant lands and to incorporate them as part of her growing commercial and colonial empire.

Secondly, England's imperial fortunes were favored by certain inherent weaknesses which characterized the peoples of the

2. Inherent weaknesses of her competitors

Continent. Eastern Europe, still landlocked and the victim of ignorance and restricted outlook, was wasting its time in petty and useless warfare. Central Europe, where one day were to rise the national states of Germany, Austria, and Italy, was still in the feudal stage despite the existence of that heritage of earlier times — the Holy Roman Empire. Even England's neighbors across the Channel were cramped in their efforts to establish colonial empires. The Dutch, for example, though thrifty, enterprising, and farseeing, were handicapped by lack of numbers and by their too great insistence on trade instead of on actual settlement. France, though having colonizing leaders and a much larger population than England, wasted her time and her resources in interminable and futile dynastic wars on the Continent and in domestic religious strife. Portugal made a gallant start in the field of colonial enterprise, but she had neither the resources nor the power to compete successfully with Britain. . And Spain, clerical and feudalistic in spirit, and administratively and financially mismanaged, early headed, as we have already observed, straight for disaster. Finally, in this connection we should not overlook the fact that English statesmen early learned how, by means of the so-called balance-of-power system, to play their continental rivals against each other, thus protecting in no small degree both England and her expanding empire.

No less important to England from the point of view of empire building than her position of insularity and the weakness of her rivals, was the advantage of having a rapidly increasing middle class — small landholders, merchants, manufacturers, money lenders, and shopkeepers. **3. An increasing middle class** This class, which even under the early Tudors began to displace the old feudal nobility in the councils of the state, increased greatly in wealth, numbers, and power during the sixteenth and seventeenth centuries. Interested primarily in profits which would enable them to better their standard of living, even to the point of having all those comforts enjoyed by the titled aristocracy, its members were from the first ardent advocates of overseas expansion. Indeed, in their opinion, no other venture afforded greater opportunity for the acquisition of money than did commerce, especially beyond the seas. It was this class, as we shall presently see, which furnished most of the leaders and managers, nearly all the capital, and many of the pioneers for the founding of England's overseas domains.

That England, more than any other European country, had by the opening of the seventeenth century a flourishing middle class which was ready and anxious to embark on **4. Absence of feudalism and serfdom** the enterprise of colonization was due in no small measure to the fact that she had rid herself of feudalism. We have noted how the backbone of the old feudal order had been broken by the Wars of the Roses. Under the absolutist régime of the Tudors the feudal aristocracy, both lay and ecclesiastical, was further subjugated. The destruction of the old order paved the way for the new, until gradually feudal ideals and feudal economy gave way to a régime that was more or less distinctly bourgeois. Accompanying this transformation was the disappearance of serfdom and the subsequent change in English rural economy. With the increase in woolen manufactures in the sixteenth century and the consequent demand for raw material, the old system of tillage gradually gave way to sheep-raising. Greedy landlords motivated more by profits than by humanitarian interests, first by judicial action and later by parliamentary legislation, extinguished the ancient rights of the peasants, thus permitting the landlords to enclose great areas of the common lands. Under these Enclosure Acts, hundreds of thousands of acres were turned into pastures, the dispossessed tenants furnishing England with a ready supply of prospective New World migrants.

Finally, by the opening of the seventeenth century England was intellectually ahead of her continental rivals with the **5. Intellectual** exception of Holland. Politically, as we shall **progress** presently note in more detail, she had abandoned in 1688 absolute for limited monarchy, dominated by the middle class rather than by feudal lords. Freedom of speech and of the press, as yet almost unheard of in Spain and France, prevailed. Profound religious changes also occurred. While a state church yet obtained, there was no such conformity as existed on the Continent, and religious restrictions on the free use of capital had become obsolete. "The printing press, the revival of pagan literature, the multiplication of books on travel, commerce, and economy, the translation of the Bible into English so that the multitude could read it and dispute over matters of interpretation, and the corroding insinuations of business and natural science produced," as Professor Beard well says, "a luxuriant variety of religious sectarianism." In comparison with their continental neighbors, Englishmen were more free to give vent to their intellectual interests. Indeed, it was not until the French Revolution that the laity of the Continent began to emancipate itself from the overwhelming control of monarch, aristocracy, and clergy. And even then the emancipation was confined chiefly to the western fringe of Europe.

Yet notwithstanding these advantages, England did practically nothing in the way of exploration and colonization for **England's** half a century after the Cabot voyages. During **tardy interest** this period she was too poor and too much absorbed **after Cabot** in domestic affairs to engage in either overseas **voyages** trade or colonial experiments. Moreover, she was, as we have already seen, debarred from any part of the newly discovered world by the papal bull of demarcation. But, thanks to hardy fishermen who with increasing frequency visited the banks of Newfoundland and to the increasing rumors about the unexplored wealth of the New World, interest in America was kept alive. And with the accession of Elizabeth to the throne and the ensuing contest with Spain, this interest grew apace. In fact, by the close of the sixteenth century expansion and colonization were uppermost in the minds of many Englishmen.

Several factors account for this changed state of affairs. In the first place, the struggle with Spain, as we have just noted, focused attention on America. Many leading Englishmen, even before the destruction of the Armada, expressed the opinion that by planting colonies in America, England would be strengthened and Spain correspondingly weakened. Thus in 1583 Sir George Peckham, after calling attention to the enormous wealth that Spain derived from the New World, declared that it was time for his countrymen to awaken "out of that drowsie dreame wherein we have so long slumbered" and to set about colonizing America. The following year Hakluyt, another leading spirit who favored colonization, in his *Discourse on Western Plantinge*, written for the enlightenment of Elizabeth, urged the government to establish between Florida and Cape Breton posts from which attacks could be made on Philip's fleets to the end of weakening his grip on America. Sir Walter Raleigh was especially outspoken "against the ambitious and bloody pretences of the Spaniards who, seeking to devour all nations, shall be themselves devoured."

Motives for English expansion

1. Desire to weaken Spain

Closely related to this desire to weaken Spain was the factor of nationalism and national prestige. The England of the sixteenth century was a very different England from that of the fourteenth or even fifteenth century. Feudal decentralization and feudal economy had given way to unification and nationhood. The spiritual overlordship from the outside had been broken by the Reformation. An insular patriotism had developed. Many Englishmen argued that increased area and population would not only strengthen England by adding to her resources, but

2. New national spirit and national prestige

would enhance her prestige and standing. It was on this ground, for instance, that Sir Ferdinando Gorges advocated expansion. "Nothinge," said he, "adds more glorie and greatness to anie nation, than the enlargement of theire territories, the multiplyinge of theire subjects."

The desire to get rich quickly, the ardent hope of every adventurer in every age, was another motive for colonization. **3. Desire for quick riches** The achievements of the great seamen, so admirably depicted by Hakluyt in his famous *Voyages*, stirred the English in much the same way as generations before the adventures of Marco Polo and the other Asiatic travelers had roused the curiosity of Europe in regard to the East. The stories of profits ranging from one hundred to four hundred per cent likewise whetted the appetite for riches. In the year 1622, for example, a consignment of goods purchased for £386,000 in India sold in England for £1,915,000. The literature of the day painted America as a land of gold and silver. Englishmen, it was believed, could find mountains of precious metals just as the Spanish had found riches in Mexico and Peru. It was this fanciful idea in part that enabled those adventurous Elizabethan gentlemen, Gilbert and Raleigh, to undertake their experiments in America. It was the same idea that enticed the first Englishmen to Virginia, "where gold and silver is more plentiful than copper is with us," — so plentiful indeed that the prisoners' fetters were reported to be made of fine gold. Even as late as 1760 Thomas Jeffreys incorporated the following item on the Far Northwest in his standard atlas of America: "Hereabouts are supposed to be the Mountains of Bright Stones mentioned in the Map of Ye Indian Ochagach." All of the earlier American colonial charters were granted on the assumption that gold and silver would be found, and each contained a clause reserving a fixed amount, usually one-fifth, to the monarch.

A fourth factor which interested a considerable number of people in colonization was the desire to see the natives of the **4. Missionary spirit** New World Christianized. English Protestants especially were stirred by the fact that "Spanish Papists" were winning the red man to God, and felt that it was their duty for the sake of the true faith to "instill into the purged

THE

THIRD AND LAST
VOLVME OF THE VOY-
AGES, NAVIGATIONS, TRAF-

fiques, and Difcoueries of the *English Nation*, and in
fome few places, where they haue not been, of ftrangers, performed within and before the time of thefe hundred yeeres, to all
parts of the *Newfound* world of *America*, or the *Weft Indies*, from 73.
degrees of Northerly to 57 of Southerly latitude:

As namely to *Engronland*, *Meta Incognita*, *Eftotiland*,
Tierra de Labrador, *Newfoundland*, vp *The grand bay*, the gulfe of *S. Lau-*
rence, and the Riuer of *Canada* to *Hochelaga* and *Saguenay*, along the coaft of *Aram-*
bec, to the fhores and maines of *Virginia* and *Florida*, and on the Weft or backfide of them
both, to the rich and pleafant countries of *Nuena Bifcaya*, *Cibola*, *Tignex*, *Cicuit*,
Quinira, to the 15. prouinces of the kingdome of *New-Mexico*, to the
bottome of the gulfe of *California*, and vp the
Riuer of *Buena Guia:*

And likewife to all the yles both fmall and great lying before the
cape of *Florida*, *The bay* of *Mexico*, and *Tierra firma*, to the coafts and Inlands
or *Newe Spaine*, *Tierra firma*, and *Guiana*, vp the mighty Riuers of *Orenoque*,
Diffekebe, and *Marannon*, to euery part of the coaft of *Brafil*, to the Riuer of *Plate*,
through the Streights of *Magellan* forward and backward, and to the
South of the faid Streights as farre as 57 degrees:

And from thence on the backfide of *America*, along the coaftes, harbours,
and capes of *Chili*, *Peru*, *Nicaragua*, *Nuena Efpanna*, *Nuena Galicia*, *Culiacan*,
California, *Nona Albion*, and more Northerly as farre as 43 degrees:

Together with the two renowmed, and profperous voyages of Sir *Francis Drake*
and M. *Thomas Candifh* round about the circumference of the whole earth, and
diuers other voyages intended and fet forth for that courfe.

Collected by RICHARD HAKLVYT *Preacher*, *and fometimes*
ftudent of Chrift-Church in Oxford.

¶ Imprinted at London by *George Bifhop* *Ralfe*
Newberie and ROBERT BARKER
ANNO DOM. 1600

TITLE PAGE OF "THIRD AND LAST VOLUME OF THE
VOYAGES"

35

myndes" of the heathen "the swete and lovely liquor of the Gospell." One Protestant writer even went so far as practically to declare that the spread of the Gospel was "the white man's burden." Supporters of earlier colonizing companies frankly asserted from time to time that the spread of Christianity was one of their chief aims. "The Kingdom of God will be enlarged," said one, "and the tidings of his truth will be proclaimed among so many millions of saveage men and women who now live in darkness in those regions." Even Captain John Smith declared that "gaining provinces addeth to the King's crown; but the reducing Heathen people to civilite and true Religion, bringeth honour to the King of Heaven." Nearly all the colonial charters, we should also note, specifically mentioned the spread of Christianity as one of the objects of settlement.

While increased money supply, expanding trade, the introduction of the wage system, and the multiplication of enclosures, Economic   noted above, made for progress, they also made and social   for social inequality. Measured by present-day inequality   standards, England in 1600 was wealthier than in 1500, but this wealth was very unevenly distributed, being almost entirely concentrated in the hands of the upper and middle classes. With the influx of precious metals prices shot upwards and the cost of living increased many fold. Beef, for instance, rose from one cent a pound in 1548 to four in 1588; pork and mutton more than doubled in price during the same period; and the cost of other food products and of clothing rose accordingly. People of moderate means with approximately fixed incomes were forced to economize in order to make ends meet. Worse yet, the wages of workingmen either did not increase or at best trailed the rising commodity prices, and thousands were reduced to beggary and vagabondage; jails were filled to overflowing and crime increased.

Contemporary authorities erroneously attributed this economic distress and its resultant social evils to overpopulation; 5. Notion that   and, as a remedy, suggested colonization. Among England was   those who urged this solution was Sir Humphrey overpopulated   Gilbert, who in 1576 pointed out that, "We might inhabite some part of these countryes, and settle there such needy people of our country, which now trouble the common-wealth, and through want here at home are enforced to commit outrageous offences whereby they are dayly consumed with the gallowes." Christopher Carleill, another staunch advocate of colonization, agreed with Gilbert, and in 1583 asserted that emigration would be a boon to "our poore sort of people, which are very many amongst us, living altogether unprofitable and often times to the great disquiet of the better sort." Hakluyt, as might be expected, entertained the same view. "These pety theves," said he, "mighte be condemned for certain yeres in the western partes." In a pamphlet entitled *Nova Britannia*, published in 1609, the author, after stating that two things — money and people — were necessary for successful colonization, declared that England had "swarmes of idle persons, which havving no meanes of labour to relieeve their misery, doe like-wise swarme in lewd and naughtie practises." It would be most profitable for England, he went on to say, "to rid our multitudes of such as lie at home, pestering the land with pestilence and penury, and infecting one another with vice and villianie worse than the plague it selfe." Still another pamphlet declared there was nothing "more dangerous for the estate of commonwealths than when the people do increase to a greater multitude and number than may justly parallel with the large-ness of the place and Countrey: for hereupon comes oppression, and diverse kindes of wrongs, mutinies, sedition, commotion and rebellion, scarcitie, dearth, povertie, and sundrie sorts of calamities, which either breed the conversion, or eversion, of cities and commonwealths." It is unnecessary for us to add further evidence. England with a population of approximately five million was not overpopulated; unequal distribution of wealth with its attendant economic and social evils created the illusion and furnished both motive and material for colonization.

This hopeless welter of selfishness, extravagance, injustice, and misery was, in the opinion of many thinkers, the fruit of the old order. The learning of the Renaissance and the 6. Desire to overseas discoveries had broadened the mental and establish ideal physical horizon of these thinkers. In the New commonwealth World they beheld a heaven wherein might dwell righteousness.

Here mankind would have plenty of space and would be secure from all the dark vistas of the past: war, hunger, cruelty, and vice. They were, therefore, staunch expansionists. Foremost among them was Sir Thomas More, who in his *Utopia* vigorously protested against the greed, injustice, and misery of the social order of his day. In the wilderness of the New World he would have man start afresh. Reasonable pleasure, both of mind and body, were to be the chief aims of his transoceanic community.

Of all the influences which inspired Old World expansion, and particularly English expansion, none was more important than **7. Desire for self-sufficing national state** the desire of the centralized national state to be economically self-sufficing and, in consequence, politically independent. According to the so-called mercantilist theory, which had come to be almost universally accepted by the close of the sixteenth century, this desire could be realized if the nation possessed a large and permanent stock of gold and silver. It was common belief that these commodities, always in demand and always acceptable in payment for services or goods, represented the wealth of a country. It was also commonly believed that the nation's strength and prosperity depended absolutely upon the amount of specie at its command. Thus Englishmen had observed, as we have already noted, that Spain was powerful and apparently prosperous as long as gold and silver flowed into her coffers from the New World. Moreover, an adequate supply of gold and silver was necessary for national defense at a time when international struggles were becoming more frequent and when credit as yet was relatively undeveloped.

Inasmuch as England did not possess rich deposits of precious metals, she was obliged either to seek possession of mines outside **Sources of specie** of Europe, or else build up her stock of gold and silver by means of privateering and favorable trade balances. Recourse was had to both means, but the imaginary picture of America as a treasure house of gold, silver, and precious stones gradually vanished, and statesmen, therefore, came more and more to depend upon commerce as a source of specie supply.

The cardinal feature of the mercantilist doctrine was ad-

mirably expressed by two seventeenth-century English writers.
The first of these, Misselden, in his *Circle of Commerce*, published in 1623, wrote as follows: "If the native com- Doctrine of
modities exported doe waigh downe and excede in mercantilism
value the forraine commodities imported, it is a rule that never
faile's, that then the Kingdom growe's rich and prosper's in
estate and stocke, because the overplus thereof must needs
come in, in treasure." The other, Thomas Mun, in a pamphlet
entitled *England's Treasure by Forraign Trade*, published in
1664, declared that "the means to increase our wealth and
treasure is by Forraign Trade, wherein wee must ever observe
this rule, to sell more to strangers yearly than wee consume of
theirs in value." In other words, the value of a country's
exports should always exceed that of her imports, and this
difference or balance of trade would be paid in money or in
additional goods. Suggestions made by the mercantilists for
fostering a favorable balance of trade were many. In general,
however, they advocated (1) a large population, that there
might be abundant labor and consumers; (2) the promotion of
trade and circulation of money within the state for the purpose
of ensuring prosperity; (3) the encouragement of home manufactures and the exportation of home-manufactured articles;
(4) the prohibition of foreign manufactures by the imposition
of high customs duties; (5) the granting of government subsidies or bonuses to infant manufactures; (6) the negotiation
of treaties favorable to the middle or commercial class; (7) the
establishment of colonies for markets and sources of raw materials; and (8) the fostering of the fishing and shipping industries
as valuable auxiliaries of trade and naval strength.[1]

At the time of Elizabeth and the first Stuarts it was not easy
for England to apply the mercantilist theory. On account of the
lack of many natural resources she had long been England's de-
compelled to import certain essential commodities pendence on
from foreign countries. Thus from the Baltic tries for staple
States, Sweden, Russia, Poland, and the Germanies commodities
came naval stores for her shipping, and potash so necessary for

[1] The doctrine of mercantilism as applied to Great Britain's colonies is
discussed in Chapter IV.

her basic industry, the manufacture of woolens. From Southern Europe came salt, sugar, and dried fruits, and the luxuries, wine and silk. Portuguese and afterward Dutch traders supplied English merchants with dyes, saltpeter, and spices from the Far East at greatly increased prices. And two-thirds of the fish, which the English consumed in considerable quantities, were purchased from foreigners, principally from the thrifty Dutch, who were firmly entrenched in this particular industry.

Not only was England dependent on her rivals for staple necessities, but the problem of finding adequate markets abroad **The problem** for her own commodities, now increasing in both **of markets** variety and volume, was becoming more difficult. Trade with Catholic Spain was extremely precarious, and the Spanish habitually confiscated English vessels that dared carry on intercourse with the Barbary States, on the ground that they brought "armour, munition, and forbidden merchandise to strengthen the infidells against these partes of Christendome." Venice opposed English commercial activities in the eastern Mediterranean; Denmark imposed onerous charges on English merchantmen passing through the sound or Danish straits; and France excluded English goods by tariffs and other arbitrary taxes. Prolonged civil strife had virtually ruined the Flanders market for English wool, and English traders in Russia no longer enjoyed exemption from customs duties. Even the privileges which English merchants had long been accustomed to in the German towns were being withdrawn in retaliation for the exclusion of the Hanse merchants from the advantages of the Steelyard in London. To make matters worse, English goods on every hand were facing competition.

To statesmen and business men there seemed to be only one remedy for both of these pressing problems, namely, commercial **Expansion for** and colonial expansion. By direct intercourse with **raw materials** India the products of the Orient might be procured **and markets** independently of the Dutch and at less cost, and new markets opened up for English goods. Similarly it was thought that colonies in America would be both a source of supply and a market for English products. No longer, they reasoned, would England be dependent on the Dutch for fish, or on the Baltic States for the all-important naval supplies, or on European markets for the sale of manufactures. Her trade henceforth would in large measure be diverted from foreign into national channels, thus she would become not only economically self-sufficient, but prosperous and strong. "Our monies and wares," wrote an advocate of colonization in 1606, "that nowe run into the hands of our adversaries or could frendes shall pass into our frendes and naturall Kinsmen and from them likewise we shall receive such things as shall be most available to our necessities, which intercourse of trade maye rather be called a home bread trafique than a forraign exchange."

Such were the motives that interested Englishmen in expansion and that led many of them to engage in colonial enterprise. Before the sixteenth century had passed ambitious gentlemen adventurers like Gilbert and Raleigh, dreaming of personal glory and wealth and a greater England beyond the seas composed of extensive feudal or proprietary estates, had made their ill-starred efforts to plant colonies in the New World. Though they failed, they inspired others; less than a century later the foundation of the British Empire was securely laid, colonies having been founded in Virginia, Maryland, New England, the Bermudas, the Bahamas, Guiana, and the lesser Antilles, and trading posts having been established along the African coast and in India. Before 1750 it had expanded to include all the territory on the Atlantic seaboard from Florida north to the Bay of Fundy, Nova Scotia, Newfoundland, the Hudson Bay region, Belize, the Mosquito Coast of Central America, Jamaica, and the lower valley of the Ganges.

The beginning of the British Empire

5. The Migration to English Colonial America

Of all the empires established in America by the countries of Western Europe that of England was to have by the middle of the eighteenth century by far the largest population. In peopling the English colonies, especially during their early years, two agencies — the chartered trading company and the proprietor — played a leading rôle.

Agencies of colonization

The trading companies which were charted by their respective governments were in reality commercial or semi-commercial corporations, modeled in part after the celebrated merchant adventurers of an earlier day. In addition to rich merchants, their membership included noblemen of high rank, gentlemen, and government officials. Thus the London Company, famed for planting the first successful English colony in America, was composed of 659 persons, including 21 peers, 96 knights, 58 gentlemen, 110 merchants, and 282 citizens. Like corporate shareholders of today, each shared in the profits of the company according to his stock subscription. Not unlike the state, the company enjoyed a greater or lesser degree of complete sovereignty in the region specified in its charter. Moreover it was continuous, elected its own officers, made its own by-laws, raised and coined money, regulated trade, disposed of corporate property, and provided for defense. On the other hand, it was by no means completely independent of its creator. It looked to the home government for many rights and privileges and constantly relied on it for protection. In return the company was expected to strengthen the nation by opening up new channels of commerce, maintaining a favorable balance of trade, supplying material for the navy, and weakening commercial and political rivals.

1. The chartered trading company

More than half a hundred of these companies were chartered by England, France, Holland, Sweden, and Denmark before 1700. By 1588 England alone had chartered six: the Muscovy, Cathay, Baltic, Turkish, Moroccan and African; and in 1600 the famous English East India Company was officially born. Many members of one company were often members of another company; 116 members of the Virginia Company, for example, were members of the East India, 13 of the Muscovy, 46 of the Bermuda, and 38 of the New England companies.

Their number

It is not our purpose to follow the history of these chartered companies.[1] As colonizing agents they furnished the money

[1] For a list of these companies, as well as an excellent discussion of their importance, see E. P. Cheyney, *European Background of American History*, chapters vii–viii.

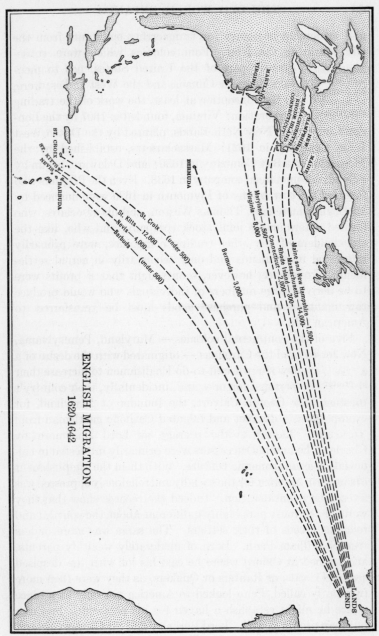

ENGLISH MIGRATION
1620-1642

VIRGINIA

MARYLAND

NEW HAMPSHIRE
RHODE ISLAND
CONNECTICUT

MAINE

MASSACHUSETTS

St. Croix — (under 500)

St. Kitts — 12,000

Nevis — 4,000

Barbuda — (under 500)

Bermuda — 3,000

Virginia — 8,000

Maryland — 1,500

Connecticut — 2,000

Rhode Island — 300

Massachusetts — 14,000

Maine and New Hampshire — 1,500

ST. CROIX

ST. KITTS
NEVIS

BARBUDA

BERMUDA

LANDS
END

43

and leadership necessary for transferring emigrants from the Old World to the New.   Four colonies which were subse-

English colo-
nies in Amer-
ica founded
by trading
companies

quently part of the United States, not to men-tion those in Canada and the West Indies, were, in their inception at least, the work of the trading corporation: Virginia, founded in 1607 by the London Company; New Netherlands, planted by the Dutch West India Company in 1621; Massachusetts, established by the Massachusetts Bay Company in 1630; and Delaware, begun by a Swedish commercial company in 1638.   Even the Pilgrims who founded the tiny colony of Plymouth in 1620 were financed by an English merchant, Thomas Weston, and his associates, who formed a terminable joint stock company, and who, like the stockholders of the other trading companies, were primarily interested in dividends and only secondarily in actual settlement.   Experience, however, soon taught that if profits were to be derived large numbers of individuals who would produce raw materials and purchase goods must be transferred to American soil.

Five of the continental colonies — Maryland, Pennsylvania, New Jersey, and the Carolinas — originated with the desire of a

2. The
proprietor

few shrewd well-to-do Englishmen to increase their personal fortunes and, incidentally, their country's prestige.   Sir George Calvert, the founder of Maryland, for example, was a discreet and talented Catholic gentleman from Yorkshire.   Raised to the peerage as Lord Baltimore by Charles I, he and his successors were primarily interested in colonization as an economic venture.   With them the establishment of a home in America for the socially and religiously oppressed was a secondary consideration.   Indeed the records show that they were for the most part highly indifferent about the political and religious creeds of their settlers.   The same was more or less true of William Penn.   Born of moderately wealthly parents, and trained at Oxford where he cast his lot with the despised sect of Friends, or Ranters or Quakers, as they were then more frequently called, Penn looked to America not only as a place where he might establish a haven for his persecuted brethren but reap profits as well.   Lord Berkeley and Sir George Carteret launched the project that led to the founding of New Jersey because they thought it promised a fortune in land speculation. Even those favorites of Charles II, who received the vast ocean-to-ocean tract known as Carolina, dreamed of immense profits from colonization as well as of contributing to the ideal of imperial self-sufficiency.

Like the trading corporations, these proprietors were free to establish whatever institutions they pleased as long as they were not in conflict with the laws and government of England. Like the trading corporations, too, they supplied the capital for establishing their overseas domains. These proprietors expected to derive their profits from the rent or sale of land, quitrents, tariffs, and a share in whatever mines might be discovered. The Penns and the Calverts, as well as less known proprietors, induced as many people as they could to settle in their "plantation" in much the same way as modern boards of trade or chambers of commerce boom their towns or cities in order, among other things, to obtain purchasers for real estate in which they, or at least some of their members, are financially interested. The following excerpt from one of Penn's Old World advertisements — for the Penns and the Calverts and the other proprietors were ingenious advertisers for settlers — does not differ materially in its psychological appeal from the advertisement of a modern real estate man: "The Richness of the Air, the navigable Rivers, and thus the prodigious Increase of Corn, the flourishing conditions of the City of Philadelphia make it [the colony] the most glorious Place . . . Poor People, both men and women, can here get three times the wages for their Labor they can in *England or Wales*."

Proprietors' interest in colonization chiefly economic

With the exception of the Penns and the Calverts all the proprietors eventually relinquished their claims, and the proprietary colonies, like the colonies founded by the commercial companies, became royal provinces. As Professor Schlesinger observes: "This trend was conditioned, in large degree, by the desire of both the English government and the colonials to participate in the vested interests possessed by the original promoters and enterprisers."

Neither commercial company nor proprietor experienced great difficulty in finding settlers for their overseas domains, for the social, economic, religious, and political conditions in Europe during the seventeenth and eighteenth centuries were such that thousands were anxious to migrate to the New World.

Causes for the first great English migration to America

We have already seen how the rapid influx of specie following the discovery of the New World affected adversely the lower classes of Europe. In England, particularly in the eastern and southeastern counties, the situation was aggravated by the great economic alteration occasioned by the enclosure movement, the alteration in the value of money, and the devastating European wars which deprived England of her cloth markets. In these counties laborers were often unable to make a bare living. The monasteries, long a haven of relief for the poor, had been destroyed. The towns and countryside swarmed with those unable to secure a livelihood, and the jails and almshouses were filled to overflowing with beggars and those who had resorted to petty thievery to gain a subsistence. Indeed, so bad were conditions during the first half of the seventeenth century that parish and village authorities frequently found it necessary to double the poor relief. "Our country," wrote Sir William Pelham, "was never in that wante that now itt is, . . . for theare are many thousands in thease parts whoo have soulde all thay have even to theyr bedd straw, and cann not get worke to earne any munny. Doggs flesh is a dainty dish. . . ."

1. Social and economic

Among poorer classes

Under such conditions it was only natural that these unfortunate unemployed regarded America as a refuge and were quick to heed the inducements offered by projectors of colonies, whether proprietors or trading companies. Often the government authorities compelled the more timid to migrate by authorizing colonial agents and patentees of land to seize for their uses men and women of the lower classes, especially paupers and prisoners. An English commission in 1633, for example, was appointed "to reprieve able-bodied persons convicted of certain felonies, and to bestow them to be used in discoveries and other foreign employments."

Even the gentry which gave England its Cromwells, Hampdens, and Pyms felt the pinch of hard times, and many of them were reduced to straitened circumstances in their Among the effort to "keep up" with the standards of enter- gentry prising traders or *nouveaux riches* who were already acquiring country estates. John Winthrop, a country squire of Suffolk, a man of modest estate and one of the famous leaders of the migration to America, complained that his "meanes heer are soe shortened as he shall not be able to continue in that place and imployment where he now iss . . ."; the standard and cost of living had so increased that "noe mans estate will suffice to keepe saile with his aequalls." Winthrop shared the current opinion that England was overpopulated. "This land grows weary of her inhabitants, soe as man iss heer of less price amongst us than a horse or sheep. All towns complain of the burthen of their poore though we have taken up many unnecessary, yea unlawful trades to maintain them. Children, servants, and neighbors (especially if they be poore) are considered the greatest burthen. We stand heer striving for places of habitation (many men spending as much labour and cost to recover or keep sometimes an acre or two of lande as would procure them many hundred as good or better in another country) and in ye mean tyme suffer a whole continent as fruitful and convenient for the use of man to lie waste without any improvement." Just as business men of the day thought of America as a place for making "twenty per cent" on their investment, so those who suffered from the social and economic maladjustment of the time thought of it as a place where they might acquire landed property and better their condition.

While the social-economic factor was undoubtedly the principal and most enduring cause for the migration of the majority of those who left the Old World for America, it was by no means the only one. Closely associated and 2. Religious often intertwined with it was the more or less constant religious incentive. With the dissolution of the feudal order, the rise of new economic classes, and the growth of nationalism and individualism, the religious unity characteristic of medieval Europe disappeared; in many western and central countries the universal church gave way to state churches. Thus by the time of Elizabeth the Anglican church had definitely become the established church of England, Lutheranism had been adopted by Sweden and many of the German states, and state churches based on Calvinistic theology had been organized in both Scotland and Holland. Many small religious sects like the Anabaptists, Moravian Brethren, Pietists, Seven Day Baptists, Dunkers, and Quakers also sprang up. Unfortunately disruption of the old religious unity was not accomplished peacefully. The printing press, revived interest in the study of pagan literature, the translation of the Bible into the several national languages, and the growing emphasis of business men and scholars upon things of this world rather than on other-worldliness, not only tended to disrupt the medieval church but to introduce a veritable flood of religious controversy and ill-will. In fact, from the day that Luther began his revolt against the Catholic church early in the sixteenth century down past the close of the seventeenth century, Europe was the scene of religious turmoil and religious persecution which, directly or indirectly, led to the migration of thousands to the New World.

In England the religious disturbances centered around the Anglican church. With the exception of the change in headship and the confiscation of ecclesiastical property, little **Church of England and dissident groups** alteration was made in the established church under Henry VIII. Before Elizabeth's reign was at an end, however, many changes were made in both administration and discipline which were unacceptable to two religious groups, namely, irreconcilable Catholics and radical Protestants. The former felt that the Anglican church had advanced too far in the direction of Protestantism and was too much tinged with leveling evangelicalism, while the latter, composed for the most part of well-to-do townsmen and lesser gentry, and strongly impregnated with Calvinistic ideas, considered that the English church still leaned too much toward Rome and the doctrines and practices of the medieval church. From the standpoint of mere numbers each group represented only a small minority of both clergy and laity.

From the day when Henry VIII definitely broke with Rome, the Catholics occupied a most precarious position. Enjoying a brief respite from persecution and martyrdom dur- **The Catholics** ing the reign of Queen Mary, they again became a proscribed body under Elizabeth. At the beginning of Elizabeth's reign laws were enacted to the effect that no Catholic (1) could hold any office or employment under the crown or any ecclesiastical office or receive a university degree; (2) attend Mass; (3) speak, write, or circulate any arguments or appeals in favor of the ecclesiastical claims of the Catholic church or in derogation of the royal supremacy or of the English prayer book. Moreover, every Catholic was required by law to attend the regular services of the established church and to help support the same. Penalties for violation of these laws varied all the way from fines to execution for treason, depending on the nature of the offense. Before the opening of the seventeenth century these legal restraints were supplemented with even more rigid legislation: Catholics who refused to take the oath of supremacy or who by word or speech supported the claims of the papacy were subject to the punishment of outlawry and confiscation for the first offense and to the penalties of treason for the second. After 1568, the date when Mary, Queen of Scots, set foot on English soil, the anti-Catholic code became even more severe; and by 1603, when James I came to the English throne, the lot of the English Catholics was, legally at least, a most unhappy one.

By 1600, many of the Catholic leaders, though keenly disappointed with the course of events, fortunately had the good sense to realize that Catholicism could not be re- **Their interest** established in England on a national basis and that **in America** the most they could ever hope for was toleration. But even toleration was denied. True, James I ordered the suspension of the anti-Catholic laws at the time when his son, Charles I, was seeking a Spanish bride, and in 1622 imprisoned Catholics were released on bail or freed completely from persecution. But when the Spanish marriage scheme failed to materialize the lid was clamped down more tightly than ever. Even Charles I's marriage with Henrietta Marie of France did not entirely serve to lift the ban against the followers of Rome, and it was not until the Restoration in 1660 that they really gained partial toleration. Meanwhile, some Catholic leaders turned to America as a home for their persecuted brethren. The number of English Catholics in America during the colonial period, however, was small, the great majority preferring the risk of persecution to migration. Several reasons account for this fact. In the first place, there is much evidence that the anti-Catholic laws were not strictly enforced; secondly, the Catholics were always in hope that the situation might change for the better. Certainly the accession of the Stuarts and the powerful interposition of Spain and France gave them cause to expect the dawn of a better day. Thirdly, the intolerance in America made them hesitate. And, finally, and in some respects most important of all, many of them were of the nobility and higher gentry and, therefore, not of the classes from which the overwhelming proportion of colonists were drawn.

The radical Protestants, or Puritans as they are usually called, were scrupulous individualists who desired to carry the Reformation to its logical conclusion. As Calvinists they believed in the absolutely unconditioned will of God as expressed in the Bible; every detail of their lives — even their clothes, the names they bore, and their most ordinary social usages — was regulated according to the Scriptures. It followed then that faith in God's will, rather than good works and compliance with a medieval ecclesiastical system, was the way to salvation. In accordance with the doctrine of predestination they regarded themselves as God's elect, foreordained to be saved by "his gratuitous mercy, totally irrespective of human merit," and all others as condemned by the Almighty to eternal torment "by a just and irreprehensible but incomprehensible judgment."

The Puritans

While differing among themselves on certain points, they were in general agreement that the Catholic church was utterly corrupt, unspeakably immoral, and an agency of the devil. All, moreover, were dissatisfied with Anglicanism, which they quite rightly held to be merely a compromise between Romanism and thorough-going Protestantism. They believed in simple forms of worship; elaborate

Opposition to High Church practices

ceremonials had no place in the Biblical Christianity which they so ardently professed. Such practices as making the sign of the cross, the celebration of saints' days, and kneeling to receive communion they regarded as likely to breed superstition. They also believed that the organization of the established church should be simplified; the power exercised by bishops and arch-bishops was, they declared, "unlawful and expressly forbidden by the Word of God," and their offices "anti-Christian and devilish and contrary to the Scriptures." Some favored limiting the power of the higher clergy, but the majority wished to abolish the episcopal organization altogether and to reorganize the church on Presbyterian lines. Lastly, the Puritans freely critcisied the lax standards of their time; prevailing immorali-ties and extravagances were bitterly attacked; many innocent and indeed beneficial enjoyments were condemned as sinful. Their virtues were mainly negations — "Thou shalt nots" of the Old Testament — as their Sabbath Day observance clearly indicated.

A Puritan minority, composed largely of humble, untutored farmers, laborers, and artisans, and known as Independents or Separatists, did not agree with the majority of The their English Calvinistic brethren in their concep- Independents tion of the church. The majority believed in the ideal of a single united national church and had no intention at first of destroying or withdrawing from the Anglican fold. Their primary aim was to gain control of the national church and then to transform it in accordance with their views. Separatist leaders like Robert Browne and John Greenwood — not to mention John Robinson, William Brewster, and William Brad-ford of Pilgrim fame — were convinced not only that the estab-lished church could not be purified but that the very idea of a national church closely united with the state was wrong. The spiritual and temporal commonwealths, they maintained, should be absolutely separate, and the church should be or-ganized on the basis of independent congregations, each with power to chose its ministers and other church officials. Unlike the majority of the Puritans, the Separatists were not particu-larly aggressive, and were tolerant even in matters religious.

Both Elizabeth and the early Stuarts attempted by means of repressive measures to make both Separatists and Puritans conform to the established church.   During Eliza-

Radical English Protestants persecuted

beth's reign two of the Separatist leaders, Barrow and Greenwood, were hanged.   Separatist teachers were silenced and imprisoned, and Separatist congregations were broken up and their property confiscated.   Indeed, before the opening of the seventeenth century only a remnant of the sect remained, its members having died or fled from the country.   In the eyes of the bishop of London they were at best religious outlaws instructed by "cobblers, tailors, feltmakers, and such-like trash."   From the standpoint

1. The Separatists

of colonization the little band of Scrooby Separatists who migrated to Holland in 1608, and who twelve years later landed on the bleak shores of New England, were destined to be somewhat less important in settling that region than their more influential radical brethren, the Puritans.

The Puritans were no more fortunate than the Separatists in escaping persecution.   At the Hampton Court Conference in

2. The Puritans

1604 James I arrogantly asserted that he would make the Radicals conform or harry them out of the land, "or else do worse."   Under Charles I, who, if anything, was more autocratic, less sympathetic, and more intolerant than his father, conditions became worse.   The suspension of the laws against Catholics, to which we have already alluded, filled the Radicals with alarm.   Matters came to a head when in 1629 Charles dissolved Parliament and, among other things, set himself through his ministers, Laud and Wentworth, to the task of destroying Puritanism in all its forms.   Harsh laws were enacted and harsher decrees promulgated.   Tireless Anglican bishops gave the nonconformists no rest, and their status became well-nigh hopeless.   As persecution grew apace thousands of Puritans, having lost all hope of ever securing control of the established church, turned to America as the only avenue of escape.   Unlike the Separatists, they belonged for the most part to the middle strata.   A few were noblemen possessing landed estates; some were merchants of considerable wealth; others were professional men and university graduates.

But by far the greater number were landed gentry and yeoman farmers — the backbone of English society.

With the overthrow of Charles I and the establishment of the Commonwealth the tide turned. The Puritans now in the saddle resolved to impose their orthodoxy on all classes of the English people. As early as 1641 orders were issued for the demolition of all images, altars, and crucifixes. Two years later the Solemn League and Covenant pledged Parliament and the Puritan leaders to extirpate "church government by archbishops, bishops, their chancellors and commissaries, deans and chapters, archdeacons, and all other ecclesiastical officers depending on that hierarchy," and to "reform religion in England" in doctrine, worship, discipline, and government according to the Word of God and "the example of the best reformed churches." Although the Commonwealth guaranteed toleration for every form of Christian belief "provided this liberty be not extended to popery or prelacy," both the Anglicans and Catholics as well as lesser religious sects were under a cloud. From 1640 to 1660, therefore, the very classes who had persecuted the Puritans found themselves persecuted. And it was this persecution plus the turmoil and ill-fortune of civil war that in turn drove high churchmen and hundreds of their followers to the New World.

The Puritan reaction (1640–1660)

The recalling of Charles II to the throne in 1660 marked the end of Puritan domination in England. The established church, which twenty years before had seemingly received a death blow, rose again apparently more vigorous and despotic than ever. Once again Puritans, Quakers, and other Protestant groups became the targets of oppression; rather than undergo continued persecution, many of them elected to join their brethren beyond the seas.

The Stuart reaction and its effect on migration

That political conditions in England during the sixteenth and seventeenth centuries also contributed to the sum total of causes for migration is unquestioned. During the greater part of the Tudor régime Parliament was conservative and willing to let the monarch take the initiative. With the expansion of commerce and the growth of an individualistic

3. Political

middle class, circumstances changed. Toward the close of
Elizabeth's reign Parliament began to assert itself and to demand a greater share in shaping the affairs of the kingdom.
The Stuarts had no notion of acceding to this demand, and
there ensued between King and Parliament a long-drawn-out
contest, essentially identical in fundamentals with the great
social transformation of the next century — the French Revolution. The House of Commons, now dominated by the commercial class, demanded not only that the King respect the
fundamental privileges of members of Parliament, namely,
freedom of elections, freedom from arrest during sessions, freedom of speech, and freedom of communication with the
monarch, but also certain ancient rights of the "people," including freedom from arbitrary arrest and imprisonment, exemption from unlawful taxation, and the right of petition. As the
contest progressed it became increasingly evident that the middle class was determined that Parliament should have complete
control over legislation and taxation, and should possess some
influence in administration, to the end that their interests as
well as those of the King and landed aristocracy should be forwarded. But many, rather than suffer the pains and tribulations
of this long process, chose the uncertainties of distant colonization.

Many of those who left England during the seventeenth
century were undoubtedly influenced by all three basic causes
for migration — religious, economic, and political
— for, broadly speaking, the Puritans, the commercial classes, and those who struggled for parliamentary government, were composed of identical
peoples. In other words, Puritanism, commercial-
ism, and parliamentarianism were respectively the religious, economic, and political phases of the same middle-class movement.

Puritanism, commercialism and parlia-mentarianism phases of same movement

While exact figures are lacking, it is safe to say that as early as
1640 there were over 65,000 Englishmen in America. Of this
number approximately 14,000 settled in Massachusetts, 1500 in Maine and New Hampshire, 300
in Rhode Island, and 2000 in Connecticut. It is
interesting to note that of these New Englanders
only about 4000 were, in a strict sense, Puritans. Although

Distribution of English immi-grants in the New World

comparatively few in number, they were sufficiently powerful in Massachusetts to found a thorough-going Bible commonwealth, a theocracy controlled by an honest but narrow-minded oligarchy which not only refused to grant religious toleration but for half a century planted itself squarely across the path of political democracy and civil liberty. Between 1620 and 1642 1500 English colonists migrated to Maryland and 8000 to Virginia. During the same period the number of Englishmen who migrated to the English West Indies was more than double the number to New England: Nevis received about 4000, St. Kitts between 12,000 and 13,000, and the Barbadoes 18,600. After 1640, as we have seen, civil war, the régime of Cromwell, and the restoration of the Stuarts sent a more or less steady stream of emigrants to the New World. New England in 1689 had about 80,000 people; Maryland, Virginia, and the Carolinas together boasted a slightly larger number; while the Middle colonies had 40,000 — in all about 200,000. The population of the English West Indian islands increased even more rapidly. Of course we must bear in mind that the increase in population, both on the mainland and in the islands, cannot be attributed to immigration alone. At the outbreak of the Revolution individuals of English parentage outnumbered all other nationalities in the colonies along the Atlantic seaboard.

Closely rivaling the English in numbers and influence were the English-speaking Scotch-Irish Presbyterians from Northern Ireland. When James I came to the English The Scotch-throne in 1603 he decided that the best way to Irish handle rebellious Ireland was to replace the Irish with English and Scotch colonists. Accordingly in 1611 the natives in the six northern counties of Ulster were stripped of all title to their property, and their lands were regranted to English speculators composed for the most part of London merchants. The majority of settlers in the confiscated region, however, were Presbyterians from the Scottish lowlands. Despite the hostility of their Catholic neighbors, frequent friction with the English government, and the vicissitudes of war, the Scotch-Irish prospered, and by the close of the seventeenth century Ulster alone boasted a Presbyterian population of over a million thrifty farmers and shrewd business men.

Unfortunately the economic and religious grievances under which the Ulsterites had long suffered now began to weigh more Their heavily. British landlords and business men, with handicaps an eye to greater profits, induced the government to enact legislation for the purpose of checking Irish competition. The Navigation Acts cut off direct trade with the colonies; heavy duties practically prohibited the importation into England of Irish exports, including stock and dairy products; the Woolens Act of 1699 forbade exportation of Irish wool; discouraging regulations and inadequate markets ruined the linen industry. Even the cultivation of tobacco was forbidden. While these restrictive measures applied to all Ireland, their effect on Ulster was especially disastrous. To make matters worse, the Ulsterites were by the Test Act of 1704 declared outlaws, their marriages questioned, their chapels closed, and the continuance of their schools forbidden. Moreover they were compelled to pay tithes for the support of the Church of Ireland, an Episcopalian organization which the vast majority cordially hated. The climax soon came when, with the expiration of many of the original leases between 1714 and 1718, the grasping absentee landlords doubled and, in some instances, trebled the rents. At the same time, prolonged droughts ruined the crops, and smallpox and other diseases took a heavy toll of life.

Angered and discouraged, thousands of the unfortunate Scotch-Irish turned to America. So great was the exodus that Their by the eve of the Revolution it is estimated that migration more than 300,000 had made new homes on the to America other side of the Atlantic. No less than fifty-four shiploads reached the port of Boston between 1714 and 1720, and an even larger number landed in Philadelphia during the same years. While these thrifty people came to all the colonies, by far the greater number settled in New Jersey, Pennsylvania, Maryland, Virginia, and the Carolinas. The settlements in New York and New England were smaller and more scattered, the most important in the former being the prosperous farming

counties of Ulster and Orange. Cheap land attracted most of
the Scotch-Irish to the colonial frontiers where, as we shall see,
they soon developed a democratic, individualistic, self-reliant
society very different from that of the older settled coast regions.

Ranking next to the Scotch-Irish in numbers were the Germans, victims, in large measure, of the brutal and devastating
Thirty Years' War (1618–1648) and of the bar-   **The Germans**
barous seventeenth-century wars of conquest of
Louis XIV, which lasted nearly fifty years. It has been estimated that as a result of the earlier conflict one German county
lost over eighty per cent of its livestock, sixty-five per cent
of its houses, and seventy-five per cent of its population.
Other sections fared little better; the Palatinate, the most
fertile province of all, was reduced to a barren desert. In
emigration to America these unfortunate people saw an avenue
of escape from the poverty, rapine, and destruction which
surrounded them on all sides, and by the opening of the eighteenth century a steady stream of German farmers and artisans
from the valley of the Rhine, South Germany, and the German
cantons of Switzerland was pouring into the colonies of the
Atlantic seaboard.

The advertising of Penn and other proprietors for settlers
was also a further inducement to the Germans. During the
reign of Queen Anne, books and other literature   **Their distri-**
were distributed through the Palatinate and other **bution in**
German provinces encouraging Germans to come to **America**
England that they might be sent to English colonies. To impress the Germans the books appeared in letters of gold reputed
to have been obtained from England's overseas possessions.
Indeed, by 1709 it is estimated that fully 15,000 Germans
migrated to London for distribution to the colonies. Between
1727 and 1754 German immigration alone totalled 54,000.
It is estimated that fully a third of Pennsylvania's pre-
Revolutionary population was German. Other thousands settled in New York, in the frontier regions of Maryland, Virginia,
the Carolinas, and in other colonies. Rhinebeck-on-the-Hudson
and Germantown, Pennsylvania, became great distributing

centers. So great was the influx that Frederick William of Brandenburg and other German princes, on the one hand, feared their lands would be depopulated, and England, on the other, that her overseas possessions would be overrun by foreigners. Attempts to limit their numbers, however, failed, and by the end of the Colonial period 200,000 Germans were in America.

To the seaboard colonies also came other peoples. Hundreds of Huguenot exiles established homes in South Carolina and in Other racial   the colonies of the North, where families like the elements   Delanoes, the Devereuxs, and the Faneuils became leaders in business and in society. A somewhat lesser number of Scotch Presbyterians settled in New Jersey and New England. Liberty-loving Welshmen — many of them Quakers — took up new abodes in Pennsylvania, the Carolinas, and even in New England, where men of the stamp of Thomas Bardin played an active and useful rôle in their respective communities. From economically distressed Switzerland came a band of six hundred hardy Swiss under De Graffenried who founded New Bern, North Carolina. Other Swiss pioneers located in Pennsylvania and South Carolina. From southern and eastern Ireland came thousands of Catholic Irish in quest of religious, political and economic freedom. Practically every colonial port town had its flourishing Jewish colony, despite the fact that legally the Jews had no right to reside in any British possession. Two other nationalities, the Swedes and Dutch, as we have already seen, contributed to the racial diversity of Colonial America.

Thus the old notion that Colonial America was peopled almost exclusively by Englishmen fails of historical substantiation. A new race   Instead of being merely a product of English expansion, the colonies were, in a very true sense, a product of Old World expansion, and as such they were peopled by both English and non-English. During the seventeenth and eighteenth centuries these diverse peoples were gradually transformed into a new race — an American race — built around the English-speaking element.

How these people and their descendants made a living, how

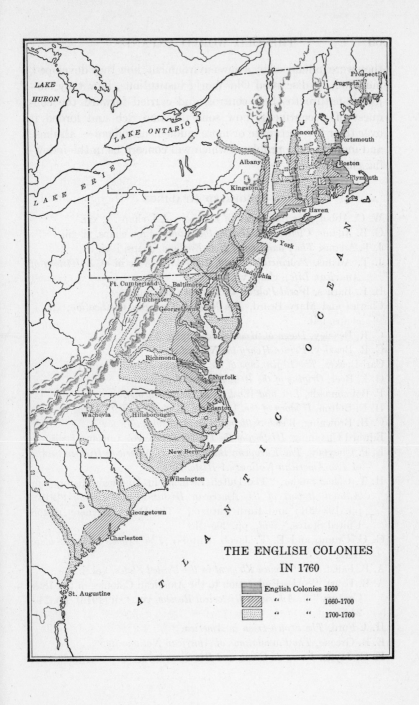

LAKE HURON

LAKE ONTARIO

LAKE ERIE

ATLANTIC OCEAN

Prospect
Augusta
Concord
Portsmouth
Albany
Boston
Plymouth
Kingston
New Haven
New York
Philadelphia
Ft. Cumberland
Baltimore
Winchester
Georgetown
Richmond
Norfolk
Edenton
Wachovia
Hillsborough
New Bern
Wilmington
Georgetown
Charleston
St. Augustine

THE ENGLISH COLONIES
IN 1760

English Colonies 1660
"   "   1660-1700
"   "   1700-1760

they were influenced by a new environment, how they developed, modified, or discarded Old World institutions, how they subjected nature to their control, and carried forward the conquest of a continent, how some became rich and lorded it over their less fortunate or more indolent neighbors — all these and more are the problems which will concern us in the following chapters.

SUGGESTED READINGS

W. C. Abbot, *The Expansion of Europe*, vol. i, chaps. x, xxi.

G. B. Adams, *Civilization During the Middle Ages*, chaps. xi–xii.

J. T. Adams, *The Founding of New England*, chaps. i–vi.

J. T. Adams, *Provincial Society*, 1690–1763 (vol. iii of *A History of American Life*), chap. vii.

H. E. Barnes, *World Politics in Modern Civilization*.

Charles and Mary Beard, *The Rise of American Civilization*, vol. i, chaps. i–ii.

C. R. Beazley, *Dawn of Modern Geography*, 3 vols.

C. R. Beazley, *Prince Henry the Navigator*.

Carl Becker, *The Beginnings of the American People*, chaps. i–iii.

G. L. Beer, *Origins of the British Colonial System*.

P. Boissonnade, *Life and Work in Medieval Europe*.

H. E. Bolton, *History of the Americas: A Syllabus with Maps*.

C. H. Browning, *Welsh Settlements in Pennsylvania*.

Edward Channing, *History of the United States*, vol. i, chaps. i–vii.

E. P. Cheyney, *The European Background of American History* (vol. i of *The American Nation: A History*).

H. T. Colenbrander, "The Dutch Element in American History" in *Annual Report of the American Historical Association* (1919), pp. 193–201; and Ruth Putnam, "The Dutch Element in the United States," *ibid.*, pp. 205–218.

G. C. Crump and E. F. Jacob (editors), *The Legacy of the Middle Ages*.

A. B. Faust, *The German Element in the United States*, vol. i.

A. B. Faust, "Swiss Emigration to the American Colonies in the 18th Century" in *American Historical Review*, vol. xxii (1916), pp. 21–24.

H. J. Ford, *The Scotch-Irish in America*.

E. B. Greene, *The Foundations of American Nationality*.

K. G. Jayne, *Vasco da Gama and His Successors*.

Amandus Johnson, *The Swedish Settlements on the Delaware*.

M. M. Knight, H. E. Barnes, F. Flügel, *Economic History of Europe*, Part i, chaps. iii–vi; Part ii, chaps. i–ii.

A. H. Lybyer, "The Ottoman Turks and the Routes of Oriental Trade" in *English Historical Review*, vol. xxx (1915), pp. 577–588.

R. B. Merriman, *Rise of the Spanish Empire in the Old World and the New*, 4 vols.

M. J. O'Brien, *A Hidden Phase of American History*.

G. B. Parks, *Richard Hakluyt and the English Voyages*.

H. I. Priestly, *The Coming of the White Man, 1492–1884* (vol. i of *A History of American Life*).

J. H. Randall, Jr., *The Making of the Modern Mind, A Survey of the Intellectual Background of the Present Age*, chaps. i–x.

G. Renard and G. Wenlersee, *Life and Work in Modern Europe*.

J. H. Rose, A. P. Newton, E. A. Benians (editors), *The Cambridge History of the British Empire*, vol. i.

Henri Sée, *Modern Capitalism, Its Origin and Evolution*, chaps. ii–vi.

W. R. Shepherd, "The Expansion of Europe" in *Political Science Quarterly*, vol. xxxiv, pp. 43–60, 210–225, 392–411.

Preserved Smith, *The Age of the Reformation*.

R. H. Tawney, *Religion and the Rise of Capitalism*.

J. W. Thompson, *An Economic and Social History of the Middle Ages (300–1300)*.

J. K. Wright, *The Geographical Lore of the Time of the Crusades*.

CHAPTER II

THE COLONIAL FARMER

COLONIAL America was a land of farmers. Indeed, as late as 1760 nine-tenths of an unevenly distributed population of approximately 1,500,000 derived its livelihood from the soil of the Atlantic seaboard. Towns and cities were as yet few in number, and in striking contrast with the present, the largest of these — Boston, New York, Philadelphia, and Charleston — could boast of only a few thousand inhabitants each. Agriculture, always the basic industry of society, with few exceptions afforded the colonists at all times a fairly certain means of subsistence. Even the colonial merchants, fur traders, fishermen, manufacturers, and shipbuilders often spent part of their time cultivating the soil, and those who did not were dependent in very large measure upon their agrarian brethren.

1. LAND, CROPS, TOOLS, AND METHODS

Of the several factors which determined the character of colonial agriculture, topography, climate, rainfall, and fertility

New England unadapted by nature for agriculture
of soil rank first. New England, for example, separated from the St. Lawrence basin by mountainous territory and from the valleys of the Mohawk and the Hudson by the Berkshires, was essentially an isolated coastal region. In fact, it was not until about the middle of the nineteenth century, with the advent of the railroad, that this comparative isolation was overcome. Unlike those of other colonies, the rivers of New England, with the exception of the Connecticut, were not navigable for any considerable distance on account of numerous rapids and waterfalls; and while they proved later to be of immense value when harnessed for waterpower, they were at best minor factors in the settlement of the section. "In the frequent harbors and bays, in the 700 miles of coast line, in the great

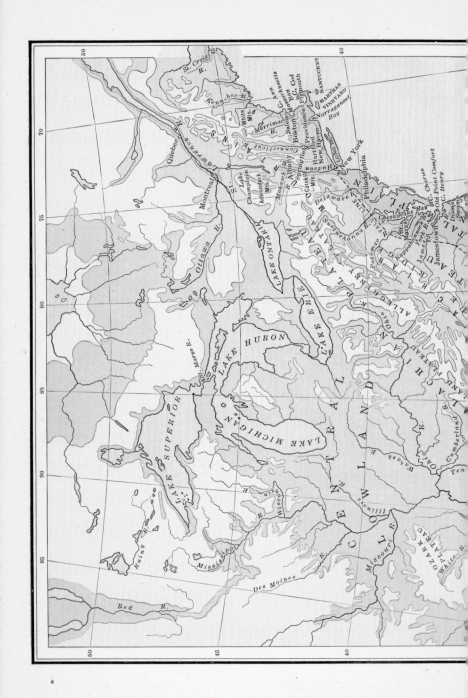

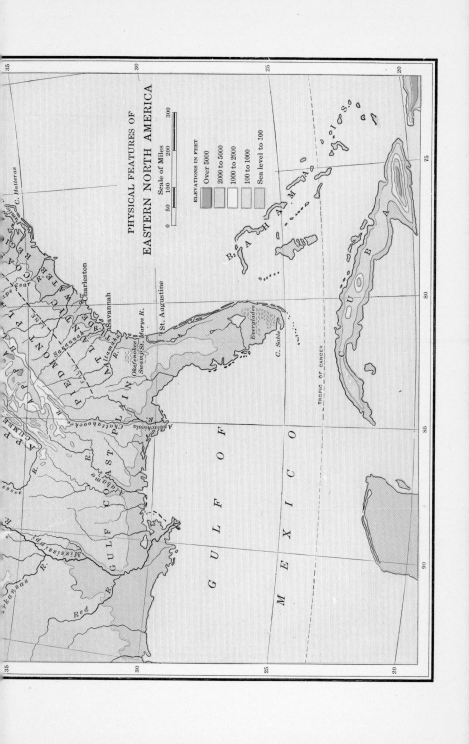

PHYSICAL FEATURES OF
EASTERN NORTH AMERICA

Scale of Miles

0   50   100   200   300

ELEVATIONS IN FEET

Over 5000
2000 to 5000
1000 to 2000
100 to 1000
Sea level to 100

C. Hatteras

C. Fear

ATLANTIC

COASTAL PLAIN

PIEDMONT REGION

APPALACHIAN

Charleston

Savannah

Savannah R.

Altamaha R.

Okefenokee Swamp

St. Marys R.

St. Augustine

Everglades

C. Sable

Chattahoochee R.

Apalachicola R.

Flint R.

Alabama R.

Tombigbee R.

GULF COASTAL PLAIN

Mississippi R.

Red R.

Arkansas R.

Tennessee R.

GULF OF MEXICO

TROPIC OF CANCER

B   A   H   A   M   A

C U B A

Sound stretching across Connecticut, and in the sounds about lower Massachusetts," to quote the historian Weeden, "were the physical features, the initiatory characteristics that controlled the destiny of New England." In other words, nature had fitted the region for commerce and not for agriculture. With the exception of a wide strip of sandy land in the southeastern part, almost useless for agriculture, it possessed little level territory. Its broken, undulating, semi-mountainous area lent itself neither to the formation of plantation estates nor to the profitable employment of slave labor so characteristic of the eighteenth-century South. Only in its central and eastern sections and in parts of the present state of Vermont did it possess land adapted to remunerative farming. Elsewhere its boulder-strewn, stubborn soil made cultivation most difficult. Little wonder then that such a topography together with long, severe winters and short summers tended to make agriculture in New England more difficult, less productive, and less profitable than in the Middle and Southern colonies.

The South, on the other hand, with its broad coastal plain stretching from the mouth of the Hudson to the swampy everglades of Florida, was especially adapted to agriculture. Between the bay-indented coast and the "fall line" or head of navigation of the numerous rivers which drained the area, lay the narrow, forest-covered lowlands destined to be the cradle of the American plantation system. Once cleared and placed under cultivation, the rich but in some places thin soil of this tidewater region afforded the settler even more than a comfortable living. Unless fertilized, however, it was easily exhausted, and new land was required. Here and there along the coast of the Carolinas and Georgia, and especially near the river mouths, were marsh lands well suited for the production of rice.

South specially adapted for agriculture

The tidewater

The rolling upland or Piedmont country, sheltered on the west by the Alleghenies and separated from the tidewater region by a belt of pine barrens, possessed soil of almost unsurpassed fertility. Moreover, in comparison with New England, the South was blessed with an almost

The Piedmont

semi-tropical climate which made it possible to produce not only wheat, oats, barley, corn, fruit, and livestock, but also the staples tobacco, rice, indigo, and cotton. Fortunately, too, the region enjoyed an abundant rainfall. Generally speaking, it may be safely said that topography and climate more than anything else ultimately made the colonial South an agrarian section. We may even venture that had it been settled by those who peopled New England, essentially the same agricultural organization and society would have developed.

Characteristics of both New England and the South were exhibited in the physical features and climate of the Middle colonies. In New York the rich productive valleys of the Hudson and the Mohawk were from the first famous for their agricultural output. Likewise the broad, sloping river valleys of Pennsylvania and New Jersey seemed to have been especially prepared by nature for the tiller of the soil. On the other hand, very considerable areas such as northeastern Pennsylvania were, like western New England, rocky and mountainous and, therefore, unfitted for profitable agricultural pursuits. Nor could the colonial farmer make much use of the extensive marshes and unfertile sandy tracts of eastern New Jersey. In New York and in the northern part of New Jersey and Pennsylvania the climate differed slightly from that of New England. In the southern half of the section, however, climatic variation was less and the season of growth longer. Like the South, the Middle colonies were blessed with an adequate rainfall.

Physical characteristics of Middle colonies

These physical differences, together with the ambition of the great majority of the colonists for landed property, were largely instrumental in shaping the character of the various colonial land systems. Following the Old World model, both commercial companies and individual proprietors receiving grants from the English crown planned at first to make America a land of great estates and tenant-farmers. As in England, land ownership by those who tilled the soil would not exist. Under the law of primogeniture every estate would remain intact, being transferred upon the death of its aristocratic owner to his eldest son. Such,

Old World plans to make America a land of great estates

indeed, had been the dream of those visionary "gentlemen" adventurers, Gilbert and Raleigh, and such in part was the scheme which their successors at first attempted to inaugurate. In the early days of Virginia, for example, the land belonged not to the settler but to the London Company, which attempted to exploit it for the benefit of its stockholders. Similarly the extensive territory of Carolina was to be carved into feudal estates; and in Maryland, a typical seventeenth century proprietary colony, sixty manors tilled by tenants were established before 1676, each containing on an average about three thousand acres. Even in New York the great feudal properties established under the Dutch régime were confirmed and, in some instances, enlarged under English rule.

Yet the various attempts to introduce into the New World an aristocratic land system in its entirety failed. Land was too cheap and too abundant for a man to become a manorial tenant. Moreover, settlers were primarily concerned in bettering their own social and economic position rather than in piling up profits for either trading company or landed proprietor. In the Old World they had learned that possession of wealth in the form of land determined one's place in the social order. There, too, they had experienced the impossibility of obtaining ownership of land already preëmpted by the few. To them, undeveloped America with its broad expanse of territory unfettered by tradition or custom appeared as a land of rare opportunity. Possession of its virgin soil, they confidently believed, could be obtained not only by virtue of birth, title, and official influence, but by dint of hard work and personal initiative. All forms of feudal tenure they therefore strenuously opposed, with the significant result that by the time of the American Revolution there had developed on this side of the Atlantic a system of landholding strikingly different from that of eighteenth-century Europe. In general, two types of ownership came to prevail: namely, the freehold and the leasehold.

Failure of manorial system to secure permanent foothold in America

In the three New England colonies of Massachusetts, Connecticut, and Rhode Island most farmers were the absolute owners of the acres they tilled. In these colonies neither large estates nor feudal tenure prevailed. "Where there is

Land system in New England

one farm in the hands of a tenant," wrote Thomas Hutchinson, "there are fifty occupied by him who has the fee of it." Most of New England was at first settled on a group basis, grants from the crown directly to individuals being the exception rather than the rule. These town or group settlements were usually authorized by the respective colonial legislatures. After sites for the village green and meeting-house had been set apart, streets were laid out and house lots for settlers designated. The order for laying out the town of Yarmouth, Maine, is typical: "That ten acres of plain land be laid out in a square lot for a meeting house, burial place, minister's house lot, market place, and school; around this ten-acre lot, a street four rods wide, and on this street house lots of half an acre each, and in some convenient place, a common field equal to six acres to each house lot."

The home lot assigned each settler and on which were located his dwelling, outbuildings, and garden, varied in size from a

Each settler's allotment

small yard to sometimes as much as thirty acres. In addition he received a share of the arable land which, following somewhat the custom of the English manor, was divided into strips. The amount of land allotted to each individual usually depended upon (1) his investment in the original enterprise, (2) his ability to use the land, and (3) the size of his family. Other things being equal, the industrious man with a large family received more than his neighbor who was less ambitious or who had a smaller family. The outlying meadows and pasture land, including woods and waste, were held in common and regulated by town ordinances. Ultimately, however, these were enclosed and disposed of to private individuals, New England thus becoming a land of compact farms. Taxes were assessed by the local authorities, but quitrents and other feudal charges, common in other parts of colonial America, did not exist. Massachusetts, it is true, did impose quitrents in Maine, but this was contrary to the prevailing practice in New England. Indeed, subject to the remote authority of Old World officials who seldom bothered him, to the dictates of some exacting creditor if he were unfortunate enough to be a debtor, and to the laws of his town and colony, nearly every New England farmer was by 1750 the supreme master of his land as far as ownership was concerned. He could sell it, will it to his relatives, add to it by purchase, or do with it what he pleased. Incidentally, the old custom of primogeniture was soon displaced in New England by the practice of equal distribution to all heirs or the reservation of only a double portion to the eldest son.

Outside of New England most of the soil was disposed of on some basis of feudal tenure. A variety of land systems prevailed. In the royal province of New York, Long Island and part of Westchester county were divided into typical New England freeholds. Along either side **Land systems in the Middle colonies** of the Hudson, however, were great semi-feudal estates like the Van Rensselaer, the Van Cortlandt, and the Livingston manors, whose broad acres were tilled not by freeholders but by tenants who paid rent to an aristocratic "Lord of the Manor." North and west of the Hudson extensive tracts were granted by royal governors to favored individuals. Thus Governor Fletcher's favorite and righthand man, Captain John Evans, received a tract of between three **New York** hundred fifty and six thousand acres. Indeed, so widespread was the practice that one of Fletcher's successors asserted that nearly three-quarters of the available land of the province had been granted to about thirty persons during Fletcher's régime. It was not until 1768 when land in the Mohawk valley was purchased from the Iroquois Indians that a settler in that section of the colony could obtain a farm in fee simple. Yet despite the existence of large estates, small farms predominated. Land distribution in the proprietary colonies of New Jersey and Pennsylvania was not markedly different from that of New York. Here and there were to be found **New Jersey and Pennsylvania** extensive manorial estates like those of Lewis Morris in East New Jersey and of the Penns on the Delaware. In both colonies, however, there was a notable tendency to divide large estates into small and manageable farms not unlike those of New England.

Quite contrary to prevailing opinion, the seventeenth-century South was not a land of great plantations. Prior to 1640 Lord Baltimore, it is true, did make grants in perpetuity for estates ranging as high as thirty thousand acres, but he soon discovered that it was much more profitable to issue grants for smaller plots. Virginia did likewise, and as a consequence the land of both colonies was parceled out to thousands of freeholders, each owning a farm varying from fifty to five hundred acres. Large plantations, which became more numerous during the eighteenth century, were comparatively few in number during the earlier period. When the London Company abandoned its communal enterprise in Virginia it made grants both to individuals and to corporations. To resident shareholders it allotted one hundred acres for each share of stock held. It further provided that these individual holdings might be increased by "head right," a system which entitled any person to an additional fifty acres if he would pay the passage of a new settler from Europe to Virginia. It was under this scheme, which was made law when the colony became a royal province, that most of Virginia's land was distributed during the seventeenth century. Even a freeman paying his own passage was entitled to fifty acres, and an additional fifty acres for his wife, and for each of his children or other members of his household. The land system in the Carolinas and Georgia did not differ materially from that of Virginia, the mass of the population being small yeoman farmers. In all the Southern colonies clergymen, physicians, and government officials were rewarded with numerous grants, and personal favorites received large tracts gratuitously. Charles Carroll, for example, was the recipient of no less than sixty thousand acres.

Land systems in Southern colonies

With the exception of the three New England colonies mentioned above, the colonial land system was feudal in character in its inception, inasmuch as all the land was at first sold or leased by an overlord who in turn had obtained his holdings from the crown. By the end of the seventeenth century the personal service of tenant to lord aspect of the feudal tenure had largely disappeared, being superseded

Quitrents

by the payment of what is generally known as a quitrent. This obligation, which varied from colony to colony, ranged all the way from the fraction of a penny to two shillings sixpence per hundred acres. Unlike ordinary rent, the amount bore no relation to the value of the land, and as long as the tenant fulfilled his obligation to the overlord the quitrent did not in any way limit the former's freedom to dispose of his acres as he saw fit. As a form of revenue it was uniformily unsatisfactory, although in some instances, notably in the case of the Penns, Baltimores, and Fairfaxes, considerable sums were collected annually. As a rule, however, the colonial farmer not only opposed it but whenever possible evaded payment; in New York and in New Jersey attempted collection sometimes led to violent resistance. Efforts to enforce the feudal practices of escheat and alienation also roused animosity. Under the former one's lands, in case he had no heirs or was convicted of treason, reverted to the crown or proprietor, and under the latter a fee sometimes as high as one year's rent was demanded on every transfer of the property.

As population increased, cheap land in the older settlements became less and less available. By the opening of the eighteenth century, therefore, farmers' sons and newcomers *The advancing* as well as the less prosperous but ambitious and *agrarian* adventurous element of the towns were turning *frontier* toward the sparsely settled frontier, despite its dangers and hardships. Here the young man who did not possess sufficient capital to buy a farm or plantation in the neighborhood in which he was reared could for a small sum acquire a tract in the unbroken wilderness. Here, too, those discontented souls who chafed under the social, economic, or religious restraints of the older communities could find freedom. Even before the beginning of the new century thousands had turned their backs to the Atlantic seaboard and were facing westward to the foothills of the Appalachians. Less than fifty years were to elapse, as we shall subsequently see, before other thousands of pioneer farmers were streaming across colonial boundaries into the fertile valleys formed by the mountains themselves. In reality they were the vanguard of that mighty host of emigrants which

was to plunge with irresistible force into the wooded valleys of
the Ohio country and sweep across the broad plains of the Mississippi and over the Rockies to the waters of the Pacific.

Affecting this movement was the mania for speculation.
Every colony had its land speculators; individuals, companies,
Land   religious organizations, and even towns obtained
speculation   large tracts of territory for the purpose of reselling
at a profit. New Englanders with surplus capital and political
influence saw in the unappropriated lands of their own section
            as well as those of other colonies opportunity for
New England
            speculative investment.   Thus in 1720 Roger
Wolcott of Windsor, Connecticut, together with others, secured
an unoccupied tract, seven by ten miles, for speculative purposes. In the same manner men like Colonel Samuel Partridge,
Jacob Wendell, Colonel Israel Williams, and Ezra Stiles acquired
immense holdings which they resold at profits which would make
a twentieth-century realtor envious.   In 1678 the people of
Deerfield, Massachusetts, complained that nearly half the best
land of the town belonged to eight or nine speculators "each
and every of which are never like to come to a settlement
amongst us. . . ." In the same colony the land of the town of
Leicester was granted to twenty-two individuals, including
Paul Dudley, the attorney-general; John Clark, a political
leader; and Samuel Sewall, son of the chief justice. Not one of
the twenty-two became inhabitants of the community. Speculators, too, secured control of the greater part of the famous
New Hampshire grants consisting of one hundred and thirty
townships in the present state of Vermont; these they disposed
of to the hundreds of eager land-seekers who poured into the
Green Mountain region after the Revolution.

Land agents and speculators were likewise active in the
Middle and Southern colonies. In New York an extraordinary
In Middle   proportion of the landed wealth was in the hands of
and Southern Sir William Johnson or representatives of those
colonies   great aristocratic families who throughout the
colonial period, and even after, dominated every phase of the
colony's institutional activity. Chief Justice Allen of Pennsylvania, a close friend of the Penns, was reputed to have been the

greatest land speculator of his time.   For years prior to the
Revolution no less a personage than Benjamin Franklin had
been engaged in land speculation.   In 1763 he, together with a
number of wealthy and influential Philadelphia merchants, had
under consideration a number of speculative undertakings in-
cluding the exploitation of western lands.   In Virginia and the
Carolinas millions of acres of the rich fertile lands of the back
country fell into the hands of speculators like Robert Beverly,
Richard Henderson, the Washingtons, the Carters, and Lord
Fairfax, who in turn disposed of them to German and Scotch-
Irish immigrants.   Even some of the newcomers like the Van
Meters soon learned to reap handsome profits from land deals.
Prominent Charleston merchants of the type of Benjamin
Whitaker dealt in houses, tenements, and plantations as a side
line, and by the time of the Revolution the sale of land in
South Carolina had become a business in itself.

Naturally the actual settler resented the activities of the land
speculator and was outspoken in his condemnation of those
officials who were instrumental in aiding the specu-   Land specula-
lator.   He could see no reason why he should be   tion resented
compelled to help enrich some "grasping and perti-   by actual
nacious capitalist" merely because the latter had   settlers
the foresight and political influence to acquire wilderness land.
The fact that speculators frequently sold him lands to which
they had no title, and that the colonial authorities often failed
to redress the wrong, also embittered him.   Legal contests and
long-drawn-out quarrels between the older and richer families
engaged in land speculation on the one hand, and the poorer inhabitants and the newcomers anxious to acquire homes and
landed property on the other, featured the history of practically
every colony throughout the colonial period.   The story of the
great land companies, the majority of which had their origin in
colonial times, will be discussed in a later chapter.

The real tiller of the soil, struggling to rear a family and
anxious to better his lot, was then as now usually too busy with
his crops, livestock, and land-clearing to engage in   Farm products
speculative enterprises.   Especially was this true of
the New England farmer who labored under so many natural

handicaps. Yet despite the character of the soil and harshness of climate, the farmers of this region by dint of hard work and the practice of thrift managed to raise many products in sufficient quantities not only for home consumption, but also for export. Of these Indian corn or maize was by far the most important. Its ease of cultivation, rapid growth, large yield, and general use as a food by both man and beast made it the staple crop of this section throughout the colonial period. From friendly Indians the early settlers learned how to plant, fertilize, cultivate, grind, and cook it. At the opening of the eighteenth century it was estimated that its production cost approximately ten dollars per acre, the yield being worth about four times this amount. Repeated cropping without adequate fertilization, however, rapidly lessened the natural productivity of the soil, **1. Grain** and the yield decreased somewhat in the older settled communities after 1700. European grains, particularly barley, oats, rye, and buckwheat were also grown extensively, but wheat was never grown in colonial New England with any degree of success. In some instances, notably in Massachusetts, it proved to be a good crop on new land for two or three years, but thereafter the yield was uncertain and usually disappointing. By 1745 it had almost passed out of cultivation, the section depending for its supply upon the Middle and Southern colonies.

Numerous other farm products such as hay, peas, beans, turnips, pumpkins, and squash, some European and some American **2. Vegetables** in origin, were produced in considerable quantities. Artificial grasses were not grown at first, practically all the hay being cut chiefly from the natural meadows and the salt marshes. English grasses were not unknown before 1700, but native grasses together with cornstalks furnished most of the forage for the livestock of New England until the eighteenth century. As population increased and the old meadows and marsh lands failed to furnish adequate hay, the practice of seeding the tilled uplands with the so-called artificial grasses became widespread. Herds' grass, or timothy as it was called after one Timothy Hansen, who introduced it from New England into New York and other colonies, was grown in considerable quantities in New Hampshire as early as 1720. Both red and white clover appear to have been introduced into New England long before 1700 but were not grown extensively until past the middle of the eighteenth century. Potatoes, which found their way into Ireland from the West Indies before 1600, from whence the name "Irish potatoes," were neither grown nor used extensively by New Englanders until after the Revolution; this was largely because of the superstitious belief that they were injurious and if eaten by a person every day for seven years would cause death. Cabbage and other vegetables of a coarser variety were grown, and the more prosperous farmers in addition raised lettuce, radishes, green corn, carrots, beets, spinach, parsnips, onions, parsley, savory, mustard, peppergrass, celery, cauliflower, and asparagus.

Fruit grew in abundance in all the colonies, but apples, pears, plums, apricots, quinces, cherries, and crab apples seemed best suited for New England. Two new varieties of apple, the yellow sweeting and the Newtown pippin, **3. Fruits** were produced in Rhode Island during the seventeenth century, and the Reverend Timothy Dwight in his *Travels in New England and New York* catalogued no less than twenty varieties for the section. Indeed, the New England farm without its orchard was rare, even though the trees were sometimes neglected, and little effort was ever made to improve the quality of the fruit. Besides those consumed in their natural state, large quantities of apples were crushed for cider, or sliced and dried for winter use. In years when there were bumper yields the surplus was often fed to the cattle and swine. Huckleberries, blackberries, strawberries, gooseberries, and grapes, both wild and cultivated, produced enormous quantities of small fruit, while maple sugar and honey furnished many a family with an ample supply of sweetening.

Livestock played no lesser rôle in the life of the New England farmer than his garden or his field. Cattle, sheep, swine, horses, poultry, and in the earlier days even goats, were raised in large numbers. New England cattle, and **4. Livestock** indeed most of the cattle of the other colonies, were derived from four main stocks: English, Danish, Dutch, and Swedish, which soon became indistinguishably blended. The number per farm varied greatly, depending upon time and location, and the same was true of other farm animals. The livestock equipment on a typical mid-eighteenth century eastern Massachusetts farm appears to have been one or two horses, one or two yoke of oxen, ten or fifteen head of cattle, about the same number of swine, and a flock of from ten to twenty sheep. As one traveled north or west from Boston, the number of livestock per farm decreased; figures for two hundred and fifteen farms in Falmouth, Maine, in 1760, for example, show an average of one horse, two oxen, three or four cows, nine or ten sheep, and one or two hogs. In a few isolated instances, notably in Rhode Island, we find much larger farms supporting twenty to forty horses, twenty-five to fifty dairy cows, and several hundred sheep each. Every New England farm produced butter and cheese for home consumption and in some cases for export as well. While severely criticising the New Englander's treatment of cattle, the author of *American Husbandry*, a keen observer, writing toward the close of the colonial period, admitted that the New England dairies, of which there were a considerable number, despite the absence of large towns and a ready market, succeeded quite as well as those of the Old World. The hogs he described as plentiful and "very large," and the mutton as "good." The horses, many of which were exported to the West Indies for use on the sugar plantations, he declared were excellent and the most hardy in the world. The sturdy ox was the staple agricultural animal for draught purposes, being much more extensively used than the horse. Not only were oxen better adapted for use in tilling the rough, stony hillsides and in ploughing out roads in winter, but they were far more serviceable than either horse or mule in connection with the lumber industry, in which practically every New England farmer was more or less engaged.

The New England farm, like the medieval manor, in large measure supplied the necessary raw materials for both tools
5. Other products and clothing. Despite severe winters and predatory enemies such as wolves and Indians, sheep raising was encouraged in every way and early became an important industry. The wool, while inferior in quality to that produced

in England, furnished material for coarse homespun. Tanned cattle hides supplied leather for boots, shoes, and harness. A field or patch of flax and usually one of hemp was to be found on every farm, and the woods abounded with timber suitable for building, for fuel, and for the manufacture of tools and furniture.

PRINCIPAL PRODUCTS OF ENGLISH COLONIES IN AMERICA

New England Colonies	Middle Colonies	Southern Colonies
Corn, oats, barley, rye, buckwheat	Wheat, corn, and other grains	Corn and wheat
Cattle		Vegetables
Fruits and vegetables	Cattle, sheep, swine and horses	Naval stores
Maple sugar in New Hampshire, Central and Western Massachusetts, and Western Connecticut		Tobacco in North Carolina and Virginia
	Clams, oysters, and fish	
Sheep and horses in Rhode Island and Connecticut	Potatoes and other vegetables	Rice and indigo in South Carolina and Georgia
Leather in Massachusetts		
Furs in Maine, New Hampshire, and Vermont	Fruits	Figs and other semi-tropical fruits in South Carolina
Whale products and fish in Rhode Island and Massachusetts	Lumber	
	Furs	
Rum in Massachusetts	Iron	Cattle
Iron products in Connecticut and Massachusetts		

Unquestionably the outstanding farmers of colonial New England were the "Narragansett Planters," a group of large land owners in southern Rhode Island who devoted most of their time to dairying and stockraising on a large scale. On the basis of size of farms, financial return, social life, and political influence, they closely resembled the holders of those vast estates in the valley of the Hudson or the planting South.

The author of *American Husbandry* was less severe in his criticism of agricultural conditions in the Middle colonies. Indeed, no section of colonial America was so favored by soil and climate for general farming as the region from the Hudson to the Potomac. In comparison with New England, a greater variety of crops were raised and the yield was usually larger. Wheat instead of corn was the important staple crop, the fields of New York and Pennsylvania, with only superficial tillage, yielding twenty to forty bushels per acre. Rye, oats, barley, and other cereals were also produced in abundance, and hay was even a better crop than in New England. Nor was there scarcity of fruit and vegetables in these "bread colonies." So plentiful, for instance, were peaches in New Jersey and Delaware that they were fed to hogs or left to waste upon the ground. In the Middle colonies, in contrast to New England, potatoes were an important article of food and, in consequence, were extensively grown. Great quantities of melons, equal in quality to those produced in Italy and Spain, were grown in the vicinity of New York. The gardens, especially those of the Dutch and German settlers and of their descendants, rivaled those of the Old World. A ready market and an abundance of hay and grain and of rich pasture lands made the production of cattle, sheep, and swine profitable. Particularly was this true of the back country where the cost of transporting grain was almost prohibitive. There livestock could be fattened and, at little expense, driven to the coast towns for sale. Philadelphia early became the colonial center of the livestock business. The region, too, was noted for its splendid horses, especially the famous Conestoga type developed by the thrifty German farmers of Pennsylvania, the name being taken from a stream in Lancaster county. The forests, like those of New England, furnished not only a great variety of timber products, but plenty of game and fur-bearing animals. The rivers, lakes, and adjacent coast waters teemed with clams, oysters, lobsters, and fish.

The Southern colonies raised practically the same kinds of grain, vegetables, and fruits as those produced by their northern neighbors. Corn, for instance, grew better in Maryland and Virginia than in New England, and both colonies during the eighteenth century were exporters of wheat. For variety and quality of product the southern gardens were rated as among the finest in the world. South Carolina produced as fine figs, oranges, and pomegranates

Southern colonies producers of staples

as one could wish for. But with the exception of the up-country regions, settled for the most part by Scotch-Irish and Germans, the South, broadly speaking, was not the home of the general farmer or the specialist in grain or fruit growing or in vegetable gardening. Rather the southern agriculturist devoted almost his entire effort to the production of tobacco, rice, or indigo. Cotton, which subsequently became the great staple crop, was during the colonial period commercially unprofitable, partly because the cleaning of the fiber was too costly, and partly because there was no great demand for it.

The colonial South, particularly Virginia, Maryland and, to a lesser degree, North Carolina, with its rich soil and favorable climate, was, as we have already noted, especially adapted for the production of tobacco, a plant of American origin under cultivation by the natives at the time of the discovery of the New World. The use of this plant, production of which was destined to influence so powerfully the social, economic, and political life of the South, was early introduced into Europe. There, however, the habit of smoking soon met with the decided opposition of king and prelate alike, who denounced it as loathsome and dangerous both to the individual and to society. But in spite of this opposition it spread rapidly and with it grew a consequent demand for the production of tobacco. The first successful crop produced in Virginia was raised by Captain John Rolfe, the future husband of Pocahontas, in 1612, and in less than half a dozen years it became the staple crop of the colony, much to the disgust of the members of the London Company who were anxious to have the settlers produce flax, cotton, indigo, and other commodities which they thought would be more profitable and more useful to the mother country. Indeed, the cultivation of tobacco spread so rapidly that in less than a quarter of a century it was raised to the exclusion of almost everything else. In 1622 Virginia exported sixty thousand pounds, or three times as much as in 1619. In 1664 Virginia and Maryland, with a population of about forty thousand, produced fifty thousand hogsheads, and two years later the yield was so enormous that it took one hundred vessels to transport one-half of it. As time went on the acreage increased

Tobacco

until by the middle of the eighteenth century the two colonies were producing over one hundred thousand hogsheads or close to fifty million pounds annually. This did not include smaller amounts raised in North Carolina, Delaware, and scattered sections of the Northern colonies.

While tobacco proved from the first to be commercially profitable, its production gave rise to a number of important conse-

Results of to- quences. In the first place, as we have just seen, it
bacco culture often was grown to the exclusion of other crops and, therefore, the planter became dependent upon the other colonies for part or all of his food supply. A few planters, it is true, early realized that it was a better paying proposition to grow corn, wheat, and other cereals on partly exhausted tobacco land than to grow tobacco. Some turned old tobacco land into pasture for sheep and cattle. As the center of population moved westward during the eighteenth century this tendency toward a system of agriculture based on grain and livestock production increased. But most farmers found it more profitable to raise tobacco than to raise food. In regard to manufactured goods, both before and after the Revolution a similar condition prevailed: it was cheaper to buy than to make them. In the past we have been prone to accept the statement that the southern laborer, whether slave or indentured servant, was too ignorant to make either tools or clothing. As a matter of fact, it was not a question of knowledge but one of dollars and cents. In the second place, the growth of tobacco rapidly exhausted the soil. The planter was obliged to fertilize his land or clear new land. Again it was a question of which course was the least expensive, and the planter, with apparently little concern for future generations, would use up one tract and then clear another. For the immediate present it was the cheaper way. Unfortunately, however, this method was not without serious drawbacks, for it put a premium upon waste and extravagance, encouraged greediness, and tended to crowd out the small yeoman farmer by the formation of larger estates. Thirdly, the cultivation of the crop created a demand for cheap labor, which was an important factor in the development of the system of negro slavery. Lastly, it ultimately gave birth to an aristocratic, landholding class,

who in the later colonial period, and long afterwards, dominated the social and political life of the entire section.

Nor were the results markedly different where the other two great southern staples — rice and indigo — were grown. While Virginians were deeply interested in the production of both of these commodities, it remained for Carolina planters to make them commercially profitable. Experiments with an inferior grade of rice had been tried during the last quarter of the seventeenth century, but it was not until after the famous Madagascar variety had been introduced that the production of the crop became a financial success. At first it was grown on the uplands, but soon it was discovered that the unhealthy swamps along the seacoast, when once drained and cleared of trees, were admirably suited for its culture, and here the great rice plantations developed. Negroes performed the work, for white men could not long endure the heat of a tropical sun or withstand the attacks of the dreaded malaria. Indeed, not infrequently even the strongest slaves fell victims to disease, their death entailing no small loss to their owner. All things considered, the production of rice was less profitable than that of tobacco; yet by 1754 South Carolina alone exported approximately one hundred thousand barrels, and her rice planters were leading lives of ease and luxury.

The cultivation of indigo, while not introduced until 1741, spread so rapidly that in 1747 the shipments to England totaled over two hundred thousand pounds. This yield gradually increased, and before the Revolution South Carolina was exporting five hundred thousand pounds a year. As in the production of rice, blacks did the work. On an average one slave could handle two acres, which would produce approximately sixteen pounds of dye; slave labor was also used in extracting the dye from the plant and in preparing it for market. Indigo, like the other southern staples, was profitable, and some of the best coast lands of Carolina were devoted to its cultivation. And the owners of these lands formed an important part of that landed aristocracy which, as we have noted, set the social standards and controlled the political affairs of the South.

During the colonial period the great staples were not extensively raised in North Carolina or in the upland sections of the
General farm-   other Southern colonies. In these regions the type
ing in North   of farming closely resembled that of New York
Carolina and
the back   and Pennsylvania. The grass-covered hills of the
country   Piedmont and the back country furnished excellent
grazing lands, and cattle raising was carried on to advantage.
In both the Carolinas, for instance, herds of a thousand head or
more were common. Enclosed pastures were rare, only the
cultivated fields being fenced; the cattle, which were usually
branded, were free to roam wherever they pleased. Unfortunately, the southerner neglected his stock, with the result that
often large numbers perished from starvation or exposure. Such
was the evidence of a careful observer who, traveling through
South Carolina in 1731, recorded that the cattle were very thin
in winter "because they can find very little to eat, and have no
cover to shelter them from the cold Rains, Frosts and Snows
which last sometimes three or four days; only the cattle designed for the Butchery are fed, and they bad enough, with
Potatoes, Straw and Grain; but they always lie in the open
Field, for there is not one Hovel in all the Country, either for
Oxen or Cows. If you object this to the Planters, they answer,
that such Houses or Hovels would do very well, but that they
have too many Affairs to think of that. The last Winter being
very severe about 10,000 horned Cattle died of Hunger and
Cold." Hogs were raised in large numbers and were easily
fattened on acorns, walnuts, chestnuts, herbs, and roots, with
which the woods abounded. Horses and sheep were also raised
both for domestic purposes and for export.

The tools and implements used by the colonial farmer were, to
say the least, primitive and extremely wasteful of man power.
Tools and   The tool most used was the hoe, of which there were
implements   several sorts. By the middle of the eighteenth
century the better equipped farmers had in addition spades,
mattocks, axes, rakes, forks, a scythe, a flail, a fanning-mill,
harrows, a wooden cart or two, and an unwieldly wooden plow.
In general, these tools and implements differed very slightly
from those used by the European peasant of the twelfth century

FARMING TOOLS OF LATER COLONIAL TIMES

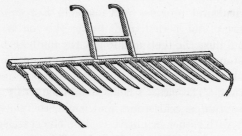

COLONIAL HORSE RAKE

or even by the Egyptian farmers in the time of Rameses II. In practically every instance they were hand-made, the woodwork being fashioned at home and the iron parts, such as plowshares, chains, axes, scythes, hoe blades, and fork tines, being hammered out by the village blacksmith. At best, the tools were heavy, clumsy, ill-contrived, and tiring to use. In the harvesting of hay or grain, for example, an able-bodied worker using a scythe would not average more than three-quarters of an acre a day. Once cut, the grain was flailed out or threshed out by driving horses or cattle over it.

Farm methods and farm management in colonial America were as primitive as the tools used. Here and there, it is true,

Methods attempts were made to apply scientific principles to the breeding of livestock and to crop production, but such instances were confined almost entirely to a few wealthy and intelligent cultivators who were abreast of the latest developments in European agriculture. With these exceptions, practically no advance in agricultural technique was made until after 1750. The European system of leaving land fallow that it might regain its fertility was widely practiced, and little or no attention was paid to scientific methods of cropping or to the art of cattle breeding. Several reasons help to account for this fact. Little agricultural progress was made in Europe during the greater part of the period, and it was only natural that the settler should use the tools and follow the methods to which he was accustomed. An abundance of cheap, fertile land discouraged the use of artificial fertilizer and the practice of careful crop rotation. The cleared fields not infrequently were filled with roots, stumps, and stones and could, therefore, be cultivated only with rather primitive tools. The scarcity and high cost of labor made it relatively unprofitable to carry on intensive farming. And the lack of adequate markets and the resultant inability of the farmer to dispose of his products at all times operated to postpone both the bettering of transportation facilities and the improvement of farm methods. Then, too, the colonial farmer was, generally speaking, isolated; he had neither time nor money for travel and observation, and no modern means of communication linked him to the outside world. Unless a member of the landed aristocracy, his whole time and energy were used in securing a livelihood for himself and his family; life was so hard that he found little leisure either for study or for thought as to how he might improve his agricultural methods. Finally, as an inheritor of the past, he was not only more or less a slave to that which was customary but, even worse, he was the victim of much that was purely superstitious. As Professor Lippincott has remarked, there was not much chance for improvement where, for instance, almost implicit faith was placed in the signs of the moon and stars as guiding principles for planting and cultivation of crops.

2. LABOR SUPPLY

The colonial farmer was always face to face with the serious problem of an inadequate labor supply. In sharp contrast to England with its widespread unemployment and Scarcity of overflowing labor market, the colonies were at all farm labor times short of laborers. On every hand help was needed to clear new land, to erect buildings, to construct roads and bridges, and to cultivate and harvest crops. Such work required human machines with sturdy bones and muscles. But in a new world where cheap land was abundant and where every free man might easily become an independent farmer, it is not surprising that a labor market did not exist. Even the few rural folks who either because of indolence or lack of means failed to engage in farming on their own account, frequently found employment in the trades or in some other industry. Wages were consequently high. In fact, as early as 1633 Winthrop, complaining of the high wages in the Massachusetts Bay colony, declared that "the scarcity of workmen had caused them to raise their wages to an excessive rate. . . ."

In the North, and particularly in New England, the farmer depended in large measure upon his family for help. The few experiments with Indian labor were very disap- Farm labor in pointing, for the red man in this capacity proved to Northern be neither apt nor willing. Sometimes during the colonies planting and harvesting seasons the farmer was able to secure hired help in the neighborhood, but such help — paid for in either money, food, clothing, or an order on the nearest country store — was all too frequently neither efficient nor very dependable. More often at these busy seasons, as well as at other times, neighboring farmers "changed works," a custom which still prevails in some sections of the country. Even the women assisted each other with such duties as the annual housecleaning, butchering, and soap and carpet making. When the framework of a barn or house was to be raised, or a school or meeting-house erected, or a new field cleared of stumps and stones, practically every person in the community, from the highest to the humblest, voluntarily turned out to form a "bee." On such occasions, which ranked high in the social life of the farmer, the women chatted and gossiped as they served rum, cider, and eatables to the men who with brain and brawn strove good-naturedly to outdo each other. Thus not only was the task in hand quickly done, but a happy break was made in the monotony of life. Group coöperation in some colonial communities was made compulsory. Artisans were also sometimes legally impressed to aid the farmer in harvest times.

In the early days little skilled labor was needed in the North, for every farmer was a jack-of-all-trades; he was his own shoemaker, cooper, carpenter, and ironworker. He laid walls, stoned up wells, butchered pigs and cattle, made axe handles and brooms, and split staves and shingles. Frequently, too, he surveyed his own land, designed his buildings, acted as his own lawyer, and prescribed medicine for the members of his family. His home was a factory and his barn a workshop wherein he and the other members of his household produced many of the articles necessary for their existence.

The nature of southern agriculture, however, made it quite impossible to depend even in a small way upon the family for Character of labor. The Virginia planter, for instance, was consouthern agri- stantly in need of a large labor force to clear new culture made labor supply lands and to cultivate and harvest his tobacco. imperative Without such labor the South, despite what we have been told about the influence of geographical environment, might well have remained a land of small peasant proprietors. Such a labor force was not lacking, for from across the Atlantic came two classes of workers — indentured servants and enslaved Africans.

We have already noted that the English workingman did not share the hard-won victories gained by the English middle class during the seventeenth century. His status re- **Old World** mained unaltered or because of changing economic **conditions give rise** conditions became even worse. By law he was in **to indentured** effect confined to his native parish, where he had **servitude** little or no opportunity to improve his lot. His wage, fixed by land-owning justices of the peace who were interested in keeping it at the lowest level, was exceedingly small and seldom enough to furnish an adequate living for himself and his family. His supplies he was obliged to purchase at arbitrary prices, and his children at an early age were forced to toil that they might contribute their bit to the meager support of the household. He was always face to face with starvation and beggary, and struggle and economize as he might he was unable to save anything for sickness or old age. The English economists of the time regarded him, as we have observed, with impatience and aversion, and as a useless weight upon the community. The New World with its opportunities to earn at least a decent living seemed to afford him the only avenue of escape from his miserable condition. To the poorer classes on the Continent as well, particularly to the Germans, America was the land of promise.

But their very poverty stood between these wretched people and the land to which they would turn in search of a happier existence. To overcome this barrier tens of thou- **Indentured** sands voluntarily sold themselves into servitude to **servants** ship captains, agents of planters, professional speculators, and others in return for the payment of the cost of their transportation, which varied from six to eight pounds sterling per person. All sorts of discomforts and even extreme hardships — overcrowding and indescribably bad sanitary arrangements, starvation and barbarous punishments — were experienced on shipboard by these indentured servants or redemptioners, as they were called, and the number who died of disease and exposure was appalling. Those fortunate enough to reach America were at once transferred to masters to work out their terms of bondage, which generally ran from two to seven years. Individuals bound to sea captains were usually advertised and auctioned off to the highest bidder, who not infrequently happened to be a "soul driver" or a person who trafficked in indentured labor. Sometimes these drivers bought "the whole and sometimes a parcel of them as they can agree, and then they drive them through the country like a parcel of sheep, until they can sell them to advantage." Many who came were, upon arrival, redeemed by friends and relatives, but in this expectation large numbers were, on the other hand, disappointed. Frequently very old or sick people came over who were unable to pay their passage and in such cases their children agreed to serve both for themselves and for their parents.

Although every colony had its bondsmen, the number was exceptionally large in the proprietary colonies where the demand for cheap labor was imperative. Without workers
Number and distribution of indentured servants to till their broad acres the Baltimores, Penns, and Carterets realized that they could not hope to reap any considerable profits and, as a business proposition, they made every effort to secure as many indentured servants as possible. So successful were they that in all probability over half of the thousands of immigrants who poured into the Middle colonies during the seventeenth and eighteenth centuries were in bondage. The number in the Southern colonies was also large during the seventeenth century, but dwindled rapidly after slavery secured a real foothold.

Not all the indentured worked out their term of servitude on farm or plantation. In ability they varied greatly. The vast
Status of indentured servants majority were ordinary laborers; a few were skilled workmen, and some were experienced artisans, tradesmen, or persons trained in the professions. But quite irrespective of their Old World background, and whether they were bound to farmer or townsman, the vast majority were little better in status than slaves. True, they were not bound to the soil like serfs of feudal times, or to unlimited servitude like slaves. By law they were protected in life

This Indenture MADE the *Twentieth* Day of *June* in the Year of our Lord one thousand, seven hundred and eighty five BETWEEN *Alexander Beard* of *Providence* in the *County* of *Philadelphia* of the one Part, and *John Dickey* of *Philadelphia* of the other Part, WITNESSETH, that the said *Alexander Beard* doth hereby covenant, promise and grant, to and with the said *John Dickey* his - Executors, Administrators and Assigns, from the Day of the Date hereof until the first and next Arrival at *Philadelphia* in America, and after for and during the Term of *three* Years to serve in such Service and Employment as the said *John Dickey* or his Assigns shall there employ *him* according to the Custom of the Country in the like Kind. In Consideration whereof the said *John Dickey* doth hereby covenant and grant to and with the said *Alex* to pay for *his* Passage, and to find allow *him* Meat, Drink, Apparel and Lodging, with other Necessaries, during the said Term; and at the End of the said Term to pay unto *him* the usual Allowance, according to the Custom of the Country in the like Kind. IN WITNESS whereof the Parties above-mentioned to these Indentures have interchangeably put their Hands and Seals, the Day and Year first above written.

Signed, Sealed, and Delivered,
in the Presence of

Alex Beard

John Dickey

A TYPICAL INDENTURE

Original in Historical Society of Pennsylvania.

and limb, and upon provocation could appeal to the courts. Moreover, upon the expiration of their time their master was legally bound to pay certain freedom dues and to provide certain articles of clothing. Despite these considerations, the vast majority undoubtedly led lives of hardship, sorrow, and suffering. The servant's limited term of servitude frequently spurred his master for economic motives to get all he could out of him while under contract. Without the master's consent he could not learn a trade or engage in business; upon his shoulders fell the hardest tasks, and if he "soldiered on the job" he courted severe punishment. Socially he was generally ostracised by his "betters," and even the opportunities for association with members of his own caste were narrowly restricted. Although both were subject to the same laws, heavier penalties were imposed upon him than upon a freeman for the same offense. Except in times of emergency he was not permitted to carry arms. In the affairs of the community he had no voice, for suffrage was denied him. If harsh treatment, or the hope of securing employment for a wage, or the spirit of adventure urged him to run away, he was advertised as a fugitive, and if apprehended was not only liable to be lashed, but his term of service was doubled and even further extended if he absconded at planting or harvest time. Fortunate, indeed, were those whose masters instead of being hardhearted and cruel were of kindly disposition; in such instances the records indicate that master and servant lived and worked together in a spirit of friendly coöperation.

The bondman as a laborer was in many instances far from satisfactory. Uppermost in his mind was not the welfare or pocketbook of his master, but the day when he would be free to labor for a wage or to secure property and engage in some enterprise for himself. Hundreds of weaker spirits perished under the hardships of the system, but the majority of those who survived were able, by the practice of thrift and industry, soon to become prosperous husbandmen and freeholders and, as a consequence, influential members of their respective communities. Many of the best people of North Carolina, for instance, were ex-servants from Virginia and other colonies to the north.

The supply of white laborers was further augmented by a considerable class of involuntary servants composed of kidnapped individuals, political and religious offenders, pau- Involuntary pers, and vagrants. Thousands of children and servitude simple-minded folk in English cities, particularly Bristol and London, fell easy victims to the wiles of professional kidnappers and agents of companies and proprietors who had Kidnapping colonies in America. Children were lured from their homes by promises of trinkets or sweetmeats and then forcibly seized and sold for long terms of servitude. As early as 1627 approximately fourteen or fifteen hundred children are said to have been sent across the Atlantic. Fifty years later it was officially estimated that not less than ten thousand persons were either forcibly or fraudulently "spirited away" to America every year. In 1671 a kidnapper openly boasted that for twelve years he had sent five hundred individuals annually to the colonies. Parents in straitened circumstances often indentured their children, and English parish authorities welcomed the opportunity of sending orphans and paupers to the New World. Many of these poor unfortunates, thus separated from friends and relatives and subjected to even greater hardships than they had been accustomed to, were early claimed by death. Those of stronger constitution, after serving their term of bondage, either became independent farmers or farm laborers or joined the growing group of artisans.

Still another group of involuntary white servants was that numerous class sometimes referred to as "criminals" or "transported prisoners." Composed almost entirely of Transported political and religious offenders and convicts from "criminals" Newgate and other British prisons, this class included some of the best and some of the worst elements of the English population. In the first category may be mentioned those who dared to criticise or even oppose the government. Among these were the Irish transported by Cromwell during his occupation of Ireland, the Cavaliers who bitterly denounced the Puritans and championed the cause of the Stuarts, the Roundheads after the Restoration, and the Scotch and English who from time to time rebelled or plotted insurrectionary movements against the

English monarchs. Several of these offenders were men of superior intelligence and training who were employed by their masters in positions of responsibility. Many of the convicts deported were in a modern sense not criminals at all, but victims of an unjust penal code, for the English calendar at this time listed no less than three hundred crimes which were punishable by death. Thus the starving poor who committed trifling offenses, such as petty thievery, for instance, found themselves in the same class as highwaymen and murderers. Debtors likewise were cast within gloomy prison walls. During the seventeenth century, however, the English courts frequently substituted transportation to the New World in lieu of the prescribed penalties. Indeed, so common did this practice become that it was legalized in 1717 by a parliamentary statute which directed that certain classes of criminals might, at the discretion of the court, be transported for a term of not less than seven years. Between this date and the outbreak of the Revolution some forty thousand persons were sent to America, some for seven years, some for fourteen, and some for life. In Maryland, which received a larger portion of them than any other colony, they formed the backbone of the servant class.

But not all of these transported convicts were petty criminals; included in their ranks were counterfeiters, robbers, and even **Real criminals sent to America** murderers; some were disease carriers, a menace alike to master and community. Several of the colonies vigorously protested against receiving these undesirables and by legislative enactment attempted to bar them out. Efforts in this direction were frowned upon by the British government and consequently in most instances came to naught.

Before the first quarter of the seventeenth century had passed, another type of laborer, the African negro, had been introduced. **Introduction of negro slavery and its slow growth during seventeenth century** In 1619 "a Dutch man-of-war with 20 Negars," so the story runs, anchored off Jamestown, where it disposed of its human freight. For a century or more prior to this time Portuguese, Spanish, and more especially Dutch traders, in their zeal for easy profit had developed a lucrative slave traffic with southwestern

Europe and more particularly with the West Indies. Throughout the seventeenth century, however, the supply of slave labor in the mainland colonies increased very slowly, not because the majority of the colonists had any moral scruples against the enslavement of human beings, but because of the Dutch monopoly of the trading stations along the African coast and the competition of the West Indies for this type of labor. The negro population of Virginia in 1671 was only two thousand, and in the colonies to the north it was even less. Thirty years later only four thousand, or about eight per cent of Virginia's total population, was slave. Indeed, with the possible exception of South Carolina, the economic system of the South throughout the seventeenth century depended upon the labor of the poor whites, both free and indentured.

But the eighteenth century witnessed an entirely different condition. For this change two important factors were, to a great extent, responsible. In the first place, English shippers and traders on both sides of the Atlantic manifested an increasing ability to engage in the slave business, and they were finally able to wring from the monopolizing Dutch a share in the trade. *Economic advantages of slaves as compared with indentured labor* Henceforth English slavers experienced little difficulty in securing slave cargoes along the West African coast from native chiefs or slave drivers, in exchange for all sorts of cheap clothing, hardware, ammunition, and rum of an inferior quality. These cargoes when sold in the New World brought high profits, and the English, therefore, were anxious to expand their markets. Secondly, as time went on the colonial planter came more and more to realize that the slave was a better investment than the indentured servant; his term was for life and not for a few fleeting years like that of the servant. He was more easily acclimated and had greater power of endurance; he required fewer clothes, thrived on plainer food, and was satisfied with humbler lodgings. As a rule he was more docile and tractable and, therefore, easier to manage. Moreover, his children were the property of his master, and there were no "freedom dues" to be paid or other contract stipulations to be observed. True, his master had to provide for him in his old age, but this expense was trifling.

No objection was made by New World planters, therefore, when in 1672 Parliament chartered the Royal African Company, Slave traffic increases an English commercial corporation, and gave it an exclusive monopoly of the slave trade with the British colonies. But English merchants, not members of the company, and traders and shipowners of Boston, Newport, New York, and Charleston did protest, with the result that in 1698 they too were allowed to participate in the business. So rapidly did the volume of the traffic increase after this concession that it was estimated that approximately two hundred and fifty thousand negroes were brought to the West Indies and to the American mainland within the next ten years. When in 1713 the famous *Asiento* was signed by England and Spain granting the former the exclusive right for thirty years of bringing African slaves into Spanish possessions, the traffic was further stimulated, shippers of New England rivaling those of Old England in the number transported and the profits obtained. Both shipper and planter preferred males from fifteen to twenty years of age, as females were physically less capable, and the older negroes were inclined to moroseness and suicide.

Space forbids any description of the capture of the blacks and the horrors of their passage overseas. The slave was considered Character of slave traffic by many to be utterly devoid of intelligence, a debased and brutal savage, no more deserving of consideration than an ox or a horse. And yet he could scarcely have been more brutal than the captain of the ship to whose deck he was chained. But then we must not forget that in any society at any time there are always individuals who seek material profits at the expense of the weaker, and so it was with the slave traffic. The slaver little heeded the preachments of that small minority who, like John Eliot, regarded the sale of "soules for money" as a "dangerous merchandise." Material gain rather than the welfare of humanity dominated his every activity; he became habituated in his cruelty, and if at times his conscience troubled him, he undoubtedly found comfort in the widely prevailing notion of the time that, after all, the negro was better off as a slave in Christian America than as a freeman in Africa.

Every colony had its slaves. In the North, ship masters sold them directly to purchasers or disposed of them through advertisements or intelligence offices. In the South, on Methods of the other hand, it was common to sell them in slave disposal batches to local merchants, who in turn sold them either singly or in groups to planters for cash, or more frequently in exchange for tobacco, rice, and indigo. Charleston merchants sometimes made the selling of negroes their sole business. Oftentimes negroes were auctioned off at fairs, the price depending upon the state of the great staple crops and market conditions.

Distribution of Negro Population, 1760[1]

Total negro population north of Maryland	87,000
Total negro population in Southern colonies	299,000
Total (approximately)	386,000

Distribution of Population in Southern Colonies

	Total	Whites	Blacks
Maryland	164,000	108,000	56,000
Virginia	315,000	165,000	150,000
North Carolina	130,000	110,000	20,000
South Carolina	100,000	30,000	70,000
Georgia	9,000	6,000	3,000
Total	718,000	419,000	299,000

Slavery distribution throughout the colonies was very uneven. In the North, as compared with the South, the blacks were, for geographic and industrial reasons, of little economic Distribution consequence; some were employed on farms, it is of slaves in true, but the majority in this section were used as colonial household servants, coachmen, boatmen, sailors, America and porters. In not a few instances northern slaveholders frankly confessed that they were financially overburdened with slaves. On the eve of the Revolution only one out of every fifty of the inhabitants of New England was a negro. In New York

[1] See Edward Channing, *History of the United States*, vol. ii, pp. 491–492; Marcus W. Jernegan, "Slavery and Conversion in the American Colonies," in *American Historical Review*, vol. xxi, p. 523, note 123.

negroes were more numerous, being approximately one in six. In Delaware and Pennsylvania, where there was a good deal of Quaker opposition to slavery, about one-fifth of the population was African. Three-fourths of the total number of four hundred thousand, however, were to be found in Maryland, Virginia, the Carolinas, and Georgia, where in some communities they equaled or exceeded the whites in number. In South Carolina, for example, where from 1733 to 1766 English ships brought in three thousand slaves annually, they formed sixty per cent of the entire population.

This rapid increase roused a good deal of opposition in many quarters. In the Southern colonies, particularly Virginia and Opposition to South Carolina, many of the leading planters slavery feared slave insurrections, especially after a serious slave uprising in South Carolina in 1729. This constant dread was well expressed by Colonel William Byrd, the famous Virginia planter, who in 1736 declared that, "these base Tempers require to be rid with a taut Rein or they will be apt to throw their Rider." Byrd also lamented the presence of so many blacks because he was of the opinion that they would "blow up the pride, and ruin the Industry of our White People who, seeing a Rank of poor Creatures below them, detest work for fear it should make them look like slaves." The fear of insurrections and riots was also shared by the commercial centers of the North. Except from the Quakers there was comparatively little opposition to slavery on moral grounds; here and there, of course, were individuals and groups of individuals both North and South who shared the opinion expressed in 1678 by the English Puritan author, Richard Baxter, that "to go as pirates and catch up poor negroes or people of another Land, that never forfeited Life or Liberty, and to make them slaves and sell them is one of the worst kinds of Thievery in the world." But the majority who opposed the institution did so for social and economic rather than for moral reasons. They thought little about abstract notions of liberty, but much about the safety of their own lives, their social position, and the protection of their property. The anxiety of New York and Newport traders to limit the traffic appears to have been solely for the purpose of keeping up the

price, and the duties levied by the Northern colonies upon
slave importation were primarily for purposes of revenue.

Many of the colonies, notably Maryland and Virginia, attempted to restrict the importation of slaves, largely because
they were overstocked and feared that further addi- Attempts to
tions from overseas would seriously reduce the curb slave
value of their chattels. But quite irrespective of importation
vetoed
motive, the attempts of the colonists to curb the by mother
slave trade were usually sooner or later vetoed by country
royal governors or the British Board of Trade, which at all
times was powerfully influenced by English merchants and shipowners. The effort of the Virginia legislature in 1710, for instance, to limit importation by imposing a duty of £5 on each
slave, was promptly vetoed by the governor. When in 1760
South Carolina absolutely prohibited importation, the Act was
summarily set aside by the home government, which for a century
had unswervingly adhered to the policy that the colonists must not
be permitted to "discourage a traffic so beneficial to the nation."

While slavery as an institution will be discussed more in detail
in a subsequent chapter, it is important that we note here that
the master had almost absolute power over his The status of
slave; he could sell him as he would a horse or cow, the slave
rent him to another owner, work him as long as he liked, and
punish him if he disobeyed. His status was carefully defined
by law and, compared with a white servant, he had few rights
which his master was bound to respect. Some effort was made
to Christianize him, but missionaries and others who devoted
their energies to this task were frequently antagonized by
masters both North and South, whose opposition was based
almost entirely upon economic and social grounds; religious
instruction, they believed, would impair the economic value of
the slave by increasing his cost of maintenance and changing
his attitude toward his work. Conversion, they further believed, would fill the negro's mind with notions of equality —
religious, social, and political — a thing to be abhorred. Indifference to religion on the part of not a few masters constituted
another obstacle to the conversion of the slaves. Peter Kalm,
the Swedish traveler, writing in 1748, declared that "it is like-

wise greatly to be pitied that the masters of the negroes in most
of the English colonies take little care of their Spiritual welfare
and let them live on in their pagan darkness." The earlier
notions acquired by the negroes were also almost insuperable
obstacles to overcome. Just how many were even nominally
converted it is impossible to say, but the number in proportion
to the entire negro population was probably very small. Like
the indentured servant, the slave sometimes ran away, and
when caught was usually severely dealt with. All things
considered, his lot in colonial America depended in no small
measure on the nature of his employment, and on his own
temperament and that of his master or overseer.

3. Home and Family

The home of the colonial farmer, like his labor supply, varied
greatly, both in respect to locality and time. The bitter struggle
The first   for existence made it quite impossible for him to
homes   construct a comfortable and permanent home.
The habitations of the majority of the earliest settlers, therefore,
were not unlike the humble dwellings which they left in the Old
World. Some were mere caves or half-faced camps; others were
uninviting wigwam affairs, flimsy huts or hovels of wattle and
clay. "For our houses and churches in these tymes," wrote the
Virginia General Assembly of these early years, "they were so
meane and poor . . . that they could not stand above one
or two yeares." But all these were, for the most part, temporary structures and were succeeded by more permanent homes
constructed of wood or, in some instances, of brick or stone.
Wood was plentiful, cheap, and usually easily accessible; the
log house, therefore, was a familiar type, particularly in the
North and along the frontier after 1660. Contrary to a prevailing notion, it was not something peculiar to America, but
was introduced by the Swedes and Finns in whose homeland it
was the ordinary form of rural dwelling, and adopted by the
English pioneers. In size it varied all the way from a cellarless
square single-room, thatched-roof cabin with a gaping stone
fireplace, to a large many-roomed structure with cellar and
spacious garret which were used for storing food. Its walls

SCOTCH-BOARDMAN HOUSE, SAUGUS, MASS.

HAMMOND HOUSE, EAST VIEW, N. Y.
TYPICAL NEW ENGLAND AND NEW YORK
COLONIAL FARM HOUSES

WESTOVER ON THE JAMES, BUILT BY WILLIAM BYRD

were neither papered nor plastered, and its floors were without carpets. In every detail it was severely plain.

As time went on the more prosperous farmers in the older settled regions erected clapboarded frame houses, much to the envy of their less well-to-do neighbors. These *Frame houses* frame houses were at first one-story buildings measuring about sixteen by twenty-four feet. Only the more prosperous farmers were able to have homes two stories high in front and sloping down to one story in the rear. Enormous chimneys of brick and stone extended through the house, affording flues for the open fireplaces. Most of these farmhouses were solidly built, with frames of heavy oak timbers and a double sheathing of clapboards. Writing about these frame houses in 1656 a contemporary observed that "although for the most part they are but one story besides the loft, and built of wood, yet contrived so delightfully that your ordinary houses in England are not so handsome, for usually the rooms are large, daubed and whitelimed, glazed and flowered, and if not glazed windows, shutters which are made very pretty and convenient." But even the frame structures were often unpainted on the outside, and the same was true of the barns and other outbuildings. The permanent home of the ordinary farmer was seldom constructed of any other material than wood.

The patroon estates of New York boasted luxurious, well-built houses of brick or stone; but the majority of the farm houses of the colony, like those of Holland, were *Homes of holders of large estates* small structures of wood or brick with stoops, sanded floors, and high, steep roofs. Although the early home of the planter was built of undressed logs, the opening of the eighteenth century saw the erection of those splendid, well-constructed mansions of which Drayton Hall on the Ashley river; Tuckahoe, the seat of the Randolphs on the James river; Westover, the beautiful residence of William Byrd; Mount Vernon, the home of Washington; and Sabin Hall on the Rappahannock, were typical. Surrounded by gardens of flowers and neatly trimmed hedges, homes like these with their broad lawns sloping down to the banks of the stream on which they were located, equaled the residences of the average English country gentleman for room, comfort, and beauty. Clustered about these spacious, stately mansions with their great halls, beautiful high rooms, and graceful staircases, one found a small village of barns, negro cabins, stables, offices, and other buildings. The homes of the lesser planters and small farmers were more in keeping with those of the northern farmer.

The huge fireplace was indispensable in most homes even though it did send "half the smoke into the apartment" and Importance of "half the heat up the chimney." Over its flames fireplace the meals were prepared and fruit and vegetables dried for preserving; on it, too, the farmer and his family had to depend for heat, for furnaces were unknown, and stoves were not used extensively except by the Germans of Pennsylvania. But even a roaring fireplace failed to provide sufficient warmth during the winter months, and the familiar saying that "one side roasted while the other froze" was all too true. Indeed, so cold were many of the farm homes of the North that sometimes the sap, forced out of the wood by the flames, froze into ice at the ends of the logs. And in this respect the town houses were no better. John Adams so dreaded spending the winter in the ill-heated New England houses that he often expressed the wish that he might hibernate from autumn until spring.

The northern farmer's house was furnished simply and almost entirely with homemade articles; bedsteads, chairs, tables, Home furnish- bureaus, kitchen utensils, and tableware were subings of north- stantial rather than ornamental. The colonial merern farmer chant might have upholstery, carved woodwork, fine linen, and silver plate, but these were luxuries which the ordinary farmer could not afford. With him and his family economy was a watchword, and furniture and utensils were used until worn out or broken beyond repair. Yankee thrift became proverbial.

The country homes of the wealthy patroons and the mansions of many of the southern planters, on the other hand, were lavishly furnished with articles from abroad. ParThe planter's ticularly was this true of the planter who exchanged home often lavishly his tobacco or rice for goods of one kind or another. furnished Not infrequently he bought on credit, mortgaging his next crop even before it was planted. From the cabinetmakers of London came chairs, tables, and settees of carved mahogany, upholstered in rich fabrics or the finest of Russian leather; walls were hung with expensive tapestries or were decorated with beautiful paintings and engravings. Costly clocks and candlesticks adorned the mantels, and the dining tables literally groaned under the weight of silver, china, and glassware. Sleeping chambers were furnished accordingly, the highboys, chests, and bedsteads being of beautifully finished oak and walnut. And a southern kitchen, in contrast with that of a northern homestead, was equipped with almost every conceivable utensil that could be used; iron pots, hard metal plates, copper kettles and pans, pewter dishes, spoons, stone bottles, crocks, jugs, and mugs, are only a few of the many that might be enumerated.

Food was everywhere abundant. In the North the farmer produced nearly everything for the table; only salt, molasses, spice, and a little sugar, tea, coffee, and rum were **Northern** bought. Most farmers' families rated sugar a **farmer's food** luxury; some used maple sugar and honey but the majority, in marked contrast to the southerners, used common molasses for sweetening. As compared with city people their food, though plentiful, was of the simplest kind and was served, as we have noted, on the coarsest of dishes. Beef, pork, mutton, salted or smoked fish, eggs, corn and rye meal in various forms, vegetables, and dried fruits, with occasionally venison and pie or pudding, made up the daily fare. Those who lived along rivers or near the coast enjoyed fresh fish. Indeed, so plentiful were shad and salmon that the former was considered fit for only the poorest families, and apprentices in binding themselves out often stipulated that the latter should not be served more than twice a week. Practically every farmer's wife was skilled in preserving fruits and vegetables; some, like apples, she dried, but others she preserved with spice in huge crocks, sealed over with paper and wax. Frequently she had not only enough for home consumption, but a surplus which was disposed of in southern and West Indian markets. Large quantities of beer, rum, and cider were consumed, and brewhouses and cider mills were general. New Englanders were especially heavy cider drinkers; it was not uncommon for a thrifty Yankee farmer to lay in an annual supply of from ten to twenty barrels; nor was it unusual for neighboring farmers to assemble for a social evening and drink a barrel of cider in a single night.

While the poorer people of the South subsisted largely on pork, rice, johnny-cake, and hominy, the planter set a sumptu-**The planter's** ous table. The meat supply was inexhaustible; **table** veal, mutton, beef, venison, fowl of every description, and the finest of ham and bacon were served in a most appetizing manner. Fish were as plentiful as in the North, and oysters and clams could be raked up by the bushel at the mouth of any tidal stream. Seldom were there less than two or three kinds of meat served at any meal, and quantities were out of all proportion to actual needs. Bread of all kinds, milk, butter, cheese, and eggs were relished as well as pies and puddings and the best of fruits; sweet potatoes and other vegetables also formed part of the daily menu. And no dinner was complete without some variety of sweetmeats or nuts. No stranger or guest ever left a planter's home with his appetite unsatisfied, nor did he go away thirsty, for no part of Europe or its frontier, America, was more abundantly supplied with liquors than the South; distilleries were not infrequent, and breweries and cider mills were numerous. Beer, apple and peach brandy, cherry fling, cherry rum, and cider were among the most ordinary liquors consumed by all classes; French, Spanish, and Portuguese wines were drunk by the poor as well as the more prosperous, while claret, Fayal, Madeira, and Rhenish wines were most often found on the planter's table. The favorite non-alcoholic beverage was chocolate, though coffee was used by some; tea did not come into use until the first quarter of the eighteenth century.

In dress no less than in furnishings and food we find a marked contrast between the poorer farmer of moderate means or even **Dress of** the farmer well-to-do and the planter. With the **poorer** exception of the wealthy owners of estates along the **farmers** Hudson and of a few "gentlemen farmers" of New Jersey and Pennsylvania, like John Dickinson, the rural population of the North dressed in plain homespun and leather, both of which were produced on the farm. During the summer months the garments were of coarse linen and towcloth; the children and many of the men went barefoot except on the Sabbath, but even then it was not uncommon for them to carry their shoes and stockings until near the church, in order to save leather and shine and, possibly, discomfort. In winter the men and boys wore heavy flannel shirts, woolen or buckskin trousers, and heavy, double-soled, calfskin or cowhide shoes or boots. Deerskin was frequently used for coats. Women and girls dressed in similar materials. Each member of the household had a "best suit" or a "best dress," which was worn only on Sunday and on special occasions. Whether for "every day" or "dress up," the clothes were stylish in neither cut nor color; but — of vastly more importance — they wore well. The same cloth was used for one member of the family after another until even the patches were worn out. We can understand, therefore, how it was possible for many a farmer to bequeath his suit of "Sunday best," which had lasted him a lifetime, to his son! By the middle of the eighteenth century many of the farmers of the North could afford to dress better, and a few, anxious to imitate their wealthier neighbors, did; by far the larger number, however, either because of habit or for economic reasons which we shall subsequently note, did not. With the exception that their clothes were of poorer quality, the indentured servants and other farm laborers in the North dressed in much the same style as their "betters."

Although the small farmer class of the South in some measure produced its own clothing and dressed in materials similar to those worn by the northern farmer, the planters copied foreign fashions and almost exclusively wore foreign fabrics. Opulent or well-to-do gentlemen like Byrd, for instance, personally or through their agents bought large quantities of clothing in the great textile towns of England and in the colonial commercial centers of the North. From the Old World they imported lawns, linens, duck, serge, silks, and poplins as well as a considerable amount of gold and silver lace. Instead of one "best suit" the planter had ten or a dozen suits of brilliant plush and broadcloth, adorned with buttons and lace. His shoes and boots were of foreign make and trimmed with shining brass, steel, or silver buckles. The dress of his wife and daughters, with their numerous articles of jewelry, was even more lavish and costly; only the families of the wealthy townsmen of the North, like the Beekmans and De Lanceys of New York, and the Boylstons and Pickmans of Massachusetts, could compare with the southern aristocracy in elegance of apparel.

In all the colonies large families were the rule. Diaries and old family Bibles record many instances of families of fifteen, twenty, **Colonial** twenty-five, and even thirty children. The Rever- **families large** end Samuel Willard, first minister of Groton, Massachusetts, for example, had twenty children and was himself one of a family of seventeen. The northern farmer, as we have already noted, looked to his family for labor; every boy and girl was expected to work, and each had his or her task in the household or on the farm. Parents considered such work not only as an economic necessity, but as the best molder of their children's characters. An abundance of cheap land made early marriage possible, and often girls were mothers long before they were twenty. Unmarried men of thirty were rare, and comely matrons were grandmothers at forty. Indeed, it was not uncommon to find father, son, and grandson working together in the same field. The traveler Kalm, in observing the rapid growth of population in the colonies, noted a number of instances where the children, grandchildren, and great-grandchildren in a single family totaled well over a hundred. The members of the family were generally affectionate toward each other in spite of the fact that the children were frequently and sometimes harshly punished. Divorce was rare, being frowned upon by both lay and ecclesiastical authorities; in case of unhappy marriage the parties usually agreed to separate.

Practically every household had its trials and sorrows. Infant mortality averaged possibly as high as forty per cent, and many **Ignorance of** a mother, called upon not only to prepare meals and **hygiene and medicine, and** rear children, but to wash, iron, spin, weave, knit, **consequent** mend, make soap, butter, cheese, pickles, preserves, **high mortality** candles, "try out" lard, "salt down" pork and beef, make sausage, care for poultry, and sometimes work in the field,

BRUSHING UP THE HEARTH

went to an early grave. Colonial tombstones bear silent testimony to this fact. Cotton Mather's first wife, for example, married at sixteen, bore him ten children, and died at the age of thirty-two. Most of the diseases and epidemics known today were as much in evidence then as now, and frequently took heavy toll. Superstition, ignorance of hygiene, and lack of competent medical assistance were, of course, largely responsible for the high death rate. Drainage and sanitation received little or no attention; bathtubs and other modern conveniences were unknown. Some of the southern planters provided bathing pools, and in summer the northern famer lad had his "swimming hole." Eyes and teeth were almost entirely neglected; fresh air, especially night air, was considered dangerous and, therefore, windows of sleeping rooms were seldom or never opened.

In case of illness the village doctor was not summoned unless the numerous home remedies and nostrums failed to bring relief, for every family had its Jerusalem oak, penny- Remedies for royal, wormwood, sweet basil, boneset, rhubarb, disease mostly salts, and calomel, not to mention patent medicines. superstitious Every springtime each member of the household was dosed with various concoctions so that the blood might be purified and "the system toned up." Many credulously resorted to superstitious practices for the curing of all sorts of ailments from smallpox to broken bones. In fever, for example, one was advised to take "two salt white herrings and slit them down the back and bind them to the soles of each of the patient's feet." Another fever remedy consisted in paring "the patient's nayles when the fever is coming on," and putting "the paringes into a little bagge of fine linen or sarenet," and tying the bag "about a live eele's necke in a tubbe of water. The eel will dye and the patient will recover." To cure a pain in the eye William Penn in his *Book of Phisick* prescribed that a white-shelled snail should be pricked and the liquid dropped into the eye several times each day. In view of such hocus-pocus it is small wonder that whole families, both in country and town, were swept out of existence by smallpox and other dread diseases. Not until the first half of the nineteenth century, as we shall see, did medical science make much progress.

4. Religious and Social Life

When the moments of sorrow and misfortune came the colonial farmer and his family turned to their God for solace and comfort. Like all agricultural peoples, the non-human hand of nature in the form of lightning, untimely frosts, destructive windstorms and floods, reinforced their religious experience or reverential relationship to the Divine. When death claimed a son or a daughter it was "God's will." If a crop failed or was destroyed, it was God's handiwork, for they had unquestioned faith in a Divine system of reward and punishment.

Colonial farmer deeply religious

Not all the colonists — either farmers or townsmen — were members of a common religious group, for the colonies, as we have seen, early became the home of many denominations. While the majority of the various Christian sects had adherents in every colony, certain denominations by the middle of the eighteenth century or earlier were more powerful in so far as membership and influence were concerned. Outside of Rhode Island, for example, New England was a Congregationalist stronghold, and in the South the Anglicans predominated. The Baptists were firmly established in Rhode Island and in certain other parts of New England as well as in South Carolina. Pennsylvania, early famed for its religious freedom, became the home of Quakers, Lutherans, Moravians, and other German sects. The Dutch Reformists centered in New York, and the Jews, of whom probably very few were farmers, were most numerous in Newport, New York, Philadelphia, and Charleston. Although the majority of the Catholics lived in Maryland, they were found in other colonies, principally in the cities. Wherever the Scotch-Irish settled one was almost certain to find Presbyterianism. Methodism did not secure a foothold until the decade prior to the Revolution; in fact, it was in 1766 that Philip Embury and Robert Strawbridge, the first two Methodist preachers in America, began their work, the former in New York City and the latter at Sam's Creek not far from Baltimore, Maryland.

Many religious groups in colonial America

Despite the existence of so many sects, there was striking similarity in the religious life and outlook of all the colonies. The Virginia planter, for example, no less than the New England farmer, was, during the seventeenth century and even after, largely under the influence of certain ideas and restrictions essentially Puritanical in character. He was expected and on occasion virtually compelled to be a church-attending and God-fearing man. In 1699 the Virginia legislature, motivated by the petitions of three counties, enacted a law compelling every citizen of the colony to attend some place of worship. To fish on the Sabbath, travel, transport or sell goods, or indulge in what today would be regarded as innocent amusement, was sinful and in most of the colonies illegal and subject to punishment. In the past historians have been too prone to differentiate between the North and South on matters religious and to describe the Southerner as a lighthearted, non-religious person. Nothing could be further from the truth, for the majority of southern families during the seventeenth century were deeply religious. This fact is amply substantiated not only by the strict regulations adopted from time to time for the proper observance of the Sabbath, but by the number of days set apart for religious devotion and thanksgiving, the testamentary evidence expressed in wills, tombstone inscriptions, private correspondence, the value attached to religious books, and the numerous instances of charitable endeavor. During this earlier period, and more especially after 1700, there were many planters who refused to take religion very seriously and who went to church largely as a matter of form or for social reasons. Others who did not believe in institutionalized religion absented themselves altogether. The flagging religious zeal of the planter may have been due in part to the fact that in the ranks of the Episcopal clergy after 1700, particularly in Maryland and Virginia, were many men of inferior ability and character who had little influence over their congregations. During this earlier period too there were people who, much to the annoyance of those more religiously inclined, desecrated the Sabbath by drinking, fighting, gambling, swearing, and "fiddling and dancing." But such

Similarity of religious life and outlook in all the colonies

Sabbath-breakers were to be found in all the colonies, even in seventeenth-century Massachusetts despite the strictness of its ethical-religious code.

The life of the country minister, particularly that of the frontier preacher, was frequently a hard one. With his parish-**The country** ioners scattered over a large territory he was often **preacher** obliged to preach in different sections. Father Mosely of Maryland, for example, cared for two congregations, one of which was ninety miles from his house. So small was the country preacher's salary that he could scarcely support himself, and on occasion he appeared in the pulpit clad in a suit of patched homespun. Dire poverty, too, practically compelled him to supplement his meager stipend by tutoring farmer boys for college or by undertaking the cultivation of a small tract of land. As a rule he was a man of great faith and believed himself divinely ordained to guard his flock; he was their leader, and for him they had profound reverence. In matters both domestic and civil he was their adviser, and his opinion carried more weight probably than that of any other individual. He comforted them in times of misfortune and sorrow and was quick to reprove them when they fell into sin or violated the customary codes of the community. His long, dry, expository sermons he read in tones that were convincing and unmistakable, and he never tired in exhorting his flock to avoid swearing, drunkenness, fornication, sleeping in church, and "other temptations of the devil."

The colonial country church, like the colonial country home, was with some exceptions a very plain structure. Sometimes **The country** unpainted, often without steeple or spire, with bare **church as a** and unattractive interior, and with little or no **social agent** equipment for either heat or light, it nevertheless played a major rôle in the farmer's life. Here he and his family had opportunity to meet friends and neighbors, and when the weather permitted it was a common practice for the men and boys to gather in little groups under the wagon-shed or in some shaded spot, or sit about on the tombstones of the churchyard and discuss crops, weather, or the "latest news" from the seaboard towns. Meanwhile the "women folks" gossiped on the porch or in the pews. In the South where towns were fewer and the isolation of the rural family was more pronounced than in the North, the church was of the greatest importance, for it afforded the people the opportunity of getting together, of meeting old acquaintances and making new ones. Both before and after the service young and old mingled together; friendships were formed, courtships begun, and vows exchanged. Church attendance likewise enabled many a man and woman to display to good advantage — and incidentally to the envy of less fortunate neighbors — a smart waistcoat, a beautiful dress, or some bit of costly finery recently imported from some British merchant. If the "meetin' house" happened to be near the farmer's home, he and his family walked to "service," otherwise they rode, sometimes long distances and over almost impassable roads. In summer those who came from afar usually brought their dinner with them, while in winter they were entertained by relatives or friends who lived near the church. Only sickness, frontier distances, or impassable roads would keep any farmer's family away. In the vast majority of the churches of colonial America, whether town or country, it is interesting to note that the better pews were usually occupied by the church officials and wealthier families, while the side seats were reserved for the poor and the less influential.

In New England as well as in some of the other colonies the country church was important politically. Local issues were freely discussed and every election had its sermon **The country** which was a source of political instruction. Indeed, **church as a** as we shall note later, many a farmer patriot at the **political agent** time of the Revolution gained his conception of liberty in part from some dissenting preacher who never tired in his opposition to all authority imposed from without, whether ecclesiastical or political. "The choice of public magistrates," said a seventeenth-century Connecticut preacher, "belongs unto the people, by God's own allowance. They who have the power to appoint officers and magistrates, it is in their power also, to set the bounds and limitations of the power and place unto which they call them." Year after year during the eighteenth century farmers and townsmen alike listened to the doctrine that people were justified in even rising against the sovereign himself in order "to redress their grievances; to vindicate their national and legal rights; to break the yoke of tyranny." Nor is it strange that these dissenting preachers should entertain such notions and dare to voice them from the pulpit. They and their forefathers had renounced Anglicanism with its hierarchy of bishops and archbishops; they had established independent self-governing congregations in the New World and, as the disciples of Milton and Locke, they had learned to cherish political liberty and to be ever ready to defend "free" institutions. Anglicanism, established by law and supported by public tax in all the colonies south of Pennsylvania, appeared to them as a giant tentacle of the octopus of English monarchism which menaced both their civil and religious liberties. As such they feared it and were fanatical in their opposition to it; we shall see later how this opposition, buttressed by the political philosophy of Locke and communicated to the rank and file of the colonial population, was strong enough when combined with economic causes and frontier conditions to effect a break in the unity of the British Empire.

The moral conduct of the colonial farmer, whether northerner or southerner, was shaped to some extent by the church. This **Moral conduct of colonial farmer partly shaped by church** was especially true of those who accepted or were inclined to accept Puritanical standards. In the eye of the Puritan this world was, of course, a place of temptation and danger where one must be ever on his guard against the buffetings and assaults of the devil and his minions. Eternal vigilance, of which a rigid code of personal conduct was the essential feature, was, therefore, prescribed not only for the Puritan himself but for his neighbor as well. In addition to rigid laws for the observance of the Sabbath, rules of conduct were formulated and enforced which today would be regarded as infringements on personal liberty. Mixed dancing, card playing, and the like were, for example, prohibited in many colonial communities. To what extent sexual immorality prevailed during the colonial period we do not know. Such records as we have would seem to indicate that it was fairly widespread by the middle of the eighteenth century. Whether it was more prevalent in the towns than in the country is also almost impossible to say. Drunkenness, as we have already noted, was a prevailing vice in all the colonies despite the fact that the church bitterly condemned it. The influence of the church together with the better economic condition of the poorer people as contrasted with the Old World was also probably responsible for the comparatively few cases of arson, rape, infanticide, and murder in colonial America; and what crime existed was confined largely to the towns.

In matters religious we must not overlook the fact that two marked tendencies were evident in all the colonies before the middle of the eighteenth century, both of which somewhat affected the farmer's life. In the first place, there was a decided trend toward the separation of Church and State, although the movement for the setting up of established churches prevailed to the eve of the Revolution. We have already seen that in the Southern colonies, as in England, the Anglican church was the state church. In Massachusetts, too, church and government were completely united until 1684, when the Puritan theocracy was legally and theoretically brought to an end by royal edict. In several of the colonies, including Rhode Island and the Middle provinces, with the exception of part of New York, a state church never gained a foothold, and in these the notion gradually developed that State and Church should be independent of each other. This idea, so different from that which prevailed in the Old World, spread to the other colonies, where it weakened the state-church establishment.

Of even greater importance was the tendency in the direction of religious toleration. Neither of the powerful groups, the Anglicans and Congregationalists, as we have noted, believed in toleration; yet in spite of this fact a better acquaintance of the sects with each other and the general decline in religious zeal tended to make for liberty of religious opinion. Freedom of worship developed so rapidly that at the outbreak of the Revolution religious persecution had ceased for all sects except the Catholics, who were still under the ban and against whom extremely harsh laws were enacted but often not strictly enforced. Under the leadership of Roger Williams complete religious liberty was decreed in Rhode Island from the outset, and tolerant tendencies were early noticeable in Plymouth and Connecticut. In 1649 Maryland granted religious freedom to all those who professed to believe in Christ; and New Jersey in 1665 provided for complete liberty of conscience, as also did the charter of South Carolina four years later. Pennsylvania in 1682 provided equal liberty for all "who confess and acknowledge the one Almighty and Eternal God to be the creator, upholder, and ruler of the world." Lastly, and in many respects most important of all from the viewpoint of liberty of conscience and the unshackling of the human mind, was the hard-won victory achieved by martyred Quaker men and women in their desperate seventeenth-century struggle with the Massachusetts theocracy.

The vast majority of colonial farmers, confronted as they were with the task of earning a livelihood, had less time at their disposal for amusements and pastimes than had the townsmen. In the average family the father rose with the break of day, kindled a fire in the huge fireplace, and then with the older sons went to the barnyard to milk the cows. The younger boys rose early, too, for they had hogs to feed and other chores to do before the breakfast was served, which was usually about six o'clock. As soon as the meal was finished each member of the family turned to the tasks of the day — the father and sons to the fields or woods, depending on the time of year, and the women to the several household duties. At the blast of the dinner horn at noon the men hurried in from the fields, "washed up," and then gathered with the other members of the family about the dinner table. The meal over, all resumed their work to labor on until sunset, when again chores had to be done. Then followed a simple supper and prayers. At the end of such a day every member of the household, with the possible exception of the very youngest, was usually too weary to want amusement; nine o'clock at the latest was bedtime.

Yet it would be a grave mistake to conclude that the colonial farmer was entirely a slave to work; holidays and the long

Colonial farmer's arduous life left little time for amusement

winter months afforded some respite from the daily routine and gave a chance for play.   In addition to games of all sorts, horse racing and cock fighting were prevalent in all the colonies but especially in the South, where they were **Amusements** the leading sports.   Virginia alone had more than a dozen race courses before 1700.   Cricket and fox hunting were also very popular diversions in the South, and so was dancing.   Hunting and fishing furnished excellent sport in all the colonies, and game of every kind was killed without thought for the future; raccoon or opossum hunting was extremely popular.   Like the Sunday "services," weddings and funerals, both of which were regarded as important social events, afforded opportunity to meet friends and acquaintances.   Drinking at funerals early became a fixed custom, and imbibing to the point of intoxication was scandalously common.   Indeed, it was this practice that caused a York county, Virginia, testator to declare: "Having observed in the daies of my pilgrimage the debauches used at burialls tending much to the dishonour of God and his true Religion, my will is that noe strong drinks be provided or spirits at my buriall."

In the way of affording diversion and amusement no agency played a more important rôle than the fairs, which closely resembled those of contemporary Europe.   Held in **Fairs** all the colonies with the exception of Connecticut from one to four times a year, and usually lasting three or four days, they were eagerly awaited by the country folk.   Here they could take part if they desired in a variety of sports ranging all the way from horse racing to catching a greased pig.   For those who desired entertainment of a less strenuous nature there were puppet shows, fortune tellers, tight-rope walkers, and the like.   These fairs not only brought people together in a social way, but served as places for the exchange of livestock and goods.   Almost every fair, for example, had cattle, sheep, hogs, horses, and other products on exhibition or for sale.   In some communities, particularly in Virginia, the fairs were utilized for collecting debts, buying and selling real estate, and obtaining bills of exchange.

Scarcely less important than the fairs in a social way were the

elections, which brought the farmer into contact with his neighbors and sometimes with the townspeople. In Virginia, as
well as in some of the other colonies, elections
Elections
afford social   were enlivened by feasting and drinking and by
outlet for   such sports as wrestling, foot racing, and shooting at
colonial farmer
the mark, for which prizes were offered. Frequently,
too, rival points of view, enforced by too much strong drink, led
to bloody rough-and-tumble fights. The seventeenth-century
Massachusetts election, though almost always preceded by
prayer and psalm singing, was often transformed into a day of
gayety by the younger generation. One good New Englander
complained that the day had been made the occasion "to meet,
to smoke, carouse and swagger and dishonour God . . ."

5. Political Interest

Every farmer was more or less interested in the government of
the locality and the colony in which he resided; his influence and
Suffrage   participation in political affairs, however, depended
restricted   in no small measure not only upon the colony in
which he lived but upon his economic status and religious affili-
ation. In Massachusetts, for instance, until 1684 suffrage was
restricted to members of the Congregational church, all dissenters being denied the right to vote; and even after that date
only freeholders of an estate worth at least forty shillings a year,
or the owner of other property to the value of forty pounds
sterling could vote. Likewise in Pennsylvania the right to vote
was limited to freeholders of fifty acres or more of land well
seated, twelve acres cleared and under cultivation, and to other
persons worth at least fifty pounds in lawful money. The
prospective voter also had to believe in Christ as the Savior of
the world. To vote in Virginia the farmer had to be a freeholder owning at least fifty acres of land if there was no house on
it, or twenty-five acres of land with a house twelve feet square.
In South Carolina the franchise was limited to communicants of
the Church of England possessing fifty acres freehold or a
personal estate of ten pounds. And so it was in the other
colonies; suffrage was strictly limited to property holders and
taxpayers and, in some cases, to communicants of some par-

ticular church. Moreover, in every colony the suffrage was
limited to the male sex.

Although these suffrage requirements worked greater hardship upon the non-propertied peoples of the towns than on the
farmers, they nevertheless excluded a considerable
percentage of the rural population. In Pennsyl-   *Participation
vania, for example, the tax lists show that only   *of small farm-
about eight per cent of the country folk were   *ers in politics
qualified to enjoy the suffrage. Election districts were large,
and means of communication inadequate. Party organization
did not exist as it does today. Moreover, the propertied
interests of the older settled regions, particularly the towns, by
refusing to apportion representation in elective bodies on the
basis of population, often dominated the government. Taking
these facts into account, we can readily understand how the
small farmer in particular would have little voice in shaping the
political affairs of his community. Such was the situation in
Virginia where, throughout the colonial period and after, control
rested with the tidewater aristocracy who feared the boisterous
democracy of the growing small farmer class. Indeed, it was
this very condition of affairs that caused Thomas Jefferson to
declare in 1780 that "19,000 men below the Falls give law to
more than 30,000 living in other parts of the State." Nor was
the condition different in Pennsylvania where, on the eve of the
Revolution John Dickinson was arguing that the colonists
should be taxed only by their own representatives, three eastern
counties elected twenty-four of the thirty-six representatives to
the Colonial Assembly with the result that a Quaker merchant
oligarchy lorded it over the German and Scotch-Irish farmers
of the other counties. Finally, we should not fail to observe
that during the colonial period many farmers, as at present,
failed to exercise the franchise because of sheer indifference.

In considering the framework of the government under which
the colonial farmer lived, it is interesting to note that while each
colony had its own peculiar institutions and tradi-   *Framework of
tions, all were strikingly similar in that each had a   *colonial
governor, a representative assembly, and a judicial   *government
system. Moreover, all had the Common Law of England which

guaranteed trial by jury, free speech, and freedom from arbitrary imprisonment. Eight out of the thirteen, namely, Georgia, the two Carolinas, Virginia, New Jersey, New York, New Hampshire, and Massachusetts, were royal colonies by 1776, each with a governor appointed by the king. In the proprietary colonies of Maryland, Pennsylvania, and Delaware executive authority was vested in the proprietor or in a governor or lieutenant-governor appointed by him. Only in Connecticut and Rhode Island, the so-called "corporate" colonies, was the governor chosen by representatives of the enfranchised voters, and in both he was little more than a figurehead in so far as functions and power were concerned.

The executive

Turning to the colonial legislatures, we note a somewhat different situation. With the exception of Pennsylvania, each colony had two legislative branches. The members of the Upper House of Councillors or Assistants, as they were called, were, with the exception of Massachusetts, Connecticut, and Rhode Island, chosen by the governor, who usually took pains to name personal favorites or at least those whom he had reason to believe would support his claims. The Colonial Assembly or Lower House, however, was in every instance chosen by the qualified voters. It did not take a farmer long to discover that the colonial governor, with his sweeping power to enforce laws, to grant reprieves and pardons, to remove councillors, to summon, adjourn, and dissolve the popular assembly, to veto measures deemed by him to be objectionable, to propose laws desired by the crown, to levy troops for defense, and to enforce martial law in time of invasion, war, and rebellion, represented aristocracy and exalted royal rights, and that he was not particularly favorable toward colonial self-government. Moreover, the favoritism shown by the governor in filling offices at his disposal and in making land grants irritated the colonists. Nor were they pleased when he granted special privileges to a select few or winked at the wrongdoings of corrupt or overbearing officials. The farmer as a taxpayer resented what he believed to be exorbitant taxation, and at all times was a caustic critic of those officials who, in his judgment, lavished spoils on favorites or were guilty of wasteful or unnecessary expenditures.

The colonial legislature

It was overtaxation, favoritism, special privilege, and general dissatisfaction with the régime of Governor Berkeley in Virginia more than anything else that led Nathaniel Bacon and his fellow-farmers in 1676 to protest as they did and to demand "fair play."

Nor was the farmer, as well as the townsman, long in learning that the Colonial Assembly, although not representative of all the people, was democratic in tendency, that it championed self-government, and that it was definitely resolved to control the colonial purse strings and to use that control for advancing the welfare of those whom it represented.   Among other things, it succeeded in stripping the appointed Upper House of all power over money bills, much in the same manner as the British House of Lords was stripped of authority over money measures in 1911. It stipulated that money grants be made annual, not permanent, and that they be paid out by a treasurer appointed by the Assembly, and by withholding, or threatening to withhold, the governor's salary it succeeded in making that official amenable to its wishes.

Colonial Assembly controls purse strings

Moreover, when during the eighteenth century the governors complained about "republican principles" exercised by the colonists and elaborated a scheme involving (1) reduction of all the colonies to the status of royal provinces, (2) freeing the royal governors from financial dependence upon the Colonial Assemblies by parliamentary imposition of taxes, (3) maintenance of a British standing army in the colonies, and (4) more frequent use of the royal veto on colonial laws, the colonists, as we shall see, became more bitter and vindictive toward royal authority and more determined than ever in their insistence that their rights of self-government be respected.   At the same time the small farmer class, restless under the domination of a powerful wealthy class composed of lawyers, capitalists, and large landowners, was equally insistent that the suffrage be extended and that the colonial government be further democratized.   Especially was this true of those German and Scotch-Irish farmers on the frontier.

Assembly champions principle of self-government

6. INTELLECTUAL OUTLOOK

Before leaving the colonial farmer we must say a word or two about his general intellectual outlook. In this respect a wide gap

Contrast in intellectual outlook between small farmer and wealthier planter

existed between the small and less prosperous farmer and the wealthier planter. Burdened with the responsibility of securing a livelihood for himself and those dependent upon him, the farmer gave little attention to things cultural; his life was of necessity wrapped up in material interests, and his best energies were expended in grappling with nature for an existence. Instead of writing poetry, building cathedrals, or studying anatomy he was busy conquering the forest, building a home, tilling the soil, harvesting crops, and fighting Indians. However much he may have had the desire for what we usually speak of as the higher things of life, he had neither time nor energy to devote to them. The planter, on the other hand, enjoyed a considerable amount of leisure and could and did devote himself to things not strictly utilitarian.

In manners, conversation, education, and intellectual outlook the planter was vastly superior to the small farmer. His reputa-

Planter culturally superior to small farmer

tion for graciousness and hospitality, for instance, was unsurpassed. He sent his children overseas or north to be educated, or obtained tutors for them from England, Scotland, or the Northern colonies. If sufficiently wealthy and interested, he had his own library where he often spent many hours in the study of literature, history, science, politics, and law. As early as 1696 the library of Colonel Nicholson of Virginia contained over two hundred volumes. Moreover, the planter's close contact with England enabled him to acquire much of the polish and urbanity of the leisure class of the Old World which, together with his wit and vivacity, helped to distinguish him from the rank and file of the colonial agricultural population.

But even among the planter class there were those who could not sign their names; indeed, both north and south there were thousands of men and women who could not sign their names. Out of 2160 jurymen in mid-seventeenth-century Virginia counties, only 1166 were able to sign their names in full. Deeds and depositions also bear testimony to the same effect. Out of 12,445 men from fourteen Virginia counties only 7,439 were able to sign their names to their deeds and depositions. Illiteracy among women in the same counties and on the same basis was even greater, only 756 out of 3,066 being able to sign their names. How many colonial farmers there were who were able to read, write, and perhaps do a little ciphering, but had no interest in acquiring further education, we do not know; undoubtedly the number was very large. In the North the majority of them, as we have noted, depended on their children for labor. In 1704, to cite a single instance, there were only six families in the whole of Westchester county, New York, who were able "to spare their children's time more than to learn to read and write."

Lack of formal education and consequent illiteracy

It is easy to understand why illiteracy was so prevalent when we consider that colonial America had no system of schools, either public or private. In a frontier community where so much emphasis is placed on things material and where little or no formal education is regarded as necessary, there is little urge for schools. The widely scattered farms and plantations in the Southern colonies made it quite impossible to establish an effective school system. Virginia, Maryland, and the Carolinas, however, boasted a number of private schools of which the "Old Field Schools" of Virginia were typical. These schools received their name because of their location in abandoned fields. They were formed by the families of a neighborhood and were taught by the wife of one of the planters, by the local clergyman or, if the families were sufficiently well off, by a more competent teacher. Grammar schools and endowed free elementary schools also existed. Some plantations had their own private tutors, and the records show that there were also endowed parish schools.

Few schools in Southern colonies

In the Northern colonies opportunities for schooling were somewhat better. In Pennsylvania a half-hearted attempt was made to make education a function of the state, and all parents were required under penalty of a heavy fine to see that their children could read. New Jersey in 1693

In the Middle colonies

authorized towns to levy taxes for the support of public schools, and a number of such appear to have been subsequently established. As late as 1756 the schools of the province of New York were described as being of "the lowest order"; this description appears to have been accurate, for not only were the schools of poor quality but the intellectual level of the people was low.

Even in New England, which in the past has been pictured by historians as the cradle of the American educational system of In New today, opportunity for schooling might have been England much better. The Puritans of Massachusetts, it is true, zealous that their children should be brought up in the faith of their fathers and trained in good citizenship as they understood it, decreed in 1642 that owing to "the neglect of many parents to train up their children in learning and labor, which might be profitable to the Commonwealth" education henceforth should be compulsory. This Act did not establish schools, but simply provided that children be taught either by their parents or otherwise to "read and understand the principles of religion and the capital lawes of the country." Five years later this Act was followed by another requiring every town of fifty families to provide for primary education by maintaining a teacher of reading and writing, and each town of one hundred families to establish a grammar (Latin) school "with a teacher able to instruct youth so as they may be fitted for the university." But it is one thing to enact legislation and another thing to carry it out. Many towns, with an eye on the purse string, failed to comply, and in 1701 the legislature complained that the law was "shamefully neglected in divers towns." That part of Massachusetts which is now the state of Maine did not have a single school until after the opening of the eighteenth century. Outside of Massachusetts the situation was even worse. Rhode Island and New Hampshire were almost entirely without schools in 1700. Connecticut, however, was somewhat better off than her northern neighbors. School attendance was not compulsory in any of the colonies, and even in those communities where school was maintained throughout the year, attendance of farmers' children was very poor.

The Bible or New Testament, the hymn book, and the almanac, the "cyclopedia of the colonial period," were the books most read by those farmers and their families who could read; few other books were to be found in the average farmer's household. Of these the Bible was regarded as fundamental, but the almanac with its fund of "information," the reliability of which the farmer never questioned, was in all probability as widely perused. From it one could secure data relative to the sun and moon and other heavenly bodies, and no almanac was a good one which did not also contain interest tables, the dates of court and freemen's meetings, distances from tavern to tavern, prophecies about the weather, texts of sermons, household recipes, lists of pills, salves, and bitters, and jokes, as well as space where the date of a neighbor's birth, wedding, or death might be recorded. Some of these almanacs also contained short stories, essays, and poems. As the eighteenth century advanced, imported books on agriculture and stockbreeding, such as John Worledge's *The History of Husbandry Discovered*, found their way to the mantels of some of the more prosperous farmers.

Books in average farmer's home

All things considered, the life of the colonial farmer, with the exception of the planter aristocracy of the South and the great landed proprietors of New York, was narrow, hard, and unchanging. Roads were poor and travel costly and hazardous and he, therefore, seldom journeyed forth except to attend a fair, go to market, or help subdue the Indians. He saw little or nothing of the outer world and naturally he was non-progressive, provincial, and more or less superstitious. To see an odd number of crows, for instance, was counted lucky, but to begin work on Friday was unlucky. Not only was he compelled to struggle with Indians, backward seasons, and numberless enemies such as wolves, grubs, and caterpillars, but he was constantly tormented either by low prices for what he had to sell, by irksome laws of a government which was not always of his making, or by the teachings of a severe theology in which the devil and eternal damnation were ever stressed.

Farmer's outlook narrow and provincial

On the other hand, we must not forget that the nature of his life made for industry, frugality, thrift, and honest work. To **Compensating factors** cope with frontier conditions left little time for play or reverie, but the very fact that his life was hard tended to develop in him a certain determination, shrewdness, tenacity, and sense of fair play — characteristics common to those who dwell on the frontier. And colonial America, after all, as we have already noted, was only the frontier of Europe. Yet in the older settled regions of this frontier there gradually emerged a trading, moneyed class with views and interests quite different from those of the colonial farmer, and it is to this class that we shall now turn our attention.

SUGGESTED READINGS

J. T. Adams, *Provincial Society, 1690–1763* (Vol. iii of *A History of American Life*). Chaps. i–iv, vii–viii.

("An American") *American Husbandry*, 2 vols.

C. M. Andrews, *Colonial Folkways* (Vol. ix of *Chronicles of America*).

J. C. Ballagh, *White Servitude in Virginia*.

J. S. Bassett, *Servitude and Slavery in the Colony of North Carolina*.

Charles and Mary Beard, *The Rise of American Civilization*, vol. i, chaps. iii–iv.

P. W. Bidwell and J. I. Falconer, *History of Agriculture in the Northern United States before 1860*.

B. W. Bond, *The Quit-Rent System in the American Colonies*.

P. A. Bruce, *Economic History of Virginia in the Seventeenth Century*, vol. i, chaps. iv–ix; vol. ii, chaps. x–xiv.

P. A. Bruce, *Social Life in Virginia in the Seventeenth Century*.

A. H. Buck, *The Growth of Medicine From the Earliest Times to About 1800*.

A. W. Calhoun, *A Social History of the American Family*, vol. i.

G. S. Callender, *Selections from the Economic History of the United States, 1765–1860*, chaps. i–ii.

Lyman Carrier, *The Beginnings of American Agriculture*.

Edward Channing, *The Narragansett Planters*.

S. H. Cobb, *The Rise of Religious Liberty in America*.

A. O. Craven, *Soil Exhaustion as a Factor in the Agricultural History of Virginia and Maryland, 1606–1860*.

St. John de Crèvecœur, *Sketches of Eighteenth Century America*.

A. M. Earle, *Home Life in Colonial Days*.

Melville Egleston, *The Land Systems of the New England Colonies.*

R. H. Gabriel, *Toilers of Land and Sea* (Vol. iii of *The Pageant of America*).

C. A. Herrick, *White Servitude in Pennsylvania.*

Meyer Jacobstein, *The Tobacco Industry in the United States,* chaps. i–iii.

Fiske Kimball, *Domestic Architecture of the American Colonies and of the Early Republic.*

L. V. Lockwood, *Colonial Furniture,* 2 vols.

Elizabeth McClellan, *Historic Dress in America, 1607–1800.*

E. I. McCormac, *White Servitude in Maryland.*

H. L. Osgood, *The American Colonies in the Eighteenth Century,* 4 vols.

U. B. Phillips, *American Negro Slavery,* chaps. i–vi.

U. B. Phillips, *Life and Labor in the Old South,* chaps. i–iii.

Philip Schaff and others, *The American Church History,* vol. 13.

L. B. Schmidt and E. D. Ross, *Readings in the Economic History of American Agriculture,* chaps i–vii.

W. B. Weeden, *Economic and Social History of New England, 1620–1784,* 2 vols.

T. J. Wertenbaker, *The First Americans, 1607–1690* (Vol. ii of *A History of American Life*). Chaps. i–v, xi–xiii.

T. J. Wertenbaker, *The Planters of Colonial Virginia.*

CHAPTER III

THE COLONIAL MERCHANT AND MANUFACTURER

WHILE hardy colonial frontiersmen were blazing new trails and clearing new farm lands, a small but increasing minority of enter-

Colonial industry becomes increasingly diversified

prising colonists were devoting their energies to trade, or to other pursuits, such as trapping, fishing, lumbering, shipbuilding, and manufacturing. Even the vast majority of farmers north of Maryland spent a considerable portion of their time in some industrial enterprise other than farming. In other words, colonial industry from the beginning became more and more diversified.

The extent of diversification, which varied greatly from colony to colony, was, like the character of colonial agriculture, largely

Extent of diversification determined by natural conditions

determined by geographical conditions and natural resources. New England with its inclement weather, its stony, hilly and not over-fertile land, its many short streams and tumbling waterfalls, its wealth of coast line, its valuable forest resources, and its great submerged coastal plain abounding in cod, mackerel, and other fish of commercial importance, enjoyed a more diversified economic life than either the Middle or Southern colonies.

South of the Chesapeake, as we have already observed, there was comparatively little economic diversification. In the early

Southern industry less diversified than northern

days of Virginia the London Company at great expense attempted to establish several industries. Men skilled in erecting iron works and in manufacturing salt were sent to the colony. A number of Dutchmen and Poles were sent over to begin the production of pitch, tar, turpentine, and potash. Likewise several Hollanders were despatched to erect sawmills, as also were a number of Frenchmen to produce wine and silk. In 1621 a company of Italians skilled in the manufacture of glassware arrived. All efforts to secure industrial diversification, however, met with trifling success, the new industries being unable to compete with the tobacco culture. In fact, adherents of the company frankly admitted in 1625 that "the Attempts of setting other stapell Comodityes as the Iron Works, Silke, Wines and many the like though persued with great constancy, charge and care, have hereunto failed by sundry mis-accedences." Nature, in other words, thwarted the company's preconceived economic system. Nor, with the possible exception of North Carolina, was it different in the other Southern colonies. Soil and climate more than any other influence destined the region for the time being to be agricultural and a producer of great staples.

The people of the Middle colonies, like the New Englanders, were engaged in more than one industrial enterprise. Here, too, climate, geography, and abundant natural resources were largely instrumental in shaping the economic life of the section throughout the entire colonial period and even after. While the region did not enjoy as many good harbors as New England, it nevertheless did possess two great estuaries of the Atlantic: the Delaware and Chesapeake bays, both extending far inland, with their river tributaries, the Delaware and the Susquehanna, tapping one of the most richly endowed agricultural sections east of the Alleghenies. In the storm-sheltered harbor of New York, which was linked with the heart of the continent by the valleys of the Hudson and the Mohawk, it could boast the finest commercial port in America. Nor was nature stingy with the region in other respects. Along the coast were valuable oyster and shad fisheries; great forests supplied the choicest of pine, spruce, and hardwoods and furnished a home for many fur-bearing animals; and beneath the surface were rich deposits of ore.

Industry in Middle colonies diversified

1. THE FUR TRADE

Of the various specialized colonial industries the fur trade was of outstanding importance. In striking contrast to the present, the forests abounded in beaver, otter, fox, mink, and other valuable fur-bearing animals, the pelts and skins of which found New England a ready market in the Old World. Eighteen years early engages before the Pilgrims landed at Plymouth, Bartholo- in fur trade mew Gosnold, the explorer, obtained furs from the savages along the coast of New England. The Pilgrims them- selves engaged in the fur business, their first cargo back to England in 1621 being composed of pelts and clapboards. In- deed, it was by means of the fur traffic that the Pilgrims bought their freedom from their merchant backers; in the five years from 1631 to 1636 Plymouth alone shipped approximately £30,000 worth of furs to London. Every early Massachusetts town had its fur-trading monopoly which it customarily "farmed out" to various persons and not always to the highest bidder; in 1657 we find the legislature of the colony declaring that the fur trade ought to be controlled by the commonwealth and not by its several communities. The trade in New England as well as elsewhere was carried on almost entirely through the medium of the Indians, the white trader or middleman receiv- ing large quantities of furs in exchange for trinkets, blankets, liquor, and ammunition. Needless to say, the industry was sub- ject to all sorts of abuse, for the New England fur trader, not unlike those of the other colonies, did not hesitate to drive a hard bargain whenever opportunity offered.

The fur traffic was no less important in the English mainland colonies outside of New England. Under the Dutch West India New York Company, which enjoyed a monopoly of the trade advantage- of New Netherland, the industry developed rapidly ously situated in the Hudson valley, where for the first two decades for fur trade of Dutch occupation it was almost the only busi- ness. So great were the profits that within a few years traders pushed farther up the valley and out along the Mohawk, which formed a natural highway between the posts on the Hudson and the thrifty and energetic Iroquois who controlled the routes to the Great Lakes and occupied the position of middlemen be- tween the whites and the more remote Indians. In 1656 Fort Orange (Albany), the Dutch trading post, exported 35,000 beaver and otter skins. Even after New Netherland passed into the hands of the English the fur traffic continued to be an important industry, 40,000 skins being exported annually to England. Toward the end of the century, however, the trade declined, only 15,000 skins being exported from the colony in 1699.

In the colonies south of New York the fur business long continued to occupy a position of importance. Pennsylvania and Virginia trappers traversed practically every valley in the eastern Alleghenies, and year after year the Potomac, the James, and the many tributaries of the Chesapeake were dotted with their fur-laden canoes. Carolina and Georgia traders did a thriving business with the Creek and Choctaw Indians. Augusta, Georgia, laid out in 1736, became from the first one of the foremost fur trade centers in America. Pack trains employing no less than six hundred horses are reported to have brought in 100,000 pounds of skins annually. It was estimated that at the same time the fur export from Charleston, South Carolina, totaled between £25,000 and £30,000 a year.

Fur trade important in colonies south of New York

As the population of the English colonies increased and fur-bearing animals became more scarce in the older settled regions, trader and trapper alike turned westward in quest of unexploited territories. No sooner had they advanced beyond the valley of the Mohawk or pushed across the Alleghenies into the Ohio country, however, than they came into conflict with the French who, as we have noted, laid claim to a vast territory stretching from the Gulf of St. Lawrence to the mouth of the Mississippi and embracing the heart of the North American continent. A wonderful system of lakes and rivers afforded easy access to the entire region, which was particularly rich in valuable furs. From 1600, when the French king, Henry IV, awarded a monopoly of the fur trade to a group of French traders and merchants, the fur business constituted France's chief source of wealth in the New World and she, therefore, stubbornly resisted any intrusion on the part of outsiders.

New France and the fur trade

Much as France desired to keep her vast empire intact and maintain a monopoly of the fur trade within her boundaries, she

was powerless to do so. In the first place, her empire was in
many respects merely an empire on paper, for as late as 1750
French   its white population totaled only between sixty and
weakness   seventy thousand, a number wholly inadequate
to develop its resources or to defend it. Pitted against this
sparse population and covetous of the domains it claimed were
the more than a million inhabitants of the thirteen English
mainland colonies. While the French colonists were spending
their time in exploring the endless forests and numerous rivers,
their English rivals were transforming the Atlantic seaboard
wilderness into farms and plantations and relentlessly pushing
westward to conquer new lands, plant new settlements, and
reap new profits.

It was inevitable, therefore, that these two peoples should
sooner or later come into conflict over the fur trade and over pos-
Fur trade and   session of the trans-Allegheny country. Indeed,
possession of   the fur trade, the fisheries (see below), and owner-
trans-   ship of the great central West were among the chief
Allegheny
sources of   causes, if not the chief causes, of King William's
international   War (1689–1697), Queen Anne's War (1701–1713),
conflict
                    King George's War (1744–1748) and the French
and Indian War (1754–1763), all four of which merely represented the American phase of that mighty struggle waged
between France and England during the seventeenth and eighteenth centuries for the colonial and commercial supremacy of
the world. It is not our purpose to give a detailed account of
each of these conflicts; it is sufficient that we bear in mind that
beginning with the closing years of the seventeenth century,
when the Hudson Bay Company loomed up as a powerful potential rival of the French, English traders and speculators increasingly menaced the trade and prestige of their ancient adversary.
In 1724 the colony of New York, for example, roused the ire of
the French by establishing a fortified trading post at Oswego on
Lake Ontario for the purpose of intercepting the Indian trade
with Montreal. A few years later De Noyan, the French com-
mandant at Detroit, bitterly complained about the intrusion of
the English and their growing influence over the Indians. The
hostility of the two rivals was further intensified when toward

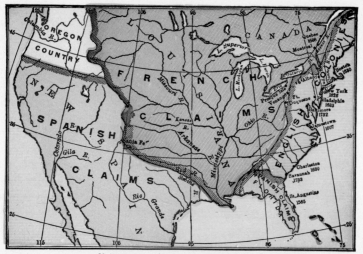

**CENTRAL NORTH AMERICA, 1755
AT THE BEGINNING OF THE FRENCH AND INDIAN WAR.**

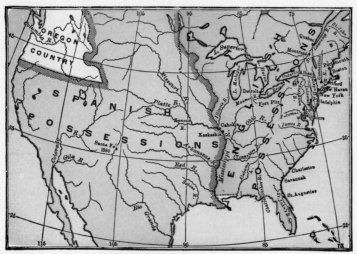

**CENTRAL NORTH AMERICA, 1763
AFTER THE FRENCH AND INDIAN WAR.**
(ACCORDING TO PEACE OF PARIS)

the middle of the century English traders established a post at Pickawillany on the Big Miami river only to have it destroyed in 1752 by a force of French and Indians.

The last of the struggles just mentioned, namely, the French and Indian War or Seven Years' War as it is sometimes called, involved all the great powers of the world. England and Prussia on the one side were pitted against France, Austria, Spain, and minor states on the other in what proved to be the decisive contest for imperial mastery. When at last peace came in 1763 *The Treaty of 1763 and the downfall of the French Empire in America* the British flag floated triumphantly over Canada and the territory east of the Mississippi with the exception of New Orleans. This city together with Louisiana, that vast region spreading westward from the Mississippi, defeated France transferred to her luckless ally, Spain. Of her former extensive territories in North America she retained only two small, rocky islands off the coast of Newfoundland. The French dream of colonial empire on the American continent was at an end. Even Spain was forced to cede Florida to England in exchange for Havana, which the British had seized during the war. With the British gains in other parts of the world we need not be concerned. Britain's triumph in America was sufficient to justify the Earl of Granville in saying that this had been "the most glorious war and the most triumphant peace that England ever knew."

But the fur traffic, even though an important cause of this momentous struggle, had been for years rapidly declining as a colonial industry. Only on the frontier and in the territory recently acquired from France did it retain *Fur traffic declines* a semblance of its seventeenth-century character; and in 1764 England ruled that henceforth all hides and skins could be exported only to the mother country. Less than $700,000 worth of furs and peltry were exported from all the North American colonies in 1770.

2. Lumbering, Naval Stores, and Shipbuilding

Of far greater economic value than the fur-bearing animals were the forests in which they lived. From Maine to Georgia the

colonists were blessed with an abundance of timber resources.
Almost all of New England was covered with magnificent forests
of cedar, spruce, and white pine, the latter so useful for masts and spars that the British authorities
regarded it as the most valuable timber in America.
Hardwoods, among them red and white oak with
their knotless trunks of fifty to seventy feet, highly prized by
every colonial shipbuilder, were also plentiful. Here, too, thrived
the sugar maple from the sap of which was made sugar to supply
many a colonial household.

Colonial New England's timber resources

Extensive forests of spruce, hemlock, fir, balsam, and white
pine covered many sections of New York; hardwoods, such as
beech, birch, ash, oak, cherry, walnut, and chestnut
abounded in all the Middle colonies and even in
Virginia and the colonies to the south. Vast tracts
of the Carolinas and Georgia were covered with forests of long
leaf yellow pine, valuable not only for its lumber but more especially for its tar, pitch, and turpentine. Cypress and mulberry
also grew extensively in the South.

Timber resources in other colonies

It is impossible to estimate with any degree of accuracy the
value of the timber destroyed during the colonial period; we do
know, however, that thousands of acres of splendid
virgin forests met destruction at the hands of the
settler. Naturally, he was not interested in conser-
vation, and with axe and fire he cleared the land that he might
raise food for himself and his family, or some staple for the
European or West Indian market. It would be a serious error,
however, to conclude that all the enormous forest resources of
the colonies were wasted. From them the great majority of the
colonists built and heated their homes, manufactured their tools
and furniture, obtained the fuel and raw materials for their
industries, and secured the bark and wood necessary for dyeing and tanning purposes. Upon them the colonial and, to
a certain extent, the British shipbuilder was dependent for
timber, masts, and naval supplies; and the sawed timbers, shingles, clapboards, staves, headings, hoops, ashes, and naval
stores which they furnished were of the greatest commercial
value.

Importance of colonial forests

TYPICAL VIRGINIA SAWMILL OF THE
SEVENTEENTH CENTURY

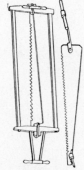

PIT SAWS WHICH
PRECEDED
SAWMILLS

While a few of the colonists devoted all of their time to lumbering, by far the larger number engaged in this industry were farmers who occupied themselves with it during the winter months.   Particularly was this true in the Northern colonies, where they were glad of the opportunity to supplement the slender income derived from the summer's toil.   During the eighteenth century an increasing number of land speculators, merchants, capitalists, and even professional men turned their attention to lumbering.   Elisha Cooke and Mark Hunking Wentworth, the latter the "lumber king" of colonial America, were typical of this group.

Lumbering carried on mostly by farmers

At first all the work was done by hand with axe and handsaw, but scarcity of labor and an increasing market for forest products made the use of machinery imperative.   Dutch artisans, as we have already noted, were sent to Virginia in 1620 to erect a sawmill, but the first successful mills in America appear to have been built in New England in the early sixteen-thirties by settlers near Piscataqua.   In striking contrast to the great lumber plants of our Northwest today, these first mills were primitive in type, consisting of a single vertical slash or blade saw pulled downward by a water wheel crank and upward by a large elastic pole.   Yet, primitive as they were, they nevertheless enabled a man and boy to turn out a thousand feet of pine lumber per day.   The Dutch also at an early date erected mills along the Hudson which were run by wind or water and, in some instances, by a combination of both.   These smaller mills, which rapidly multiplied in number, were usually individual enterprises costing from five hundred to a thousand dollars.   Larger mills using gang-saws and representing a larger capital outlay came into use toward the close of the seventeenth century.   In 1700, for instance, a Dutch mechanic installed a gang of twelve saws in one of the Livingston mills in New York, and on the eve of the Revolution mills with twelve and fourteen saws were in operation in the Mohawk valley and in New England.   The majority of these larger mills were owned on shares or were the property of some manufacturing or commercial concern using large quantities of sawed timber.

Methods

Limited capital and the expense of building a dam and race-way confined the early colonial mills to creeks and to the smaller rivers. Lack of adequate transportation likewise was partly responsible for limiting the industry to the costal areas of the New England and Middle colonies, with the result that these districts were early denuded of merchantable timber.   Indeed, as early as 1670 a Plymouth law recited that several towns "are already much straightened for building timber"; even Boston soon had to depend on Maine for its firewood.   Because of the rapid exhaustion of the seacoast forest resources of the Northern colonies before 1700, the center of the lumber industry tended to shift to the frontier and to the southern provinces, particularly to the Carolinas, after that date.   Before the Revolution recourse was had to the device of securing timber in the back country and floating the logs down the numerous streams to the mills which were located near the coast.

Lumber industry confined to costal areas

The products of the colonial forests commanded a wide market, including not only Britain but Spain and Portugal as well as the West Indies.   The towering masts of many a British man-of-war, for example, came from some New England hillside; to the mother country, whose forests had been exhausted in the iron industry, also went spars, sawed timber, naval stores, and potash to bleach her woolens.   Irish peasants packed their butter and salt provisions in buckets and tubs made of coopers' supplies from Pennsylvania;   Spanish and Portuguese shipbuilders planked their vessels with timber from Maine and New Hampshire; and West Indian planters shipped their sugar and molasses in barrels and hogsheads manufactured from materials of the American forests.

Wide market for colonial forest products

The production of naval stores was of prime importance both to the colonists and to the mother country.   From the first many Englishmen, as we have seen, warmly advocated colonization on the ground that it would bring to England definite economic advantages.   Most potent and fundamental of all these, they believed, would be the tapping of new sources of supply that would render her independent of foreign nations.   Among the supplies that she was forced to import were

Importance of naval stores

tar, pitch, turpentine, flax, hemp, and cordage, essential alike to merchant marine and navy. For years, as we have noted, she had depended on the Baltic countries for these indispensable naval stores — a source at best costly and liable at any time to be cut off by war, embargo, or blockade. Accordingly, strenuous efforts were made to secure these products from the colonies.

At first it was confidently expected that New England, glowing accounts of which told of an "abundance of Turpentine, Pitch, Tarre, Masts and other materials for building Naval store both of Ships & Houses," would supply the mother production country with these products. But such expectations were all too sanguine, for local shipbuilders consumed nearly all the tar, pitch, and turpentine produced by the section. From the South, however, and especially from the Carolinas, she obtained great quantities. Between 1701 and 1718, for instance, shipments of tar from America to England increased from 177 to 82,084 barrels, and of this amount South Carolina alone furnished 32,000 barrels. It is also significant that at the latter date colonial tar constituted nearly ninety per cent of all the British imports from America. In 1724 South Carolina was exporting 52,000 barrels of pitch, tar, and turpentine per year; but this remarkable increase did not continue. In 1768 the total importations into Great Britain from all the colonies amounted to a little more than 135,000 barrels. Two years later it had fallen to 102,169 barrels. In addition, approximately 6,000 barrels found their way into other countries.

During the eighteenth century Great Britain attempted to stimulate the production of naval stores by means of bounties. Thus in 1705 Parliament provided for a bounty of Great Britain £4 a ton on pitch and tar imported from the colo- attempts to nies, £3 per ton on rosin and turpentine, £1 a ton on stimulate production of masts, yards, and bow-sprits, and £6 a ton on naval stores hemp. This Act, although somewhat modified, was by bounties in force for nearly fifty years, during which bounties on naval stores to the amount of £1,458,762 were paid. While bounties failed to increase materially the output of these articles in the Northern colonies, they unquestionably promoted their production in the South and especially in the Carolinas, for as soon as this encouragement was removed or even minimized those engaged in the business turned their attention to other pursuits.

Of all the specialized colonial industries, shipbuilding was in many respects the most important of all. Without a colonial Shipbuilding: fleet the products of forest, farm, and sea would its prime have had to depend upon outside interests for disimportance tribution. Ships were built in every colony, but the industry was confined chiefly to New England and the Middle group. By recourse to bounties, the Southern colonies endeavored from time to time to develop the industry but without success. High freight rates, for instance, induced Virginia in 1661 to offer bounties for sea-going vessels built and permanently owned in the colony. And in 1711 and again in 1753 we find South Carolina offering similar inducements to persons building ships and to shipwrights settling in the province. But the shipwrights did not come, and in 1754 the law of the previous year was repealed.

The launching of Governor Winthrop's little 30-ton sloop, the *Blessing of the Bay*, New England's first sea-faring vessel, in In New 1631, marked the beginning of her shipbuilding England career. Cheapness of building materials and a ready market for the sale of the ships caused the industry to grow rapidly, and in less than thirty years the coast was dotted with shipyards. At Newburyport, Ipswich, Gloucester, Salem, Boston, New Bedford, Newport, Providence, New London, and New Haven, shipwrights and master builders busily plied their trade. Villages far up navigable streams and even inland towns engaged in the business. Stimulated by the English Navigation Acts, which confined colonial commerce to English and colonial vessels, building grew apace. In 1676 Edward Randolph, an unfriendly but accurate English observer, who subsequently became British collector of customs for New England, declared that Massachusetts had up to that time built 730 vessels. But the golden age of New England shipbuilding dates from 1700 to 1735, a period in which she sold vessels to every part of the Atlantic world. Indeed, in no other country were ships built so skillfully and inexpensively; timber was plentiful and easily available, and its cheapness more than offset the cost of labor, which was a little higher than in Europe. So rapidly did the business grow that in 1724 several master builders of London petitioned the Lords of Trade to restrain New England competition, a request which was not granted.

The thrifty and ambitious New Englanders, however, had no monopoly of colonial shipbuilding. Early in the seventeenth century the Dutch launched a vessel at New Amsterdam, and for years the shipyard of Rip Van Dam, located on the river front back of Trinity churchyard, was the scene of bustling activity. Even after the colony passed into the hands of the English the industry did not slacken, and during the eighteenth century busy yards at Albany and Poughkeepsie turned out vessels to handle the trade of the province. But it was Pennsylvania that most closely rivaled New England. Both Philadelphia and Wilmington had extensive shipbuilding yards, and their ships formed no inconsiderable part of the colonial merchant marine. Many vessels were also built on the eastern shore of Maryland. Yet so great was the leadership of New England that she built annually twice as great a tonnage as all the other continental colonies combined.

The colonial ships varied greatly both in size and type. By far the larger number of colonial-owned vessels were small, being usually of twenty to fifty tons burden and constructed for use in the fisheries and the West Indian and the intercolonial trade. The construction of ocean-carriers of a hundred tons burden or more, built on order or speculation for the English market, continued throughout the colonial period. Of the 7,694 ships engaged in the commerce of Great Britain in 1775 almost a third were built in American yards. "America," declared the British writer, Champion, "was able to supply us with ships 30 per cent cheaper than they could be built in Great Britain."

While all sorts of vessels were turned out by the colonial shipbuilder, four rather distinct types of vessels were built: (1) giant three-masted square-rigged ships, or pinks as they were sometimes called — the ocean freighters of their day; (2) snows and barks, also three-masters and, except for rigging, differing little from the pinks; (3) ketches, brigs, brigantines, and schooners, all two-masters but of different sizes; (4) sloops, shallops, and smacks, single-masters built especially for the fisheries and the coasting trade. In addition, every port had its flotillas of mastless hog-boats, fly-boats, wherries, rowboats, and canoes.

Every ship built not only gave employment to dozens of ship carpenters but stimulated other industries and helped increase **Other indus-** the store of capital. Timber had to be cut and **tries aided by** sawed; nails, anchors, rope, and sails manufac- **shipbuilding** tured; and food and clothing provided for workers and crew. The sailors were recruited in part from English seaports, but mostly from the youth of the American seaboard. The glamour of the sea with its possibility of wealth and adventure lured many a lad from a colonial fireside. For a New England youth a sea voyage, to quote Professor Morison, offered "an easy escape from the strict conventions and prying busybodies of New England towns." On the broad sea he was beyond the jurisdiction of strait-laced Puritan preachers; the Cotton Mathers might bewail that it was a "matter of saddest complaint that there should be no more Serious Piety in the Sea-Faring Tribe," but he heard them not.

3. FISHING AND WHALING

Ranking in importance with shipbuilding was the fishing industry. Long before the Pilgrims set foot upon the New World **Early impor-** English, Dutch, Portuguese, and French navigators **tance of** were exploiting the rich fishing grounds extending **fisheries** from Long Island to the Grand Banks of Newfoundland. Indeed, as early as 1540 the American fisheries were mentioned in an Act of the English Parliament, and fifty years later Sir Walter Raleigh declared that they were the "stay and support of the west counties of England." By the close of the sixteenth century the Newfoundland fisheries alone were employing two hundred vessels and ten thousand men and boys. Four years after the Pilgrims landed at Plymouth Captain John Smith reported that "there hath been a fishing, this year upon the coast [of New England], about fifty English ships." Smith

WHALING IN THE ARCTIC OCEAN

SPERMACETI WHALE OF THE SOUTHERN OCEAN

was right when he predicted that the fisheries would be invaluable. "Let not the meannesse of the word Fish distaste you," said he, "for it will afford as good gold as the mines of Guiana and Potassie with less hazard and charge, and more certaintie and facility."

Although carried on to some extent in all the colonies, it was only in New England, however, that fishing developed into a leading industry. Here many a Puritan early turned to the sea, where with net and harpoon he reaped without sowing. Boston exported fish in 1633, and in a few years thereafter the entire region began to realize the commercial importance of this seemingly inexhaustible economic resource. Soon every port had its fishing fleet which brought in cod, mackerel, bass, herring, halibut, hake, sturgeon, and other deep-sea fish. To encourage the industry the General Court of Massachusetts in 1639 exempted all vessels and other property employed in the business from all duties and public taxes for seven years; to the same end, fishermen and shipbuilders were excused from military duty. The result of this legislation was early apparent, for Governor Winthrop reported that in 1641 three hundred thousand dried fish had been sent to market, and before the end of the century New England merchants were shipping cargoes of fish to the West Indies.

Fishing industry limited to New England

As the industry expanded the fishermen pushed northeastward to the coast of Nova Scotia, the Gulf of St. Lawrence, and to the Grand Banks of Newfoundland. In these, the richest of American fishing waters, they at once came into conflict with the French. As collisions and quarrels became more frequent the New Englanders began to clamor for the expulsion of their rivals, who by 1680 had not only laid claim to all the territory east of the Kennebec, but were levying tribute on foreign vessels engaged in fishing on the Acadian coast and inciting the Indians to attack outlying English settlements and murder crews of New England fishing boats frequenting the coast of Maine. When, therefore, war broke out between England and France in 1689, the business men of New England — fishermen, shipbuilders, and merchants — welcomed the chance

Conflict with the French

to send a successful expedition against Port Royal, Nova Scotia, the base of the French privateers. Bitter was their disappointment, however, when by the Peace of Ryswick, 1697, concluded at the close of King William's War, the French were left in possession of all the coast islands and fishing grounds north from the Penobscot river, with the exception of the eastern half of Newfoundland, which was retained by England.

But King William's War was merely the opening scene of the American phase of the struggle between France and England which was to continue for another hundred years. When the contest was renewed in 1702 the New Englanders again hailed the opportunity of expelling the French from the fishing grounds of America. "It grieves me to the heart," wrote Subercase, the French governor of Acadia, "to see Messieurs les Bastonnais enrich themselves in our domain; for the base of their commerce is the fish which they catch off our coasts, and send to all parts of the world." Notwithstanding his plea for support, Nova Scotia was again captured in 1710 by a combined colonial and English force. By the terms of the peace concluded at Utrecht, 1713, which marked the termination of Queen Anne's War, all of Newfoundland and the Hudson Bay country came into possession of England; Nova Scotia also remained in the hands of the English, and the French were prohibited from fishing within thirty leagues of its coast from Sable Island to the southwest. France, however, was allowed to retain possession of Cape Breton Island, the Gulf of St. Lawrence, and the islands lying within its mouth. Her fishermen, moreover, were to enjoy the privilege of catching and drying fish on certain parts of the coast of Newfoundland.

Queen Anne's War and partial expulsion of French from fishing grounds

New Englanders rejoiced. While their rivals had not been excluded entirely from the fisheries, their sphere of operation nevertheless had been greatly curtailed. England now had exclusive possession of many of the richest grounds and an equal chance, it was thought, to compete with the French in the non-monopolized territory. The rejoicing, however, was of short duration, for much to the dis-

Rivalry of French continues

may and even chagrin of the colonists, the French immediately
colonized Cape Breton, and under the protection of the bristling
walls of the fortress of Louisburg their fisheries became more
flourishing and prosperous than ever before.

More than thirty years elapsed before another chance came to
the New Englanders to rid themselves of the menace of French
competition. It is quite unnecessary for us to re-   French prac-
count the story of the capture of Louisburg, the   tically ousted
stronghold of the French position; we need simply from fishing
                                                    grounds by
note that by the Treaty of Aix-la-Chapelle, 1748,   treaty of
which concluded King George's War, Cape Breton   1763
Island was handed back to France, and the fisheries question
remained unsettled. Indeed, it was not until 1763, when the
French colonial empire crumbled and practically disappeared,
that the business interests of New England had the satisfaction
of seeing France dispossessed of all her territory in the northern
fishing grounds with the exception of the two small islands of
Miquelon and St. Pierre.

But neither French competition nor three-quarters of a
century of intermittent warfare prevented the New England
fisheries from making a remarkable growth. In   Growth of
1731, almost exactly a hundred years after its estab- fishing
lishment, the industry employed between 5,000 and industry
6,000 men; Gloucester alone had a fleet of seventy vessels, and
fishing developed so rapidly in Marblehead that a fisherman's
reproof to an exhorting preacher that "our ancestors came not
here for religion. Their main end was to catch fish," seemed
literally true. Salem, Ipswich, Yarmouth, Plymouth, and
Chatham all had their cod-fleets which plied the teeming northern waters. It is estimated that 665 vessels carrying approximately 4,400 men were annually employed in cod-fishing during
the ten years prior to the Revolution. Altogether the industry
in 1765 furnished employment to 10,000 men, yielded a product
worth approximately $2,000,000 per year, and kept 350 vessels
busy carrying fish to the markets of Europe and the West Indies.
As Professor Morison has expressed it, "Puritan Massachusetts
derived her ideals from a sacred book; her wealth and power
from the sacred cod."

The better grades of cod were salted and dried and sold in the Catholic countries of Portugal, Spain, and Italy or exchanged for salt, lemons, oranges, raisins, and wines for the English and colonial markets. Considerable quantities of middling grades of dried codfish, easy to keep and prepare, were sold to the Portuguese islands and to colonial farmers. The lower grade of dried fish, "refuse fish" as it was sometimes called, together with pickled mackerel, bass, and alewives were shipped to the West Indies for slave consumption.

Markets

Closely allied with the fishing business, and sometimes considered a part of it, was the whaling industry. As early as 1614 Captain John Smith had visited the New England coast "to take whales and make tryalls at a myne of gold and copper." Richard Mather, who came to Massachusetts in 1635, related that he had seen off the New England coast "mighty whales spewing up water in the air like the smoke of a chimney . . . of such incredible bigness that I will never wonder that the body of Jonah could be in the belly of a whale." At first those engaged in the industry depended entirely upon the occasional drift whales cast ashore by the sea; they soon learned the art, however, of harpooning the whales from small boats along the coast. By the close of the seventeenth century Plymouth, Salem, Nantucket, and the fishing towns on the eastern end of Long Island were doing a profitable whaling business, and New England merchants were exporting considerable quantities of whale products.

Early whaling

But the heyday of colonial whaling came after 1715. In that year a Nantucketer, Christopher Hussey by name, fitted out a vessel to pursue sperm whales and tow them ashore. Less than a dozen years later arrangements were made for extracting the oil on shipboard; thus the Macys, Coffins, Folgers, Husseys, and other Nantucket whalers were enabled to extend their cruising radius to the coast of Brazil and to the Arctic ocean. Whalers of other New England towns soon followed their example, and by 1774 no less than 360 vessels were engaged in this perilous industry. Of these, at least 120 belonged to Nantucket, 180 to other Massachusetts ports, and the remainder to Connecticut, Rhode Island, and

Heyday of whaling after 1715

New York. Well might Edmund Burke exclaim in the House of Commons:

Look at the manner in which the people of New England have of late carried on the whale industry. Whilst we follow them among the tumbling mountains of ice and behold them penetrating into the deepest frozen recesses of Hudson's Bay and Davis's Straits, while we are looking for them beneath the Arctic Circle, we hear that they have pierced into the opposite region of polar cold, that they are at the antipodes and engaged under the frozen serpent of the South. . . . Nor is the equinoctial heat more discouraging to them than the accumulated winter of both poles. We know that, whilst some of them draw the line and strike the harpoon on the coast of Africa, others run the longitude and pursue their gigantic game along the coast of Brazil. No sea but what is vexed by their fisheries. No climate that is not witness to their toils. Neither the perseverance of Holland nor the activity of France nor the dexterous and firm sagacity of English enterprise ever carried this most perilous mode of hard industry to the extent to which it has been pushed by these recent people.

And Burke did not exaggerate. Climate, topography, forest, and sea made New England a maritime section — a veritable nursery of seamanship. Fishing, shipbuilding, and commerce, rather than farming, were her key industries and the fundamental sources of her prosperity and wealth.

4. HOUSEHOLD MANUFACTURES

Significant as were the industries just described, we should not allow them to overshadow the importance of the numerous commodities produced in the colonial household. Four groups of household manufactures Roughly, these may be grouped as follows: (1) wearing apparel and textile supplies; (2) furniture and utensils; (3) farm tools and implements; (4) necessities and comforts. Each of these groups deserves brief mention.

Despite the fact that the colonists were expected to secure their clothing and other manufactures from the mother country, they nevertheless early engaged in the household production of textiles. Money was so scarce, the cost of transportation so high, and prices so excessive that many of the colonists were unable to buy imported clothing. Particularly was this true of those northern farmers who had little or nothing to send to England in exchange for manufactured goods except grain, which the English corn laws rigidly excluded. Even the British authorities were cognizant of this fact, for in 1705, in explaining the reason why the colony of New York was engaging in manufacturing, Lord Cornbury said that "the want of wherewithal to make returns to England" made it necessary. Again, as late as 1731–32 the Board of Trade in a report to the House of Commons declared that the colonies north of Maryland had "no staple commodities of their own growth to exchange for our manufactures, which puts them under great necessity, as well as under great temptation, of providing them for themselves." Indeed, it would seem that whatever manufacturing was done in the home and on the plantation prior to 1765 was done chiefly from necessity rather than from desire and was more or less local in character.

Necessity rather than desire accounts for textile manufacture prior to 1765

At first flax and wool, the principal raw materials used in textile manufacture in colonial times, were scarce and costly. Flax had been introduced into New England in 1629, but it was not until after the middle of the century that it was raised in sufficient quantities to satisfy the demands of home consumption. The British government, in accord with its mercantile principles, prohibited the exportation of sheep or fleece from the mother country, and so forced the settlers to depend upon Spain for their wool supply.

Textile material scarce and costly at first

Neither British restrictions, nor wolves, Indians, or severe winters, however, prevented the colonists ultimately from producing their own wool. The first sheep were brought to Jamestown in 1609, and by 1648 there were 3,000 in Virginia alone. Sheep were also early introduced into New England where, in spite of unfavorable conditions, every effort was made to encourage the industry. With the outbreak of the English civil war in 1640 the steady stream of Puritan immigrants to the New World ceased. For more than a decade these newcomers had brought with them money and manufactures which, upon their arrival, they exchanged for

Inrceased wool supply

provisions. All was now changed. Hard times ensued, and the New England farmer found himself without a market for his expanding stock of food-stuffs. "Corn," wrote Winthrop, "would buy nothing. Cows that cost last year £20 now sold for £4 or £5. No man could pay his debts, nor the merchants make return unto England for their commodities, which occasioned many there to speak evil of us."

Under such circumstances New England farmers were virtually compelled to produce their own clothing. In 1643 the author of *New England's First Fruits* wrote: "They are making linens, fustians, dimities, and look immediately to woolens from their own sheep." Two years later the General Court of Massachusetts appealed to the towns to increase and preserve the number of sheep. This appeal, together with certain stringent measures taken by the Massachusetts authorities, bore results quickly, for so rapidly did the number increase that by 1662 sheep were worth only one-fourth as much as in 1645. Connecticut also enacted legislation for increasing the supply of wool. In order that the flocks might be adequate to clothe the people at least with every-day wear, sheep were exempted from taxation in 1666 and given exclusive pasture rights on part of the land. Every male citizen, moreover, was obliged to work one day each year clearing away underbrush so that the area of sheep-pasture might be extended. Somewhat later New Hampshire exempted sheep from taxation for a period of seven years and made it a crime to kill ewes. Even little Rhode Island no less than her adjoining neighbors was interested in the industry and before 1650 was exporting sheep to Connecticut for breeding purposes. Before 1700 New England was producing enough wool for her domestic manufactures.

In the Middle colonies, too, the production of wool was of major importance, but the section did not pursue so consistent a policy of encouraging its production as did New England. The Dutch settlement of New York boasted the possession of sheep as early as 1625, and the wives and daughters of the Swedes on the Delaware from the beginning employed "themselves in spinning wool and flax and many in weaving." Maryland, too, began to raise sheep. Pennsylvania and New Jersey endeavored to stimulate sheep raising by means of bounties, and we find that in 1701 the former ordered every one owning forty acres of cleared land to keep at least ten sheep. As late as the middle of the eighteenth century, however, there was a shortage of wool in Pennsylvania, which was made up by importations from neighboring provinces. In Virginia and her sister colonies to the southward flocks of sheep were common, although scarcity of pasture land was a serious drawback to their increase.

Before the Revolution cotton was also available as a textile material; indeed, as early as 1678 New England imported over 54,000 pounds of cotton from the British West Indies, and New York in the same year received 2,290 pounds from the Barbadoes. But this fiber, so indispensable in later years, was, in comparison with flax and wool, little used during the colonial period. Cattle and buffalo hides and the skins of the deer, squirrel, raccoon, rabbit, bear, wolf, fox, cat, woodchuck, and beaver were also used for wearing apparel as well as for robes and covers.

Other materials used for wearing apparel

Of the raw materials used by the colonists in the manufacture of textiles flax and hemp ranked next to wool. By the end of the seventeenth century all the colonies were producing flax in considerable quantities. The valleys of the Merrimac and Connecticut in New England, the Hudson valley near Albany, the Delaware valley, northern New Jersey, and the Maryland upland back of Baltimore, were famous centers of production. Hemp was also produced in several of the colonies.

Flax production

Once supplied with adequate raw materials, the majority of the colonists made their own textiles, especially the coarser grades. Soon every northern farmhouse became a busy workshop where during the fall and winter months the women "spun and wove the serges, kerseys, and linsey-woolseys which served for common wear." Nor were the southern plantations an exception to the rule, for newspapers, wills, advertisements, and governors' reports and messages bear testimony to the fact that slaves were taught to spin and weave. By the eighteenth

Adequate raw material makes possible increased production

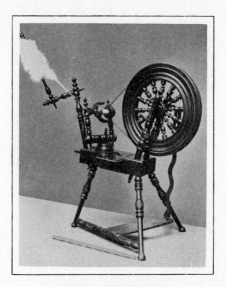

SPINNING WHEEL

Courtesy of the South Kensington Museum

MODEL OF HAND LOOM

century wool-cards and spinning-wheels were found in every planter's inventory, and the records show that many a plantation owner had a special spinning-room or separate building devoted to this purpose.

At first all the processes of textile manufacture were carried on in the home. In the case of woolen fabrics, for example, the sheep were sheared by hand; the wool was then cleaned, carded, and combed and made into rolls. It was then spun into thread, dyed, and knit or woven. Finally the cloth was fulled or softened by wetting it with warm soap-suds and pounding it vigorously with heavy oaken mallets. Indigo, the juices of various plants and flowers, and the bark of certain trees such as sumach, dogwood, oak, hickory, and butternut were used for dyes. The cards, spinning-wheels, reels, looms, and other tools used were the products of the family work-bench or of the village cabinet-shop. Little specialization was noticeable until toward the middle of the eighteenth century when, with the increase in population and the slight development in mechanical improvements, mills began to be erected for the more difficult processes of dying, carding, and fulling. Some families, of course, continued all the processes as before, but an increasing number sent their wool to the mills to be carded and fulled even though it was to be spun and woven at home. Indeed, in the years just prior to the Revolution, it was no uncommon sight to see some red-cheeked New England farmer's lass on the way to or returning from a carding-mill with a bundle of wool towering up behind her bigger than her horse. Professional spinners and weavers also began to offer their services during the eighteenth century.

While most of the textiles produced in the colonial home consisted of linsey-woolsey, jeans, and towline, numerous other varieties, such as ducking, fine linen, and fustian, were manufactured. In addition to wearing apparel, coverlets, counterpanes, towels, tablecloths, sheets, pillowcases, bedcovers, bedticks, lace, and sailcloth were made in the colonial household. The designs and ornamentation of colonial textiles pay tribute to the ingenuity of colonial women.

As the volume of domestic textiles increased, a good many weavers in New England, much to the alarm of the British Colonial textile woolen interests, began to export homemade cloth manufacture to the Southern colonies and to the West Indies. alarms British For generations before the establishment of the colonies, English wool-growers, manufacturers, and merchants had reaped splendid profits by exporting fine woolen goods. In supporting the colonial movement they confidently expected to retain and even to increase this foreign trade, for in keeping with the economic philosophy of the time they had every reason to believe that the colonies would be a source of supply and a market for the mother country's manufactures. Even as early as 1584 Richard Hakluyt enthusiastically declared that "if her Majestie take these Westerne discoveries in hande, and plante there, yt is like that in shorte time wee shall vente as great a mass of clothe yn those partes as ever wee did in the Netherlandes, and in time moche more." English business men never lost sight of this argument, and when, therefore, the New Englanders, instead of buying, began to export cloth, the powerful English woolen interests showed great concern. In fact, during the century prior to the Revolution they repeatedly petitioned the Board of Trade to prohibit and restrain the activities of their colonial rivals.

The production of leather and leather goods was almost as important as textile manufacture. Every colony was fortunately Leather and amply supplied with hides, oak or hemlock bark, leather goods and other raw materials. Tanneries were early established, the first one in New England being erected at Lynn in 1629, and by the middle of the century Massachusetts was shipping saddlery and shoes to her sister provinces. New York and New Jersey, too, at an early date had tanneries turning out leather for local consumption. And so rapidly did the industry develop in the Carolinas that we find them shipping leather to Pennsylvania and New England. Like the weaving of cloth, the working up of leather was, during the greater part of the period, largely confined to the home, where not only boots and shoes were made but also coats, vests, breeches, skirts, stockings, aprons, and other durable articles of wearing apparel. By the middle of the eighteenth century, however, there were many instances where the production of leather goods, particularly shoes, was on a shop basis, and certain northern towns like Lynn, New Haven, Newark, and Philadelphia had gained fame as producers of leather goods. In 1768 approximately 13,000 pairs of American made shoes were shipped to various parts of the English continental colonies; of this number Massachusetts alone exported nearly 9,000 pairs.

Of the hats and caps worn by the colonists the majority were of American make; only plantation owners and certain of the townspeople preferred those of British manufacture. Hats of both fur and wool were manufactured in New England, New York, and Pennsylvania and shipped in large quantities not only to the Southern colonies and the West Indies, but to Ireland and Southern Europe where they came into competition with English made goods. As the woolen manufacturers had done before them, the English hatters also appealed to their government for protection. In response Parliament, after an inquiry (1731) revealing that 10,000 hats were produced annually in New England and New York, enacted the law of 1732 prohibiting the exportation of hats from one colony to another, forbidding the employment of negroes in the industry, and requiring that substantially the same apprenticeship rules be observed in the colonies as in England, namely, an apprenticeship of seven years and the employment of not more than two apprentices by any master. Contrary to the oft-repeated dictum that this measure practically ruined the business, it appears that, with the notable exception of New York, the colonies evaded or disregarded the law, and the industry continued to thrive.

Until the cabinetmaker definitely established himself, practically every household made its own furniture. Tables, cupboards, benches, chairs, bedsteads, cradles, and stools were built from timber cut from the adjoining forest or farm wood lot. And the same was true of such common household utensils as brooms, trays, trenchers, bowls, platters, noggins, lamps, buckets, tubs, churns, firkins, baskets, doormats, breadtroughs, cheese-ladders, butter ladles, washboards, graters, hominy blocks, and the like. Many households also appear to have been expert in the production of copper, brassware, plaster, and pottery.

Before the blacksmith, carpenter, and harness-maker became permanently established, practically every farmer, as we noted **Farm tools and** in the previous chapter, made his own wagons, **implements** plows, harrows, forks, rakes, flails, shovels, ox-yokes, sleds, axe, hammer and hoe handles, scythe-snaths, trees, harnesses, clips, clevises, nails, and other necessary tools and articles. In the North many of these were made in winter when the farmer, unless engaged in the lumber business, had little else to do. Many southern plantations were also self-sufficient as far as implements were concerned. About a dozen of Thomas Jefferson's younger slaves made approximately a ton of nails a month.

Numerous household necessities and comforts were regularly produced by members of the colonial family. Chief among these **Household** were food, drink, and light. Of the food products **necessities** by far the most important were hominy, meal, **and comforts** cheese, dried fruits, maple syrup and sugar. The drinks included beer, cider, and more than two score other beverages. Candlewood, bayberry, and candles, the latter made chiefly from soft-soap and potash, furnished light. Lye, necessary for the production of soft-soap, and the soap itself were among the commonest products manufactured in the home.

5. IRON AND OTHER MANUFACTURES

One of the earliest and in course of time most widespread of colonial industries was working iron. The colonies had plentiful **Beginnings of** deposits of bog iron ore from which iron of good **colonial iron** quality was readily produced. Thanks to the busi- **business** ness sagacity of the younger John Winthrop, who secured capital and skilled laborers from England, Massachusetts Bay was able to establish a forge and a furnace at Lynn in **In New** 1643, only fifteen years after the founding of **England** Boston. Within a short time the capacity of this plant reached eight tons per week, thus comparing favorably with that of some of the larger establishments of the Old World.

For a quarter of a century Lynn supplied the farm tools, pots, kettles, and other domestic utensils for the growing communities of eastern Massachusetts. Furnaces and foundries were subsequently erected in other parts of the colony, including Raynham (1656), Great Barrington (1731), and Lenox (1765). Nor were the other New England colonies one whit behind their enterprising neighbor. Joseph Jenks, an immigrant from Hammersmith and a mechanic of remarkable ability, erected an iron foundry at Pawtucket, Rhode Island. By 1658 both New London and New Haven had begun the smelting of iron, and the opening up of valuable deposits of hematite ore in the hills of Litchfield county a few years later soon enabled Connecticut to outrank Massachusetts as an iron producing colony. The first steel produced in America was probably made in Connecticut in 1722. By the middle of the eighteenth century Massachusetts had four slitting-mills, Connecticut eight iron and steel mills, and New Hampshire one bar-iron plant. In addition to supplying iron for local needs, New England sent insignificant quantities of pig-iron to England and shipped some edged tools and other implements of iron to other colonies.

Little iron appears to have been produced in New York until after the middle of the eighteenth century, when both the Livingstons and Schuylers shipped bar-iron as well as cop- *In the Middle* per to the mother country. In New Jersey, on the *colonies* other hand, iron works were erected at Shrewsbury in 1675, shortly after the founding of the colony. In Pennsylvania, too, the industry early gained a firm foothold, Penn himself being an interested promoter. By 1750 the center of the industry had shifted from New England to Pennsylvania, and the wealthy iron masters of the valleys of the Delaware and Susquehanna had joined hands with the merchant princes of Philadelphia in dominating the colony.

The year that witnessed the introduction of slavery saw also the beginning of the iron industry in Virginia. But these early ironworks erected along the James river were destroyed by the Indians just as they were nearing *In the South* completion in 1622. Tobacco culture proved so profitable that a hundred years elapsed before the business was resurrected under

the auspices of Governor Spotswood, who soon gained the significant title of the "Tubal Cain" of the Old Dominion. Under
his direction new furnaces were built and the industry placed
on a firm foundation. A small portion of the Virginia output
was used for domestic purposes, but the greater part was shipped
across the Atlantic. The same was true of the Maryland
product, most of which came from the four furnaces of the
Principio works located at the head of Chesapeake Bay and
owned by an English company.

From what has been said about the colonial iron industry it
would be erroneous to conclude that iron manufactures were not
Colonies imported from Great Britain. During the seven-
partially teenth century the most prosperous colonial iron
dependent ventures were at best small undertakings, erected
on England
for iron goods and owned by private individuals. Several places
of manufacture were little more than enlarged blacksmith shops,
and many a country smithy upon occasion turned out small
quantities of iron and iron goods. The Principio plant, as we
have just seen, as well as the neighboring Virginia furnaces in
which Governor Spotswood was interested, and many of the
works erected in New Jersey and eastern Pennsylvania after
1700, were company enterprises financed either entirely or in
part by British capital. Undoubtedly the colonists found it unnecessary to import many common commodities like nails and
tacks, as these were produced in abundance in the mills and farm
households of the North. New Jersey, Pennsylvania, and
Maryland, we know, shipped considerable quantities of pig-iron
to New England, principally to Massachusetts, where it was cast
into pots, kettles, and implements which were reshipped to the
Middle and Southern colonies and to the West Indies. The
records show, too, that on the eve of the Revolution iron tools
and agricultural implements made in Philadelphia were sold
extensively in American markets, including the West Indian
plantations.

That the colonial industry was steadily growing is evidenced
by the fact that soon after 1700 English business men became
actively interested in it. Their interest manifested itself in
two diametrically opposite directions. In the first place, the

known supply of English ore was rapidly nearing exhaustion, the famous Sheffield furnaces, for instance, being already dependent upon Russia and Sweden for part of their raw material; from time to time, therefore, the English manufacturer of iron goods warmly urged Parliament to enact legislation encouraging the colonial production of bar- and pig-iron. On the other hand, however, he was even more anxious to restrict the colonial manufacture of finished iron products, for they came into competition with his own. *England encouraged colonial production of pig- and bar-iron, but opposed colonial manufacture of finished iron products. The Act of 1750* In light of this fact it is easy to understand why in 1719 a bill was introduced to prevent the colonists from manufacturing hollow-ware or other castings or erecting forges for refining iron. Although the measure failed of enactment, the agitation for restriction continued, and in 1737 another bill was introduced. It was not until 1750, when an interruption of the Baltic trade curtailed the supply of imported iron, that an Act was passed allowing the free importation into England of colonial pig-iron and, at the ports of London and Bristol, bar-iron, but prohibiting the future erection in America of slitting or rolling mills, tilt hammers, or steel furnaces. In other words, the colonial iron masters were henceforth to produce iron for British manufacturers and to cease manufacturing it into tools, implements, and hardware. Under this law, shipments of pig-iron to the English market increased, but colonial manufactures, for reasons which we shall note in the following chapter, instead of diminishing or being abolished, continued to thrive.

Another industry of primary importance in the economic life of the colonists was the distillation of rum from cheap West Indian molasses. Beginning in New England before the middle of the seventeenth century, the *Rum manufacture* business from the first proved to be most lucrative, the product sometimes selling as high as a dollar per gallon. Long before the Revolution it became New England's chief manufacturing industry; in 1774 the sixty-three distilleries of Massachusetts alone produced 2,700,000 gallons. In the North rum replaced beer and cider as the favorite beverage for the rank and file of the population, and by many it was considered almost as much of a necessity as flour. Not only were large quantities of it consumed at home, but it soon came to be regarded as indispensable for the fishing fleets, the Indian trade, and the slaving business. Long before the Revolution the foundations of many a New England fortune had been laid from profits derived in part from this flourishing industry.

Space forbids any detailed account of the numerous other manufacturing enterprises engaged in and developed by the Other manu- colonists to meet their increasing needs. Among factures these the most important were the manufacture of flour, paper, brick, tile, cordage, twine, pot and pearl ashes, and sailcloth. Other products included salt, spiritous and malt liquors, candles, glass, pottery, firearms, gunpowder, brass, copper, and tinwares. Practically all of the goods turned out in these industries were for local consumption.

6. Effect of Colonial Manufacturing on Great
Britain and on the Colonies

To what degree the colonial market for British manufacture was impaired by these colonial enterprises it is impossible to say. Northern farm Certain it is, however, that in the provinces north of communities Maryland, and particularly in New England, by largely self- sufficing as far the greater majority of farmer folk purchased far as few foreign commodities. Some notion of the manufactured goods were extent to which the colonial farm community was concerned self-sufficing may be gained from the following list of articles which the Moravian Brethren proposed to contribute to a store opened by them in 1753 on the forks of the Delaware:

Apron-skins, powder-horns, glue, shoes, slippers, shoe-lasts, wooden and horn heel pieces, saddle-trees, saddles, horse-collars, bridles, halters, saddle-bags, girths, pocket-books, martingales, straps, stockings, caps, gloves, socks, hats, felt caps and felt slippers, spinning-wheels, reels, boxes, guns, tea-caddies, writing-desks, deer and calf skins dressed for breeches, buckwheat groats, oat-groats, malt, millet, dried peaches, dried apples, dried cherries, rusks, ginger-bread, cakes,

iron banks for chests, nails, plows, axes, hatchets, grubbing hoes,
corn-hoes, grind-stones, whet-stones, punk, flint and steel, pipe-stems,
pipe-heads, shirt-studs, pewter plates, tea pots, lanterns, tallow candles,
soap, starch, hair-powder, sealing wax, wafers, tobacco boxes, buttons,
buckles, spoons, bowls, shovels, brooms, baskets, wheat, flour, butter,
cheese, handkerchiefs, neck-cloths, garters, knee-straps, linen, white,
blue and checked woolens, currant-wine, beer, whiskey, tar, potash,
turpentine, pitch, lamp-black, sulphur-matches, vinegar, flaxseed, lin-
seed oil, rape seed and oil, nut oil, oil of sassafras, ammonia, rasped
deer's-horn, bush-tea, medicine chests, brushes, shovels and tongs,
chafing-dishes, combs, currycombs, glove-leather, leather breeches,
ropes, blank-books, soft-soap, rakes, knives, drawing-knives, guitars,
violins, tobacco and tobacco-pouches, snuff, oil of turpentine, hemp,
flax, buckets, milk pails, tubs, pottery, cotton yarn, cord, hatchels,
oven forks, linen nets, augers, hammers, pincers, candlesticks, tinware,
chisels, mill-saws, homespun, boots, whips, harness, wheelbarrows,
wagons, coffee-pots, chains, canoes, boards, bricks, roofing-tiles, lime,
preserves and pickles, quills and slate pencils.

Even in the plantation colonies many of the estates before the
outbreak of the Revolution were to a remarkable degree self-
sustaining. Every large plantation numbered Many planta-
among its working force blacksmiths who could tions self-
forge rough iron into nails, chains, and hoes; opening of the
coopers who made casks for the tobacco crop, Revolution
barrels for flour, and vats and tanks for brandy and cider; and
tanners who prepared leather for the cobblers to fashion into
shoes for the slaves. Those southern communities settled by
Germans or Scotch-Irish produced not only enough for themselves but often sent goods of home manufacture to other parts
of the colonies. Of course some estates manufactured very
little. Thus a 1721 report on Maryland asserted that "the
Inhabitants wear the like Cloathing and have the same furniture
within their houses with those in this Kingdom. The slaves are
cloathed with Cottons, Kerseys, flannels and coarse linnens all
imported; & it is computed that this province consumes of
British Manufactures to the value of £20,000 per annum."
Testimony regarding manufactures in South Carolina was
similar; here there was practically no manufacturing except
during hard times, when a little negro-cloth was made.

The records of colonial commerce, though somewhat unsatisfactory, indicate that in 1698, when the population of the colo-

Decreasing imports per capita of colonial population
nies numbered a little less than 272,000, the original official value of goods imported from Great Britain totaled $2,034,000 or about $7.10 per capita. Twenty years later, when the population had increased to nearly half a million, the actual value of the imports from the mother country was approximately $2,220,000 or only $4.20 per inhabitant. During the first three years of the reign of George II, who ascended the throne in 1727, the imports averaged $2,320,000 per year, or about $4 for each of the estimated population of 580,000. But the low-water mark was reached during the five years ending with 1748, when a population of almost a million imported on an average only $3,095,000 worth of goods, a little over $3 worth per person. Between 1768 and 1774, the closing years of the colonial period, when the number of people had increased to almost 2,750,000, the annual purchase of British goods amounted to $12,130,000 or about $4.40 for each inhabitant.

While these figures are indicative of the amount of foreign goods consumed by the colonists at several periods and also

Factors influencing colonial purchase of foreign manufactures
throw light upon the volume of domestic manufactures, we must, nevertheless, not forget that colonial purchases abroad fluctuated greatly from season to season because of poor crops, low prices for American produce, or the interruptions of war. Nor should we overlook the fact that as the seacoast towns increased in size and wealth during the eighteenth century the market for the finer goods of foreign manufacture was considerably enlarged. "Most of the furniture in the homes of the trading towns," wrote Governor Bernard of Massachusetts in 1763, "is of British manufacture; nails, glass, lead, locks, hinges, and many other materials for homes are wholly imported from Great Britain." Only a few years earlier Josiah Wedgewood, the father of the English porcelain industry, frankly admitted that the British consumption of white stoneware was "very trifling in comparison with what is sent abroad; and the principal of these markets are the Continent and Islands of North America."

To the continental colonies, he said, was sent "an amazing quantity of white stoneware and some of the finer kinds." And so it was with many other manufactured commodities of British origin. The proportion of British manufactures among goods shipped from the mother country to America increased from 66 per cent in 1698 to 76 per cent in 1721 and 81 per cent during the six years ending with 1774. Generally speaking, the finer goods of British manufacture — the kind consumed by the prosperous merchant and well-to-do planter — dominated the American market during the entire colonial period. The coarser and more essential manufactures, on the other hand, were, as we have just observed, largely produced by the colonists.

In engaging in manufacturing enterprises, household and otherwise, the New World settlers either consciously or unconsciously laid the foundation of American economic independence. While favored with an abundance of raw materials they, nevertheless, faced baffling obstacles. The country was new, land was abundant and cheap, labor was scarce, scattered, and costly, free capital was lacking, and the means of communication and transportation were strikingly inadequate. *Obstacles to colonial manufacturing*

To encourage the colonists to overcome these natural and artificial handicap and to engage in manufacturing, the colonial governments from time to time enacted various measures giving direct assistance in the form of bounties, premiums, subsidies, land grants, loans, tariffs, and monopolies. Lotteries to obtain money for establishing or fostering new industries, or to relieve manufacturers who had lost their property by fire or similar disaster, were legalized. Frequently both manufactures and materials for manufacture were exempted from taxation and, in many instances, both were made legal tender. Such action not only relieved the lack of money but promoted industry as well. Shipbuilders and owners were aided by special tonnage laws. Yet notwithstanding all this favorable legislation, location and natural resources more than anything else shaped the history of colonial manufacturing. *Manufacturing encouraged by colonial governments*

7. COMMERCE AND TRADE

The importance of sea-faring and trade in colonial life can scarcely be overestimated. Many of the colonists, deriving the

Importance of trade to colonists

greater part of their wealth and profits from the ocean, devoted no small fraction of their time to commercial pursuits. Especially was this true of the colonies north of Maryland, where the men of the prosperous trading centers, as we shall see, dominated every phase of colonial life. The colonial merchant did not confine his activities to his local community or even to the narrow fringe of coast from Maine to Georgia; his interests radiated not only to every part of the North Atlantic but practically to every part of the known world.

In general, three types of colonial trade may be distinguished, namely, local, intercolonial, and foreign. Local trade was

Agencies of local trade

1. Shops and stores

carried on chiefly by means of stores and shops, markets and fairs, and itinerant peddlers. In the towns the shops were the main channels of distribution and were, of course, fairly easy to reach. As early as 1700 they had become more or less differentiated as to the goods they sold, depending somewhat upon the size of the town. Every colony had its cross-roads merchant, and in many localities the inn-keeper carried on merchandizing as a side line. In the Southern colonies where both towns and cross-roads were fewer, the store was often kept by a planter. These stores, like the country stores of today, were usually stocked with a multiplicity of different articles. Those stores nearer the frontier carried a supply of goods suitable for the Indian trade.

In Pennsylvania and the colonies to the north provisions and other goods such as craft products were distributed by means of

2. Markets and fairs

markets not unlike those which had long existed in the Old World. These markets, held at designated places on certain days of the week, enabled the producer and consumer to eliminate the middleman, for no dealer could buy until householders had had opportunity to purchase what they wanted. The Act establishing the Boston market in 1696, for example, stated explicitly that "it was principally intended for the benefit of housekeepers." Naturally, merchants and shop-keepers and even some farmers were outspoken in their opposition to the markets. Incidentally the markets helped link the towns with the surrounding country. The fairs, held from one to four times a year, depending on the locality, did not differ materially in either organization or purpose from those in contemporary Europe.

In the country districts of the North the itinerant peddler — the forerunner of the tin-peddler of a later day — often did a thriving business despite the fact that shop-keepers **3. The itin-** and merchandizing inn-keepers waged incessant **erant peddler** warfare against him. In some communities peddling was absolutely prohibited under penalty of heavy fine, but such laws were difficult to enforce, and the traffic continued. From the standpoint of distribution of goods the peddler, without doubt, performed a real service, and the opposition to him was based upon the desire to eliminate him as a competitor.

In addition to providing for markets the colonies, southern as well as northern, enacted legislation from time to time for the benefit of the consumer. This legislation was **Economic** usually either directly or indirectly concerned with **regulation by** price fixation of both goods and services and with **colonial governments** an adequate supply of both for the colony. Thus **for benefit of** we find on the statute books of every colony laws **consumers** regulating the weight and measure and price of such commodities as bread; embargoes on foodstuffs in time of scarcity; the stimulation of production by means of bounties, monopolies, and exemption from taxation; apprenticeship; and enforced division of labor. Many of these laws were crude and ineffective, but their passage is significant.

Intercolonial trade, which originated when the older settlements began to furnish provisions to their newer neighbors, was carried on almost entirely by water. In striking **Intercolonial** contrast to the splendid highways of today, roads **trade** were few and bad and at times almost impassable; **Colonial roads** often they were little more than widened Indian **few and bad** trails, for the colonists had neither the men nor the money to level the hills, drain the marshes, or bridge the streams. During the eighteenth century, as population increased and settlers pushed farther west, more attention was paid to the development of internal improvements. Inland farmers with grain and other food stuffs to market were naturally keenly anxious to have bridges built and roads improved, and by the eve of the Revolution the Indian trails in the upland country from New York to Georgia were gradually taking shape as passable highways. But, at best, overland transportation throughout the entire colonial period was slow, difficult, and costly; and merchants and shippers, therefore, were forced to make use of the sea with its many harbors and tributary waterways. The ocean, rather than any broad macadam or concrete surfaced highway, linked Boston, New York, Philadelphia, and the Southern colonies.

By far the greater portion of the continental intercolonial commerce and, indeed, of all colonial shipping was in the hands of enterprising Northerners who, with hundreds of small craft, penetrated every harbor, bay, estuary, and navigable river. Several reasons may be mentioned to account for this fact; in the first place, the northern colonists, instead of supplementing the economic system of the mother country by supplying her merchants and manufacturers with necessary raw materials, produced few native commodities which could be sold in England. Stark necessity drove them to market their surplus lumber, beef, and fish wherever they could, and as an inevitable consequence many engaged in trade as a means of securing a livelihood. Then, too, fishing, as we have already pointed out, tremendously stimulated shipbuilding, and both of these industries together with local manufacturing and small farm agriculture were in no slight degree responsible for the growth of thriving and prosperous commercial towns. The South with its lack of numerous harbors and with a ready foreign market for its staples — tobacco, indigo, and rice — failed to develop navigation and shipping. To the southern planter large-scale agriculture appeared vastly more profitable than commerce. English merchants sent their fleets to his door to transport his products, and he manifested little or no interest in shipbuilding. South of Maryland, therefore, few cities arose,

Greater portion of continental intercolonial commerce in hands of Northerners

and the number of merchants and traders remained relatively small. Last of all, distance from the Old World relieved the northern colonist from the competition of British merchants and carriers, and he was thus enabled to monopolize the inter-colonial trade.

Merchandise of all sorts, both domestic and foreign, was distributed by the colonial coasting vessels. Scores of small New England vessels went to Newfoundland and Annap-olis with rum, salt, and provisions. Rum, tools, and imported wares from New England were ex-changed for the breadstuffs raised on the farms of the Middle colonies. Philadelphia sent large consignments of starch to Massachusetts and leather and iron goods to the distant Carolinas. Pennsylvania stoves were advertised in Boston, and New England woodenware in Maryland. Yankee vessels laden with grain, livestock, liquors, hardware, fish, and imported cloth anchored in southern ports where they traded their cargoes to good advantage for tobacco, rice, raw leather, and naval stores. Hundreds of sloops piled high with goods collected at the larger commercial centers like Boston, Newport, New York, and Philadelphia, visited the smaller ports and river towns to trade with local merchants whose stocks included furs, raw materials, and the surplus products of the neighboring farm.

Character of coastwise trade

During the eighteenth century this business of collecting and distributing articles of commerce greatly expanded. Indeed as early as 1716, according to an English economist of that century, "the domestic commerce which those northern provinces carried on with each other was now nearly equal to that with the parent coun-try." That such a statement had basis is evident when we consider that of the 259 vessels which entered at the port of Boston between May, 1704, and May, 1705, 147 were from coast ports. Of this number 12 came from the Carolinas, 14 from Virginia, 23 from Pennsylvania, and 25 from New York. Again during the three years, June 24, 1714—June 24, 1717, no less than 390 sailed from Boston to other continental ports. Taking a somewhat longer period, we find that between 1705 and 1732 the number of vessels entering Boston from other continental

Colonial coastwise trade expands after 1700

ports increased 231 per cent as against an increase of only 221 per cent for those from overseas. The volume of the coastwise shipping as compared with the volume of foreign trade carried on by the colonies in 1769 is given in the table on page 159.

It will be noted that the figures in the fourth column, which give the volume of the tonnage engaged in intercolonial trade, include not only the thirteen colonies but Newfoundland, Canada, Nova Scotia, Florida, Bermuda, and the Bahamas. To obtain the volume for the thirteen colonies only 25,000 tons should be deducted. Practically one-half the total tonnage of Rhode Island and Connecticut and more than one-third that of Massachusetts was devoted to the coastwise business.

Although the intercolonial trade was advantageous in that it furnished a source of capital, enabled many a colonist to make a *Oceanic commerce of colonies* living, and served to make the colonies acquainted, it was not as important as the oceanic commerce of the colonies which, long before the Revolution, rivaled that of European nations. For the transatlantic trade the Southern colonies furnished tobacco, rice, wheat, indigo, and *Trans-Atlantic trade of Southern colonies* naval stores, receiving in return cargoes of manufactured goods. Having no overseas shipping of their own, they depended upon English merchants and northern carriers for the transportation of their commerce. Each year about Christmas time scores of English merchantmen set sail for the Chesapeake, where they delivered their manufactured goods, taking in return thousands of hogsheads of tobacco. The tobacco fleet alone in 1706 numbered no less than 300 sails. Not more than a fourth of the colonial leaf was consumed in England, and vessels laden with the American product found their way into the ports of France, Holland, Spain, and the distant marts of Sweden and Russia.

With the exception of Pennsylvania all the colonies north of Maryland carried on a certain but not very extensive trade with *Transatlantic trade of Northern colonies* England. From these colonies the mother country received greater or lesser quantities of fur, fish, raw hides, lumber, whale fins, whale oil, naval stores, wheat, flour, hops, and iron. These exports were supplemented by tobacco, sugar, molasses, rum, cocoa, hard-

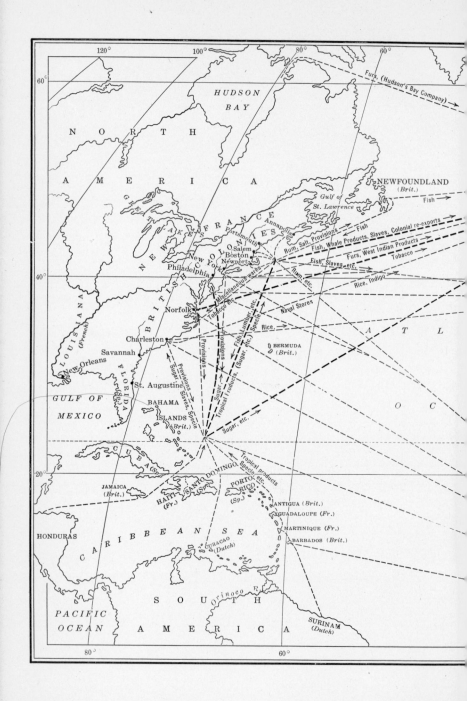

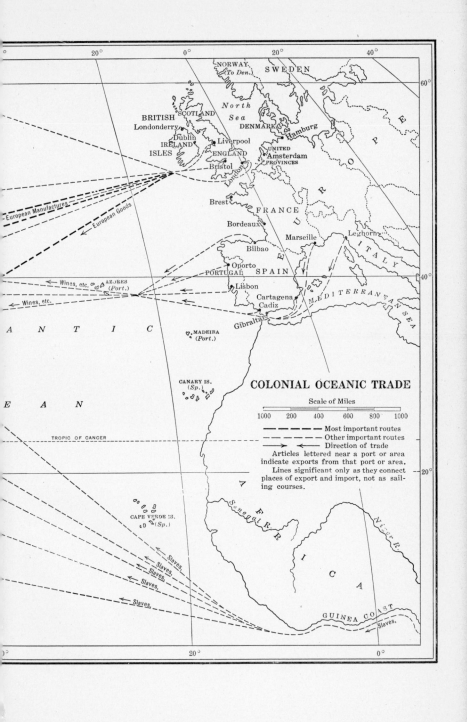

COLONIAL OCEANIC TRADE

Scale of Miles

1000   200   400   600   800   1000

———— ———— Most important routes
— — — — — Other important routes
←———— Direction of trade
Articles lettered near a port or area
indicate exports from that port or area.
Lines significant only as they connect
places of export and import, not as sail-
ing courses.

GROSS REGISTERED TONNAGE OF THE VESSELS ENTERED AND CLEARED AT THE PORTS OF EACH COLONY IN 1769

Colony	Entered from —					Cleared to —				
	Great Britain and Ireland	Southern parts of Europe and Africa	British and foreign West Indies	Continent of America, Bahamas, etc.	Totals	Great Britain and Ireland	Southern parts of Europe and Africa	British and foreign West Indies	Continent of America, Bahamas, etc.	Totals
New Hampshire	915	480	9,500	5,551	16,446	2,822	170	12,878	3,874	19,744
Massachusetts	14,340	6,595	17,898	27,618	66,451	14,044	5,102	17,532	26,988	63,666
Rhode Island	415	226	5,958	10,237	16,836	540	863	6,060	10,312	17,775
Connecticut	150	105	7,790	9,971	18,016	580	200	9,201	7,985	17,966
New York	5,224	2,730	6,964	11,714	26,632	6,470	3,483	5,466	11,440	26,859
New Jersey	....	25	257	654	936	....	....	555	538	1,093
Pennsylvania	9,309	10,745	12,521	12,453	45,028	7,219	12,070	11,959	11,738	42,986
Maryland	15,486	4,095	4,533	6,574	30,688	16,116	6,224	3,358	5,298	30,996
Virginia	20,652	4,600	11,612	10,373	47,237	24,594	7,486	11,397	8,531	52,008
North Carolina	6,415	700	6,702	9,259	23,076	7,805	1,030	6,945	7,333	23,113
South Carolina	15,281	3,325	6,893	5,608	31,107	15,902	5,773	6,377	5,803	33,855
Georgia	2,523	525	4,288	2,357	9,693	3,029	200	4,654	1,358	9,241
Total	90,710	34,151	94,916	112,369	332,146	99,121	42,601	96,382	101,198	339,302

Emory R. Johnson, T. W. Van Metre, C. G. Huebner and D. S. Hanchett, *History of Domestic and Foreign Commerce of the United States*, vol. i, p. 92.

woods, and dyewoods obtained in the coastwise trade. As a rule, all of these products were carried in colonial ships which brought back cargoes of manufactured goods. While all the principal northern ports carried on trade directly with England, Salem, Newport, and New York were preëminent.

TRADE OF GREAT BRITAIN WITH COLONIES, 1700

	British Imports from Colonies			British Exports to Colonies			Total		
	£	s	d	£	s	d	£	s	d
New England	41,486	11	9	91,918	14	6	133,405	6	3
New York............	17,567	10	0	49,410	15	0	66,978	5	0
Pennsylvania	4,608	9	8	18,529	6	2	23,137	15	10
Virginia and Maryland	317,302	12	11	173,481	10	4	490,784	3	3
Carolina	14,058	14	6	11,003	12	4	25,062	6	10
Total..............	395,023	18	10	344,343	18	4	739,367	17	2

TRADE OF GREAT BRITAIN WITH COLONIES, 1769

	British Imports from Colonies			British Exports to Colonies			Total		
	£	s	d	£	s	d	£	s	d
New England........	223,695	11	6	142,775	12	9	366,471	4	3
New York...........	75,930	19	7	113,382	8	8	189,313	8	3
Pennsylvania........	204,979	17	4	28,112	6	9	233,092	4	1
Virginia and Maryland	714,943	15	8	759,961	5	0	1,474,905	0	8
Carolinas...........	327,084	8	6	405,014	13	1	732,099	1	7
Georgia.............	58,340	19	4	82,270	2	3	140,611	1	7
Total.............	1,604,975	11	11	1,531,516	8	6	3,136,492	0	5

Emory R. Johnson, T. W. Van Metre, C. G. Huebner and D. S. Hanchett, *History of Domestic and Foreign Commerce of the United States*, vol. I, pp. 74, 92.

A study of the appended table shows (1) the comparative value of the trade between the mother country and the colonies in 1700 and 1769; (2) that the imports and exports of the Southern colonies were more than double those of all the other colonies; and (3) that it was the Southern rather than the Northern colonies that did the

Colonial trade with Great Britain

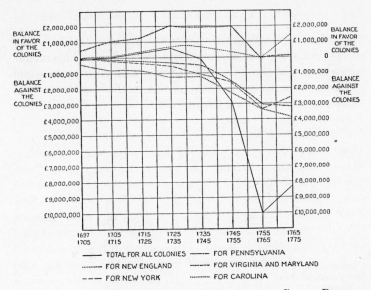

BALANCE OF TRADE BETWEEN THE COLONIES AND GREAT BRITAIN
BY DECADES, 1697–1775

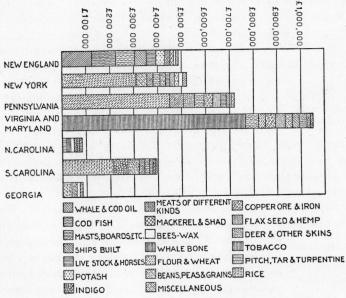

ANNUAL AVERAGE OF COLONIAL EXPORTS, 1763–1773

lion's share of the business with Great Britain. In 1769 about seven-ninths of the exports from Virginia and Maryland, five-sevenths of those from the Carolinas, and over five-sixths of those from Georgia went to the mother country. The Northern colonies afforded a striking parallel, for Great Britain received only one-fourth of New England's total exports, and less than half of New York's and Pennsylvania's. Likewise, Virginia and Maryland obtained nearly seven-eighths of their imports from Great Britain, the Carolinas three-fifths, and Georgia over five-sixths. New England, on the other hand, secured only two-fifths of her imports from the mother country, New York less than half, and Pennsylvania only a very small fraction.

With the Azores and the Continent the Northerners carried on a very considerable trade. Quantities of fish were marketed **Colonial trade** in ports from the Baltic to the Mediterranean, and **with continent** beef, pork, lumber, oil, and rice were exchanged **of Europe** with the countries of Southern Europe for wines, wool, spices, fruits, salt, and iron. While ships rarely went up the Adriatic to Venice, a few appear to have crept through the Danish straits into the Baltic. Occasionally some daring captain even piloted his vessel to India.

But the West Indies rather than either the mother country or Europe furnished the key to the commercial and industrial **Great import-** prosperity of the northern colonists, for the West **ance of West** Indian trade, including that with the French, **Indian trade** Dutch, and Spanish islands, enabled them to utilize **to colonists** their fisheries, forests, and fertile soil, expand their manufactures, supply cargoes for their merchant marine, build up their towns and cities and, above all, secure the necessary money for their goods and bills of exchange with which to pay their adverse English trade balances.

Several factors favored the development of this trade. In the first place, the sugar islands, as the West Indies were often **Factors favor-** called, afforded an excellent market. Producing by **ing develop-** far the larger portion of the world's sugar supply by **ment of West** means of slave labor, they were forced partly by the **Indian trade** natural order of things to import nearly every necessity of life. From New England they obtained lumber for their houses, "refuse" fish for their slaves, horses, dairy products, oil, and goods of both domestic and British manufacture. In return, the New Englanders received cargoes of sugar and cheap molasses for the distilleries of Massachusetts and Rhode Island. Practically all the grain, flour, bread, vegetables, and potatoes for the sugar islands were supplied by New York, Pennsylvania, Maryland, and Virginia. Pennsylvania led in furnishing beef, pork, hams, and livestock, but her exports in this respect were supplemented by those of Virginia and North Carolina. Like the New Englanders, the merchants of the Middle colonies received in return sugar, molasses, and other tropical products including coffee, cotton, ginger, pimento, indigo, and often Spanish coin or bills of exchange. Even the Carolinas shipped staves of red oak for sugar hogsheads, white oak for rum casks, yellow pine for siding, and cypress for shingles. In connection with the island trade, northern vessels brought quantities of mahogany and logwood from Central America for reshipment to Europe.

1. Caribbean Islands dependent on outside world for commodities

The second factor favoring the development of trade with the West Indies was that the Northern colonies were unable to market their commodities in the mother country. Of the salable commodities Great Britain at first welcomed only furs, forest products, and ships; colonial cereals, meats, and fish were not wanted, for they were supplied by English producers who were protected by tariff legislation. The enactment of the Corn Law of 1689, for instance, practically prohibited the importation of grain. Similar duties were levied on fish, and the importation of salted beef and pork was forbidden altogether. Unable to market the bulk of their surplus commodities in the mother country or the neighboring Continent, northern merchants and shippers turned, therefore, to the British and foreign West Indies where, as we have just noted, the products of forest, farm, and sea found a ready market and were sold for cash or exchanged for a variety of tropical products. The value of colonial exports to the West Indies in 1770 totaled £844,178. New England vessels engaged in fisheries during the summer months often became Caribbean traders during the winter, frequently wandering from port to

2. Available market for northern commodities

port without prearranged plans, their captains reaping profit as occasion offered.

Scarcely less important was the dependence of certain northern industries, particularly rum manufacturing, fishing, and **3. Dependence of northern industries on West Indian products** shipbuilding, on West Indian products. Without molasses it would have been quite impossible for Massachusetts to have maintained her principal manufacturing industry, and thus indirectly both the fishing and shipbuilding industries would have suffered. Of the £949,656 worth of West Indian products imported to the thirteen mainland colonies in 1770, more than half was accounted for by rum; molasses ranked next, and sugar third; the three together made up four-fifths of the total.

Most of the early West Indian trade was carried on with the British possessions. It was not long, however, before the colonists, despite mercantilist regulations, began to **4. Dependence of colonies on West Indian trade for specie supply** trade with the French and other foreign West Indies. The inducements to do so were great. The unwise colonial policy of France with its numerous trade restrictions, together with the greater fertility of the soil of her colonies, premiums on the importation of slaves, better methods of cultivation and, hence, larger production, made it possible for a French West Indian planter to undersell his British rivals from 25 to 50 per cent. He also needed the food products, horses, and lumber which New England and the Middle colonies wished to market. Even more important, this trade, though carried on illegally, enabled New England and the Middle colonies, as we have noted, to secure an adequate supply of specie with which to make good their adverse trade balances with the mother country.

Finally, the West Indian trade was inextricably bound up with the traffic in African slaves, for practically all the slaves sold in **5. West Indian trade closely connected with slave traffic** the American market were first brought to the West Indies. New England vessels, especially those of Newport as well as ships from other colonies, laden with rum, sailed for the Guinea Coast where they exchanged their cargo for slaves which they in

PINE TREE SHILLING — OBVERSE AND REVERSE

MASSACHUSETTS PAPER MONEY

From originals in the collection of the Massachusetts
Historical Society

turn disposed of in the slave markets of the West Indies at a handsome profit. The vessels were then loaded with sugar, molasses, rum, indigo, and other West Indian products which in turn were sold in the mainland colonies or in Europe. There were many deviations in this triangular trade, but the West Indies with their slave markets and their tropical products so needed by the Northern colonies constituted the all-important angle. Without them the rum industry would have been seriously crippled, and without rum the slave traffic, in all probability, would have been adversely affected.

The West Indian trade, as well as the coastwise and transatlantic, faced many obstacles. Among them were the obstructive tactics of royal officials in their administration of the customs and navigation laws, war, depression, lack of adequate credit facilities, storms, and piracy. Of these, the last named was in some respects the most serious. Every sea was infested with buccaneers who preyed on merchant ships — capturing, pillaging, burning. In some colonies, notably Rhode Island, New York, and South Carolina, the pirates entered into deals with merchants and officials whereby they received protection in return for a share of the spoils. So serious was the situation and so loud the complaints that in 1699 the mother country passed an Act for the suppression of piracy. This legislation, however, brought little relief. Swarms of desperate characters continued to sail the sea, and it was not until the eighteenth century, when the royal navy had become more effective, that the menace was reduced. Some of the risks encountered by the shipping interests were offset by insurance, but insurance companies did not make their appearance in the colonies until after 1720. *Obstacles encountered by colonial shipper*

Throughout the colonial period both merchant and manufacturer were hampered by lack of capital and by the absence of a uniform system of money and adequate credit facilities. For this condition of affairs four reasons may be noted. First, the colonies were without gold or silver mines, and the unfavorable balance of trade with Great Britain, to which we have already alluded, drained them of what specie they were able to acquire. *Colonial merchant handicapped by lack of money and credit facilities*

The Southern colonies, it is true, thanks to their staples, enjoyed a favorable balance, but this was usually spent for additional manufactured goods or for an increased labor supply. In the second place, credit institutions, by means of which the bulk of our business is transacted today, were largely wanting, and merchants and others were obliged, therefore, to make their payments for the most part in money or kind. Thirdly, the exportation of coin from the mother country was forbidden by law. Lastly, the colonies had no common currency of their own.

In default of an adequate supply of coin the colonists were compelled at first to resort to an extensive system of barter or payment in kind; thus bead money or wampum redeemable in beaver skins passed as currency in New England and the central colonies until about the beginning of the eighteenth century. Staple commodities like corn, cattle, peltry, and wheat were declared by law to be legal tender in payment for merchandise, labor, and taxes. For many years Harvard students paid their tuition in produce, livestock, and meat, and "occasionally with various articles raked up from the family closets of student debtors." In the Southern colonies tobacco and rice as well as other commodities were used as currency, the "crop notes" issued, calling for the delivery of certain quantities of these commodities, passing from hand to hand. Even as late as 1730 the Virginia Assembly provided for the establishment of warehouses for the storage of tobacco, the owners receiving transferable notes similar to the present day gold and silver certificates which might be used to satisfy debts, public and private, in the county or district wherein they were issued. This primitive system continued until the middle of the eighteenth century in North Carolina, where as many as twenty commodities, aside from tobacco, had been used as legal tender. Unfortunately the articles used in barter had no staple value; not only did they vary in price from time to time, but they constantly fluctuated with reference to each other. All things considered, barter, though necessary and useful, failed to meet the needs of the colonists.

We have already noted that some hard money of foreign denomination reached the colonies as a result of trade, but even the ratio of value between the English and non-English coin varied from colony to colony despite all attempts of the home government to establish a common rating. The Spanish "piece-of-eight" (silver coin of eight reals), for instance, was generally rated as worth four shillings six pence of English money, but in New York and North Carolina it was equivalent to eight shillings; in New Jersey, Pennsylvania, Maryland, and Delaware to seven shillings six pence; in New England and Virginia to six shillings, and in South Carolina and Georgia to four shillings eight pence. And the same variation extended to subsidiary coins. Sometimes, too, the value of the coins was impaired by clipping or reduced in weight by "sweating," the process of removing small particles of silver or gold by violently shaking a number of coins together in a bag. Massachusetts was the only colony to establish a mint, which issued small pieces of silver known as pine tree shillings. In 1684 this mint was closed by order of the crown. The serious disadvantages of such conditions in making intercolonial exchanges may be readily imagined.

Foreign coin inadequate and unsatisfactory

From what has just been said it is easy to understand why the colonies had recourse to paper money as a circulating medium. First adopted by Massachusetts in 1690 to meet the expenses of the disasterous expedition against Quebec, the practice was soon followed by the other New England colonies and by South Carolina, New York, and New Jersey. Ultimately all the colonies, with the exception of North Carolina, resorted to this easy but dangerous means of supplying an adequate currency. Even such eminent individuals as Colden and Franklin staunchly defended the use of paper money on the ground of necessity. "There is a certain proportionate quantity of money," wisely remarked Franklin, "requisite to carry on the trade of a country currently and freely; more than which would be of no advantage in trade, and less, if much less, exceedingly detrimental to it."

Paper money

It is wholly unnecessary for us to study the history of the numerous issues, for all were more or less alike in purpose and in result.   Some bore interest while others did not;   some were made legal tender for payments of all sorts, while others could

Its deprecia-
tion

be used for future obligations but not for past debts; some could be used for all public payments but not for business transactions between private individuals; some were made payable on demand and others were not. The source of funds pledged for their redemption varied greatly. Some were retired promptly, according to the terms of their issue, but others were not; some were irredeemable. All depreciated and, therefore, tended to drive "good" money out of circulation.   Silver in Massachusetts, for instance, rose to a premium of 1100 per cent between 1700 and 1750.

The reaction of the colonists to paper money is worth noting. At first it had the enthusiastic support of the great majority, for

Reaction of
colonists to
paper money

it gave promise of supplying a crying need of both people and government. As soon as it began to depreciate and commodity prices began to climb, however, business men, especially money-lenders and merchants, became lukewarm in their approval and finally bitterly denounced its further issuance in any form. The manufacturer, too, aligned himself with merchant and money-lender.   At first paper inflation stimulated manufacturing enterprises, but when depreciation set in the cost of production increased rapidly.   The situation in New England was typical: in 1736 a vessel could be built more cheaply on the Thames than in Massachusetts; and the quantity of molasses distilled annually in Boston between 1735 and 1742 fell off one-third. Wage-earners as well as those with fixed incomes complained about the high cost of living.   Pointing out that inasmuch as their incomes had not increased in proportion to the cost of living, a Massachusetts pamphleteer declared with great truth that "Salary Men, Ministers, School-Masters, Judges of the Circuit, President and Tutors at College, Widows and Orphans, &c., are pincht and hurt more than any."   After stabilizing her currency in 1749 Massachusetts enjoyed commercial and industrial prosperity, business picked up; while Rhode Island, which continued to be submerged in a deluge of depreciated paper, lost a large part of her West Indian trade; at the same time her distilling and manufacturing industries languished. But the farmers with goods to buy as well as those who were obliged to borrow money, were staunch supporters of cheap currency even though they too sometimes found fault with the prices they received for their produce. Its use, as we shall see in the next chapter, was at first curtailed and finally forbidden by Parliamentary action.

8. TOWNS AND TOWN LIFE

Simultaneously with the growth of trade and industry there sprang up along the coast, particularly of the Northern colonies, a number of thriving commercial centers which by **Growth of** the eve of the Revolution rivaled many of the lead- **towns** ing ports of the mother country both in population and wealth. Ranking first as the greatest emporium of British America was Philadelphia, with about 25,000 people at the end of the colonial period. Boston stood second with a population of slightly over 20,000, and New York — the commercial capital of the territory around the mouth of the Hudson — was close on the heels of her New England rival. Charleston with about 10,000 inhabitants, the fourth town in size, was not only the largest port in the South but the center of social life for a considerable number of South Carolina planters. Newport, a prosperous manufacturing and commercial center and outranked only by Boston among the New England ports, stood fifth with a population of approximately 7,000. Baltimore, Norfolk, Portsmouth, Salem, Providence, New London, and New Haven were promising commercial towns. With the increase of population during the eighteenth century a number of inland towns became industrially and commercially important. Among these may be mentioned Albany, at the junction of the Hudson and Mohawk valleys; Lynn, Massachusetts, the center of colonial shoe manufacture; Hartford, Connecticut; and the substantial Pennsylvania towns of Lancaster, York, and Germantown, the latter with its one "Main street" nearly two miles long. A number of towns like Richmond, Virginia; Reading, Pennsylvania; and Springfield, Massachusetts, destined to become great inland urban centers, were straggling villages of a few score houses at the outbreak of the War of Independence.

Notwithstanding the fact that these towns housed only one-tenth of the population, they exercised a tremendous influence **Importance** in colonial affairs largely because they were centers **of towns** of wealth and communication. Here lived the prosperous merchant princes, the Whartons, Pembertons, Willings, and Morrises of Philadelphia; the Amorys, Faneuils, Hancocks, and Boylstons of Boston; the Lows, Livingstons, Crugers, and Waltons of New York; the Redwoods, Lopezes, and Wantons of Newport; the Browns, "Nicky, Josey, John, and Mosey," of Providence; and the merchant-planters, Manigaults, Mazycks, Laurens, and Rutledges of Charleston. Owners not only of stores and merchant ships but of wharves, warehouses, fishing craft and whalers; speculators in town real estate and frontier lands, private bankers and underwriters of marine insurance, they, together with the proprietors of the estates along the Hudson and the southern planters, formed the backbone of eighteenth-century colonial aristocracy that virtually ruled colonial society and politics. In the commercial colonies petty shop-keepers, vendue-masters, rope-makers, sail-makers, sailors, coopers, caulkers, smiths, carpenters, and fishermen were dependent upon the merchants for a livelihood. Even the northern farmers, as we have seen, "felt the ebb and flow of sea-borne commerce," for they looked to the merchant to market their surplus goods. "If the merchant trade be not kept on foot," wrote a contemporary historian, "they fear greatly their corne and cattel will lye in their hands."

Like the men of the great estates, the merchant aristocracy of the colonies lived well. Many, like those of the present day, **The merchant** owned a spacious town mansion of wood or brick and **aristocracy** a country house as well, both of which were lavishly furnished with the finest imported articles. In sharp contrast to the poorer families, their wives and daughters wore gowns of costly broadcloths, silks, and linens, modeled after the latest London fashions. Feasts and pageants, dinners and dances at some country inn were of common occurrence. Speaking of the merchants of Boston in 1740 an English traveler declared that both "ladies and gentlemen dress and appear as gay, in common, as courtiers in England on a coronation or birthday." And this

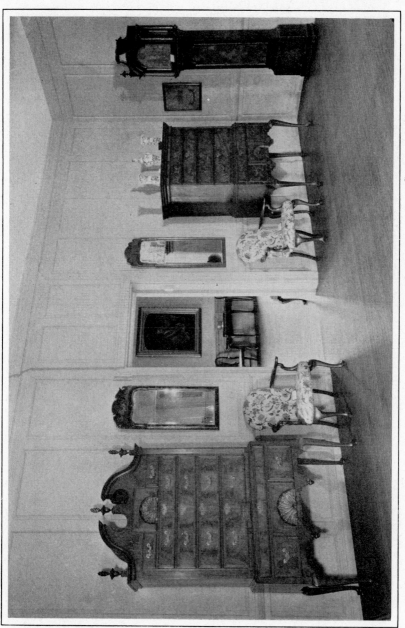

INTERIOR OF A 1750 TOWN HOUSE

was equally true of the rich merchants' families of the other seacoast towns.

Individually and as a class the merchants jealously guarded their interests against both over-zealous officials and "radical" majorities. More intent on business than politics, they nevertheless were quick to enter the political arena when their interests were jeopardized or they desired to secure some particular end through legislation. "Few town meetings have been held near tidewater," writes Professor Morison, "where the voice of shipowner, merchant, and master mariner did not carry more weight than that of fisherman, counting-room clerk, or common seaman. Society in seaboard New England was carefully stratified, and the Revolution brought little change save in personnel. The 'quality' dressed differently from the poor and middle classes, lived in finer houses, expected and received deference and 'ran' their communities because they controlled the working capital of ships and goods. The only difference from Old World society lay in the facility in passing from one class to another." Outside of New England this cleavage between rich and poor was everywhere apparent and became more distinct with the passing years.

Class cleavage

As centers of communication the commercial towns were scarcely less important than as centers of wealth. During the early years the American settlements were in large measure cut off from the Old World and from each other. Such roads as existed were, as we have noted, poor affairs at best. Bridges and ferries were as yet a thing of the future. Few vehicles were to be had. Practically the only means of travel was by foot, horseback, or water. Every community had its inns or taverns, but many of them were cheerless, ill-kept places. There were no newspapers, and only with the arrival of some vessel from overseas or some coastwise trader was news of the outside world to be had. A postal system did not exist; indeed, it was not until 1691, when postal service between Massachusetts, New York, and Pennsylvania was established, that the semblance of a postal system came into being. Under such conditions it was impossible to

Towns centers of communication

break down the barriers of provincialism or to develop anything like a common intellectual life.

By 1750, however, there was marked improvement. While roads over which a wheeled conveyance might pass with safety were as yet comparatively few, there were many highways and postroads connecting the several colonies with each other. In fact, there were enough roads as early as 1732 to warrant publication of the first American guidebook which, along with other useful information, gave the roads and the distances between the more important towns. Regular "lines" of stagecoaches and stageboats were beginning to operate between such places as Boston and New York, and New York and Philadelphia. Travel by water was also considerably easier because of the increased size of the vessels. The inns, too, improved decidedly. Under the direction of Benjamin Franklin and William Hunter of Virginia, who were appointed deputy postmasters-general in 1753, the postal service was reorganized and expanded.

Means of travel and communication improved by 1750

Of all the agencies intimately associated with the towns which ultimately helped to make them centers of communication and shaped the intellectual outlook of the colonists, probably none was more important than the press. The first printing press in English America was set up in Massachusetts in 1639, yet not a single newspaper was published in North America at the close of the seventeenth century. A three-page pamphlet entitled "Public Occurrences, both Foreign and Domestick," published in Boston in 1690, was promptly suppressed by the authorities for uttering "reflections of a very high nature" on a current political problem. Another attempt, more successful than the first, was made in 1704 when the first number of the *Boston News-Letter*, the first regular newspaper in the colonies, appeared. By judiciously refraining from criticizing the authorities, and by printing only belated news from Europe, customs house clearings and entries, this dull, tiny four-page, two-column sheet managed to live, but fifteen years elapsed before it had a rival in any of the colonies. In 1719 the *Boston Gazette* was started, as was also *The American Weekly Mercury* in Philadelphia. Shortly after-

The beginning of colonial journalism

ward James Franklin, brother of Ben, began the *New England Courant* in spite of the advice of his friends, who assured him that America did not need another newspaper! By 1765, however, no less than forty-three newspapers had been established, three of which were in German.

Some of these papers were, of course, short-lived. All were small-sized weeklies whose make-up was much the same. Considerable space was allotted to local news and Make-up of gossip and to advertisements. All frequently ran newspapers letters, domestic and foreign, sermons, poetry, essays, and reprints of English articles. Cartoons were few, but some, as in the case of Franklin's snake cut into eight pieces and entitled "Join or Die," an appeal to the colonies to unite at the time of the French and Indian War, were very effective. With improvement in communication and manifestation of greater interest in what the other colonies were doing, items such as legislative Acts, speeches of governors, and brief notes about crimes and accidents were copied from other papers. A few were bold enough to print editorials of a very independent and unbiased character; others, however, and especially those controlled by some royal official or wedded to some political party or group, were more guarded and circumspect in what they had to say. In literary quality there was much variance. The *South Carolina Gazette*, for example, excelled in the quality of its original verse, while the prose articles of the *Virginia Gazette* were quoted in all the colonies. The old tradition of the literary preëminence of the colonial press of New England is without foundation.

In addition to the newspapers a number of magazines began to be published toward the middle of the century. The first of these was founded by Franklin in 1741 under the Magazines title *The General Magazine and Historical Chronicle for all the British Plantations in America*, and contained general news, lengthy extracts from new books, and reprints of original poems and prose essays from colonial newspapers. This magazine is doubly significant. In the first place, it represented an effort to produce something culturally American and intercolonial in scope. Its content was entirely American; the poems and essays instead of being copied from English journals were American productions. Likewise the "Accounts of or Extracts from New Books, Pamphlets, &c., Published in the Plantations" was, as the title implied, a department devoted exclusively to the review of publications from the colonial press. The reprints were not selected from the papers of any one colony but from the press of all the Anglo-American provinces, insular as well as continental. Secondly, the catholicity and character of its content was indicative of the intellectual change which the colonies were undergoing, a topic to which we shall presently devote attention. Of the other literary magazines two merit mention. The *American Magazine and Historical Chronicle*, a Boston monthly which ran from 1743 to 1746, published reprints of the best essays appearing in England and in the colonies. The other, the *American Magazine*, made a very successful start under the editorship of the Reverend William Smith, provost of the University of Pennsylvania, but suspended publication after a year when that distinguished gentleman returned temporarily to England.

Numerous pamphlets and broadsides supplemented the papers and magazines, and their contents furnished material for a considerable amount of conversation and debate. The town market-place, the grog-shop, the drawing-room of the merchant were alike forums for the discussion of all sorts of questions and, along with pulpit, town meeting, and fireside, were the clearing houses of public opinion.

Pamphlets and broadsides

It is difficult to overestimate the significance of the colonial press. The newspapers, of course, were far more important than the magazines; while vastly inferior in comparison with the metropolitan daily of today, the colonial sheets were powerful factors in shaping colonial opinion. Indeed, no phase of colonial life — social, economic, religious, political, cultural — escaped the notice of their editors. Many persons who never saw the inside of a classroom and who never listened to the thunderings of the clergy, or paid little heed to them, read a colonial newspaper and were influenced by it. That some read more than their local paper is evidenced by the

The significance of the press

fact that in 1758 the colonial post office, which had long carried newspapers free of charge, was compelled to fix a rate on the ground that the "Newspapers of the several Colonies on this Continent, heretofore permitted to be sent by the Post free of Charge, are of late years so much increased as to become extremely burthensome to the Riders."

Yet important as the press was in disseminating information and affording a medium for the expression of opinion, it was frequently subjected to censorship and restraint. Press censorship Following English precedent, Puritan Massachusetts established a system of official licensing for presses which lasted until 1755. And in all the colonies any publisher who dared to criticize the government, or even inadvertently printed anything displeasing to the officials, was liable to arrest. In 1722 James Franklin, editor of the *New England Courant*, spent four weeks in jail for insinuating in rather peppery fashion that the government had neglected to do its utmost to capture a piratical ship hovering off the coast. Similar sentences were meted out to other editors for trivial offenses.

Fortunately the advocates of free speech won a great victory in 1735 when John Peter Zenger, a German immigrant and editor of the *New York Weekly Journal*, was brought The Zenger to trial on the charge of criminal libel preferred trial against him by Governor Cosby of New York. Shortly before, Cosby had removed the chief justice of the province for rendering an adverse decision in a matter in which the former was personally interested. Articles appearing in Zenger's paper sharply criticizing the governor's action led to the editor's arrest. The new chief justice, a tool of the governor, ruled that the jury had to decide only whether Zenger had published the articles or not, thus leaving to the court the decision as to their libelous character. But Andrew Hamilton of Philadelphia, probably the most brilliant and distinguished lawyer in America, argued that the jury enjoyed the right to decide whether the statements in question were false and libelous. This argument, together with his clever handling of the case and his eloquent appeal for free public discussion as a safeguard for free government, won the jury, and Zenger was acquitted. The verdict was everywhere received with delight, Gouverneur Morris afterward hailing it as "the morning star of liberty which subsequently revolutionized America."

9. Towns and Culture

If the commercial towns were the centers of wealth and communication, they were no less the centers of things cultural and **Colonial** scientific. During the greater part of the seven-**culture and** teenth century the colonists had not the time, **science cen-** **tered in com-** energy, or money to devote to the finer aspects of **mercial towns** civilization. "These first Americans," to quote Professor Wertenbaker, "were pioneers in opening to civilization a vast continent, not pioneers in chemistry, anatomy, zoölogy, engineering, or literature. From Maine to the Carolinas we look in vain for a single figure of note in such matters, one standing out above the level of mediocrity. This does not mean that the New England trader or the Virginia planter was inferior in natural capacity to the men they left behind in England. It means rather that their energies turned to the practical problems of clearing the forests, building homes, planting crops, constructing ships, trading and fishing; to the subtleties of Indian warfare, to the increasing political struggle with the Crown."

The only persons who had leisure for study and reflection were the clergy, but they were so immersed in narrow theological **Theology over-** doctrines that they spent their time and energy in **shadowed** discussing the Old and New Testament, preparing **other intellec-** long sermons, or writing "treatises on religious **tual interests** **during the** melancholy," and telling others what they must and **seventeenth** must not do if they were to save their immortal **century** souls. This was especially true of New England where, to quote Professor Wertenbaker again, "The intellectual streams were in large measure dried up in the arid wastes of theological disputation." Instead of books on science and art the section produced such wordy treatises as Norton's *The Orthodox Evangelist* and Cotton's *Ecclesiastes and Canticles.* Even though one had the inclination to buy or write something that did not strictly conform to the Puritan standard, he was frowned upon, throttled, or asked to migrate to other parts.

TAKEN up aſtray in Dorcheſter, ſome time ſince, ~~a dark coloured hay mare, with two~~ ~~marks, in which mare~~ ~~ſeveral Mackeril and ſome pieces~~ of ſalt Fiſh &c.   The Owner by applying to Mr Matthew Pymer of Dorcheſter aforeſaid, may have the Mare &c again, paying Charges.

TO be Sold a likely Negro Boy about 18 Years of Age, ſpeaks good Engliſh, and hath been uſed to almoſt all ſorts of Buſineſs either in Town of Country ; whoever inclines to purchaſe ſaid Negro let them inquire of the Printer hereof.

RAN-away from his Maſter Nathanael Holbrook of Sheiburn, on Wedneſday the 19th of Sept laſt. an Indian Lad of about 18 Years of Age, named John Pitteme : He is pretty well ſett and of a guilty Countenance, and has ſhort Hair : He had on a grey Coat with Pewter Buttons, Leather Breeches, an old tow Shirt, grey Stockings, good Shoes and a Felt Hat.

Whoſoever ſhall take up the ſaid Servant, and convey him to his Maſter in Sherburn, ſhall have Forty Shillings Reward, and all neceſſary Charges paid.   We hear the ſaid Servant intended to change his Name and his Clothes.

ANY Perſon that has a Hat and Cane which is none of their Own, are deſired to bring or ſend them to the Printing-Houſe in Newbury-Street, and ſhall Receive Ten Shillings as a Reward.

AL'L Perſons that have any Demands on the Eſtate of John Buttolph, late of Boſton, Wine Cooper, deceas'd are deſired to apply to his Relict Widow and Adminiſtratrix Mehitable Buttolph for Payment ; and thoſe Indebted to ſaid Eſtate are deſired to make ſpeedy Payment to ſaid Adminiſtratrix, as they would avoid further Trouble.

A Wet Nurſe, with a good Breaſt of Milk, that would go into a Family, may be heard of by enquiring of the Printer.

STolen out of a Houſe in this Town, on Tueſday the 25th of September paſt, ſeveral Yards of printed Linnen two Pair of Childrens ſcarlet Broad Cloth Shoes, ſeveral Peices of Quality Bindings   Whoever will inform the Printer thereof, ſo that the Perſon who ſtole them may be brought to Juſtice, ſhall have Forty Shillings Reward.   And if ſuch Goods be offered to be Paw'd or Sold, it is deſired they may be ſtopt and notice given as aforeſaid.

WHEREAS Dr. Tucker, who lately dwelt at the North End of Boſton has removed to his Farm at Chelmsford, and his Wife Martha refuſes to dwell with him ; he therefore cautions all Perſons againſt harbouring or entertaining his ſaid Wife as they would avoid the Trouble of a Law Suit ; and he deſires that none would give Credit to his ſaidWife on his Account for he declares he will not pay any Debts contracted by her, while ſeparated from him

ADVERTISEMENTS FROM "BOSTON NEWS–LETTER"
FOR OCTOBER 4–11, 1739

While the situation outside New England was somewhat better it was, nevertheless, pretty shabby intellectually. In Virginia, for example, Sir William Berkeley in 1671 thanked God that the colony had neither free schools nor a printing press and expressed the hope that it would have neither for a hundred years. Moreover, we should not forget that what culture there was in seventeenth-century America was not created by the colonists, but brought with them from the Old World, and that it changed very slowly under the influence of the wilderness frontier.

By the opening of the eighteenth century, however, conditions were altering. The towns had emerged from the hardships of the pioneering period. Among the clergy a broader *Culture changing by opening of eighteenth century* spirit was noticeable; sectarian prejudices, while still strong, were less pronounced. Contact with the main currents of Western European progress was increasing; facilities for education were improving; the number of professional men was larger and, most important of all, a wealthy merchant class with leisure and a taste for intellectual pursuits had come into existence. Under these influences the transplanted seventeenth-century culture gradually disappeared and was replaced by a distinctly colonial culture which bore fewer earmarks of clericalism.

One of the many evidences of this change is found in the growing interest in science. While the theologians on both sides of the Atlantic were thundering about the sins of *Growing interest of Europeans in science* this world and eternal damnation, others were heeding the dictum laid down by Sir Francis Bacon in his *Novum Organum* that man could master nature by observation and experimentation, and that the conquest of nature and a knowledge of this world were far more important than speculations about the hereafter. Space forbids even brief mention of the accomplishments of those seventeenth-century intellectual giants, Descartes, Leibnitz, Harvey, Malpighi, and Newton, to cite only a few, who did so much to break the backbone of the monopoly which the theologians had so long held over things intellectual. Suffice that their work ushered in a new day which in course of time was to revolutionize man's outlook on life.

Reverberations of what was taking place in the Old World naturally spread to all civilized quarters of the globe, and the colonists, therefore, soon felt the impact of the new forces. Interest in science increased, and here and there a colonist was stimulated to engage in scientific research. Indeed, the writings of the eighteenth-century colonists abound in observations relative to geography, climate, and natural resources.

Scientific achievements in colonial America

In New England, which from the beginning had been the theological stronghold, the new movement did not make as much headway at first as it did elsewhere. The Reverend Jared Eliot of Connecticut who, as we noted in Chapter II, was one of the outstanding men of his day, was deeply interested in science, and his *Essays on Field Husbandry* were based on thirty years of experimentation. John Winthrop, descendant of the first governor of Massachusetts and professor of mathematics and natural philosophy at Harvard from 1738 to 1779, was perhaps the greatest scholar and lecturer of his day. His researches in the field of science gained for him international fame. Professor Isaac Greenwood gave "astronomical lectures" in Boston in 1734, and a few years later Edward Bromfield, a Harvard graduate, was making lenses with which he was experimenting. Even many of the clergy, including no less a personage than Cotton Mather, were zealous students of natural history; Governor Joseph Dudley of Massachusetts and his son Paul were especially devoted to the subject, and several papers by the latter appeared in the *Philosophical Transactions*.

In New England

But it was in the Middle and Southern colonies that the greatest advance was made; here much scholarly work was done in the fields of botany and zoology, although nothing was done in the field of geology. James Logan of Philadelphia, for instance, carried on a number of experiments on maize, his published results supporting the Linnaean theory of sex in plants. Cadwallader Colden of New York was also deeply interested in botany and became a correspondent of Linnaeus. So important was the work of John Bartram, the Quaker naturalist who started his famous botanical

In Middle and Southern colonies

garden in Philadelphia in 1718, that he won from Linnaeus the praise of being "the greatest natural botanist in the world." A considerable part of the flora and fauna of Virginia was described and catalogued by John Banister, a correspondent of the English naturalist, John Ray. Another Virginian, John Mitchell, a doctor of medicine, wrote the first American treatise on the principles of science and also contributed a number of scientific articles to the British Royal Society which had been founded in 1662. Mitchell's principal scientific investigation was in connection with an epidemic of yellow fever in 1737. Other Virginians who won fame for their scientific work included John Tennent, John Clayton, and William Byrd. Perhaps the leading scientific publication of the period was Mark Catesby's *Natural History of Carolina, Florida, and the Bahama Islands*, which appeared in 1731. *Observations on the Weather of Charlestown*, by Dr. John Lining of Charleston, should also be mentioned.

But greatest of all in forwarding the cause of science was Franklin. While Jonathan Edwards, idealist, preacher, and metaphysician, was heralding anew the tenets of Calvinism and depicting the terrors of hell, the distinguished Philadelphian was proposing the formation of the American Philosophical Society for the enlargement of human knowledge. "The first drudgery of settling new colonies," said he, "is now pretty well over, and there are many in every province in circumstances that set them at ease, and afford leisure to cultivate the finer arts and improve the common stock of knowledge." The outgrowth of a literary-scientific club called the Junto, the new society had as its purpose the promotion of the applied sciences and practical arts and the encouragement of "all philosophical experiments that let light into the nature of things, tend to increase the power of man over matter, and multiply the conveniences and pleasures of life." Included in its membership were virtually all the principal representatives of secular learning in the colonies as well as a number of eminent Old World scientists, such as Buffon, Linnaeus, Condorcet, Raynal, and Lavoisier. Franklin's brilliant achievements in the field of science soon won for

Franklin's contribution to scientific movement

him membership in the Royal Society and an international reputation. "We are waiting with the greatest eagerness to hear from you," wrote Buffon and his fellow physicists from France in 1754. At home his enthusiasm inspired others to new scientific endeavor.

That the colonists or at least some of them were fully aware of the importance of science and of the change in outlook being

Scientific movement gives colonists new outlook

wrought by it is evident from the following excerpt taken from an article which appeared in the *Virginia Gazette* in 1737 and reprinted in the *American Magazine* in Boston in 1743:

The World, but a few Ages since, was in a very poor Condition, as to Trade and Navigation. Nor, indeed, were they much better in other Matters of useful Knowledge. It was a Green-headed Time, every useful Improvement was hid from them; they had neither look'd into Heaven nor Earth; into the Sea, nor Land, as has been done since. They had Philosophy without Experiment; Mathematics without Instruments; Geometry without Scale; Astronomy without Demonstration. . . . They went to Sea without Compass; and sail'd without the Needle. They view'd the Stars without Telescopes; and measured Latitude without Observation. . . . They had Surgery without Anatomy, and Physicians without the Materia Medica. . . . As for Geographic Discoveries, they had neither seen the North Cape, nor the Cape of Good Hope. . . . As they were ignorant of Places, so of Things also; so vast are the Improvements of Sciences, that all our knowledge of Mathematics, of Nature, of the brightest part of humane Wisdom, had their Admission among us within the last two centuries. . . . The World is now daily increasing in experimental Knowledge, and let no Man Flatter the Age, with pretending we are arrived to a Perfection of Discoveries.

Turning to the institutions of higher education in the colonies, we find that the evidences of cultural change are present but

The colleges and cultural change

less manifest than in science. Harvard, the first college in the colonies, was authorized by the General Court of Massachusetts in 1636 and endowed two years later by John Harvard, a Charlestown minister. Established principally for the purpose of training men for the ministry, this institution for more than fifty years enjoyed the

COLLEGE OF WILLIAM AND MARY

After a print made early in the eighteenth century

proud distinction of being the only one of its kind in America. In fact, it was not until 1693, after more than thirty years of endeavor, that William and Mary, the second in point of time, was founded. Lack of enthusiasm on the part of many planters, together with the opposition of English officialdom, were chiefly responsible for the long delay in establishing the Virginia insti- The older   tution. Even after its principal sponsor, the institutions   Scottish churchman, James Blair, commissary of the bishop of London, had secured a royal charter and funds for its endowment, Attorney-General Seymour emphatically de- clared that there was not the slightest need for such an institu- tion. Blair reminded him that the principal purpose of the college was to educate young men for the ministry that the souls of the colony might be saved. "Souls! Damn your souls," was the heated rejoinder; "make tobacco." But despite opposi- tion and many misfortunes the college managed to survive. In 1729 its faculty consisted of President Blair and six profes- sors, but its work was that of an academy rather than a college. Though not as influential as Harvard, it nevertheless trained a large proportion of the men who played an important rôle in Virginia politics and in the struggle for independence. The third collegiate institution, Yale, was chartered a few years later (1701) in part as a protest against the growing religious liberalism of Harvard and, in part, to meet the demand of the wealthier element of New Haven for a college of their own. Endowed by Elihu Yale, a son of Massachusetts who had made a fortune in East Indian trade, the institution soon be- came the stronghold of the strictly orthodox type of Calvinism, much to the satisfaction of the Mathers and their friends.

Six other institutions of collegiate rank were established before 1775, four of which were primarily for sectarian purposes. Of The younger   these, the College of New Jersey (Princeton), colleges   founded in 1746, was Presbyterian in inspiration; King's College (Columbia), chartered in 1754, was Anglican; Brown, established in 1764, was Baptist; and Rutgers, founded in 1766, was Dutch Reformed. Brown, it should be noted, soon revealed a tendency to be heretical. Of the other two, Dart- mouth, chartered in 1769, was an outgrowth of Wheelock's

Indian school which was established in 1754 for the purpose of training Indians as missionaries, but it subsequently became an institution where the sons of New England farmers might prepare to teach, preach, or practice law. The Philadelphia Academy, forerunner of the University of Pennsylvania and established by Benjamin Franklin in 1751 for the purpose of training young men for social and political leadership, was undoubtedly the most liberal institution of higher learning in the colonies.

In many respects all of these colleges, with the exception of the last mentioned, were more or less alike in organization, curriculum, and student body. All were largely under church control, and most of the professorships were filled by clergymen. Student life was also very similar, one's position being determined by the wealth and social eminence of his family. As in the Old World, entrance was based almost entirely upon a knowledge of Latin and Greek. Thus Harvard as early as 1643 stated that "when any scholar is able to understand Tully or such like classical Latin author *extempore*, and make and speak true Latin in verse and prose, . . . and decline perfectly the paradigms of nouns and verbs in the Greek tongue, let him then, and not before, be capable of admission into the college." The course of instruction was deeply rooted in the past and, in fact, did not differ basically from that of the medieval university. Although arithmetic, geometry, physics, astronomy, ethics, politics, and divinity were included in the course of study, the chief emphasis was placed upon the classics and sometimes Hebrew. At Harvard one was counted unfit to receive his degree until he was "found able to read the originals of the Old and New Testament into the Latin tongue, and to resolve them logically." Only in the Philadelphia Academy was there any marked attention paid to the study of English and the sciences. Such vitalizing subjects as history, literature, geography, government, and political economy found no place outside of the Philadelphia institution; and even there the astute Franklin was forced to compromise with those who favored the traditional scheme of things. The classics and the other scholastic subjects were provided for those who wished to train for law, medicine, or the church, but Franklin insisted that for the man who wanted to follow some other calling, or who desired a liberal education, there should be courses such as applied mathematics, accounting, science, physics, chemistry, agriculture, natural history, history, ethics, government, trade, international law, and modern languages.

Culturally and intellectually Franklin was ahead of his time. To him college was a place where young men were to be encouraged to drink deep from the font of knowledge and be stimulated to independent thinking. Outside of Franklin's institution, however, the opposite tendency prevailed; dogma rather than experiment ruled; to have an inquiring mind was to be damned. Occasionally some instructor like William Small, professor of mathematics and philosophy at William and Mary, dared to teach doctrines which unsettled the minds of his students and challenged their creative intelligence; but in general the colonial colleges tended to be strongholds of tradition and conservatism.

Colleges strongholds of conservatism

More indicative of the cultural change after 1700 was the growing interest in books and the increasing number of private and public libraries. Many of the first settlers, especially those trained in the universities, brought their libraries with them and subsequently added to them. Thus William Brewster at the time of his death in 1643 had nearly four hundred volumes, and Miles Standish about fifty. John Winthrop, Jr., boasted a library of over a thousand volumes. Likewise inventories of seventeenth-century Virginians show that there were many persons who possessed sizable libraries. Many of these libraries were composed very largely of theological literature, and the neglect of contemporary writers is especially noticeable.

Books and libraries in seventeenth century

That the colonists possessed more books and that more books were being read by 1750 is clearly evident from the increased number and size of private libraries, the larger production and importation of books, the increased number of booksellers, the more frequent book advertisements in the press, and the growth of the public library movement. Not only did clergymen have con-

Evidences of increased reading by 1750

siderable collections, but the wealthy merchants and many of the prominent lawyers were accumulating libraries. Charleston, South Carolina, claims the distinction of having the first library supported by public funds. Through the initiative of Franklin, a public subscription library was founded in Philadelphia in 1731; similar institutions were soon opened in Boston, Newport, New York, and Charleston. The Philadelphia library, Franklin tells us, "soon manifested its utility, was imitated by other towns and in other provinces, . . . reading became fashionable; and our people, having no publick amusements to divert their attention from study, became better acquainted with books, and in a few years were observ'd by strangers to be better instructed and more intelligent than people of the same rank generally are in other countries. . . . The libraries have improved the general conversation of the Americans, made the common tradesmen and farmers as intelligent as most gentlemen from other countries, and perhaps have contributed in some degree to the stand generally made throughout the colonies in defense of their privileges." Between 1745 and 1763 no less than seventeen subscription libraries were founded. Books were included in the endowments of the colonial colleges, notably of Harvard and Yale. The interest of the reader had greatly broadened since the previous century; instead of heavy theological tomes he was now delving into the newest scientific books and into the writings of Dryden, Milton, Locke, Swift, Montesquieu, Voltaire, and Rousseau.

The changes in learned professions, especially law and medicine, also illustrate the intellectual and cultural metamorphoses through which the colonies were passing. It is difficult for even the ordinary layman of today to imagine the ignorance and superstition regarding the human body that prevailed during the seventeenth century among the most enlightened. Modern physiology was practically unheard of. The colonial doctors were sadly deficient in both education and skill, for there were no facilities for medical training on this side of the Atlantic except apprenticeship to a doctor. Where barbers were surgeons and hospitals did not exist, where quackery was rampant, and where

The learned professions and cultural change

reputable physicians prescribed from superstition rather than science, it is small wonder that the death rate was high. The following prescription is significant. To cure small-pox and plague: "In the month of March take toads as many as you will alive, putt them in an earthen pott, so that it may be half full; cover it with a broad tyle or iron plate; then overwhelme the pott so that the bottom may be uppermost; put charcoales around about it. . . . Sett it on fire and lett it burn out and extinguish of itself; when it is cold take out the toades, and in an iron mortar pound them very well . . . moderate the dose according to the strength of the partie."

Seventeenth-century medical practice

With the spread of the scientific movement conditions began to improve. European medical centers such as Edinburgh, Leyden, and Paris saw an increasing number of Americans in attendance, and in 1765 the first medical school on the American continent was established at Philadelphia. Of even greater signifi-cance was the tendency to abandon the idea that disease was the work of the devil and that the sick could be made well by driving out the evil spirits. Moreover, inoculation for smallpox, intro-duced in Boston in 1721 and accepted after a bitter conflict with some of the reactionary clergy, marked a change for the better. Quackery, however, was still widespread at the eve of the Revolution. Dissection was also still frowned upon, and obstet-rics as yet found no place in the doctor's studies or practice.

Slight gains in medical practice during eighteenth century

The legal profession made better progress than did the medical. At the close of the seventeenth century the law was still in its formative stage in the colonies. There were practically no English-trained lawyers in the provinces and, therefore, the work of drafting and administer-ing codes devolved upon laymen. By 1750 the situation had changed markedly, for every important town had its coterie of able practitioners, most of whom were closely united by social and business ties with the townsmen of wealth. In 1729 six of the leading lawyers of New York City formed a bar association for the purpose of raising the standards of the profession. The following year the judges of the Supreme Court of the colony

The law

ruled that an apprenticeship of seven years would be required of all candidates who wished to practice before them, indicating that they also shared the professional consciousness that was seemingly gathering momentum within the ranks.

Lastly, the change in religious outlook and the growing spirit of humanitarianism, both of which were so much in evidence by the middle of the eighteenth century, serve to show that the colonial mind was undergoing an intellectual transformation. Prior to 1700 and perhaps until somewhat later religion in Europe as well as in the colonies was largely formalized. The first revolt against this formalism and, in a larger sense, against continued Puritan absolutism, followed the horrible Salem witchcraft tragedy of 1690–92, in the course of which two hundred persons were accused of being in league with the devil, one hundred and fifty imprisoned, and twenty put to death. Witchcraft, which is grounded in a belief in the supernatural, was no new phenomenon. In the period after the Protestant revolt, for instance, large numbers of unhappy wretches, some of them helpless old women, were put to death as witches in the Old World. The penalty of death for those having "dealings with Evil Spirits" remained on the statute books of England from 1603 to 1735. Even in the colonies over a score of persons were executed as witches prior to 1690. But the superstitious delusion was doomed by the rising forces of rationalism. The terrible Massachusetts calamity had scarcely ended before men began to be skeptical about the guilt of the accused and to doubt the words of that group of fanatical Puritan divines who had fostered and engineered it.

The second revolt against the old order came a generation later. With the increase in economic opportunities and responsibilities and the growth of the scientific movement, many persons on both sides of the Atlantic began to turn away from the old doctrines. This abandonment, partial in some cases and complete in others, so significant in itself, was emphasized by the Great Awakening, a long-continued Calvinistic evangelical movement which swept

Changing religious outlook and growing spirit of humanitarianism evidence of cultural change

Salem witchcraft a boomerang to old order

Decline of formal orthodoxy

over the colonies like wildfire in the late thirties and early forties. It is unnecessary for us to go into the details of this movement; its leaders, George Whitefield and Jonathan Edwards, the latter one of the greatest intellects America has produced, stirred the colonists, emotionally and intellectually, to the very depths. As a consequence the grip of the religious formalists or "Old Lights," as they were called, was broken. For many, religion henceforth was something more than an empty "shell of orthodoxy." Moreover, the Great Awakening quickened the spirit of humanitarianism, as is evidenced by the renewed attempts to minister to the Indian and to treat him more fairly, attempts to reform prisons and the penal codes, and the greater concern for the poor and unfortunate.

Closely related to and, indeed, in some respects an integral part of colonial culture, was the esthetic aspect of colonial life. **The fine arts** Inasmuch as the first settlers were practically compelled by circumstances to devote all their time and energy to the business of making a living, they enjoyed little or no leisure for music, painting, sculpture, and the like. Whatever passion, therefore, they had for beauty had to be expressed in the homes they built, the tools and furnishings they made, and the other tasks they performed. Moreover, they showed little originality, either borrowing freely or slavishly imitating Old World patterns.

Nowhere is this fact better demonstrated than in seventeenth-century colonial architecture. The Dutch, for example, closely **Architecture** followed the models familiar to them. "New Amsterdam," as Lewis Mumford points out, "was a replica of the Old World port, with its gabled brick houses and its well-banked canals and fine gardens." The simple, square, frame house that sheltered the New Englander, with its large fireplace and single chimney, as well as the gabled structures of the South, were based on medieval designs. Likewise the Puritan meetinghouse and the Anglican church were copied after their respective English models. With increasing prosperity, however, both the colonial townsman and the well-to-do planter discarded the more informal house for a spacious Georgian mansion modified to meet local needs. These better

REVEREND JONATHAN EDWARDS

homes were built of both brick and wood, although after 1720 the former material was used in the South almost exclusively. But quite irrespective of material or size, the colonial homes possessed a grace and simple beauty which have never been equaled in the history of American architecture.

House furnishings, like the house itself, were usually patterned after those of the homeland, their elegance depending upon the owner's income. Like the colonial **Furnishings** planter, the wealthy townsman imported practically all his furnishings, and London cabinetmakers were kept busy turning out desks, highboys, chests, chairs, and bedsteads for their overseas customers. Only the finest grades of oak, walnut, olive wood, and mahogany were used, and after 1700 there was a notable tendency to buy not only the most costly but the most comfortable furnishings. Upholstered chairs, for example, began to replace chairs with wooden or hard leather seats, and pewter began to give way to china. A few of the wealthy households in the North patronized the home craftsman skilled in metal working. Little appears to have been done in brass until after the Revolution, but dozens of silversmiths — the majority of Dutch and French extraction — were doing work that was the equal of anything done in Europe.

Colonial painting during the earlier period was confined to portraits. Nearly all the colonies appear to have had artists at work, the most important of whom included the **Painting** Evert family of New York, Christopher Witt of Philadelphia, and Tom Child and Joseph Allen of Boston. During the eighteenth century not only did the number of painters multiply but interest in painting increased. Among those who gained considerable renown during the earlier half of the century may be mentioned Jeremiah Theuss, the painter of the Ravenels, Porches, Manigaults, Izards, Allstons, and other prominent social leaders of Charleston; Gustavus Hesselius and Robert Feke. But these were far outstripped by four others who had risen to high distinction by the eve of the Revolution: John Singleton Copley, Benjamin West, Charles Wilson Peale, and Gilbert Stuart. The pre-Revolutionary years also saw the first exhibition of colonial paintings (New York, 1757), and a growing interest in European painting on the part of some of the wealthier colonists.

Sculpture, as might be expected, lagged behind the other fine arts and did not make its appearance until 1752 when a few

Sculpture

plaster-paris figures were mentioned in the inventory of the estate of John Smibert, Boston portrait painter and art importer. Somewhat later portrait busts were being imported, and in 1759 we find Washington placing an order for busts of a number of distinguished Old World military leaders.

Turning to music, it is interesting to note that no organized musical life existed prior to 1700, due partly to clerical opposition

Music

and partly to lack of funds. What music there was consisted in vocal and instrumental renditions in private homes, taverns, and at dances and fairs. Popular ballads, much to the disgust of the New England clergy, as well as hymns were sung, congregational singing was prevalent throughout the North, and the Swedes and Germans had their folksongs. Musical instruments such as violins, flutes, spinets, and virginals were to be found in all the colonies. Pipe-organs were installed in Philadelphia and Port Royal, Virginia, around 1700; but Boston did not get its first pipe-organ until 1713. Boston and Charleston were the outstanding musical centers, although the Moravian settlement of Bethlehem, Pennsylvania, was famed for its Bach renditions. The first song recital in America was given in Charleston in 1733, and the first ballad opera in the same place two years later.

Another art, the drama, made rapid strides during the last half of the eighteenth century. Throughout the earlier century

Drama

New England was openly hostile, and little progress was made elsewhere. A theatre opened at Williamsburg sometime between 1720 and 1725 was not successful. *The Beaux Stratagem* and *The Busybody* were among the performances given in New York between 1732 and 1734. Charleston also opened a theatre in 1735. It was not until 1750, however, with the arrival of the distinguished stage artists, Mr. and Mrs. Lewis Hallam, from London, that the success of the theatre was assured. Their performances enabled the colonists outside of

New England to see everything that the London stage had to offer, and their company became famed for its excellence.

From what has been said it is evident that all of these cultural influences contributed to the development of colonial nationalism. By the middle of the eighteenth century Franklin was not considered merely a Pennsylvanian, but an American; King's College enrolled students from other colonies, and Boston papers, as we have noted, were read in New York and Charleston. But none of these influences, nor the vigorous struggles with France, important as the latter were in this respect, completely welded the colonies into a nation. Unity in no small measure was achieved as a result of a revolution in the British Empire in which colonial merchant and manufacturer were vitally concerned. To the causes of this revolt we will now turn.

Changing culture contributes to colonial nationalism

SUGGESTED READINGS

J. T. Adams, *Provincial Society, 1690–1763* (vol. 3 of *A History of American Life*), chaps. iii, v, vii, ix–xi.

R. G. Albion, *Forests and Sea Power.*

A. V. G. Allen, *Jonathan Edwards.*

F. W. Bayley, *The Life and Works of John Singleton Copley.*

Charles and Mary Beard, *The Rise of American Civilization*, vol. i, chap. iv.

F. H. Bigelow, *Historic Silver of the Colonies and its Makers.*

J. L. Bishop, *A History of American Manufactures, 1608–1860*, vol. i.

J. B. Brebner, *New England's Outpost Acadia Before the Conquest of Canada.*

P. H. Bruce, *Economic History of Virgina in the Seventeenth Century*, chaps. xii, xiii, xv, xviii.

V. S. Clark, *History of Manufactures in the United States, 1607–1860*, chaps. i–viii.

A. H. Cole, *The American Wool Manufacture*, vol. i, chaps. i–iii.

E. C. Cook, *Literary Influences in Colonial Newspapers.*

J. S. Davis, *Essays in the Earlier History of American Corporations.*

J. C. Duniway, *The Development of the Freedom of the Press in Massachusetts.*

A. M. Earle, *Stage Coach and Tavern Days.*

H. D. Eberlein, *The Architecture of Colonial America.*

Edward Eggleston, *The Transit of Civilization*.

Edward Field, *The Colonial Tavern*.

L. H. Gipson, *Jared Ingersoll*.

E. B. Greene, *Provincial America, 1690–1740* (vol. vi of *The American Nation: A History*), chaps. xvi–xvii.

T. F. Hamlin, *The American Spirit in Architecture* (vol. xiii of *The Pageant of America*), chap. i–ix.

E. P. Hohman, *The American Whaleman, A Study of Life and Labor in the Whaling Industry*, chaps. i–iv.

Arthur Hornblow, *A History of the Theater in America*, vol. i., chaps. i–vi.

J. F. Jameson, *Privateering and Piracy in the Colonial Period*.

E. R. Johnson, and others, *History of Domestic and Foreign Commerce of the United States*, vol. i, chaps. i, ii, v, ix, x.

A. B. Keep, *The Library in Colonial New York, 1698–1776*.

M. S. Kier, *The March of Commerce* (vol. iv of *The Pageant of America*), chaps. i–ii.

E. L. Lord, *Industrial Experiments in the British Colonies of North America*.

Raymond McFarland, *History of the New England Fisheries*, chaps. i–vii.

C. H. Maxson, *The Great Awakening in the Middle Colonies*.

J. H. Morgan, *Early American Painters*.

S. E. Morrison, *Maritime History of Massachusetts, 1783–1860*, chaps. i–ii.

F. L. Mott, *History of American Magazines, 1741–1850*, chaps. i–ii.

F. R. Packard, *The History of Medicine in the United States before 1800*.

J. B. Pearse, *A Concise History of the Iron Manufacture of the American Colonies to the Revolution*.

W. R. Rugg, *Unafraid, The Life of Anne Hutchinson*.

O. G. Sonneck, *Early Opera in America*.

J. M. Swank, *History of the Manufacture of Iron in All Ages*.

Isaiah Thomas, *The History of Printing in America*, vol. i.

C. F. Thwing, *A History of Higher Education in America*, chaps. i–vi.

W. P. Trent and others, *The Cambridge History of American Literature*, vol. i, chaps. i–ix.

R. H. Tryon, *Household Manufactures in the United States, 1640–1860*, chaps. i–iii.

W. B. Weeden, *Economic and Social History of New England, 1620–1789*, 2 vols.

Richard Wright, *Hawkers and Walkers in Early America*.

CHAPTER IV

THE CONFLICT OF INTERESTS

THE revolt in the British Empire popularly known as the American Revolution was not caused by "a wicked, stubborn, German king," George III, for individuals, no matter how important, do not, as Professor Andrews well says, create or stop revolutions. Moreover, it was not a conflict the causes of which can be summarized by the time-worn statement that "Taxation without representation is tyranny." Nor was it a spontaneous uprising of the entire colonial population, for we have fairly conclusive evidence that fully one-third of the colonists opposed the movement in all its stages, and that another third remained at times lukewarm or indifferent. Furthermore, it was not a "sedate and gentlemanly affair" carried on only by scholarly, refined, and conservative people. Instead, it was in large measure an outgrowth of ignorance, misunderstanding, and opposing ideals, and, above all, of deep-seated conflicting interests between groups within the Empire. In this chapter we shall consider in brief outline the nature of these factors and the part played by them in bringing about the secession of Great Britain's wealthiest and most advanced overseas domain.

Nature of the American Revolution

1. MERCANTILISM AND ECONOMIC FRICTION, 1650–1763

Foremost of the half dozen fundamental factors in which the Revolution was rooted was the clash of economic interests between the colonists and the mother country. At the bottom of this economic friction lay the doctrine of mercantilism. According to this doctrine, as we have already noted, a state to be wealthy, independent, and powerful must possess a large and permanent stock of gold and silver. If it be without rich deposits of precious metals — as was England — then it must seek possession of mines in other

Mercantilism and colonies

parts of the world or build up its stock of gold and silver by means of favorable trade balances. To help insure the latter the state ought to (1) protect and aid home agriculture in order that sufficient foodstuffs may be produced for its people; (2) encourage the production of raw materials for home manufacture; (3) protect and stimulate home industry; (4) encourage native shipping in every possible way; and (5) provide an efficient navy. Any state possessing colonies was, according to mercantilism, specially blessed, for colonies would (1) supply the mother country with necessary raw materials which it did not produce and would otherwise have to buy; (2) furnish a market for home manufactures; (3) afford home merchants and shipowners a means of additional profits; and (4) directly or indirectly add to the wealth of the nation by increasing its specie supply.

Every essential tenet of the mercantilist philosophy was applied to the English colonies by the mother country. Dominated throughout the seventeenth and eighteenth centuries by an exclusive, privileged, autocratic, moneyed middle class whose main interest was in trade, and by politicians who for the most part did its bidding, England used the colonies, first, for the promotion of home interests, and, secondly, for the welfare of the Empire. From first to last she operated on the theory that the prosperity and independence of the entire Empire depended on her own well-being, and at no time did she, as we shall see, become the tail to the economic kite of any colony. To have done so would have been contrary to the chief purpose for which the colonies were founded as well as to the main thesis of mercantilism and to the spirit of the times.

England applies doctrine of mercantilism to colonies

In applying the mercantilist theory to the colonies, England first endeavored by a series of laws and ordinances to regulate colonial trade. Among the most important of these regulatory measures were the so-called Navigation Acts, the first of which was applied to the colonies soon after the importation of tobacco began. It was not until the days of Cromwell, however, when England and Holland were engaged in a life-and-death struggle

Trade regulations: the Navigation Act of 1650

for the commercial supremacy of the seas, that more drastic and sweeping legislation began to be enacted. In 1650, for instance, when the bulk of the British colonial trade was in the hands of the Dutch, Parliament forbade foreign vessels "to come to, or Trade in, or Traffique with" any of the English colonies in America unless licensed by Parliament or by the Council of State. At the same time the colonies were forbidden to have "any manner of Commerce or Traffique with any people whatsoever." In other words, the colonies were to carry on commercial intercourse solely with England. It mattered not if the Virginia planter could derive a greater profit by doing business with the Dutch; the interests of the British carrier and the mother country were paramount, and these demanded the elimination of foreign competition and a monopoly of the Empire's shipping.

This measure, so unmistakable in its meaning, was followed the next year by the famous Navigation Act of 1651. Less comprehensive as far as the colonies were concerned, it provided (1) that all goods grown or manufactured in Asia, Africa, or America and imported into England or its possessions must be brought in English-owned and English-manned ships; (2) that European goods could be imported into England or its possessions only in English ships or in vessels belonging to the country where the goods were produced or whence they were usually shipped for transportation; (3) that, with few exceptions, no foreign goods should be brought into England except from the place of production or from the usual port of shipment; (4) that salted fish, fish oil, or whale fins could not be imported into England unless caught by English vessels, and that no fish should be exported from England or its possessions except in English ships; (5) that the English coastwise trade should be completely closed to foreign vessels. It is evident that this Act, which incidentally placed English and colonial shipping on an equal footing, was not only aimed at the Dutch but that it sought to further the growth of the English merchant marine and the fishing industry.

The Acts of 1650 and 1651, although only partially enforced, occasioned serious complaint in the colonies. Virginia planters, for example, asserted that the measures worked great hardship and that their passage was due to "the Avarice of a few interested persons, who endeavor to rob us of all we sweat and labour for." Even Governor Berkeley declared that those who sponsored the legislation "would faine bring us to the same poverty wherein the Dutch found and relieved us; would take away the liberty of our consciences and tongues, and our right of giving and selling our goods to whom we please." In 1655 the legislature of the colony resolved that "all freedom of trade shall be maintained, and all merchants and traders shall be cherished." Massachusetts condemned the seizure of a Dutch vessel in its waters, and the legislature of Rhode Island went so far as to declare that in times of peace, commerce with the Dutch was lawful. The English West Indies, where the laws were more strictly enforced, were also outspoken in their opposition to them.

Colonial reaction to Acts of 1650 and 1651

Offensive as they may have been to the colonies, these laws were only a beginning. In 1660 the Restoration government, faced by a lean treasury and hard pressed by the mercantile and industrial classes for protection and assistance, passed an "Act for the Encouraging and Increasing of Shipping and Navigation." It stipulated in the first place that goods imported into or exported from any British colony must be carried in ships built, owned, and manned by Englishmen. Not only would this give English shippers a monopoly of the carrying trade of the Empire, but it would encourage shipbuilding both in the mother country and in the colonies. Secondly, it ruled that certain "enumerated" articles — sugar, tobacco, cotton, wool, ginger, indigo, fustic, and other dye woods — grown or manufactured in the colonies could not be sold directly to foreigners, but must first be sent to England or to some other part of the British Empire. This list was subsequently extended; rice, molasses, and the naval stores — tar, pitch, turpentine, hemp, masts, and yards — being added in 1706; copper ore, beaver, and other skins in 1722; whale fins, raw silks, hides, pot and pearl ashes, pig- and bar-iron, lumber, coffee, pimento, and cocoanuts in 1764. Up to 1766

The Navigation Act of 1660

non-enumerated articles, including a number of the more important colonial commodities such as fish, grain, and rum, could be disposed of directly to any part of the world, unless of course their sale in this way was prevented by foreign restrictions. In that year, however, the mother country, hoping to keep the colonists from purchasing manufactured products from her European competitors, forbade the shipment of colonial goods of every description to any foreign country north of Cape Finisterre. By adopting the process of "enumeration," England sought (1) to supply her manufacturers with needed raw materials; (2) to enable the home merchants to reap a profit as middlemen or distributors; and (3) to increase her revenue (specie supply), since all goods imported from the colonies were, as a rule, like goods from foreign countries, subject to heavy duties.

The Act of 1660 did not prevent the colonists from importing staples directly from foreign countries. Articles manufactured in Holland or in France, for instance, might be **The Act of** brought directly to Virginia or Massachusetts in **1663** English ships and there disposed of at a lower price than like goods of English manufacture. Moreover, the merchants of the mother country, unless the owners of the ship, derived no profit from such transactions. To remedy this situation and to keep the colonies "in a firmer dependence upon it [England] and rendering them yet more beneficial and advantageous unto it," Parliament in 1663 provided that all European goods bound for the colonies must first be sent to England and from there reshipped in English ships to colonial ports. The only exceptions to this rule were salt from Spain for the New England fisheries, wines from Madeira and the Azores, and a few commodities from Ireland and Scotland. In reality the Act practically gave the mother country a monopoly over the colonial import trade and enabled its merchants to collect profitable commissions on all European goods consumed in the colonies. It also enabled the home government to increase its revenue and in this way lessen the burden of direct taxation.

Like their predecessors, the Acts of 1660 and 1663 roused determined opposition in the colonies and, for want of adequate

enforcement machinery, were constantly evaded. Prior to
1672 colonial merchants sent shipload after shipload of enumerated articles direct to Europe without landing
them in England, under the pretense that they were
destined for some other port of the Empire. In
that year, however, Parliament endeavored to put
an end to this practice by providing that every outbound vessel
carrying enumerated articles must give a bond that it would
land the articles in England or else pay specific export duties
equal in amount to the import tax levied on such articles by the
home country. It also authorized the appointment of colonial
customs collectors to supervise and enforce the Act. But these
officials made little headway, the colonists regarding them as
busybodies interfering with what was none of their business.
Evasions continued at an increasing rate, some of the colonists
even going so far as to dispose of their commodities direct to
Europe through privateers and pirates.

Acts of 1660 and 1663 opposed and evaded

Naturally these infractions did not please the business men of
the mother country, and with passing years their clamor for the
more strict enforcement of the Navigation Acts
became louder and louder. Finally in 1695 merchants of Bristol, Liverpool, and London petitioned
the House of Commons for action. The result was
the passage the following year of the "Act for preventing Frauds and regulating Abuses in the Plantation Trade." By it all the earlier navigation laws were
reaffirmed; in addition it ruled that all English vessels, whether
owned in England or in the colonies, must be registered; that
all colonial laws at variance with the Acts of trade were null and
void, and that all colonial governors must take an oath to enforce the Navigation Acts or suffer penalty of fine and loss of
office. To the delight of zealous imperial officials it also
authorized collectors and inspectors to visit and search ships,
wharves, and warehouses, and to seize unlawful merchandise.
Furthermore, cases involving penalties could be brought before
colonial admiralty courts. Up to this time it had been almost
impossible to secure convictions in revenue cases from colonial
juries. For a few years after its passage the Act of 1696 was

The Act of 1696. Home merchants demand stricter enforcement of navigation laws

fairly effective, and by 1701 the balance of trade, long in favor of the mainland colonies, stood in favor of England.

Of all the trade regulations none roused the ire of the colonists more than the famous Molasses Act of 1733. We have already noted that the Northern colonies, deprived for the most part of a market in the mother country for their ever-increasing surplus products, turned to other quarters, and particularly to the West Indies, where they readily exchanged their provisions, horses, cattle, timber products, and cargoes of African slaves for rum, sugar, molasses, and money or bills of exchange. By far the greater part of this West Indian trade, however, was carried on with the non-British islands, especially with the French, who on account of the richness of their soil, premiums on the importation of slaves, and other factors were able to undersell their British competitors from twenty-five to fifty per cent. In addition, the English West Indian planters suffered through the "enumeration" of sugar, for the home country was unable to consume the entire British West Indian output or to market the surplus profitably to the producer. It was most natural, therefore, that the planters should seek relief. In 1730 and again the following year they petitioned the Privy Council to prohibit trade with the foreign islands. Failing to gain assistance, they carried the matter into Parliament, where it was debated at length. Spokesmen for the Northern colonies pointed out that any interference with the West Indian trade would paralyze the commercial provinces, for it, more than anything else, enabled them to utilize their fisheries, forests, and fertile soil and, above all, to secure the necessary money with which to satisfy their English creditors. The rich absentee planters, members of Parliament, on the other hand, backed by a powerful lobby, relentlessly pressed their case. Many persons both in and out of Parliament asserted that while the dispute grew out of a clash of interests within the Empire, it was in reality part of the greater contest going on between France and England for commercial supremacy. The Northern colonists, they also declared, though promoting their own interests, were violating one of the main tenets of mercantilism by enriching foreign sugar

The climax in trade regulation: the Molasses Act of 1733

colonies and impoverishing those of their own Empire. And it was on this broader ground that the matter was in a large measure decided. In its final form the Act was, in theory at least, restrictive rather than prohibitory. It imposed a duty of nine pence a gallon on rum, six pence a gallon on molasses, and five shillings a hundredweight on sugar imported from the non-English West Indies.

The argument that the Act was aimed primarily at France failed to impress the commercial provinces. In both New England and the Middle colonies, merchants and distillers regarded it as a piece of class legislation which would enable "a few pamper'd Creolians" to "roll in their gilded equipages through the streets" of London at the expense of two million American subjects. But England was without adequate customs service to enforce the law and, as many had anticipated, it was practically ignored, trade with the foreign islands going on as before. Had it been enforced it would in all probability have ruined, or at least seriously crippled, not only northern commerce but all northern industry as it then existed. Even though it was evaded, the law was not without effect. In the first place, because it failed to take account of the growing economic democracy — of what the colonists regarded as their right to develop the natural resources of their country and to utilize them as they saw fit — and sought to keep the colonists in the narrow and subordinate place assigned them in the mercantilistic scheme, it constituted a perpetual grievance against the mother country. Secondly, it irritated the colonists to have their interests subordinated to those of a small coterie of West Indian sugar planters. Finally and, in many respects, most important of all, it made, to use Mr. J. T. Adams's words in his *Revolutionary New England, 1691–1776,* "a large section of the colonial population smugglers and law breakers by necessity, it lowered the moral tone of the community and decreased the respect for law."

Its effect on the mainland colonies

A second source of friction between the mother country and the colonies, growing out of the application of the mercantilistic theory, was the attempted restriction of colonial manufacturing. During the seventeenth century and the earlier part of

Anno sexto

Georgii II. Regis.

An Act for the better securing and encouraging the Trade of His Majesty's Sugar Colonies in *America*.

VVEREAS the Welfare and Prosperity of Your Majesty's Sugar Colonies in America are of the greatest Consequence and Importance to the Trade, Navigation, and Strength of this Kingdom : And whereas the Planters of the said Sugar Colonies have of late Years fallen under such great Discouragements, that they are unable to improve or carry on the Sugar Trade upon an equal Footing with the foreign Sugar Colonies, without some Advantage and Relief be given to them from Great Britain : For Remedy whereof, and for the Good and Welfare of Your Majesty's Subjects, we Your Majesty's most dutiful and loyal Subjects, the Commons of Great Britain assembled in Parliament, have given and granted unto Your Majesty the several and respective Rates and Duties herein after mentioned, and in such Manner and Form, as is herein after expressed ; And do most humbly beseech Your Majesty that it may be enacted,

B b b b a

THE MOLASSES ACT OF 1733

Reduced facsimile

Anno vicesimo quarto

Georgii II. Regis.

An Act to regulate and restrain Paper Bills of Credit in His Majesty's Colonies or Plantations of *Rhode Island*, and *Providence* Plantations, *Connecticut*, the *Massachusets Bay*, and *New Hampshire* in *America* ; and to prevent the same being legal Tenders in Payments of Money.

Wereas the Act of Parliament made in the Sixth Year of Her late Majesty Queen Anne, intituled, An Act for ascertaining the Rate of Foreign Coins in Her Majesty's Plantations in America, hath been intirely frustrated in his Majesty's said Colonies of Rhode Island and Providence Plantations, Connecticut, the Massachusets Bay, and New Hampshire in America, by their creating and issuing, from time to time, great Quantities of Paper Bills of Credit, by virtue of Acts of Assembly, Orders, Resolutions, or Votes, made or passed by their respective Assemblies, and making legal the Tender of such Bills of Credit in Payment for Debts, Dues, and Demands ; which Bills of Credit have, for many Years past, been depreciating in their Value, by means whereof all Debts of late Years have been paid and satisfied with a much less Value than was contracted for, which hath been a great Discouragement and Prejudice to the Trade and Commerce of his Majesty's Subjects, by occasioning Confusion in Dealings, and lessening of Credit in those Parts · Therefore, for the more effectual preventing and remedying of the said Inconveniencies, may it please your

6 13 D most

ACT OF 1751 TO RESTRAIN IS-
SUE OF PAPER MONEY

Reduced facsimile

the eighteenth, conditions in the colonies were, as we observed in the previous chapter, far from favorable for industrial pursuit. Land was plentiful and cheap and agriculture profitable, and the person who essayed to engage in manufacturing on any considerable scale was handicapped by lack of capital, a stabilized currency, and an adequate labor supply. In spite of these obstacles, however, many lines of manufacture, as we have seen, were undertaken, especially in the New England and Middle colonies. This of course was contrary to the mercantilistic theory, which regarded colonies not only as sources of raw materials but as markets to be monopolized and exploited by home interests. The development of rival industries in the colonies curtailed the market for English manufactures, and the English merchant and manufacturer, therefore, turned to Parliament for protection, as the American manufacturer today asks Congress to safeguard his interests by tariff legislation.

Attempted restriction of colonial manufacturing a second source of friction

The passage of the Woolens Act in 1699 marked the first important step in the direction of restraint on colonial manufacture. At the time of its enactment all of the Northern colonies were producing considerable quantities of woolen goods on a small scale, and one, Massachusetts, supplied a large part of its own needs and even exported woolen goods to other colonies. The English woolen manufacturer naturally opposed this colonial enterprise, for every skein of woolen yarn and every yard of woolen cloth produced in America lessened his market. Moreover the landed classes who produced the raw material, the persons who fabricated it, and the merchants who handled the finished product were all affected adversely by this colonial competition. Consequently they supported the manufacturers in their contention that an industry affecting over a million of England's population and accounting for nearly half of her exports, as the woolen industry did, ought not to be endangered even by some other part of the Empire. The Act of 1699, passed by Parliament in response to the urgent protests of these affected groups, provided under heavy penalty that no woolen goods of any description could be sent from one colony to another or from any colony to a

1. The Woolens Act, 1699

foreign country. The Act, it should be noted, was far from prohibitory, for any colony could still manufacture for consumption within its borders.

A second law restricting colonial manufacture was enacted in 1732. Favored by an abundance of beaver and unhampered by government regulations, New Yorkers and New **2. The Hat** Englanders had for several years been manufactur- **Act of 1732** ing beaver hats in increasing quantities. Because of their peculiar advantages they were often able to undersell the British manufacturer not only in the colonies but in foreign lands, particularly Spain and the West Indies. The home interests complained about this competition, and in 1731 asked the Board of Trade to suppress the manufacture of hats in the colonies. A parliamentary inquiry, disclosing the fact that New York and New England were turning out no less than 10,000 hats annually, resulted in legislation. The Hat Act of 1732, as it was called, provided (1) that no American-made hat could be exported from one colony to another, or from the colonies to England and Europe; (2) that no master could have more than two apprentices and that each must serve for not less than seven years; and (3) that no one should engage in the manufacture of felt hats unless he had served a seven-year apprenticeship. The employment of negroes in the industry was forbidden.

A third restrictive law applied to the iron industry. The mother country, as we have seen, was anxious to have the colonists augment her supply of bar- and pig-iron, but **3. The Iron** she had not the slightest desire to see the colonists **Act of 1750** engage in the manufacture of finished iron products. In fact, as early as 1719 a bill was introduced in Parliament prohibiting the manufacture in America of hollow-ware and castings and the erection of forges for refining iron. Twenty years later the project was renewed, but it was not until 1750 that the desired legislation was enacted. In that year a law was passed providing (1) that bar- and pig-iron should be admitted to Great Britain duty free, but (2) absolutely prohibiting under penalty of £200 the erection in the colonies of slitting or rolling mills, plating forges, or steel furnaces. Such establishments already in operation were allowed to continue. From this law we can readily see that the British iron interests who were chiefly responsible for its passage intended, in accordance with the mercantilistic theory, that the colonial iron-masters should furnish them with raw material but should not compete with them by manufacturing bar- and pig-iron into tools, implements, and hardware.

Although these restrictions on colonial manufacturing in all probability did not entail any serious economic loss upon the colonists, they nevertheless caused friction. In fact, many colonists entertained the notion that the colonies were being exploited for the benefit of a little group of home manufacturers. Thus Benjamin Franklin, in discussing the causes of American discontent, declared that the interests of British tradesmen and artificers were regarded as more important then the interests of the colonists. "The hatters of England," said he, "have prevailed to obtain an Act in their own favor restraining that manufacture in America, in order to oblige the Americans to send their beaver to England to be manufactured, and purchase back the hats, loaded with the charges of a double transportation. In the same manner have a few nailmakers, and a still smaller body of steel-makers (perhaps there are not half a dozen of these in England), prevailed totally to forbid by an Act of Parliament the erection of slitting-mills, or steel furnaces, in America; that the Americans may be obliged to take all thêir nails for their buildings, and steel for their tools, from these artificers, under the same disadvantages." These laws, like the Acts restricting trade, were to a great extent ignored by the colonists, for the imperial authorities had no adequate machinery to enforce them.

Attitude of colonists toward restriction

Closely connected with the laws on colonial trade and manufactures were the restrictions on the lumber industry. From the very first the mother country depended upon the magnificent forests of the Northern colonies, particularly New England, for masts for the royal navy and at an early date took steps to reserve the larger trees for that purpose. Thus the last clause of the new charter granted Massachusetts in 1691 reserved for the crown all trees

Restrictions on lumber industry

of not less than twenty-four inches in diameter at the base not growing on private lands. About a decade later a parliamentary statute provided a penalty of £15 for the felling of such trees anywhere in the colonies of New York, New Jersey, and New England. In 1711 the penalty was raised to £100, and surveyors of the "King's Woods" were appointed to mark suitable trees with a broad arrow, thereby signifying that they were reserved for the use of the navy. Still later Parliament ruled that no white pine trees outside the bounds of a township should be cut without a royal license. Evasion of this statute led the mother country to enact that no white pine trees might be felled unless they were on the property of private persons.

Inasmuch as lumbering was one of the most important of the colonial industries, these restrictive measures and the unpopular officials who endeavored to enforce them were a *Restrictions a source of perennial friction.* Colonial lumber interests, whether frontier chopper or seaboard merchant, anxious for private gain, constantly broke the laws by ruthlessly cutting forest giants reserved for masts and sawing them into planks or splitting them into shingles. Arrests were made, but convictions were impossible, for judge and jury alike were on the side of the law-breakers. In 1720 the Massachusetts Assembly advanced the absurd claim that the timber described as belonging to the crown was royal property only while standing, and that as soon as it was cut it belonged to the colony. The Lords of Trade labeled this fantastic doctrine a "scandalous evasion" of the law. Colonial land speculators joined lumbermen in defying the restraints, some even going so far as to declare that Parliament had no right to infringe on the economic liberties of the colonists.

Frequent controversy over land titles and quitrents constituted a fourth source of friction between the colonies and the mother country. Opportunity to acquire free land *Controversy over land titles and quitrents a fourth source of friction* was, as we have seen, a factor of prime importance in attracting settlers to America, and they and their descendants vigorously resisted every move that threatened their absolute ownership. In New England, for example, popular feeling was roused when, during the administration of Governor Andros, the home authorities questioned the validity of all land titles on the ground that the original companies who had made the grants to the towns, which in turn had bestowed them on individuals, had no power to do so. Moreover, Andros was instructed to dispose of all lands "yet undisposed of" and others which had not yet received royal confirmation for a quitrent of not less than two and a half shillings for every hundred acres. Although the quitrent was small and Andros was cautioned not to molest any man's "Freehold or Goods," this move on the part of the mother country was bitterly resented by the colonists as unjust and uncalled-for meddling and interference. Outside of New England, attempts to alter land titles in favor of home interests, or to levy and collect quitrents, met with opposition. In fact, from Maine to Georgia conflicts over land titles and quitrents undoubtedly strengthened the hand of those who were thinking in terms of "natural rights" and of those who later were to create defenses and revolution by appealing to the "rights of man."

A fifth source of conflict, not only between Great Britain and the colonies but between classes within the colonies, growing out of a clash of economic interests, was the parliamentary regulation respecting colonial currency and credit. During the first quarter of the eighteenth century British merchants repeatedly informed Parliament that many of the colonies enacted laws favoring colonial creditors but seriously impeding British creditors in the collection of debts lawfully due them. In asking for redress they characterized some of the discriminatory legislation as "bare-faced fraud." As a result of the merchants' representations Parliament in 1732 provided that the affidavit of a resident in Great Britain should have the same weight as evidence given in open court in the colonies. Lands, tenements, and slaves owned by the colonists were made liable for debts in much the same way as was real estate in England. Spokesmen for the unthrifty and less fortunate colonists upon whom this regulation weighed most heavily condemned it on the ground that Parliament was interfering with the internal affairs of the colonies.

Parliamentary regulation of colonial currency and credit a fifth source of friction

Vastly more important as a source of conflict than this law regarding credit were the parliamentary regulations respecting colonial currency. Hard pressed for a circulating Paper money medium, all the colonies with the exception of and banks North Carolina, as we observed in the previous chapter, resorted to the issuance of paper money. During the decade 1730–1740 not only did several of the colonial governments, particularly those of New England, add large quantities of paper currency to the amount already in circulation, but groups of private individuals, motivated partly by selfish aims and partly by a desire to enable farmers and others to secure money at reasonable rates, formed "banks." As early as 1722 Pennsylvania had established a loan office which issued and loaned bills not exceeding twenty shillings secured by land of double the value. "The poor middling people who had any land or houses to pledge," says Keith, "borrowed from the loan-office, and paid off their usurious creditors. The few rich men who had before this given over all trade, except that of usury, were obliged to build ships and launch out again into trade." In 1732 the New London Society United for Trade and Commerce was started in Connecticut. It had a short and stormy career but in many respects served as the model for the more famous Land Bank of Massachusetts, which came into existence in 1740.

Organized in response to a resolution of the Massachusetts Assembly requesting the submission of proposals for supplying the colony with "more money" and "an additional The Massa-medium of trade," this so-called bank, which had chusetts Land no capital stock, planned to issue £150,000 in Bank paper money notes to be secured by land. Artificers and traders not owning land were to be allowed to make loans of not over £100 each on personal security provided they had proper sureties. The notes, which were not to be redeemed for twenty years, might be paid off in commodities.

This scheme and others like it, as well as the demand for paper money, had at all times the almost solid backing of the debtor class — of the farmers and frontiersmen, the me- Debtors vs.chanics and laborers — in a word, of those who creditors bought goods on credit, or who were in debt for land, or who on

occasion had to borrow money. Like the Greenbackers and the
Populists of a later day, they believed that land banks and cheap
money would remedy their economic ills. The creditor class,
on the other hand, composed for the most part of money-
lenders, merchants, manufacturers, and their lawyer-allies —
of the wealthy, the educated, and the socially superior classes
— opposed the issuance of paper money and bitterly fought
the debtor banks at every turn. For them rival banks
and increasing issues of paper currency meant competition,
inflation, and possible ruin. In Massachusetts they endeavored
to counter the Land Bank scheme by setting up a bank of their
own known as the "Silver Bank," which undertook to issue
notes based on silver. Similar action was taken in Rhode
Island and New Hampshire. They also tried to induce the
Massachusetts Assembly to veto the Land Bank plan, but that
body, being dominated by the debtor element, declined; whereupon the governor with the advice of the Council, both of whom
favored the creditor group, issued a proclamation cautioning all
persons not to use the Land Bank notes on the ground that they
tended "to defraud men, to disturb the peace, and to injure
trade." Shortly afterward an address signed by one hundred
and thirty prominent merchants of the colony further warned
the public to have nothing to do with the scheme.

But entreaties and warnings were without avail, and in desperation many of the creditor group joined with the London
The Massa- merchants, who were also suffering from abuses of
chusetts Land colonial paper inflation, in asking the Privy Council
Bank throttled for relief. Drastic action followed: all persons
were forbidden to pass Land Bank bills, certain classes of officials
found guilty of doing so were threatened with removal, military
officers were forced to ascertain whether their subordinates had
passed the bills, and registrars of deeds were ordered to return
all Land Bank mortgages. In spite of these edicts, however, the
Land Bank bills continued to circulate. Finally in 1741 Parliament, at the earnest solicitation of the creditor group, suppressed
the institution. This suppression brought ruin to many of its
supporters, including among others the father of Samuel Adams
of Revolutionary fame.

Not content with the destruction of the Land Bank, Parliament in 1751, in response to the loud complaints of the English merchants "that many fair creditors and other persons not in debt lost half or three-fourths of what was due to them, and of their personal estate" on **Parliament forbids use of paper money** account of the immoderate issues of paper money by New England, passed an Act forbidding the governments of that section to issue any additional legal tender bills of credit. In 1764 Parliament forbade the use of legal tender paper money in all the colonies on the theory that it was "false in its principles, unjust in its foundations, and manifestly fraudulent in its operations."

At this point we need not stop to consider the effect of this legislation on the relations of the colonial debtor-creditor groups. That we shall discuss later. Here we are primarily concerned with its effect on the relations between the mother country and the colonies. Generally speaking, the colonial business interests approved the action of the home government, while the debtor class almost savagely condemned it. Especially was this true in the case of the suppression of **Action of English government respecting paper money and Land Banks embittered colonial debtors** the Land Bank, which had the whole-hearted support of nearly two-thirds of the Massachusetts Assembly. In fact John Adams, writing in 1774, was of the opinion that its suppression was more important than the Stamp Act in "creating ferment" and rousing opposition in Massachusetts to British authority. Franklin entertained similar notions, and in 1766 informed British leaders that one of the principal reasons for American ill-feeling toward England was the prohibition of paper money.

While the colonists objected to all restrictive enactments and repeatedly asserted that it was their "natural right" to engage in any sort of industry and to trade with whom they wished, we should not forget that the mother country did much to ameliorate the effect of these restrictions and to promote the well-being of the colonies. In the first place, she gave them preferen- **Disadvantages of restrictive legislation partly balanced by advantageous measures** tial treatment in the matter of customs duties. The rates on colonial tobacco, for example, were much less than those on

Spanish tobacco. Similarly the rates on colonial indigo, iron, whale oil, hemp, lumber, silk, ginger, pot and pearl ashes, and molasses were less than those on foreign commodities. England, it may be argued, adopted this preferential system because she needed these products, but this should not blind us to the fact that these particular commodities enjoyed an especial advantage in the British market. Secondly, the duty on many commodities exported to the colonies by way of England was refunded in part or entirely, so that in some instances, as in the case of Dutch linens, the colonists could purchase them more cheaply than they could be purchased in England. These refunds or drawbacks were not granted to iron and steel products, cordage, sailcloth, and paper of foreign manufacture. Thirdly, the mother country sought by means of bounties and other financial inducements to encourage the production of certain commodities. We have already observed how for many years prior to the seventeenth century England not only had been dependent on the Baltic countries for naval supplies, but also had been the victim of an adverse balance of trade totaling well over £500,000. In the hope of remedying this state of affairs, Parliament in 1705 passed a measure granting bounties on naval stores imported from the colonies — £4 per ton on pitch and tar, £6 a ton on hemp, £3 a ton on rosin and turpentine, £1 a ton on masts, yards, and bowsprits. Increased production and a rapid decline in the price of these commodities, however, led to a considerable reduction of the bounties during the reign of George II. To free England from dependence on French indigo, a bounty of 6d. a pound on indigo imported directly into England from her overseas possessions was provided in 1748. Furthermore, colonial tobacco growers were aided by the parliamentary prohibition of tobacco-growing in England and Ireland. Finally, the colonies as part of the British Empire enjoyed, in addition to the advantages already enumerated, military and naval protection, free or privileged trade with other parts of the Empire, and the benefit of Great Britain's commercial treaties.

As is often the case where interests clash, many of the colonists either did not recognize these advantages or else regarded them as of little or no importance. Separated from the mother

country by three thousand miles of ocean and surrounded by
conditions markedly different from those of the Old World,
the colonists, as we have already stated, developed
from the outset a spirit of independence. They
desired to do as they pleased, especially where
economic interests were involved. To them mercantilism with its numerous restrictions was an essentially
selfish policy which sacrificed the interests of the colonies to
those of the mother country. Or, to put it differently, the self-
interest of the English mercantilist clashed with the self-interest
of the colonist. Each consulted his own wishes and catered to
his own needs. Inevitable conflict resulted, featured by misunderstanding, evasion of the law, and growing bitterness. It
was not until the years 1763-1776, however, when the mother
country attempted to tighten her imperial grip on her overseas
possessions, that the issues at stake became more sharply defined and that the storm clouds of revolution began to loom on
the horizon.

*British mer-
cantilism and
colonial self-
interest clash*

2. Plans for Reform, 1750-1763

By 1750 many British statesmen were convinced that England's colonial policy was badly in need of reform. Like Topsy,
the Empire had "just growed," and no systematic
plan of administering it had ever been evolved.
Separated from each other during the early years
by almost impassable forests or by long stretches of
water, each colony had within certain limits developed its own
institutions, traditions, customs, and usages to which the home
government in so far as possible adapted itself. Instead of regarding them as organic parts of the English body politic, the
mother country to a great extent treated them as disconnected
autonomic political entities. Indeed, so loose was England's grip
on her overseas colonies that the citizens of each regarded themselves not as Englishmen, nor even as Americans, but as Virginians, New Yorkers, or Marylanders, as the case might be. Most
important of all from the standpoint of administration was the
fact that as virtually self-governing units, each had developed

*The colonies
under the old
colonial
"system"*

its own land policy, its own method of dealing with the Indians, its own system of administration.

By the middle of the eighteenth century, however, conditions on both sides of the Atlantic had so greatly changed that the mother country felt that for her own benefit and **Proposed changes in colonial policy** that of the Empire as a whole, the time had come (1) for centralized control of the trans-Allegheny country; (2) for a closer association of the colonies for administrative purposes; (3) for imposing a greater share of the expense of colonial defense and administration upon the colonists themselves; and (4) for compelling the colonists to adhere more strictly to the principles of the mercantile system. Inasmuch as all of these proposed changes ran counter to the interests of the majority of the colonists and ultimately led to armed conflict within the Empire, let us briefly examine the motives back of each of them.

The proposal for centralized control of the western country was advanced for two major reasons. In the first place, the home authorities were alarmed over the Indian **1. Centralized control of West** situation. Under the régime of the several colonies **Protection of Indians** the natives had been shamefully maltreated by unscrupulous traders and eager land-grabbers who made constant use of liquor to facilitate their fraudulent transactions. Their lands had been stolen, their children kidnapped, and their hunting grounds destroyed. Time after time their spokesmen had pleaded in vain with the individual colonies for just treatment. Failing to secure redress for past wrongs or any cessation on the part of the whites of the practices so distasteful to them, the outraged savages were daily becoming more embittered toward the English. In view of the possibility of Indian warfare and of the foreseen continuation of the life-and-death struggle with France, the friendship and support of the Indians, and especially of the Iroquois tribes, was a matter of vital importance to Britain. No longer could she afford to entrust the problem of administering the natives to the jurisdiction of the colonies. One centralized system of Indian administration which it was hoped would be competent to defend the rights of the savages and retain their allegiance was, therefore, planned to replace thirteen separate, selfish, and oftentimes conflicting Indian policies.

The second major reason for centralized control of the West was intimately bound up with the first. Both the home authorities and many of the colonists desired to substitute   Desire for for the chaotic colonial control of the frontier uniform land domain some sort of uniform policy which would policy eliminate, or at least minimize, the numerous squabbles and hard feelings arising out of its disposition. To frame such a policy, however, was not an easy task, for both in the colonies and in England there were two distinct economic groups diametrically opposed to each other on the question of the West.

Included in the first group were all those who for any reason whatsoever opposed the opening up of the West to settlement. It numbered (1) those who maintained that the Conflicting colonies were chiefly valuable for furnishing the economic mother country with the necessary raw materials groups for home manufacture; (2) men of fortune in both America and Great Britain who had invested heavily in lands east of the Alleghenies and who, therefore, did not relish the prospect of transmontane competition; and (3) the Indians and those whites who believed that neither the natives nor their hunting grounds should be encroached upon. This group desired to keep the trans-Allegheny country an untenanted wilderness — a place where the fur-bearing animal and the Indian hunter might continue to thrive and from which England might continue to receive its cargoes of peltries. Opposed to this group in interest and in principle were (1) all those who held that the colonies were chiefly valuable not as sources of raw materials but as markets for British manufactured goods; (2) those who saw glowing opportunities for profits by speculating in land beyond the Alleghenies; and (3) those who regarded the colonies as a dumping ground for surplus population, and especially for English "radicals" and other malcontents. These groups wanted the rich acres in the trans-Allegheny region to become populated as rapidly as possible — the manufacturers that they might have more consumers for their products, and the speculators more buyers for their land.

The task of devising a land policy that would satisfy these two conflicting groups was well-nigh impossible. The problem was aggravated by the fact that several of the colonies, including Massachusetts, Connecticut, Virginia, the Carolinas, and Georgia, laid claim by virtue of their charter rights to extensive tracts of land beyond the mountains. Many citizens of these colonies, particularly Virginia, were keenly aware of the possibilities of great wealth which these western lands offered. Naturally they were loath to accept any plan, imperialistic or otherwise, that would curtail or impede the exploitation of these domains. On the other hand, colonies without western lands jealously pointed out that if the colonies having western territory were allowed to retain this territory, the latter would soon overshadow their less fortunate neighbors in wealth and power. Many English leaders also felt that the mother country might well ignore the original charter grants, reclaim these immense western tracts, carve them into new colonies, and control the sale of the land to the enrichment of the imperial treasury. Regarded from any angle the formulation of a workable policy satisfactory to all was by no means a simple matter. It was one thing to see the need for it but quite another to formulate it, as we shall see.

Claims of certain colonies to western lands render formation of land policy more difficult

The motives which prompted British statesmen to advocate a closer association of the colonies for administrative purposes were many. All, however, sprang from the conviction that the colonies were in reality no longer isolated units, each with its own peculiar problems, but one continuous settlement confronted with common problems and dangers. The seventeenth-century wilderness barriers which separated one colony from another had in large measure disappeared. The colonists, it is true, still thought of themselves as Virginians or New Yorkers, but their problems were strikingly alike. Virginia had an Indian problem, a military problem, a financial problem, but so had each of her sister colonies and, in many cases, the action of one respecting these problems affected all. In view of this fact many spokesmen on both sides of the Atlantic were of the opinion that the

2. Closer association of the colonies

old policy of each colony's dealing separately with these common problems should be abandoned in favor of concerted action. With the renewal of the struggle with France continually impending, the argument for closer association of the colonies gained ground. "The French," wrote Dinwiddie of Virginia, "too justly observe the want of connection in the colonies & from them conclude (as they declare without Reserve) that although we are vastly superior to them in Numbers, yet they can take & secure the Country before we can agree to hinder them." In the interest of all concerned, it seemed clearly evident that the colonies ought not to remain, as Governor Glenn of South Carolina put it, "a Rope of Sand, loose and unconnected."

The agitation for closer association and concerted action on the part of the colonies culminated in the Albany Congress of 1754. Summoned for the purpose of negotiating a treaty of alliance between the colonies and the Indians, partly in response to instructions from the British Board of Trade and partly in response to the almost passionate pleadings of a number of the *An abortive attempt to form a union: the Albany Congress of 1754* ablest colonial governors, twenty-five delegates representing the New England colonies and New York, Pennsylvania, and Maryland met at Albany on June 19, 1754. Incidentally two of the colonies, Virginia and New Jersey, which had been invited to send delegates, failed to respond to the summons, though the former was represented by DeLancey, the lieutenant-governor of New York. Although an alliance with the Indians was the primary subject before the Congress, it soon became obvious that it was inextricably bound up with the more fundamental question of permanent colonial union, and after lengthy discussion the delegates reached the unanimous conclusion, first, that a union of the colonies was "absolutely necessary for their preservation," and, secondly, that such a union could be established only by parliamentary action.

When it came to the matter of actual union, however, it was far from smooth sailing. In the first place, there was a question as to just what form such a union should take and what powers it should enjoy. After considerable *The proposed plan of union* parley in which Benjamin Franklin and Governor Shirley of

Massachusetts figured prominently, the plan previously drafted by Franklin was adopted with slight modifications. In brief outline it provided for (1) a chief executive (president-general) to be appointed and supported by the crown; (2) a legislature (grand council) of forty-eight members to be chosen by the several colonial assemblies largely on the basis of population and wealth. The legislature was to exercise general control over Indian affairs, including the purchase of Indian lands in the name of the crown, raise and equip a colonial army and navy, erect forts, and make laws and levy taxes necessary for the execution of its policies. All acts of the legislature, however, were subject to the veto of the executive, and to be effective had to be approved by the crown.

Inasmuch as none of the delegates, with the exception of those from Massachusetts, were empowered to enter any form of **Its reception by colonies** union, the plan was submitted to the respective assemblies. If approved by them it was to be transmitted to Parliament. To the keen disappointment of all those who hoped for its favorable acceptance the plan met with a cool reception, the colonial assemblies in every instance either rejecting it outright or failing to ratify it. While sharing in the disappointment, Franklin and Shirley, chief proponents of the plan, were not much surprised by its rejection. Indeed, both more or less expected it. "All the Assemblies in the Colonies," Franklin wrote, "have, I suppose, had the Union Plan laid before them, but it is not likely, in my Opinion, that any of them will act upon it so far as to agree to it, or to propose any Amendments to it. Every Body cries, a union is absolutely necessary, but when they come to the Manner and Form of the Union, their weak Noddles are perfectly distracted."

Three outstanding reasons account in large measure for the colonial rejection of the Albany plan. First of all, the colonists **Causes for its rejection** were still psychologically particularistic and provincial. Despite the fact that they formed one continuous settlement along the Atlantic seaboard and were faced, as we have just observed, with common problems, they were extremely narrow in outlook and extremely jealous of their prerogatives. Local pride and local patriotism were strong, and no colony was willing to surrender any part of its power or authority to any other colony or to any central government such as was set up under the Albany plan. Secondly, the colonists knew very well that the mother country, as we shall presently see, was anxious to have the colonists bear a greater portion of the cost of colonial defense. That indeed had been one of the leading reasons why the Board of Trade had advocated colonial union and, moreover, it was clearly envisaged in the Albany plan itself. To accept the Albany plan, therefore, would, in the opinion of the colonists, mean additional taxation and taxation by an authority other than the local legislature, both of which the colonists opposed. Furthermore, many of the colonists were convinced that if they took no steps in the direction of shouldering a greater share of the expense, the mother country would have to continue the task of defending them. And why, they asked, should they make any move to increase their own financial burden for the sake of helping the British taxpayer? Thirdly, the colonial assemblies in rejecting the Albany plan were undoubtedly influenced by "special interests," particularly by those concerned with western lands. Thus the records clearly indicate that the official action of Connecticut was influenced by the stockholders of one of the great land organizations, the Susquehanna Company, which did all within its power to block the plan for union.

Although Parliament was not called upon to ratify the Albany plan, it was not favorably impressed with it, largely, it would appear, because it was too democratic in **The mother** nature and because it did not provide effectively **country's plan** against the immediate dangers which confronted **of union** the colonies on their western frontier. As a matter of fact, even before the fate of the Albany plan had been determined, the home authorities had formulated a plan of union of their own. According to it each colonial assembly was to appoint a commissioner and these commissioners together were to agree upon the necessary military establishments of the colonies and to apportion the expense thereof among the colonies according to their wealth and population. This board of commissioners or intercolonial assembly could be reconvened whenever emergency demanded. Moreover, the defense of the colonies and the management of Indian affairs was to be placed under the control of an official named by the crown. This plan of union, which was essentially a military one, was never offered to the colonies. The fact that neither this nor the Albany plan was adopted did not, as we shall see, remove the need for closer colonial association.

Closely bound up with the question of colonial union was the many-sided problem of imperial defense. From the beginning the burden of protecting the Empire had been borne primarily by the mother country. The navy, for example, whose importance to the colonists can scarcely be overestimated, was financed entirely by the British taxpayer. During the four years of 1708 to 1711 nearly £2,000,000 was added to England's debt solely for naval protection for the colonies. Theoretically each colony was supposed to provide for its own military defense except when war disturbed Europe or when a situation arose which endangered the Empire as a whole. In reality, however, the mother country was frequently called upon to erect forts, to send arms and ammunition, and even troops. Thus the refusal of the colonies to coöperate for defense against the Indians compelled the home authorities to station garrisons in the two most exposed colonies, New York and North Carolina. Moreover, the mother country was obliged to spend large sums annually for presents for the Indians in an effort to retain their friendship. With the national debt standing at approximately £72,500,000 in 1750 and the English landowner paying six and a half shillings per pound, or about thirty per cent of his income, not including tithes and poor-rates, the British government realized that something had to be done to lighten what the British taxpayer claimed — and not without reason — to be an excessively high tax burden.

To accomplish this end it seemed that the most logical thing to do was to require the colonists to share a greater portion of the cost of imperial defense. Indeed various proposals for a direct parliamentary tax upon the colonists, apart from the impositions levied in connection with the trade regulations, had

3. Imperial defense and the burden of taxation

been made prior to 1750. Sir William Keith, for example, suggested a stamp tax as early as 1728, but the proposal was rejected on the ground that the colonies would oppose it. By the middle of the century, however, the matter of imposing some form of tax upon the colonies with the object of relieving the home taxpayer was widely discussed in both press and pamphlet.

Beginning of British agitation for direct parliamentary tax on colonies

Only brief mention need be made at this point of the mother country's reasons for desiring stricter enforcement of the mercantilistic system. (1) She wanted to weld the various parts of the Empire more closely together and at the same time stamp out as far as possible the growing spirit of arrogance and independence which in more ways than one was beginning to manifest itself in her self-willed and self-reliant overseas domains. (2) She aspired to weaken her ancient rivals, France and Spain, by preventing, or at least discouraging, her colonies from trading with their island possessions in the Caribbean. (3) She wanted the home business man, whether carrier, merchant, or manufacturer, to benefit in fullest measure from the colonies. (4) She hoped to acquire additional revenue, which at this time she so sorely needed. In all her plans for compelling the colonies to adhere more closely to the mercantilistic regulations, the mother country, as we shall see, continued to be actuated by self-interest. Either she did not realize or else did not want to realize that the colonies had grown in wealth and power and that they felt fully competent to manage their own affairs.

Stricter enforcement of mercantilism

While the French and Indian War to a large extent delayed the inauguration of the proposed changes in colonial policy which we have just discussed, it also emphasized, from the standpoint of Great Britain, the glaring need for reform. In the first place, it brought out in striking fashion the inherent weaknesses in the prevailing system of imperial defense. Inasmuch as the colonies had refused to accept the Albany plan of union and had also failed to take any concerted action for their common defense, the mother country was forced to rely during the war on the old

French and Indian War emphasizes need for new colonial policy

decentralized requisition system. During the first two years of the conflict the total military expense of the colonies was estimated at £170,000, an amount which Parliament voted to refund "as an Encouragement to exert themselves for the future in their mutual and common Defense." In 1757 the British authorities informed the colonies that all they were expected to do was to levy, clothe, and pay the provincial soldiers, and that the home government would furnish provisions and equipment. The colonists were furthermore told that if they showed the proper vigor in raising troops they would in all likelihood be compensated for any expenses they might be put to.

But despite these inducements the results were far from satisfactory. Only three colonies, Massachusetts, Connecticut, and

1. Lack of unity and inadequate defense

New York, made anything like the expected contribution. In fact these three, although they contained only about one-third of the colonial white population, furnished seven-tenths of all the colonial troops. Georgia, New Hampshire, and North Carolina were too poor to do much; but Maryland and Pennsylvania, both wealthy and populous, did almost nothing. Loudoun, the commander-in-chief during 1756 and 1757, declared that Rhode Island was unwilling to do her share and that Virginia had failed to furnish its quota. The Maryland Assembly refused to let what few troops it did raise serve under Loudoun. Indeed, it went so far as to specify when, where, and under whose direction they should serve. So bad was the situation during these years that Loudoun declared that it was "the constant study of every Province here to throw every expence on the Crown, and bear no part of the expence of this War themselves." Often the colonial levies were so late in arriving at the place of assembly as to delay seriously military operations. General Amherst, for instance, complained in 1760 that "the Sloth of the Colonies in raising their troops and sending them to their Rendezvous made it impracticable for me to move the Troops on as soon as I could have wished." Frequently, too, internal political disputes interfered. This was notably the case in Pennsylvania, where a heated contest over taxing proprietary estates overshadowed everything else. Virginia and New York were both in a quarrel with their respective governors.   Then there were disputes about the conditions and duration of service.   All in all, the war strengthened the growing conviction of the home authorities that the colonies could not be relied upon to defend themselves and that the system of requisition was a bad one.   In other words, it convinced them that some system of centralized colonial control for purposes of defense was imperative.

The need for reform was demonstrated in the second place by the colonial wartime trade with the French.   According to British law, all trade between any part of the Empire and the enemy was absolutely prohibited in wartime.   But this principle, which had been flagrantly violated by the colonies during the earlier struggles between England and France, was again openly ignored during the French and Indian War. The French forces in Canada, for example, were supplied with beef, pork, and other provisions from Pennsylvania, New York, and New England.   Part of these provisions went over land, and part went by sea to Cape Breton, whence they were sent to Quebec and other points.   No less important was the trade which the colonies carried on either directly or indirectly with the French West Indies.   Northern skippers, especially Rhode Islanders and Pennsylvanians, operating openly or under thinly veiled disguises, did a flourishing business. As a general rule their vessels were protected from seizure by licenses granted by French officials, who naturally welcomed the illicit intercourse, or by flag-of-truce passes issued by colonial governors theoretically for facilitating the exchange of prisoners of war.   Some were armed with both.   The flag-of-truce passes were from the outset in great demand, and their sale by certain governors soon became nothing short of scandalous.   Governor Denny of Pennsylvania sold them at first in small numbers at high prices.   Later, as the number issued increased and their value declined, he resorted to the practice of selling blank ones for £20 each.   Even speculation in flag-of-truce passes became common in port towns.   In 1759 and 1760 the Delaware River at Philadelphia swarmed with vessels unloading cargoes of French commodities received in exchange for provisions.   In fact, a

2. Colonial wartime trade with enemy and inadequate enforcement of mercantilist system

great majority of the Philadelphia merchants were interested in this illegal trade. Exactly what portion of the trade with the French was carried on by way of neutral Spanish and Dutch ports we do not know. The records, however, indicate that it was large. Down to 1761 the Spanish port of Monte Cristi, to cite a single instance, was literally filled with colonial vessels which exchanged their cargoes of provisions, lumber, British manufactures, and war supplies for sugar, molasses, indigo, and specie. On February 5, 1759, there were no less than twenty-eight ships ranging from thirty to one hundred and fifty tons burden in Monte Cristi harbor; seven were from New York, eight from Rhode Island, eight from Massachusetts, four from Connecticut, and one from Virginia. Again out of fifty-two British vessels in the same harbor on May 31, 1761, fifteen were from Massachusetts, ten from Rhode Island, nine from New York, and one each from Connecticut and North Carolina. Often a single day would witness over a hundred North American vessels in this port alone. Practically all of Monte Cristi's imports were destined for the adjoining French colony of Haiti, and its exports were likewise of French origin.

As the war progressed it became increasingly evident that by continuing this illegal trade the colonial merchants were seri-

Trade with enemy prolongs war ously thwarting the efforts of the British military and naval authorities. In the first place, by furnishing the French islands with an ample supply of provisions and a ready market for their produce they enabled these islands to hold out for a longer time than they otherwise could have done. Secondly, by indirectly supplying French privateers with necessary provisions they made it possible for them to continue their depredations on English commerce. Thirdly, by draining the colonies of provisions they made it necessary for the mother country to send supplies from England to the English armies operating in America, thus adding to the difficulty and expense of prosecuting the war. This trade naturally roused the ire of the military and naval commanders. General Crump in his communications with Pitt bitterly denounced it. Admiral Cotes called it "iniquitous," and Commodore Moore stigmatized those engaged in it as "traitors to

By His EXCELLENCY,

Joseph Dudley Esq.

Captain General and GOVERNOUR in Chief, in and over
His Majesties Provinces of the *Massachusetts-Bay* and
New-Hampshire in *New-England.*

A PROCLAMATION

Against a Commerce & Trade with the *French* of *Canada,*
Cape *Breton,* &c.

WHEREAS the Articles of Commerce betwixt the Subjects of the Crown
of **Great Britain,** and those of **France,** upon the late Treaty of
Peace, are not yet fully Adjusted and Settled ; And His Majesty's Commands
in that Regard not yet Arrived.

I have therefore thought fit, by and with the Advice of His Majesties Council, to put forth this Proclamation, strictly to forbid all Persons whomsoever of holding any Correspondence, Commerce, Trade and Dealings in any manner of wise with the French of Canada, Cape Breton, or of any other Parts or Places ; Or of carrying or sending any Provisions, Lumber or other Supplies to them of what kind so ever, until His Majesties Pleasure shall be known therein, as they Tender their Allegiance and Duty to His Most Sacred Majesty, and on Pain of His Majesties Displeasure, and of Suffering such other Pains, Penalties and Forfeitures as may be Lawfully inflicted on them.

Given at the Council Chamber in *Boston,* upon Tuesday the 29th Day of *March,* 1715:
In the First Year of the Reign of Our Soveraign Lord, GEORGE, by the Grace
of GOD of *Great Britain, France* and *Ireland* KING, Defender of the Faith, &c.

By Order of the Governour,
with the Advice of the Council,   *J.* DUDLEY.

Joseph Hiller, Cler. Conc.

GOD Save the King.

BOSTON: Printed by *B. Green,* Printer to His Excellency the GOV. & COUNCIL. 1715:

PROCLAMATION AGAINST COMMERCE AND TRADE, 1715

their country." Even Pitt himself in calling upon the colonial governors to suppress it, declared that the enemy was "principally, if not alone, enabled to sustain and protract this long and expensive war" by means of it. Indeed, this illegal commercial intercourse, perhaps more than any other aspect of the war, forcibly demonstrated the fundamental weakness of the British system of colonial administration and the pressing need for its reform.

The outcome of the war was even more important than the struggle itself as far as the question of colonial administration
Guadaloupe or Canada and the West was concerned. After wide discussion and protracted debate between those who asserted that colonies were chiefly valuable as sources of raw materials and those who maintained that they were chiefly worth while as markets for English manufactures, Great Britain, to the utter disgust of the former, retained Canada and the West, and East and West Florida, in 1763, in preference to the rich French sugar-planting island of Guadaloupe and the Spanish island of Porto Rico. This decision, we should note, resulted in part from the opposition of the British West Indian planters, who strongly opposed the acquisition of additional sugar-producing territory lest it destroy their monopoly of the home market. It was also in part the result of the fact that as England was becoming less and less an agricultural and more and more a manufacturing nation, the temperate zone colonies with their rapidly expanding population afforded a better market for manufactured goods than the tropical possessions with their fewer numbers. The relative value of the two types of colonies in this respect is shown by the tables on the next page.

The decision to retain Canada and the West brought with it a number of perplexing problems, of which some were old and
3. The problem of the West some new. What, for instance, should be done with the immense territory beyond the Alleghenies? Should the half dozen seaboard colonies which claimed the region be allowed to administer it as they pleased, or should it be administered by the mother country? Should it be left as a hunting ground for the Indians, as was advocated by the influential Hudson Bay Company and others interested in

EXPORTS FROM ENGLAND TO TROPICAL COLONIES [1]

	1746–1747	1751–1752	1756–1757	1761–1762	1766–1767
Antigua......	£ 44,487	£ 68,185	£113,308	£125,323	£119,740
Barbadoes....	95,107	172,822	156,932	213,177	145,083
Bermudas....	3,891	11,767	2,890	7,786	12,133
Jamaica......	215,283	351,475	352,797	460,631	467,681
Montserrat...	1,650	5,307	18,069	23,895	23,071
Nevis........	583	10,442	15,420	9,066	11,875
New Providence	......	......	1,013	......	14,986
St. Christopher	27,743	83,917	116,549	102,627	106,162
West Indies in general.....	345,348	......	......	......	763
Domenica....	......	......	......	......	30,863
Tortola......	......	......	304	2,052	27,010
St. Vincent...	......	......	......	......	14,822
Grenada......	......	......	......	119	89,767
Guadeloupe...	......	......	......	170,226	......
Havana......	......	......	......	116,777	......
Martinique...	......	......	......	166,196	......
Total	£734,092	£ 703,915	£777,282	£1,397,875	£1,063,956

EXPORTS FROM ENGLAND TO MAINLAND COLONIES

	1746–1747	1751–1752	1756–1757	1761–1762	1766–1767
New Foundland	£ 49,021	£ 46,995	£ 23,537	£ 34,387	£ 53,550
Carolina......	95,529	150,777	213,949	194,170	244,093
Hudson's Bay	2,994	3,380	4,033	4,122	4,981
New England.	210,640	273,340	363,404	247,385	406,081
New York....	137,984	194,030	353,311	288,046	417,957
Pennsylvania .	82,404	201,666	268,426	206,199	371,830
Virginia and Maryland..	200,088	325,151	426,687	417,599	437,628
Georgia......	24	3,163	2,571	23,761	23,334
Nova Scotia..	4,408	19,310	70,600	25,071	25,094
Florida.......	......	......	......	......	30,963
Total......	£783,092	£1,217,812	£1,726,518	£1,440,740	£2,015,511

[1] From George Louis Beer, *British Colonial Policy, 1754–1765*, p. 138.

the development of the fur trade, or should it be opened up to settlement so as to serve as soon as possible as a market for British manufactures?   If the latter, should the colonists be left free to derive all the profits which were sure to ensue from land sales, or should the disposition of the territory be regulated so as to give land speculators in every part of the Empire an opportunity to share?   How should Canada, with its eighty thousand French inhabitants, and Florida, with its Spanish population, be governed?   Now that the French had been ousted, what steps would be necessary to keep the colonies loyal and prevent them from seeking complete independence?   William Burke, kinsman of the famous statesman, in opposing the retention of Canada, declared that while it remained in French hands it bound the North American colonies to Great Britain. "A neighbor," said he, "that keeps us in some awe," is not always the worst of neighbors.   Great Britain had no adequate colonial machinery to grapple with the problems which these questions involved.   To cope with them, new methods had to be devised and new policies formulated.

Finally, the enormous expense occasioned by the Seven Years' War greatly emphasized the need of overhauling the British **4. Increased** colonial system.   The conflict cost England over **expense and** £82,000,000, of which £60,000,000 was added to **need for in-** **creased** the already existing national debt of seventy-odd **revenue** million pounds.   Moreover, the mother country was convinced that it would be necessary to keep a standing army of ten thousand men in America for the purpose of protecting both the old and the recently acquired parts of the Empire.   It was estimated that such a force would cost yearly about £300,000, an increase of approximately £220,000 over the pre-war period.   In addition about £1,500,000 had to be raised annually for the navy.   For the mother country to bear the whole burden of this expense was almost out of the question. The British landowner, as we have seen, was already weighted down with taxes, and in view of the growing unrest on the part of the English laboring class the government deemed it unwise to shift the added expense to the shoulders of the wage-earner. It was only natural, therefore, that it should turn to the colonies for revenue. The war, it reasoned, had been fought in part in their defense; the standing army was to protect them against possible French and Indian attacks; the navy was to be used in part to safeguard their commerce. Under the existing system of colonial administration the colonies, in the opinion of many British leaders, had demonstrated both their inability and their unwillingness to bear their share of the military burden. Reform was clearly necessary if the mother country was to derive a dependable income from American sources.

3. DARKENING SKIES, 1763–1774

Before turning to the story of the new British colonial policy which began to take shape in 1763 and to the conflict to which it gave rise, let us glance for a moment at the political situation in Great Britain at the close of the Seven Years' War. First of all, instead of two major parties, Whig and Tory, as in the mid-nineteenth century, we find some half dozen factions, nearly all of Whig origin, and composed of individuals who were motivated almost entirely by personal ambitions and interests. *The British political situation in 1763*

Of these the faction known as the Old Whigs was in some respects the strongest and in some the weakest. Composed for the most part of the representatives of some of the former great Whig families, it opposed royal prerogative and stood for reform in a mild way. Lord Hardwicke, the Duke of Newcastle, and the Marquis of Rockingham were prominent figures in the group, but its outstanding leader was the gifted Edmund Burke, a man of lofty ideals, vast knowledge, and rich imagination, although at times irritable, tactless, and partisan. *1. The Old Whigs*

Closely allied to the Old Whigs were the followers of the Duke of Cumberland. They included the former coterie of Robert Walpole and the adherents of George II. This faction perhaps more than any other was absolutely without constructive policy and, in addition, lacked coherence and solidarity. Its spokesman and most brilliant member was Henry Fox, a shifty politician who was chiefly responsible for the faction's disruption. After the death of the Duke of Cumberland in 1765 it ceased to exist. *2. The Cumberland faction*

The strongest of the Whig factions in point of numbers was the Bedfordites. Their leader, the Duke of Bedford, a landed mag-

3. The Bed-fordites
nate, was personally a man of ideals, conservative in outlook, and extremely able. His followers, how-ever, did not on the whole measure up to his standards. In fact they were popularly known as the "Bloomsbury Gang," their chief ambition being the attainment of office.

From the standpoint of popularity and ability of its member-ship, the faction presided over by William Pitt was by all odds

4. The Pitt faction
the most notable. Numerically weaker than some of the other factions, it counted among its adherents some of the ablest English statesmen of the day. To the Pittites, for example, belonged Lord Camden, the Duke of Grafton, and, above all, the Earl of Shelburne who as president of the Board of Trade and Secretary of State was closely in touch with colo-nial affairs. Although they constituted a faction themselves, Pitt and his followers disliked partisanship and opposed govern-ment by faction. Above all they denounced those who sought to further their own selfish ends at the expense of the crown's prerogatives or the interests of the nation at large. More than any other faction, they formulated definite principles and lived up to them. The Pittites and the Old Whigs were on the whole more sympathetic toward America than the other fac-tions.

The "Grenvillites," as the followers of George Grenville, Pitt's brother-in-law, were called, were up to 1761 allied to Pitt.

5. The Gren-villites
In that year, however, they refused to follow Pitt's example in resigning office, and rallied round Gren-ville. The faction, which was small, included, among others, the Earl of Egremont and Sir George Sackville. Grenville himself, although overbearing, narrow-minded, ungracious, and utterly lacking in tact, was upright and industrious and not without ability, especially in the field of finance.

Finally there was the court faction composed of four rather sharply defined groups: (1) The "King's Friends," somewhat

6. The court faction
sordid in their ideals and without political principles except that of the predominance of the king. They were supposed to be the king's intimate advisers, even being

spoken of by their contemporaries as a sort of inner cabinet. (2) The Independents or unattached Whigs, who were mainly interested in obtaining office. Less devoted to the king than the members of the previous group, they refused at times to do the king's bidding, much to his annoyance. (3) The Scotch representatives in Parliament who, like the Independents, supported the crown largely because they were liberally rewarded with jobs. (4) The adherents of the old Tory party, supported by landed interests and, with few exceptions, loyal to the crown. Each of these four groups had its own peculiar interests and did not always act as a unit in Parliament. In a general way the Earl of Bute and Lord North may be regarded as the spokesmen for the court faction.

George III, who came to the throne in 1760, was primarily concerned with increasing his own prerogatives. Naturally, therefore, he had no use for either parties or factions, for he honestly believed that both were interested in purely selfish ends at variance with his own ambitions and the welfare of the people. On this point two factions, the Pittites and the Grenvillites, more or less agreed with him, but a family feud between the two, along with other factors, made it impossible for the king to unite both of them at the same time with the court faction and thus command a safe majority in Parliament. Consequently throughout the period under consideration weak coalition ministries, made up of representatives from at least three of the warring factions, were necessary. In fact, from the close of the Seven Years' War to the close of the Revolution England had no less than four ministries: the Grenville ministry, 1763–1765; the Rockingham ministry, 1765–1766; the Grafton-Pitt ministry, 1766–1770; and the North ministry, 1770–1782. All four of these ministries, we should remember, had to work with a Parliament which represented almost exclusively landed and moneyed interests — interests which thought of the colonies only in terms of profit, of raw materials and markets, of national strength. Upon the shoulders of the first of these ministries rested the burden of inaugurating Britain's new colonial policy.

George III's ambitions and coalition government

When the Grenville ministry came into office in 1763 it at once set to work to do three things: (1) to establish some sort of unified and efficient control over Britain's newly conquered territory; (2) to readjust and tighten the British trade laws; and (3) to lighten the financial strain on the English taxpayer by raising revenue in the colonies. All three were merely phases of the general plan for the reorganization of the Empire.

The Grenville ministry, 1763-1764, and its objectives

Even before Grenville became prime minister the problem of the West had reached an acute stage. Canada and the Floridas with their alien populations had to be provided for. Then, too, pioneers from the older settled colonial regions were staking out claims in the wooded valleys of the Ohio country. Speculative land companies and colony promoters, who before the war had, as we have observed, turned their attention to the trans-Allegheny country, were again renewing their interest in the region. Thus in 1763 George Washington and other Virginian soldiers, to whom Governor Dinwiddie in 1764 had promised 200,000 acres "of His Majesty the King of Great Britain's lands on the east side of the River Ohio," in part compensation for their services, pressed their claims in a petition to the king. In the same year the Ohio Company, which as early as 1747 had petitioned for 500,000 acres on the upper Ohio, sent a special agent to London to protect their interests. In the same year, also, a new concern, the Mississippi Company, composed of fifty prominent Virginians and Marylanders, including George Washington, the Lees, and the Fitzhughs, memorialized the king for a grant of 2,500,000 acres on the east bank of the Mississippi. Incidentally, each promoter, according to the plan, was to receive 50,000 acres for himself. In New York, Pennsylvania, and other colonies, companies of speculators eagerly hoped for slices of the great valley territory.

The problem of the West becomes acute

1. Settlement and speculation

Coupled with the problem of settlement was the question of the Indians. We have already noted that the British policy of leaving the question of the natives and their trade to the several colonies had resulted in dismal failure. Indeed, so bad had the situation become that in 1761 the English

2. The Indians

government took complete charge and appointed two commissioners to have control and supervision over all Indian affairs. While these imperial officials labored indefatigably to eradicate the numerous abuses heaped upon the unsuspecting aborigines by the whites, their task was so herculean that they had made little headway when the Grenville ministry came into power. English settlers and land speculators continued to steal the red man's lands and to defraud him of his furs. To make matters worse, the British military authorities had abandoned the practice of giving the natives presents of guns and clothing. In fact, General Amherst did his best to prevent them from receiving ammunition and rum, at the same time approving a plan to supply them with blankets which had been used by smallpox patients!

Such treatment was bound, sooner or later, to result in bitter hatred and open rebellion. Aroused by the tales of the French fur traders, who led them to believe that France Pontiac's was about to regain control of the Mississippi conspiracy valley, the Indian tribes of the Old Northwest, under the leadership of the Ottawa chief Pontiac, organized a great confederacy. By May, 1763, they were on the warpath, and within a few weeks every British post west of Niagara, with the exception of Detroit, had been either captured or destroyed. Months of warfare followed. It was not until the spring of 1764 that a semblance of peace was restored. The details of this uprising need not concern us; it is sufficient to remember that it hastened the action of the British government respecting the West.

Fortunately for the Grenville ministry a policy for the West had already been formulated by Lord Shelburne, president of the Board of Trade, before that ministry came into The Proclamation of 1763 office. This policy with certain modifications constituted the famous Proclamation of 1763. By its terms boundaries were established for three new mainland crown colonies — Quebec, East Florida, and West Florida. All other lands "lying to the westward of the sources of the rivers which fall into the sea from the west or the northwest" which had not been acquired by the British government from the natives, either by cession or purchase, were "for the present" reserved to the

Indians. In other words, all territory between the crest of the Alleghenies and the Mississippi from Florida to 50° north latitude was for the time being at least closed to settlers and land speculators. Moreover, the sale of Indian lands, except to the crown, was prohibited, and all those who had inadvertently settled within the reserved region were ordered to withdraw. Henceforth no person could carry on trade with the Indians unless he was licensed by the governor or commander-in-chief of some colony. This license incidentally involved giving bond to observe such regulations as "we shall at any time think fit to . . . direct for the benefit of the said trade." Fugitives from justice taking refuge in the reserved territory were to be apprehended and returned.

No sooner was the Proclamation of 1763 announced than it became a source of conflict. The colonists, not understanding that in the mind of its framers the measure was regarded

Proclamation of 1763 a source of conflict and one of the leading causes of the Revolution

as a temporary expedient designed primarily to pacify the red man and allay his fears, looked upon it as an arbitrary and unnecessary obstacle to their natural expansion westward. Ambitious pioneers, colony promoters, and venturous speculators who had either already secured claims to thousands of acres along the Ohio and its tributaries, or who planned to obtain domains beyond the mountains, were especially vexed. Veterans of the Seven Years' War and members of the Ohio and Mississippi land companies voiced their opposition to the measure in no uncertain terms. Six of the older colonies questioned its validity on the ground that it involved territory over which they had prior claim. Of all the acts of the imperial government which in any way contributed to the disruption of the Empire, none perhaps was of greater importance than this proclamation. Certainly it, as much as any other factor, was responsible for alienating the influential colony of Virginia. To Virginians, part of the lands beyond the mountains were theirs by charter rights; Virginia men and Virginia money had helped win them from France, and they could see no good reason why they should be excluded from them. And when in 1774 there seemed likelihood that the rich lands of the Ohio and Kentucky country would be

granted to the British Walpole Company, sponsored by Grenville and managed by the Whartons of Philadelphia, their anger
knew no bounds. Men who hitherto had been loyal to the
mother country now became staunch supporters of revolutionary doctrines, largely because they believed that Virginia was
being exploited in favor of court favorites, politicians, and Old
World speculators.

The proposals to tighten the British mercantilistic regulations
and to raise revenue in America were closely intertwined. As
Chancellor of the Exchequer, Grenville calculated
that the colonists ought to be responsible for at least
one half of the £300,000 estimated as necessary
annually for the defense of Britain's American possessions. Partly for the purpose of raising about
one-third of this £150,000 and partly for the purpose of rendering the colonies more useful to the mother country
commercially, he suggested that immediate steps be taken for
the strict enforcement of the old mercantilistic regulations. The
Navigation Acts, particularly the Molasses Act of 1733, which,
as we have seen, had been passed under pressure from the West
Indian interests, had been notoriously evaded. Many customs
officials in the colonies either turned smugglers themselves or
were bribed by smuggling merchants and carriers. The few who
conscientiously attempted to perform their duties were either
hampered or completely blocked by numerous methods. "If
conniving at foreign sugar and molasses, and Portugal wines and
fruit," wrote Governor Bernard of Massachusetts in 1764, "is to
be reckoned corruption, there was never, I believe, an incorrupt
Custom House official in America till within twelve months."
Indeed so laxly enforced were the various Trade Acts that the
Board of Trade admitted that it had cost £7,600 a year to collect
£1,900. In the majority of the colonies smuggling had become
eminently respectable long before 1763.

In Parliament, where Grenville's proposals were favorably
received, immediate action was taken. Additional revenue cutters were sent to American waters, naval commanders were permitted to act as customs officials, the jurisdiction of courts of
admiralty in revenue cases was enlarged, colonial governors were

Proposals to tighten trade laws and to raise revenue in colonies closely related

ordered to see that all trade laws were strictly enforced, and the use of "Writs of Assistance," or general search warrants,

Efforts to en-
force Trade
Laws: the
Sugar Act,
1764 which, without specification as to goods or place, gave the holder the right of search and seizure, was authorized. Moreover, the Molasses Act, which was about to expire, was reënacted in modified form and supplemented in 1764 by a new measure known as the Sugar Act. Imposed for the express purpose of "defraying the necessary expenses of defending, protecting, and securing the British colonies and plantations in America," this new legislation lowered the duty on foreign molasses brought into the colonies from six to three cents a gallon, raised the duty on refined sugars, forbade the importation of foreign rum, and placed a heavy tax on Oriental and French textiles and Portuguese and Spanish wines, coffee, and pimentos unless shipped by way of England. It also provided that henceforth, with few exceptions, no drawbacks should be allowed. Furthermore, it listed stricter regulations for the registration of vessels.

Inasmuch as the prosperity of the Northern or commercial colonies depended on the foreign molasses trade, the Grenville

Colonial and
Old World
opposition to
the Sugar Act measures caused a furor. The proposal to enforce the Molasses Act, Massachusetts merchants asserted, marked the end of trade in the provinces, since the rum distilleries, the fisheries, and the slave trade were absolutely dependent upon it. The trade had been "sacrificed to the West Indian planters," and every prudent man might as well, they said, get out of debt with Great Britain as fast as he could and "betake himself to husbandry." John Hancock wrote that "the times are very bad" and "will be worse here, in short such is the situation of things here that we do not know who is and who [is] not safe." Rhode Island and Connecticut merchants were equally discouraged and apprehensive. Leading citizens of New York bitterly complained about the restrictions and the dwindling trade. Clement Biddle of Philadelphia, writing to Samuel Galloway on June 13, 1764, declared that "the restrictions we are lay'd under by the Parliament puts us at a stand how to employ our vessels to any advantage, as we have no prospects of markets at our own islands and cannot send elsewhere to have anything that will answer in return." Merchant organizations in nearly all the commercial provinces drafted formal protests. In Rhode Island the Assembly, in a remonstrance to the Board of Trade, demonstrated by a wealth of facts and figures that the colony could not exist without the foreign West Indian trade. Of the 14,000 hogsheads of molasses imported annually for the distilleries, for example, only about 2,500 could be procured from the British islands. As time went on and attempts were made to enforce the legislation the complaints became more insistent and more frequent. Even the English merchants, whose trade with the colonies began to decline as a result of the new legislation, lifted their voices in opposition.

But Grenville paid little attention to the rising storm of protest and proceeded to carry out the remainder of his program. All duties and forfeitures under the Sugar Act, he **The Currency** declared, had to be paid in gold or silver. The **Act, 1764** colonists were in a quandary; they were without mines of precious metals and their principal source of specie supply, the foreign West Indies, was at least partially cut off by enforcement of the Trade Acts. To make matters worse, Grenville, at the earnest solicitation of British creditors, induced Parliament in 1764 to pass the Colonial Currency Act which, as we have already seen, forbade further issue of paper money in the colonies and prevented colonial debtors from settling their accounts in depreciated currency. Money in any form became scarce and bitter complaint and discontent followed.

Grenville's third measure was the famous Stamp Act. To raise the remaining two-thirds of the £150,000 which, as we have just noted, was the amount he proposed to obtain **The Stamp** from the colonies, he suggested that a direct tax **Act, 1765** in the form of "certain stamp duties" be levied. Far from acting in a tyrannical manner, he informed the colonists a whole year in advance that if they did not like this method of raising the necessary funds he would be glad to have them "signify" a more satisfactory means. Failing to get any reply except a proposal to try the old requisition system again, and petitions and remonstrances denying the right of Parliament to tax the colonies at all, Grenville, with little opposition, pushed the stamp bill through Parliament in March, 1765. By its terms revenue stamps, ranging from a half-penny to ten pounds, were to be placed on commercial and legal documents, liquor licenses, pamphlets, newspapers, almanacs, advertisements, playing cards, and dice. Infractions of the law were to be punished by heavy fines and forfeitures which, at the option of the informer or prosecutor, might be collected through the vice-admiralty courts. Certain cases involving forgery and counterfeiting were punishable by death.

Less than a month later Grenville, still intent on cutting down expenses, induced Parliament to pass the Quartering Act. It **The Quartering Act, 1765** provided that in case the colonial barracks were insufficient to house the proposed army of ten thousand men, public hostelries were to be used. If more room was needed, vacant houses, barns, and other buildings were to be rented. The Act also directed the colonists to furnish the troops with fuel, candles, vinegar, salt, bedding, cooking utensils, and small quantities of beer, cider, and rum. Persons furnishing quarters and supplies were to be reimbursed by the province in which the troops might be stationed. Rates for transporting troops or supplies from one colonial point to another were fixed in the Act. Any excess of these rates had to be borne by the colonies.

The opposition to the Sugar and Currency Acts was mild in comparison with the storm which followed the passage of the **Colonial reaction to Stamp and Quartering Acts** Stamp Act and the Quartering Act. From Maine to Georgia the cry went up that both being in the nature of a direct tax were unconstitutional. Newspaper publishers, pamphleteers, lawyers, bankers, and merchants, on whom the Stamp Act fell most heavily, were especially outspoken. Northerners like James Otis of Massachusetts and Stephen Hopkins of Rhode Island declared that such legislation was nothing short of tyranny and asserted that the mother country had no right to tax the colonies without their consent. The Virginia House of Burgesses, led by the fiery back-country orator, Patrick Henry, passed a series of resolutions to the effect that the inhabitants of the colony could not be bound by any law or ordinance imposing any tax upon them unless imposed by the Virginia Assembly. A Stamp Act Congress, composed of delegates representing nine colonies, meeting in New York in October, 1765, issued a declaration of rights and grievances drafted by John Dickinson of Pennsylvania, in which it was argued that the colonists were entitled to the inherent rights and liberties of native-born Englishmen — petition, trial by jury, and self-taxation. The Congress also drafted petitions to the king and to each of the two houses of Parliament requesting repeal of the Stamp Act and of other obnoxious legislation.

But the fundamental question at stake was not constitutional but social and economic. Thousands of colonists who condemned the Stamp Act and the other Grenville Real issues measures were either unfamiliar with or else did at stake social and economic not disturb themselves with such questions as parli- rather than amentary representation, the inherent rights of constitutional man, and other legal and metaphysical subtleties and arguments which were advanced by Otis, Hopkins, Dickinson, and others. Such discussions were confined to a relatively small group. Even the Stamp Act Congress, familiar to every American schoolboy today, was scarcely mentioned in the newspapers at the time it was held. The vast majority of the colonists were concerned rather with the effect of the Grenville legislation on their business, their pocketbooks, and their standard of living. Philosophical arguments, as Professor Andrews says, were beyond the mental range of many of the colonists, but not so money and the means of subsistence. Indeed, the main burden of protest was social and economic, rather than constitutional, in tenor. Thus John Hancock wrote: "Under this additional Burthen of the Stamp Act, I cannot carry it [trade] on to any profit and we were before Cramp'd in our Trade & sufficiently Burthen'd, that any further Taxes must Ruin us." Dickinson voiced the apprehensions of the Pennsylvania merchants when he questioned whether any merchant could bear "the payment of all the taxes imposed by the Stamp Act on his policies, fees with clerks, charter parties, protests, his other notarial acts, his letters, and even his advertisements." Franklin, even before the Stamp Act went into effect, thought it would fall "particu-

larly hard on us lawyers and printers"; and John Adams, who
with his fellow lawyers had agreed that all legal business should
be suspended until the Stamp Act was repealed, complained
when his fees began to fall off that "this long interval of indolence and idleness will make a large chasm in my affairs."
"I have groped in dark obscurity till of late," he continued,
"and had but just known and gained a small degree of reputation when this project was set on foot for my ruin as well as that
of America in general."

From the economic and psychological point of view, the
mother country could scarcely have chosen a more inopportune
time to launch its new policy. During the greater
part of the struggle with the French the colonists
had enjoyed widespread prosperity. With the
termination of war, however, came business depres-
sion. Business in general fell off rapidly, the price of farm products declined, land values tumbled, shipping decreased, and
incomes diminished. Everywhere the pinch of hard times was
felt. Each one of the Grenville measures accentuated the situation. The Sugar Act tended to ruin the West Indian trade and
thus cut off the supply of hard money and increase unemployment; the Currency Act forbade the issuance of paper money;
the Stamp Act increased the need for gold and silver; the
Quartering Act added a new item of expense; and, to cap the
climax, the Proclamation of 1763 closed the West to those who
would repair thither to start life anew or mend their broken
fortunes. To the colonists, who were already hard pressed
economically, each succeeding parliamentary measure seemed
specially designed to bring about their complete ruin.

Grenville legislation launched in a period of depression

Had the colonists been content with congresses, constitutional
discussions, protests, remonstrances, and memorials, the Grenville legislation might have remained unchanged.
So important were the issues at stake and so deep-
seated the feeling of discontent, however, that opposition of a more formidable character began to
manifest itself even before the Stamp Act went into effect.
This opposition, which in a very true sense marked the beginning
of the ten-year struggle between the mother country and the

Colonies re-sort to more formidable opposition

mainland colonies immediately preceding the withdrawal of the latter from the British Empire, took two forms: (1) Boycotting England by means of non-importation and non-consumption agreements; and (2) violent resistance.

The use of the boycott was, in its inception, almost accidental. The depression following the French and Indian War plus the Grenville legislation forced the colonists to econo- 1. The boymize. Certain articles of food were eliminated, cott fashionable mourning was simplified, domestic sage, sassafras, and other herbs were used in place of imported tea, and homespun took the place of British textiles. To the alarm of the British merchant and manufacturer British imports began to fall off rapidly, and the colonists soon perceived that in nonimportation and non-consumption they possessed weapons which could be used to good advantage for the repeal of the obnoxious measures. Accordingly, four days before the Stamp Act went into force two hundred New York merchants agreed not to purchase European goods until the Sugar Act had been modified and the Stamp Act repealed. A week later, more than four hundred Philadelphia merchants agreed to make all their orders for British merchandise contingent upon the repeal of the Stamp Act. Less than a month later, Boston merchants made a similar agreement, and smaller New England towns followed suit.

The effect of these agreements was soon felt in the mother country. English exportations to the commercial colonies declined from £1,410,372 in 1764 to £1,197,010 in Its effect on 1765, and from £515,192 to £383,224 in the tobacco England colonies. Moreover, it was said that the mainland colonists owed British business men between £4,000,000 and £6,000,000. British merchants, manufacturers, and workingmen in distress flooded Parliament with petitions praying for the immediate repeal of the Stamp Act. Benjamin Franklin, being in England at the time, was summoned to appear before the House of Commons for interrogation on the attitude of the Americans. He declared that "the restraints lately laid on their trade, by which the bringing of foreign gold and silver into the colonies was prevented; the prohibition of making paper money among themselves; and then demanding a new and heavy tax by stamps; taking away at the same time trials by jury, and refusing to receive and hear their humble petitions," accounted for their action. The colonists, he asserted rather bluntly, would never submit to the Stamp Act unless compelled to do so, and compulsion might mean revolution.

Meanwhile the radical element in the colonies — the unenfranchised, the poorer, the less educated, and the less responsible **2. Violent** — who, as we shall see presently, enjoyed little in **resistance** common with the privileged mercantile-planting class, organized societies known as "Sons of Liberty." Led by men from their own ranks or sometimes, at first, by men higher up, they expressed their opposition to the Grenville legislation by a series of popular demonstrations. Parades were held, stamp collectors were intimidated, burned in effigy, and forced to resign, and stamps and property of the stamp collectors and others who favored the Grenville measures were destroyed. Thus in Boston, a mob incited by those who were most seriously affected by the Sugar and Stamp Acts, and led by a shoemaker named Mackintosh, burned the stamp collector Oliver in effigy, tore down a new building of Oliver's which it was thought he intended to use as a stamp office, partially destroyed the Oliver home, and attacked the houses of the registrar of the admiralty and the comptroller of the customs, destroying the records of the admiralty courts. Oliver resigned and merchants forced the sheriff who arrested Mackintosh to release him.

While events of this nature were occurring in both the mainland and West Indian colonies, the king and Parliament, vexed **The Grenville** by the troubled state of American affairs, forced the **legislation** Grenville ministry out of office. The new ministry, **modified:** led by the young and inexperienced Marquis of **repeal of the** **Stamp Act,** Rockingham, did not know which way to turn. On **1766** the one hand, it was bombarded with petitions and remonstrances asking for the immediate repeal of the Stamp Act and modification of the other Grenville measures. The majority of those who wanted to avoid high taxes at home, who regarded the colonies in a narrow mercantilistic fashion, and who were angered by the action of the American radicals, were

Glorious News:

Conſtitutional LIBERTY Revives!

NEW-HAVEN, Monday-Morning, May 19, 1766.

Mr. *Jonathan Lowder* brought the following moſt agreeable
Intelligence from *Boſton.*

BOSTON, Friday 11 o'Clock, 16th May, 1766.
THIS Inſtant arrived here the Brig Harriſon, belonging to John Hancock, Eſq; Captain Shubael
Coffin. in 6 Weeks and 2 Days from LONDON, with important News as follows.

From the London Gazette.

Weſtminſter, *March* 18th, 1766.

THIS day His Majeſty came to the Houſe of Peers, and being in his royal robes ſeated
on the Throne with the uſual ſolemnity, Sir Francis Molineux, Gentleman Uſher of the
Black Rod, was ſent with a Meſſage from His Majeſty to the Houſe of Commons,
commanding their attendance in the Houſe of Peers. The Commons being come thither accordingly, His Majeſty was pleaſed to give his Royal Aſſent to An ACT to REPEAL an Act made
in the laſt Seſſion of Parliament, intitled an Act for granting and applying certain Stamp-Duties
and other Duties in the Britiſh Colonies and Plantations in America, towards further defraying the
Expences of defending, protecting and ſecuring the ſame, and for amending ſuch parts of the ſeveral Acts of Parliament relating to the trade and revenues of the ſaid Colonies and Plantations,
as direct the Manner of determining and recovering the penalties and forfeitures therein mentioned.
Alſo ten publick bills, and ſeventeen private ones.
Yeſterday there was a meeting of the principal Merchants concerned in the American trade, at
the King's Arms tavern in Cornhill, to conſider of an Addreſs to his Majeſty on the beneficial Repeal of the late Stamp-Act.
Yeſterday morning about eleven o'clock a great number of North-American Merchants went in
their coaches from the King's Arms tavern in Cornhill to the Houſe of Peers, to pay their duty to
his Majeſty, and to expreſs their ſatisfaction at his ſigning the Bill for Repealing the Stamp-Act,
there were upwards of fifty coaches in the proceſſion.
Laſt night the ſaid gentlemen diſpatched an expreſs for Falmouth with fifteen copies of the act,
for repealing the Stamp-Act to be forwarded immediately for New-York.
Orders are given for ſeveral Merchantmen in the river to proceed to ſea immediately on their re-
ſpective voyages to North-America, ſome of whom have been cleared ſince the firſt of November laſt.
Yeſterday meſſengers were diſpatched to Birmingham, Sheffild, Mancheſter, and all the great
manufacturing towns in England, with an account of the final deciſion of an auguſt aſſembly relat-
ing to the Stamp-Act.
⁂ BOSTON. ⁂
When the King went to the Houſe of Peers to give the Royal Aſſent, there was ſuch a vaſt Con-
courſe of People, huzzaing, clapping Hands, &c. that it was ſeveral Hours before His Majeſty
reached the Houſe.
Immediately on His Majeſty's Signing the Royal Aſſent to the Repeal of the Stamp-Act, the
Merchants trading to America, diſpatched a Veſſel which had been waiting, to put into the firſt
Port on the Continent with the Account.
There were the greateſt Rejoicings poſſible in the City of London, by all Ranks of People, on
the TOTAL Repeal of the Stamp-Act. The Ships in the River diſplayed all their Colours, Il-
luminations and Bonfires in many Parts. In ſhort, the Rejoicings were as great as ever was known
on any Occaſion.
It is ſaid the Acts of Trade relating to America would be taken under Conſideration, and all
Grievances removed. The Friends to America are very powerful, and diſpoſed to aſſiſt us to the
utmoſt of their Ability:
It is impoſſible to expreſs the Joy the Town is now in, on receiving the above great, glorious
and important News. The Bells in all the Churches were immediately ſet a Ringing, and we
hear the Day for a general Rejoicing will be the Beginning of next Week.

Extract of a Letter from New-London, *to* New-Haven, *dated* May 17, 1766.
"I give Joy on the total Repeal of the Stamp-Act. We have the news at New-London Satur-
day Night 9 o'clock, at 10 the Guns in the Fort are firing on the Joyful occaſion ; Drums beating,
&c. I am now with the Gentlemen of the Town on the Occaſion."
N. B. *Like Rejoicings now* (Monday Morning) *in* New-Haven.

NEW-HAVEN: Printed by *B. Mecom,* for the Entertainment of the People
in general, and his good Cuſtomers in particular.

*Mr. Lowder having rode very hard to bring the above Glorious Tidings, it is not doubted the Sons of
Liberty will be generous in helping to defray his Expences. 'Tis deſired that ſuch Donations be left at Mr.
Beers's Tavern*

just as stoutly opposed to repeal or modification. The merchant-manufacturing interests, however, finally triumphed. The Stamp Act was repealed, the tariff on molasses was reduced to one pence per gallon, and certain other customs duties were lowered. To appease the opposition and to safeguard itself, Parliament issued a Declaratory Act asserting its right to tax the colonies at any time.

The passage of the remedial legislation occasioned great rejoicing in America. The non-importation movement quickly **America rejoices** collapsed, local manufacturing declined, and British goods again began to flow into the colonies. Toasts were drunk to King George and on every hand there were festive celebrations. The merchant class alone was not entirely satisfied, for the remedial measures failed to restore the commercial system as it existed in the palmy days before 1764.

But it did not take British taxpayers long to discover that the modification of the Grenville legislation did not in the least **The Townshend Acts, 1767** lighten their financial burdens. Accordingly the Rockingham ministry was ousted in July, 1766, and was succeeded by the Pitt-Grafton coalition. The central figure in the new cabinet was the brilliant but erratic and irresponsible Charles Townshend. Like Grenville, he maintained that the colonies were and ought to be subordinate to the mother country, and that they ought to contribute to the support of the Empire. As Chancellor of the Exchequer he had little difficulty in inducing Parliament in 1767 to pass a series of Acts which bear his name. Of these the most important was a new revenue bill which imposed duties on glass, lead, painters' colors, tea, and paper; the duties were to be collected by British commissioners stationed in American ports. Writs of Assistance were declared legal, and infractions of the law were to be tried in courts without juries. The revenue derived from the Act was to be used not only for the upkeep of the military establishment but for "defraying the charge of the administration of justice, and the support of civil government in such provinces where it shall be found necesary." Another Act suspended the New York Assembly for refusing to comply fully with the provisions of the Quartering Act.

The passage of the Townshend Acts was the signal for renewed colonial opposition. Still suffering from the post-war business depression and from the effects of the Currency American Act of 1764, the colonists were both discouraged and opposition discontented. On every hand men complained of "high taxes," the "unfavourable balance of trade," the "deluge of bankruptcies," the "alarming scarcity of money," the "stagnation of trade," and the "load of restrictions." Many regarded the Townshend legislation as a deep-rooted plan to embarrass them further. Few of the colonists understood Britain's financial dilemma. Indeed, the vast majority thought that the mother country was not only bent on crushing them economically, but on curtailing what they had long regarded as their right of self-government.

The opposition manifested itself in many forms. Lawyers and those pamphleteers who had opposed the Grenville legislation on constitutional grounds were again outspoken. 1. On con Otis declared that the colonies "must instantly, stitutional vigorously and unanimously unite themselves . . . grounds to maintain the Liberty with which Heaven itself hath made us free." John Dickinson of Pennsylvania in his celebrated *Letters from a Farmer*, while urging the colonists to refrain from the use of force, asserted that the Townshend measures were unjust, un-English, and dangerous for the future well-being of the colonies. "Let us," said he, "consider ourselves as . . . freemen . . . *firmly bound together* by the *same rights, interests,* and *dangers.* . . . What have these colonies to *ask*, while they continue free; Or what have they to *dread*, but insidious attempts to subvert their freedom? . . . They form *one* political body, of which *each colony* is a *member*." Samuel Adams, that "master agitator" who was vastly more interested in his native land than in the welfare of the British Empire, induced the Massachusetts Assembly to send a *Circular Letter*, which he penned, to the other colonial assemblies urging them to coöperate in defending their natural and constitutional rights. Several of the colonies passed sympathetic resolutions in reply, and Virginia issued a circular letter calling upon the other colonies to support Massachusetts in her petition which she addressed to the British authorities praying for redress.

But in so far as America was concerned, the steady stream of colonial pamphlets and resolutions was not half as effective in **2. The re-** securing the repeal of the Townshend Acts as was **newed boycott** the renewal and extension of the commercial boycott. In 1767 leading Bostonians agreed not to purchase certain imported articles, of which they had made a long list. Interest in home manufacture revived, and the newspapers were filled with reports pertaining to the increase and perfection of local manufacturing. Harvard graduates wore homespun and printed their theses on paper manufactured in a nearby town. In 1770 the *Boston Gazette* declared that the "very impoverishing custom of wearing deep mourning at Funerals is now almost entirely laid aside in the Province." New York, Philadelphia, and the lesser commercial centers were following a similar custom by 1769. Even the Virginia planters, headed by Washington, formed a non-importation association. While some of the colonists, including many of the merchants, failed for one reason or another to live up to these non-importation agreements, both the English merchant and manufacturer were well aware of their existence. Indeed, in a single year imports from Great Britain fell off by more than £740,000. Fortunately for the British, the loss of their American market was more than made up by the increased demand for woolens in Germany as well as by other circumstances, and for this reason non-importation was less effective than when used to bring about the repeal of the Grenville legislation. It was effective enough, however, to disturb the peace of mind of the English business man and to open the eyes of the government.

One form of opposition, namely violence, not only aggravated Britain but alarmed the more conservative colonists as well. In **3. Violence** Boston, for example, the radical element became so menacing that the new customs commissioners asked for a warship and a regiment of soldiers to protect them. After repeated requests the British authorities in 1768 sent the man-of-war *Rommey*. Soon after its arrival the sloop *Liberty*, one of John Hancock's vessels, sailed into Boston harbor with a cargo composed in part of Madeira wine on which there was a heavy tax of seven pounds sterling per ton. When the customs

CHARLES TOWNSHEND

Chancellor of the Exchequer. After the portrait by Sir Joshua Reynolds

BOSTONIANS PAYING THE EXCISE MAN
OR TARRING AND FEATHERING
After a print published in London in 1774

official went on board he was "hoved down" into the cabin, the wine was taken ashore, and a false entry made. A few days later the *Liberty* was seized by the customs officers and, to prevent its rescue, was moored under the guns of the *Rommey*. Infuriated by this action, a mob soon terrorized the town. One of the customs officials was assaulted, a small boat belonging to the service was burned, and the homes of the comptroller and collector were damaged. The frightened commissioners, fearing for their lives, took refuge on the *Rommey* and later in Castle William. A short time afterward when the inspector-general, who had been away from Boston, returned he was roughly handled by a small mob. In the other commercial colonies similar events took place. In Providence a customs official was tarred and feathered, and at Newport a revenue cutter was destroyed. In New York and in New Jersey mobs were much in evidence, and in Philadelphia a mob stole smuggled wine which the customs officers had seized, and assaulted a protesting official.

To British mercantilists and imperialists such action on the part of what they regarded as subordinate dependencies was not to be tolerated. With few exceptions, they main- British government resorts to force to quell violence and to assert its authority tained that colonial radicalism should be suppressed and that, above all, the colonies should be compelled, by force if necessary, to accept any law or policy which the mother country might see fit to devise. Accordingly the ministry, heeding the requests of the customs officials for more adequate protection, and the almost impassioned entreaties of Governor Bernard of Massachusetts for troops "to rescue the Government out of the hands of a trained mob," resolved to station a military force in Boston. Despite the fact that regular garrisons were already maintained in more than a score of places in Britain's colonial possessions in America, rumors that troops were to be sent caused great excitement. The various acts of the British officials were roundly denounced in the *Boston Gazette*, and at a town meeting a convention of delegates from all the towns of the colony was summoned to take proper steps for safeguarding the colony's interests. Governor Bernard, however, refused to call the

Assembly, which he had prorogued, or to receive petitions prepared by the convention reciting the colony's grievances.

When the first contingent of soldiers arrived from Halifax on September 28, 1768, the Boston selectmen, in open defiance of The "Boston the Quartering Act (renewed in 1767), refused to Massacre" provide food and shelter for them within the limits of the town, and in almost every other conceivable way let it be known that they were not welcome. But this was not all. During the next few months the radicals, urged on by the tireless Samuel Adams, did all they could to stir up trouble between the citizenry and the soldiers. Both officers and privates were dubbed "Red Coats," "Lobsters," and "Bloody Backs," and on several occasions were pelted with oyster shells, snowballs, and the like. Many conservative Bostonians — property owners and business men — hated and feared the mobs more than they did the soldiery, but were powerless to prevent trouble. Late in February, 1770, an informing customs official, while being dragged from his home by a mob, fired into the crowd, killing an eleven-year-old boy named Seider. It is difficult to imagine how any event could have better served the purpose of the radicals. Not only was the unfortunate official arrested and, in spite of the order of the court, found guilty of murder, but Seider was pictured as a martyr to the cause of liberty. Feeling ran high, and stories soon began to circulate that civilians were being insulted by the soldiery. Finally on March 5, a sentry on guard at the customs house after having been repeatedly hazed and snowballed by a crowd, called for assistance. A sergeant and six men were sent to his relief, whereupon the crowd began to assault them with sticks and stones, daring them to fire. The soldiers, however, refrained from action until one of them was knocked down with a club; the guard then opened fire, killing three outright and wounding several others. This was the celebrated "Boston Massacre." Captain Preston, the commander of the guard, immediately surrendered to the civilian authorities, and the other members of the squad were arrested. Although a Boston town meeting promptly labeled them "murderers," the accused, after a very fair trial in which they were defended by John Adams and Josiah Quincy, Jr., were,

The true Sons of Liberty

And Supporters of the Non-Importation Agreement,

ARE determined to refent any the leaft Infult or Menace offer'd to any one or more of the feveral Committees appointed by the Body at Faneuil-Hall, and chaftife any one or more of them as they deferve; and will alfo fupport the Printers in any Thing the Committees fhall defire them to print.

☞AS a Warning to any one that fhall affront as aforefaid, upon fure Information given, one of thefe Advertifements will be pofted up at the Door or Dwelling-Houfe of the Offender.

NOTICE POSTED BY THE SONS OF LIBERTY, 1770

with the exception of two who were convicted of homicide, found not guilty. Needless to say the radicals refused to accept the verdict with equanimity and in every possible way kept the incident alive in the minds of the populace.

Between 1770 and 1773 the gathering storm temporarily subsided. Three factors account for this interval of calm. In the first place, the Townshend Acts, with the exception of the duty on tea, were repealed. This action resulted partly from the effect of the colonial boycott on British goods, partly from the fact that the Acts, while yielding little revenue, had increased the military establishment in America and had brought the colonies to the brink of rebellion, and partly because Lord North, who became prime minister in 1770, maintained that the taxation of British goods was contrary to the best principles of mercantilism. The tax on tea was retained on the ground that the colonies should be at all times fully aware of British authority. "The properest time to exert our right of taxation," said North, "is when the right is refused."

The gathering storm subsides

1. Repeal of Townshend Acts

Secondly, the six lean years of economic depression following the close of the French and Indian War gave way in 1769–1770 to better times. Restrictions, depression, panics, and non-importation were forgotten, or at least lost sight of. The merchant class, as Professor Schlesinger points out, turned "with a sense of profound relief to the pleasant task of wooing the profits of commerce." Thanks to non-importation, the net balance of trade stood in favor of the commercial colonies in 1770, and the American merchants were able therefore not only to pay off their standing debts in England but to secure considerable quantities of gold. So rapidly did business pick up that British importations into such centers as New York and New England multiplied from three to five fold. "Commerce," a Massachusetts official reported, "never was in a more flourishing state." And this was equally true of domestic as well as of overseas trade. With conditions so favorable to his welfare, the merchant was content to let well enough alone, and for the time being he had little or nothing to say about the "tyrannous

2. Economic depression gives way to material prosperity

supremacy of Parliament, the rights of man, and encroachments on liberty."

Thirdly, fear on the part of the merchant class that the non-mercantile, non-propertied masses might become too powerful, socially and politically, if the agitation against the   **3. Fear of** mother country continued; tended to check the dis-   **popular up-** content. "All men of property," said Colden of   **heaval** New York, "are so sensible of their danger from riots and tumults that they will not rashly be induced to enter into combinations which may promote disorder for the future, but will endeavor to promote due subordination to legal authority." In the mind of the merchant the doctrine of individual rights, so stressed in the controversy with England, was never intended to apply to the rank and file. Indeed, the prospect of a social and political revolution, which would in all probability greatly curtail or minimize their own social and political power, was the last thing in the world that the merchants desired.

For three years, therefore, comparative calm prevailed. Everywhere men of property seemed to have things well in hand. Extreme radicals, it is true, were unwilling to let   **Radicals con-** sleeping dogs lie. Spurred on by restless leaders,   **tinue agitation** like Samuel Adams, they did their best to keep alive the flames of opposition by recourse to the old cries about British oppression and colonial rights. Adams, hoping for complete independence, declared that the rank and file of the people were not dependent upon "merchants or any particular class of men"; and William Lee advised his brother in Virginia not to "trust anything to the merchants for, in general, gain is their God; but force them to coöperate with the wishes of the people." The alliance between the merchants and masses was, for the time being, clearly at an end.

While the radicals did not make as much headway as they wished during these years, one event played directly into their hands, namely, the *Gaspée* affair. For some time,   **The *Gaspée*** prior to 1770 the English East India Company had   **affair** been running behind financially and to make up for the losses had advanced the price of tea on the London market. This, of course, led to widespread smuggling on the part of the American merchants, who could buy tea in Holland much more cheaply than in England, and at the same time avoid paying duty. England resolved to enforce the law, and accordingly its revenue cutters and customs officials became extremely active. Riotous scenes occurred in Falmouth and in Philadelphia in 1771. But it was in Rhode Island, with its numerous inlets and islands, a veritable haven for smugglers, that the chief trouble occurred. Among the revenue boats sent to apprehend the illicit trading was the *Gaspée*, commanded by Lieutenant Dudingston. In the eyes of the colonists Dudingston was more than over-zealous. He stopped and searched vessels without adequate pre-text, seized goods illegally, and fired on market boats as they entered Newport harbor; he treated the farmers living on the islands shamefully, ruthlessly cutting down their trees for fuel and seizing their sheep for meat. The chance for revenge came when on June 9, 1772, the *Gaspée* ran aground seven miles below Providence. At midnight the boat was attacked by a mob of men and boys headed by John Brown, the richest merchant of Providence. Dudingston was wounded, he and his crew were put ashore, and the vessel was burned. English officialdom con-demned the act as treasonable and directed that those respon-sible for it should be apprehended and sent to England for trial.

The *Gaspée* affair, together with the report in 1772 that judges' salaries would henceforth be paid by the mother country out of Committees of revenue derived from colonial customs, furnished correspondence Adams and his fellow radicals with new fuel. By means of newspaper and pamphlet they kept up a running barrage of agitation against England. Everywhere the people were urged to consider whether they wanted to be "freemen or slaves," whether they wanted to submit everything "dear and sacred" to the decisions of "pensioned hirelings." Adams, fully realizing the changed attitude of the merchants and the necessity of keeping the people roused, was especially vindictive. Whether in town meeting, on the street corner, or in tavern or grog-shop, he constantly advocated the need for union and com-mon action. Finally in November, 1772, he moved in the Boston town meeting that a committee of twenty-one be appointed "to state the Rights of the Colonists and of this province in particular, as men, as Christians, and as Subjects; with the Infringements and Violations thereof that have been or from time to time may be made"; and to communicate and publish the same to the several towns of Massachusetts and to the world as the sense of Boston, also requesting of each town "a free communication of their Sentiment on this Subject." This resolution, passed without a dissenting voice, in reality provided for the establishment of a radical agency which was to be used to stir up popular sentiment in favor of revolution and to resist the will and authority of the British ministry. By January, 1773, more than eighty Massachusetts towns had similar committees. Two months later the Virginia Assembly appointed a standing committee of correspondence, and the majority of the other colonies followed suit. We should note that the radicals now had both an issue and the beginning at least of an organization divorced from control of the merchant class.

At the beginning of the year 1773, however, the moderates and conservatives, whether merchants or landed proprietors, still dominated the situation. With few exceptions they flatly opposed revolution and complete independ-   **Radicals not in control** ence, both of which were now being openly advocated by the radicals. For their own advantage it was better, they believed, to pursue a policy of expediency and passive resistance. Even the merchant John Hancock, who in the dark days prior to 1770 had backed Adams with both funds and influence was, as Professor Schlesinger says, "adverse to any further agitation by the radicals while the golden fruits of commerce invited picking."

Just at this stage, when the outlook for more peaceful relations between the mother country and the colonies seemed so encouraging, Lord North and his colleagues commit-   **The mother country attempts to aid the English East India Company** ted a fatal blunder. The advance in the price of tea in England did not materially aid the East India Company, and at the beginning of the year 1773 the company found itself on the verge of bankruptcy with seventeen million pounds of tea in its warehouses in England, and its dividends cut in half. The stock-holders, some of whom were government officials, were at their wits' end. In an effort to aid the company financially and at the same time increase the revenue of the government, North induced Parliament in May, 1773, to enact a measure which practically gave the company a monopoly of the tea trade in America. By its terms the company was to all intents and purposes relieved of the entire tea duty in England and at the same time permitted to send its tea directly to the colonies in its own ships and to dispose of it to retailers through its own agencies. Thus the British and colonial importer — both middlemen — were eliminated. Although the company had to pay the three-penny customs tax in the colonies it was able, nevertheless, to reduce the price twenty-five per cent and thus undersell both the honest merchant and the dealer who trafficked in smuggled tea.

Angered by the granting of a monopoly to what seemed to them to be a powerful, grasping corporation, and by the pros-
Effect on pect of the loss of profits from a lucrative trade, and
colonists fearful lest other articles should be similarly monopolized by the East India Company or like concerns, the merchants again joined with the radicals. In so doing they had no intention of supporting the radical demand for complete independence. High sounding statements about "liberty" and the "rights of man" did not concern them half so much as the prospect of economic loss. If the trade and commerce of the colonies should be monopolized then, as one of their number said, America might be prostrated before a monster that might "be able to destroy every branch of our commerce, drain us of all our property, and wantonly leave us to perish by thousands." Possible trade ruin, in other words, was the great issue at stake as far as the merchants were concerned, and they were willing to enter into almost any sort of an alliance to avoid such a catastrophe. Moreover, we should note that in joining with the radicals they apparently thought that they could control the situation as they had done on previous occasions. This, as we shall presently see, they were unable to do.

Long before the East India Company's ships arrived at the colonial ports, the question of what steps ought to be taken to "safeguard" colonial interests was discussed. Everywhere the general consensus prevailed that the tea should not be allowed to land, but the radicals and merchants were by no means always in agreement as to just what procedure should be followed to prevent its being landed. The more conservative merchants as well as the moderates were inclined to resort to the old method of economic boycott, and to bring pressure to bear on the company's consignees to resign. The radicals, on the other hand, determined to make the most of the situation, advocated sterner measures. In Boston, where they soon gained the upper hand, tarring and feathering and other forms of violence became the order of the day. The company's consignees, among whom were the two sons and the nephew of Governor Hutchinson, were labeled "Traitors to their Country, Butchers," who were "doing everything to Murder and destroy all that shall stand in the way of their private Interests." The obstinate refusal of the Massachusetts governor to allow the tea ships to leave the harbor, and the no less plain refusal of the consignees to resign at the repeated request of the merchant-controlled town meeting, opened the way for Samuel Adams to summon a great mass meeting. This body, in which the rank and file greatly outnumbered the merchants and conservatives, not only refused to obey the governor's order to disperse, but unanimously adopted a resolution to the effect that the tea should not be landed and that the duty on it should not be paid. The governor, however, was equally determined that the tea should not leave the harbor until it had first been landed and the duty on it paid. The result was the famous Boston Tea Party. On the night of December 16, 1773, a band of men disguised as Indians boarded the company's vessels and dumped £18,000 worth of tea into the harbor while a great crowd on shore looked on. The deed was performed quietly and no other damage was done. Among the "Indians" were merchants who toiled "side by side with carpenters, masons, farmers, blacksmiths, and barbers."

[margin note: Colonial reception of the tea: the Boston Tea Party]

In the other colonies the East India Company met with opposition also. In Philadelphia eight thousand citizens, representing all walks of life, adopted resolutions directing Captain Ayers, commander of the company's tea ship, not to enter his cargo at the customs house and to resail at once for England. Ayers wisely obeyed. In New York, as in Philadelphia, all classes were opposed to the company's tea shipments, and a document entitled "The Association of the Sons of Liberty" denounced as enemies and declared a boycott against all persons who in any way should aid in bringing dutied tea into port. Furthermore, the radicals of the city held a meeting and appointed a committee of correspondence to communicate with the other colonies. Many conservative merchants, thoroughly alarmed, took steps to hold the radicals in check, but soon found themselves powerless to stem the tide. Fortunately for the company, its consignees, realizing the state of public opinion and having no desire for a repetition of the Boston Tea Party, not only resigned but advised the captain of the company's tea ship to return to sea "for the safety of your cargo, your vessels, and your person. . . ." In Charleston, where the radicals, composed mostly of planters and mechanics, found it more difficult to secure the coöperation of the merchants in opposing entry of the tea, resistance was less marked than in the northern ports. Here the tea was unloaded and placed in the government warehouses where it remained until it was auctioned off three years later for the benefit of the new revolutionary government.

Other colonies opposed to East India Company

The tea episode, especially the Boston Tea Party, led to two very important results. In the first place, all the colonists who regarded private property as sacred and who feared the consequences of radical rule, condemned the use of violence. Conservatives, for example, denounced the Boston Tea Party as a "diabolical" act, contrary to the best interests of the country. Even liberal-minded men like Franklin and Dickinson disapproved of it, the former labeling it "an act of violent Injustice" for which the East India Company ought to be fully compensated. Only the

Effects of the tea episode

1. On colonies

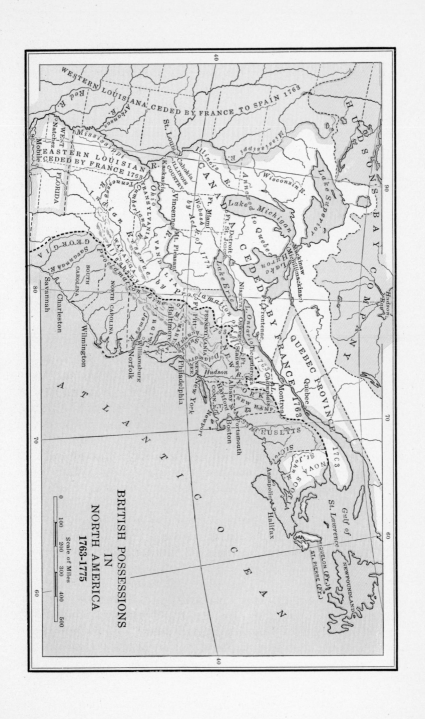

BRITISH POSSESSIONS
IN
NORTH AMERICA
1763-1775

Scale of Miles

0
100
200
300
400
500

extremists approved of it, and throughout the colonies their cause was, for the moment at least, injured by it.

In the second place, it precipitated the crisis which had long been brewing between the colonies and Great Britain. In the eyes of the British ministry and British leaders 2. On Great generally, the refusal of the colonists to accept the Britain East India Company's tea and the lawless assaults on the company's property, coupled with the refusal of the radicals to obey the crown officials, was nothing short of open defiance. In other words, they frankly asserted that British authority had been flouted and that the time had arrived for coercive action. Only Pitt and Burke and a few others thought otherwise, and in the spring of 1774 Parliament at the request of Lord North passed the so-called Intolerable Acts.

The first of these, the Boston Port Bill, closed the port of Boston until such time as the British authorities were satisfied "that the trade of Great Britain may safely be The British carried on there, and His Majesty's customs duly reply to the collected." It also stipulated that the port should Boston Tea Party: the not be opened until the inhabitants of Boston had Intolerable made restitution to the East India Company for Acts the destruction of its property. The Massachusetts Government Act practically reduced that province to the status of a crown colony, while the Administration of Justice Act ordered that all persons indicted for murder or other capital crimes be sent to England or to some other colony for trial in case the governor or his lieutenant were of the opinion that such persons could not obtain an unbiased trial in the colony. A fourth measure, a new Quartering Act, provided that if ample barracks were not ready for troops within twenty-four hours after they had been ordered, the local authorities must find suitable quarters for them. Finally, the Quebec Act, though not a punitive measure, extended that province by adding to it the great stretch of territory west of the old colonies and north of the Ohio. It furthermore provided that government should be by officials appointed by the Crown. The privilege of self-taxation was denied and trials were to be without jury. Moreover, all Catholics were to enjoy complete religious toleration.

As a further means of asserting Britain's authority and of "putting the rebels in their places," General Gage, commander-in-chief of the armed forces in America, was appointed governor of Massachusetts, and four additional regiments were despatched to the disaffected New England area. Belief in England was general that the colonists would not and could not resist. Hutchinson and some of his more conservative brethren entertained this opinion, and Gage himself informed George III that the Americans "will be Lyons whilst we are lambs but if we take the resolute part they will undoubtedly prove very meek." But events were to prove that Gage was wrong as were the great majority of the colonists, who ignorantly believed that England would not resort to armed coercion.

The passage of the Intolerable Acts and the administrative measures taken for their enforcement widened and deepened the chasm of misunderstanding and hard feeling between the colonies and the mother country. The North ministry, instead of adopting a conciliatory policy and sending a commission of inquiry to America to ascertain the exact state of affairs, chose to treat the colonies as mere mercantilistic dependencies whose citizens should be punished for disobeying the edicts of the mother country and resorting to mob violence. The colonists, motivated by self-interest and having for a hundred and fifty years enjoyed a wide degree of home rule, bitterly resented the North measures. Henceforth, as we shall see, the struggle, which from the first had been basically economic, was to become essentially political. Even more important, as we shall also see, the coercive acts of 1774 resulted in a sharper cleavage between the radical and conservative elements in the colonies.

4. OTHER INSTITUTIONAL DIFFERENCES GENERATE FRICTION

Although diverging economic interests constituted the principal cause for conflict within the British Empire, they were by no means the only agency of friction. Other forces — social, intellectual, religious, and political — operating during the entire colonial period, were contributing factors.

Socially many Britishers regarded the colonists as inferior and treated them as such. Not only did they frequently snub them when occasion offered, but they often referred to them in harsh language. A London pamphleteer, for example, wrote that the English ministry might well dub the Americans "a race of dastardly cowards, sprung from our bastards, our swindlers, and our convicts." Bostonians were characterized as "people of coarse, insolent manners," and New Englanders in general as little short of slaves, the only difference being "that they were not bought and sold." Even General Wolfe, the hero of Quebec, declared that the Americans "are in general the dirtiest, most contemptible, cowardly dogs that you can conceive." With apparently little thought for the feelings of others, many spokesmen in the mother country seemed to gain a peculiar satisfaction by constantly stressing the poverty of the colonists and by poking fun at their dress, manners, speech, and customs.

Colonists regarded as socially inferior by British

But such tactics were by no means monopolized by the British. Many of the colonists, unacquainted with the English countryside, thought and spoke of Great Britain as a den of iniquity given over to every species of luxury and dissipation. Henry Laurens and other Americans who had visited eighteenth-century England were astonished at the frivolity and immorality of the ruling class. "Chastity," wrote Laurens in 1772, "is certainly out of fashion in England."

Colonial conception of England

Such characterizations did not tend to knit the Empire more closely together. Loose talk and flippant generalizations about their heritage and their mode of life, whether true or not, embittered the colonists and roused within them a rebellious spirit. Moreover, those familiar with conditions in the English metropolis raised the question whether the colonists ought to render obedience to a government controlled by "licentious and unprincipled men."

Social differences provoke hard feelings

No less important as a source of friction was the great intellectual gulf between the colonies and the mother country. Intellectually eighteenth-century even more than seventeenth-century America was a pioneer community. Its population, as

Intellectual gulf a source of friction

we have seen, was chiefly concerned with things material — with the conquest of forest and savage and with gaining a livelihood. In comparison with England it could boast few men of fortune and leisure. Largely as a consequence it was without the magnificent specimens of architecture, painting, and other forms of art which abounded in England. No great cathedrals, art galleries, or museums graced its landscape. It had no rivals to Gainsborough, Romney, or Reynolds. Its colleges were weaklings compared with Oxford and Cambridge, and of professional schools it had practically none. In the appreciation of music and literary attainment it also trailed far behind England. Colonial officials and English travelers repeatedly called attention to the American's careless use of English and to his grammatical errors. Only in acquaintanceship with political literature were the colonists on a par with the English, and this disparity in intellectual attainment, like the social differences, was constantly emphasized.

Religious and sectarian forces, perhaps more than social or intellectual differences, helped to create ill-feeling and enmity in

Religious and sectarian forces produce discord

the colonies. Indeed, John Adams asserted that the religious question served "as much as any other cause to arouse the attention, not only of the inquiring mind, but of the common people, and urge them to close thinking on the constitutional authority of parliament over the colonies." In general these forces contributed to the spirit of revolt in two fairly distinct ways.

The first of these was the apprehension aroused by the repeated attempt to spread the Anglican faith in the colonies at

Anglican ambitions arouse apprehension

the expense of the Presbyterians, Quakers, and other sects, and by the scheme to establish an Anglican Episcopate in America. The stronghold of Anglicanism, as we have already noted, was in the plantation provinces. South of Pennsylvania and in three New York counties it had legal establishment. Naturally Anglican leaders dreamed of the time when it would be the dominant faith in all the colonies. The dissenting groups were well aware of this fact, and in 1763 the famous Massachusetts divine, Jonathan Mayhew, launched a bitter attack against the Anglican Society for the Propagation of the Gospel in Foreign Parts, on the ground that it was trying to "root out Presbyterianism." This opinion, widespread among the Dissenters in the North, was strengthened by recurrent rumors that an episcopate was to be founded in the colonies. After 1750 opposition to the plan was universal outside the ranks of the Established Church. New England Congregationalists declared that with its establishment the colonies would be deluged in a flood of episcopacy and victimized by "right reverend and holy tyrants." An American bishopric, they warned, would mean additional taxes, priest-controlled courts, and the assumption of secular functions by episcopal authorities. Even Arthur Lee of Virginia regarded the scheme "as threatening the subversion of both our civil and religious liberties." Discord and apprehension were bound to develop where Dissenters labeled all officials appointed by the British government as "ruffle-shirted Episcopalians" and tools and allies of "tyrannical monarchialism," and where Anglicans retorted in turn that all Dissenters were steeped in "republican principles."

Closely connected with the opposition to Anglicanism was the tremendous influence of the dissenting clergy in shaping the political ideals of the rank and file. Year after year, especially at election time, Presbyterian and Congregational preachers directly or indirectly taught the ideas of Locke and Milton. In the course of their sermons they not only dwelt upon the origin and nature of government, but even asserted that people had a right to rebel against a government that took their money or property without their consent. Patrick Henry, who declared that government was "a conditional compact between king and people," and that "a violation of the covenant by either party discharges the other from obligation," was taught in his youth by a Presbyterian divine that the British Constitution was "but the voluntary compact of sovereign and subject." And this was typical of every Calvinistic community. The dissent-

Calvinist preachers undermine royal authority

ing preachers' sermons, usually printed in pamphlet form, were virtually political textbooks. Moreover, at the meetings called to protest against the British measures, the preacher, mingling freely with lawyer and mechanic, was no uncertain force in helping to mold sentiment adverse to the British authorities.

Last, but not least of the several forces making for the disruption of the Empire, were the numerous misunderstandings and conflicts which arose in connection with the government and administration of the colonies, and which, for want of a better term, may be called political. Let us review them briefly.

Political differences a disruptive force

First of all may be mentioned the almost constant struggle between the colonial legislatures and the executive officials appointed by the crown. Each of the thirteen colonies, as we have observed, had a representative assembly elected by property owners. Small and feeble at first, they developed until by the middle of the eighteenth century each was a miniature House of Commons, claiming and exercising the right to levy and collect taxes, borrow money, raise troops, regulate trade with the Indians, issue currency, fix the salaries of government officials whether appointed by the crown or otherwise, and appoint agents to represent the colony in its dealings with England. Naturally these assemblies were not primarily concerned in promoting the interests of the ruling class in Great Britain or of the colonial officials appointed by it; rather their efforts at all times centered around achieving their own ends and ambitions and protecting the interests of those who elected them. The executive official, on the other hand, was not chiefly concerned with the social and economic welfare of the colonists. Schooled in the tenets of mercantilism, anxious to enlarge his own private fortune or to secure a lucrative post for some dependent relative or friend, he regarded the colonial assembly as a troublesome barrier. A clash was inevitable.

The colonial legislature *versus* royal-appointed executive officials

Perhaps nowhere was this constant strife between the colonists and the representatives of the home government more in evidence than in the case of the royal governor. Eight of the colonies, we will remember, were royal provinces by 1752, and the

governor of each was, therefore, appointed by the Crown.   This
in itself was a cause of friction, for some of the royal colonies
aspired to the same degree of self-government as   The colonial
was enjoyed by Rhode Island and Connecticut   governor a
where the governor was elected.   Selected for the   source of strife
most part from the English middle class, the royal governors
differed greatly in culture, training, and ability.   Some were
efficient administrators, while others were notorious failures.
Some were needy politicians, spendthrifts, and adventurers.
Indeed, the historian Bancroft went so far as to assert that
America was "the hospital of Great Britain for its decayed
members of Parliament and abandoned courtiers."   Nearly
all were alike in that they used their office to enrich themselves
and others by means of sinecures, patronage, land grants, and
the acceptance of bribes.   Furthermore, nearly all of them
gained the reputation of being overbearing.   "Their office,"
wrote Franklin, "makes them insolent; their insolence makes
them odious; and being conscious that they are hated, they
become malicious; their malice urges them to continual abuse
of the inhabitants in their letters to Administration, representing them as disaffected and rebellious, and (to encourage the use
of severity) as weak, divided, timid, and cowardly.   Government believes all; thinking it necessary to support and countenance its officers.   Their quarreling with the people is deemed a
mark and consequence of their fidelity.   They are, therefore,
more highly rewarded, and this makes their conduct still more
insolent and provoking."

Of course, it may be argued in defense of these royal appoint-
ees that bribery, corruption, and the awarding of spoils was the
prevalent custom in eighteenth-century Europe;   Governor and
that in the colonies honesty received little or no   Assembly in
financial reward, and that the office of colonial   constant
governor was not such as to attract men of high   struggle
ideals.   But this is not the point.   The colonists looked upon the
royal governor as an outsider; were envious of his power, which
they increasingly sought to curtail, and aspired to control the
many offices which he filled with his henchmen.   Naturally,
therefore, he was the object of constant criticism and was

virtually compelled to carry on an incessant struggle with the colonial assembly, for it, as we have noted, held the purse strings, and without money the governor was all but powerless.

The governorship, however, was not the only piece of British administrative machinery, the workings of which stirred up the colonists. The Board of Trade and Plantations, which first took definite form in 1660 as a committee of the Privy Council and which was reorganized in 1696, was a powerful engine of colonial supervision and control. It met almost daily and scanned every detail of colonial affairs — social, economic, religious, political. Practically nothing escaped its scrutiny. All colonial legislation was subject to its review. It recommended that the crown veto or disallow any act of a colonial assembly contrary to the laws of England, or threatening to the maintenance of the royal prerogative, or jeopardizing the property rights of any citizen of the Empire; and its recommendations were almost without exception accepted. The Board also heard complaints. Any colony, for example, could present any grievance it might have through its agent resident in England, and any British merchant or manufacturer, on the other hand, was equally free to lodge objections against any colonial authority and to make suggestions which he thought would prove to his advantage. Although the percentage of laws disallowed was not great, the colonists mistrusted and disliked the Board, and not without reason, for its decisions were not only tardy but sometimes unjust. Above all, many of the colonists thought of it as simply another agency created to limit their freedom of action for the benefit of grasping English business men.

Work of Board of Trade and Plantations causes resentment in colonies

For the same reasons they held in no high regard other administrative agencies. Among these were: (1) the Privy Council which, serving in the capacity of a court of appeals, often declared colonial acts unconstitutional and, therefore, null and void; (2) the Secretary of State in charge of colonial affairs, who appointed the royal governors and to whom complainants appealed as a last resort; (3) the Commissioners of Customs, who appointed the

Other administrative agencies disliked by colonists

customs collectors and the two American surveyors-general, and who kept an eagle eye on illegal commerce; (4) the Treasury, which had control of royal revenues and expenses in the colonies; (5) the Admiralty and War Office, which had to do with colonial defense on land and sea and which also coöperated with the customs officials in suppressing illegal trade; and (6) the Bishop of London, who exercised control over the Anglican church in the provinces.

Division of authority and jurisdiction between the various administrative offices led to confusion and delay which often affected the colonists adversely. Colonial matters were sometimes regarded lightly and thrust aside. Colonial papers, for example, were pigeon-holed for years at a time, while the anxious colonists awaited a decision. Added to this was the careless handling of colonial mail; ship captains frequently gave it little attention, with the result that it was sometimes lost or destroyed; if it were fortunate enough to reach England it often lay in the customs house for weeks or even months before delivery. Naturally, such a state of affairs did not make for harmony.

Division of authority affects colonists adversely

Out of the conflict occasioned by the social, economic, religious, intellectual, and political forces which we have briefly summarized in this chapter, came the American Revolution. These forces, to paraphrase a figure of speech used by Mr. J. T. Adams in his *Revolutionary New England*, were the tiny streams, the rivers, the innumerable lakes that furnished the waters from which flowed the mighty cataract of civil war within the British Empire. In the next chapter we shall see how the colonies, as a result of this conflict, completely severed their constitutional and legal relations with Great Britain and united to form a new nation.

SUGGESTED READINGS

J. T. Adams, *Revolutionary New England, 1691–1776.*
C. W. Alvord, *The Mississippi Valley in British Politics,* 2 vols.
C. M. Andrews, *The Colonial Background of the American Revolution.*
E. A. Bailey, *Influences Toward Radicalism in Connecticut 1754–1775.*
A. M. Baldwin, *The New England Clergy and the American Revolution.*

Charles and Mary Beard, *The Rise of American Civilization*, vol. i, chap. v.

Carl Becker, *The Eve of the Revolution* (Vol. ii of *Chronicles of America*).

G. L. Beer, *The Old Colonial System, 1660–1754.*

G. L. Beer, *British Colonial Policy, 1754–1765.*

Edward Channing, *History of the United States*, vol. iii, chaps. i–v.

V. S. Clark, *History of Manufactures in the United States, 1607–1860*, chap. ii.

H. J. Eckenrode, *The Revolution in Virginia.*

H. E. Egerton, *The Causes and Character of the American Revolution.*

S. G. Fisher, *The Struggle for American Independence*, 2 vols.

W. W. Henry, *Patrick Henry; Life, Correspondence and Speeches*, 3 vols.

G. B. Hertz, *The Old Colonial System*, chap. iv.

F. G. Hinkhouse, *The Preliminaries of the American Revolution as Seen in the English Press, 1763–1775.*

J. K. Hosmer, *Samuel Adams.*

G. E. Howard, *Preliminaries of the Revolution, 1763–1775* (Vol. viii of *The American Nation*).

E. R. Johnson and others, *History of Domestic and Foreign Commerce of the United States*, vol. i, chap. iii.

W. E. H. Lecky, *History of England in the Eighteenth Century*, vol. iii.

E. I. McCormac, *Colonial Opposition to Imperial Authority During the French and Indian War.*

William Macdonald, *Documentary Source Book of American History, 1606–1926.*

C. H. McIlwain, *The American Revolution: A Constitutional Interpretation.*

L. B. Namier, *The Structure of Politics at the Accession of George III.*

F. W. Pitman, *Development of the British West Indies.*

A. M. Schlesinger, *The Colonial Merchants and the American Revolution.*

A. M. Schlesinger, *New View Points in American History*, chaps. iii, vii.

P. H. Silburn, *The Colonies and Imperial Defense.*

G. O. Trevelyan, *The American Revolution*, 4 vols.

M. C. Tyler, *Literary History of the American Revolution, 1763–1783*, 2 vols.

C. H. Van Tyne, *The Causes of the War of Independence.*

CHAPTER V

REVOLUTION AND INDEPENDENCE

WE have already noted how, during the century and a half preceding the American Revolution, two fairly distinct social and economic classes developed in Colonial Amer- Two social ica. One, the conservatives, composed of the rich and economic and the well-born — of merchants, large landhold- colonial ers, and money-lenders — dominated every phase America of colonial life. It owned or controlled the economic resources of the colonies — the bulk of the land, forests, fishing grounds, the agencies of commerce, and the fluid capital. By means of property qualifications for voting and office holding, and by recourse to the devices of wire-pulling, log-rolling, and bossism, it was able to limit greatly the political power of the 1. The con- rank and file. Socially, its members considered servatives themselves superior to the common people, toward whom they assumed a snobbish attitude. Indeed, unless one had money or was a member of an "old respectable" family or was well educated or had served the state in some prominent capacity, he was regarded as socially inferior. Even at Harvard College students' names, to the eve of the Revolution, were arranged in the order of the "respectability of their parentage."

In sharp contrast to the conservatives were the radicals. Recruited for the most part from the ranks of the poorer people — small farmers, mechanics, shopkeepers, and 2. The frontiersmen — this class was ever conscious of the radicals barrier which separated it from the advantages of wealth, education, and social position enjoyed by the conservatives. Partly because of this fact and partly because it aspired to substitute "the rule of the many for the rule of the few," it waged unrelenting warfare against privilege of every kind. Primogeniture and entail, quitrents, tax systems favoring the rich, an established church, unequal representation, restricted suffrage, and economic monopolization were constantly attacked. Neither the privileged class in the colonies nor royal officials nor Old World profiteers were spared.

For obvious reasons the conservatives, not unlike the privileged orders of England and France against which the common people of these countries rose during the eighteenth century, did not sympathize with the desire of the radicals for change. On the contrary, they staunchly defended the existing order, at the same time belittling as much as possible all radical assertions and thwarting all radical demands. On occasion these antagonistic groups, as we have observed, coöperated against Great Britain, but at no time did the conservatives have any intention of releasing their grip on colonial affairs or of removing the barrier separating the two classes. The momentous decision of the British government, however, to apply drastic measures to the colonies not only paved the way for a real test of strength between the two factions, but opened the gates, as we shall now see, to the pent-up waters of revolution and civil war.

Conservatives opposed to radical proposals

1. The Radicals Triumph

Although the vast majority of the colonists bitterly condemned the passage of the Intolerable Acts, there was sharp division of opinion among them as to what course of action they should pursue. The more extreme radicals, defiant and uncompromising, and bent on obtaining colonial self-government or even independence, advocated a strong retaliatory policy. Not only did they flatly oppose any restitution to the East India Company, but they wanted the colonies to suspend all commercial intercourse with Great Britain and with the British and foreign West Indies. The conservatives, on the other hand, anxious to reach a peaceful understanding with the mother country and, above all, to avoid any move that would strengthen the radicals, hesitated to endorse the radical program.

Radicals and conservatives disagree on policy toward Great Britain

In the midst of the heated discussion between the two factions a movement, largely spontaneous in origin, for an intercolonial congress to discuss the situation, gathered headway. On May

17, 1774, a Providence town meeting proposed such a congress and a few days later a similar suggestion came from the New York and Philadelphia committees of correspond- First Con ence and from the Virginia House of Burgesses. tinental Con Finally, on June 17, the Massachusetts Assembly, gress called inspired by Samuel Adams, who was keenly aware of the grow ing sentiment for an intercolonial gathering, invited the other colonies to send delegates to a Continental Congress to be held at Philadelphia the next September. The delegates, the invitation ran, were "to consult upon the present state of the colonies, and the miseries to which they are and must be reduced by the operation of certain acts of Parliament respecting Amer ica, and to deliberate and determine upon wise and proper measures to be by them recommended to all the colonies, for the recovery and establishment of their just rights and liberties, civil and religious, and the restoration of union and harmony between Great Britain and the colonies, most ardently desired by all good men." The delegates, it was suggested, might be chosen by the colonial assemblies, by popularly elected conven tions, or by committees of correspondence.

Realizing that the great issue between them would in all prob ability be decided by the forthcoming Congress, both radicals and conservatives sought to control its personnel. Congress con Bitter contests, therefore, ensued in each province. trolled by When the irregularly elected Congress assembled radicals on September 5, every one of the thirteen colonies except Geor gia, where the royal governor prevented the selection of dele gates, was represented. Of the fifty-six delegates who eventually appeared only eleven were merchants, and these Professor Schlesinger records were "more addicted to politics than to trade"; over two-thirds were lawyers, but many of these fre quently derived a large part of their income from agriculture; many of them, especially those from the Southern colonies, were among the ablest men in America; and, most important of all, while every shade of opinion in the colonies was represented, the Congress was controlled by the radicals.

The first test of strength between the antagonistic groups came on the opening day when the Congress declined the invita-

tion of Joseph Galloway, a wealthy Pennsylvanian and leader
of the conservatives, to meet in the state house, and voted to
Radicals score hold its sessions in Carpenter's Hall, to the great
first victories satisfaction of "the mechanics and citizens in general." The radicals also scored a second victory by securing the
election of Charles Thomson as secretary despite the fact that
Galloway deemed him "one of the most violent Sons of Liberty
(so-called) in America."

These radical victories were of minor consequence in comparison with the set of resolutions known as the Suffolk Resolves,
Congress en- which the radicals induced the Congress to endorse
dorses Suffolk on September 17. These Resolves, adopted a few
Resolves days before by Suffolk County, Massachusetts,
declared in bold language that the Intolerable Acts were unconstitutional and void, and that the government of Massachusetts,
as then established, was illegal. The Resolves furthermore advised the people of the province to organize their own civil
government to which all taxes should be paid, to raise troops for
defense, and to suspend all commercial intercourse with Great
Britain, Ireland, and the West Indies.

Alarmed at this action, which they asserted was nothing
short of a "complete declaration of war," the conservatives,
Conservative partly for the purpose of nullifying its effect and
plan of union partly to test the real intentions of the Congress,
rejected submitted a plan prepared by Galloway for a new
form of union between the colonies and the mother country.
This plan, which in reality was the platform of the conservatives,
provided for a crown-appointed president-general and a council
of deputies chosen every three years by the colonial legislatures.
Parliament might veto acts of the council, and acts of Parliament relating to the colonies might, in turn, be vetoed by the
council. Although the plan was warmly supported by Jay and
Duane of New York and by other men of wealth, the radicals
managed to defeat it. "Measures of independence and sedition," said Galloway long afterward, "were . . . preferred to
those of harmony and liberty."

The rejection by the radicals of the conciliatory conservative
plan did not prevent the two factions from agreeing to a Dec-

SAMUEL ADAMS — RADICAL LEADER

After the portrait by J. I. Copley

WE, his Majesty's most loyal subjects, the Delegates of the several Colonies of New-Hampshire, Massachusett's Bay, Rhode-Island, Connecticut, New-York, New Jersey, Pennsylvania, the Three Lower Counties of Newcastle, Kent, and Suffex, on Delaware, Maryland, Virginia, North-Carolina, and South-Carolina, deputed to represent them in a continental Congress, held in the city of Philadelphia, on the fifth day of September, 1774, avowing our allegiance to his Majesty, our affection and regard for our fellow-subjects in Great-Britain and elsewhere, affected with the deepest anxiety, and most alarming apprehensions at those grievances and distresses, with which his Majesty's American subjects are oppressed, and having taken under our most serious deliberation, the state of the whole continent, find, that the present unhappy situation of our affairs, is occasioned by a ruinous system of colony administration adopted by the British Ministry about the year 1763, evidently calculated for inflaving these Colonies, and, with them, the British Empire. In prosecution of which system, various Acts of Parliament have been passed for raising a Revenue in America, for depriving the American subjects, in many instances, of the constitutional trial by jury, exposing their lives to danger, by directing a new and illegal trial beyond the seas, for crimes alledged to have been committed in America: And in prosecution of the same system, several late, cruel, and oppressive Acts have been passed respecting the town of Boston and the Massachusett's-Bay, and also an Act for extending the province of Quebec, so as to border on the western frontiers of these Colonies, establishing an arbitrary government therein, and discouraging the settlement of British subjects in that wide extended country; thus by the influence of civil principles and ancient prejudices to dispose the inhabitants to act with hostility against the free protestant Colonies, whenever a wicked Ministry shall chuse so to direct them.

To obtain redress of these grievances, which threaten destruction to the lives, liberty, and property of his Majesty's subjects, in North-America, we are of opinion, that a non-importation, non-consumption, and non exportation agreement, faithfully adhered to, will prove the most speedy, effectual, and peaceable measure: And therefore we do, for ourselves and the inhabitants of the several Colonies, whom we represent, firmly agree and associate under the sacred ties of

Thirteenth. THAT all manufactures of this country be sold at reasonable prices, so that no undue advantage be taken of a future scarcity of goods.

Fourteenth. AND we do further agree and resolve, that we will have no trade, commerce, dealings or intercourse whatsoever, with any colony or province, in North America, which shall not accede to, or which shall hereafter violate this association, but will hold them as unworthy of the rights of freemen, and as inimical to the liberties of their country.

And we do solemnly bind ourselves and our constituents, under the ties aforesaid, to adhere to this affociation until such parts of the several Acts of Parliament passed since the close of the last war, as impose or continue duties on tea, wine, molasses, syrups, paneles, coffee, sugar, piemento, indigo, foreign paper, glass, and painters colours, imported into America, and extend the powers of the Admiralty courts beyond their ancient limits, deprive the American subject of trial by jury, authorise the Judge's certificate to indemnify the prosecutor from damages, that he might otherwise be liable to from a trial by his peers, require oppressive security from a claimant of ships or goods seized, before he shall be allowed to defend his property, are repealed---And until that part of the Act of the 12. G. 3 ch. 24. entitled, "An Act for the better securing his Majesty's dock yards, magazines, ships, ammunition, and stores," by which, any persons charged with committing any of the offences therein described, in America, may be tried in any shire or county within the realm, is repealed---And until the four Acts passed in the last session of Parliament, viz. that for stopping the port and blocking up the harbour of Boston---That for altering the charter and government of the Massachusett's-Bay ---And that which is entitled, "An Act for the better administration of justice, &c."---And that " For extending the limits of Quebec, &c." are repealed. And we recommend it to the provincial conventions, and to the committees in the respective Colonies, to establish such farther regulations as they may think proper, for carrying into execution this Affociation.

THE foregoing Affociation being determined upon by the CONGRESS, was ordered to be subscribed by the several Members thereof; and thereupon we have hereunto set our respective names accordingly.

In Congress, Philadelphia, October 20, 1774.

Peyton Randolph President

Jno Sullivan } *New Hampshire*
Nath: Folsom

Thomas Cushing }
Samuel Adams } *Massachusetts*
John Adams } *Bay*
Robt. Treat Paine

laration of American Rights. This manifesto, adopted on October 14 and remarkable for its clarity and dignity, declared, among other things, that Parliament had imposed unjust taxes on the colonies, had burdened them with standing armies in times of peace, had dissolved their assemblies when they attempted to deliberate on grievances, and had treated their petitions for redress with contempt. The Intolerable Acts were characterized as "impolitic, unjust, and cruel, as well as unconstitutional." The colonists, the Congress asserted, were "entitled to life, liberty, and property and . . . had never ceded to any foreign power whatever, a right to dispose of either without their consent." Inasmuch as they were not represented in the British Parliament they were "entitled to a free and exclusive power of legislation in their several provincial legislatures where their right of representation can alone be preserved, in all cases of taxation and internal policy. . . ." These ideas were embodied in addresses to the king, to the British people, and to the inhabitants of the Province of Quebec.

The Declaration of Rights

But the radicals wanted something more than finely expressed declarations and well-worded petitions. Accordingly they succeeded after a hard struggle in pushing through a scheme known as the Association — a non-importation, non-consumption, non-exportation agreement — by means of which they hoped to paralyze Great Britain commercially and thus force the British ministry to accede to their demands. Beginning with December 1, 1774, no goods of any description were to be imported from the British Isles, directly or indirectly; if this failed to bring redress, then all exportation of colonial goods to Great Britain, Ireland, and the West Indies was to cease September 10, 1775. Anticipating the situation which would ensue from these coercive measures, the Congress agreed that "utmost endeavors" would be made to meet it. Agriculture, particularly the breeding of sheep, was to be stimulated. Local arts and manufactures were also to be encouraged, and profiteering was to be forbidden. Extravagance and dissipation, "especially all horseracing, and all kinds of gaming, cock-fighting, exhibitions

Congress adopts coercive measures: the Association

of shows, plays, and other expensive diversions and entertainments" were to be discouraged. Even the luxury of mourning was to be curtailed as in the days of 1765–1766.

Inasmuch as the Congress itself had been chosen in a highly irregular manner and was, therefore, an extra-legal body, it could not give legal sanction to its acts. But the radicals readily overcame this difficulty by decreeing that the Association covenant applied not only to its signers, but to every person in the colonies, and by providing detailed machinery for its enforcement. This machinery consisted of committees of "safety and inspection" in every county, city, and town, chosen by those qualified to vote for representatives in the colonial legislature. Each committee was to see that the Association covenant was complied with, and they were publicly to boycott and brand as an enemy of American liberty any one who dared violate its provisions. Goods imported by any one were to be seized by the committees and either stored or sold. If necessary, an entire province might be boycotted.

Radicals provide machinery for enforcement of Association covenant

The publication of the Association document met with a storm of protest from the conservatives who fully realized its revolutionary character. Merchants everywhere raised the question of why they should be compelled to sacrifice their trade for the benefit of farmers and mechanics and designing men of the stamp of Samuel Adams. Not a few declared that the conservative members of the Congress had been outwitted and out-manœuvered by the radicals. "You had all the honors," wrote one, "you had all the leading cards in every suit in your own hands, and yet, astonishing as it may appear to by-standers, you suffered sharpers to get the odd trick." In certain colonies, particularly New York and Connecticut, the conservatives held protest meetings and adopted resolutions derogatory to both Congress and the Association.

Conservatives condemn Association

But protest was well-nigh useless; the radical tide was too strong to stem. Between November, 1774, and the following June one after another of the colonies approved the work of the Congress, some ratifying the Association unanimously. Enforcement machinery was quickly set up in every colony but

Georgia, most of the committees, as might be expected, being composed of radicals. The New York, Philadelphia, and Boston committees, the conservatives asserted, were made up of "nobodies" and "unimportant persons." Governor Wright of South Carolina went so far as to declare that the Savannah committee was merely "a Parcel of the Lowest People, Chiefly Carpenters, Shoemakers, Blacksmiths, &c. . . ." But the committees, even though composed of the rank and file, functioned well, and the Association was vigorously enforced. In fact, English imports fell from £562,476 in 1774 to £71,625 in 1775 in the New England colonies; from £437,937 to £1,228 in New York; from £625,652 to £1,366 in Pennsylvania; from £528,738 to £1,921 in Maryland and Virginia; and from £378,116 to £6,245 in the Carolinas. In other words, import trade from England in 1775 declined almost ninety-seven per cent in comparison with the preceding year. English business men having financial interests in America bombarded Parliament and the British ministry with petitions praying for repeal of the obnoxious legislation of 1774.

Association ratified and enforced

But Lord North and his conservative followers, ignorant of the real situation in America and above all of the fact that the silent pressure of environment had given rise to a distinct American mind, were in no mood to listen to petitions and declarations. The colonists, they asserted, by refusing to obey the laws of Parliament and by creation of revolutionary agencies, such as the Association, had openly rebelled. And open rebellion must be suppressed even though it worked hardship for the time being on the British merchant and manufacturer. "An enemy in the bowels of a Kingdom," said Solicitor-General Wedderburn to the House of Commons, "is surely to be resisted, opposed, and conquered; notwithstanding the trade that may suffer, and the fabrics that may be ruined." Even the eloquence and arguments of Pitt and Burke, both of whom urged the repeal of the Intolerable Acts and the adoption of a conciliatory policy, were largely in vain. "Every motive of justice and of policy, of dignity and of prudence," warned Pitt before the House of Lords, "urges you to allay the ferment in America; by the

Attitude of Lord North and British conservatives

removal of your troops from Boston, by a repeal of your Acts of Parliament, and by a display of amicable disposition toward your colonies. On the other hand, every danger and every hazard impend to deter you from perseverance in your present ruinous course. Foreign war hanging over your head — by a slight and brittle thread; France and Spain watching your conduct and waiting for the maturity of your errors, with a vigilant eye to America and the temper of your colonies."

But the British conservatives, bounded intellectually by the immediate present and determined to have their way, refused to

Lord North's "olive branch" reso-lutions and the Restrain-ing Act heed this prophetic advice. Lord North, it is true, sponsored a set of "conciliatory resolutions," February 27, 1775, offering to relieve from parliamentary taxation any colony that would assume its share of imperial defense and make provision for the support of local officers of the Crown. This plan, however, was nullified (1) by an address to the king assuring him of support at all hazards in suppressing the rebellion, and (2) by the Restraining Act of March 30, 1775, which was designed to destroy the commerce of New England. By the terms of the Restraining Act the people of New England were cut off from the northern fisheries and their trade confined to Great Britain, Ireland, and the British West Indies until "the trade and commerce of His Majesty's subjects may be carried on without interruption." Less than a month later the Act was extended to New Jersey, Pennsylvania, Delaware, Maryland, Virginia, and South Carolina. Thus, wittingly or unwittingly, British conservatives coöperated with colonial radicals in closing the door against conciliation.

The situation already tense now became dangerous. While Parliament was listening to the entreaties of Pitt and Burke and

The situation becomes dangerous others and adding to its coercive measures, the triumphant radicals were busy strengthening their organization, enforcing the Association, stirring up a spirit of resistance among the people by means of inflammatory propaganda, drilling troops and gathering military supplies, and gaining a firmer foothold in the existing provincial governments or setting up governments of their own. The conservatives, defeated and bewildered, were on the defensive, while the great majority of the middle-grounders, without organization or program, knew not which way to turn. With the extremists on both sides of the Atlantic in control, and with each determined to coerce the other into submission, armed warfare was sooner or later inevitable.

The first blow was struck on April 19, 1775, when General Gage, military governor of Massachusetts, attempted to arrest two of the radical leaders, Samuel Adams and John Hancock, and to destroy military supplies which the radicals had collected at Concord. It is unnecessary for us to recount the exploits of Paul Revere and William Dawes who warned the countryside of Gage's intended action, or to describe the reception which the British regulars received at the hands of the colonial "minute men" at Lexington and Concord, for both are known to every American schoolboy. It is sufficient to keep in mind that these momentous events made the British conservatives more resolute and furnished the radicals with additional fuel for propaganda. Indeed, in every hamlet and town from Maine to Georgia Gage and his British redcoats were represented as "massacrers of innocent people," "butcherers," and the agents of "tyrannous despoilers of liberty."

The extremists come to blows: Lexington and Concord

While reports such as these were being circulated to the southward, thousands of New England troops, collected for the most part by the radical committees appointed to enforce the Association, began to pour into Cambridge just outside of Boston. In fact it was now evident that the extremists, especially those of New England, were determined to supplement peaceful coercion with military force, and that to this end they would leave no stone unturned to gain support from the Second Continental Congress which, according to resolution of the First Congress, was to assemble at Philadelphia on May 10, 1775.

Northern radicals determine to supplement peaceful coercion with military force

Similar to its predecessor in the irregularity of its election and in the fact that it included all shades of opinion, the new Congress was, nevertheless, much more radical in personnel. There were a few out and out conservatives, but these had no leader of the caliber of Joseph Galloway. Nearly all the delegates had had more or less political experience either in their local com-

The Second Continental Congress munities or in their colonial legislatures. Among them were a large majority of those destined to be the outstanding leaders of the Revolution: Washington, Jefferson, Harrison, Wythe, Richard Henry and Francis Lightfoot Lee from Virginia; Samuel and John Adams, Hancock, and Gerry from Massachusetts; Franklin and Morris from Pennsylvania; Reed and Rodney from Delaware; Sherman and Wolcott from Connecticut; and Rutledge from South Carolina. By far the greater number of them had been adversely affected economically by British policy.

With the election of John Hancock as president it was evident at the outset that the radicals were in control. But the more

Congress controlled by radicals and moves in direction of war and independence extreme leaders were compelled to proceed slowly at first, for the conservatives, though out-numbered, strenuously opposed every move away from conciliation and in the direction of independence. "Every important step," wrote John Adams, "was opposed and carried by bare majorities." Indeed, it was largely because of the conservative belief that the force of public opinion together with commercial coercion would force the British authorities to yield, that the Congress shortly after convening again petitioned King George III for a redress of grievances. But the move was in vain, and thereafter the Congress moved steadily in the direction of civil war and independence. Lord North's offer of peace was rejected on the ground that the obnoxious Acts had not been repealed or the right of Parliament to tax renounced; steps were taken to raise and equip an army, and Washington was appointed commander-in-chief, and plans were made for (1) encouragement of privateering and a fleet, (2) protection of the frontiers, (3) alliances with the Indians, (4) the more stringent enforcement of the Association, (5) securing assistance of outsiders, particularly England's European rivals, (6) a system of currency and credit, and (7) a national postal system.

Outside the Congress the idea of absolute independence spread rapidly from the closing weeks of 1775. Strengthened by the

course of events in both Great Britain and America and impatient of halfway measures, the radicals employed every means at their disposal to advance the scheme of complete separation. Press, pulpit, tavern, and provincial assembly were fertile seed-beds for its propagation. Conservative apologists who never tired of emphasizing the necessity for loyalty to the mother country were literally smothered by radical pamphleteers. None of these pamphleteers, not even Samuel Adams, approached Thomas Paine in effectiveness and influence.

Idea of complete independence gathers momentum

Radical propaganda

Born in England of Quaker parentage, Paine was in his thirty-seventh year when he first set foot on American soil in December, 1774. Already he had gained the reputation of being a social misfit and an enemy of all things aristocratic and monarchial, and it is not surprising, therefore, that he at once threw himself wholeheartedly into the colonial dispute. In January, 1776 — thirteen months after his arrival — he published his famous pamphlet, *Common Sense*, in which he set forth in brilliant fashion the economic and political arguments for complete independence. Sweeping aside the legal quibble which had long befogged the questions at issue, he went straight to the root of the matter. Government, he asserted, was merely a means to an end, and governmental policies always rested squarely on economic foundations. Whether the colonies ought to remain a part of the British Empire or not should be determined not on the basis of legal or constitutional precedents but on the ground of whether it was economically profitable for them or not. Commenting on this point he maintained with some disregard for fact that the colonies had from the first suffered economically and that whatever prosperity they enjoyed had been won in spite of English hostility and English exploitation. The mother country, he further maintained, had never shown generosity in its dealings with the colonies and instead of helping them had hampered their development by a meshwork of paternal restrictions. "America," said he, "would have flourished as much, and probably much more, had no European power taken any notice of her. The commerce by which she hath enriched herself are

Thomas Paine's Common Sense

the necessaries of life and will always have a market while eating is the custom of Europe. As Europe is our market for trade we ought to form no partial connection with any part of it. It is the true interest of America to steer clear of European connections, which she never can do while by her dependence on Britain she is made the makeweight in the scale of British politics." Single-handed he attacked the British constitution, which conservatives and radicals alike had lauded to the skies, and pointed out wherein he believed it was inadequate to colonial needs. It was nonsense, he declared, to assume that England was the mother of the colonies: "Europe and not England is the parent country of America. This new world hath been the Asylum for the persecuted lovers of civil and religious liberty from every part of Europe. Hither they have fled, not from the tender embraces of the mother but from the cruelty of the monster." It was absurd, he said, that an island three thousand miles away should control a continent. The Crown and all that it symbolized was likewise mercilessly flayed, for the king, Paine asserted, could only make war and give away places. "A pretty business, indeed, for a man to be allowed eight hundred thousand sterling a year for, and worshipped into the bargain! Of more worth is one honest man to society, and in the sight of God, than all the crowned ruffians that ever lived." The colonies, he concluded, should abandon their petitions and their expressions of loyalty and formally declare their independence.

The effect of *Common Sense* on colonial public opinion was amazing. Many men who up to the time of its publication were

Effect of Common Sense more or less governed in their attitude and action by a sense of loyalty to the king and by reverence for English traditions, saw things in a new light. Bitter antagonism and even hatred replaced the old feelings of loyalty and sentimental attachment for things British. Especially was this true of the rank and file, for Paine phrased his arguments in language that the ordinary man could understand, and hundreds of thousands of his pamphlets were sold.

That Paine's work as well as that of the other radical pamphleteers, the news of the Restraining Act, and the numerous military encounters between the British and the colonists, were bearing fruit for the radicals was soon evident by the pronounced drift of public opinion in favor of independ- Provincial assence during the early months of 1776. Nowhere, semblies favor perhaps, was this tendency more apparent than independence in the action of the provincial assemblies. As early as 1774 all the colonies except New York and Georgia, where the conservatives were strongly entrenched, had laid the foundations for complete revolutionary governments in the form of provincial congresses, conventions, or conferences. By the autumn of 1775 the old colonial governments had in large measure disappeared, their power being taken over by the new-born but vigorous revolutionary governments. Though usually controlled by the radicals, these new governments were at first somewhat slow in deciding for complete independence. In fact, the five Middle colonies specifically instructed their delegates to the Second Continental Congress to oppose any move in the direction of independence, and as late as January, 1776, not more than a third of the members of the Congress were willing to vote for a definite break with the mother country. By the spring of 1776, however, the tide was flowing strongly in the opposite direction. Massachusetts led the way by informing her delegates at Philadelphia that she was in favor of independence. In April North Carolina explicitly approved such a step, and about a month later Virginia instructed her representatives in the Congress to propose independence. Thus one after another the several colonies fell into line until by the end of June even the more reluctant, like Maryland, had given their assent.

Only a semblance of the old governmental régime remained, and sentiment in favor of separation was strong and daily growing stronger. Radicals both in and out of Congress Congress votes openly declared that the hour had come to break for separation completely with Britain and to embark on the uncharted sea of absolute independence. They had not long to wait, for on June 7 Richard Henry Lee, on behalf of the Virginia delegation, moved that "these united colonies are, and of right ought to be free and independent states," that a plan of confederation be prepared, and that effectual measures be taken to secure

foreign alliances. John Adams, in seconding the motion, argued
for an immediate declaration. But the conservatives and even
some of the middle-grounders held back. The people, they
asserted, had not yet demanded such a measure and the Middle
colonies "were not yet ripe for bidding adieu to British connection." After considerable debate final decision on the question
was postponed for three weeks, and a committee consisting of
four radicals, Thomas Jefferson, Benjamin Franklin, John
Adams, and Roger Sherman, and one moderate, Robert R.
Livingston, was appointed to prepare a formal declaration.
When the motion was again brought before the Congress on
July 1 nine colonies voted for it, Pennsylvania and South Carolina opposed it, the Delaware delegation was tied, and New
York was excused from voting. On the following day, however,
when the final vote was taken all except New York cast their
ballots in the affirmative. On July 4 the final draft of the Declaration was formally adopted, although it was not signed until
some weeks later.

Written under high emotional pressure and purposely designed to inspire and to win for the radical cause the support of
liberals on both sides of the Atlantic, the Declaration of Independence consists of two principal
parts: a preamble and a list of grievances. The
preamble, an eloquent statement of the Lockian philosophy of
natural rights applied to New World conditions, held as "self-
evident truths" that "all men are created equal, that they are
endowed by their Creator with certain inalienable Rights; that
among these are life, liberty, and the pursuit of happiness. That
to secure these Rights, governments are instituted among men,
deriving their just powers from the consent of the governed;
that whenever any form of government becomes destructive to
these ends, it is the right of the people to alter or to abolish it,
and to institute new government, laying its foundation on such
principles, and organizing its powers in such form, as to them
shall seem most likely to effect their Safety and Happiness."
Of the list of grievances, the majority of which concerned
George III, thus making him "the scapegoat for the Parliament
and the Ministry of Great Britain," some were overstated and

The Declaration of Independence

THOMAS PAINE

After the portrait by Romney

others difficult to prove. "The history of the present King of Great Britain," so ran the indictment, "is a history of repeated injuries and usurpations all having in direct object, the establishment of an absolute tyranny over these states." By refusing to give his assent to laws passed by the colonial legislatures, by repeatedly dissolving representative bodies, and by obstructing the administration of justice, he had, the document asserted, done all in his power to destroy local self-government. Moreover, he was charged with having "erected a multitude" of new offices in the colonies and of filling them with his henchmen, of quartering troops on the colonists, cutting off their commerce, arbitrarily imposing taxes on them, plundering and burning their towns, and murdering their people. Against such acts warnings, petitions, and remonstrances had been in vain and had been "answered only by repeated injury." "A Prince whose character is thus marked by every act which may define a Tyrant, is unfit to be the ruler of a free People."

Three or four days after its formal adoption, the Declaration was publicly read in Philadelphia and copies of it soon appeared in every community from Maine to Georgia. Its publication was doubly significant. It marked the complete triumph of the radicals; and it put an end to all hope of adjustment and conciliation. In England those who favored the American cause were powerless to effect any change in the policy of the administration; and in America the radicals, as we have seen, wanted no conciliation. To the moderates — those who had aligned themselves with neither conservatives nor radicals, and who had hoped that some sort of a compromise would be effected — the adoption and publication of the Declaration was almost tragic, for it meant that the hour had arrived when they must make the momentous decision of either casting their fortunes with the radicals, becoming "Patriots" and helping establish a new order, or remaining within the fold of the British Empire. Henceforth party lines were to be more sharply drawn. Outwardly at least one had to be either a patriot or a loyalist — and if the latter, he was in the eyes of the former an enemy and a traitor. From this time on, as we shall now see, the Revolution more clearly assumed a

Publication of Declaration marks complete triumph of radicals

double character: (1) A conflict between the imperial government and thirteen revolting provinces, and (2) a conflict between two American parties or groups — patriots and loyalists.

2. CIVIL WAR

From the standpoint of physiographic factors, economic interests, social customs, religious views, political ideals, and mental attitudes, colonial America on the eve of the Revolution, instead of being made up of thirteen separate units, was in reality composed of three diverse geographical areas: (1) The commercial North, extending from the port towns of Maine to the Chesapeake; (2) the tidewater region from Maryland to Georgia; and (3) the rather indefinite frontier stretching from Canada southward, bounded on the east by the older settled districts and on the west by the Alleghenies. Two questions regarding each of these areas are all-important. In the first place, what elements of the population in each of these three sections supported the Revolution and why? In the second place, to what extent were the supporters of the movement homogeneous?

Colonial America composed of three diverse geographic areas

In the commercial North, by far the greater part of the population, as we have noted, was composed of small tradesmen, mechanics, and yeoman farmers. Socially, economically, and politically they ranked beneath the ruling merchant class. They were individualistic, ignorant, and exceedingly narrow-minded. Franchise qualifications rather severely limited their participation in governmental affairs. In comparison with the great landholders and the merchants to whom they were usually in debt, they owned little property, and yet on their shoulders often fell the burden of taxation. Toward them, both the English official and the wealthy colonist assumed a snobbish attitude. Indeed, Cadwallader Colden of New York was not far wrong when, in 1765, he declared that they were "the most useful and the most moral, but allwise . . . the dupes" of the wealthier classes. Yet they were democratic and more or less enthusiastically supported the Revolution in the hope that by so doing they might destroy the

Supporters of the Revolution in commercial North

1. Small tradesmen, mechanics, and yeoman farmers

social, economic, and political grip both of England and of the ruling colonial group.

For the wealthy and conservative merchant class which had long dominated the commercial provinces, the question of supporting the Revolution was most perplexing and The crucial. On the one hand, they feared (1) that in- merchants dependence might lead to the establishment of a radical régime which would operate to their disadvantage; and (2) that complete separation from the Empire might seriously interfere with their customary trade operations, which constituted the chief source of their profits. On the other hand, pressure of environment and a large measure of economic freedom had developed in them a vigorous spirit of liberalism and home rule, both of which had been severely jolted by the British policy in effect since 1763. Moreover, many of them undoubtedly realized that opposition to the Revolution might mean ruin for their business, ostracism, imprisonment, confiscation of their wealth, and even banishment. Finally, the radical propaganda that independence would materially benefit the merchant as well as other men of means was not without its effect. One writer, for example, declared that independence would probably mean "a free and unlimited trade; a great accession of wealth, and a proportionate rise in the value of land; the establishment, gradual improvement, and perfection of manufactures and science; a vast influx of foreigners . . .; an astonishing increase of our people from the present stock." "Some think they say everything against a state of independence," wrote another, "by crying out that in a state of dependence we enjoyed the protection of Great Britain. . . . But do we not pay dearly for this protection? The restriction of our trade alone is worth ten times the protection, besides the sums we pay in customs and other duties to the amount of more than a million annually. The customs of the port of London alone are worth £2,000,000 per annum. Let us for once suppose an independency, that we may observe the consequence. We should then trade with every nation that would trade with us. . . . Suppose we were attacked by some foreign power in this state of independency, for this is the bugbear: what then? The nation that would be fool enough to do it would raise a hornet's nest about its ears. Every nation which enjoyed a share of our trade would be guarantee for the peaceable behaviour and good conduct of its neighbors . . . To ask what we should do for fleets to protect our trade, is as absurd as to ask if timber grows in America . . . Our trade will protect itself. It will never be the interest of any nation to disturb our trade while we trade freely with it, and it will ever be our interest to trade freely with all nations. As long as the wide Atlantic Ocean rolls between us and Europe, so long will we be free from foreign subjection were we once clear of Great Britain." It was with arguments such as these that the radicals bombarded the doubting merchants, and in the end many of the latter came to the conclusion either to endeavor to steer a middle course or heartily support the American cause.

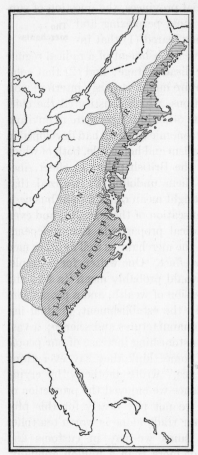

GEOGRAPHIC-ECONOMIC SECTIONS OF COLONIAL AMERICA AT THE EVE OF THE REVOLUTION

In the tidewater region, long controlled by an aristocratic planting class, the question of complete independence led to sharp divisions. In Georgia the great majority opposed the movement, for the colony was less affected by the new imperial policy of the mother country and was still dependent on the home government for subsidies and for protection against the Indians. For somewhat different reasons more than half the people of South Carolina were not in favor of creating an untried and, as they thought, radical democracy. Virginia, on the other hand, which was socially and religiously more akin to England than any of her sister colonies, was, like New England, a patriot stronghold. Three economic factors explain in large measure why the Lees and Washingtons and other Virginians of their stamp, who imitated the manners and tastes of the English nobility, who educated their sons in English universities and supported the Anglican Church, joined hands with the radicals of the commercial provinces and the liberty-loving frontiersmen in the revolt against the mother country.

Question of complete independence causes sharp division in tidewater region

The first of these factors was the land problem. Wasteful methods of cultivation and the rapid increase in population resulted in a fairly sharp advance in the price of meadow-lands in the tidewater and Piedmont sections between 1750 and 1775. Indeed, as early as 1759 Governor Dinwiddie had informed the Board of Trade that the best lands of the colony had already been preëmpted, and by 1774 the available supply east of the Proclamation Line of 1763 had practically all been taken. To colonial planters and speculators, who coveted the fertile expanses beyond the Alleghenies, the Proclamation of 1763 was nothing more or less than a selfish policy designed to promote the interests of Old World court favorites, politicians, and speculators. The proposal of the home government, for example, to hand the Kentucky and Ohio country over to the Walpole Company — an English organization including Lord Camden and the Earl of Hertford and sponsored by George Grenville — instead of granting it to Virginia land companies, angered and alarmed the Virginians. Their ire was also roused by the refusal of the mother country to permit the survey of certain transallegheny bounty lands which George Washington and other far-seeing Virginians had purchased. Nor did the somewhat tardy decision of the British ministry to open the West for settlement placate the irate

Economic factors alienate loyal Virginians

1. Ownership of land

colonials, for free land grants were prohibited, a new system of surveys preventing indiscriminate locations was prescribed, all lands were to be sold at auction, and quitrents were doubled. For that part of the agricultural South which was interested in western lands complete independence would mean an end of all such restrictive measures as the Proclamation of 1763 as well as of the entire quitrent system. Before the Revolution was over Washington and many other Virginians had secured title to the lands denied them a few years earlier by the British government. Moreover, of approximately four thousand western land grants made before the conflict ended, four-fifths were issued to Virginians.

Less important perhaps than the land question in winning planter support for the Revolution was the problem of the **2. Public finance** public finances. Virginia secured its revenue from three principal sources: (1) quitrents, (2) customs duties, (3) poll taxes. While the total public income from these sources varied from year to year, there was usually a substantial balance after current expenses, including the salaries of royal officials, had been taken care of. Thus in 1773 there was a favorable balance from the quitrents and the customs of nearly £10,000. But all balances from these two sources instead of being at the disposal of the colonial assembly went into the royal treasury. With the cost of local government mounting annually it was, therefore, necessary for the assembly to increase the poll tax. Naturally, the planter, fully cognizant of the situation, did not view it with complacency. As in the case of the western lands, he felt that he was being victimized for the benefit of the mother country. And the rapid curtailment of the currency during the ten years preceding the Revolution greatly added to his discontent and unrest.

Finally, the vast majority of the great landed proprietors of the tidewater were head over heels in debt to British merchants, **3. Indebtedness** a condition which arose primarily from their wasteful system of marketing. Jefferson estimated that the Virginia planters owed at least £2,000,000 and that "these debts had become hereditary from father to son, for many generations, so that the planters were a species of property annexed to certain mercantile houses in London." In 1791 a group of British merchants submitted a statement to their government listing the debts due them from American customers in 1775. The total principal and interest amounted to £4,930,656, and of this £4,137,944 — over five-sixths — was due from states south of Pennsylvania; Virginians alone owed £2,305,408. John Randolph's father, for example, owed the London firm of Capel and Osgood Hanbury £11,000 and was also a heavy debtor to Jones and Farrell. Archibald Cary owed the Hanburys over £7,000 and Archibald Lidderdale and Company nearly £3,000. Jones and Farrell of London and Kippen and Company of Glasgow held bonds against Thomas Jefferson for approximately £10,000. Benjamin Harrison, Edmund Pendleton, the Lees, Flemings, Marshalls, and others, were also heavy debtors. With their plantations, slaves, and sometimes their furniture and ungrown crops mortgaged beyond their actual value, it seemed in 1775 that nothing less than virtual repudiation could save them. Indeed, between 1750 and 1775 the provincial assemblies passed a series of lax Bankruptcy Acts as well as other measures detrimental to non-resident creditors. Although these laws were nearly always killed by royal veto, they nevertheless indicate the ends to which the planter debtor was willing to go to extricate himself from a precarious financial state. Even before the complete break with the mother country came, Jefferson and Patrick Henry made the sweeping proposal in an extra-legal meeting of the Virginia Assembly that all payments on British debts be stopped; subsequently a statute was passed which confiscated these debts and provided that they might be paid into the Virginia treasury. During the war more than five hundred Virginians paid off their sterling debts due to British merchants in depreciated paper currency. In other words, the Revolution afforded at least a temporary cure for their financial ills.

These three economic factors, coupled with a deep aversion to any encroachment upon what seemed to them to be their civil and political rights, were the chief agencies which transformed the planters psychologically from loyalists to patriots.

The merchant class in the tidewater region, small in compari-

son with that of the commercial provinces, was composed for the
most part of factors and agents for British trading houses and

Majority of tidewater merchant class not in favor of Revolution

was, therefore, opposed to the Revolution. It had
nothing in common with the northern radicals; the
continental Association was injurious to its business,
and the commercial policy of the mother country,
which the northern provinces had attempted to
break down, was beneficial to it. Consequently no effort was
made to win its support, the radical writers concentrating on
the point that complete independence would free the planters
from the financial grip of the factors and the British mercantile
houses. "You are without merchants, ships, seamen, or shipbuilders," wrote one; "your trade is confined to a single spot on
the globe, in the hands of the natives of a distant island, who fix
the market for all commodities at their pleasure, and we may be
very sure will rate yours at the lowest, and their own at the
highest prices, they will in any conscience bear. Every article of
merchandise, that is not the produce of Britain, must first pay
its duties to the Crown, perhaps must be increased in the price
a very large advance per cent there, and then be re-exported to
Virginia, and undergo an additional advance of seventy-five,
and sometimes near one hundred and fifty per cent there." By
buying from the factors, he went on to say, the Virginians were
losing £200,000 annually. Of the fifty foreign houses that he
estimated had control of the trade of the colony, each it was
"not unreasonable to say" made £15,000 a year net gain
"which will be just so much saved to the colony whenever its
own natives shall become its merchants." Virginia tobacco, he
declared, for which the factors paid a mere pittance, yielded
their houses an enormous profit. He concluded that, all told,
dependence on the factor system cost Virginia not less than
£5,987,500 annually, all of which could be saved by casting free
from Britain.

The third section, the long-drawn-out frontier, settled mostly
by German and Scotch-Irish freeholders, not only favored the
American cause but gave it impetus. By training and environment its inhabitants were democratic. Nearly all were Dissenters, and no social or economic tie, such as influenced the

merchant and planter classes, bound them to England. Like the voteless mechanics and artisans of the older settled regions they believed in equality and keenly resented the social, economic, and political domination of the seaboard aristocracy, whether merchants, clergy, or professional men of New England, Quaker oligarchy of Philadelphia, holders of manors on the Hudson, or tobacco and rice planters of tidewater Virginia and South Carolina. They gladly arrayed themselves, therefore, on the side of revolution, hoping thereby, like the unenfranchised proletariat of the coast towns, to secure that complete independence and freedom of action for which they were so valiantly struggling.

Majority of frontiersmen favor American cause

It would be a grave mistake for us to conclude from what has just been said that the great majority of the colonists at all times actively supported the Revolution. Just how many were back of it heart and soul at any stage we do not know. John Adams was of the opinion that not more than one-third of the people opposed it at any time. On the other hand, Joseph Galloway, Tory exile from Pennsylvania, testifying before a parliamentary committee in 1779 declared that at the beginning of the struggle less than one-fifth of the entire colonial population favored independence, and that even after three years more than four-fifths of the colonists favored union with Great Britain "upon constitutional principles" rather than independence. Both Adams and Galloway probably exaggerated, for both were biased. Moreover, they failed to take into account that opinion was easily swayed by the fortunes of war. Lecky, the English historian, was probably much nearer right in his statement that "the American Revolution, like most others, was the work of an energetic minority who succeeded in committing an undecided and fluctuating majority to courses for which they had little love, and leading them step by step to a position from which it was impossible to recede."

Revolution the work of an energetic minority

If the actual number of active supporters of the movement at any particular time was not large it was not the fault of the more radical patriots. From first to last they worked almost incessantly for the American cause, and there was no community from Maine to Georgia that was not flooded with their propa-

Propaganda and the Revolution   ganda. From pen and printing press came hundreds of pamphlets, letters, newspaper articles, and cartoons, all calculated to inform, encourage, and inspire. The private house, tavern, and grog-shop were alike patriot strongholds and the scenes of heated debate and discussion. Even the pulpit played its part, patriot preachers everywhere losing no opportunity to denounce "British oppression" and advance the cause of independence. "The few that pretend to preach," complained the Tory diarist, Nicholas Cresswell, "are mere retailers of politics, sowers of sedition and rebellion, who serve to blow the cole of discord and excite the people to arms. The Presbyterian clergy are particularly active in supporting the measures of Congress from the rostrum, gaining proselytes, persecuting the unbelievers, preaching up the righteousness of their cause, and persuading the unthinking populace of the infallibility of success!" The carefully reasoned arguments justifying the revolt on constitutional grounds and on the basis of natural rights which were still advanced, doubtless won some converts for the radicals, but for the rank and file of the colonists fine-spun theories often obscured the real issues. For them the cartoon, the lampoon, or the plain speech of a Thomas Paine was vastly more effective than dozens of legalistic, philosophical tracts or speeches. Indeed, it was the passionate plea or the threats of social boycott or violence couched in everyday language that usually stirred the lukewarm and the sluggish to action.

But many of the colonists could not be persuaded, either by propaganda or threats, to forsake their loyalty to Great Britain.

The Loyalists   In the past, historians and others have unjustly described the Tories or Loyalists as despicable cowards and king-worshippers, whose only ambition was to enjoy the spoils of political office. That a few may have been of this stamp is beyond question, but the vast majority were men of the highest character and principle. Included in their ranks were (1) great landowners such as the Van Cortlandts, Crugers, De Lanceys, De Peysters, Jessups, and Philipses of

New York; (2) rich merchants like the Whartons, Penningtons, and Pembertons of Philadelphia, and the Higginsons, Chandlers, and Hutchinsons of Boston; (3) large numbers of professional men — lawyers, physicians, and college authorities; (4) many prosperous farmers; (5) the majority of crown officials; (6) many of the Anglican clergy and laity; (7) those who aped the English aristocracy and who for one reason or another hated radicalism and democracy; and (8) some from the lower ranks of society who depended on Loyalist merchant or landowner for a livelihood. In all probability the Loyalists comprised at least one-third of the entire population of the thirteen revolting colonies; in three — New York, Pennsylvania, and South Carolina — they were easily in the majority. Many of the Loyalists suffered from arbitrary acts of Parliament and were as anxious for reform as the most ardent patriot, but insisted, as we have noted, that whatever the wrongs, they should be righted by petition and compromise and not by violence and mob rule. In the opinion of the Loyalists the Revolution was a conspiracy and the conspirators, in the words of one of the Loyalist leaders, "an infernal, dark-designing group of men . . . obscure, pettifogging attorneys, bankrupt shopkeepers, outlawed smugglers, . . . wretched banditti, . . . the refuse and dregs of mankind."

Against the Loyalists, who lacked both the organization and aggressiveness of the Revolutionists, the Patriots waged warfare that was even more bitter and relentless than that carried on against Great Britain. During the conflict great numbers of Loyalists flocked to the royal colors or, in a few instances, organized militia companies of their own under commissions from the crown. New York alone furnished fifteen thousand men. Much to the disappointment of the British authorities, however, their military service was not commensurate with their numerical strength, their expedition against the coast towns of Connecticut which burned Fairfield and Norwalk and their coöperation with the Indians in the cruel Wyoming and Cherry Valley massacres being their outstanding exploits. Many loyalist privateers did injury to patriot shipping. Nor should we overlook the almost savage

Their military service to Great Britain

guerilla warfare between Patriot and Loyalist that characterized the history of the South during these hectic years.

Those Loyalists not under the immediate protection of the British armies suffered all sorts of hardship. No sooner had the Treatment of conflict with the mother country begun than the cry Loyalists was raised for punishment of all those who refused to declare themselves on the side of the Revolution. Even before the Declaration of Independence was signed revolutionary committees in every colony were warning the Loyalists to be quiet, depriving them of their arms, and compelling them to adhere to the Association. As the struggle progressed and it became evident that some of the Loyalists could not be intimidated or coerced into supporting the patriot cause, the Revolutionists resorted to more drastic measures. All who refused to take an oath of allegiance were denied the rights of citizenship; they could neither vote, hold office, nor enjoy court protection. In many cases they were even forbidden to pursue their professions or to acquire or dispose of property. Free speech was denied them, and they were forbidden to travel, or go near or trade with the British armies. When many of these laws failed to accomplish their purpose the more ardent Loyalists were jailed, sent to detention camps, banished, tarred and feathered, or otherwise cruelly treated, or even put to death.

How many Loyalists were banished we do not know. Nearly all of the new state governments enacted legislation banishing Banishment those who for any reason refused to swear allegiance to the revolutionary governments. In September, 1778, Massachusetts banished about two hundred and sixty, including fifty-three merchants, sixty "esquires," twenty-four mariners, and a number of former state and crown officers. In the same year New Hampshire exiled thirty "gentlemen," eight merchants, four doctors, and others. In 1779 New York banished a number of her wealthy and prominent citizens, and the next year Rhode Island did likewise. In the South, particularly in the Carolinas, where an intensely bitter struggle between the two factions ensued, banishment was the order of the day. Before the war was over probably more than a hundred thousand Loyalists died or were exiled — a great number of able citizens for a struggling frontier community to lose.

To banishment was added confiscation of property. The conflict had scarcely begun when Thomas Paine, the vigorous and resourceful author of *Common Sense*, advised the Patriots to appropriate the property of the Loyalists for the purpose of defraying the expenses of the war. Several of the states soon took up the suggestion. Any fears which they may have entertained respecting the wisdom of their action were quickly dispelled when late in 1777 Congress advised the states to confiscate and sell the real and personal property of those who had forfeited "the right to protection" and to invest the proceeds in Continental certificates. Though some of the more conservative Patriots protested that confiscation was unjust and "contrary to the principles of civil liberty," statutes of condemnation and forfeiture were enacted in all the former colonies before the war was over. Many of these Acts placed the Loyalist completely at the mercy of those who labeled him a traitor. In Massachusetts, for example, mere publication in a local newspaper that his property was to be seized was sufficient, and if he did not appear, trial by jury was omitted from the proceedings. The property of those who had been banished or who had fled could thus be taken over without their knowledge. Many persons were the unfortunate victims of those who had a grudge against them, and evidence abounds that in every state the execution of the sequestration laws was frequently attended with scandal and corruption. The amount of property seized is somewhat problematic; claims totaling over £10,000,000 were filed with the commission established by the British Parliament, and of these less than £1,000,000 were disallowed.

Faced with the opposition of both the Loyalists and the imperial government and without an army or navy, a national treasury, or even a well-organized central government, the Patriots at the outset were confronted with baffling obstacles. To make matters worse, each of the thirteen states not only regarded itself as absolutely independent, but was jealous of both its sister states and the

Continental Congress.   Each was more concerned with its own civil and military problems than with those growing out of the common cause.   Within each there was often utter lack of unanimity, even among the Patriots.   That the patriot leaders were able to cope with these obstacles and others of similar character and to carry the Revolution through to a successful conclusion is fitting testimony to their character and ability.

Of all the troubles with which the inexperienced Continental Congress, upon whose reluctant shoulders fell in no small measure the fiscal, military, and diplomatic burdens of the struggle, had to contend, none perhaps was more perplexing than the raising of money.   Created in an emergency and regarded merely as the instrument of thirteen sovereign states, the Continental Congress did not enjoy the power of taxation.   Consequently it was compelled to resort to other sources in order to secure the revenue necessary for carrying on the many activities connected with the war.

Financing the Revolution

By far the most productive of these expedients was paper money.   Although the practice of issuing paper money had been checked, as we have seen, by the British Parliament in 1764, Congress authorized an issue of $2,000,000 less than a week after the battle of Bunker Hill. Before the end of the year 1779, when Congress voted to limit the amount of bills in circulation to not more than $200,000,000, no less than forty issues totaling $241,552,780 were authorized, as follows:

1. Paper money

Year	Number of resolutions authorizing issues	Amounts
1775	3	$6,000,000
1776	4	19,000,000
1777	5	13,000,000
1778	14	63,500,300
1779	14	140,052,480
Total	40	$241,552,780 [1]

[1] Davis Rich Dewey, *Financial History of the United States*, p. 36.

PHILIPSE MANOR IN 1784
The beautiful estate of a leading Tory

To the continental issues the several states added no less than
$209,524,776 in paper notes, making a grand total of over
$450,000,000. Nearly all of the paper put out by the states
was issued by Virginia and the Carolinas. Both the state and
continental notes were frequently counterfeited by both the
English and the Americans, although Congress and the states
repeatedly took steps to suppress the counterfeiting.

Inasmuch as Congress did not have the power to tax, it felt
that it could neither redeem the continental notes, which incidentally ranged in denomination from one-sixth of   Redemption
a dollar to sixty-five dollars, nor declare them to be   and accept-
                                                          ance of paper
legal tender. Accordingly it recommended that   as legal
they be redeemed by the states on a basis of popu-   tender
lation, and that the several states enact the necessary legislation
to make them legal tender for all debts. It did, however, go so
far as to resolve that if any person should "be so lost to all
virtue and regard for his country" as to refuse to accept the
notes, he should be "deemed an enemy of his country." The
states heeded the legal tender suggestions but paid little attention to the recommendations for redemption. In 1780 Congress
recommended that the Continental paper money already issued
be exchanged for new five year interest-bearing notes redeemable in specie. Under this law $119,400,000 of the old notes were
received and cancelled. Under the Funding Act of 1790, the old
notes were accepted in payment for government bonds at the
rate of one hundred to one. Only $6,000,000 of the $78,000,000,
the amount estimated to be outstanding, was received, the rest
probably having been lost or destroyed.

Since its value rested wholly on the success of the struggle and
the willingness of the states to redeem it, so much unsecured
paper inevitably depreciated. At first the de-   Depreciation
preciation was not great, but by 1779 it had be-   and its effect
come marked. By January, 1781, it took one hundred dollars in
paper to acquire one dollar in silver; less than six months later
the paper was practically worthless and had all but ceased to
pass as currency. Indeed, one writer, Breck, declared that its
annihilation was so complete that barbershops were papered in
jest with the bills; and the sailors, being paid off in bundles of

this worthless money on returning from their cruises, had suits of clothes made of it and with characteristic light-heartedness turned their loss into a frolic by parading through the streets in decayed finery, which in its better days had passed for thousands of dollars. In fact, to be "not worth a continental" was equivalent to being utterly worthless. As might be expected, prices shot upwards and many persons soon found it extremely difficult to pay their debts. In 1781 a pair of shoes cost $100 in paper money, a bushel of corn $40, a pound of tea $90, and a barrel of flour $1,575. Speculators with an eye to profit attempted to control the market by purchase of the available supply or else by buying up the goods before they reached the market. "One great reason," resolved a Boston town meeting in 1778, "of the present Excessive Price of Provisions in this Town arises from the Avarice, Injustice, and Inhumanity of certain Persons within Twenty Miles of it, who purchase great Part of the same of Farmers living at a greater Distance and put an exhorbitant Advance upon it." In some of the states the monopolizers and engrossers were not only denounced but fined and imprisoned. The New England states, as well as several of the others, held conventions where the cognate questions of currency, taxes, and prices were discussed. At the suggestion of Congress attempts were made to fix the price of both labor and commodities, but generally speaking they availed little. Had the majority of the colonists been wage or salary earners instead of farmers, the distress occasioned by the depreciation and rising prices would undoubtedly have been appalling.

In its desperate effort to secure funds Congress also resorted to requisitions. This method, however, was little more success-

2. Requisitions ful than when employed by Great Britain in earlier times. The four requisitions between November, 1777, and October, 1779, for a total of $95,000,000 in paper money yielded only $54,667,000, which in specie was equivalent to the small sum of $1,856,000. The three specie requisitions of August, 1780, November, 1780, and March, 1781, for $3,000,000, $1,642,988, and $6,000,000 respectively, a total of about $10,643,000, brought returns of only $1,592,222. The net revenue obtained from all the requests upon the states for money up to January 1, 1784, was only $5,795,000 in specie. Each state, ignorant or indifferent to the facts, insisted that it had paid more than its share, or at least was afraid that it might do so. Congress also resorted in 1780 to requisitioning commodities, the states being called upon for corn, flour, beef, pork, hay, and other supplies. In return for these the army quartermasters issued certificates. It has been estimated that the value of these certificates in gold specie totaled $16,708,000. While considerable quantities of supplies were obtained by this means, it soon became evident that it was both wasteful and inefficient. Grain and flour, for example, spoiled for lack of money to transport them, or they were stolen outright. Often when horses and wagons were impressed into service the owners would secrete their horses and render their wagons useless by removing a wheel or some other indispensable part. The method of requisitioning supplies, Washington informed Congress, was the "most uncertain, expensive, and injurious that could be devised."

Domestic and foreign loans constituted the third device used by Congress to secure funds. Indented certificates, similar to modern coupon bonds, in denominations ranging **3. Loans** from $300 to $1,000 and bearing from four to six per cent interest were disposed of in each of the states through loan offices set up for that purpose. Between sixty and seventy million dollars in paper was subscribed, which in specie **Domestic** was worth approximately $7,500,000. In addition to the loan office certificates, a mass of certificates were issued by quartermasters and other military officers and agents for food, clothing, horses, wagons, and other necessities for the army. Alexander Hamilton, first Secretary of the Treasury, estimated that these obligations outstanding in 1790 totaled $16,708,000. Short-time and temporary loans for small amounts were also obtained during the closing years of the war from the new Bank of North America. The foreign loans, though less in face value than the domestic, were in all probability **Foreign** more than equal in specie value to all the coupon-bearing certificates sold at home. During the first years of the war small subsidies were secured from France and Spain. Beginning in 1777 these were supplemented by government loans as indicated in the accompanying table.

FOREIGN LOANS TO UNITED STATES DURING REVOLUTION [1]

Year	France	Spain	Holland
1777	$181,500		
1778	544,500		
1779	181,500		
1780	726,000		
1781	1,737,763	$128,804	
1782	1,892,237	45,213	$720,000
1783	1,089,000		584,000
Total	$6,352,500	$174,017	$1,304,000

[1] Davis Rich Dewey, *Financial History of the United States*, p. 46.

Private Dutch bankers were also induced to lend over a million dollars during the last years of the struggle when victory for the patriot cause was assured. All these foreign loans were indefinite in length, or else for periods of not over fifteen years; practically all of them bore five per cent interest. Most of the money obtained from the foreign loans was used to purchase supplies in the Old World; some of it, however, reached this side of the Atlantic, one installment from France being used to pay interest on the domestic loans, and another to furnish the specie necessary for the founding of the Bank of North America. It is difficult to see how the patriot cause could have carried on without financial aid from abroad.

The total cost of the Revolution from the standpoint of funds to carry it on has been variously estimated; in all probability it Total cost of was slightly over $100,000,000. That any appreci-Revolution able part of this amount could, at the time, have been raised by taxation is doubtful. A large part of the moveable wealth of the country, as the Beards point out, was in the possession of the Loyalists who fled the country. With some exceptions, the farmers who made up the bulk of the population had little or no money with which to pay taxes. Moreover, the fact that in the minds of the people the question of taxation was one of the major aspects of the Revolution itself was not without its psychological effect. Finally, those ignorant of basic economic principles could see no reason why taxes should be assessed when the printing presses, as one member of Congress said, could turn out paper money by the wagon load.

The fiscal machinery set up by Congress during the Revolution was such as to invite chaos. Because of persistent jealousies in the Congress itself and among the states, and **Administra-** because of fear of centralized authority, an inde- **tion of finances** pendent treasury was not established until the Revolution was almost over. At the outset it experimented with two treasurers, both appointed by majority vote, one to receive and the other to pay out the public funds. This arrrangement soon gave way to a financial committee of thirteen congressional delegates, which in turn was supplemented in 1776 by a treasury board of five members. Three years later this treasury board was set aside to make way for a new one of five members, three of whom could not be congressional delegates. Finally, early in 1781, Congress abolished this board and provided for a superintendent of finance. For this position Robert Morris, an experienced Philadelphia merchant and financier, was chosen.

On paper Morris was given wide powers, but state pride, jealousy, and bickering faced him at every turn. He wrestled with the situation for three years, during which he **Robert Morris** endeavored to increase the requisitions from the states, to put new life into the loan policy, both domestic and foreign, to create a national revenue, and place the currency of the country on a specie basis. Discouraged with the results of his labors and by the many charges that he was using his office to further his private interests, Morris resigned in 1783. Whether he was guilty of irregularities in his accounts and of speculating with public funds — two of the most serious charges leveled against him — is to this day a matter of dispute. Morris himself indignantly denied the accusations, which he answered in great detail. His friends also staunchly asserted his innocence. Others, including those who have delved into the matter, are of the opinion that he knowingly allowed his private interests to become entangled with public affairs and that he was not, therefore, impartially devoted to the welfare of the public. Be that as it may, one thing seems certain: Morris did vastly more than had previously been done to bring order out of chaos.

The blundering manner in which the Second Continental Congress handled the financial side of the Revolution was characteristic of the way it dealt with every other aspect of the struggle. From first to last its evident lack of experience, authority, and ability to get things done and done quickly was manifest on every hand. What it did do was often done in a seemingly half-hearted manner. Under the circumstances, however, it is doubtful if it could have done differently. Most of its members were extremely provincial in outlook and had no conception of the magnitude of the struggle on which they had embarked. Jealousy was rampant, and with a divided population there was lacking the unity of purpose and whole-hearted coöperation essential in the prosecution of all great enterprises. Moreover, and in some respects most important of all, real power and authority rested, as we have noted, with each state; the Congress labored under an almost insuperable disadvantage in executing and accomplishing when authority to do so was wanting.

Shortcomings and handicaps of Continental Congress

On the military side there were perhaps two additional reasons for the dilatory manner in which the Congress acted during the first years of the conflict; namely, the underrating of British strength and the feeling that Great Britain would yield rather than engage in a fight to the finish — both of which inferences might be drawn on the basis of British conduct during the Intercolonial Wars. But Britain was no weakling, and she had no intention of yielding. At the outset her military leaders reasoned that inasmuch as New England was the hotbed of rebellion they would isolate it by sending expeditions up from New York along the Hudson and down from Canada by way of Lake Champlain, and then crush it by means of an army operating from Boston. But this plan was given up as impossible of execution, and was succeeded

Military plans of Great Britain

by another by which British naval forces would occupy and bottle up all the principal colonial ports, using these ports as centers from which to destory colonial shipping. Fortunately for the Patriots' cause this plan was not put into execution; in fact, it was abandoned in favor of a scheme for occupying colonies like New York, Pennsylvania, and South Carolina where the Loyalists were numerically strong. It was this plan that made easier Washington's task of forcing Howe out of Boston and which accounts for Clinton's attack on Charleston and the British occupation of New York and Philadelphia during the years 1776–1777.

The colonists were pitifully unprepared to meet these plans. Without a seasoned army or the means of supporting one, and fearful lest a powerful armed force might mean Inadequacy of military dictatorship, it was nevertheless virtually the continental army compelled by circumstances to transform the motley array that had rushed to besiege the British in Boston into the continental army with Washington as commander-in-chief. A few months later it supplemented this action by advising the states to enroll in the militia all able-bodied men between sixteen and fifty. The enormousness of Washington's task can hardly be imagined. The supply of arms and ammunition was scarce, and the men were raw, undisciplined, mercenary, and inclined to desert on the slightest provocation. "Such a dearth of public spirit, and want of virtue, such stock-jobbing, and fertility in all the low arts to obtain advantages of one kind and another, . . . I never saw before, and pray God I may never be witness to again," wrote the commander-in-chief. "Such a dirty, mercenary spirit pervades the whole I should not be at all surprised at any disaster that may happen." In February, 1776, when he found that instead of twenty thousand troops he had less than half that number, he urged Congress to abandon the militia and to create a national army, a step which that body failed to take until eight months later, when it voted to raise eighty-eight battalions totaling 63,000 men. Even then it was unable to secure recruits, despite the fact that it offered a bounty of twenty pounds and a hundred acres of land, and was obliged to "advise" the states to fill their quotas by draft. At no time did the army have ready for service more than a small part of its paper enrollment. And what was true of men was equally true of necessary equipment and supplies. Furthermore, by listening to Horatio Gates, Thomas Conway, Thomas Mifflin, and Charles Lee — a group of designing men anxious to curb Washington's authority and perhaps oust him from command — and by establishing a military board of control, the Congress undoubtedly handicapped and embarrassed Washington in his movements.

The weakness of the patriot army and the dilatoriness of Congress, as well as British strength, were reflected in the operations of 1776–1777. Washington met defeat in his campaign about New York and at the battles of Brandywine and Germantown. Three of the leading ports — Newport, New York, and Philadelphia — passed into the hands of the British. And worst of all, the opening of the year 1778 found Washington at Valley Forge with an almost naked, half-starved, unpaid army which had dwindled to less than three thousand mutinous-minded men. Only Washington's brilliant achievement at Trenton late in 1776 and the disastrous defeat of Burgoyne and the surrender of his entire force at Saratoga in the autumn of 1777 lightened the gloomy outlook and bolstered up the sinking hearts of the patriot leaders. But in spite of these victories it was obvious that unless allies could be found the American cause was doomed.

The gloomy years, 1776–1777

Long before the beginning of the war, men like Franklin, John Adams, John Jay, and Thomas Jefferson, versed in the history of contemporary Europe, were fully aware of the rivalry which had long existed between Great Britain and the continental powers, particularly France, for the commercial and imperial supremacy of the world. They knew, for example, that France, still smarting from her defeat in the Seven Years' War and the loss of her magnificent American empire, was watching every opportunity for revenge. They knew too that Holland, France, and Spain had long carried on a lucrative trade with the colonists and that these states would undoubtedly welcome any chance of increasing that trade at the expense of Britain. A few of the more

The background of foreign aid

far-sighted British leaders like Chatham also knew these things and repeatedly warned their countrymen to take the Bourbon powers into consideration in their plans for coercing the colonies. It was only natural that the Patriots should turn to Britain's ancient rivals for aid.

At the outset of the revolt, Congress, therefore, created a secret committee to correspond with foreign powers and direct negotiations with them. Early in 1776 it des- Steps taken to patched Silas Deane of Connecticut to Paris and a secure foreign few months later sent Franklin and Arthur Lee to be aid his collaborators at the French court. Subsequently John Jay was sent to Spain, John Adams to Holland, and other agents to the other leading European capitals. Despite the fact that practically no aid was secured from Vienna, Berlin, and St. Petersburg, the Bourbon states from the first lent a sympathetic ear to the American envoys. American ships were sheltered in their ports, where their cargoes were disposed of and the vessels reloaded with manufactured goods. In a single year the Spanish firm of Gardoqui and Sons shipped to the Americans at the expense of its government 11,000 pairs of shoes, 18,000 blankets, 41,000 pairs of stockings, and as great quantities of shirtings, tent-cloth, and medicines. In France the dashing Beaumar-chais, author, publisher, courtier, musician, shipowner, manufac-turer, and financier, acted as go-between for the struggling rebels and his government; and under his direction an almost steady stream of supplies destined for America poured out of French ports in spite of British protests.

But the American representatives desired something more than funds and supplies; they wanted an alliance that would bring armed assistance. France was the one state The French that seemed most likely to enter into such an ar- alliance rangement, and on her, therefore, the Americans centered their efforts. For a time the French government, despite the wiles of Franklin and the pressure of French sentimentalists like Beau-marchais, was unwilling to come out openly in favor of the revolutionists. Several reasons induced France not to do so; with the philosophy back of the American revolt she was not in sympathy, her finances were sadly disordered, open recognition would mean war with England, and to date the progress of American arms was far from promising. But the surrender of Burgoyne swept aside these drawbacks, and on February 6, 1778, treaties of alliance and commerce were signed whereby France recognized the independence of the United States and openly declared war on Great Britain. Spain, fearing that the independence of the English provinces would set a bad example for her own colonies, refused to become an ally of the revolutionists. Her feverish desire, nevertheless, to strike a blow at England in retaliation for destroying the Armada, despoiling her treasure ships, violating her commercial codes, and stealing away Gibraltar, caused her to enter the struggle on the side of France in 1779. The Dutch also became a party to the conflict. Motivated by trade inducements, they had from the first been extremely friendly to the Americans, furnishing them quantities of ammunition and other supplies in exchange for tobacco or on credit. This was more than Great Britain could stand, and accordingly she declared war on Holland in 1780, thus making it easier for Adams to negotiate a favorable treaty and to induce the private Dutch bankers to make the loans to which we have already alluded.

With the participation of France in the conflict the tide turned. In April, 1778, the French admiral, Comte D'Estaing, The tide turns set sail for America with a fleet and several regiin favor of the ments of soldiers. The British, realizing that the Patriots conflict with her colonies was fast blossoming into a general European war, at once laid new plans. Howe, who had been inactive in Philadelphia during the winter of 1778, was replaced by Sir Henry Clinton, who was instructed to evacuate the city, attack the French in the West Indies, devastate the coast of New England, and center his operations at New York. Commissioners were also despatched to America by the North ministry with a peace proposal which, however, proved to be unacceptable. By the end of the year 1778 it was clear that the British had abandoned their earlier plans of conquering the northern provinces and that they were shifting their attention to the South. In fact, the only military events of importance in the North and, indeed, in the entire country, were the ill-fated expedition against Newport, the battles of Monmouth and Stony Point, the defection of Benedict Arnold, and the operations in the transallegheny Northwest.

Although the French alliance, the entrance of the Bourbon powers into the conflict, and the shifting of British plans undoubtedly brightened the prospects of the patriot cause, the situation at the opening of the year 1781 was still precarious. The financial situation was desperate; Washington's army showed no improvement, and many who heretofore had loyally supported the patriot leaders were becoming apathetic and indifferent. More assistance was necessary if the revolutionists were to triumph. More assistance needed

No one in America sensed this fact more than did the young French nobleman, Marquis de Lafayette, who at an early age tendered his services to the Patriots. He, along with John Kalb and the Prussian, Baron von Steuben, and a few others, stood out from the dozens of European officers who swarmed to America and who, as Washington wrote, had "nothing more than a little plausibility, unbounded pride and ambition, and a perseverance in application not to be resisted but by uncommon firmness, to support their pretensions; men who in the first instance, tell you they wish for nothing more than the honor of serving so glorious a cause as volunteers, the next day solicit rank without pay, the day following want money advanced to them, and in the course of a week want further promotion, and are not satisfied with anything you can do for them." In the winter of 1779–1780 Lafayette returned to France for the purpose of inducing the French government to send an army to continental America. A force of 5,500 of the finest troops France had, and commanded by the experienced soldier, Comte de Rochambeau, was the result. Lafayette secures added assistance

It is unnecessary for us to follow the military events of the closing years of the struggle, which terminated in the surrender of Cornwallis at Yorktown. Despite the brilliant performance of General Greene in the southern campaigns of 1781–1782, it is difficult to see how the Patriots could have triumphed without the assistance which Lafayette secured. The French troops resisted The coming of the French army and the triumph at Yorktown every attempt of Cornwallis to dislodge them, and their bravery and discipline helped to inspire the Americans. Even more important, without the aid of the French army the successful siege of Yorktown would have been impossible.

Finally, in evaluating foreign aid we should always keep in mind the assistance rendered to the American cause by the **Assistance of allied fleets** fleets of France, Spain, and Holland. During the war American naval vessels under the command of such daring leaders as John Paul Jones, James Nicholson, and others, won many hard-fought engagements to the embarrassment of the British navy, but these brilliant exploits in last analysis were insignificant in comparison with the damage the Americans wrought to British shipping. "The success of the American cruisers has given a prodigious wound to the British Trade," ran one account. "It is computed in England that £1,500,000 sterling has been taken in the West Indian trade alone. The consequence has been several capital houses in England have failed for large sums, and more are expected to share the same fate." But the work of the fleets of the continental allies was even more important, for they were powerful enough to cripple Britain and to force her to change her plans repeatedly. Indeed, had Britain's mastery of the sea gone unchallenged it is conceivable at least that the outcome of the Revolution might have been very different.

Closely allied to the work of the navy and more intimately connected with the everyday life of the people on both sides of **Privateering supplements work of navy** the Atlantic were the operations of the privateers. Commissions were issued both by Congress and by many of the states, and it is estimated that no less than 2,000 vessels were commissioned during the period of the war. Of this number probably nearly one-half came from Massachusetts; Rhode Island had almost 200, and even the closely watched towns bordering Long Island Sound engaged in the business. Privateers swarmed in the West Indies; they lay in wait off Spanish ports for British vessels laden with fish; they even frequented the British Channel and the North Sea in quest of British merchantmen. No less than 250 English vessels, valued at £1,800,000, were captured in the year 1776. Although

BENJAMIN FRANKLIN

After the Duplessis portrait

the risks were tremendous and capture by the enemy frequent, these disadvantages were more than offset by the opportunity for adventure and the possibility of enormous profits. Elias Hasket Derby of Salem realized £1,000,000 from privateering. Nathaniel Tracy of Newburyport, who was said to have lost 140 vessels in 1777 and to have been on the verge of bankruptcy, made a fortune before the war was over; he was the principal owner of twenty-four ships which captured prizes selling for just under $4,000,000. Profits were usually split on a fifty-fifty basis between the owner and the crew. Prizes taken in American waters were brought home at once, but those captured elsewhere were usually taken to some European port and sold or exchanged for merchandise. The work of the American privateers was in part offset by enemy privateers; by the end of the war American shipping in Long Island Sound, for example, had been wiped out. As might be expected, privateering boosted insurance rates skyward.

3. PEACE

For some time prior to the surrender of Cornwallis at Yorktown it was evident that Britain was losing in the struggle to which she was a party. Her merchants and manu- British facturers, finding it increasingly difficult to market difficulties their goods, began to clamor more loudly. In spite of increased taxes the national income decreased, while expenditures during the course of the war exceeded those of peaceful days by over £100,000,000. The growth of the British debt during the same period was even greater, for it increased no less than £120,000,000. Government loans could be floated only at ruinous rates. Along with all this the administration had to endure the relentless hammering of the growing opposition in England, headed by Edmund Burke, which advocated the termination of the conflict with the Americans. Despite this apparently desperate situation those who had preached coercion of the colonies, still hoping that by some means the allies might be defeated and the Empire saved, were reluctant to yield. In the spring of 1782, however, British emissaries began to put out peace feelers. But a year was to elapse before the

Treaty of Paris, by which Great Britain acknowledged the triumph of the Patriots and the political independence of her former colonies, was signed.

The story of the negotiation of the treaty need not detain us. The shrewd American commissioners, Franklin, Jay, and John

Peace negotiations

Adams, wide awake to the fact that neither France nor her ally Spain had entered the contest for the sake of establishing a powerful republic in America, but rather to get revenge and regain American territory, conveniently ignored for the time being the Treaty of Alliance with France and their instructions to include her in any treaty negotiation, and agreed upon the general terms of peace with the British agent, Oswald, without consulting either of the Bourbon powers. This procedure naturally angered the French, for they were deeply concerned about the unsatisfied desires of Spain; and Vergennes, the French minister, took Franklin to task; but that astute gentleman, with his abounding knowledge of human nature and his unsurpassed ability to meet difficult situations, was equal to the occasion. The American envoys, he said, had been guilty of bad manners, but they hoped that all that had been accomplished as a result of the struggle with Great Britain would not be undone by "a single indiscretion." That Vergennes' feelings could not have been very deeply wounded, or else that Franklin's suavity had appeased him, is evident from the fact that a few weeks later he made, at Franklin's solicitation, another loan of 6,000,000 livres to the United States.[1]

By the terms of the final draft of the treaty Great Britain acknowledged the independence of the United States and her

The Treaty of Peace: its terms

claim to the territory west to the Mississippi, north to Canada, and south to the Floridas. She also agreed that the people of the new republic should continue to enjoy unmolested the right to fish on the banks of

---

[1] Some authorities, notably the French historian, Professor Bernard Faÿ, contend that in assisting the United States France was not motivated by any desire to weaken England or to regain any part of her American territory, but rather by a burning desire to help the United States gain her independence. Those who may wish to examine this argument more in detail should consult Professor Faÿ's *The Revolutionary Spirit in France and America.*

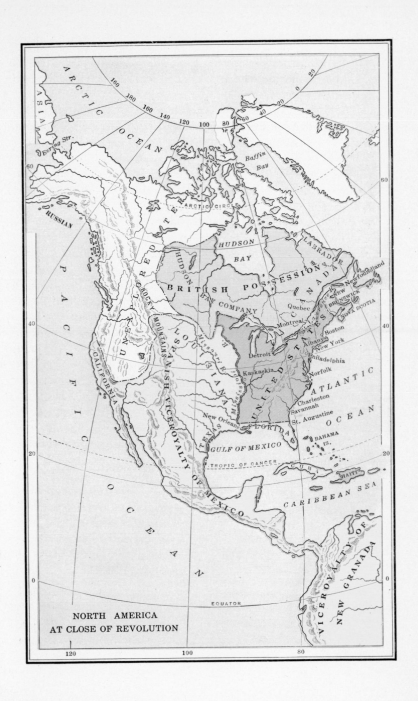

NORTH AMERICA
AT CLOSE OF REVOLUTION

Newfoundland, and that they should have the liberty of participating in the inshore fisheries of all the British dominions in America as well as "to dry and cure fish in any of the unsettled bays, harbors, and creeks of Nova Scotia, Magdalen Islands, and Labrador so long as the same shall remain unsettled." Furthermore, she agreed to evacuate the territory of the United States without carrying off American property. The United States, on the other hand, promised that no lawful impediment should be thrown in the way of British creditors in recovering their debts from American debtors, that there should be no further persecution of the Loyalists, and that Congress should recommend to the legislatures of the states the restitution of the property taken from them. The navigation of the Mississippi from its source to its mouth was to remain forever "free and open to the subjects of Great Britain and the citizens of the United States." Efforts of the American negotiators to secure Canada and Nova Scotia and to induce Great Britain to agree to a commercial treaty failed. If the terms of the treaty were liberal to the Americans, as many Englishmen at the time claimed they were, it was undoubtedly because Great Britain desired to weaken as much as possible the existing relationship between her Bourbon rivals and the young American republic. Certainly it was to her interest to do so.

4. Social and Economic Conditions in Wartime

In the preceding sections we have been chiefly concerned with the methods employed to win independence. Let us now briefly ascertain what was going on in a social and economic way in America while the war was in progress.

In the first place, the civilian population suffered much less privation and want than did the men in the army. During the Revolution the majority of the people, unlike the urban dwellers in the complex industrial society of today, were farmers who were to a very great extent self-sustaining in so far as the necessities of life were concerned. As they had done before the outbreak of hostilities, they raised their own food, made their own clothing, and manufactured their own tools. Indeed, with the

Overwhelming majority of people self-sustaining during Revolution

exception of certain manufactured articles, some luxuries, and a few articles of food such as sugar and tea, the population, urban as well as rural, managed to produce the needed essentials.

However, it would be most erroneous to conclude from what has just been said that the non-combatant population, or at least Scarcity of   part of it, did not feel the pinch of war.   In many food   towns food was at times scarce and costly.   The coast towns of Massachusetts, for example, suffered severely on account of their exclusion from the cod-fishery on which they depended partly for food.   "Food is getting scarce and money scarcer," wrote a New Englander early in 1777; two years later the same writer declared that the seaboard towns of Massachusetts "will soon have nothing to eat."   Rhode Island and Connecticut towns, where the heavy hand of the British was especially felt, also suffered.   "Nearly one-quarter of the best plow-land is now in possession of the enemy," wrote Governor Greene of Rhode Island in 1779, "and other considerable tracts are so exposed that the occupiers have not dared, nor been able, to plant them for two years past."   How much reduction was made in the amount of food consumed we do not know, but there is evidence that curtailment and substitutes were urged. The situation in the Middle states was not markedly different from that which prevailed in New England; in the South, where few towns existed, the war was only slightly felt until 1780.   While the war, by drawing upon the farm population for men, may have lessened food production slightly, the real difficulty was undoubtedly caused by lack of adequate means for getting the food from the producer to the consumer.   In several states embargoes were laid from time to time on the export of food.

Perhaps more important in accounting for the suffering of the people than scarcity of food was the enhancement of prices. Enhancement   Salt, for example, which sold for eighteen cents a of prices   bushel in 1774 cost six dollars a bushel in specie in 1781, and a similar change took place in the cost of practically every other commodity.   This advance in prices, while due in part to decreased production and increased demand, was in large measure occasioned by other factors, such as the increased cost of doing business, speculation, and, above all, the depreciation of paper money. The skyrocketing of prices is admirably illustrated by an extract from a letter written by Mrs. John Adams to her husband: "I blush whilst I give you a price current. All butcher's meat from a dollar to eight shillings per pound; corn twenty-five dollars, rye thirty per bushel, flour fifty pounds per hundred, potatoes ten dollars a bushel, . . . labor six and eight dollars a day; a common cow from sixty to seventy pounds; and all English goods in proportion. . . . I have studied, and do study, every method of economy in my power; otherwise a mint of money would not support a family." The numerous attempts on the part of various state and local governments to regulate prices have already been touched upon.

As in every war, luxury and extravagance existed side by side with hardship. Private letters, ship records, and merchants' advertisements in newspapers abound in evidences Luxury and of luxurious and extravagant living, especially extravagance during the later years of the war. Servants, lavish dinners, and parties multiplied; sales of laces, silks, velvets, and the like increased prodigiously. "I am weary to death of this dreadful war," wrote Dr. Orne, Salem physician, to Colonel Pickering. "It is attended with such irregular distribution of property, such evasion of order, such decay of morals, so much public distress and private extravagance." Money flowed freely. "You can scarcely form an Idea of the increase and growth of extravagance of the People in their demands for labour and every article for sale," said a letter to John Adams in 1778. "Dissipation has no bounds at present; when or where it will stop, or if a reform will take place, I dare not predict." Others spoke of the "inordinate extravagance" of the times. Even Samuel Adams complained about the "Superfluity of Dress and Ornament" of the people at a time when the army was half starved and semi-naked, a sentiment repeatedly echoed by Washington and others. Nor was the extravagance confined to New England. Newspapers, diaries, and travelers' accounts are replete with stories of dancing, horse racing, and gay living in the Middle and Southern states.

Like other wars, the Revolution was characterized by changes in the social structure. We have already noted that even before Changes in so- the outbreak of hostilities, colonial society was cial structure more or less stratified. During the war this stratification, although continuing, underwent considerable modification. Particularly was this true in the North where the economic confusion occasioned by the war was much more pronounced. Many old families, for example, whose fortunes had been derived from and were being maintained by the fisheries or by trade, suddenly found themselves reduced to the verge of bankruptcy. Others at the top of the social ladder, whose incomes came from fixed investments, were not much better off. Many from the lower ranks of society, on the other hand, vastly improved their social and economic position. Former laborers, shopkeepers, peddlers, and small farmers were numbered among the *nouveaux riches* who now rose to the top to the consternation and dismay of those older established families who had long held sway.

Privateering, speculation, and army contracts were among the most lucrative means of acquiring wealth. Of these, the Profiteering last named afforded splendid opportunity for the and the new acquisition of big profits. How many persons piled rich up fortunes as army contractors we do not know. The number seems to have been sufficiently large to have led Congress to complain in 1777 that in every state there were those "instigated by the lust of avarice" who were endeavoring to enrich themselves at the expense of the public. Many starting with little or nothing were rich men before the war was over. "The war," wrote one observer, "has thrown property into channels where before it never was and has increased little streams to overflowing rivers; and what is worse, in some respects by a method that has drained the sources of some as much as it has replenished others. Rich and numerous prizes, and the putting six or seven hundred per cent on goods bought in peace times, are the grand engines." Profiteering by means of army contracts was not confined to the newcomers. Old mercantile establishments — Otis and Andrews of Boston, for example — were reaping profits of fifty to two hundred per cent or more on army clothing at the very time when Washington's

naked and half-starved troops were stationed at Valley
Forge.

The amount of suffering caused by the partial suspension or,
in some cases, utter ruin of certain industries such as the New
England fisheries is difficult to ascertain. Likewise Suffering
it is impossible to calculate the anguish that visited
hundreds of homes when father or son, who put to sea in a
privateer, never returned. The army, too, took its toll. Some
communities lost as many as one-third of their able-bodied
male population. The little village of Gloucester, Massachusetts, alone lost over 300 in killed and missing, and the fishing town of Marblehead at the close of the war had 458 widows
and 996 fatherless children.

The economic upheaval which the war occasioned caused
practically no change in agriculture in so far as tools and
methods were concerned. Considerable informa- The war and
tion about European improvements, it is true, was agriculture
disseminated by those who came from across the Atlantic, but
this apparently had little immediate effect. The derangement
of trade during the first years of the war and those just preceding stimulated the production of wool and cotton. Mutton
disappeared from butcher-shops and from the tables of Patriots
in order that the wool supply might be increased. At an early
date the legislatures of Maryland, Virginia, and South Carolina
urged that more cotton be grown; so promising was the result
that we find Alexander Hamilton enthusiastically asserting in
1775 that several of the Southern colonies could in the course
of a couple of years "afford enough to clothe the whole continent." Production of the two leading staples of the South,
tobacco and rice, went on as usual. The first mill operated by
water for the cleaning of rice was erected on the Santee river in
1778. The indigo industry which, as we observed in an earlier
chapter, developed rapidly after 1750, declined during the war,
mainly because of the removal of the British bounty. Scarcity
of farm labor, as we have noted, was in a measure responsible for
a somewhat lesser yield in some communities, but this decrease
as well as any loss caused by the depredations of the armies may,
to some extent, have been compensated for by the increase in

price of what the farmers had to sell. The farmers, of course, like others who had goods to dispose of, were accused of being extortioners. "The illiberal Spirit of the Farmers," wrote a New Englander in commenting on prices, "is beyond Belief, loosing even first principles." However, when increase in taxation and other expenditures which they had to meet over the entire period of the war are considered, it is doubtful if the farmers as a class benefited as much in an economic way as did those engaged in non-agricultural pursuits, with the possible exception of labor. Certainly the small farmer, as James Truslow Adams points out in his *New England in the Republic, 1776-1850*, was growing restive before the end of the war, an indication that all was not well with him economically.

The effect of the war on manufacturing was much more apparent than on agriculture. The Revolution, sudden stoppage **Revolution** of English goods, and urgent demand for war sup-**stimulates** plies, coming close on the heels of the period of non-**manufactures** importation, naturally tended to stimulate greatly the manufacturing enterprises in existence during those years. Every patriot's home was a factory which produced not only enough homespun for his family, but a surplus for sale. Wealthy New England and Middle states' merchants and southern planters who, up to this time, had dressed in imported fabrics now wore garments that came from the home spinning wheel and loom. Many states offered bounties and prizes and encouraged the formation of societies which in turn would encourage manufacturing and the mechanic arts. Thus in 1775 the United Company of Philadelphia for Promoting American Manufactures was formed. Not until the privateers began to place their cargoes on the market and foreign goods began to come in through new channels, was there a decline in the household output. Many northern towns had small manufacturing establishments outside the home before the Revolution; as early as 1767 Haverhill, Massachusetts, for example, had forty-four workshops and nineteen mills. Paper mills, potteries, and like establishments multiplied during the Revolution, the capital coming mainly from the mercantile class. In this connection the loss of the Loyalists with their capital and industrial experience was keenly felt. In some cases pre-war establishments were closed for want of managers and workmen, so great were the demands of the army and the privateers for men. Except shipbuilding, commercial iron manufacture was the only important industry ante-dating the war to decline, but the decline was offset in part by the increased manufacture of steel.

Great interest centered in the manufacture of munitions and other war supplies. Gun factories sprang up at Sutton, Massachusetts; Waterbury, Connecticut; and North **Manufacture** Providence to supplement the small gun factories **of munitions** already in existence in such places as Lancaster, **and other war** Pennsylvania. At Springfield, Massachusetts, the **supplies** home of the present day Springfield rifle, Congress in 1778 established a munitions plant where cannon were cast. Powder mills were established at Andover, Stoughton, Bradford, Morristown, and other points. Some lead was obtained from Connecticut and Virginia, but by far the greater amount needed for military purposes came from abroad or from the melting down of such home commodities as roofs and window weights. Several of the states offered bounties for the manufacture of guns and other materials needed for war, as they did for the manufacture of textiles.

Little need be said about the internal trade of the struggling states. It is sufficient to keep in mind that, as in the days preceding the Revolution, it was seriously handicapped **Internal and** for want of adequate means of transportation, a **coastwise** uniform and stable monetary system, and a central **trade** authority with power to regulate interstate commerce. This state of affairs, which had long existed, was to continue, as we shall see, long after the war was over. Trading with the enemy was not permitted, but the records indicate that many a patriot farmer and shopkeeper carried on business with the British armies. Indeed, as between the British and the Americans as customers they preferred the former, for they paid cash and their money was sound. The coasting trade was practically ruined by the depredations of the British privateers.

Foreign trade underwent considerable change, especially during the early years of the conflict. No longer restricted by mercantilistic tenets, the rebellious provinces at the outset threw open their ports to all traders except the British, and even this

Foreign commerce exception was subsequently waived. The colonial warehouses were almost bare of foreign goods, and the merchants of France, Holland, and Spain jumped at the opportunity of securing a lucrative market at the expense of their hated rival. Soon many ships laden with continental goods destined for America were on their way across the Atlantic. That not all reached their destination, however, is evident from the fact that the British admiralty reported the capture of no less than 570 vessels between 1776 and 1779. Yet in spite of the vigilance of the British naval authorities and the activities of enemy privateers, an increasing number of foreign cargoes made their way to American ports. Indeed, by 1778, and perhaps earlier, there was little or no lack of foreign merchandise. In return for their goods the foreign merchants received tobacco, rice, flour, and other commodities. Indirect trade with Britain, although forbidden prior to 1780, was nevertheless carried on. Twenty-four million pounds of Chesapeake tobacco, for instance, passed through British customs houses in the years 1777–1778. Commerce with the British West Indies, on the other hand, was seriously injured by the war, for the British navigation laws automatically excluded the Americans from trade with any other part of the Empire.

Before leaving this section we should perhaps observe that the Revolution, like every other war, had its "sunshine patriots"

"Sunshine patriots" and propaganda and its propagandists. Many, inspired by real love of country, gave unstintingly of themselves and their possessions throughout the conflict. They bore their sufferings heroically, never lost faith in the righteousness of their cause, and struggled on until independence was won. Others talked loudly about the duty which devolved upon every able-bodied man to join the army, but it appears that often those who talked loudest were the ones who failed to volunteer and when drafted were among the first to secure substitutes or, in lieu thereof, pay a fine. In their ranks too were those who speculated in soldiers' notes and profiteered at public expense. The propagandists, in their efforts to rouse the people and to keep them buoyed up, appealed to all the emotions that are so easily stirred in times of war. The British were depicted as tyrants and the Patriots as saints. British soldiers were charged with the crimes of rape, thievery, and murder; widely circulated reports said they were purposely spreading such dread diseases as smallpox and wantonly digging up bodies from the cemeteries, stripping them of their burial clothes, and leaving them exposed naked to the public eye. Wrong-doing on the part of the Patriots was carefully smothered, and only stories that would make a good impression were circulated.

5. The Aftermath of War

In its consequences the Revolution was vastly more than a mere political revolt within the British Empire which resulted in the birth of a new commonwealth. In its larger and more fundamental aspects it was, as Dr. J. Franklin Jameson has shown,[1] a great social movement which transformed or modified every phase of American life. In this section it is our purpose to indicate in somewhat brief fashion the effects of the Revolution in this broader sense. *Revolution a social movement*

In the first place, the Revolution gave added momentum to those political changes which were already under way when hostilities began. The years 1774–1777 witnessed the elimination of the British ruling class, the destruction of the old colonial governments, and the emergence of popular government. While complete political democracy was not realized, and while the extent of popular representation and control varied greatly from state to state, the desire of the irrepressible but hitherto voteless proletarian element of the towns, and the frontier settler who had long been deprived of his full political rights by unjust discrimination in the matter of representation, came nearer to realization.[2] Indeed, so great was the "leveling" surge to which the Revolution lent full force, *Political changes*

[1] J. Franklin Jameson, *The American Revolution considered as a Social Movement*

[2] For a statement of the property qualifications for voting and office-holding incorporated in the new state constitutions see Allan Nevins, *The American States During and After the Revolution, 1775–1789*, p. 170.

that conservative planters, merchants, and large landholders within the patriot ranks who honestly believed that restricted suffrage was absolutely essential to the best interests of property owners and those who had wealth, were filled with alarm. "Every one who has the least pretensions to be a gentleman," exclaimed Samuel Johnston of North Carolina, "is borne down *per ignobile vulgus* — a set of men without reading, experience, or principles to govern them." The suffrage, another conservative lamented, was being extended "to every bi-ped of the forest." By emphasizing the doctrine of equality several of the new state constitutions, especially those of Virginia and Pennsylvania, seriously undermined the grip of the old order and paved the way for the democratic reforms of a generation later. Moreover, the Revolution, by effecting British withdrawal from the arena of American domestic politics, narrowed the struggle for political control and left the former colonists free to work out their own political salvation and to institute such changes and reforms as they saw fit.

The permanent transformations wrought in the realm of economic life were far-reaching. Standing at the head of the list Transformation in land-holding was the emancipation from British control of all the vacant lands within the boundaries of the United States. Henceforth no royal edicts such as the Proclamation of 1763 could keep fur-trader, settler, or land speculator out of the region beyond the Alleghenies. No longer would surveyors or other royal agents set aside trees for the British navy. The quitrent system, under which farmers and planters paid annually hundreds of thousands of dollars to the king and to the Penns and Baltimores, was abolished. In a word, all restrictive British legislation as far as land was concerned was swept aside and the crown lands were vested in the hands of the state legislatures. The sale in small parcels of the confiscated estates of the Tories, such as those of Sir William Pepperrell in Maine, the Phillipses and Sir John Johnson in New York, the Penns in Pennsylvania, Lord Fairfax in Virginia, and Sir James Wright in Georgia, to enterprising farmers tended powerfully to break up the system of large landed properties. Thus Roger Morris's 5,000 acres in Putnam county, New York, went to no less than two hundred and fifty persons; while the number of farms carved out of that of James De Lancey reached two hundred and seventy-five.

Closely related to the changes in landholding just noted was the abolition of the system of entail and primogeniture. For a long time pillars of aristocracy and cordially hated by every believer in equality, these Old World institutions had become deeply rooted in American soil, particularly in the South where the founders of the great families with wide estates desired to perpetuate their name and influence. Just before the Revolution began Maryland abolished primogeniture and South Carolina did away with entail; elsewhere, however, both institutions flourished, though in some states in somewhat modified form. Pennsylvania and Delaware and the four New England states, for example, allowed the eldest son a double share. The offensive against both institutions was led by Thomas Jefferson who, less than three months after penning the Declaration of Independence, introduced a bill in the Virginia legislature for the complete abolishment of entail within the bounds of the Old Dominion. The landed aristocracy, angered and in a belligerent mood, fought the proposal to the last ditch only to be beaten by the rising tide of democracy. It is estimated that the new law "released from entail at least half, and possibly three-quarters, of the entire 'seated' area of Virginia." A few years later the cognate institution of primogeniture was also swept away. So rapidly was Virginia's example followed that every state except two abolished entail within ten years after the signing of the Declaration of Independence, and five years later every state, without exception, had wiped out primogeniture and provided in some form for equality of inheritance. All save two — New Jersey and North Carolina — placed daughters on an absolute equality with sons in the inheritance of landed property.

In addition to the changes in landholding and the changes in agriculture which occurred during the war, which are briefly summarized in the preceding section, the Revolution gave impetus to the formation of much-needed agricultural societies. The first of these organizations in the

United States — the Society for the Promotion of Agriculture — was founded at Charleston, South Carolina, in August, 1785. Later in the same year a similar society came into being in Philadelphia; others soon followed, New York boasting such an organization in 1791, and Massachusetts and Connecticut in 1792. While by far the majority of the members of these societies were theorists rather than "dirt" farmers, the societies, nevertheless, rendered most valuable service by carrying on and encouraging experimentation and by spreading information about tools and methods. The introduction and greater use of such implements as the cast-iron plow, the cradle, and the like, as well as the various efforts to improve livestock, are to be attributed in part to these organizations. Nor should we forget that the Americans learned much about farming from the Europeans with whom the war brought them into close contact.

If the Revolution profoundly affected land ownership and property inheritance it no less profoundly affected industry and commerce. At the outset the thirteen provinces were, as we have so many times pointed out, merely parts of the British Empire and, as such, were forbidden to emit bills of credit, to make paper money, to engage in certain manufacturing pursuits, or to carry on trade with whom they pleased. Their economic life, in short, was completely subordinated to that of the British merchant, manufacturer, and landowner. This state of affairs the Revolution completely altered; the annoying restrictions were swept away, and the former colonists were no longer compelled to be "hewers of wood and drawers of water" for the British business man, but were now at liberty to organize and develop their industry and commerce as they saw fit, subject only to internal limitations, such as the lack of capital, and to external circumstances over which they had little or no control.

Church as well as State felt the leveling hand of the Revolution. When the Revolution broke out nine of the colonies, as we noted in a previous chapter, had established churches. In New England, outside of Rhode Island, the Congregational church was established by law and supported by general taxation, and the same was true of the Anglican church in Virginia,

Maryland, New York, the Carolinas, and Georgia. In but two colonies, Pennsylvania and Rhode Island, did complete religious freedom prevail. In the former, Quakers, Lutherans, Presbyterians, Baptists, Moravians, Dunkards, Mennonites, and Catholics lived in peace; and in the latter, Baptists, Quakers, Anglicans, Congregationalists, and a few Jews and Catholics flourished undisturbed. Taking all the colonies together there appear to have been no less than 3105 religious organizations; of these 658 were Congregational, 543 Presbyterian, 498 Baptist, 480 Anglican, 295 Quaker, 261 German and Dutch Reformed, 151 Lutheran, and 50 Catholic.

Religious situation at beginning of Revolution

While the Revolution did not greatly reduce the number, and not at all the variety, of religious organizations, it enormously strengthened two movements which, as we have seen, were already under way long before the outbreak of hostilities, namely, the tendency toward equality of religious sects and freedom of conscience. The Revolution was not many months old before an attack was launched against the established churches, with the result that in all the states except Virginia the Anglicans were soon dispossessed of their privileges and immunities and placed on an equal legal basis with the Baptists, Quakers, and other non-established groups. In Virginia, where the Anglicans were most firmly entrenched, a bitter struggle ensued, and it was not until 1786 that Jefferson's long cherished and much debated "Statute of Virginia for Religious Freedom," divorcing Church and State, was carried through. In New England, where the Congregationalists enjoyed supremacy, the fight for disestablishment was even more bitter and long-drawn-out; and it was not until the nineteenth century that this last stronghold of church privilege was forced to yield — disestablishment taking place in New Hampshire in 1817, in Connecticut in 1818, and in Massachusetts in 1833.

Effect of Revolution on church equality

Although the Revolution contributed little in the way of legal enactment to the cause of religious toleration aside from the separation of Church and State, it helped, directly or indirectly, to weaken the old bigotry and narrow-mindedness of the people. To what extent this greater spirit of tolerance was due to the

Revolutionary atmosphere of liberty and freedom is, of course, difficult to say.   Infidelity and indifference, both of which were

Increased religious toleration on the increase when the Revolution began, undoubtedly played a part.   Also, in this connection, we should not forget that contact with the Europeans, many of whom were imbued with deistic ideas, had a liberalizing influence.   Finally, the utterances of men like Franklin, Jefferson, and Madison, whose religious platform was embodied in Jefferson's "Statute of Virginia for Religious Freedom" which provided that "no man shall be compelled to frequent or support any religious worship, place, or ministry whatsoever; nor shall be enforced, restrained, molested, or burdened in his body or goods, nor shall otherwise suffer on account of his religious opinions or belief; but that all men shall be free to profess, and by argument to maintain, their opinions in matters religious," were not without weight.

From what has just been said we must by no means conclude that the Revolution brought complete religious freedom.   Re-

Religious tolerance not complete ligious backbiting and mud-slinging still continued, many people feeling that their religion, and theirs alone, afforded the only channel to eternal salvation. No less significant was the fact that despite the growing movement for complete separation of Church and State, the opinion still prevailed that the state could not live without the aid of religion.   At the close of the war no man could take any office in Massachusetts or Maryland without subscribing to a declaration that he believed in Christianity.   In Pennsylvania he had to declare in addition that he believed the Scriptures to be divinely inspired; and in Delaware a Trinitarian test was required.   In New Jersey and the Carolinas he had to be a Protestant.   "No person," ran the constitution of North Carolina, "who shall deny the being of God, or the truth of the Protestant religion, or the divine authority either of the Old or New Testaments, or who shall hold religious principles incompatible with the freedom or safety of the State, shall be capable of holding any office or place of trust or profit in the civil department within this State."   Interestingly enough, there were no religious qualifications for service in the army!

Aside from losses occasioned by the growth of free thought and of indifference, the various religious organizations suffered many hardships on the material side as a result of the Revolution. Decrease in income, depreciation of paper money, and destruction of property brought anguish to many a clergyman and his congregation. Indeed, in some instances congregations were broken up or abandoned by their ministers, particularly in Anglican communities in the North. Many preachers became war chaplains, leaving no one at home to fill their places. Thus in Hampshire and Berkshire counties in western Massachusetts thirty-three towns had ministers, whereas thirty-nine had none. Lack of large public buildings forced the military authorities, both British and American, to convert churches into hospitals, barracks, prisons, and storehouses. Many edifices were desecrated; Old South Church in Boston, for example, was converted into a riding-school for the British cavalry. The records show that more than fifty churches were destroyed by the enemy during the course of the conflict, and probably several Anglican edifices suffered a like fate at the hands of the Patriots who regarded them as strongholds of Toryism.

Revolution worked hardship on religious organizations

Immediately following the Revolution practically all of the various religious groups attempted to improve both their spiritual and material fortunes. Several reorganized their forms of government. The Anglicans, feeling that they could no longer continue to be a part of the diocese of the Bishop of London, established an American episcopate with Bishop Seabury at its head. The Catholic clergy, who had hitherto been under the control of the Vicar Apostolic of London, finding themselves in much the same predicament as their Episcopal brethren, held a meeting in Maryland in 1783 to discuss plans of organization. The following year the Catholic church in the United States was erected into a distinct body with Father John Carroll at its head; in 1790 Father Carroll became Bishop of Baltimore. Likewise the Methodists found it increasingly difficult to remain under Old World control, and in 1784 Francis Asbury was on the authority of John Wesley ordained as superintendent of the American

Religious groups in postwar years

Methodists, a title which was shortly superseded by that of bishop. All the other religious groups, with the exception of the Congregationalists, also showed the influence of the Revolution by developing more independent and comprehensive organizations. Thus in 1789 the first General Assembly of the Presbyterian church in the United States convened at Philadelphia. The Dutch Reformed church held its first General Synod in 1792, and the Universalists their first General Convention in 1786. The influence of the Revolution on American religion was further seen in the fact that of the religious bodies which gained most rapidly in membership during these years, four out of five were anti-Calvinistic; these were the Methodists, Universalists, Unitarians, and Freewill Baptists.

The Revolution with all the emphasis it placed on liberty and equality could not help but affect man's treatment of man, **Penal code reform** although in this connection we must be careful neither to overrate the influence of the Revolution nor underrate the effect on America of the writings of Beccaria or the labors of John Howard, the two great humanitarian reformers of Europe. We have already alluded to the severity and even barbarity of the English penal code which was still in effect throughout the British Empire at the outbreak of the Revolution. In a few of the colonies, notably in Pennsylvania, attempts had been made to liberalize this code, and though they had been successful they were disallowed by the crown. Consequently when the Declaration of Independence was issued the penal codes of the several colonies presented a sorry spectacle. In New York sixteen crimes were punishable by death on the first offense, and for many second offense felonies a similar punishment was meted out. Delaware listed twenty crimes for which death was the penalty. Connecticut had fifteen and Rhode Island somewhat less. Inspired by Jefferson, who was familiar with the efforts of Beccaria to improve the criminal laws of Europe, Virginia led the movement for reform, but it was not until 1796 that it adopted a new code which made only treason and murder capital offenses. Two years earlier Pennsylvania had completed the revolutionizing of her criminal code, death being reserved only for deliberate homicide. Reform in the criminal law of the other states was more dilatory, and in one, Massachusetts, it was made more severe in 1785 when robbery, rape, burglary, and sodomy were added to the list of crimes punishable by death, arson by life imprisonment, and manslaughter by prison and branding.

Imprisonment for debt was another Old World institution which had been brought to America and was sadly in need of reform when the Revolution broke out. Every-*Imprisonment* where men of all ages were lodged behind prison *for debt* walls for inability to pay even trifling sums. In 1787, for example, ten men whose combined debts totaled only £24 were languishing in a New York prison without hope of release. Elsewhere the situation was equally bad. There was considerable agitation in all the states for reform, but little was accomplished before the nineteenth century. In New York the Society for the Relief of Distressed Debtors furnished food, blankets, and fuel to many of the unfortunates and even succeeded in securing the release of some of them. Maryland in 1787 enacted a one-year law which enabled an insolvent debtor to secure his freedom through bankruptcy proceedings, but the measure failed of reënactment. Sometimes an unhappy debtor had recourse to advertising as a means of securing aid. The following from the Pennsylvania *Packet* is typical:

Old Gaol, Feb. 28 [1783]

Now confined for debts, about £40, one who can make over, on security, a house which rents for £20 per annum, exclusive of ground rent. Whoever shall be so humane as to lend the above sum, will not only relieve me from a cold gaol and unmerciful creditors' cost of suits (as I paid last summer near £4, now have the same sum to pay for the same debt) but likewise save my property, and enable me to follow my trade, to help support myself in my old age, being now sixty-three.

Intimately associated with penal law and debtors' reform was the agitation for prison reform. Prison conditions the world over at the time of the Revolution were almost un-*Prison condi-* speakable. The ragged, half-starved inmates were *tions during* forced to live in dark, ill-ventilated, vermin-ridden, *Revolutionary* non-heated rooms or cells. Little or no provision *period* was made to segregate the sexes or to weed out the petty offender from the real criminal. Disease swept hundreds to death. The jailers were frequently brutish individuals who, caring nothing about either the woes or reform of those they supervised, robbed every newcomer of what he had, trafficked in liquor, and profiteered on the food supply. The following description of a Philadelphia prison in 1786 gives an accurate picture of the horrible conditions which prevailed:

No separation was made of the most flagrant offender and convict, from the prisoner who might perhaps be falsely suspected of some trifling misdemeanor; none of the old, hardened culprits from the youthful, trembling novice in crime; none even of the fraudulent swindler from the unfortunate and possibly the most estimable debtor; and intermingled with all these, in one corrupt and corrupting assemblage, were to be found the disgusting object of popular contempt, besmeared with filth from the pillory; the unhappy victim of the lash, streaming with blood from the whipping post; the half-naked vagrant; the loathesome drunkard; the sick, suffering from various bodily pains, and too often the unaneled malefactor, whose precious hours of probation had been numbered by his earthly judge.

That reform was urgent goes without saying. Pennsylvania made the beginning when in 1776 the Philadelphia Society for Assisting Distressed Prisoners was founded. The British entry into the city forced its disbandment, but in 1787 a similar organization, the Society for Alleviating the Miseries of Public Prisons, came into being. Tench Coxe and Benjamin Rush were among its early members. This society memorialized the legislature in the interest of reform and on request of the executive council of the state prepared in 1788 a detailed report of the existing abuses. As a result, an Act was passed in 1790 which, among other things, provided for (1) the classification of prisoners; (2) the prohibition of drink; (3) abolition of thievery and extortion on the part of jailers; (4) removal from public view of prisoners at hard labor; (5) the furnishing of adequate food and clothing; and (6) religious instruction. While this Act attracted widespread attention, few of the states followed Pennsylvania's lead until the next century, although Virginia, to her credit, attempted to do so. New England trailed at the end of the procession, the famous Newgate

Prison reform

dungeon near Granby, Connecticut, one of the worst places of confinement in the world, being used during the entire Revolutionary period.

On education the Revolution had a double effect. In the first place, it took the minds of the people away from things cultural and, with demand for men and money, tended to The Revolution and drain the existing educational institutions of both tion and teachers and funds. Common schools everywhere, education both public and private, as well as some of the institutions of higher learning, were forced to close or to curtail their activities. Schools in New York City, for example, went out of existence. Counterbalancing this disastrous effect, however, was the fact that the schools which disappeared were primarily religious in character and conducted after Old World models rather than designed to fit American conditions. The Revolution made the basis of the new schools which rose on the ruins of the old primarily political; men like Jefferson, Madison, and John Adams were imbued with the idea that education rather than religion was essential to liberty and to the preservation of the state. "Above all things," wrote Jefferson, "I hope the education of the common people will be attended to; convinced that on their good sense we may rely with the most security for the preservation of a due degree of liberty." Writing in 1776 about the content of the new state constitutions then in process of formation, John Adams expressed a somewhat similar view. "Laws for the liberal education of youth," said he, "especially of the lower class of people, are so extremely wise and useful that, to a humane and generous mind, no expense for this purpose would be thought extravagant."

Yet despite the concern of Jefferson, Adams, and the others, seven of the first state constitutions said nothing about schools or education. The four which did were Georgia, Educational North Carolina, Pennsylvania, and Massachusetts. growth The first constitution of Vermont also made provision for an educational system from town to university. Prior to 1789 little legislation affecting the common school was enacted by any state, although there was considerable agitation for it in Virginia, Pennsylvania, and New York. On the other hand, the period witnessed the establishment of several academies of which Phillips Andover (1778) in Massachusetts and Phillips Exeter (1781) in New Hampshire were perhaps the most outstanding. Before 1790 eight new collegiate institutions were added to those already in existence; these were Dickinson in Pennsylvania; Washington, St. John's, Georgetown, and Abington in Maryland; Washington, and Hampden-Sidney in Virginia; and Charleston in South Carolina. The last decade of the century saw the addition of more than a half-dozen others. Meanwhile a medical department had been added to Harvard in 1783, and the first law school in America had been opened at Litchfield, Connecticut, in 1784, by Judge Tappan Reeve. Finally in connection with education we should bear in mind that the Revolutionary period ushered in a new era in the production of American textbooks. Of these the two most notable were Noah Webster's spelling book, published in 1783, of which ultimately fifty million copies were sold, and Jedidiah Morse's geography which appeared the following year.

While the Revolution undoubtedly broadened the intellectual horizon of many it also, like all wars, served to concentrate the **Effect of Revolution on fine arts** attention and energy of the people upon things non-cultural. Little or no advance, for instance, was made in art, music, architecture, and the like. Reading appears to have declined and what was read largely concerned politics. Of course the apparent standstill of the arts is to be accounted for in large measure by the departure of the Loyalists, who constituted the cultural backbone of many a community.

Every war, great or small, tends to upset the moral fabric of those affected by it, and the Revolution was no exception. The **The Revolution and morals** younger generation showed a hearty disrespect for tradition and authority. Restlessness was everywhere manifest. Intemperance, vice, and crime increased. Church attendance, even where church property had not been destroyed, declined. Indeed, so bad was the situation in the eyes of many of those whose social and moral outlook had been fashioned in pre-Revolutionary days that they freely prophesied all sorts of dire results, little realizing that the Revolution was ushering in a new social order and a new outlook on life.

Finally, and in some respects most important of all, the Revolution strengthened that growing spirit of independence and liberalism which, as we have seen, had been con- Revolution sciously or unconsciously developing from the day strengthens independence, when the English planted their first permanent liberalism, and settlements on American soil. Henceforth the nationalism former colonists, though some might copy Old World customs and manners, were to think and feel more strongly than ever before in terms American. And America at the close of the Revolution was psychologically at least vastly different from the America of the beginning of that conflict. The radical triumph was now doubly complete, and it seemed definitely settled that America was to be neither a playground for a colonial aristocracy nor a mere field to be exploited by British business men. Monarchism had given way to republicanism, aristocracy to democracy, conservatism to liberalism. In a word, the destinies of America had passed into the hands of farmers and middle-class people whose outlook and ways of doing things were markedly different from those of the colonial aristocracy and the royal officialdom which they had supplanted. Although many citizens of the new republic were still extremely provincial in their point of view, the spirit of nationalism long manifest was fast making inroads on the old strongholds of particularism and foreshadowing the day when the dozen or more independent commonwealths would be knit together into a federal union. That the Revolution, despite the lukewarmness and apathy of many Americans, strengthened this movement toward centralization is beyond question.

In the chapter which follows we shall set forth the more salient features of that titanic struggle for the control of the young republic which ensued between the forces of agrarianism and capitalism — a struggle which was already looming on the horizon even before the Revolution had begun.

Suggested Readings

J. T. Adams, *New England in the Republic, 1776–1850*, chaps. i–iii.

R. A. Bayley, *History of the National Loans of the United States* (*Tenth Census* of the United States).

Charles and Mary Beard, *The Rise of American Civilization*, vol. i, chap. vi.

C. L. Becker, *The Eve of the American Revolution*.

C. L. Becker, *The Declaration of Independence*.

W. C. Bruce, *Benjamin Franklin, Self-revealed*, 2 vols.

C. J. Bullock, *Finances of the United States from 1775 to 1789*.

G. S. Callender, *Selections from the Economic History of the United States*, chap. iv.

Edward Channing, *A History of the United States*, vol. iii, especially chap. xiii.

V. S. Clark, *History of Manufactures in the United States, 1607–1860*, chap. x.

E. S. Corwin, *French Policy and the American Alliance of 1778*.

D. R. Dewey, *Financial History of the United States*, chap. ii.

E. G. Dexter, *A History of Education in the United States*.

Bernard Faÿ, *The Revolutionary Spirit in France and America*.

Felix Flügel and H. W. Faulkner, *Readings in the Economic and Social History of the United States*, chap. i.

J. W. Fortescue, *History of the British Army*, vol. iii.

E. B. Greene, *The Foundations of American Nationality*, chaps. xviii–xxiv.

I. S. Harrell, *Loyalism in Virginia, Chapters in the Economic History of the Revolution*.

L. C. Hatch, *The Administration of the American Revolutionary Army*.

Rupert Hughes, *George Washington, the Savior of the States, 1777–1781*.

J. F. Jameson, *The American Revolution Considered As A Social Movement*.

E. R. Johnson and others, *History of Domestic and Foreign Commerce of the United States*, vol. i, chap. vii.

C. H. Lincoln, *The Revolutionary Movement in Pennsylvania*.

Edward McCrady, *South Carolina in the Revolution*.

William MacDonald, *Documentary Source Book of American History, 1606–1926*.

E. S. Maclay, *A History of American Privateers*.

J. T. Morse, *John Adams*.

Allan Nevins, *The American States During and After the Revolution, 1775–1789*.

E. P. Oberholtzer, *Life of Robert Morris.*

V. L. Parrington, *Main Currents in American Thought,* vol. i (*The Colonial Mind, 1620–1800,* Book ii).

G. W. Pellew, *John Jay.*

A. M. Schlesinger, *New Viewpoints in American History,* chap. vii.

G. O. Trevelyan, *The American Revolution,* 4 vols.

C. H. Van Tyne, *Loyalists in the American Revolution.*

C. H. Van Tyne, *The War of Independence: American Phase.*

W. B. Weeden, *Economic and Social History of New England, 1620–1789,* vol. ii, chaps. xx–xxi.

CHAPTER VI

THE STRUGGLE FOR CONTROL

ALTHOUGH the Revolution emphasized democracy and equality and witnessed the passing of British officialdom and a large part of the old colonial aristocracy, it by no means saw the end of class distinction and class rivalry in America. Indeed, one does not have to look far to discover that the same social-economic groups which had more or less definitely emerged prior to the war persisted throughout the conflict and for generations after its close. In one group, it will be remembered, were the propertied interests — owners of large estates, merchants, shippers, money lenders, speculators, and many members of the professional classes. While its personnel by 1783 had changed considerably on account of the exodus of the Loyalist element and the advent of the *nouveaux riches*, its philosophy of the sacredness of private property and government by the well-born and well-to-do was nevertheless the same. Opposed to this group were those owners of little or no property — small farmers, mechanics, shopkeepers, and ordinary laborers — who, as we have noted, championed liberty and equality, battled against privilege of every sort, and put humanity above possessions. Between these two groups a long and acrimonious contest ensued for the control of the destinies of the young republic and of the several states of which it was composed. It is the purpose of this chapter to picture the social and economic background of this struggle and to indicate briefly the intellectual and cultural changes accompanying it.

1. HARD TIMES AND UNREST

The Revolution, like practically every other movement of its kind, was followed by hard times. The situation, however, was **Post-war depression** doubly difficult, for the former colonies had to shift not only from a war to a peace basis, but from a colonial to an independent basis. The short business boom immediately following the war, during which even the poor went head-over-heels in debt in imitating the extravagances of the rich, soon collapsed; and the new republic found itself in the throes of a depression lasting until 1787, and most severe in 1785–86. Even before the Treaty of Peace was signed there were indications that economic activity was slackening. "The full confidence all Ranks of People put in this news of Peace," wrote the mercantile firm of Thurston and Jenkins of Rhode Island, "has stagnated business exceedingly." Army contracts and privateering came to an end, demand for goods decreased, debts remained unpaid, and by the opening of 1784 many business men found themselves in financial straits. The non-propertied group also felt the pinch. Farmers, unable to market their surplus products, had difficulty in meeting their taxes and interest charges. Soldiers returning from the army were obliged to sell their wage certificates at one-eighth of their face value. Ex-privateers as well as thousands of artisans and laborers found it next to impossible to obtain employment. On every hand the buoyant optimism which had characterized the boom days gave way to uncertainty, distress, and discontent.

Of the propertied-business group none perhaps suffered more during this economic depression than the American manufacturer. With the country on practically a free trade basis and with Great Britain determined to retain her American market at all costs, he was powerless either to keep his monopoly of the domestic market or to withstand the merciless competition to which he was subjected. During the months immediately following the signing of the Treaty of Peace Great Britain literally glutted the former colonies with cheap manufactured goods. In desperation the home producer petitioned Congress, but that body was unable to help. His efforts to get his state to do something met with more success, for between 1783 and 1788 all the states with the exception of Connecticut, New Jersey, and Delaware levied tonnage dues upon British vessels or discriminatory tariffs upon British goods. Unfortunately the effect of this action on the part of the several states was minimized or completely neutralized by the fact that the duties were not uniform, and the British vessels therefore used the free or cheapest ports.

Helpless situation of American manufacturer, 1783–1789

Scarcely less desperate was the situation of the American shipper. We have already noted that at the time peace was

Desperate plight of American shippers concluded Great Britain absolutely refused to negotiate a commercial treaty with the United States despite repeated efforts on the part of the American envoys to induce her to do so. While she continued to encourage the former colonists to send her needed commodities, and placed the United States on an equal footing with European nations in so far as British importations from America were concerned, she nevertheless closed her doors to American fish-oil, whale fins, blubber, and spermaceti. She also forbade the United States to participate in the carrying trade of her West Indian possessions, or to send salt meats or fish to them even in British vessels. It is difficult to imagine the disastrous effects of these restrictions on the American shipper. American whalers were ruined, for England constituted their only market. The exclusion of the United States from trade with the British Caribbean territories cost her a trade worth $3,500,000 a year. To make matters worse, France and Spain also closed their West Indian islands to shippers of the new republic. Consequently the only West Indian markets left were the Dutch, Swedish, and Danish islands, and these were wholly inadequate.

Naturally the interruption of the West Indian trade seriously interfered with the coastwise trade and the slave traffic, both of

West Indian trade greatly curtailed which were intimately bound up with it. Of vastly greater importance, it made it impossible for the Americans to secure the much-needed specie and bills of exchange with which to pay for their foreign goods. Finally, it severely handicapped such domestic manufactures as the rum industry and shipbuilding. Massachusetts, for example, launched about 125 vessels annually before the war, but this number dwindled to 15 or 20 by 1785. Ultimately the loss of the West Indian trade was largely compensated for by the building up of a lucrative commerce with Russia and the Far East. These new trade areas, however, which were a source of wealth to the Derbys of Salem, the Peabodys and Cabots of Boston, and the Girards of Philadelphia, brought little relief to the American shipper during the dark days of depression. Prior to the adoption of the Federal Constitution only four European states were willing to make commercial agreements with us: France (1778), Holland (1782), Sweden (1783), and Prussia (1785). Of these only the last two guaranteed reciprocal commercial privileges.

American merchants were also hard hit during the lean years. In the first place, they, like their fellow manufacturers, had to compete with the British who, not content with flooding the country with their goods, undertook their distribution. As a consequence every town of any importance had its British agents or factors. "Those infamous paricides, the Refugees and English factors," said the *Massachusetts Centinel* in April, 1785, "are permitted quietly to contaminate the air of a land of *Freedom* — to impede the wheels of government with their gold and to ruin our merchants and tradesmen by their Importations, our Trade is suffering every restriction, and as a nation we are treated with every indignity and insult that ignorance, ingratitude, or voraciousness can invent." A little later in the same month Boston merchants, following pre-war precedent, held a meeting in Fanueil Hall where they (1) voted to petition Congress "for laws putting our commerce on an equality," (2) made arrangements to communicate with committees in other colonies, and (3) pledged themselves not to do business with British factors and, in so far as possible, to prevent others from doing any. In this connection they agreed not to lease warehouses to the British and not to employ any person who helped the British. This anti-English feeling was widespread in the northern states. The British retention of the trading posts in the Northwest, contrary to the provisions of the Peace Treaty, naturally deprived the Americans of a large share of the profits of the fur trade and added to the feeling against Great Britain.

Lack of a uniform national currency and governmental machinery for facilitating interstate trade also worked great hardships on the domestic merchant. The monetary situation described in an earlier chapter remained unchanged. The heavy importation of foreign goods in 1783–84 drained the country of most of its

American merchant suffers

Other factors handicap merchant

specie, and what was left was debased in value, for clippers and counterfeiters flourished everywhere. Paper currency with its constant fluctuations was hated by every business man, for he could never be quite certain of its value. New Jersey paper money, for instance, was practically worthless in New York. The slight improvement in the means of carrying on interstate commerce was more than offset by the numerous and conflicting state tariffs. Levied for the purpose of obtaining revenue, protecting home manufactures, checking the consumption of what were regarded as useless or injurious articles, and retaliating against the commercial restrictions of rival colonies or European countries, these measures were a source of constant dispute and bitter wrangling and, above all, a most serious impediment to interstate commerce. A few examples will perhaps help to make this fact clear: in 1786 Massachusetts forbade the importation of fifty-eight articles; so high were New York's duties and so irritating her methods in collecting them that she was cordially despised by her sister commonwealths; North Carolina paid handsome royalties in the form of customs to both Virginia and South Carolina; in 1783 Madison estimated that Philadelphia and Baltimore merchants made from thirty to forty per cent on Virginia's imports and exports. Dozens of such illustrations might be cited. Equally numerous were the measures which handicapped the merchant in the collection of his debts; these ranged all the way from laws making depreciated paper legal tender to stay laws closing the courts to creditors.

The money-lender and speculator likewise felt the effects of depression. At the beginning of 1784 the indebtedness of the several states was approximately $21,000,000, while that of the national government totaled close to $40,000,000. Although the latter sum was slightly reduced during the next few years by the receipts from the sale of public lands, the interest on it remained unpaid. Furthermore, the national treasury expended in the neighborhood of $4,500,000 from 1784 to 1789, of which about half came from foreign loans and the remainder from requisitions on the states. In 1786, when the depression was seemingly at its worst, the national financial system broke down com-

Financiers adversely affected by depression

pletely. Loans, either domestic or foreign, could be obtained only with the greatest difficulty; requisitions were of slight avail, and efforts to secure funds by means of a national tax failed. Holders of government bonds, whether original subscribers or speculators who had acquired them at greatly reduced figures, were thoroughly alarmed. Moreover, the money-lenders, like the merchants, were sorely afflicted by the abuses growing out of the widespread use of paper money and the enactment of legislation adverse to the creditor class.

The economic situation in which the propertied-business group found itself during these post-war years was the more unhappy, first, because of the character of the national government and, secondly, because many of the state governments were in the hands of the radicals, namely, small farmers and their non-propertied allies. The first Federal Constitution — the Articles of Confederation — had been drafted by a committee of the Second Continental Congress and submitted to the legislatures of the several states in November, 1777, for their approval. It was explicitly understood that it was not to be effective until every state had ratified it. Several of the states gave it their approval within a short time, but it was not until March 1, 1781, when Maryland ratified it, that it was finally adopted. Under the Articles of Confederation the United States was merely a league of sovereign commonwealths. The federal government consisted of a Congress in which each state enjoyed equal power. The Congress in turn was composed of delegates chosen annually by the states. No provision was made for three separate governmental departments — legislative, executive, and judicial. The Congress was empowered to declare war, make peace, send and receive diplomatic representatives, make treaties, regulate the value of coin both of the United States and of the several states, borrow money and emit bills of credit, raise armies, build a navy, control Indian affairs, fix weights and measures, and establish post offices. It, however, had no power to levy taxes or to regulate commerce. Moreover, no amendment could be added to the Articles unless it was first approved by the Congress and then ratified by every

Governmental situation adverse to propertied-business class

Articles of Confederation

state. To secure adoption practically every important congressional measure had to have the assent of nine states.

We can readily see why the propertied-business men opposed such an arrangement. With sovereignty vested in the states the central government, even if so disposed, was powerless to aid them. It could not, for example, raise funds with which to pay holders of public securities either their interest or principal, for under the Articles Congress was forced to fall back on the requisition system in much the same manner as England was compelled to rely on it in colonial days and with the same disappointing results. During the years 1782–83 Congress asked the states for $10,000,000, but received less than $1,500,000. As early as 1781 the weakness of the central government in so far as the propertied-business class was concerned was strikingly shown when Congress, acting on the suggestion of "divers inhabitants of the state of Pennsylvania," proposed that the Articles be amended so as to authorize the levy by the federal government of a five per cent duty on imports, the proceeds to be used toward liquidating the interest and principal of the national debt. But this and other similar proposals were blocked by the dissenting voice of Rhode Island and New York. And what was true of the attempts to secure revenue was likewise true of efforts by Congress to prevent the several states from enacting conflicting and oftentimes prohibitory tariffs so detrimental to interstate commerce. What the propertied-business group wanted and what it early began to agitate for, as we shall presently see, was a strong centralized government controlled by it and capable of protecting and promoting its interests.

Propertied-business class not benefited by Articles of Confederation

Failure to provide a strong central government at the outset was due to several reasons. In the first place, we must not forget that the Revolution was a double conflict: a struggle on the part of the colonists for local self-government against the external and centralized control of Great Britain, and a struggle on the part of the radical element in the colonies for social, economic, and political advantages. The very nature of this double struggle and the philosophy back of it would naturally

Reasons for failure to establish a strong central government at the outset

retard the establishment of a stable and efficient central government. Secondly, the spirit of localism or particularism was too strong and that of nationalism too weak to make possible the early formation of a highly centralized government. No one who examines the writings of the leading men of the period or inquires into the nature of the numerous quarrels which ensued between the states over boundaries, trade, currency, tariff, religion, political views, manners, and war burdens, can doubt that the spirit of union was greatly outweighed by that of localism. Thirdly, the social and economic upheaval which war of necessity occasioned was not conducive to the establishment of a powerful centralized government. Finally, and in some respects most important of all, the radicals did not want a strong federal government established for fear that it might deprive them of all that they had gained as a result of the Revolution.

Radical-controlled state governments were as distasteful to the propertied-business group as the weak central government set up under the Articles of Confederation. Lack Propertied-of space forbids any detailed account of the long business class dislike radical-and intense struggle which took place between the controlled radicals and conservatives for control of the former governments colonies. Suffice that during the ten-year period, 1775–1785, the radicals gained either full or partial political control or constituted a very powerful political minority in all the northern states except Connecticut, New Jersey, and Delaware, and in North Carolina and Georgia. Consequently they were instrumental in shaping much of the legislation enacted by these commonwealths — legislation which, as might be expected, was not always to the liking of the conservatives. During the dark years of 1785–86, pinched farmers, small retailers, laboring men, and debtors generally, found themselves unable to meet their obligations; their slim possessions, even to their bed and food, passed into the hands of tax gatherers and creditors by means of foreclosure and seizure, and they themselves were thrown into prison. Then it was that they resorted to drastic measures. Stay laws, impairment of contracts, legal tender acts, increased issues of paper money, and the closing of the courts to suits for debt were among the more important legislative steps taken to ward off harassing sheriffs. These attempts were sometimes supplemented by acts of violence; mobs in Windsor and Rutland counties, Vermont, for example, tried to prevent the courts from holding sessions, and the courthouse at Plymouth, New Hampshire, was burned.

But it was in Massachusetts that the unrest and resentment on the part of the radicals manifested itself to the greatest degree. From the seventeenth century on the cleavage between the aristocratic-propertied-conservative and the democratic-non-propertied-radical classes had become more and more sharply pronounced. The former, believing that it had a monopoly on political wisdom, was outspoken in its opposition to the participation of the common people in government. Only the well-born and the well-to-do, as we have noted, were in its opinion qualified to rule and it, therefore, discountenanced every effort of the rank and file to make itself felt in a political way. It was fear of the non-propertied element with its demands for equality and for increased participation in the affairs of Massachusetts, for instance, that had caused the propertied-business interests to hesitate in taking action against Great Britain prior to the Revolution; and it was likewise fear of radical domination which motivated the same interests in drafting the state constitution of 1780 to double the property qualification for voting. The revolutionary principles of liberty and equality which had been dinned into the ears of every son of Massachusetts were either forgotten or ruthlessly thrust aside; the sanctity of property outweighed all other considerations.

Unrest and resentment of radicals more pronounced in Massachusetts

The situation in Massachusetts was already tense when in 1786 the legislature, acting on the suggestion of the new governor, James Bowdoin, a representative of the propertied-business group, voted a tax of £311,000, an average of about twenty dollars for every household of five. The proceeds of this tax, which fell more heavily on farmer than on merchant and money-lender, were to be used in part to pay off the state's revolutionary debts which had passed largely into the hands of speculators. But this tax together

Heavy taxes and scarcity of money

with the indebtedness incurred during the boom period was more than the poorer families of the state could pay. Local retailers and money-lenders, however, pressed by Boston merchants, who in turn were being crowded by British creditors, had to have money. Foreclosures and lawsuits grew apace. Thousands of unfortunate debtors lost everything, even their scanty household furnishings, and the jails overflowed with prisoners confined for debt.

The wrath of the common people, particularly in the central and western portions of the state, was soon at fever heat. Town and county conventions, hurriedly called by the discontented, bitterly complained that the common people were being reduced to beggary and misery, and prayed the legislature to redress their grievances. These included the question of the continued existence of the state senate and some of the higher courts, notably the Court of Common Pleas, the method of representation, exorbitant fees, the method of paying the state debt, unequal taxation, and the lack of currency. Above all things, they wanted the state debt scaled down, the special privileges enjoyed by property eliminated from the Constitution, additional paper currency issued, and the lot of the debtor, whether farmer or townsman, made easier. "Their creed is," wrote the conservative General Knox to Washington, "that the property of the United States has been protected from the confiscation of Britain by the joint exertions of all; and, therefore, ought to be the common property of all; and he that attempts opposition to this creed is an enemy of equality and justice, and ought to be swept from the face of the earth. In a word, they are determined to annihilate all debts, public and private, and have agrarian laws, which are easily effected by the means of unfunded paper money, which shall be a tender in all cases whatsoever. . . . We shall have a formidable rebellion against reason, the principle of all government, and against the very name of liberty." The creditor class heaped abuse and vituperation on the debtors for refusing to recognize the gravity of the situation and for not attempting to alleviate it. "Instead of cheerfully paying as far as they are able their own private debts, retrenching their idle,

Pleas of debtors for relief unheeded

unnecessary expenses, and contributing their portion to support a government of their own making," wrote a member of this class, "we see them assembling conventions to do acts treasonable to the State." Continuing, he declared that their leaders were "destitute of property, without reputation, hardy and factious in their tempers, and eminent only for their vices and depravity." Still another member of the ruling group labeled them "bankrupts and sots who have gambled or slept away their estates" and a "multitude of tavern-haunting politicians" — the worst men in the commonwealth.

Thus condemned by those higher up and unable to secure redress from the legislature, the debtor element — agrarians, Shays's mechanics, and laborers — rebelled. In August, Rebellion 1786, a strong band of insurgents seized the court house in Northampton and forcibly prevented the court from sitting. Less than a week later another insurgent band took possession of the court house in Worcester and compelled the court to adjourn. A little later a mob not only prevented the court from sitting at Great Barrington but released all the imprisoned debtors. Similar disturbances occurred in other disaffected areas. Alarmed at the turn of events, Governor Bowdoin summoned a special session of the legislature; that body, however, having several members more or less in sympathy with the insurgents, failed to get at the heart of the difficulties, although it promised to redress grievances and took steps to protect the courts. Meanwhile an insurgent force led by Daniel Shays, who had fought at Lexington, Bunker Hill, Saratoga, and Stony Point, and who had been made a captain and lauded for his bravery, forced an adjournment of the court at Springfield. Late in 1786 General Benjamin Lincoln was despatched with a force of 4,000 troops to suppress the insurrection, and during the winter of 1787 succeeded in quashing the revolt. Despite the desire of certain conservatives that the rebels be severely punished, the legislature, wisely sensing majority opinion, granted amnesty to all — even to Shays. Law and order had triumphed, but so deep-seated was the feeling on the part of the rank and file that Governor Bowdoin was decisively defeated when he stood for reëlection.

2. Establishment of a Strong Federal Government

The economic depression with its resultant unrest and discontent, the inadequacies of the federal government under the Articles of Confederation, and violent outbreaks such as Shays's Rebellion, so alarming to men of property, were all laid at the door of the radicals by the propertied-business group. Leaders of this group like Alexander Hamilton asserted that all the ills suffered by the young republic during the post-war years were attributable to too much agrarianism, which in turn resulted from too much democracy. As long as small farmers, mechanics, and laborers were allowed to control the states and the states were permitted to dominate or ignore the central government there was, they said, not the slightest chance for the country to be prosperous and its citizens happy and contented. "Democracy," to quote Professor Parrington, "was pictured as no other than mob rule, and its ultimate purpose the denial of all property rights." Rhode Island, where populism prevailed, was held up to the country as a commonwealth poisoned by democracy and popular rule. And Shays's Rebellion with its armed attack upon lawyers and courts, its intimidation of legislators, its appeal for the repudiation of debts, was cited as certain evidence that the rank and file was not fit to govern.

Propertied-business group blames radicals for ills of depression

In short, the propertied-business class did not want the common people to control America in 1787 any more than it wanted them to control it in pre-Revolutionary days. In place of a central government which was at the beck and call of radical-controlled sovereign states, it wanted to establish a centralized government which would itself be sovereign and which would be controlled by merchants, money-lenders, manufacturers, and property holders. In other words, it wanted a government that would pay the debts of the country past and present, get rid of paper money and establish a sound currency, regulate commerce, protect manufactures, properly distribute the western lands, carry out treaty agreements, protest against the menace of aggressive foreign nations, and guarantee the

Propertied-business class aspires to political as well as social and economic control

sanctity of private property. The radical-non-propertied group was content with natural rights theories, local sovereignty, and the Articles of Confederation, and blamed the propertied-business interests for whatever ills befell the country and the common man in particular. The propertied-business class, on the other hand, was composed of realists; its members in their desire for a strong centralized government were motivated not by high-sounding phrases about liberty and equality, but by a desire to promote their economic interests.

The movement for a stronger central government had its beginning, however, even before the depression years following **Beginnings of** the close of the war. As early as 1780, before the **movement for** Articles of Confederation were adopted, Alexander **stronger union** Hamilton, then only twenty-three years of age, had pointed out their defects: "The idea of an uncontrollable sovereignty in each state . . .," he wrote, "will defeat the other powers given to Congress, and make our union feeble and precarious. . . . Congress should have complete sovereignty in all that relates to war, peace, trade, finance." During the next two years Hamilton in a series of papers known as *The Continentalist* enlarged upon what seemed to him to be the shortcomings of the Articles and urged that the federal government be given the powers of taxation, regulation of commerce, and disposal of ungranted land. In 1783 Pelatiah Webster, a Yale graduate and a merchant and economist of some note, published *A Dissertation on the Political Union and Constitution of the Thirteen United States of North America* in which he elaborated a scheme of government which from the standpoint of the business man was a vast improvement over that existing under the Articles of Confederation. In 1785 Noah Webster, author of the famous spelling book and dictionary to which we have already alluded, wrote a tract entitled *Plan of Policy for Improving the Advantages and Perpetuating the Union of the American States*, in which he made an earnest appeal that the federal government be modeled after the pattern of the state governments. In the same year Governor Bowdoin of Massachusetts, fully aware of the discontent in his own state which was soon to burst forth into open rebellion, suggested the necessity of a stronger union,

ALEXANDER HAMILTON

whereupon the legislature of the commonwealth adopted a resolution declaring the Articles of Confederation to be inadequate and recommending that a convention be called to revise them. But it was perhaps Shays's Rebellion more than anything else that quickened the movement for a more powerful centralized system. "This dreadful situation," wrote General Knox, ". . . has alarmed every man of principle and property in New England. Our government must be braced, changed, or altered to secure our lives and property. . . . The men of property and the men of station and principle . . . are determined to endeavor to establish and protect them in their lawful pursuits. . . . They wish for a general government of unity, as they see that the local legislatures must naturally and necessarily tend to retard the general government. . . . Every friend to the liberty of his country is bound to reflect, and step forward to prevent the dreadful consequences which shall result from a government of events. . . ."

While the Massachusetts disturbances were alarming propertied-business men in every part of the country Alexander Hamilton, James Madison, and others were skill- The Annapolis fully laying plans for a convention which they Convention hoped would create a strong national state that would be subservient to the interests of the property holders and business men. As early as 1784 the Virginia legislature had adopted a resolution framed by Madison appointing commissioners to meet with those of Maryland for the purpose of formulating plans respecting the navigation of the Potomac. On the invitation of Washington who, as a large holder of western lands, was anxious to increase their value by improving water communication between the East and the West by way of the Potomac, the delegates from the two states met at Mount Vernon in 1785. Out of this conference there emerged a second conference — the Annapolis Convention of 1786 — which was called by Virginia to discuss commercial conditions and "to consider how far a uniform system in their commercial regulations may be necessary to their common interests and their permanent harmony." All the states were asked to send representatives; nine states appointed delegates, and of these only five, Virginia, Delaware,

Pennsylvania, New Jersey, and New York, were actually represented.

Whether Hamilton, Madison, and other leaders of the propertied-business group who were leaving no stone unturned in their efforts to gain their ends merely planned this convention as a gesture preliminary to the more famous Philadelphia Convention of the following year we do not know. There is some reason, however, for believing that they did. Indeed, the French minister to the United States wrote home that they "had no hope, nor even desire, to see the success of this assembly of commissioners, which was only intended to prepare a question much more important than that of commerce. The measures were so well taken that at the end of September no more than five states were represented at Annapolis, and the commissioners from the northern states [New England] tarried several days in New York, in order to retard their arrival." Whatever may be the facts, we know that the convention did nothing in the way of carrying out the express purposes for which it was called. Instead, a report penned by Hamilton pointing to the critical situation in the states and advising them to send delegates to another convention to meet in Philadelphia in May, 1787, was adopted. In wording his resolution, the astute Hamilton was extremely careful not to rouse the ire of those opposed to a strong centralized system. Consequently he merely recommended that the forthcoming convention "devise such further provisions as shall appear to them necessary as to render the constitution of the federal government adequate to the exigencies of the union." He also shrewdly attempted to allay the suspicions of the farmer-controlled state legislatures by adding that any amendment which the Philadelphia Convention might agree to must in accordance with the Articles be submitted to the states for their approval.

The Hamiltonian proposal was at once forwarded to the state legislatures and to the Congress, and the latter on February 21, 1787, issued a call for the convention. In doing so it was even more explicit than Hamilton in stating that the sole and express purpose of the convention was the revision of the Articles. Fortunately for the sponsors of the convention, neither the Annapolis gathering nor the Congress specified the manner in which the delegates were to be chosen, and in no instance was recourse had to popular election. By May, 1787, all the states with the exception of New Hampshire and Rhode Island, acting through their legislatures, had chosen delegates. New Hampshire subsequently sent two delegates after John Langdon, a wealthy Portsmouth merchant, offered to defray the expenses of its delegation. In Rhode Island, however, where the propertied-business group had lost control of the legislature, the farmer government having already repudiated its financial obligations to the Confederacy, absolutely refused to participate in the convention.

The Philadelphia Convention of 1787 was strikingly different from the First or even the Second Continental Congress. Of the sixty-two delegates appointed, fifty-five attended the sessions with more or less regularity, and thirty-nine put their names to the final draft of the new Constitution. Though not an "assembly of semi-gods," as Jefferson once said, the convention nevertheless contained the cream of the leadership of the propertied-business group, "the representatives," as the Beards so well say, "of the conservative wing of the old Revolutionary party." Fiery radicals of the Patrick Henry, Samuel Adams, Thomas Paine type were conspicuous by their absence; and small farmers, mechanics, and laborers were in reality not represented. By far the greater majority were lawyers with experience in public life; seven, for example, had been state governors; nearly thirty had served in Congress, and eight had affixed their names to the Declaration of Independence. Washington, probably the wealthiest and certainly one of the most highly respected men in America, was unanimously chosen president of the convention. Those who sat under him, among whom were Robert and Gouverneur Morris, John Dickinson, James Wilson, Charles and General Charles Cotesworth Pinckney, Benjamin Franklin, Alexander Hamilton, James Madison, Roger Sherman, Elbridge Gerry, Edmund Randolph, Nathaniel Gorham, John Langdon, John Rutledge, and George Wythe, were not theorists but men of affairs — holders of government securities, merchants,

Dominated by propertied-business interests

money-lenders, lawyers, and land speculators — who honestly believed that the only way to promote their own economic interests and to save the country from ruin and possible civil war lay in establishing a strong centralized system of government.

Deliberating behind closed doors and bound to secrecy, keeping no official record of their debates, and only the slightest memoranda of the propositions which came before the convention and the votes for and against them,[1] and ignoring their instructions merely to amend the Articles of Confederation, this historic assembly in the course of four months drafted a new Federal Constitution. It is not our purpose to trace the detailed story of its formation.[2] Rather, we are concerned with (1) the extent to which the members of the convention were in agreement on the great economic objects so dear to the hearts of every owner of property and every business man; (2) the nature of the machinery set up by the convention to obtain the ends desired by the propertied-business group; and (3) the struggle which ensued over the ratification of the new instrument.

Convention drafts new Federal Constitution

In the past historians and others, seemingly captivated by the dictum that "history is past politics," have pictured the Philadelphia Convention as a house divided against itself and the Constitution as a compromise of wrangling factions. Nothing could be further from the truth so far as the great economic questions of taxation, regulation of commerce, payment of the national debt, the coining and borrowing of money, disposal of western lands, defense, and the protection of private property were concerned. With the small-farmer-non-propertied class to all intents and purposes not represented in the convention, there was general unanimity on practically all the economic and protective provisions included in the final draft of the Constitution. By it

Little disagreement in Convention on great economic questions

[1] Fortunately Madison took copious notes of the debates. These were acquired by Congress in 1836 and were published in 1840. They constitute our chief source of information on the drafting of the Constitution.

[2] The best brief account of the making of the Constitution is that by Robert Livingston Schuyler, *The Constitution of the United States: An Historical Survey of Its Formation.*

Congress was given power to lay and collect taxes, duties, imposts, and excises, coin and borrow money, regulate interstate and foreign commerce, fix the standard of weights and measures, provide for patents and copyrights, establish post offices, raise and support armies, maintain a navy, and pay all debts contracted by the United States prior to the adoption of the Constitution. To safeguard against radical state legislation, the states were forbidden to coin money, emit bills of credit, make anything but gold and silver coin a tender in payment of debts, make any law impairing the obligation of contracts, lay imposts or duties on imports or exports or on tonnage. In other words, the ends so much desired by the propertied-business group were unmistakably written into what was designed by them to be the fundamental law of the land.

In setting up a form of government capable of carrying out these ends, however, the convention was far from unanimous, and compromise after compromise was necessary. Nearly all agreed that democracy was a dangerous thing and that the majority will should be limited as far as possible. Just how to restrain it and at the same time secure popular approval of their handiwork was, therefore, the besetting problem which the members faced. At the outset the convention agreed — six states to one, and one divided — that "a national government ought to be established consisting of a supreme legislative, executive, and judiciary." While the word "national" was eliminated from the resolution for strategic reasons, the separation-of-powers idea with its implied system of check and balance formed the basic framework around which the governmental machinery provided for in the Constitution was built. *Lack of unanimity on structure of government*

Of the plans of government submitted, that of Virginia was the most representative of the larger states. Briefly, it provided for a two-house legislature composed of members apportioned among the states on the basis of quota of contribution or free white population; the members of the lower house were to be elected by the people of the several states and those of the upper house were to be chosen by the lower house out of persons nominated by the *Various plans of governmental structure submitted* state legislatures. An executive — either an individual or a group of men — was to be chosen by the legislature and to be ineligible for a second term. The judiciary was to consist of a supreme court and inferior courts. The acts of the legislature, which was authorized to pass on the constitutionality of state laws, were subject to review by a council of revision consisting of the executive and part of the judiciary. Counterbalancing the Virginia plan was the New Jersey or small-state plan fathered by Paterson of New Jersey. Federal rather than national in spirit, it called for a single chambered Congress in which each state was to enjoy one vote, a plural executive chosen by Congress, and a supreme federal judiciary.

While neither the Virginia nor New Jersey plan was adopted, features of each appeared in the final draft of the new Constitution. For example, it provided for a two-house legislature, members in the House of Representatives or lower house being apportioned among the states largely on the basis of population, elected biennially by popular vote, and paid from the national treasury. In the Senate or upper house each state was allotted two members to be elected for a six year term by its legislature. Unlike the members of the Congress of the Confederation, each senator could vote individually and received his compensation from the national treasury. Executive authority was vested in a president chosen for a term of four years and eligible for reëlection by electors who in turn were designated by each state in such manner as its legislature might direct. Each state was entitled to as many electors as it had senators and representatives in Congress. In case the electors failed to give a majority to any one person, the choice of a president then devolved upon the House of Representatives, where each state should have one vote. Judicial power, which under the Confederation had been exercised entirely by state courts, was vested in a strong, independent, federal judiciary headed by a Supreme Court, the members of which were appointed by the president with the advice and consent of the Senate for life or during good behavior. Provision was made for such inferior courts as might from time to time be deemed necessary.

Framework of new government

Such, in brief, was the governmental structure which the members of the convention wrought. In creating it they were not governed by fine-spun political theories, but by the hard realities of the problems with which they had to contend. Madison, Hamilton, Martin, and others, it is true, were versed in the history of government and political theory, but such excursions as were made into these fields were, as Professor Schuyler so aptly says, "purple patches" — embellishments as it were — rather than integral parts of the proceedings. Uppermost in their minds at all times was the desire to provide the kind of government which would function best for the ends they had in view. As representatives of the propertied-business group they naturally endeavored to erect a governmental structure which, in so far as possible, would be controlled and operated not by the small-farmer-non-propertied class, but by men of property and standing. *Governmental structure determined by economic considerations rather than by political theories*

This desire to create a government in which men of affairs, rather than the rank and file, would predominate was responsible for the numerous utterances in the convention about the dangers of democracy. Gerry of Massachusetts, for instance, opposed the election of the House of Representatives by popular vote. "The evils we experience," said he, "flow from the excess of democracy," and he decried "the danger of the levelling spirit." William Livingston of New Jersey declared that "the people ever have been and ever will be unfit to retain the exercise of power in their own hands." Charles Pinckney of South Carolina so distrusted the common people that he proposed high property qualifications for federal office holders. Edmund Randolph of Virginia was even more skeptical of the political wisdom of the untutored and propertyless. All the distress which property had suffered during the post-Revolutionary years was to be attributed, he asserted, to "the turbulence and follies of democracy." In like manner Roger Sherman of Connecticut advocated reducing popular influence in the new government to a minimum. Alexander Hamilton of New York elaborated upon the "imprudence of democracy." "All communities," he exclaimed, *Fear and dislike of democracy manifested in Convention* "divide themselves into the few and the many. The first are the rich and well-born, the other the mass of the people" who "seldom judge or determine right." Accompanying these expressions of popular distrust were all sorts of proposals for restraining the masses by means of property qualifications for voting and office holding.

When after prolonged debate it became obvious that this proposal was fraught with serious drawbacks, the framers of the new government then had recourse to a system of so-called checks and balances as a means of accomplishing their purpose. The legislative department was checked by its division into two houses, by the president's veto, and by the power of the judiciary to declare its acts null and void. Even though the small-farmer-non-propertied class should get control of the lower house, as Madison feared it would,[1] there seemed little likelihood, therefore, that it could put upon the statute books legislation detrimental to propertied-business interests. The executive, removed from the passions of the populace by the method of selection, was checked by the Senate in the matter of treaties and appointments. Finally, the Supreme Court, the members of which were, as we have noted, appointed for life by the President with the approval of the Senate, was far removed from the people. They had little or no voice in its selection; any Acts such as stay laws which they might induce their state legislature to pass, could be declared unconstitutional by this highest court of the land. To cap the climax, the several states, as we have just noted, were forbidden to enact legislation detrimental

Marginal note: System of checks and balances devised as barrier to political domination by common people

---

[1] Madison expressed his view on this point as follows: "The landed interest, at present, is prevalent, but in process of time . . . when the number of landholders shall be comparatively small . . . will not the landed interests be overbalanced in future elections? and, unless wisely provided against, what will become of our government? In England, at this day, if elections were open to all classes of people, the property of landed proprietors would be insecure. An agrarian law would take place. If these observations be just, our government ought to secure the permanent interests of the country against innovation. Landholders ought to have a share in the government, to support these invaluable interests, and to balance and check the other. They ought to be so constituted as to protect the minority of the opulent against the 'majority." Cf. *Elliot's Debates*, vol. i, pp. 449–450.

to the propertied-business interests, and the president was empowered, upon call from the state authorities, to send troops to
suppress domestic insurrection. Thus no stone was left unturned to guard against possible domination by the masses.

The Constitution drafted, the next great problem which faced
its makers was to secure its ratification. Fearful lest the popularly controlled state legislatures, hotbeds of local- The problem
ism and state sovereignty, might be unwilling to of securing
accept the new instrument of government with its the adoption
                                                    of the
numerous restraints on state activity, its framers Constitution
sent it to the existing Congress under the Confederation with
the advice that that body in turn transmit it to the state
legislatures to be submitted by them to special state conventions.
Moreover, as a further aid to the success of their undertaking,
they boldly cast aside the old provision in the Articles of Confederation that the fundamental law of the land could not be
altered or amended without the unanimous consent of the
states and inserted in the new Constitution a provision that it
should go into effect as soon as it received the approval of nine
states. No single radically controlled state could, therefore,
prevent its adoption.

The submission of the Constitution to the several states for
ratification led at once to the liveliest kind of a campaign between those who favored its adoption and those who The hostile
opposed it. The former, styling themselves Federal- groups:
                                                       Federalists
ists, were, with few exceptions, the very same and Anti-
propertied-business men and their lawyer satellites Federalists
who had labored so indefatigably for a central government
capable of promoting their interests. The content of the host of
pamphlets and newspaper articles, as well as the correspondence
which featured the campaign, amply support this fact; David
Humphreys of New Haven, for example, wrote to Washington
that "all the different classes in the liberal professions will be in
favor of the proposed Constitution. The Clergy, Lawyers,
Physicians & Merchants will have considerable influence on
Society. Nor will the Officers of the late Army be The Federal-
backward in expressing their approbation." Gen- ists
eral Knox, another correspondent of Washington's, declared

in October, 1787, that the new Constitution was "received with great joy by all the commercial part of the community." Shortly afterward Madison wrote Jefferson that in New England "the men of letters, the principal Officers of Government, the judges and lawyers and clergy and men of property furnished only here and there an adversary." And Hamilton, surveying the situation at the close of the Philadelphia Convention, felt certain that the new Constitution had "the good will of the commercial interests throughout the states which will give all its efforts to the establishment of a government capable of regulating, protecting and extending the commerce of the Union, . . . the good will of most men of property in the several states who wish a government of the Union able to protect them against domestic violence and the depredations which the democratic spirit is apt to make on property; — and who are besides anxious for the respectability of the nation — the hopes of the creditors of the United States that a general government possessing the means of doing it will pay the debt of the Union."

The Anti-Federalists, as the opponents of the Constitution were called, were, on the other hand, almost entirely recruited The Anti-Federalists from the small-farmer-non-propertied group. Here and there, of course, men of property like George Clinton of New York were numbered among those who wanted to see the Constitution rejected. The Anti-Federalists hated or distrusted men of superior education and property. They championed government by the common man and decentralization. "An apprehension that the liberties of the people are in danger, and a distrust of men of property or Education," wrote Rufus King to Madison in January, 1788, "have a more powerful Effect upon the minds of our Opponents than any Specific Objections against the Constitution." Shortly afterward he asserted that the opposition arose chiefly "from an opinion that is immovable that some injury is plotted against them — that the system is the production of the rich and ambitious, that they discover its operations and that the consequences will be the establishment of two orders in the Society, one comprehending the opulent and the great, the other the poor and illiterate." The opposition in New Hampshire, a citizen of that state informed Washington, "was composed of men who were involved in debt, and in consequence would be averse to any government which was likely to abolish their tender Laws and cut off every hope of accomplishing their favorite plan of introducing a paper currency." In like manner Hamilton pointed out that among those who would oppose the adoption of the new Constitution were "*inconsiderable* men in possession of considerable offices under the state governments who will fear a diminution of their consequence, power, and emolument by the establishment of the general government and who can hope for nothing there." He also added that "some *considerable* men in office possessed of talents and popularity who partly from the same motives and partly from a desire of *playing a part* in a convulsion for their own aggrandisement will oppose the quiet adoption of the new government." To these causes there should be added, he said, "the disinclination of the people to taxes and of course to a strong government — the opposition of all men much in debt who will not wish to see a government established one object of which is to restrain the means of cheating Creditors — the democratical jealousy of the people which may be alarmed at the appearance of institutions that may seem calculated to place the power of the community in few hands and to raise a few individuals to stations of great prominence."

Between the Federalists and Anti-Federalists were many middle-grounders who, as in the early days of the Revolution, knew not which party to support. It was this The middle-group which Richard Henry Lee had in mind when grounders in discussing the new Constitution in his *Letters from the Federal Farmer to the Republican* he wrote as follows: "One party is composed of little insurgents, men in debt, who want no law, and who want a share of the property of others; these are called levellers, Shaysites, &c. The other party is composed of a few, but more dangerous men, with their servile dependents; these avariciously grasp at all power and property; you may discover in all the actions of these men, an evident dislike to free and equal government, and they go systematically to work to change, essentially, the forms of government in this country; these are called aristocrats, moneyites, &c. Between these two parties is the weight of the community; the men of middling property, men not in debt on the one hand, and men, on the other, content with republican governments, and not aiming at immense fortunes, offices and power. In 1786 the little insurgents, the levellers, came forth, invaded the rights of others, and attempted to establish governments according to their wills. Their movements evidently gave encouragement to the other party, which in 1787 has taken the political field and with its fashionable dependents, and the tongue and the pen, is endeavoring to establish in a great haste, a politic kind of government. These two parties are really insignificant, compared with the solid, free and independent part of the community." The Federalists, on whose shoulders fell the burden of securing the adoption of the new instrument, made every effort to obtain the support of this unattached majority.

Though inferior in numbers, the Federalists enjoyed marked advantages over their opponents. In the first place, the very *Federalists enjoy advantages in struggle for ratification* fact that they were property holders and business men, and had as allies the professional classes and the majority of the more influential newspaper proprietors, enabled them to exercise greater influence than would otherwise have been possible. They were the inheritors, for example, of the long established tradition that propertied rather than non-propertied interests should rule. Secondly, they were better organized, had by far the greater number of the leaders of public opinion on their side, and possessed the financial resources necessary for waging a strenuous campaign. Moreover, they had the powerful backing of Washington and the militant Order of Cincinnati earlier established by ambitious Revolutionary officers. Finally, they were on the whole better educated and better informed and, therefore, better able to propagandize the public than were the Anti-Federalists.

During the campaign the country from Maine to Georgia was flooded with oratory and pamphlet literature. On every hand *Bitterness of campaign* there were slashing and acrimonious attacks and counter-attacks. Bitter invectives were heaped upon the heads of agrarians and paper money advocates by capitalistic New Englanders. A group of Hartford, Connecticut, Federalists, for example, sharply satirized farmer-controlled Rhode Island in a mock epic poem entitled *The Anarchiad,* a bit of which follows:

Hail! realm of rogues, renown'd for fraud and guile,
All hail! ye knav'ries of yon little isle.
There prowls the rascal, cloth'd with pow'r,
To snare the orphan, and the poor devour;
The crafty knave his creditor besets
And advertising paper pays his debts;
Bankrupts their creditors with rage pursue,
No stop, no mercy from the debtor crew.
Armed with new tests, the licens'd villain bold
Presents his bills, and robs them of their gold;
Their ears, through rogues and counterfeiters lose,
No legal robber fears the gallows noose.
Look through the State, the unhallow'd ground appears
A pen of dragons, and a cave of bears;
A nest of vipers, mixed with adders foul;
The screeching night-bird, and the greater owl:
For now unrighteousness, a deluge wide,
Pours round the land in overwhelming tide;
And dark injustice, wrapp'd in paper sheets,
Rolls a dread torrent through the wasted streets;
While net of law th' unwary fry draws in
To damning deeds, and scarce they know their sin.
New paper struck, new tests, new tenders made,
Insult mankind, and help the thriving trade.
Each weekly print new lists of cheats proclaims,
Proud to enroll their knav'ries and their names;
The wiser race, the snares of law to shun,
Like Lot from Sodom, from Rhode Island run . . .

Some of the Anti-Federalist rejoinders were equally cutting and vindictive.

For sagacity and insight into the stuff of government and politics, none of the literature produced during the struggle for ratification equaled *The Federalist,* a collection of eighty-five essays, most of which were written by Hamilton and Madison and a few by Jay, or *Letters from the Federal Farmer to the Republican,* by Richard Henry Lee, to which we have already alluded. The *The Federalist and Letters from the Federal Farmer to the Republican*

former, considered by the Federalists as an unanswerable defense of the Constitution, is remarkable for its comprehensiveness, cogency, and simplicity of statement; while the latter, which voiced the principal objections to the new instrument, is equally noteworthy for its calmness and fair-mindedness.

Of the *Federalist* essays number ten, penned by Madison, admirably summarizes practically the entire Federalist theory of

Economic foundation of government according to *The Federalist* political science. "The diversity in the faculties of men, from which the rights of property originate" is, according to Madison, "an insuperable obstacle to a uniformity of interests. The protection of these faculties is the first object of government. From the protection of different and unequal faculties of acquiring property, the possession of different degrees and kinds of property immediately results; and from the influence of these on the sentiments and views of the respective proprietors, ensues a division of the society into different interests and parties." The most common and durable source of factions or parties, Madison goes on to say, has always been the "various and unequal distribution of property." "Those who hold and those who are without property have ever formed distinct interests of society. Those who are creditors and those who are debtors fall under a like discrimination. A landed interest, a manufacturing interest, a mercantile interest, a moneyed interest, with many lesser interests, grow up of necessity in civilized nations, and divide them into different classes actuated by different sentiments and views." The regulation of these various and interfering interests, Madison held, formed the principal task of modern legislation and involved the spirit of party and faction in the "necessary and ordinary operations of government."

While far more restrained than many of his Anti-Federalist compatriots who, like Elbridge Gerry, for example, declared

Principal Anti-Federalist objections to Constitution that the new Constitution was the outcome of a conspiracy hatched in secret, Lee in his *Letters from the Federal Farmer* stated the principal objections of the opponents to the Constitution. Chief of these was the accusation that it was undemocratic, that it was planned to serve the interests of a propertied minority, and that it in no wise reflected the judgment and wishes of the rank and file of the country's population. "Every man of reflection," said Lee, "must see that the change now proposed is a transfer of power from the many to the few." Lee also took exception to what he thought to be the unseemly haste with which Hamilton and others were urging the adoption of the Constitution. The people, he maintained, should have time to examine it fully and to deliberate about its several provisions before being called upon for their final decision. Although Lee did not emphasize the fact, many opposed the Constitution because it contained no bill of rights.

Four of the smaller and less powerful states — Delaware, Connecticut, New Jersey, and Georgia — promptly ratified the new form of government. In Pennsylvania, where the The Constitution opponents of the Constitution in the legislature tion ratified sought to gain more time for deliberation by absenting themselves, and thus making it impossible to summon a ratifying convention for lack of a quorum, a Federalist mob dragged two of the absentees back into the assembly room where they forcibly detained them. The legislature now having a quorum at once made provision for the election of delegates to the convention. The convention, in which the Federalists outnumbered the Anti-Federalists two to one, approved the new government on December 12, 1787, less than a week after Delaware, the first state to ratify, had registered its approval. In Massachusetts, where the opponents of a stronger federal government were powerfully represented in the convention, the Federalists wisely delayed an early vote; as it was, the margin of victory for the Federalists was uncomfortably close, the final vote being 187 to 168. In Maryland and South Carolina those in favor of ratification won rather sweeping victories. In Virginia, on the other hand, they were successful by the narrow margin of ten votes, 89 delegates voting "yes" and 79 "no." Had it not been for the influence of Washington, Marshall, and other leaders of repute who favored the adoption of the new Constitution, it is doubtful whether the Federalists would have carried the day. Two of the states, New Hampshire and New York, returned majorities against ratification. When the New Hampshire convention met

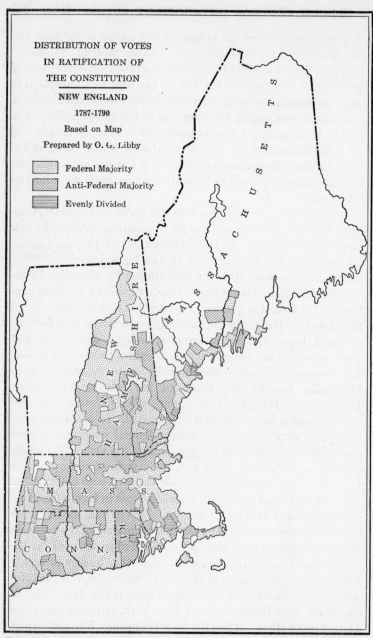

DISTRIBUTION OF VOTES

IN RATIFICATION OF

THE CONSTITUTION

NEW ENGLAND

1787-1790

Based on Map

Prepared by O. G. Libby

Federal Majority

Anti-Federal Majority

Evenly Divided

From McLaughlin's *The Confederation and the Constitution*. Permission of Harper & Brothers

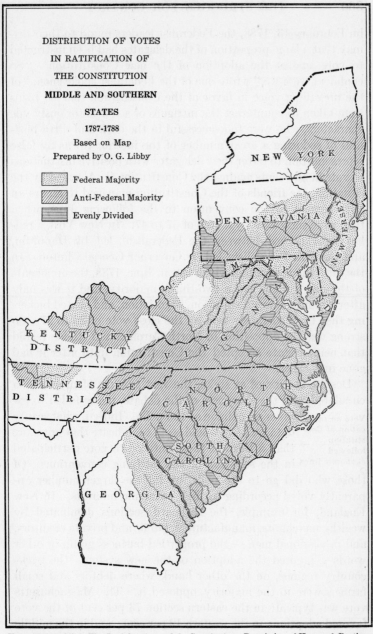

DISTRIBUTION OF VOTES
IN RATIFICATION OF
THE CONSTITUTION
MIDDLE AND SOUTHERN
STATES
1787-1788
Based on Map
Prepared by O. G. Libby

Federal Majority
Anti-Federal Majority
Evenly Divided

NEW YORK

PENNSYLVANIA

NEW JERSEY

MARYLAND

KENTUCKY
DISTRICT

VIRGINIA

TENNESSEE
DISTRICT

NORTH
CAROLINA

SOUTH
CAROLINA

GEORGIA

From McLaughlin's *The Confederation and the Constitution.* Permission of Harper & Brothers

on February 13, 1788, the Federalist leaders found to their dismay that a large proportion of the delegates had been instructed to vote against the adoption of the new Constitution. "So confident were we," wrote one of the Federalist spokesmen, "of the prevailing voice in favor of the Constitution that no pains were taken to counteract the intrigues of a few notoriously vile characters, who were too successful in the dark and dirty business of seducing a great number of the interior towns by false representation to fetter their delegates with positive instructions to vote in all events against the Constitution." Alarmed by the situation, the friends of the Constitution managed to secure an adjournment of the convention to the following June, when they were successful by a vote of 57 to 47. In New York a redhot fight ensued between the Federalists, led by Hamilton, and the Anti-Federalists, led by Governor George Clinton. In the ratifying convention which met in June, 1788, the opponents of the new system had a two-thirds majority, and it was only after a month of argumentation, negotiation, and heated bickering that the Federalists won by the close vote of 30 to 27. So strong was the opposition in North Carolina and Rhode Island that neither state accepted the Constitution until after it had gone into effect.

Despite the issues at stake, the vast amount of propaganda circulated, and the sharpness of the debate, many failed to express an opinion at the polls. Indeed, what scanty data we have would seem to indicate that not more than a third of those entitled to vote participated in the selection of the ratifying conventions. Of those who did go to the polls, by far the larger number apparently voted according to their economic interests. In New England, for example, the seaboard sections dominated by wealthy merchants, manufacturers, public and private creditors, and professional men — the propertied-business group in other words — favored the adoption of the new system; the back-country regions, on the other hand, where debtors and small farmers were in the majority, opposed it. The Massachusetts vote was typical: in the eastern section 73 per cent of the vote favored adoption; in the western 42 per cent; and in the middle

Vote on ratification of Constitution followed economic lines

— the scene of Shays's Rebellion — only 14 per cent. In like manner the strength of the Federalists in the Middle states lay in the seacost towns. Of the fifty-six members of the Pennsylvania convention, for whom we have more or less data respecting their economic status, thirty-eight favored adoption and eighteen were opposed. Of the thirty-eight who voted for the Constitution, four were merchants, eight lawyers, two doctors, two clergymen, ten farmers, and twelve capitalists. Of the eighteen opposed to ratification, all but five represented agrarian interests primarily. In Virginia the new Constitution was adopted through the efforts of the tidewater planters and the German and Scotch-Irish element of the Shenandoah Valley; the Piedmont section, whose interests were almost entirely agrarian, was strongly Anti-Federal. In South Carolina the friends of the Constitution lived in Charleston and along the coast; the back portions of the state, settled mainly by small farmers, was overwhelmingly opposed to ratification.

3. THE NEW GOVERNMENT CONTROLLED BY PROPERTIED-BUSINESS MEN

While the adoption of the Constitution was the occasion for rejoicing on the part of propertied-business men, their leaders fully realized that the battle was only half won. Propertied-business men realize necessity of controlling new government. Complete victory would result only if those who had framed the new government and had secured its ratification were to put it into operation. If the small-farmer-non-propertied element should obtain control it might adopt measures which would completely nullify all that the Federalists had done and thereby defeat the purposes they had in view. Indeed, it was the thought that the new government might fall into unfriendly hands that prompted Washington to write as follows: "As the period is now rapidly approaching which must decide the fate of the new Constitution, as to the manner of its being carried into execution and probably as to its usefulness, it is not wonderful that we should all feel an unusual degree of anxiety on the occasion. I must acknowledge that my fears have been greatly alarmed, but still I am not without hopes. . . . There

will, however, be no room for the advocates of the Constitution
to relax in their exertions; for if they should be lulled into security, appointments of Anti-Federal men may probably take
place; and the consequences which you so justly dread be
realized." Many others shared Washington's apprehensions.

That the Anti-Federalists were keenly aware of the Federalist
intention to secure control of the new government is apparent
from their many utterances to that effect made during the months preceding and following the ratification of the Constitution. "These lawyers, and
men of learning, and moneyed men that talk so
finely, and gloss over matters so smoothly, to make
us poor illiterate people swallow down the pill," exclaimed a
rural delegate to the Massachusetts ratifying convention,
"expect to get into Congress themselves; they expect to be the
managers of this Constitution, and get all the power and all the
money into their own hands, and then they will swallow up all
us little folks, like the great leviathan, Mr. President; yea, just
as the whale swallowed up Jonah. This is what I am afraid of."
The debates in the Virginia ratifying convention were also
clearly indicative that the opponents of the new government
were fearful lest the Constitution become merely an instrument
for the promotion of propertied-business class interests.

With each side thus distrustful of the other, and with each
bent on securing control of the new government, it was only
natural that a bitter campaign to fill the offices
under the new system should ensue. In fact, it is
almost impossible to determine any demarcation
between the struggle for ratification and the heated
contest for control of the new government. "The agitation"
[over ratification], wrote John Marshall, "had been too great to
be suddenly calmed; and for the active opponents of the system
to become suddenly its friends, or even indifferent to its fate,
would have been a victory of reason over passion, or a surrender
of individual judgment to the decision of the majority, examples
of which are rarely given in the progress of human affairs."
Marshall then went on to point out that in some of the states a
disposition to acquiesce in the decision which had been made

[marginal notes:]

Anti-Federal-
ists fear that
Constitution
might become
instrument of
class control

The struggle
for control of
the new
government

and to await the issues of a fair experiment of the Constitution
was avowed by the minority; that in others, the chagrin of defeat seemed to increase the original hostility to the instrument,
and that in "all those states where the opposition was sufficiently formidable to inspire a hope of success, the effort was
made to fill the legislature with the declared enemies of the
government, and thus commit it in its infancy to the custody of
its foes." In every state, with the exception of Georgia, the
Anti-Federalists put up congressional candidates, and in many
communities the fight was no less hot than had been the
conflict over ratification.

When the smoke of battle had cleared, however, it was found
that the Federalists had again won another great victory. Of
the twenty-four Senators no less than eleven — all   Personnel of
of them Federalists — had been members of the   first govern-
Philadelphia Convention; and of the fifty-five   whelmingly
members of the first House of Representatives, nine   Federal
or about one-sixth had been members of the body which drafted
the Constitution. Of the seventy-eight members of the first
Congress forty-four had been members of the Philadelphia Convention or of the state ratifying conventions, of whom all but
seven had supported the new system. Moreover, Washington,
though unanimously chosen President, was extremely careful to
fill the administrative offices at his disposal with friends of the
Constitution. For the extremely important post of Secretary of
the Treasury he turned first to Robert Morris, staunch Federalist and a member of the Philadelphia Convention, and when he
declined, to Alexander Hamilton, the "giant of Federalism."
General Knox of Massachusetts, another ardent Federalist, was
made Secretary of War, and Edmund Randolph of Virginia, a
Federalist convert, Attorney-General. Thomas Jefferson, who
was named Secretary of State, was the only person not over
enthusiastic about the Constitution to receive an appointment,
and even he had favored its adoption and was not at this time
identified with anti-federalism. The judicial branch of the
government was filled entirely by those who had helped draft the
Constitution or who had worked for its subsequent adoption.
All the minor offices, including those in the diplomatic, consular,

and customs service, were also filled with partisans of federalism. In a word, the government that began with the inauguration of Washington on April 30, 1789, instead of being non-partisan, was made up in large measure of those active spirits who had labored so hard to make the Constitution and to secure its approval.

The new government lost no time in fulfilling its mission, which embraced among other things restoration of the public credit, building up of adequate revenues, payment of the national debt, promotion of trade and commerce, protection of home industries, strengthening the defenses on land and sea, creating a nation-wide judicial system, and allaying in so far as possible opposition to the new order of things. Fortunately for those in power, these several tasks were made easier by the fact that the economic depression and accompanying hard times out of which the movement for a stronger central government developed had given way by 1790 to more prosperous conditions. While the Constitution did not create this prosperity except in so far as it tended to increase the confidence of the propertied-business class, it fell heir to all the benefits that immediately flow from an upward trend of the business cycle. Federalists on every hand enthusiastically but erroneously gave the new system entire credit for the return of better times. No one was more cognizant than Washington that the country now was enjoying renewed prosperity. Writing to Jefferson as early as August, 1788, he said there was occasion for rejoicing "that the people have been ripened by misfortune for the reception of a good government. They are emerging from the gulf of dissipation and debt, into which they had precipitated themselves at the close of the war. Economy and industry are evidently gaining ground. Not only agriculture, but even manufactures, are much more attended to than formerly. Notwithstanding the shackles under which our trade in general labors, commerce to the East Indies is prosecuted with considerable success. . . . This year the exports from Massachusetts have amounted to a great deal more than their imports." Jefferson, too, was fully aware that the return of prosperity would help the new govern-

Constitution floated in on wave of prosperity

ment, for in 1791 he wrote: "In general our affairs are proceeding in a train of unparalleled prosperity. This arises from the real improvements of our government, from the unbounded confidence reposed in it by the people, their zeal to support it, and their conviction that a solid nation is the best rock of their safety, from the favorable seasons which for some years past have coöperated with a fertile soil and a genial climate to increase the productions of agriculture, and from the growth of industry, economy, and domestic manufactures; so that I believe I may say with truth, that there is not a nation under the sun enjoying more present prosperity, nor with more in prospect." Had the country been less prosperous there would undoubtedly have been far less enthusiasm for the Constitution and for the measures enacted under it during Washington's administrations.

The directing mind and the person above all others most responsible for the success of the new government was Alexander Hamilton, the real spokesman of the propertied-business class. Born in the West Indies, trained at **Alexander Hamilton** King's College (Columbia), where he distinguished himself as a brilliant student, and equipped with a scintillating mind and a charming personality, he proved himself before his untimely death to be a great lawyer, a skillful orator, a master organizer, a pamphleteer *par excellence*, and a statesman of the first rank. By temperament he loved and respected aristocracy and throughout his life despised democracy and republicanism. His ideal of government was rule by landed gentlemen, wealthy merchants, and prosperous professional men backed, if necessary, with standing armies. He never knew the small farmer and the villager who were obliged to earn their living by the sweat of their brow and, what was more, he did not want to know them. Practical to the last degree, he hated theorists and idealists and based his political philosophy on economic realities. "That power," said he, "which holds the purse-strings absolutely must rule." For him no government was worth the mention that did not reflect the wishes of property. Adam Smith's *Wealth of Nations* was his political prayer book, but he had little use for the writings of the French revolutionary "fanatics," as he called them. Humanitarianism and democratic liberalism were foreign to him. Unlike his great compeer — Jefferson — he conceived America in capitalistic rather than agrarian terms, as we shall see.

Before assuming office Hamilton had clearly in mind those economic measures which he believed were absolutely necessary for the promotion of the interests of the propertied-business class and for the stability and permanence of the federal government. They included (1) the funding of the entire national debt — principal and interest — at face value irrespective of whether the old bond and stock certificates were held by the original subscribers or had been acquired by speculators and others at a discount; (2) the assumption at face value of the debts of the several states by the national government; (3) the establishment of a national bank and a mint; (4) the levying of customs duties for the purpose of protecting and encouraging American manufactures and commerce; (5) the disposal of the public lands, the proceeds to go toward liquidation of the national debt; and (6) the establishment of a sinking fund for the purchase of public securities in the open market from time to time. This program, it will be noted, was in keeping with Hamilton's belief that no government could long endure without the confidence and support of propertied and business men, and it embodied the basic foundation for the later capitalistic development of the United States.

The Hamiltonian program

Hamilton's *Report on the Public Credit*, the first of those famous documents in which he elaborated his program, was more than a mere device to liquidate the debts of the United States. Submitted to Congress in January, 1790, it presented a detailed plan for funding the debt and increasing the fluid capital of the country. In brief, it proposed that the old bonds and certificates, the principal and interest of which at face value totaled approximately $50,000,000, should be called in and replaced with new securities. Part of the new bonds were to draw six per cent, part three per cent, and still another part no interest until ten years had elapsed, after which it would draw six per cent. Furthermore, Hamilton proposed that the national government assume

The first Report on the Public Credit

at face value the debts of the several states, incurred for the most part during the Revolution. These amounted to about $20,000,000, and he reasoned that their assumption would, among other things, make for orderliness and stability and bind the Union more closely together; that inasmuch as the states had been deprived of the right to levy import duties, it was logical that the central government should relieve them of their debt burden; and, most important of all, that assumption would force all public creditors to depend upon the federal government rather than upon the states for the sums due them.

Hamilton also fathered a sinking fund which the Secretary of the Treasury could use to buy securities in the market when in his judgment it was to the best interests of the gov- *Sinking fund* ernment and the holders of public securities to do *proposal* so. He planned that the money for this sinking fund, as well as for interest on the new securities and for their ultimate retirement, should come from (1) import duties, and (2) the proceeds of the sale of public lands in the West.

Hand in hand with the funding and assumption plans was the scheme for a central banking agency which Hamilton outlined in his *Report on the National Bank*. Long before *Report on* the adoption of the Constitution he had dis- *National Bank* cussed with Robert Morris the necessity and possibility of such an institution. A national bank, he argued, would, in the first place, augment the productive capital of the country by increasing the number of notes in circulation, by putting them to greater use, and by gathering up what otherwise might well be idle funds. Secondly, it would enable the government to obtain loans more easily; and, thirdly, increased circulation of money and the greater opportunity to make loans would facilitate the collection of taxes. Of the capital stock of $10,000,000 one-fifth was to be subscribed by the government and the remainder by the public — one-fourth in specie and three-fourths in new six per cent federal bonds.

In still another report Hamilton dealt exhaustively with the vexatious and much debated subject of the coinage. While expressing a preference for gold he, nevertheless, recommended that both gold and silver should be minted in the ratio

of 1 to 15 — a proportion corresponding to the bullion values
of the time. He also advocated the use of the decimal system
Hamilton's coinage recommendation of coinage, and proposed that the dollar, the monetary unit, should consist of 24¾ grains of pure gold
or 371¼ grains of pure silver. He further recommended the coinage of ten-dollar gold pieces, silver dimes, and
one cent and one-half cent copper pieces.

It requires no great stretch of the imagination to realise that
the Hamiltonian program tended not in the slightest to heal the
Propertied-business and small-farmer-non-propertied groups diametrically opposed to each other on Hamiltonian program breach which had existed between the propertied-business class and the small-farmer-non-propertied
group long before the outbreak of the Revolution.
Members of the former, especially the financial,
commercial, and industrial interests, were happy
almost beyond words over the likelihood that the
measures which they had long cherished would soon
become law. The latter, on the other hand, fully convinced that
the enactment of the Hamiltonian proposals would burden the
farmer and even the planter with taxation for the benefit of the
capitalist group, raised its voice in opposition.

The agrarians first leveled their guns on Hamilton's funding
proposals. A large part of the old bonds — both state and
continental — they rightly declared, had been
Opposition to Hamilton's funding scheme acquired by shrewd and enterprising capitalist
speculators at ridiculously low prices. Soldiers,
farmers, and cross-roads merchants — poor, igno-
rant of the significance of the adoption of the federal Constitution, and unaware of the Hamiltonian funding scheme — had
fallen an easy prey to the slick-tongued capitalistic agents who
scoured the country in quest of depreciated paper. When,
therefore, the funding measure came before Congress some of
the opposition leaders, contending that the debt represented
goods bought at greatly inflated prices, services rendered at
exhorbitant rates, or loans of depreciated paper, proposed that
it be scaled down from face to market value. Great was the
rejoicing on the part of those who held securities when this
proposal was voted down. Another congressional group headed
by Madison, no less eager than Hamilton and his immediate

followers to restore the credit of the nation, was especially anxious to do justice to both the original investor and the speculator. Accordingly, Madison advanced a plan which in reality was in the nature of a compromise between those who wanted the debt refunded at face value and those who would refund it at market value. In brief it provided that the specu-lator be paid the highest price that had prevailed on the market and the original holder the difference between the face value and the market price. While aware that this plan did not do full justice to all concerned, Madison felt certain that it was far superior to the other two. "The original sufferers," said he, "will not be fully indemnified; but they will receive from their country a tribute due to their merits, which if it does not en-tirely heal their wounds, will assuage the pain of them." But Madison's plea fell on deaf ears in so far as those who argued for funding at face value were concerned, and on February 22, 1790, the Congress rejected his proposal by a vote of almost three to one. A few months later Hamilton's proposal was adopted. Incidentally twenty-nine of the sixty-four members of the House of Representatives at the time were security holders.[1]

Opposition to the assumption of the debts of the several states by the national government was bitter and uncompro-mising. Representatives of the agrarian South *Opposition to* declared the proposal to be merely another move in *assumption of* Hamilton's well laid plan to enrich the capitalists *state debts* *bitter and un-* of the North at the expense of the rest of the *compromising* country. The opposition of the South was the greater because their debts in proportion to population were much less than those of the North. Moreover, some of the southern states had already taken care of their debts, and their citizens could see no reason, therefore, why they should be taxed to help pay the debts of the North. The Hamiltonians worked day and night to stem the rising tide of opposition, but when the vote on the measure was taken in the House of Representatives on April 12, 1790, they met defeat by two votes. Speculators who for months had been scouring the back country of the Carolinas

---

[1] For details on this point consult Charles A. Beard, *The Economic Origins of Jeffersonian Democracy*, chap. vi.

and Georgia, buying up state securities on the assumption that they would be funded at face value, were almost beside themselves with disappointment and anger, while the opposition gloried in their discomfiture. "Last Monday Mr. Sedgwick," [1] tauntingly wrote one of the opposition, "delivered a funeral oration on the death of Miss Assumption. . . . Her death was much lamented by her parents, who were from New England. Mr. Sedgwick, being the most celebrated preacher, was requested to deliver her funeral eulogium. It was done with puritanic gravity. . . . Sixty-one of the political fathers of the nation were present and a crowded audience of weepers and rejoicers. Mrs. Speculator was the chief mourner and acted her part to admiration; she being the mother of Miss Assumption, who was the hope of her family. . . . Mrs. Excise may have cause to rejoice because she will be screened from much drudgery — as she must have been the principal support of Miss Assumption as well as of her mother and all her relations. Mrs. Direct Tax may rest more easy in Virignia as she will not be called into foreign service."

The rejoicing of the opposition, however, was short lived, for, following a favorable motion to reconsider, Hamilton and his **Hamilton wins** cohorts redoubled their efforts. Finally, after **battle for** weeks of ceaseless negotiations and meticulous **assumption** diplomacy, Hamilton seized upon the idea of bargaining with the agrarian South over the site of the permanent capital. The North wanted assumption and the South wanted the capital. Here, surely, he reasoned, was opportunity to effect an arrangement which would satisfy both sections. Fortunately for Hamilton, Jefferson, who had just returned from France to take up his new duties as Secretary of State, and who was soon to become Hamilton's chief antagonist, listened to his plea for assistance. At a dinner party arranged by Jefferson it was agreed that two members who had previously voted against assumption should change their minds and vote for it, and that the friends of assumption in return should see to it that the national capital was located on the banks of the Potomac

[1] Thomas Sedgwick, a representative from Massachusetts, who was himself a heavy speculator in public securities.

in territory set off from Virginia and Maryland. The feelings of the Pennsylvanians, who also wanted the capital, were assuaged by providing that Philadelphia should be the seat of the national government for ten years. "And so," wrote Jefferson long afterwards, "the Assumption was passed, and twenty millions of stock divided among favored states and thrown in as a pabulum to the stock-jobbing herd." While the action of the Congress in providing for the redemption of the old bills of credit issued during the Revolution by the Continental Congress in the ratio of one cent to the dollar was a hard blow to the speculators, the assumption victory was a real triumph. Indeed, we can well imagine with what satisfaction the Hamiltonians answered the satirical article on the death of Miss Assumption with the following verses:

> The wit who bastardized thy name
> •   And croaked a funeral dirge
> Knew not how spotless was thy fame —
> How soon thou would'st emerge.

With Hamilton on the crest of success, it was inevitable that his recommendations for a national bank and a mint should be accepted. But the bank proposal was not adopted without a fight, for as soon as the bill for its establishment came before the Congress the agrarians attacked it as a capitalistic measure. "This plan of a national bank," said Jackson of Georgia, the famous champion of agrarianism, "is calculated to benefit a small part of the United States, the mercantile interests only; the farmers, the yeomanry, will derive no advantage from it." The measure, he went on to say, sought to create a monopoly and was wholly contrary to the spirit and intent of the Constitution. Even Madison, who had labored so indefatigably for the establishment of a strong federal government, opposed the bank as unconstitutional. The opposition, however, was not strong enough to prevent the passage of this measure. It is significant that of the twenty votes cast against the measure in the House, nineteen were those of southern members. The bank, which was chartered for twenty years, opened for business in Philadelphia in

Establishment of national bank and mint

December, 1791; branches were subsequently established in Boston, New York, Baltimore, Washington, Norfolk, Charleston, Savannah, and New Orleans. The Mint Act of 1792 also closely followed Hamilton's suggestions; it made no provision, however, for the coinage of the gold dollar.

Hamilton's proposals for internal revenue and a tariff were likewise strenuously opposed by the agrarians. Anxious not to **The excise** alienate the propertied-business class by the impo- **tax** sition of direct taxes, he recommended an excise tax on spirituous liquors. Congress, following this suggestion, enacted early in 1791 a fairly sweeping excise law. While eastern distillers were affected by this measure their business was of such a character that they easily shifted the burden of the tax to the consumer. Frontier farmers, who on account of bad roads and high transportation costs were transforming their grain into whisky, were less fortunately situated. Much of their liquor was for domestic use, and the excise duty, therefore, fell on them as a direct tax; even those who sent part of their manufactured product to market were unable to shift the tax as did the eastern distillers.

News of the passage of the excise measure created a veritable hornets' nest on the frontier. Indeed, so great was popular dissatisfaction in Virginia and North Carolina that **Agrarian op-** **position: the** open rebellion threatened. Alarmed by the extent **Whisky** of the opposition, Congress in 1792 put through **Rebellion** supplementary legislation abolishing the tax on the smaller stills. Even this modification of the law failed to placate the irate frontier farmers of Pennsylvania. Shut off from the more populous East by densely wooded mountains and unable to understand why they should be taxed for the benefit of propertied-business men, they resorted to resistance. As in the Revolution, meetings, resolutions, and protests became the order of the day. Passive resistance, however, soon gave way to more drastic action: men refused to pay the tax, government collectors were intimidated, and persons who gave information or other aid to revenue officers were summarily dealt with. Finally, in 1794, when a United States marshal attempted to serve warrants on those who had been indicted for refusal to pay the tax an open insurrection, known as the Whisky Rebellion, broke out. The disaffected portions of the population were at once pictured by the propertied-business groups as an ignorant, vicious, unpatriotic, despicable lot. Hamilton, anxious to strengthen the hand of government and to teach the rank and file respect for law and order, advised Washington to treat them severely. Milder counsel, however, prevailed and with the approach of a considerable military force led by Washington and Hamilton the revolt quickly melted away. Several of the ringleaders were arrested and marched to Philadelphia where they were jailed; only two were subsequently convicted, and they were pardoned by the President. Propertied-business men everywhere rejoiced over the triumph of the government. Yet few of them apparently realized that both the excise law and the revolt to which it gave rise weakened their cause and strengthened the opposition. Only a few years were to elapse, as we shall see, before the reins of the federal government were to pass into the hands of the very men whom the Hamiltonians labeled as pernicious, malignant, contemptible, and vile.

Hamilton's arguments in favor of a protective tariff — arguments which have been advanced in every national political campaign from the beginning of the Republic to the present day — are set forth in his notable *Report on Manufactures* of 1791. While these arguments, as well as other features of the report, will be considered in a subsequent chapter, it is important to note here that the proposal for a tariff to protect American industry, which took form in the Revenue Act of 1792, met with the opposition of the agrarians. Any protective measure, they asserted, was bound to be a burden laid upon the farmer and laborer for the benefit of manufacturers and capitalists. "The policy of protecting duties to force manufacturing," wrote John Taylor of Virginia, philosopher and statesman of agrarianism, "is of the same nature and will produce the same consequences as that of enriching a noble interest, a church interest, or a paper interest; because bounties to capital are taxes upon industry and a distribution of property by law. And it is the worst mode of en-

Agrarian opposition to protective tariff

couraging aristocracy, because to the evil of distributing wealth at home by law, is to be added the national loss arising from foreign retaliation upon our own exports. An exclusion by us of foreign articles of commerce will beget an exclusion by foreigners of our articles of commerce, or at least corresponding duties; and the wealth of the majority will be as certainly diminished to enrich capital, as if it should be obliged to export a million of guineas to bring back a million of dollars or to bestow a portion of its guineas upon this special interest."

To the propertied-business class the adoption of the Hamiltonian program in its entirety was a fitting climax to its earlier dreams and aspirations. Through its efforts the struggling agrarian-controlled young republic of 1783 had undergone changes which were destined to affect profoundly its later development. A constitution had been drafted and ratified, a government, the overwhelming majority of whose personnel represented propertied and business interests, had been selected, and the foundations for the future capitalistic industrialization of America had been laid. Small wonder that Hamilton should be idolized by merchants, shippers, and moneylenders. He had set the house in order; the great obstacles which beset the path of the business man in the dark days following the Revolution had been cleared away.

Adoption of Hamiltonian program fitting climax to aspirations of propertied-business class

4. The Agrarian Challenge

But if Hamilton and those who were heaping adulation upon him in the hour of triumph entertained the notion that the backbone of the agrarian opposition had been broken and that control of affairs was to remain permanently in the hands of capitalists and business men and their allies in the professions, they were fated to be disillusioned. Scarcely had the last of the Hamiltonian proposals become law before certain forces began to undermine the group in power and thus to pave the way for its political downfall. Chief among these were (1) the continued feeling on the part of the common people that the Hamiltonian legislation — the funding of the debt, the bank, the excise law,

Forces destined to undermine Hamiltonians

and the protective tariff — was designed to aid the wealthy at the expense of the farmer and laborer; (2) hostility of private soldiers of the Revolution and others whose securities had passed into the hands of speculators or their agents; (3) condemnation of democracy and equalitarianism by Federalist leaders and Federalist press; (4) the French Revolution; (5) Federalist foreign policy, particularly the Jay Treaty; (6) attempts of Federalists to curb Anti-Federalists by means of the so-called Alien and Sedition laws; and (7) Thomas Jefferson, agrarian leader and philosopher-politician, who with endless patience welded together an organization democratic in character and imbued with the idea that government should exist not for the benefit of the few — the well-born and the wealthy — but for the welfare of all the people.

Opposition of farmer, mechanic, and common soldier was intensified when, following the passage of the Hamiltonian measures, they beheld those who were profiting from the new legislation building finer homes, dressing more lavishly, and in other ways displaying their increasing wealth. As this show of wealth increased the rumblings and grumblings in the coffeehouses and taverns and along the highways and byways grew in intensity. Agrarian spokesmen, like John Taylor, repeatedly gave expression to this growing hostility on the part of the rank and file. In his pamphlet entitled *An Enquiry into the Principles and Tendency of Certain Public Measures*, which appeared in 1794, Taylor attacked the Hamiltonian program as a capitalist device to enrich the wealthy and impoverish the poor. A year earlier "A Farmer" in an anonymous tract bearing the title *Five Letters Addressed to the Yeomanry of the United States* declared that the laws of the Union were stained with (1) mercantile regulations highly injurious to the agricultural interests of the country; (2) funding systems by which the property and rights of poor but meritorious citizens were sacrificed to wealthy gamesters and speculators; (3) the establishment of banks "authorizing a few men to create ficticious money, by which they may acquire rapid fortunes without industry"; and (4) excise laws which disturbed domestic tranquillity and prevented the farmer from enjoying

1. Continued opposition of rank and file

the fruits of his industry. Somewhat later Callender, another agrarian pamphleteer, expressed much the same opinion in his *Sedgwick & Co., or a Key to the Six Per Cent Cabinet.* Pamphlets of lesser importance and newspaper articles also voiced the opposition of the common people to the existing order.

Instead of calmly considering the criticisms and complaints which poured in from all sides, the Federalists either arrogantly
Federalists ignore agrarian complaints ignored them or else denounced those who made them as "ignorant," "malevolent," "spiteful," "envious," "vulgar," "infamous," and "low-lived Democrats" — "desperate, embarrassed, unprincipled, disorderly, ambitious, disaffected, morose men," to quote one anti-agrarian leader. Federalist leaders never tired of heaping vituperation upon all those who disagreed with them, and every agrarian critic was pictured as a propertyless leveller, the spiritual heir of Daniel Shays, and the enemy of his country. "As to property, I have none," wrote a Federalist champion posing as an apostle of agrarianism, "thank heaven I have divested myself of all yellow dirt, all filthy lucre. . . . Property . . . is the mother of aristocracy. . . . A Numarian law would be a rich blessing. Oh, how it would gladden the hearts and gild with pleasure the faces of the true disciples, to serve once more on committee, whose business it should be, at least once in three years, to inspect the chests and coffers of the overgrown purse-proud man or the paltry muck-worm, who toiled with the dirty view of 'laying up pelf against a rainy day,' and divide their ungodly spoil amongst the pure lovers of liberty." "A Numarian law," he continued, "is not an object to be despaired of. In order to gain the landholders it is only necessary to convince them that it is their interest to pare commerce to the quick. . . . That the landed interest is one thing and the monied is another, is very plain. . . . I have heard it reported that there is one State in the Union of no mean size, that would not suffer land to be touched by that harpy of the law. If this is true, it is a glorious example, a noble policy. A new-made landed-man laughs his monied dupe creditor in the face with virtuous scorn, . . . View the American Court and tremble. The head of the system and all coadjutors ought speedily to be ostracised and

banished. . . . For a beginning it would remove the Secretary of the Treasury and appoint some Young Broker in his place. . . . For Secretary of War, I would chuse their worthy re-inflated fellow citizen, Daniel Shays, Esq." In some instances Federalist writers thought it better policy to be less vindictive and satirical in refuting the allegations of their agrarian opponents.

While the controversy resulting from the adoption of the Hamiltonian program was raging, the French Revolution — that mighty social-political upheaval destined to affect so profoundly both the Old World and the New — engulfed Europe. The French Revolution This event, so far-reaching, was in reality an aspect of the titanic struggle between the privileged and unprivileged which had been increasing in intensity from the close of the Middle Ages, and of which the seventeenth-century revolutions in England were the first unmistakable manifestation.

The privileged class, composed for the most part of the wealthier nobility, and the higher clergy and constituting only a very small minority of the population, fell heir to prac-tically all the advantages, privileges, and immuni-ties of the medieval aristocracy. The privileged order Its members monopolized the higher offices in the state, army, and church, enjoyed exemption from taxation, and frequently were pensioned. Above all, they esteemed themselves as inherently superior to the rank and file: they lived in finer homes, wore better clothes, set luxurious tables, performed no menial tasks, and expected and received deference from the common people. Unlike the feudal nobility, however, the privileged order of the seventeenth and eighteenth centuries rendered little or no service to the lower social classes. In fact, many of its members, if not the majority, idled away their lives in the growing cities or at the royal court while their flint-hearted agents squeezed money from the less fortunate.

Upon the shoulders of the unprivileged class, which included within its ranks the *bourgeoisie*, the country gentry, the artisans and laborers, the peasantry, and the lesser clergy, fell the chief burdens of the day. They tilled the The unprivileged soil, carried on the manufacturing, did the merchandising, performed all sorts of manual work, and paid most of the taxes. They bore no high-sounding titles, high social and official distinctions were not heaped upon them, and the rich sinecures of church and state were generally closed to them. In the eyes of the privileged class their chief mission was to make the existing state of the higher aristocracy more easy and secure.

With the discovery of the New World and the subsequent expansion of commerce and trade, and the accompanying intellectual changes, the unprivileged were no longer content with the old order of things. Viewing society as dynamic and progressive rather than static and fixed, the leaders of the unprivileged began to agitate for change. They could see no reason why they should continue to be considered social underlings by foppish spendthrift nobles whose only claim to greatness rested on ownership of a moldy castle, a worm-eaten patent of nobility, a family tradition, or the knowledge that they were favorites of a royal household. Moreover, they were no longer satisfied to have the government conducted by absolute monarchs and the privileged class in the supposed interest of rulers, nobility, and clergy. They were tired of seeing royal funds obtained from taxing the unprivileged wasted on extravagant enterprises, squandered on dynastic wars, or handed over outright to the nobility in the form of gifts or pensions. They wanted participation in the affairs of government to the end that their own interests might be promoted and safeguarded even at the expense of the privileged class. In a word, they desired social and political equality, and when in 1788–89 France, due to a profligate court, an expensive foreign policy, and a corrupt administrative system, stood face to face with bankruptcy the hour was at hand for the overthrow of the old order.

The dramatic story of the Revolution itself — of the summoning of the Estates General or National Parliament for the first time in more than one hundred and fifty years, of the metamorphosis of the third estate into a national assembly controlled by the *bourgeoisie*, of the sweeping reforms embodied in the famous Declaration of the

The unprivileged challenge the old order

The French Revolution in summary

JOHN JAY

After the portrait by Stuart and Trumbull

JOHN ADAMS

Rights of Man, of the transformation of absolute monarchy into limited monarchy, of the ascendency of the proletariat, the growth of anti-monarchial feelings, the calling of a new assembly and the establishment of the first French Republic, of the combined efforts of France's powerful neighbors to suppress the Revolution and restore the old order, of the merciless anti-monarchist campaign, of the execution of Louis XVI and Marie Antoinette, of the radical reforms enacted, of the reaction, of the emergence of Napoleon Bonaparte and of his rise and fall — need not be told here. It is sufficient that we bear in mind that the echoes of this conflict which rent asunder the old order reverberated to every corner of the civilized world. Everywhere conservatives, fearful lest everything they held dear be lost, struggled desperately to stem the floodtide of democracy and radicalism. In England, for example, Edmund Burke in his *Reflections on the French Revolution* and in other writings thundered against what he held to be the work of "monsters and outlaws" who had perpetrated the worst of "frauds, impostures, violences, rapines, murders, confiscations, compulsory paper currencies, and every description of tyranny and cruelty."

But it is with the effect of the French Revolution on the young American republic that we are chiefly concerned. From Maine to Georgia the news that in France the old order with all its trappings had been overturned and that the aristocracy of Europe under the leadership of the Duke of Brunswick had been turned back by the embattled Revolutionists on the French frontier, was greeted with wild enthusiasm by the common people. To them the Old World upheaval was a replica of their own struggle against wealth and privilege. Discontented with their social and economic position they had left their farms, their workbenches, and their firesides to fight for "the rights of man" only to be disappointed and disillusioned. News of the French Revolution, therefore, was like a powerful shaft of sunlight piercing the heavy clouds of restlessness and discontent; perhaps, after all, that larger life with its promise of greater social, economic, and political equality, of which they

Rank and file of America wildly enthusiastic over the French Revolution

had dreamed and for which they had fought, would be realized. Everywhere there were festivals, songs, speeches, and riotous parades. French ideas, French modes of speaking, and French fashions became the order of the day. Liberty poles were erected and liberty caps worn. Conversation centered around topics concerning "liberty, equality, and fraternity." Titles such as "Sir," "The Honorable," and "His Excellency" were discarded as too aristocratic, and "Citizen" and "Citizeness" replaced "Mr.," "Mrs.," and "Miss." Even the theatres caught the spirit and Shakespeare and Sheridan gave way to *Tyranny Suppressed* and the *Demolition of the Bastille*. Streets whose names were associated with aristocracy or monarchialism were rechristened; thus Royal Exchange Alley in Boston became Equality Lane, and Kings Street in New York was renamed Liberty Street.

Thomas Paine, trenchant pamphleteer of the American Revolution, reënforced this enthusiasm in his *Rights of Man*, a brilliant and eloquent reply to Burke's *Reflections*.

Paine's *Rights of Man* and rise of democratic clubs

"Every age and generation," he contended, "must be free to act for itself in *all cases* as the ages and generations which preceded it. The vanity and presumption of governing beyond the grave is the most ridiculous and insolent of all tyrannies. . . . Every generation is, and must be, competent to all the purposes which its occasions require. It is the living, and not the dead, that are to be accommodated." Paine's preachments stimulated the formation of secret democratic clubs which, modeled after the revolutionary clubs (Jacobin) of Paris, sprang up from one end of the country to the other. Resolutions galore, embodying democratic and equalitarian sentiments and especially endorsing the work of the French radicals and condemning the efforts of the Old World reactionaries to stamp out the Revolution, were passed by these societies. Ominously for those in power, the activity of these newly formed organizations was not confined to the events of Europe. From the outset an increasing number were interested in local politics; indeed, many explicitly stated that their avowed purpose was to discuss and disseminate information about domestic affairs.

To the Hamiltonians the French Revolution with its exalta-
tion of the common man, its defiance of tradition and constituted
authority, its challenge of privilege, and its emphasis on democracy, was from the beginning a-   Hatred of
nathema. They hated it and did all within their   Hamiltonians
                                                   for French
power to neutralize or destroy its popularity and Revolution
influence in America. As the movement gathered headway and
control passed from the moderates into the hands of the
radicals, the Hamiltonian leaders became almost hysterical
lest the "rabble" in America should overturn the government
and destroy the Constitution. Like cornered animals fighting
for their lives, they savagely attacked every sympathizer of the
Revolution as a "Jacobin" intent on destroying the social
order. Every sympathizer of the French Revolution, a New
England clergyman shouted, was guilty of spreading "atheis-
tical, anarchial and, in other respects, immoral principles. . . .
The editors, patrons, and abettors of these vehicles of slander
ought to be considered and treated as enemies to their country.
. . . Of all traitors they are the most aggravatedly criminal;
of all villains they are the most infamous and detestable."

For what end, raved Timothy Dwight, president of Yale and a
Federalist spokesman, should respectable people be connected
with French revolutionists and democrats who   Federalist
were nothing more than atheists, blasphemers, and condemnation
sappers of Christian morals and good government.   of French
"Is it," he inquired, "that our churches may be-   sympathizers
come temples of reason, our Sabbath a decade, and our psalms
of praise Marsellaise hymns? Is it that we may change our holy
worship into a dance of Jacobin phrenzy and that we may behold
a strumpet personating a goddess on the altars of Jehovah? . . .
Is it that we may see our wives and daughters the victims of
legal prostitution, soberly dishonoured; speciously polluted, the
outcasts of delicacy and virtue, the loathing of God and man?
. . . Shall our sons become the desciples of Voltaire and the
dragoons of Marat; or our daughters the concubines of the
illuminati?" Others were no less bitter and vindictive in
denouncing what many of them honestly believed to be a loathsome social scourge.

The Federalist onslaught on the democratic clubs was even more vitriolic. In fact, on every hand the cry was raised, **Democratic societies condemned** "Down with the Democratic clubs!" Federalist leaders seemingly vied with each other in condemning these organizations as "demoniacal societies," "nurseries of sedition," and "hot-beds of treason." Even Washington, influenced probably by Hamilton, insinuated that they were back of the Whisky Rebellion, and attacked them as secret and self-created bodies ignorantly or wilfully engaged in the dissemination of propaganda designed to undermine the government.

While the two opposing groups were warring over the character and status of the Democratic clubs, Citizen Genêt, representative of revolutionary France, arrived in the **Citizen Genêt** aristocratic city of Charleston. Young, handsome, elegant in manner, eloquent and entertaining in conversation, and friendly in bearing, he was received with great acclaim by the Anti-Federalists. Indeed, his month's journey northward to Philadelphia was a continuous ovation. Everywhere he was greeted as a conquering hero by the multitudes who paid tribute to France and the principles of the Revolutionists. The rank and file of the capital city, almost frenzied with joy over his arrival, gave him round after round of thunderous applause. Such a reception was enough to turn the head of almost any man, and the impulsive Genêt was, therefore, greatly angered when in presenting his credentials to Washington he was received with stern formality. Believing that the administration did not represent the people and that the latter would support him in case of conflict with the government, he very unwisely embarked upon a policy which soon not only got him into trouble but strengthened the hand of the Federalists.

Prior to Genêt's arrival Washington, fully aware that the new plenipotentiary would leave no stone unturned to drag the **American neutrality** United States into the European embroglio on the side of France, asked his cabinet for advice and suggestions. Hamilton unhesitantly argued that the treaties of 1778 between France and the United States were obsolete because they had been negotiated with the Bourbon monarchy, which the Revolutionists had overthrown. Even if in force, he contended that there would be no obligation on the part of the American republic to come to the assistance of France, for the treaties stipulated that only in case of a defensive war was help to be given. Jefferson, on the other hand, just as warmly maintained that treaties are negotiated between nations rather than between governments, and that the pacts of 1778 were still binding. Washington inclined toward the Hamiltonian point of view and in 1793 issued his neutrality proclamation in which he announced to the European belligerents that the United States would not be a party to the conflict and warned all American citizens to refrain from any act which might be considered hostile by the states involved.

But the proclamation of neutrality meant nothing to Genêt. Even before presenting his credentials he planned, with American assistance, to organize two expeditions in the United States, one against Louisiana and the other against Florida. He attempted to use American ports as bases of operation for French privateers and commissioned American vessels to prey on British commerce. When Jefferson, who was still Secretary of State, took him to task and endeavored to reason with him, he flew into an insolent rage and denounced the administration as cowardly and unrepresentative. Finally the government, unable to tolerate longer his abuse and interference, asked for his recall. Genêt, knowing that his return to France would probably mean his execution, decided to remain in America. Accordingly he went to New York, married a daughter of George Clinton, and lived quietly until his death in 1835.

Genêt's high-handed acts and his recall

Genet's presence in America and his high-handed methods were of three-fold importance. In the first place, they served to accentuate the bitterness between the Federalists and Anti-Federalists. Secondly, they momentarily weakened the Anti-Federalists and correspondingly strengthened the Federalists. Jefferson was well aware of this fact and was extremely relieved when the obnoxious minister was officially unhorsed. Even the Democratic clubs agreed with Madison's characterization of Genêt's conduct

Three-fold importance of Genêt's ministership

as that of a madman. Thirdly, Genêt's actions did not help the cause of the French Revolution; many Americans who had been inclined to be sympathetic now became indifferent to the Revolution or its out-and-out enemies.

Whatever advantage the Federalists may have gained from Genêt's blundering was more than offset by their apparent pro-British attitude. No sooner did England and France become involved in war in 1793 than English naval commanders promptly proceeded to destroy the French merchant marine. This action left France and her West Indian islands, with which she carried on about two-thirds of her overseas trade, in desperate straits, for both needed vital food supplies. Thus faced by economic necessity, France lifted her old mercantilistic barriers and opened her commerce to the neutrals of the world. Americans rejoiced, for here was opportunity to reëstablish their lucrative West Indian trade. But their rejoicing was of short duration for the British government, anxious to cut France off from all relief and to prevent the development of a rival merchant marine, at once ruled that all ships of neutrals were liable to capture if engaged in carrying enemy-owned goods. Even more damaging to the Americans was her insistence that a trade closed in time of peace could not be opened in time of war. To cap the climax, she issued an order in June, 1793, authorizing the seizure of all vessels laden with grain and flour. Hundreds of American ships with their crews soon fell into the hands of the British, and American newspapers were filled with accounts of the losses sustained by American shippers and with stories of the cruel treatment suffered by American sailors who had been thrown into prison.

Anglo-French rivalry and American shippers

The effect of this British action on the people of the United States was far-reaching. Shipbuilding decreased and unemployment spread in this and in allied industries. Farmers, who had looked hopefully to the West Indies as a market for their surplus grain and meat, bitterly complained that they were unable to get rid of their produce. Sympathizers of France, overlooking the fact that French men-of-war and privateers were also harassing

Effect of British maritime restrictions on United States

American vessels, expressed their hatred for Britain in no uncertain terms. Federalist leaders, though detesting France, were placed in an embarrassing position, for the large southern planting interests, who up to this time had been loyal Federalists, now welcomed trouble with Great Britain in the hope that debts still due to British creditors might be extinguished. Moreover, these same interests were not unmindful of the fact that the British had failed to compensate them for the thousands of slaves which they asserted the British had carried off at the conclusion of the Revolution. Sensing the situation and hoping to gain further at the expense of the Federalists, the Anti-Federalists demanded that drastic measures be taken against Great Britain. In consequence, proposals were made ranging all the way from sequestration of British debts and non-importation to a declaration of war. In the meantime a sixty-day embargo was proclaimed.

Despite the attitude of the southern planters and the fact that the British action worked great hardship on the commercial interests of the country, the Hamiltonians did not want war with Great Britain. The federal government, they declared, was still in the experimental stage and in no position to embark upon a costly and hazardous war. Nearly ninety per cent of the imports from which was derived practically all of the national income came from Great Britain. Severance of relations would, therefore, mean impairment of the public credit and the probable destruction of the fiscal edifice which Hamilton had so arduously constructed. Moreover, war would mean irreparable loss to the American producer and merchant and would close the door to the English investor who, as Beard points out, not only advanced credit for trade and money for land speculation and industrial enterprise, but was a heavy purchaser of government bonds and bank stock. In addition, the Hamiltonians desired to avoid hostilities with Great Britain in the hope that they might induce the British to relinquish their grip on the posts in the Northwest. These posts had been held by the British since the close of the Revolution in retaliation for the non-payment of debts to British creditors; as a result land speculators had been impeded by Indian hostility, and a fur trade worth approximately £100,000 a year had been diverted to Canada instead of flowing through United States posts. Finally, the Federalists had not the slightest desire to go to war with any country engaged in curbing "Jacobinical" France.[1]

Though hard-pressed, the Federalists, powerfully supported by Washington, succeeded in preventing a break with Great

The Jay Treaty   Britain. To ease the situation, Washington sent John Jay, the Chief Justice of the Supreme Court, to England for the purpose of concluding a treaty which would secure the British evacuation of the Northwest posts, redress of grievances, indemnification for American losses, and the removal of conditions impeding the peaceful commercial relations of the two countries. The military weakness of the United States, together with Jay's failure to make the best case possible, enabled the British to drive a hard bargain. The New England boundary line and indemnities for shipping seized were to be adjusted by joint commissions; the Northwest posts were to be evacuated by June 1, 1796, and in return the Mississippi was to be opened to British trade. While not a word was said about compensation for the slaves carried off by the British army, the old pre-Revolutionary British debts were to be assumed by the federal government and principal and interest paid in specie. Commercially the principle that "free goods make free ships" was abandoned, and the contraband list was extended. Nothing was said about the impressment of American seamen; and the all-important West Indian trade, which Jay was specifically instructed to secure, was opened to American ships of seventy tons burden only, and on the express condition that American vessels should not carry molasses, sugar, coffee, cocoa, or cotton, no matter where produced, to any other ports in the world except their own. The East Indian trade was opened to Americans subject to certain conditions. As a slap at France and at the French sympathizers in America, British trade with the United States was placed on a most-favored-nation basis, thus precluding such

---

[1] For a more detailed account of the controversy between the two American economic groups respecting the action of Great Britain see Charles A. Beard, *Economic Origins of Jeffersonian Democracy*, chap. x.

retaliatory and discriminatory measures as the Anti-Federalists had been proposing.

When the terms of the Treaty were made public a howl of rage swept over the country. Everywhere Jay was burned in effigy; the British minister was openly insulted; Hamilton, trying to defend the Treaty, was hissed and stoned; marching mobs and mass meetings condemned it as a "nefarious plot against the liberties of the people." "His Excellency, John Jay, . . . may he and his treason be forever politically damned," was a typical toast. "Damn John Jay! Damn every one who wont damn John Jay! Damn every one who wont put out lights in his windows and sit up all night damning John Jay," expressed the feeling of the rank and file. Even some of the Federalists like John Rutledge and John Langdon denounced the Treaty as the sum total of all villainies. "Never had the people," writes Claude Bowers in his *Jefferson and Hamilton,* "been more agitated or outraged. Whenever two men met, whether bankers or brokers, the Treaty was the topic of their talk. In taverns, where travelers were promiscuously packed like sardines in a box, the quarreling made night hideous and sleep impossible. In the bar-rooms, men, in their cups, disputed and fought. The stage-coaches were a forum, the crossroads store a battle ground." *Ferocious attack on Jay Treaty*

Alarmed at the ferocity of the public protest Hamilton, writing under the pen name of "Camillus," came to the rescue of the Treaty. In a series of thirty-eight essays he not only brought out its more favorable aspects, but showed with remarkable clarity that the controversy over the treaty was merely a phase of the conflict between the propertied-business class and the small-farmer-non-propertied group — in short, between capitalism and agrarianism — which began in pre-Revolutionary days. The agrarians, he said, had merely seized upon the Treaty in order to discredit the Federalists and their work. He alienated the large landed interests of the South by asserting that the southern claim of compensation for slaves taken by the British was "a very doubtful one," and by arguing that the debts owing to British creditors ought to be paid. Other Federalist leaders, *Economic aspect of controversy over Jay Treaty* among them Fisher Ames of Massachusetts, labored unceasingly in behalf of the condemned treaty. Ames, in denouncing those merchants who joined with the Anti-Federalists in opposing the Treaty, said he could not disguise his "contempt for the blindness and gullibility of the rich men who so readily lend their strength to the party which is thirsting for the contents of their iron chests." To the great relief of the Federalists the Treaty, minus the article dealing with the West Indian trade, was ratified by the Senate in June, 1795. The controversy over it, however, severely weakened the Hamiltonian group.

The grip of the propertied-business class was further lessened when in 1796 Washington, who had been in public life for almost half a century, announced that he would retire at the end of his second presidential term. For a dozen years or more he had been at the beck and call of the Federalists, with whom he had definitely aligned himself. He had, as we have observed, thrown all his weight and influence into the movement for the Constitution. Moreover, during his presidency he had done everything in his power to promote the welfare of the group of which he himself was a member. His great name and the respect in which he was held by the overwhelming majority of his countrymen undoubtedly made it easier for Hamilton and the other Federalist leaders to accomplish all that they did. On more than one occasion, for example, unpopular Federalist measures had been saved by recourse to the appeal, "Stand by Washington." In his Farewell Address of September, 1796, he cautioned his countrymen to avoid sectional jealousies, partisan strife, and foreign entanglements and alliances. His retirement opened wide the door to the opposition; men who up to this time had hesitated to say what they thought now gave widest expression to their pent-up feelings. "If ever there was a period for rejoicing," wrote a grandson of Benjamin Franklin in referring to Washington's retirement, "this is the moment — every heart, in unison with the freedom and happiness of the people, ought to beat high with exultation that the name of Washington from this day ceases to give a currency to political iniquity and to legalize corruption."

Washington's retirement a blow to the Federalists

The social and economic philosophy of John Adams, who succeeded Washington to the presidency, was not of the brand to satisfy the critics of the propertied-business or capitalist class. A stolid, pragmatic, unimaginative realist, Adams had no use for high-sounding idealisms or humanitarian panaceas. As a young man *Social and economic philosophy of John Adams* he had staunchly defended human rights, but with maturing years he became an even more ardent defender of property rights. Society, he maintained, consisted of economic classes — the rich and the poor — which were always contending with each other for control. Warfare between these diametrically opposed classes, he held, could be prevented only by a government which, on the one hand, safeguarded the poor against exploitation by the rich; and, on the other, protected the rich against the leveling attacks of the populace. While he advocated rule by the well-born and the educated, he did not believe that government should be controlled too absolutely either by agrarians or capitalists. It was probably for this reason in part that Hamilton disliked him. Personally he was unattractive, and this together with his refusal to be a victim of mob psychology, his colossal vanity, and his blundering tactlessness, did not make him a popular figure.

Adams on assuming office at once found himself face to face with many of the same problems that had vexed Washington. Among them was the question of America's attitude toward the European upheaval then in progress. During the last years of Washington's administration James Monroe, who sympathized with the French radicals, *American neutrality and France* had been recalled as Minister to France and Charles Coatsworth Pinckney, a thorough-going Federalist, named to take his place. This action together with Washington's treatment of Genêt and the Jay Treaty angered the Directory at Paris. The Washington government was labeled as pro-British; Pinckney, instead of being received, was first placed under surveillance as a suspicious character and then ordered out of the country; the American alliance of 1778 was declared at an end; French vessels were authorized to seize and confiscate all American vessels bound to or from British ports or engaged in carrying British goods, and Adet, the French Minister to the United States, was recalled. The Federalists, bristling with resentment, loudly clamored for war; but Adams, fully realizing what armed conflict with France might mean, refused to do the bidding of the more extreme Federalists, and instead of talking war to avenge national honor he announced to a special session of Congress that he would attempt to settle the difficulty by negotiation. Accordingly a committee of three — Pinckney, Marshall, and Gerry — were sent to France for the purpose of restoring friendly relations.

When the three commissioners arrived in Paris Talleyrand, in charge of foreign affairs for the French government, not only **The X Y Z papers** refused to receive them officially but subjected them to all sorts of insolence. Negotiations were carried on informally by means of certain agents designated by Talleyrand. As a price for peace these agents demanded, first, that the United States apologize for its past conduct — in other words, for what the French called its pro-British policy; secondly, that it extend to the French government a large loan; and, finally, that the "Prince of Liars" — a title which Talleyrand justly deserved — and his fellow plunderers receive a *douceur* of $240,000! After months of vain haggling, during which the American representatives were the victims of fresh insult, the commissioners broke off negotiations and reported the situation to Adams. Fully aware that the French treatment of the American mission would strengthen both himself and his fellow Federalists and weaken the opposition, Adams in March, 1798, submitted a summary of the negotiations to Congress, referring to the French agents as Mr. X, Mr. Y, and Mr. Z.

Immediately the country became almost hysterical with excitement, and the Federalist leaders, not only anxious to dis- **Federalist propaganda** credit the French Revolution but to destroy democracy at home, sought to make the most of the opportunity. Homes and offices of editors of democratic or Anti-Federalist sheets were attacked; Benjamin Franklin, dead only a half dozen years, was denounced as a democrat and his statue in Philadelphia was smeared with mud. Democrats everywhere were labeled as infidels by Federalist preachers, who urged their

JOHN MARSHALL

After the portrait by J. Paul

WASHINGTON AND JEFFERSON

From a cartoon published in 1807

congregations to hate the name of revolution. Hamilton and William Cobbett filled the Federalist press with infamous propaganda: French troops, the gullible public was informed, had already landed at Charlestown and were destroying farmhouses; negro slaves were being armed and incited to insurrection by French revolutionary agents; everywhere men should get ready to protect themselves, their wives and daughters, their property, from the horrors of the invasion which was close at hand! Even some of the courts, which were strongholds of Federalism, took occasion to denounce democracy in all its forms.

In the face of all this it is not surprising that many of the agrarian Democratic group came over temporarily at least to the banners of Federalism. Much as they hated capitalism and disliked many of the Federalist leaders, they could not withstand the emotional appeal to avenge an insult to their country. The Federalist propaganda was bearing fruit and the elated Federalists, well aware of this fact, prepared for war. The army was increased, and Washington, Hamilton, and Knox, to the consternation of the democrats, were summoned to take command. A Navy department was also organized, and fighting on the high seas was soon in progress even though no formal declaration of war had been made by either France or the United States. Adams, though gaining considerable satisfaction by being placed in the limelight by the X Y Z affair, was still opposed to war and sent a new commission to Paris. This body found Napoleon Bonaparte rather than the corrupt Directory in control, and in 1800 a Convention was signed officially abrogating the treaties of 1778 and proclaiming the principle that free ships make free goods. No provision was made, however, for indemnifying property of shippers illegally seized. The Anti-Federalists rejoiced, but their opponents, especially those who thought they saw in a war with France a prospect of discrediting democracy forever, disappointedly damned Adams for his pacifist tendencies.

In the course of the excitement occasioned by the difficulties with France a few outstanding Anti-Federalists like Jefferson refused to be intimidated or to fall prey to the Federalist propaganda. Indeed, some, more outspoken than others, in-

Federalists prepare for war

sisted from first to last that the break with France was in large
measure due to Federalist dislike of the French Revolution and
Background of democracy in general. Naturally the Federalists
of Alien and did not like to hear such accusations nor did they
Sedition Acts welcome the bitter invectives hurled at them by
the democratic press. They were particularly incensed by the
writings of the Frenchman, Philip Freneau, who at the instiga-
tion of Madison and other Virginians had established the
National Gazette in Philadelphia in the early seventeen-nineties.
No Federalist escaped Freneau's vitriolic pen, and his editorials
and articles were widely copied in the Anti-Federalist press.
Moreover, Freneau, as well as some of his democratic friends in
America, championed the cause of those Irish patriots who at
this time were rebelling against British rule in Ireland. To make
matters worse, Irish immigration to America was increasing
rapidly, the newcomers aligning themselves with the Anti-
Federalists. In view of all this the more radical Federalists
made up their minds that the time had come to silence the
critics of the existing order and, in so far as possible, to destroy
the party of democracy.

Accordingly in 1798 the Federalists pushed through Congress
four drastic measures known in American history as the Alien
The Alien and and Sedition Acts. The first of these, a new
Sedition Acts naturalization law, changed the residence requirement from a minimum of five years to fourteen years. The
second, the Alien Act, authorized the President to banish at any
time such aliens as he should judge "dangerous to the peace and
safety of the United States," or that he had "reasonable
grounds to suspect are concerned in any treasonable or secret
machinations against the government." This measure was supplemented by the Alien Enemies Act empowering the President
in case of war or predatory incursion to restrain, imprison, or
remove all alien enemies whose continued presence might en-
danger the public safety. The fourth law, the Sedition Act,
which was aimed at the democratic press, was even more severe.
It prescribed a fine not exceeding $5,000 and imprisonment of
not less than six months nor more than five years for any persons who might unlawfully combine or conspire "to oppose any

measure or measures of the government of the United States
. . . or to impede the operation of any law of the United States,
or to intimidate or prevent any person holding a place or office
. . . from undertaking, performing, or executing his trust or
duty." Persons who counseled, advised, or attempted "to procure any insurrection, riot, unlawful assembly, or combination"
were to be deemed guilty of a high misdemeanor and, if convicted, were liable to the same severe punishment. Moreover,
any person who should "write, print, utter, or publish . . . any
false, scandalous, and malicious writing or writings against the
government of the United States" or against any officer thereof
for the purpose of bringing him into disrepute or to excite the
hatred of the people for him should, upon conviction, be liable
to a fine not exceeding $2,000 and to a maximum imprisonment
of two years.

The Alien Acts, though not enforced, caused bitter resentment, and many persons, apprehensive lest a deluge of Federalist
persecutions be let loose, left the country. The **Alien and
Sedition Acts
in force** vigorous enforcement of the vicious and partisan
Sedition Act resulted in a veritable reign of terror.
Anti-Federalist papers were literally combed for evidence, and
in a comparatively short time no less than twenty-four editors
were placed under arrest. Among these were Thomas Adams of
the *Independent Chronicle* of Boston, David Frothingham of the
Argus of New York, Benjamin Franklin Bache of the *Philadelphia Aurora*, and James Thompson Callender of the *Richmond
Examiner* — four of the ablest and most distinguished democratic journalists in America. Of the dozens of others who fell
victims to the obnoxious law, Matthew Lyons, Congressman
from Vermont, was perhaps the most prominent. He was
sentenced to four months in jail and fined a thousand dollars for
asserting that President Adams had turned men out of office for
party reasons and for referring to the President's "continual
grasp for power" and his "unbounded thirst for ridiculous
pomp, foolish adulation, and selfish avarice." Jedidiah Peck,
an eccentric but kindly surveyor-preacher, was dragged from
his bed in Otsego, New York, placed in manacles and marched
two hundred miles to New York, where he was tried for sedition

for merely having circulated a powerful and somewhat vitupera-
tive petition for the repeal of the Sedition Act. Even worse was
the case of David Brown, an illiterate and irresponsible Revolutionary soldier of Dedham, Massachusetts. Hostile to the administration, Brown was in part responsible for the erection of a
liberty pole bearing the inscription: "No Stamp Act, no Sedition, no Alien Bills, no Land Tax; downfall to the Tyrants of
America, peace and retirement to the President; long live the
Vice-President, and the minority; may moral virtue be the basis
of civil government." Fisher Ames, Federalist guardian of the
existing order, at once took steps to apprehend this trumpeter of
sedition who was telling everybody the sins and enormities of the
government. After a farcical trial Brown was sentenced to
eighteen months' imprisonment and a fine of $400. Unable to
secure the money, he remained in prison for two years until
pardoned by Jefferson, President Adams having twice ignored
his petition for release.

The Alien and Sedition laws instead of accomplishing the
purpose of their designers proved a boomerang to the Federalists.
Everywhere the common people as well as some
higher up the social-economic ladder vigorously protested against what they maintained were outrageous departures from the fundamental law of
the land and from the American tradition of liberty. Not only,
they declared, was the spirit of the Federal Constitution violated,
but the first Amendment to that document, forbidding Congress
to make any law restricting freedom of speech and press, had
been maliciously and despotically transgressed.

Alien and Sedition Acts a boomerang to Federalists

Of the numerous protests the Kentucky and Virginia Resolutions were the most famous. The Kentucky Resolutions,
drafted by Jefferson and slightly modified by the
Kentuckian John Breckenridge, were presented to
the Kentucky legislature in November, 1798. They
declared that government exists by compact and that certain very
definite powers are reserved to each state. Any Act, they further
maintained, contrary to the Constitution, as were the Alien and
Sedition laws, was null and void and of no force. These resolutions were adopted, signed by the governor, and sent to the

The Kentucky and Virginian Resolutions

legislature of the several states as an expression of Kentucky's creed. Similar resolutions drawn up by Madison condemned the obnoxious laws in somewhat briefer and milder form. The passage of these resolutions served to center public attention on the hated Acts, which at once became the subject of heated debate, agitation, and newspaper controversy. Everywhere the Anti-Federalists made the Resolutions the occasion for denouncing the Acts, while the Federalists on the other hand made them the pretext not only for justifying the Acts but for defending the Constitution and their administration of the national government. One rabid New England Federalist paper even went so far as to declare that should the federal government pass into the hands of the agrarians and New England thereby lose its influence in national affairs, the section would secede from the Union and establish a government of its own!

The person most responsible for the formulation of the Kentucky and Virginia Resolutions, and the one destined to weld the discontented and restless agrarians and non- *Thomas Jef-* propertied artisans into an organization strong *ferson and his faith in* enough to oust the Federalists from control of the *the com-* national government, was Thomas Jefferson. Born *mon man* and reared on the frontier and ever conscious of its influence, an idealist who had rubbed elbows with the French Revolution, a close student of nature and of civilization past and present, he more than any other notable American of his day had an abiding faith in the common people and in democracy. "Man," he held, "was a rational animal, endowed by nature with rights and with an innate sense of justice; and that he could be restrained from wrong and protected in right, by moderate powers, confided to persons of his own choice and held to their duties by dependence on his own will." At the very time when Hamilton and his fellow Federalists were most vehement in expressing contempt for popular government, Jefferson was contending that men "habituated to think for themselves and to follow their reason as their guide would be more easily and safely governed than with minds nourished in error and vitiated and debased . . . by ignorance, indigence, and oppression." He was unalterably opposed to government by the well-born and the well-to-do, for their rule, he asserted, was certain not only to be unresponsive to the will of the majority, but to be autocratic and tyrannical.

Economically Jefferson wanted America to be a land of small land-owning farmers. Schooled in the philosophy of Quesnay **Jefferson's** and the Physiocrats rather than in that of Adam **economic** Smith, Jefferson at the opening of the nineteenth **philosophy** century was an outspoken opponent of capitalistic economy. Consequently he was bitterly hostile to the capitalistic edifice designed and erected by Hamilton. Instead of developing great urban communities with their exploiting captains of industry and exploited proletariat, he would keep America agrarian. His thought on this point is admirably set forth in the following passage taken from his *Notes on Virginia:*

The political economists of Europe have established it as a principle that every state should endeavor to manufacture for itself; and this principle like many others we transfer to America. . . . But we have an immensity of land courting the industry of the husbandman. Is it best then that all our citizens should be employed in its improvement, or that one-half should be called off from that to exercise manufactures and handicraft arts for the others? Those who labor in the earth are the chosen people of God, if ever he had a chosen people, whose breasts he has made his peculiar deposit for substantial and genuine virtue. It is the focus in which he keeps alive that sacred fire, which otherwise might escape from the face of the earth. Corruption of morals in the mass of cultivators is a phenomenon of which no age nor nation has furnished an example. It is the mark set on those, who not looking up to heaven, to their own soil and industry as does the husbandman, for their subsistence, depend for it on casualties and caprice of customers. Dependence begets subservience and venality, suffocates the germ of virtue, and prepares fit tools for the designs of ambition. . . . Generally speaking the proportion which the aggregate of the other classes of citizens bears in any state to that of its husbandmen, is the proportion of its unsound to its healthy parts, and is a good enough barometer whereby to measure its degree of corruption. While we have land to labor then, let us never wish to see our citizens occupied at a workbench or twirling a distaff . . . for the general operations of manufacture, let our work-shops remain in Europe. It is better to carry provisions and materials to work-men there, than bring them to the

provisions and materials, and with them their manners and principles.
. . . The mobs of great cities add just so much to the support of pure
government, as sores do to the strength of the human body. It is
the manners and spirit of a people which preserve a republic in vigor.
A degeneracy in these is a canker which soon eats to the heart of its
laws and constitution.

His opposition to industrialism and his thorough-going distrust of an urban proletariat was even more explicitly set forth in a letter to John Jay written in the summer of 1785: *His opposition to industrialism*

We have now lands enough to employ an infinite number of people
in their cultivation. Cultivators of the earth are the most valuable
citizens. They are the most vigorous, the most independent, the most
virtuous, and they are tied to their country and wedded to its liberty
and interests by the most lasting bonds. As long, therefore, as they can
find employment in this line I would not convert them into mariners,
artisans or anything else. But our citizens will find employment in this
line till their numbers, and of course their productions, become too great
for the demand, both internal and foreign. This is not the case as yet,
and probably will not be for a considerable time. As soon as it is, the
surplus of hands must be turned to something else. I should then,
perhaps, wish to turn them to the sea in preference to manufactures;
because, comparing the character of the two classes, I find the former
the most valuable citizen. I consider the class of artificers as panders of
vice, and the instruments by which the liberties of a country are
generally overturned.

While Jefferson later modified his ideas about industrialism,
he was in 1800 unquestionably an agrarian democrat with a
deep abiding faith in the farmer and in the farmer's fitness to
maintain a government which would afford equality to all.

Jefferson's opposition to capitalism and to government by and
for capitalists represented merely a phase of his deep-seated dislike of everything that smacked of oppression and
tended to deprave humanity. "I have sworn upon
the altar of God," he wrote in 1800, "eternal
hostility against every form of tyranny over the
mind of man." He advocated a system of universal secular education, rejected orthodox Christianity in favor of deism, cham- *Jefferson an eighteenth-century liberal*

pioned freedom of press and speech, and urged all to criticise the existing order of things with a view to its improvement. When the University of Virginia was founded under his leadership he declared that the institution would be based "on the illimitable freedom of the human mind. For here we are not afraid to follow the truth wheresoever it may lead or to tolerate any error so long as reason is left free to combat it." His fascinating personality and rare intuition made him a masterly leader of men and a skilled propagandist.

Under his leadership the agrarians swept the Federalists from power in the presidential election of 1800. Here we are not con-

The agrarian victory of 1800 cerned with even the major events of that momentous battle. Fundamentally it marked another milestone in the great contest which had long raged and which continued to rage between capitalism and agrarianism. Once in office the agrarians proceeded as rapidly as possible to effect those changes which they believed would be beneficial to themselves and to the country at large. These included the reduction, through payment, of the funded debt, the abolition of the excise tax, simplification of the civil service, the curtailment of the army and navy, nullification of the Sedition Act and repeal of the law providing for new district judges, even though the judges had already been appointed during the "midnight hours" of Adams's administration.

If Jefferson or his more radical followers hoped to undo entirely the work of Hamilton and to keep America as a land of

Agrarians thwarted by John Marshall simple agrarianism they were doomed to disappointment. In the first place, they at all times had to reckon with that staunch defender of Federalism — John Marshall. As Chief Justice of the Supreme Court of the United States from 1801 to 1835, he fought the agrarians at every turn and did all in his power to magnify and strengthen the sovereignty of the national state and to safeguard the interests of private property. Both of these concepts, so stressed by Hamilton, are outstanding features of Marshall's decisions in Marbury vs. Madison, McCulloch vs. Maryland, Cohen vs. Virginia, the Dartmouth College Case, and in the other famous cases which came before him. Utterly devoid of

THOMAS JEFFERSON

social and humanitarian interests and opposed to democracy and and its levelling influences, he was in the eyes of the Jeffersonians a thorough-going reactionary. Be this as it may, no one who studies his life and ponders his decisions will deny that he ran counter to the wishes of the agrarians or that he was powerfully instrumental in shaping the later history of his country.

Even more important than Marshall's thwarting influence was the fact that capitalism was too deeply planted on the Atlantic seaboard to be ruthlessly uprooted and cast aside by the Jeffersonians. Indeed, at the very moment of Jefferson's triumph the forces destined ultimately to transform America from a land of farmers into a paradise for the business man were already at work. Before considering these forces we shall pause to note the intellectual and cultural changes which were taking place in the United States while capitalism and agrarianism were struggling for control.

Jeffersonians unable to uproot capitalism

SUGGESTED READINGS

C. F. Adams, *Diary and Autobiography of John Adams; Works of John Adams.*

J. T. Adams, *Hamiltonian Principles; Jeffersonian Principles.*

J. T. Adams, *New England in the Republic, 1776–1850*, chaps. ii–ix.

J. S. Bassett, *The Federalist System* (vol. 11 of *The American Nation*).

F. G. Bates, *Rhode Island and the Formation of the Union.*

C. A. Beard, *An Economic Interpretation of the Constitution of the United States; Economic Origins of Jeffersonian Democracy; The Supreme Court and the Constitution.*

Charles and Mary Beard, *The Rise of American Civilization*, vol. i, chap. vii.

S. F. Bemis, *Jay's Treaty: A Study in Commerce and Diplomacy.*

A. J. Beveridge, *Life of John Marshall*, 4 vols.

E. J. Bogart and C. M. Thompson, *Readings in the Economic History of the United States*, chap. v.

C. G. Bowers, *Jefferson and Hamilton, The Struggle for Democracy in America.*

G. S. Callender, *Selections From the Economic History of the United States, 1765–1860*, chap. v.

Edward Channing, *A History of the United States*, vol. iv, chaps. i–x.

E. S. Corwin, *John Marshall and the Constitution* (vol. 16 of *The Chronicles of America*).

D. R. Dewey, *Financial History of the United States*, chaps. iii–iv.

Jonathan Elliot, *Debates on the Federal Constitution*, 5 vols.

Jonathan Elliot, *The Biographical Story of the Constitution.*

Max Farrand, *Records of the Federal Convention*, 3 vols.; *The Framing of the Constitution.*

P. L. Ford (Editor), *Writings of Thomas Jefferson*, 10 vols.

W. C. Ford (Editor), *The Federalist; Writings of George Washington*, 14 vols.

J. C. Hamilton, *Life of Alexander Hamilton.*

S. B. Harding, *The Contest Over the Ratification of the Constitution in the State of Massachusetts.*

C. D. Hazen, *Contemporary American Opinion of the French Revolution.*

W. W. Henry, *Patrick Henry, Life, Correspondence and Speeches.*

Gaillard Hunt, *Life of James Madison.*

C. R. King, *Life and Correspondence of Rufus King.*

O. G. Libby, *Geographical Distribution of the Vote of the Thirteen States on the Federal Constitution, 1787–1788.*

H. C. Lodge, *George Washington; Works of Alexander Hamilton.*

E. S. Maclay, *The Journal of William Maclay.*

A. C. McLaughlin, *The Confederation and the Constitution* (vol. 10 of *The American Nation*).

J. B. McMaster, *History of the People of the United States*, vol. i.

J. B. McMaster and F. D. Stowe, *Pennsylvania and the Federal Constitution.*

C. E. Miner, *The Ratification of the Federal Constitution by the State of New York.*

S. E. Morison, *Maritime History of Massachusetts, 1783–1860*, chap. iii.

J. T. Morse, *Benjamin Franklin.*

D. S. Muzzey, *Thomas Jefferson.*

E. P. Oberholtzer, *Robert Morris, Patriot and Financier.*

V. L. Parrington, *Main Currents in American Thought*, vol. i (*The Colonial Mind, 1620–1800*), book iii.

G. W. Pellew, *John Jay.*

G. S. Roberts, *Foreign Commerce of the United States during the Confederation.*

R. L. Schuyler, *The Constitution of the United States: An Historical Survey of its Formation.*

J. P. Warren, "The Confederation and the Shays Rebellion," *American Historical Review*, vol. xi, No. 1 (Oct. 1905), pp. 42–67.

W. B. Weeden, *Economic and Social History of New England, 1620–1789*, 2 vols.

CHAPTER VII

THE TURN OF THE CENTURY

THE American republic in 1800 was still a frontier community. Two-thirds of its total population of approximately four and a half million whites and nearly a million blacks clung America a to the Atlantic seaboard. The center of population frontier com- was about ten miles southwest of Baltimore, less munity in 1800 than half a million persons having as yet gone into the great valley beyond the Appalachians. Even east of the mountains vast stretches of territory awaited settlement. Western New York, for example, was still a wilderness.

1. THE SOCIAL ORDER

By far the greater portion of the republic's population was of native birth, the whites being of English, Dutch, German, French, Irish, Scotch, Swedish, Swiss, and Welsh Character of stock. The white inhabitants of New England and population the South were largely of English extraction. One-fourth of the population of Pennsylvania were Germans, and there were also many in New Jersey, Virginia, and New York. Descendants of French Huguenots were to be found in New York and South Carolina. There were Dutch in New York, New Jersey, and Pennsylvania; Irish and Scotch-Irish in New York, Pennsylvania, New Jersey, Virginia, North and South Carolina, and Kentucky; a few Scotch in New Hampshire, New York, New Jersey, and North Carolina; Swedes in Delaware, New Jersey, Pennsylvania, and Maryland; Welsh in New York and Pennsylvania, and Swiss and French in Indiana Territory. English was the universal language, although the Germans in Pennsylvania spoke their own tongue. Almost all of the blacks lived in the South, for slavery was fast dying out in the North. Between seventy and eighty thousand Indians, it was estimated, were still east of the Mississippi. Immigration was at

401

a low ebb. In fact, from 1790 to 1800, and for some time after, probably not more than four or five thousand newcomers arrived annually. Old World industrial and military needs, fear of British impressment, heavy emigration fees, and the widespread circulation in Europe of false reports concerning American climatic conditions and economic opportunity tended to discourage the migration of those who might otherwise have come. Of those who did come, the English, Irish, and Germans were the most numerous.

Population, instead of being concentrated in urban communities, was overwhelmingly rural. Indeed, the number of those who lived in towns of eight thousand or over totaled only 200,000. Dissemination rather than concentration of population prevailed, migration from land to town not having as yet begun. Sectionally the West was gaining in numbers at the expense of the older settled regions, particularly New England and the South. The most populous state in the Union was Virginia, with 880,200 people; Pennsylvania ranked second with 602,365, and New York pressed close behind with 589,051. North Carolina had 478,103, while Massachusetts had 422,845. Large cities were few. Philadelphia, long the metropolis of America, was about to yield leadership to New York; both had less than 75,000 persons each. Boston, Baltimore, Charleston, Salem, Providence, and Newport were the other leading urban communities in so far as population was concerned. Inland towns like Albany, Richmond, and Springfield were as yet little more than prosperous frontier agricultural and commercial centers.

Population disseminated and overwhelmingly rural

People traveled little. Habit and the pressure of gaining a livelihood made the majority of the farm population "stay-at-homes." Many farmers avoided the cities, believing them to be dens of luxury, vice, and crime, ruinous alike to the health and morals of those who frequented them. Moreover, means of communication were only slightly better than before the Revolution. Practically no improvement in ocean navigation had been made for more than half a century, and river and coastwise traffic were still slow, vexatious, and costly. A week to go from New York to Providence by way of

Poor communication

Long Island Sound was a common experience, and the voyage from Europe to America was, in the opinion of some travelers, comparatively more comfortable and regular than the river trip from New York to Albany. Travel by land was more arduous. Tolerably good highways ran from New York to Boston, Philadelphia, and Baltimore, and over these regular stagecoach lines carried passengers and mail. South of the Potomac the roads were so poor as to be almost impassable except in the most favorable weather. Bridges were rare, especially in the South and West. "Of eight rivers between here [Monticello] and Washington," wrote Jefferson in 1801, "five have neither bridges nor boats." At best stagecoaching was not only fatiguing but expensive, averaging in the neighborhood of ten cents a mile including inn or hotel charges. Travel by horseback was the easiest and quickest and, in some places, the only way possible.

Poor transportation facilities naturally hampered the postal service. When Washington became President of the newly formed Union there were but seventy-five post-masters in the entire country. By 1800, however, approximately nine hundred post offices and more than twenty thousand miles of post road served the young republic. One route — the principal one — ran from Maine to Georgia. Unless conditions were extremely favorable, more than twenty days were necessary for mail to go from one end of this route to the other. Two branch lines extended westward from the main route: one from New York to Canandaigua by way of the Hudson and Mohawk valleys; and the other from Philadelphia to Nashville by way of Lexington, Kentucky. High postage rates as well as lack of adequate transportation facilities made communication by mail expensive and difficult. To send a letter weighing a quarter of an ounce a distance of not more than thirty miles cost eight cents; over thirty and not more than eighty miles, ten cents; over eighty and not more than one hundred and fifty miles, twelve and a half cents; over one hundred and fifty and not more than four hundred miles, eighteen and a half cents; over four hundred miles, twenty-five cents. Rates for greater weight were proportionately higher. It cost one cent to send a newspaper one hundred

Postal service hampered by poor transportation and high rates

miles, and a cent and a half for longer distances. The charge for pamphlets and magazines was likewise high. Every one grumbled at this slow and costly service and, whenever possible, avoided paying postage by sending letters by travelers.

From an economic point of view the America of 1800 was little different from the America of colonial days. The vast majority of its people still gained their livelihood from agriculture. While more acres of that enormous forest-covered, untamed area of 1750 had been conquered and put under cultivation, and while total production had increased, neither the farmer's mode of life, nor his tools, methods, or habits had changed. He lived in the same type of house, wore the same sort of clothes, and ate the same kind of food as did his father before him. The clumsy wooden plow, the hoe, sickle, cradle, and flail were still in general use. Only in a very few instances had better implements, such as the grain drill and the threshing machine, been introduced. With few exceptions stock was unimproved and neglected. The treatment accorded cattle in New England and parts of the South as late as 1850 would today result in arrest and imprisonment. Drainage, fertilization, and crop rotation were uncommon. New England farmers were known to remove their barns on account of the manure accumulated round them instead of spreading the manure on their impoverished soil. The same field was cropped with corn year after year, not because it was specially well adapted to corn, but because its owner's father or grandfather had designated it as *the* cornfield. Only in Pennsylvania and a few other localities, such as the Connecticut and Shenandoah valleys, was there evidence of agricultural progress and prosperity.

Agriculture still the leading occupation

Nor had the life of the townsman undergone any fundamental change in a material sense since pre-Revolutionary days. While towns had increased in number and population, they were for the most part without improvements such as today are regarded as indispensable. In fact, only Philadelphia could boast of having well paved and well lighted streets, drainage, and a water system. New York, which in 1800 covered only the lower tip of Manhattan Island,

Unchanged character of towns

was called the city of "feasts and fevers." Its streets, with open sewers running along or across them and piled high with filth and refuse, were overrun with unsightly, malodorous hogs which, it was claimed, acted as scavengers. Roadways, from which rose clouds of germ-laden dust in dry weather, became quagmires with every rain. The privately owned reservoir which supplied the city with water was frequently polluted by bathers and laundry women. Sanitary ordinances were few and, for the most part, went unheeded. Zoning was unheard of, and consequently such nuisances as slaughter houses existed in the midst of residential sections. The homes of the plebeian element in the northern part of the city were wretched habitations at best; even the houses of the well-to-do were without the conveniences and hygienic improvements of the present day. Police and fire protection were in their infancy. Conditions in Boston, Baltimore, and the lesser towns were only slightly better, and in some instances they were worse.

The means by which those who dwelt in the towns in 1800 gained their livelihood had not altered in the course of fifty years. Shipping, seafaring, merchandising, and Occupations money lending occupied many; others dealt in real of townsmen estate or followed some profession such as the law. Still others engaged in manufacturing, which was as yet almost entirely on a handicraft basis. A considerable number were proprietors of inns, coffeehouses, or places of amusement. All towns had their hucksters and peddlers who on every street and practically at every door sought to sell, as the New York *Evening Post* complained, "almost everything that can be named, from a lady's leghorn hat to a shoestring, from a saddle to a cowskin, from a gold ring to a jewsharp." Liquor dealers and professional and amateur gamblers plied their trade. But the bulk of the urban population was composed of artisans and unskilled laborers who earned their living by the sweat of their brow.

While the Revolution wrought marked changes in the American social structure, it did not by any means alter it completely. Social classes based on birth, wealth, and official Social classes position, though not as sharply differentiated as in the Old World, continued to exist much as they did in 1750 or even earlier. At the top of the ladder stood the planters and other great landholders and the wealthy merchant-bankers who, as we shall see in subsequent chapters, reaped the lion's share of the profits from land speculation and domestic and foreign trade and controlled the credit of the country. Like their colonial predecessors, they seldom missed an opportunity for economic gain, lived amid more costly surroundings, exercised greater political influence, and enjoyed certain social and cultural advantages denied to the rank and file. Ranking next in the social order were those engaged in the professions, especially the lawyers and the clergy. Intelligent, industrious and, in the North, practitioners of pinching economy, they were as a rule closely allied with the landed-mercantile class and were stout defenders of vested interests. Occupying a lower rung in the ladder were the small farmers, artisans, and laborers — carpenters, cordwainers, typesetters, hodcarriers, draymen, sailors, ditch diggers, to mention only a few. Hampered by ignorance, without political power, often exploited by their employers, victimized by speculators, gamblers, dispensers of strong drink, and liable to imprisonment for debt, their lot was far from being an enviable one. At the bottom were the negro slaves.[1]

Unlike Europe, if a person found himself in a lower social class in America it did not mean that he was fated to remain **Rigid class** always in that particular class. Sparseness of **barriers absent** population, the enormous expanse of cheap land, **in America** abundant natural resources, the growing prevalence of the notion that one person was as good as another, and the

---

[1] A distinguished French visitor, Bayard, describing Philadelphia's citizenry in 1797, wrote as follows: "The inhabitants of Philadelphia, like all citizens of the United States, are classified by their fortunes. The first class is composed of carriage folk. Almost all these gentry, whatever their origin, have their coats of arms painted upon their carriage doors. The son of a deported thief has liveried servants just like everybody else. Nobility having been abolished by the Constitution alone, it is not astonishing that so many individuals pretend to be descended from ancient English families. This fad has become a sort of mania in mercantile cities. The second class is composed of merchants, lawyers, and business men without carriages, and doctors who pay their visits on foot. In a third class are found people who exercise the mechanical arts. Ladies who possess carriages never so far forget themselves as to receive in their homes those of the third class."

absence of rigid class barriers made it possible for him, unless he was held in permanent bondage, to climb higher socially. This movement from one social stratum to another, dating from earliest colonial times, was very much in evidence in 1800. Indeed, some of those who dwelt in "Quality Row," as the mansions overlooking New York Bay were known, or in the stately structures in Derby and Chestnut streets, Boston, had started at the bottom. A relatively small group composed of some of the older families did not countenance these transitions from one social class to another. For them society was fixed, static, and unchanging, and should remain so.

While perhaps better educated than her grandmother, woman's place in the American social structure of 1800 was much the same as it had been a hundred years earlier. The home rather than the business or professional world was supposed to be her realm. She was expected to be skilled in all the domestic sciences, including nursing. Daughters of the well-to-do were taught to sing, dance, and play the lute or harpsichord; some received instruction in painting. They were also taught to cultivate the art of conversation and to be pleasing in manner and appearance. When a woman married she was expected to devote herself unstintingly to her family and her home. Legally, socially, and intellectually she was regarded as inferior to man. Unchastity was considered as "superlatively criminal in woman," but in men was "viewed in a far less disadvantageous light." For a woman to meddle in politics or public affairs was anathema. "A female politician," said *The Female Friend*, a little book published in 1809, "is only less disgusting than a female infidel." Early marriages continued to be the rule; divorce was rare and the method of granting it was by legislative enactment. Although Mary Wollstonecraft's *Vindication of the Rights of Women in England* (1791), in which she pitilessly arraigned women for remaining complacent in their degradation, and men for selfishly making woman inferior, was republished in Philadelphia in 1794, it apparently had little or no effect on American public opinion. The days of equality for women were still far in the future.

The place of woman in the social structure

Though a few of the many foreigners who visited America at the opening of the nineteenth century were of the opinion that Social life of the majority of its citizens were primarily inhigher classes terested in making money, they did not overlook the fact that the money makers found time for social diversion. This was especially true of those above the rank and file. Men's clubs, so prevalent today, were not yet in existence, but shops and coffeehouses in the larger cities were popular meeting places. The famous Tontine coffeehouse in New York, for example, was a favorite mecca for the city's leading men. Formal and informal dinners, graced by the witty raconteur and the cultivated conversationalist, were frequent affairs. Practically all the more important towns had foreign dancing masters who taught "polite" society the cotillion, the waltz, and other steps. Balls and dancing parties were sponsored by the well-to-do in every urban community. In 1802 the Washington Dancing Assembly was organized by a group of prominent Washingtonians, including Samuel Harrison Smith, founder of the *National Intelligencer*. Similar organizations, supported and managed by men of standing, soon appeared in all the larger towns. Horse racing, which outside of New England was on the increase, numbered many of the wealthy and more aristocratic families among its patrons. The concert and the theatre, though opposed on moral and religious grounds by probably seven-eighths of the population, were not without upper-class support.

Undoubtedly the social life of the leisure class was profoundly affected by contact with the Old World and especially with French influ- France. "The alienation from England," to quote ence on Howard Mumford Jones,[1] "the French alliance, American life the going abroad of Americans like Silas Deane, Franklin, Jefferson, Jay, and the Adamses, the coming to America of French representatives, of French army officers and volunteers, who came directly into contact with this leisure class, the outbreak of the Revolution in France and the West

---

[1] *America and French Culture, 1750-1848*, pp. 243-44. See also, Dixon Ryan Fox, Culture in Knapsacks, New York State Historical Association *Quarterly Journal*, Vol. IX, No. 1, January, 1930, pp. 31-52.

Indies which drove cultured emigrés to America by the thousands — these were the direct contacts by which French manners were assimilated in America." And Professor Jones might have added, as he does elsewhere in his pages, the names of those distinguished American women — Mrs. Ralph Izard, Mrs. Benjamin Rush, Mrs. John Jay, Mrs. J. Q. Adams, and others — who were French visitors during the last decade of the eighteenth century. The consequences of this French influence on the well-to-do were evident on every hand — in the architecture of the home, its furnishings, food and drink, raiment, manners, conversation, and amusements.

Whether farmer or town laborer, the common man shared many of the pleasures enjoyed by those higher up in the social scale. Quilting parties, husking bees, barn raisings, and other coöperative enterprises were as much in vogue in 1800 as in colonial times. So were fishing and hunting, quoits, skating and sleighing, cock fighting, wrestling, and rough-and-tumble fist fights. Many villages had bowling greens. Showmen, acrobats, and magicians of all sorts wandered from town to town furnishing entertainment to both town and countryside. People came in droves, for example, to see an elephant — the first in the United States — dance, draw corks, and perform various other stunts; or to witness such exhibitions as an automaton execution of Louis XVI and Marie Antoinette. *Amusements of lower class*

People of every class gambled. They bet on horse races, wagered on card games, and "backed" their favorite in a cock fight. But the most common form of gambling was the lottery. Lotteries in 1800 were not new. *Gambling: the lottery* From the beginning of colonization this Old World importation had been used to raise funds for almost every conceivable purpose — schools and colleges, churches, bridges, docks, canals, turnpikes, poor relief, and even government buildings. Washington and other men of note were purchasers of lottery tickets from time to time. Jefferson, eager to rehabilitate his fortune, sold some of his land by lottery. Harvard College raised approximately $15,000 a year by lottery, and other institutions, such as Dartmouth, and William and Mary, somewhat lesser amounts by the same device. Practically all newspapers carried lottery advertisements. Frequently farmers, artisans, tradesmen, and merchants who had purchased tickets in the hope of acquiring quick and easy fortune neglected their business to watch the lottery drawings. So serious did the situation become that several of the Northern states took steps to curtail the lottery system. Even some of the newspapers which were benefiting financially from lottery advertisements had the courage, before the first quarter of the nineteenth century had passed, to denounce lotteries and demand their abolition. One of these was the New York *Evening Post*, whose editor was moved to action by the losses of the poor. "Look at the crowd of poor ragged wretches," said he, "that beset the office-keeper's doors the morning after the day's drawing is over, waiting with their little slips in their hands, to hear their fate, and the yesterday's earnings ready to be given to the harpies that stand gaping for the pittance." The first third of the nineteenth century was to pass, however, before the widespread campaign against the lottery began to bear fruit.

All classes of society in all sections of the country, but particularly the working class, were addicted to the use of

Indulgence in strong drink. As in colonial times, the more opu-
strong drink   lent drank imported wines; they also on occasion partook of whisky and even cider and rum. For the common people — small farmers, laborers, sailors, and the rest — rum or whisky was the universal beverage. The day was begun with an "eye opener" and closed with a "nightcap." Some were partially under the influence of liquor at all times, and for many intoxication was an everyday occurrence. Even prisoners in jails and relatives and friends at funerals were served with liquor. In every community there were those who took pride in their capacity for drinking and who boasted of the amount of liquor they had consumed. New York City alone had 1500 grog shops, to say nothing of its numerous taverns. Well-to-do families frequently spent hundreds of dollars a year for drink, and it is estimated that a part of nearly every ordinary man's earnings went for intoxicants. Already, however, there were those who were urging reform in drinking habits. Chief among

them was Dr. Benjamin Rush of Philadelphia, who as early as 1784 had published a pamphlet, *An Inquiry into the Effects of Spirituous Liquors on the Human Body and Mind*. Largely through his influence the first temperance society in the United States was organized near Saratoga Springs, New York, in 1808.

Duelling was in the opinion of many almost as reprehensible as gambling and drunkenness. While this mode of settling personal differences, so prevalent in the Old World, had found some vogue in colonial times, it was not **Duelling** until after the Revolution that it came into more general use.[1] By 1800 duelling was rife among naval officers, congressmen, and frontiersmen. Practically every family of the planter aristocracy had one or more duels recorded in its annals. Provocations which today seem childish and even silly were deemed sufficient for challenge to mortal combat. Age mattered little. In 1801 Alexander Hamilton's eldest son Philip, a lad of nineteen years, was mortally wounded on the field of honor at Weehawken, New Jersey; three years later the elder Hamilton himself fell on the same spot by the hand of Aaron Burr. No section of the country was free from the practice, and its increase at the turn of the century led to insistent demands that it be terminated. A generation or more was to pass, however, before it began to disappear.

2. RELIGION AND HUMANITARIANISM

To the casual observer the religious scene in America in 1800 was much the same as at the beginning of the Revolution. The overwhelming majority believed in the divine origin of the Bible, in the miraculous creation of the world, **Outwardly religious scene in America unchanged** and in the actual existence of heaven and hell. While Jefferson's interest in prehistoric animals and his correspondence with Buffon probably foreshadowed Darwinism, modern evolution was unheard of and the belief that all things, animate and inanimate, were the handiwork of the

---

[1] To what extent the presence of foreign troops on American soil during the Revolution encouraged duelling we do not know. There can be little doubt, however, that their presence helped to strengthen the institution on this side of the Atlantic.

Almighty and that from the beginning they had remained substantially unchanged was, with certain notable exceptions, well-nigh universal. New England was still a Congregational stronghold, though the Unitarians, as we shall see presently, had gained a firm foothold. Dutch Reformists, Episcopalians, Baptists, and Methodists were the prevailing groups in New York; Lutherans, Quakers, Moravians, and Episcopalians dominated in Pennsylvania and New Jersey; Baptists, Methodists, and Episcopalians were the most numerous sects in the South; Maryland had many Catholics; and the Methodists, Baptists, and Presbyterians boasted strength in the West. The Jews, while less powerful numerically than any of the Christian groups, were gaining considerable foothold in the seaboard cities, chiefly Newport, Providence, New York, Philadelphia, Charleston, and Savannah.

Theologically most of the denominations had seemingly undergone little or no change from earlier times. With one or two exceptions they held rigorously to the doctrine *Denominations decidedly orthodox* that God is omnipotent, absolute, unchanging, perfect in his attributes, holy, just, merciful, and good; that because of the fall of Adam and Eve man is stained with sin and, unless cleansed, is doomed on a judgment day to suffer eternal punishment in a hell of torment; that man should deny himself the pleasures of this world which are sinful or which might lead him into sin; and that he should at all times do everything in his power to honor and glorify God to the end that he may at death enter into eternal bliss with his Heavenly Maker. While differing somewhat in regard to methods by which man could be saved, nearly all the traditional sects were in agreement on these fundamental principles of orthodoxy.

As in colonial days, morals were intimately bound up with religion, and the denominational groups, therefore, regarded *Religious groups makers and conservers of morals* themselves as the makers and conservers of both private and public standards of conduct. As a rule the minister, irrespective of denomination, was held in high repute. In the meetinghouse and in the homes of his parishioners, where he was an honored guest, he constantly reminded his flock of their spiritual and moral obligations and of the necessity of avoiding the wickedness and snares of the devil. Rare indeed was the orthodox preacher who occasionally failed to follow that apostle of traditional theology, Jonathan Edwards, in portraying in lurid colors "the landscape of hell." That these preachers were powerfully influential in shaping the moral and religious standards of their time no one will seriously deny, but in emphasizing the depravity and pre-destination of man and minimizing his excellence and free will, they were, in the opinion of many critics, guilty of imposing on the mind of the vast majority needless fears and exaggerated worries over their soul's salvation.

So widespread was the notion that religion and morals were welded together and that there could be no virtue without religion, that many people were convinced that Religion and religion should be supported by the state. Inas- the state much as the first amendment to the Federal Constitution explicitly forbade Congress to make any law "respecting an establishment of religion or prohibiting the free exercise thereof," the national government, even if inclined to do so, was powerless either to establish an official religion or to assist financially any religious sect. The situation in several of the states, however, was far different. The constitution of Massachusetts, after expressly declaring that the happiness of any people and the preservation of government essentially depend "upon piety, religion, and morality, and as these cannot be generally diffused through a community but by the institution of the public worship of God and of public instruction in piety, religion, and morality," directed the legislature to require the people of the state to make suitable provision for public worship and for the "support of public Protestant teachers of piety, religion, and morality." In making similar provision, New Hampshire asserted that morality and piety, "grounded on evangelical principles," were the best security to good government. Connecticut, long a stronghold of theocracy and intolerance, allowed taxation for religious purposes. The Maryland Declaration of Rights empowered the legislature at any time "to lay a general and equal tax for the support of the Christian religion." New Jersey made "belief in the faith of any Protestant sect" a requirement for eligibility to office. In North Carolina no person could hold office who "should deny the being of God or the truth of the Protestant religion or the divine authority either of the Old or New Testament." And in Delaware and Pennsylvania a person had to believe in God, a future life, and the inspiration of the Scriptures to qualify as a legislator.

But all these outward appearances, which might lead us to conclude that religiously America in 1800 was substantially the same as a half century earlier, should not blind us to those mighty Old World intellectual currents undermining not only religious orthodoxy, but the entire established order. Ranking first was scientific skepticism. Contrary to widespread opinion, the Protestant Revolt and the Catholic Reformation following it strengthened rather than weakened doctrinal orthodoxy. Even the attempts of the humanists to induce the theologians to regard man not as an impotent and depraved being, but as a person of moral and intellectual worth, proved abortive. Lutherans, Calvinists, Anglicans, and Catholics continued their old and ofttimes bitter theological controversies. The end of the seventeenth century, however, saw the theologians on the defensive. The new science — the fruit in large measure of the Copernican and Cartesian revolutions — with its emphasis on nature, scientific method, and scientific ideals, challenged authority in every field. Religion did not escape, and traditional beliefs and practices were subjected to rigid scrutiny from the standpoint of human standards of right and reasonableness.

Old World intellectual currents undermining religious orthodoxy

While the multitudes at first took little notice of and were scarcely affected by this new rationalistic spirit, the more confident middle class became its ardent champions. The more radical, known as the Deists, weary of the theories of divine sovereignty, infinite punishment, the atonement, and supernatural grace, rejected revelation entirely and held that natural religion with its insistence

Deism and its spread to America

on good citizenship and rational morality met the moral and spiritual needs of man much more satisfactorily than did the traditional religious structure. Making rapid headway in England, where it numbered among its apologists Lord Herbert of Cherbury, John Locke, David Hume, and Matthew Tindal, Deism spread to the Continent. Here it was quickly embraced by nearly all those who had come under the spell of the new science, including Rousseau and Voltaire. Only a short interval elapsed before English deistic literature found its way to America, where it was eagerly read by laymen and fashionable clergymen. "The perusal of Shaftesbury and Collins," wrote Franklin referring to his early youth, "had made me a skeptic." By the outbreak of the American Revolution Franklin, Jefferson, Madison, Ethan Allen, Paine, and Washington, as well as many persons of lesser prominence, had come under the influence of the Deists, although some of them, notably Franklin and Washington, conformed sufficiently to keep on good terms with their orthodox neighbors. Converts to Deism were most numerous in the Middle and Southern states.

Against the Deists the orthodox clergy leveled their heaviest guns. Ethan Allen, Revolutionary patriot, whose *Reason, the Only Oracle of Man* appeared in 1784, became the target of a most vitriolic attack. When a fire, said to have been caused by lightning, destroyed all but about thirty copies of the entire edition of his book, the orthodox construed it as a judgment from heaven. Even more savage were the ceaseless onslaughts against Thomas Paine and his *Age of Reason*, which began to appear in America in 1794. With more heat than light clergymen of the stamp of Jedidiah Morse and Timothy Dwight poured out their vials of wrath and execration. Orthodox laymen expressed their horror that such a scandalous and irreligious publication should be permitted to circulate. College authorities bitterly lamented the unsettling influence which Paine and his writings would have on the youth of the land; to counteract it every Harvard undergraduate was presented with a copy of Bishop Watson's *Apology for the Bible*. Paine, generous and sentimental friend of humanity, was characterized as an "atheist" and a "dirty infidel,"

Deism savagely attacked by orthodox clergy

an odium which later was again unjustly heaped upon him by none other than Theodore Roosevelt.[1]

But all the ranting of the orthodox theologians and their staunch supporters could not throttle Deism or those other liberalizing influences emanating from the Old World as well as from American society. The more violent the protests and the more vigorous the attempts to repress "the infidel and irreligious spirit," the more insidiously and rapidly it seemed to spread. The colleges, former strongholds of orthodoxy, had by the turn of the century become "dens of the infidelity of Voltaire and his coadjutors." Of the seventy-six members of the Yale class of 1802, only a few were orthodox Christians at the time of graduation. At Harvard the cause of liberalism stood in high favor among both faculty and students. The University of Virginia was strongly agnostic; and so were other southern institutions of higher learning. No section of the country was left untouched by the new ideas. The orthodox had good reason to be frightened.

Deism and other liberalistic tendencies spread

Although the struggle between the orthodox religionists and the rising forces of liberalism extended to all parts of the young republic, it was in Calvinist New England that the battle was most fiercely fought. Here during the middle of the eighteenth century a number of young preachers, of whom Jonathan Mayhew, Charles Chauncey, and Lemuel Briant were outstanding, began to substitute rationalistic doctrines for the old Calvinistic dogmas. They proved to be the forerunners of the Unitarian revolt, which by the end of

The Unitarian revolt

[1] Paine expressed his confession of faith as follows: "I believe in one God, and no more; and I hope for happiness beyond this life. I believe in the equality of man, and I believe that religious duties consist in doing justice, loving mercy, and endeavoring to make our fellow creatures happy. I do not believe in the creed professed . . . by any church that I know of. My own mind is my own church. . . . All national institutions of churches . . . appear to me no other than human inventions set up to terrify and enslave mankind and monopolize power and profit. I do not mean . . . to condemn those who believe otherwise. They have the same right to their belief as I have to mine. But it is necessary to the happiness of man that he be faithful to himself. . . . It is impossible to calculate the moral mischief . . . that mental lying has produced in society."

the century bade fair to split the Congregationalist churches into two opposing groups. Reversing the thought processes of the Calvinists, the Unitarians instead of regarding man as a depraved, helpless creature, subject to God's wrath, looked upon him as God's child, made in His image, and the object of His love. The doctrines of original sin and unconditional predestination were brushed aside and man's reason and conscience made the divine witnesses to truth and light. Like the sixteenth-century Socinians, the Unitarians thought of Christ as the "Son of God" but not as God himself, and they tried to prove this by the Scriptures. At the same time they attacked the orthodox theory of atonement and emphasized the benevolence of God and the ultimate salvation of all men (Universalism).

Warmly received by the wealthier business interests, the politicians, and the lawyers of eastern New England, the new creed spread rapidly. As early as 1785 King's Its spread and Chapel, Boston, formerly in the hands of the influence Episcopalians, became Unitarian. Congregational churches in Worcester, Portland, and Plymouth speedily followed suit, and by 1800 the ministerial ranks of the trinitarian Calvinists in Boston were almost deserted. By 1803, when William Ellery Channing, guiding spirit of the movement, took charge of the Federal Street Church, Boston, it was a foregone conclusion that the breach with the orthodox camp was not to be healed. In 1805 David Tappan, Hollis professor of Divinity at Harvard, was succeeded by Henry Ware, a Unitarian. The Calvinists retaliated by establishing a theological school of their own at Andover in 1808. But the orthodox theologians were powerless to stem the tide, and before a quarter of a century had passed the Unitarians had their own divinity school at Harvard, an organized publication society and a nation-wide association. More important, their influence, along with that of the Deists, in humanizing and rationalizing American Protestantism was incalculable.

The outcome of the French Revolution caused a severe crisis and reaction in America as well as in England. Intellectually and religiously the conservative rationalism of New Eng-

land, which had been little influenced by French thought, held its ground. In the South and the West, however, the more radi-
Revivalistic cal tendencies of Paine and Jefferson were crushed
reaction by a violent and sentimental crusade against infidelity and anarchy akin to Jonathan Edward's Great Awakening, which left the Presbyterians, Baptists, and Methodists in complete control, and undermined for a whole century to come the genuine interest in "natural philosophy," republicanism, and secular science which the French Revolution had inspired.

Of all the revivalists none were more important than the Methodists. Methodism which, as we have seen, appeared in
the New World prior to the Revolution, owed its
Methodism beginning in large measure to the brothers Charles and John Wesley. Charles, mystic and poet, wrote its songs: "Jesus, Lover of My Soul," "Hark! The Herald Angels Sing," "Come, Thou Almighty King," and hundreds of others. John made its laws and rules and formulated its characteristic teachings. Turning his back upon science and reason and rejecting in its entirety the conception of natural religion, he emphasized the divine power of grace through faith in Jesus Christ and through personal communion with him as the only means of salvation. Revealed religion, with its traditional doctrines of original sin and Christ's redemption and atonement, was, he held, the very foundation of Christianity, but he tried to put it in practice not by theological argument, but by intense personal devotion to Christ and hence by abandoning card playing, dancing, and other worldly pleasures.

Under the energetic guidance of Francis Asbury, the leading spirit in founding the Methodist Episcopal Church in Amer-
Francis ica, Methodism made tremendous strides. In the
Asbury and single year 1805 it gained 6,000 adherents; and
the growth of when in 1816 Asbury passed to the great beyond
Methodism
in America after forty-four years of ceaseless effort on American soil, he had, in the words of the Beards, traveled "more than two hundred and fifty thousand miles through villages and towns, through thickly settled country districts and dark frontier forests, claiming finally three hundred thousand converts and four thousand ordained clergymen." Writing in his journal

near the close of his life, he records that he had crossed the Allegheny Mountains probably not less than sixty times. Like Jonathan Edwards before him, Asbury was a master in the art of arousing human emotions, his vivid portrayals of the love of Christ, the torments of hell and the joys of heaven stirring his listeners to the very depths.

Because of its emotionalism plus its emphasis on Biblical literalism and supernaturalism, and its lack of sympathy with science and secular culture in general, Methodism **Methodism** did not attract intellectuals of the Jefferson and **appealed to** Madison type. It reaped its harvest on the fron- **frontiersmen and urban** tier and among the rank and file of the older settled **proletariat** regions where many persons for one reason or another were growing lax religiously. The simplicity and sentimentality of Methodism, compared with Catholicism, Anglicanism, or even Calvinism, appealed to the common man. Its ministers sermonized in language which the lowly and humble could understand. By encouraging oratory, mass enthusiasm, and religious conviction among the people, it perhaps more than any other creed contributed to the growth of that crude but confident democracy which Andrew Jackson marshaled in his struggle with the forces of aristocracy and capitalism.

In addition to warring on skepticism, profanity, immorality, intemperance, and Sabbath breaking, the Methodists as well as nearly all the older denominations were deeply **Missionary** interested in two other fields of endeavor: mis- **enterprise** sionary enterprise among the Indians and pagan peoples overseas, and humanitarianism. The task of carrying the Gospel to the aborigines, undertaken on a large scale by both the Catholics and the Protestants during the seventeenth and eighteenth centuries, was zealously continued in the nineteenth. Increasing information about the "heathen peoples" of Asia, Africa, and the South Seas which began to filter into America even before 1800, and the publicity given it by church journals, was in no small degree responsible for American missionary interest in foreign lands. By 1814 more than twenty Baptist missionary societies had been organized to do work in foreign fields. In 1817 the United Foreign Mission Society, backed by the Presbyterian and Reformed churches, was established to "spread the Gospel among the Indians of North America, the inhabitants of Mexico and South America, and in other portions of the heathen and anti-Christian world." The Methodists delayed sending missionaries overseas, contenting themselves with efforts among the Indians and the Spanish and French inhabitants west of the Mississippi. Indeed, it was not until 1832 that Melville Cox was sent to Liberia as Methodism's first foreign missionary. The Moravians and other pietists also participated in the missionary movement.

Although the great majority of the clergy condemned in no uncertain terms those liberalistic forces tending to undermine the long-established order of things, most of them, **The clergy and humanitarianism** heeding the Gospel admonition to love one's fellows, were humanitarians and warm supporters of all sorts of benevolent schemes. Evangelists like Asbury and dogmatic Calvinists of the Samuel Hopkins and Timothy Dwight brand denounced slavery, imprisonment for debt, and war no less than did Jefferson and Thomas Paine. Like the non-denominational humanitarians too, they sponsored orphanages, asylums for the insane and for the deaf and dumb, temperance, and prison reform. Some few would even abolish capital punishment. If their congregations failed to act on their humanitarian utterances and paid mere lip service to their principles of social justice and betterment, it was usually because economic realities were stumbling blocks to pious hopes.

Of all the humanitarian undertakings none perhaps received greater attention than prison reform. At the close of the American Revolution the prisons, as we have seen, were **Prison reform** little more than seminaries of crime. Against this condition of affairs the humanitarians vigorously protested. Individual writers and workers — Caleb Lowndes, Mathew Carey, Edward Livingston, and others — and organizations like the Society for Alleviating the Miseries of the Public Prisons in Philadelphia, the Massachusetts Society for Prison Discipline, and the Society for the Prevention of Pauperism in New York, maintained that every prison should be a corrective institution, where the criminal would be transformed into a self-respecting,

REVEREND FRANCIS ASBURY

law-abiding citizen. Responding to the urgent pleas of the humanitarians, Pennsylvania not only overhauled its criminal code, but in 1790 introduced the penitentiary system which provided, among other things, separate cells for each prisoner. Other states soon followed Pennsylvania's example and by 1821 fourteen had penitentiaries. While the penitentiary system had certain inherent weaknesses and was handicapped by the politicians, who often insisted on naming untrained and incompetent keepers, it was a distinct advance over the barbaric penal system of the earlier period.[1]

Paralleling the movement for prison reform was that for more adequate care of the poor and unfortunate. Although the United States was, as Mathew Carey said, The poor and "a country far more prosperous than any other unfortunate portion of the habitable world," it nevertheless had its physically incapacitated and poverty-stricken. In colonial times, when life was less specialized than today, the poor and unfortunate were cared for by their neighbors or by the churches. In fact, direct ministration was considered a virtue. In some communities, notably Pennsylvania, the law could be invoked to compel families to care for their own dependents. For those without friends or family ties or kindred the local governmental unit — town, county, or city — generally made legal provision. Almshouses accommodating not only paupers but a variety of unfortunates — orphans, foundlings, the blind and insane — were numerous by 1800.

Those who demanded prison reform were equally insistent that the evils of indiscriminate association within the poorhouses be terminated. The founding of orphan asylums was the first step in this direction. In 1806 the Orphan Orphanages Asylum Society of the City of New York was organized, being

---

[1] Edward Livingston's Criminal Code for Louisiana was outstanding and gained for him an international reputation as a social scientist of the first rank. In addition to incorporating the chief features of the Pennsylvania system, it provided for houses of detention where the suspected and unconvicted should be confined until their guilt or innocence was determined; and houses of refuge and industry where prisoners who had shown signs of regeneration might find employment and subsistence after leaving prison and before being given absolute release.

the first in the United States. An outgrowth of the Society for the Relief of Poor Widows with Small Children, the first women's charitable organization in New York, it at once filled a much needed want. In 1817 the Roman Catholic Church opened an orphanage in New York, and thereafter orphan asylums multiplied rapidly. All were started by private benevolence, although some were assisted with public funds.

Old age pensions were unheard of, and there were few institutions, outside of the churches and almshouses, to look after Relief agencies for the indigent old the indigent old. The Female Charitable Society of Providence, organized in 1802, the Washington Benevolent Society of Massachusetts, founded in 1812, and the Association for the Relief of the Respectable, Aged, Indigent Females, formed in New York City in 1813, were the most important of the charitable agencies functioning in behalf of the needy aged.

The first quarter of the nineteenth century passed before the reformers were able to accomplish much for the blind or the The blind, and the deaf and dumb deaf and dumb. In 1817 two schools for deaf mutes, one in Hartford and the other in New York City, were opened, but there were no others for many years. The first institution for the blind was not started until 1831.

The task of segregating the insane and of providing treatment for them was also slow of realization, partly because of Treatment of the insane social inertia and partly because no one knew just what ought to be done. Up to 1800 and even after, the violently insane were sent to jail, and those considered harmless were allowed to roam at large. The idea of having separate hospitals for the demented had not yet materialized, although the hospitals founded to care for the physically sick usually admitted a limited number of patients suffering from insanity. Well-to-do families sent their afflicted members to hospitals or to private keepers or kept them at home. Those less able financially cared for their own insane or sent them to the almshouses. The insane who were allowed their freedom were often the victims of insult and even brutality; indeed, a crazy person followed by a tormenting crowd of boys and men was a common sight on almost any village or city street. Treatment, though well-intentioned, was frequently barbaric in the extreme. Practically no state made provision for the insane until well toward the middle of the nineteenth century.

3. Science and Invention

While evangelists and other champions of orthodoxy were lashing Deism, atheism, and agnosticism, and campaigning against crime, profanity, Sabbath desecration, in- The new temperance, and pauperism, science and scientific science inquiry and application were making remarkable headway in the young republic. Here again, as in the case of religion, Old World influence was pronounced. During the seventeenth century, when the foundation stones of the future America were being laid, a galaxy of Europeans — Galileo, Descartes, Torricelli, Harvey, Boyle, Hooke, Huygens, Leibnitz, Newton, and others — were opening up new intellectual vistas to mankind. Astronomical views were recast, the principles of mechanics laid down, new branches of mathematics, especially analytical geometry and calculus, were formulated, the fundamental theory of fluids was established, the geometrical and physical theories of light were worked out in considerable detail, and the fundamental problems of vibratory motion and acoustics were being attacked. Advances were also made in some of the non-physical sciences. Moreover, the same century witnessed the founding of academies in Naples, Rome, Florence, London, Paris, Leipzig, Bologna, and Venice devoted to the cultivation of science and the encouragement of research.

Despite the opposition of those who professed to see in science a menace to religion and who prophesied social disaster as a result of man's attempts to peer into the mysteries Rapid scientific advances during eighteenth century of nature, the scientific movement of the seventeenth century gathered momentum in the eighteenth. Combining experiment with mathematics, Europeans of genius whose names are now written large on the pages of history continued the work of their predecessors by delving further into nature's repositories. Cavendish, Rutherford, Priestley, Lavoisier, Davy, Gay-Lussac, and the Italian

Avogadro laid the real foundations for modern chemistry. Sir Charles Bell and Bichat, both talented physiologists, put histology and pathological anatomy on a scientific basis; Lamarck, Cuvier, and Linnaeus were indefatigable workers in the field of botany and zoölogy; in geology, Werner, Hutton, and William Smith paved the way for the later epoch-making theories of Lyell. Nor should we overlook the great French *Encyclopédie* edited by Diderot, or Buffon's famous *Natural History*, both of which emphasized and popularized the new scientific ideas at the expense of traditional intellectual interests.

American intellectuals, as we have already seen, were not unaware of this Old World scientific advancement; a few,

America aware of Old World scientific movement notably Franklin, Benjamin Rush, and James Woodhouse, deeply imbued with the scientific spirit, fully appreciated the unlimited possibilities of man's conquest over the material world. Indeed, in 1781, the many-sided Franklin, writing from the American legation in France to the English chemist Priestley, declared it was "impossible to imagine the height to which may be carried in a thousand years, the power of man over matter. We may perhaps learn to deprive large masses of their gravity and give them absolute levity, for the sake of easy transport. Agriculture may diminish its labor and double its produce; all diseases may by sure means be prevented or cured, not excepting that of old age, and our lives lengthened at pleasure even beyond the antediluvian standard." Time was to prove that Franklin was not a mere visionary.

Thanks to Franklin's inspiring leadership, Philadelphia was even before 1800 America's scientific center. Here Dr. Rush,

Philadelphia America's scientific center often referred to as the father of chemistry in America, was teaching chemistry at the University of Pennsylvania. So also were Dr. Woodhouse and Dr. Robert Hare, the latter the inventor of an oxyhydrogen blow pipe. Joseph Priestley, discoverer of oxygen and close friend of Franklin and Jefferson, persecuted in his native England because of his liberalistic views, migrated to Philadelphia, where he carried on his researches until his

BENJAMIN RUSH

death in 1804. Benjamin Silliman, having been appointed in 1802 to the first professorship of chemistry and natural history at Yale and feeling the need for instruction, came to Philadelphia because it "presented more advantages in science than any other place in our country." It was in Pennsylvania's capital city, too, that the picturesque scientist and cosmopolite, Constantine Rafinesque, published the first of his four hundred-odd papers which were to earn for him a reputation as one of the greatest of the pioneers in natural science.

But all scientific advancement in America was not monopolized by Philadelphia. In every section of the country there were those who were anxious to unravel nature's secrets. At the College of New Jersey (Princeton) the chemical researches of Dr. John MacLean attracted widespread attention. In 1802 Nathaniel Bowditch, Harvard mathematician, published his *American Practical Navigator*, and shortly afterward began the translation into English of Laplace's *Mecanique Céleste*. Dr. Samuel Latham Mitchill, elected to the chair of chemistry and natural history in Columbia College in 1792, was engaged in many lines of scientific investigation. He was one of the first to analyze the waters of the mineral springs at Saratoga. Thomas Cooper, Old World refugee, eminent for his versatility of talent and extent of knowledge, held professorships of natural science successively in Dickinson College, the University of Pennsylvania, the University of Virginia (where he never served), and the College of South Carolina. For nearly half a century he labored, as the Beards so well say, "at chemistry, mineralogy, geology, and political economy, combining disputes with the theologians over the authenticity of the Pentateuch, and equally bitter controversies with Federalist politicians over policies of government." [1]

Scientific workers outside of Philadelphia

[1] News of Cooper's appointment to the faculty of the University of Virginia in 1819 caused a terrific outcry that "atheism was to be publicly taught, that the state would become bankrupt, that the good old times were gone forever, and that war was being waged against the manhood and virtue of Virginia by the arch-scoffer of Monticello, seconded by his deistical follower (Cooper) of Montpellier." See W. P. Trent, *English Culture in Virginia*, p. 22. In South Carolina Cooper was brought to trial in 1834 for his "shameful atheism."

The first two volumes of his *Emporium of Arts and Sciences* appeared in 1812–1814; in 1815 he brought out his *Practical Treatise on Dyeing and Calico Printing*. Three years later Silliman established the *American Journal of Science and Arts*. Beyond the Alleghenies there was also considerable interest in the new science. In 1819 Rafinesque was appointed professor of modern languages and natural science at Transylvania University, a post which he held for seven years. Meanwhile, another Old World figure, J. J. Audubon, merchant, traveling painter, and dancing master, having first set foot on American soil in 1803, had begun his career in the transallegheny as an ornithologist.

Even agriculture caught the spirit of the new science. Influenced by the work of Arthur Young, leader of the widespread
Science and agriculture movement for agrarian reform in England, those Americans who visioned better farming than that which so widely prevailed formed societies for promoting agriculture. The earliest of these, founded in Philadelphia in 1785, formed the pattern for similar organizations in New York, Charleston, Boston, and elsewhere. Papers and essays covering practically every phase of agriculture were read and discussed. Richard Peters, for thirty years president of the Philadelphia society, contributed an astounding number of essays, as also did Robert R. Livingston of New York and others. To stimulate agricultural experimentation and improved methods, prizes and medals were offered and exhibitions of new tools or of new breeds of livestock were encouraged. The experience of Elkanah Watson, one of the organizers of the Berkshire [Massachusetts] Agricultural Society, was typical. Under date of 1820 he wrote as follows:

In the Fall of 1807 I procured the first pair of Merino sheep that had appeared in Berkshire. . . . I was induced to notify an exhibition under the great elm tree in the public square in Pittsfield of these two sheep on a certain day. Many farmers and even women were excited by curiosity to attend my humble exhibition. . . . The farmers present responded to my remarks with approbation. We became acquainted, and from that day to the present, agricultural societies, cattle shows, and all in connexion therewith have predominated in my mind.

Dissemination of information about improvements in other countries was one of the primary objects of all these societies. Incidentally, the Berkshire society which, unlike its earlier sister organizations, was composed of actual farmers, fostered social intercourse. At the close of its exhibition the people assembled in the largest village church, where amid impressive ceremonies the prizes and other honors were distributed. The general assembly in turn was often followed by a "pastoral ball."

On the inventive and engineering side the early republic was not without its men of genius. Whitney, Fitch, Evans, Latrobe, Livingston, Barlow, Stevens, and Fulton were Invention and members of that great company which included engineering Hargreaves, Arkwright, Watt, and other Old World luminaries whose revolutionary accomplishments were to alter radically the conditions of life for millions of human beings. The cotton gin, the multitubular boiler, the screw propeller, and the steamboat were their principal contributions to that wonderful movement which transformed a tool-using world into a world of machines.

Notwithstanding their enthusiasm, those interested in scientific advancement met with many obstacles. Religionists who feared their disturbing influence opposed them; Obstacles to most of the rank and file were ignorant and indif- scientific ferent; associations for arousing and stimulating progress interest in scientific research were few; the colleges were destitute of laboratories and laboratory equipment. Silliman, for example, tells us that the apparatus at the University of Pennsylvania was "humble," that the instructors did not have "proper" assistants, and that the work was "imperfectly" done. Even Silliman's own laboratory at Yale was for a long time a makeshift affair in a basement room. The inventor Fitch, characterized by the populace as a "crazy man," ended his life apparently because he could not secure adequate financial backing for his scientific projects.

But the obstacles confronting both scientist and inventor were, in a measure, counterbalanced by the stimulating efforts of the American Philosophical Society. Founded in Philadel-

phia prior to the Revolution, as we have observed, this organization, remarkable for its distinguished membership, which in-
American
Philosophical
Society
encouraged
science
cluded all the leading thinkers of both America and Western Europe, and for its catholicity of interest, rendered splendid service to the cause of scientific advancement on this side of the Atlantic. Through its several committees it gathered information about almost every conceivable subject that had any scientific bearing. To it came copies of all the principal scientific and philosophical books and tracts appearing in the Old World. At its sessions the leading scientific questions and problems of the day were seriously discussed. To its members and others it sent its publications embodying the fruits of research in both Europe and America. Inspired by the work of the Philadelphia organization those in other parts of the country who were interested in science established similar societies. Notable among these earlier scientific bodies were the American Academy of Arts and Sciences founded in Boston in 1780; the Connecticut Academy of Arts and Sciences begun in New Haven in 1799; and the New York Lyceum of Natural History started in 1817, which later became the New York Academy of Sciences.

4. THE PROFESSIONS

Of the several professions practiced in America in 1800 none, with the possible exception of engineering, was more affected
Backward
state of
science of
medicine in
1800
by the new science than medicine. Prior to the Revolution and even after, as we have seen, the science of medicine made slow growth. The three leading medical schools in the country — that at the University of Pennsylvania founded in 1765 by Dr. John Morgan; the College of Physicians and Surgeons of New York, the direct descendant of the medical school organized as a part of King's College; and the Harvard Medical School, which began its long and honorable career in 1783 — graduated a very small number each year. Indeed, from 1792 to 1811 only thirty-four received degrees from the New York institution. A shortage of trained physicians therefore existed. Moreover,

the physician overburdened with practice found little or no time for research.

Even those who were well trained at home or in some foreign center such as Edinburgh were ignorant of both the cause and cure for most diseases. Rheumatism, which was widely prevalent, was considered an external disease occasioned by cold and damp. Diphtheria was treated as croup. Fevers, classified as remittant, malignant, or yellow, and chronic or nervous, were attributed to marsh odors, decayed vegetable matter, rotting timber, stagnant water, bad sewerage, and lack of drainage. Doses of mercury, calomel, jalap, rhubarb, and Peruvian bark were freely administered irrespective of what the disease might be. Blistering and bloodletting or bleeding were thought by the great majority of doctors and laymen to be most efficacious for every sort of illness — fever, pulmonary consumption, diabetes, gout, asthma, idiocy, hysteria, madness — in short, for everything. Washington, for example, when attacked with what doctors now call acute laryngitis, was given an emetic, purged, bled, and blistered, but his larynx was neither examined nor directly treated. Bleeding, generally performed by a barber rather than by a physician, was freely practiced until about 1850. Dentistry was still in its infancy, and the suffering and disease occasioned by decayed teeth must have been enormous.

To make matters worse, the popular mind was enveloped in credulity and superstition. All sorts of foolish and even harmful methods of healing the sick and the physically incapacitated were eagerly tried. Rubbing wens or tumors with dead toads; warding off disease by burying a piece of pork under the eaves of a house; poulticing a bruise or a sore with dung, viper's tongue soaked in wine, or the brains of this or that animal; blowing ashes of a coal-black cat's head, burnt in a new pot, into the eyes for cataract; administering spider's web for fever and ague, and pills of rattlesnake poison mixed with cheese for palsy and rheumatism, as well as dozens of other equally senseless remedies were in common use. Charlatans peddled recipes for various nostrums from town to town, thus reaping profits by their audacity. A friend or any sick person could be induced to part with money or commodities in exchange for mixtures the secrets of which had been begged or stolen from the Chinese, the Arabians, or the American Indians.

Scores of patent medicines, to which the most astounding curative powers were ascribed, were everywhere for sale. The **Patent** very mystery surrounding their manufacture made **medicines** it more possible for the vendor to play on popular credulity. Nor were audacious and industrious distributors of these patent concoctions wanting. A Philadelphia quack, for example, filled half a page of the *Aurora* day after day with announcements of his remedies and certificates of his cures. Among them were Robertsons' Stomachic Elixir of Health, alleged to cure anything from a cough to dysentery; Robertsons' Vegetable Nervous Cordial or Nature's Grand Restorative, intended to dispel all nervous disorders as well as syphilis, barrenness, scurvy, and diseases arising from the immoderate use of tea; for children he advocated Robertsons' Infallible Worm Destroying Lozenges. Hamilton's Grand Restorative was "invaluable" for the speedy relief and permanent cure of "nervous disorders, constipation, impure blood, hysteria, cramps, gout, inward debility, and indigestion." Hahn's Genuine Eye Water, it was claimed, would cure all eye diseases.

With the science of medicine backward, and credulity and superstition widespread, small wonder that influenza, smallpox, **Epidemics** diphtheria, typhoid and yellow fever epidemics frequently scourged the country taking heavy toll. Yellow fever, largely because of its virulence and recurrent character, was especially dreaded. No port town from Portland to New Orleans escaped it. In 1793, for example, it swept 4,000 Philadelphians to their graves; five years later it claimed 3,500 of the same city's population. In New York in 1795 yellow fever deaths totaled 732; in 1798, 2,086; in 1803, 606; and in 1805, 262. As soon as the disease made its appearance people in the affected area became terror stricken. All who could fled the country; those unable to do so shut themselves up in shutter-closed houses. No one ventured abroad unless it was absolutely necessary; offices were closed and newspapers ceased circulation; the hearses in the streets made the only sounds of travel. To prevent infection everyone — children as well as adults — became heavy smokers; others chewed garlic or put it in their shoes; many burned gunpowder, tobacco, and niter in their houses and sprinkled them with vinegar. Some, doubting the remedies prescribed by the physicians, bitterly attacked them. Even Dr. Rush was not spared. "The Israelite slew his thousands," cried William Cobbett (Peter Porcupine), "but the Rushites have slain their tens of thousands." So scurrilous were Cobbett's diatribes against the noted Philadelphia physician that the latter sued for libel and recovered five thousand dollars damages.

Many persons were of the opinion that much of the disease and many of the physical ailments of the time were attributable to over-indulgence in eating and drinking. "The inhabitants," said one of the editors of the *Medical Repository*, "are almost constantly in a state of repletion, by stuffing and cramming, and by the use of stimulating drink. The consumption of animal food is probably much greater in the Fredonian [i.e., United] States, than in any other civilized nation; and it ought likewise to be observed, that the quantity of ardent spirits drank by our people, exceeds anything of the kind, that the world can produce; the appetite for inebriating drink seems to be increasing and insatiable." Some authorities are of the opinion that ill-cooked food was responsible, in part, for the inordinate drinking of rum and whisky. Salted meat, especially salt pork, was one of the principal items of diet of nearly every rural dweller and of many who lived in urban communities, and this probably gave rise to thirst. Moreover, American cooking, with some exceptions, was not conducive to good digestion. Nearly everything was fried, because that was the easiest and quickest way of preparing food for the table. Hot breads — rolls, muffins, and biscuits — buckwheat cakes, and flapjacks were eaten in immoderate quantities, contrary to the advice of physicians.

[margin note:] Over-indulgence in food and drink considered a cause of disease

Leading American physicians at the turn of the century, fully aware of the shortcomings of their profession, did their *Efforts to improve medical profession* best to improve it. To this end they kept abreast of every advance in European medical science. Thus in 1800 Dr. Benjamin Waterhouse of the Harvard Medical School and Dr. David Hosack of the College of Physicians and Surgeons of Columbia introduced vaccination as a safeguard against smallpox. Successful attempts were also made to raise the standard of medical education. Nine out of every ten practicing physicians had acquired their medical schooling in doctors' offices and had had no collegiate training.

That almost every district of our country [wrote Dr. Hosack in 1813], abounds with individuals who set up to exercise the duties of practitioners of medicine, need scarcely be stated; how great is the number of them who are totally ignorant of the first principles of their profession and who degrade the noblest of studies into the meanest of arts cannot have escaped the attention of any who at all regard the interests of society. . . . Though they differ from beasts of prey . . . yet they wage war with equal success as it regards the destruction of their objects. . . . The inroads and depredations which they commit bid defiance to all calculation. . . . The necessity of something like medical reforms is obvious, and the learned and the liberal in every quarter are called upon in behalf of so beneficial an undertaking. The degraded state of medical science renders necessary the united exertions of all if we wish to restore the healing art to its wonted dignity.

Dr. Hosack's remedy for the ills that beset his profession was more thorough education and elimination of the quack and the incompetent.

While the legislators were too busy with the material needs of their rapidly expanding communities, or too engrossed in *Standards in medical profession improve* their own affairs to concern themselves much about matters pertaining to higher education or to the professions, with the possible exception of the law, standards in the medical profession improved both ethically and educationally. In addition to the medical schools at Harvard, Columbia, and the University of Pennsylvania, heretofore mentioned, the first quarter of the nineteenth century saw the establishment of new schools at Dartmouth, Yale, Brown, the University of Maryland, Transylvania University, Bowdoin, Cincinnati, and Castleton, Vermont. Between 1810 and 1819 nearly 1400 physicians were graduated. State medical societies which set the requirements for medical education were established in every state. Philadelphia, New York, Boston, Baltimore, Cincinnati, and other cities had their medical periodicals, all of which contributed to the improvement of the profession. Of these the *Medical Repository*, a New York quarterly and the first medical journal in America, was perhaps the most important. Founded by Samuel Latham Mitchill, professor of chemistry at Columbia, and by Elihu Hubbard Smith and Edward Miller, both physicians, it enjoyed a high reputation at home and abroad. Dr. Rush, who labored zealously and fruitfully for the betterment of the medical profession, was a frequent contributor. While medicine and subjects relating thereto filled most of its pages, space was given to other sciences, notably agriculture, geography, and natural history.

The professions closely related to medicine, namely, surgery, dentistry, and pharmacy, were still in their infancy in 1800. Surgery was severely limited because there was Surgery and no anesthetic, it not being discovered until 1846. dentistry The only surgeons were the doctors, although one, Dr. Philip Physick, often called the father of American surgery, devoted the major part of his time to surgical work. Patients who were operated upon were held forcibly upon the operating table by strong attendants. Despite the excruciating pain, daring operations, including amputation of limbs, were successfully performed. Midwifery, long on the borders of respectability, was largely in the hands of old women, which probably accounts in large degree for the high percentage of women who died in childbirth. Dentistry was chiefly confined to teeth extraction, a function performed either by the doctor or by the blacksmith. A few dentists, some of whom had come from France, were practicing in New York and Philadelphia. John Greenwood, one of the early New York dentists, made a set of artificial teeth for George Washington in 1790 and again in 1795. The

Baltimore Dental College, the first dental school in America, was not established until 1839.

With few exceptions doctors were their own apothecaries. Most of them imported their medicines direct from London, although some secured supplies from Philadelphia, **Pharmacy** the leading manufacturing center in America of pharmaceuticals and medicinal chemicals. Young men wishing to prepare themselves for the "practice of physic" became apprentices to a physician, where they qualified themselves to engage in the unregulated and unlicensed business of pharmacy. The early vendors of drugs supplemented their stock of medicines with paints, oils, glass, fruits, brimstone, glue, beeswax, and a large variety of other merchandise.

The treatment of sick paupers in the almshouses led to the establishment of hospitals. The new almshouse opened in **Hospitals and** New York at Bellevue in 1816 included two hos- **dispensaries** pital pavilions, whence came Bellevue Hospital. The Philadelphia Hospital,[1] opened about 1812, was also part of an almshouse. Largely because they were charitable institutions and were overcrowded and unsanitary, the hospitals were little patronized by persons of means. Dispensaries developed alongside the hospitals, Philadelphia opening one in 1796 and New York in 1805. In 1811 the New York dispensary treated 1446 patients; 1016 received free vaccination.

Of all the professions in America in 1800 the law, with the exception of the ministry, was most firmly established. "In no country perhaps in the world," said Edmund **Legal profes-** Burke in his famous speech for conciliation with **sion in** **America prior** the colonies, "is the law so general a study." **to Revolution** This opinion was supported by General Gage who, when he became governor of Massachusetts, averred that "all the people in his government" were "lawyers or smatterers in law." Both writers might have added that the lawyers in seventeenth-century colonial America were as a class not popular, and that the majority of the people, including the

[1] The Philadelphia Hospital should not be confused with the Pennsylvania Hospital. The latter, founded in 1732, existed apart from the almshouse, and most of its patients paid for their treatment.

clergy, agreed with John Milton that "most men are allured to the trade of law, grounding their purposes not on the prudent and heavenly contemplation of justice and equity which was never taught them, but on the promising and pleasing thoughts of litiguous terms, fat contentions, and flowing fees." As the struggle for independence drew nearer and the burden of defending colonial rights fell increasingly on the shoulders of the lawyer class, this antagonistic feeling gradually disappeared.

Unfortunately for the legal profession, however, the old prejudice and popular dislike of lawyers revived after the Revolution. Two outstanding reasons account for this. In the first place, many of the ablest lawyers, being Royalists, left the country or retired from practice; others equally able gave the major portion of their time to politics; much of the practice of law, therefore, passed into the hands of lawyers of inferior ability. Secondly, and much more important, was the social unrest arising from the economic depression and the hard times following the war, already noted in an earlier chapter. With creditors of all sorts insisting on enforcing contracts and the payment of debts, the law business increased to unheard of proportions. Those unable to pay their debts were clapped into jail and the jails were filled to overflowing. People at large, not understanding the real causes for the situation, attributed their plight to the creditor class and the lawyers. Everywhere throughout the land lawyers were denounced as banditti, charlatans, demagogues, bloodsuckers, windbags, smooth-tongued rogues, and political tricksters. Some communities even went so far as to demand the complete abolition of the legal profession. "We humbly request," voted a town meeting in Braintree, near Boston, in 1786, "that there may be such laws compiled as may crush or at least put a proper check or restraint on that order of Gentlemen denominated Lawyers, the completion of whose modern conduct appears to us to lend rather to the destruction than the preservation of the town." Indeed, so great was the popular odium against the legal profession that the youthful lawyer John Quincy Adams, writing his mother in 1787, declared, "I am sometimes almost dis-

Legal profession unpopular after Revolution

couraged and ready to wish I had engaged in some other line of life."

With few or no safeguards, it was easy in colonial days and even after for men of inferior character and competence to get Early legal into the legal profession. Anyone who aspired to training be a lawyer usually entered the office of some practicing attorney of note who had a library. Here by study, observation, and occasionally by direct discussion with his senior he absorbed the principles of the law. For this privilege he paid usually one hundred to five hundred dollars, depending upon his financial status and the prominence of the lawyer in whose office he labored.[1] Whether he learned much or little often depended upon his own aptitude and fitness and upon the time and inclination the lawyer had to give him advice, information, and instruction. An admirable picture of this type of training was painted by the noted lawyer Benjamin D. Silliman, in his address to the graduating class of the Columbia Law School of 1887:

Widely different have been, with few exceptions, the opportunities of legal instruction in this country until within a comparatively recent period. The student was required to enter the office of a practicing attorney and there to pursue his studies. He was at once engaged in the practice of that of which he had not learned the principles. He became familiar by daily observation and as a copyist, with the forms of conveyancing and the phraseology of pleadings, without understanding their reason. The proper order of his instruction was inverted. Blackstone's Commentaries and, at a later period, Kent's were placed in his hands for perusal in the intervals of office business; but there was perceptible to him little relation between their contents and the daily routine of his clerical duties. As a general rule it was impossible for the attorney in whose office the student was engaged to give any material attention to his studies, and his progress and attainments, therefore, lacked system and were slow, confused and uncertain. A formal and superficial examination at length passed him to the bar,

[1] The following is an interesting illustration: "Phila., March 22, 1782. I promise to pay James Wilson, Esq. or order on demand one hundred guineas, his fee for receiving my nephew Bushrod Washington as a student of law in his office. G. Washington." Cf. Charles Warren, *History of the Harvard Law School and of Early Legal Conditions in America*, vol. I, p. 133.

and he could rarely feel at home in his profession until he had acquired, by subsequent laborious and anxious practice, a knowledge of very much that he should have attained at the outset. He was thus obliged, at great disadvantage, to lay a large part of the foundation of his house after he had toiled long upon the superstructure.

Prior to the Revolution the American lawyer was severely handicapped by lack of books. Up to 1776 only thirty-three law books were printed in America, and of this number eight were revised editions of the same book. With few exceptions all were manuals for the use of justices of the peace, sheriffs, and other petty officials, or treatises on the general rights of Englishmen.[1] A few of the wealthier and more prominent lawyers possessed small collections of law books. An inventory of Patrick Henry's library in 1799, for example, disclosed sixty-three law volumes. The library of most lawyers, however, could easily stand on the mantel. Practically no law books were to be found in either the college or public libraries before the Revolution; neither were court reports to be had on this side of the Atlantic. Students were obliged, therefore, to gain as much knowledge as possible from whatever books there were in the office in which they were serving their apprenticeship. Blackstone's *Com-*

Colonial lawyer handicapped by lack of books

---

[1] The following are fairly illustrative of these earlier volumes: Sir John Hawles, *The Englishman's Right*, a *Dialogue between a Barrister at Law and a Juryman, plainly setting forth the antiquity, the excellent designed use and office and just privileges of juries by the laws of England* (Boston, 1693).

Cotton Mather, *Lex Mercatoria Or the Just Rules of Commerce Declared. And Offences Against the Rules of Justice in the Dealings of Men with one another selected* (Boston, 1705).

Nicholas Boone, *The Constable's Pocket Book: Or a Dialogue between an old Constable and a new, being a guide in their Keeping the peace* (Boston, 1710).

George Webb, *The Office and Authority of a Justice of the Peace. And also the duty of Sheriffs, Constables, Coroners, Church Wardens, Surveyors of Highways, Constables & Officers of Militia. Together with precedents of warrants, judgments, executions and other legal process, issuable by magistrates within their respective jurisdictions, civil or criminal, and the method of judicial proceedings before justices of the peace in matters within their cognizance out of sessions, collected from the common and statute laws of England and acts of assembly now in force; and adapted to the Constitution and practice of Virigina* (Williamsburg, Va., 1736).

mentaries, the rigorous Coke on Littleton, Comyn's *Digest*, Bacon's *Abridgement*, and a brief book or two on pleadings and practice were about the only legal volumes in the office of the average country lawyer at the end of the eighteenth century.

That some embryonic lawyers enjoyed a broader course of study is evident from Chancellor James Kent's description of the beginning of his legal education:

When the college [Yale] was broken up and dispersed in July, 1779, by the British, I retired to a country village and finding Blackstone's *Commentaries* I read the fourth volume. Parts of the work struck my taste and the work inspired me at the age of sixteen with awe and I fondly determined to be a lawyer. In Nov., 1781, I was placed by my father with Mr. (now called Judge) Benson who was then attorney general, at Poughkeepsie. There I entered on law and was the most modest, steady, industrious student that such place ever saw. I read the following winter Grotius and Puffendorff in large folios and made copious extracts. My fellow students who were gay and gallant thought me very odd and dull in my taste; but out of five of them four died in middle life drunkards. . . . In 1782 I read Smollett's *History of England,* and procured at a farmer's house where I boarded *Rapin's History* (a large folio) and read it through, and I found during the course of the last summer among my papers my MSS. abridgement of *Rapin's Dissertations on the Laws and Customs of the Anglo-Saxons.* I abridged Hale's *History of the Common Law* and the old books of practice and read parts of *Blackstone* again and again. The same year I procured Hume's *History* and his profound reflections and admirable eloquence struck most deeply on my youthful mind. I extracted the most admired part, [and] made several volumes of MSS.

After the Revolution and particularly after the depression of the eighties, more attention was paid to legal education. King's
Law professorships　College, the first in America to do so, founded a professorship of law as early as 1773. In 1779 Jefferson was instrumental in creating a professorship of law at the College of William and Mary. Ten years later the College of Philadelphia appointed its first professor of law. Chairs of law were subsequently established at a number of other collegiate institutions, including Brown, Dartmouth, Transylvania, Middlebury, and Maryland. Those who filled these

CHANCELLOR KENT IN HIS LIBRARY

OLD BUILDING AT LITCHFIELD, CONN.

Here the first law classes in the United States were conducted

professorships were expected to cover a wide range of material. Thus James Kent, unanimously elected to the professorship of law at Columbia in 1793 at a stipend of two hundred pounds sterling per year, was supposed to give

. . . a brief review of the history, the nature, the several forms, and the just ends of civil government — a sketch of the origin, progress, and final settlement of the United States — a particular detail of the organization and duties of the several departments of the general government, together with an examination of such parts of the civil and criminal codes of the federal jurisprudence, as shall be the most susceptible of illustration and most conducive to public utility. The courts of the several states and the connection they bear to the general government will then be considered, and the more particular examination of the Constitution of this State, the whole detail of our municipal law, with the relation to the rights of property, and of persons, and the forms of administering justice, both civil and criminal, will then be treated fully and at large.

Several private law schools — forerunners of our modern institutions for legal training — were founded toward the close of the eighteenth century. Of these, the school established at Litchfield, Connecticut, by Judge Tappan Reeve has the distinction of being the first law school in America. During the fifty years of its existence it was attended by over a thousand students representing every section of the country. Describing the school in his *Travels in New England*, Timothy Dwight wrote:

> Law schools

It would not it is believed do discredit to any country. Law is here taught as a science, and not merely nor principally as a mechanical business; not as a collection of loose independent fragments, but as a regular well compacted system. At the same time the students are taught the practice of being actually employed in it. A court is constituted, actions are brought and conducted through a regular process, questions are raised and the students become advocates in form. Students resort to this school from every part of the American Union.

Lawyers and others were of the opinion that students could gain more in one year at this school than in three to five years under the ordinary method of apprenticeship. Numerous other law schools modeled after the Litchfield institution sprang up during the first two decades of the nineteenth century. In 1817 the Harvard Law School was founded.

Perhaps more important than the law schools in elevating the ethical and educational standards of the legal profession were the bar associations. Organized on a county or state basis, these associations established rigorous rules and requirements for office study by students desiring to become lawyers. Sometimes these rules were prescribed by a court or by statute. The profession was not without its periodicals, although most of them were short-lived. Probably the earliest and most notable of these was the *American Law Journal* of Philadelphia, edited by John E. Hall. The *American Jurist and Law Magazine*, famous during the thirties and early forties, was not founded until 1829.

Bar associations and legal periodicals

The clergy as well as the lawyers and physicians had their professional schools. As early as 1778 the Congregationalists had established a seminary at Andover, Massachusetts. In 1784 the Dutch Reformed Church opened a divinity school in New York City. St. Mary's Academy for training students for the Catholic priesthood was established in Baltimore in 1791. Three years later the Presbyterians founded a divinity school at Chambersburg, Pennsylvania; nearly twenty years after (1812) Princeton Theological Seminary opened its doors. The first seminary for the Baptists began its work at Hamilton, New York, in 1817; and that for the Episcopalians at New York City in 1817. In addition nearly all the colleges offered courses in which the Bible and theology were taught and the New Testament read in Greek.

Divinity schools

5. LITERATURE AND JOURNALISM

If science and the professions were making headway in the America of 1800 so also were letters and art. Handicapped by lack of wealthy patronage and subsidization enjoyed by European artists, actors, musicians, and *littérateurs*, and compelled to labor in a frontier nation, ninety-five per cent of whose inhabitants were provincial-minded farmers with little or no time or interest

Literary atmosphere in America in 1800

for things intellectual or esthetic, we can readily appreciate the difficulties confronting the New World artist and writer. But the American writer could not complain for want of stirring themes. The struggle with England, the unrest following the Revolution, the French upheaval, the consciousness of national independence, the battle between the forces of capitalism and agrarianism, westward expansion, humanitarianism, and a score of lesser social, economic, religious, and political items drawn from the world of reality afforded dramatist, novelist, poet, and pamphleteer ample raw material.

The drama which, as we have seen in a previous chapter, made its appearance in America in pre-Revolutionary days was hard hit when in 1774 the Continental Congress advised the colonists to "discountenance and discourage all horse racing and all kinds of gaming, cockfighting, exhibitions of shows, plays, and other expensive diversions and entertainments." With few exceptions the wishes of Congress were respected. During the early years of the struggle with Great Britain, however, both Patriot and Tory resorted to dramatic propaganda. Tory officeholders and British soldiers were painted in very unflattering colors by Mrs. Mercy Warren in *The Group*, and by John Peacock in *The Fall of British Tyranny*. The Loyalists replied in kind in such products as *The Americans Roused in a Cure for the Spleen.* Whether any of these were staged we do not know, though the title page of *The Group* represented it "as lately Acted, and to be Reacted, to the Wonder of all Superior Intelligences Nigh Head Quarters at Amboyne." Imperfect in its literary qualities, Mrs. Warren's satire admirably portrays the intensity of feeling between the hostile groups in the struggle which was to end triumphantly for the patriot cause.

Dramatic satire during Revolution

At the close of the war many persons opposed the theatre on moral and patriotic grounds. The clergy, almost to a man, attacked it as the "Devil's Chapel." In many instances the press was also unremitting in its opposition. In New York a memorial under date of 1785, signed by seven hundred persons, asked the legislature to abolish theatres. So uncongenial was the

Opposition to theatre at close of Revolution

atmosphere in the City of Brotherly Love that in 1785 the performances were advertised "gratis" and the plays were disguised by moral captions; *She Stoops to Conquer* thus became *Improper Education; Hamlet, Filial Piety; Richard III, The Fate of Tyranny*. In Boston, where acting had been forbidden by law since 1750, an audacious group, taking matters in their own hands, put on in 1792 an exhibition which today would be characterized as vaudeville. Emboldened by success, they next attempted dramas, which they advertised as moral lectures, but the county sheriff unexpectedly made his appearance and arrested the offenders.

Despite all this opposition the theatre was not without its friends, and the drastic laws against the playhouse were soon softened or repealed. Little of importance was *The Contrast* produced until 1787, when Royall Tyler's comedy, *The Contrast*, was given in New York. Contrasting the simple and homely manners and customs of the American agrarian with the frivolous and luxurious standards of the urbanite who aped Old World fashions and ways, this amateurish play stressed both patriotism and nationalism as well as the virtues of republican simplicity. Its prologue gives the cue to its theme:

> Exult, each patriot heart! — This night is shewn
> A piece, which we may fairly call our own;
> Where the proud titles of "My Lord! Your Grace!"
> To humble Mr. and plain Sir give place.
> Our Author pictures not from foreign climes
> The fashions or the follies of the times;
> But has confin'd the subject of his work
> To the gay scenes — the circles of New York.
> On native themes his muse displays her pow'rs;
> If ours the faults, the virtues too are ours.
> Why should our thoughts to distant countries roam,
> When each refinement may be found at home?
> Who travels now to ape the rich or great,
> To deck an equipage and roll in state;
> To court the graces, or to dance with ease
> Or by hypocrisy to strive to please?
> Our free-born ancestors such arts despis'd;
> Genuine sincerity alone they priz'd;

Their minds with honest emulation fir'd,
To solid good — not ornament — aspir'd;
Or, if ambition rous'd a bolder flame,
Stern virtue throve, where insolence was shame.

But modern youths, with imitative sense,
Deem taste in dress the proof of excellence;
And spurn the meanness of your homespun arts,
Since homespun habits would obscure their parts;
Whilst all, which aims at splendor and parade,
Must come from Europe and be ready made.
Strange! we should thus our native worth disclaim,
And check the progress of our rising fame.
Yet one, whilst imitation bears the sway,
Aspires to nobler heights, and points the way,
Be rous'd my friends! his bold example view;
Let your own Bards be proud to copy you!
Should rigid critics reprobate our play
At least the patriotic heart will say,
"Glorious our fall, since in a noble cause
The bold attempt alone demands applause."

* * * *

Thus does our Author to your candour trust;
Conscious, the free are generous, as just.

Colonel Manly, patriot soldier, willing to sacrifice everything
for his country, decried profiteering and luxury because it
"renders a people weak at home and accessible *The Contrast*
to bribery, corruption, and force from abroad." **exalts repub-**
The Greeks, he declaimed, were "a great, a free **lican virtues**
and a happy people" — the "cherishers of arts and sciences,
the protectors of the oppressed, the scourge of tyrants, and the
safe asylum of liberty" so long as they knew "no other tools
than the ax and the saw." But when foreign gold and foreign
luxury came it "sapped the vitals of their virtue," made them
envious, suspicious, small-minded, selfish, and jealous — evils
which the Revolutionary colonel hoped his country would be
spared. Manly's servant, Jonathan, a shrewd, uncultivated
New England Yankee who would rather have "twenty acres
of rock, the Bible, the cow, Tabitha, and a little peaceable

bundling" than an eighteenth-century city belle who laughs at old-fashioned morals and boasts that with one flirt of her skirt she can bring more beaux to her feet in a week than in a lifetime by sighing fine sentiments, indicates the leveling tendencies at work in America in his assertion that "we don't make any great matter of distinction in our state between quality and other folks." The play ends triumphantly for republican virtues. Dimple, the snobbish, flattering, Anglomaniac money-seeker, after challenging Manly, the hero, to meet him on the field of honor, takes leave, bidding all to contrast between a "gentleman who has read Chesterfield and received the polish of Europe and an unpolished, untraveled American." In retort the hero exclaims: "I have learned that probity, virtue, honor, though they should not have received the polish of Europe, will secure to an honest American the good graces of his fair countrywomen, and I hope the applause of The Republic."

Tyler's other dramatic writings include *May-Day in Town, or New York in an Uproar*, a comic opera; *A Georgia Spec, or Land in the Moon*, a three act comedy ridiculing the mania for speculating in the newly acquired Yazoo country; and *The Farm House, or The Female Duellists*, a farce. Of these, *May-Day*, like *The Contrast*, severely satirized American urban life. Historically Tyler's dramatic work is significant, not because his productions have any great literary merit but for the insight it affords of American life at the time. Moreover, to Tyler belongs much of the credit for the change in public attitude toward the theatre. Members of every social class who formerly had condemned the theatre began to see, thanks to Tyler's efforts, that it was a worthy institution which could be used to reflect and perpetuate national traits and genius.

Tyler's historical significance

Somewhat overshadowing Tyler was William Dunlap, the first American to make the writing of plays a profession. Born in New Jersey in 1766 of Loyalist parents, he early manifested a catholicity of interest and versatility of talent for things cultural. Returning to America in 1787 after a three-year sojourn abroad, where he studied painting under Benjamin West and

William Dunlap, "Father of the American Drama"

witnessed "all Shakespeare's acting plays" and some of the best contemporary comedy, he turned to writing. A seemingly untiring worker, he wrote over sixty plays including tragedy, comedy, melodrama, farce, opera, and interlude, an accomplishment which earned for him the title "Father of the American Drama." More than half were originals, the others being translations or adaptations of French and German works. For fourteen years, 1796–1805 and 1806–1811, he was a theatrical manager as well as a writer. His taste for good music and gorgeous display in costume and stage furnishings plus difficulties with his companies and the low state of culture of the theatre-going public, which wanted novelties and cheap amusement rather than high grade productions, forced him into bankruptcy. He then turned to miniature painting and became the leading spirit, as we shall see, in organizing the National Academy of Design. In 1832, seven years prior to his death, he crowned his literary work by publishing his invaluable *History of the American Theatre*.

Space forbids even a brief summary of Dunlap's numerous productions. Of those with distinctly American themes two, perhaps, deserve mention. The first, a comedy *The Father,* on manners and morals, entitled *The Father, or or American* *American Shandyism*, inspired by *The Contrast,* *Shandyism* made its appearance at the St. John's Street Theatre, New York City, in 1789. From its prologue it is obvious that its purpose was not only to amuse but to exemplify republican ideals:

> The comic muse, pleas'd with her new abode
> Steps forth in sportive, tho in moral mode:
> Proud of her dwelling in our new made nation
> She's set about a serious reformation
> For, faith, she'd almost lost her reputation.

Cartride, a servant, extols the virtues of Colonel Duncan, the hero. The medical science of the day is severely satirized through the personage of the amusing Dr. Quiescent or Tattle. The play, Dunlap tells us, was received with great applause.

André, built around the Arnold-André conspiracy and performed for the first time at the Park Theatre, New York City,

André

in 1798, glorifies the Revolution, nationalism, patriotism, and the utopian blessings which idealists believed the new republic would shower on mankind. All these are rather admirably set forth in the first act by three of Dunlap's characters — the General, M'Donald, and Seward — who are companions in arms:

> *General.* Mankind who know not whence that spirit springs,
>> Which holds at bay all Britain's boasted power,
>> Gaze on their deeds astonish'd. See the youth
>> Start from his plough and straightway play the hero;
>> Unmurmuring bear such toils as veterans shun;
>> Rest all content upon the dampsome earth;
>> Follow undaunted to the deathful charge;
>> Or, when occasion asks, lead to the breech,
>> Fearless of all the unusual din of war,
>> His former peaceful mates. O Patriotism!
>> Thou wondrous principle of Godlike action.
>> Wherever liberty is found, there reigns
>> The love of country. Now the self-same spirit
>> Fill'd the breast of the great Leonidas
>> Swells in the hearts of thousands on these plains,
>> Thousands who never heard the hero's tale
>> 'T is this alone which saves thee, O my country!
>> And, till that spirit flies these western shores,
>> No power on earth shall crush thee.

> *Seward.*   'T is wondrous!
>> The men of other climes from this shall see
>> How easy 't is to shake oppression off;
>> How all-resistless is a union'd people;
>> And hence, from our success (which, by my soul,
>> I feel as much secur'd as though our foes
>> Were now within their floating prisons hous'd,
>> And their proud prows all pointing to the East),
>> Shall other nations break their galling fetters,
>> And re-assume the dignity of man.

> *M'Donald.* Are other nations in that happy state,
>> That, having broke Coercion's iron yoke,

ANDRÉ;

A *TRAGEDY*, IN FIVE ACTS:

AS PERFORMED BY THE OLD AMERICAN COMPANY,

NEW-YORK, MARCH 30, 1798.

TO WHICH ARE ADDED

AUTHENTIC DOCUMENTS

RESPECTING

MAJOR ANDRÉ;

CONSISTING OF

LETTERS TO MISS SEWARD,

THE

COW CHACE,

PROCEEDINGS OF THE COURT MARTIAL, &c.

COPY RIGHT SECURED.

NEW-YORK:

Printed by T. & J. SWORDS, No. 99 Pearl-street.

—1798.—

TITLE PAGE OF WILLIAM DUNLAP'S "ANDRÉ"

They can submit to Order's gentle voice
And walk on earth self-ruled? I much do fear it.
As to ourselves, in truth, I nothing see,
In all the wondrous deeds which we perform,
But plain effects from causes full as plain.
Rises not man forever 'gainst oppression?
It is the law of life; he can't avoid it.
But when the love of property unites
With sense of injuries past and dread of future,
Is it then wonderful that he should brave
A lesser evil to avoid a greater?

Seward.   Hast thou no nobler motives for thy arms
Than love of property and thirst for vengeance?

M'Donald.   Yes, my good Seward, and yet nothing wondrous.
I love this country for the sake of man.
My parents, and I thank them, cross'd the seas,
And made me native of fair Nature's world,
With room to grow and thrive in. I have thriven;
And feel my mind unshackled, free, expanding,
Grasping with ken unbounded mighty thoughts,
At which, if chance my mother had, good dame,
In Scotia, our revered parent soil,
Given me to see the day, I should have shrunk
Affrighted. Now, I see in this new world
A resting spot for man, if he can stand
Firm in his place, while Europe howls around him,
And all unsettled as the thoughts of vice,
Each nation in its turn threats him with feeble malice.
One trial, now, we prove; and I have met it.

In the second act Seward, after expressing the wish that an
impassable barrier might separate America from the Old World,
exclaims:

Then might, perhaps, one land on earth be found,
Free from th' extremes of poverty and riches;
Where ne'er a scepter'd tyrant should be known,
Or tyrant lordling, curses of creation; —
Where the faint shrieks of woe-exhausted age,

Raving, in feeble madness, o'er the corse
Of a polluted daughter, stained by lust
Of viand-pampered luxury, might ne'er be heard.

But M'Donald would have no such barrier, for he wanted America to have full benefit of the best that Europe had to offer:

From Europe shall enriching commerce flow,
And many an ill attendant; but from thence
Shall likewise flow blest science. Europe's knowledge,
By sharp experience bought, we should appropriate;
Striving thus to leap from that simplicity,
With ignorance curst, to that simplicity,
By knowledge blest; unknown the gulf between.

To Seward's plaint that all this is mere theoretic dreaming, M'Donald replies:

I'll to my bed, for I have watch'd all night;
And may my sleep give pleasing repetition
Of these my waking dreams! Virtue's incentives.

Contemporary with Dunlap were a number of lesser dramatists who drew freely upon the historical events of the Revolutionary and early national periods for Dunlap's con-themes. Indeed, almost every great event from temporaries the Boston Tea Party to the War of 1812 was dramatized. David Humphrey's *The Yankey in England*, John D. Burk's *Bunker Hill*, and Susanna H. Rowson's *Slaves in Algiers, or a Struggle for Freedom, The Volunteers*, and *The Female Patriot* are typical of the work of those who during this period contributed to the beginning of native drama.

Somewhat younger than Dunlap were three other personages who stand out prominently in the history of American drama. The first of these, James N. Barker (1784–1858), James N. son of a Democratic mayor of Philadelphia and a Barker thorough-going Jeffersonian, based all of his plays on native themes. His first play, *The Spanish Rover*, as well as his second, *America*, "a brief one-act piece, consisting of poetic dialogue, and sung by the genius of America, Science, Liberty, and attendant Spirits," were never performed. *Tears and Smiles*, a comedy on American life based on *The Contrast*, appeared in the Chestnut Street Theatre, Philadelphia, in 1807. It was followed by *The Indian Princess or La Belle Sauvage* (1808), the earliest play on the Pocohantas tale; *The Embargo or What News* (1808), *Marmion, or The Battle of Flodden Field* (1812), an intense expression of American nationalism growing out of the events just prior to the outbreak of the War of 1812, *The Armourer's Escape or Three Years at Nootka Sound* (1817), and *Superstition* (1824), based upon colonial history and up to the time of its appearance the best play that had been written in America.

Mixing politics and literary endeavor as did Barker, and next to him the most important playwright during the first **Mordecai M.** quarter of the nineteenth century, was Mordecai M. **Noah** Noah (1785–1851). A Philadelphian by birth, he early manifested an interest in drama, using at first foreign themes. In 1819, however, his play *She Would be a Soldier, or the Plains of Chippewa* was given in New York. *Marion or the Hero of Lake George* (1821), giving the background of the Battle of Saratoga, and *The Grecian Captive or the Fall of Athens* (1822), prompted by American sympathy for the Greek War of Independence, were Noah's other most important dramatic works. That he fully appreciated the cultural and political situation in the America of his time is evident from the following excerpt from a letter penned to Dunlap: "My line, as you well know, has been in the more rugged paths of politics, a line in which there is more fact than poetry, more feeling than fiction; in which, to be sure, there are 'exits' and 'entrances' — where 'prompter's whistle' is constantly heard in the voice of the people; but which in our popular government almost disqualifies us for the more soft and agreeable translation to the lofty conceptions of tragedy, the pure diction of genteel comedy, or the wit, gaiety, and humor of broad farce."

The third member of the trio, John Howard Payne (1791–1852), in sharp contrast to Barker and Noah, used foreign **John Howard** themes for the most part and developed his dra- **Payne** matic art abroad. Born in New York City but carefully reared in Boston, where he received his early schooling under the direction of his father, Payne at the age of thirteen announced his intention of becoming an actor. Horrified by the thought of his son being associated professionally with an institution whose reputation was still very unsavory, especially in New England, the father sent him to a New York mercantile house, but to no avail. His first play, *Julia or the Wanderer*, a comedy, was staged in New York in 1806 when Payne was not yet fifteen. After two years at Union College, 1806–1808, he made his début as an actor in old Park Theatre, New York. Not entirely satisfied with his success, he welcomed the opportunity in 1813 to go abroad. There he remained until 1832 acting and writing. Of the sixty-odd plays which he wrote or adapted from English, French, or German sources, *Brutus*, a tragedy, played first in London in 1818, and *Charles the Second or the Merry Monarch*,[1] also presented first in London in 1824, probably represent his most finished work. The song "Home, Sweet Home," by which Payne is best remembered by most Americans, was sung for the first time in London in 1823 in his opera *Clari or the Maid of Milan*. The music for the song was borrowed from a Sicilian air.

The economic, social, religious, and political conditions at the turn of the century furnished the novelist as well as the dramatist with inspiration and abundant material. The novel and While many Americans appear to have acquired its pioneers the fiction-reading habit prior to the Revolution, the novel faced almost savage opposition for many years after the close of that conflict. From one end of the country to the other moralists painted it in the darkest colors. Not only, they contended, did it serve no virtuous purpose, but worse — it lied, softened one's mind, crowded out better books, made adventure too romantic and love too vehement, and tended to confuse and dissatisfy the youth of the young republic. Despite such rigorous censure native novelists soon made their appearance. Interestingly enough, the pioneers were women. In 1789 Mrs. Sarah Wentworth Morton (1759–1846) of Boston produced *The Power of Sympathy*, our first regular novel. Three

---

[1] Washington Irving collaborated with Payne in the preparation of this play.

years later Mrs. Susannah H. Rowson (1762–1824) brought out her *Charlotte Temple;* designed as a warning to inexperienced girls, it proved to be one of the most popular novels ever published in America. Indeed, the fact that it has gone through more than one hundred editions bespeaks its popularity. *The Coquette* by Mrs. Hannah Webster Foster (1759–1840), based upon a New England scandal, appeared in 1797, and before its author's death it had passed through thirteen editions.

Like the dramatists, the early writers of fiction arranged themselves, to borrow a phrase from the Beards, "according to their sympathies with the tendencies of their age." Leaning well over to the conservative right was Royall Tyler (1757–1826), author of *The Contrast*. A son of Boston, Harvard graduate, soldier in the army sent to suppress Shays's Rebellion, poet, wit, jurist, and playwright, Tyler published in 1797 a two-volume novel called *The Algerine Captive*. In the first volume many aspects of American social life, ranging from education at Harvard and the state of the medical profession to paper money and the shortcomings of the clergy and the Jeffersonian gentry, are good-naturedly satirized. But more important historically is the preface bearing testimony to the growing popular demand for fiction which the hero of the story, by way of emphasis, describes at length:

Royall Tyler's The Algerine Captive

When he left New England books of Biography, Travels, Novels, and Modern Romances were confined to our seaports; or, if known in the country, were read only in the families of Clergymen, Physicians and Lawyers; while certain funeral discourses, the last words and dying speeches of Bryan Sheheen, and Levi Ames, and some dreary somebody's Day of Doom formed the most diverting part of the farmer's library. On his return from captivity he found a surprising alteration in the public taste. In our inland towns of consequence social libraries had been instituted, composed of books designed to amuse rather than to instruct. . . . All orders of country life, with one accord, forsook the sober sermons and Practical Pieties of their fathers for the gay stories and splendid impieties of the Traveller and the Novelist. The worthy farmer no longer fatigued himself with Bunyan's Pilgrim up "the hill of difficulty" or through the "slough of despond" but quaffed wine with Brydone in the hermitage of Vesuvius, or sported with Bruce on the fairy land of Abyssinia; while Dolly, the Dairy maid, and Jonathan, the hired man, threw aside the ballad of the cruel step-mother, over whom they had so often wept in concert, and now amused themselves into so agreeable a terrour, with the haunted houses and hobgobblins of Mrs. Ratcliffe, that they were both afraid to sleep alone.

To the left of Tyler and occupying middle ground was Hugh H. Brackenridge (1748–1816). A western Pennsylvanian of Scotch birth, graduate of Princeton in the class with James Madison, lawyer, and free-lance demo-crat, Brackenridge in his novel *Modern Chivalry*, our first important back-country book, satirized what seemed to him to be the shortcomings and absurdities of the young republic. Vigorously individualistic, friendly to all honest liberalisms, and firm believer that the hope of re-publican government rested upon intelligence and education, he took both "monocrats" and "levellers" to task. Lawyers, city speculators, slave-owners, and even members of Congress were as sharply hit as republican demagogues and office seek-ers. His opinion of electorate methods on the frontier is ad-mirably depicted in the following description of a contest between an honest deacon and an ignorant Scotch-Irishman:

Hugh H. Brackenridge and Modern Chivalry

When they looked upon the one [the deacon] they felt an inclination to promote him. But when, again, on the other hand, they saw two kegs which they knew to be replenished with a very cheering liquor, they seemed to be inclined in favor of the other. The candidates were called upon to address the people, and the grave person mounted the stump of a tree, many of them standing round, as the place was a new clearing. His harangue was listened to by some of the older and more sedate, and one man, hard of hearing, seemed to take great effort to catch the sounds. As soon as the man of the two kegs took a stump, he was surrounded by an eager crowd. — "Frinds," said he in the native Scotch-Irish, "I'm a good dimicrat and hates the Brattish. — I'm an elder of the meetin', forby, and has been overseer of the roads for three years; — An' ye all know that my mammy was kilt o' the Ingens — now all ye that's in my favor come forit an' drenk." Ap-petite, or rather thirst, prevailed, and the voters gave their votes to the man with the two kegs.

In the same satirical vein he caricatured the business-controlled city election:

The candidates were all remarkably pot-bellied; and waddled in their gait. The captain inquiring what were the pretensions of these men to be elected; he was told, that they had all stock in the funds, and lived in brick buildings; and some of them entertained fifty people at a time, and ate and drank abundantly; and living an easy life, and pampering their appetites, they had swollen to this size. "It is a strange thing," said the captain, "that in the country, in my route, they would elect no one but a weaver or a whisky-distiller; and here none but fat squabs, that guzzle wine, and smoke segars." . . . "No, faith," (said his friend), "there is na danger of Teague [a bog-trotting servant] here, unless he had his scores o' shares in the bank, and was in league with the brokers, and had a brick house at his hurdies, or a ship or two on the stocks. . . . All is now lost in substantial interest, and the funds command everything."

In such fashion did Brackenridge attempt to purge the existing order of that which he so honestly considered silly, vulgar, and detracting to the best interests of democracy.

More radical than Brackenridge was Charles Brockden Brown (1771–1810), the outstanding novelist of his time in the English-speaking portion of the New World. Charles Brockden Brown Born in Philadelphia of Quaker stock, Brown as a youngster displayed a precocious acquisitiveness for knowledge. By the age of sixteen he had, at the sacrifice of his health, not only mastered the classics but had read widely and deeply in other fields. His family, anxious for him to be a lawyer, placed him in a law office. A sentimentalist and a dreamer, he soon abandoned the law for writing. Profoundly influenced at first by Rousseau and later by Voltaire and the English radicals, especially Mary Wollstonecraft and William Godwin, he wanted the young republic to serve nobler social ends than did the Old World, debased in his opinion by selfish ambitions. In perfect agreement with the French philosophers that the ills of society were traceable to social and political maladjustments and to human nature, he decried the struggle of the Hamiltonians for power. Indeed, he even went so far as to oppose the adoption of the Constitution, partly because that document did not include the Declaration of Independence. A state where reason and justice would at all times prevail was his ideal. Professor Parrington's summary of Brown's social philosophy is admirable:[1]

America confronted a future unmortgaged to the past; why should it repeat the old follies and mistakes that had reduced Europe to its present level? Here the pressure of vicious institutions was light as yet. Here the appeal to reason and justice was less hampered by selfish preëmptions. Let social commendation be bestowed on the uncorrupted heart, on generous impulses, on native integrity of character. Let education be a natural unfolding of humane instincts, not a sharpening of wits to overreach one's fellows. Let rewards go to frank, outspoken truth, rather than to chicanery and deceit. Inspired by such sentiments, Brockden Brown proposed to make fiction serve social ends. He would spread the gospel of Mary Wollstonecraft and Godwin by means of popular tales.

This gospel Brown first elaborated in *Alcuin: A Dialogue*, published in 1797, in which he boldly argued that women should enjoy equality with men socially, indus- *Alcuin: A trially, and politically. Pleading her own case, Dialogue* one of his characters, a highly intelligent woman, condemns the existing social order for denying woman the advantages of a college education, subjecting her to the discipline of the common law, and excluding her from many professions and pursuits which might give to her in common with men the means of subsistence and independence. To the question, "Are you a Federalist?" she replied, "What have I as a woman to do with politics? Even the government of your country, which is said to be the freest in the world, passes over women as if they were not. We are excluded from all political rights without the least ceremony. Law-makers thought as little of comprehending us in their code of liberty as if we were pigs or sheep." In his *Clara Howard*, which appeared in 1801, he anticipates twentieth-century feminism by portraying the independent thinking and acting woman.

[1] V. L. Parrington, *The Romantic Revolution in America, 1800–1860*, p. 189.

Of Brown's other works, *Arthur Mervyn* best displays perhaps his conception of what America should be. Throughout,
Brown's   the hero, a Godwinian figure, emphasizes the ideal
other works of justice and, by implication if not directly, criti-
cises all that is mean and sordid. In his *Wieland: or The
Transformation*, produced in 1798, Brown strongly advocated
rationalism as a sure cure for all the ills growing out of superstition and credulity. In addition to fiction Brown published
several brief memorial sketches and many political pamphlets
setting forth his social ideals. He was also a magazine editor
of some repute. His books, highly commended in the English
reviews, found many overseas readers, including Scott, Godwin,
and Shelley. Unfortunately his elaborate geographical and
historical works, on which he was laboring at the time of his
death, were never published. While his works are today seldom
read, Brown's place in the annals of American literary development is secure. Historically the forerunner of James Fenimore
Cooper and Nathaniel Hawthorne, his career in all probability
greatly interested young Washington Irving who, like Brown,
was fascinated by literature rather than by the law. Irving,
born in 1783, had already embarked on his literary ventures
before Brown's death, his *Salmagundi* papers, humorously
picturing the social life of New York at the turn of the century,
appearing serially in 1807-08, and his famous *History of New
York* being published in 1809. But Irving as a literary figure
really belongs to that great company of American fictionists
of the so-called middle period, and we shall, therefore, meet
him again in a subsequent chapter.

While verse in the young republic was largely imitative of
English poetry in style, its motivating factors did not differ
Character of   from those which prompted early American drama
poetry of early and fiction. Nationalism with its attendant pa-
republic   triotism and the bitter and absorbing struggle between Federalist and Democrat furnished poets and would-be
poetasters with ample material for their couplets. Judged by
present-day standards much that was written at the time as
poetry would now hardly pass muster; historically, however,
it is of prime importance, for it eloquently reveals the hopes

and fears, the ambitions and animosities of those in whose hands the destinies of the new-born nation rested.

The struggle for independence itself gave rise to hundreds of patriotic ballads, songs, and odes. Indeed, practically every poet between 1775 and 1810 composed at least one patriotic composition in which some phase of the Revolution was featured. *Patriot's Appeal, Liberty's Call, Columbia's Glory, or British Pride Humbled*, and *McFingal* — the last mentioned by John Trumbull, classmate of Timothy Dwight at Yale — are typical. *McFingal*, a thirty-eight-hundred-line political satire, is a glorification of the patriot cause: **Revolution inspired verse-making**

> Forthwith the crowd proceed to deck
> With halter'd noose M'Fingal's neck, . . .
> Then lifting high th' pond'rous jar,
> Pour'd o'er his head the smoking tar . . .
> And spreads him o'er with feathers missive,
> And down upon the tar adhesive; . . .
> Then on the two-wheel'd car of state,
> They raised our grand Duumvirate . . .
> And hail'd great Liberty in chorus,
> Or bawl'd, Confusion to the Tories.

In Joseph Stansbury, a Philadelphia merchant, and Jonathan Odell, a New Jersey preacher, the Tories had two able champions who in song and ode stoutly defended the Loyalists. "Rats," "dirty reptiles," "poltroons," "maggots and lice," are but a few of the choice terms used in characterizing the Patriots. Stansbury's *Town Meeting* especially deserves passing mention, although he was perhaps not as virulent and relentless a satirist as Odell.

In the struggle for control following the Revolution both Federalists and Democrats had their coterie of poetic spokesmen. Standing head and shoulders above all others in the ranks of Federalism were the Hartford Wits to whom allusion was made in the previous chapter. **The Hartford Wits** Provincial in outlook and representative of the New England oligarchical upper class, this group, which included John Trumbull, Timothy Dwight, Joel Barlow, Lemuel Hopkins, David

Humphreys, Richard Alsop, and Theodore Dwight, hated every form of equalitarianism.

They were, [to quote Parrington,] the literary old guard of the expiring eighteenth century, suspicious of all innovation, contemptuous of every idealistic program. They stood stoutly by the customary and familiar. The nineteenth century was knocking at their door, but they would not open to it. And as they saw that new century coming in the guise of revolution, exciting to unheard of innovations in the fields of politics and economics, and religion and letters, giving rise to Jacobin Clubs and Jeffersonian democracy, they set themselves seriously to the work of barring its progress through their own little world. They conveniently associated the economic unrest of postwar days, that gave birth to a strange progeny in Rhode Island and New Hampshire and Massachusetts, with the contamination of French atheism, charged all unrest to the account of democracy, and hastened to put it down in the name of law and righteousness. They hated new ways with the virtuous hatred of the well-to-do, and dreamed of a future America as like the past as one generation of oysters is like another.[1]

Of the three major works produced in collaboration by the Wits — *The Anarchiad, The Echo,* and *The Political Greenhouse* — the first which we have already cited [2] is undoubtedly most outstanding.

More virulent than the Hartford Wits in his denunciation of democracy was Thomas Green Fessenden (1771–1837). In *Democracy Unveiled, or Tyranny Stripped of the Garb of Patriotism,* he roundly — even indecently — abused Jacobinism, democracy, and Jefferson in particular. Almost equally abusive of the newer tendencies was the indefatigable Timothy Dwight, who in his *Triumph of Infidelity* ironically attempted to refute the arguments of the eighteenth-century "infidels," including Voltaire. Other lesser self-appointed custodians of Federalism gave free rein to anti-Jeffersonian passions, but they are insignificant in comparison with Fessenden and the Hartford Wits.

Anti-Jeffersonian poetasters

---

[1] V. L. Parrington, *The Colonial Mind, 1620–1800,* p. 358. Every person interested in understanding the history of American civilization should read the Parrington volumes.

[2] See Chapter VI, p. 00.

Of the Jeffersonian poets, Philip Freneau (1752–1832) was without peer. Born in New York of Huguenot ancestry, graduated from Princeton in 1771, and serving the Philip Patriot cause with great distinction, Freneau early Freneau became a leading exponent of Jeffersonian republicanism. Endowed with romantic imagination and love of natural beauty, he might, in all probability, had he chosen to stand apart from the social and political turmoil of his day, have made himself the indisputable founder of American poetry. But he was too wrapped up in the cause of freedom and liberalism to do this. His poems, aggregating twelve hundred pages, cover many themes. In nearly all of them one finds, as in his prose writings, the strain of democracy and opposition to tyranny in any form. An equalitarian, he, like other Jeffersonians, wanted the new republic to be and to remain a land of justice, free from tyrannous cankers. In his opinion an ambitious and moneyed domestic aristocracy was as dangerous as George III and his Tory supporters. Against the aristocratic-propertied class — the Hamiltonians — he therefore waged grim, unsparing, and deadly warfare. No word or phrase was too stinging or too scurrilous for his onslaughts against the enemies of his ideals. Indeed, we can readily understand why he was referred to by Washington as "that rascal Freneau," by Irving as "a barking cur," and by Timothy Dwight as "a mere incendiary, or rather . . . a despicable tool of bigger incendiaries [Jefferson in particular], and his paper [*National Gazette*] . . . a public nuisance."

Critics agree that Freneau's best lyrics were written between 1775 and 1790. These include *Libera Nos Domine*, *The British Prison Ship*, *The Political Balance*, *The House of* Freneau's *Night*, *The Indian Burying-Ground*, *The Wild* poetry *Honeysuckle*, *Eutaw Springs*, and *The Beauties of Santa Cruz*. So fine were some of these that even Sir Walter Scott deigned to borrow from their lines. But Freneau's lesser poems and odes, where he dipped his pen deep into the gall of partisan politics, were the ones that roused the immeasurable ire of the Federalists. Among them were *To all the Great Folks in a Lump; To Atlas*, an attack on Hamilton; *To a Select Body of*

Great Men, a lampoon on the United States Senate; *To a Would-Be Great Man*, directed at John Adams; and *On False Systems of Government*. That Freneau was more than a mere partisan and not without sweetness of heart is evident from the following lines from *The Brook in the Valley*, one of his best poems:

> The world has wrangled half an age,
> And we again in war engage,
> While this sweet sequestr'd rill
> Murmurs through the valley still . . .
>
> But, with all your quiet flow,
> Do you not some quarrels know!
> Lately, angry, how you ran!
> All at war — and much like man.
>
> How you settled with the rock!
> Gave my willows such a shock
> As to menace, by its fall,
> Underwood and bushes, all:
>
> Now you are again at peace:
> Time will come when you will cease;
> Such the human passions are;
> — You again will war declare.
>
> Emblem, thou, of restless man;
> What a stretch of nature's plan!
> Now at peace, and now at war,
> Now you murmur, now you roar;
>
> Muddy now, and limpid next,
> Now with icy shackles vext —
> What a likeness here we find!
> What a picture of mankind!

Of the other Jeffersonian verse-makers Joel Barlow deserves to rank next to Freneau. Born a Connecticut Yankee, brought up **Joel Barlow** in accordance with the best New Enland conventions, ambitious for fame and fortune, he was in the course of his lifetime lawyer, politician, journalist, poet, preacher, and speculator. Parting company with the Hartford Wits in 1788 when he went to France as agent for the notorious Scioto Land Company, Barlow soon became a strong partisan of democracy. In 1793 he was made a citizen of France and during the succeeding years made his fortune by speculating in French funds. In 1805 he returned to America and established a delightful country home on the outskirts of Washington which became a mecca for liberals. Characterized by John Adams as a worthless person of the Tom Paine type, he was in reality a warm-hearted humanitarian with a passion for improving the lot of mankind by means of education.

In 1787 he published a philosophic poem, *The Vision of Columbus*. Twenty years later this was reworked, enlarged, and republished as *The Columbiad*. From a lit- *The* erary point of view the result was an unhappy one, *Columbiad* the product being merely a "geographical, historical, political, and philosophical disquisition." Barlow's purpose in transforming *The Vision of Columbus* is set forth in the preface:

[The] real object of the poem is to inculcate the love of national liberty, and to discountenance the deleterious passion for violence and war; to show that on the basis of republican principle all good morals, as well as good government and hopes of permanent peace, must be founded; and to convince the student in political science, that the theoretical question of the future advancement of human society, till states as well as individuals arrive at universal civilization, is held in dispute and still unsettled only because we have had too little experience of organized liberty in the government of nations, to have well considered its effects.

Throughout the poem Barlow's sensitive social conscience is apparent; especially is this so in those stanzas where he denounces war, slavery, monarchy, and what to him appear to be a host of other social and political evils. In the concluding lines he visions a golden age of international good will when all nations shall draw together and

> . . . cloth'd majestic in the robes of state,
> Moved by one voice, in general congress meet
> The legates of all empires.

Like Barlow, William Cullen Bryant, a New Englander by birth and training, also shifted to the side of democracy. Apparently encouraged by his father, a physician of violent Federalist tendencies, Bryant in 1808, when only fourteen, made a scurrilous attack on Jefferson in *The Embargo*. About the same time he took Napoleon to task in a series of heroic couplets for conduct contrary to the standards of New England respectability. Yet in spite of these early writings which seemed to indicate that he would in all probability follow along well-trodden paths of Federalism, Bryant, in face of great environmental obstacles, became, as we shall see, an outstanding liberal. Indeed, his *Thanatopsis*, written in 1811, contained more than slight evidence that he was already veering away from ultra-conservative influences.

William Cullen Bryant joins ranks of democracy

Newspapers, magazines, tracts, and pamphlets no less than "polite" literature mirrored the changing scene at the turn of the century. Scarcely a town of any size existed in any part of the country that did not have its printing press and its newspaper. By 1810 the list of American newspapers had increased from forty at the close of the Revolution to over three hundred and fifty. Magazines also multiplied from five in 1794 to twelve in 1800, and to about forty in 1810; by 1825 the number had reached almost a hundred. Essays, generally dealing with English fashions, manners, morals and, above all, politics, abounded; nearly a hundred appeared in New England alone between 1785 and 1800.

Journalism mirrors changing scene

The newspapers varied greatly in character and in circulation. The majority were weeklies, but some came out semiweekly and a few triweekly. The first daily, *The Pennsylvania Packet and Daily Advertiser*, began its career in Philadelphia in 1784, and a number of other dailies soon made their appearance; by 1809 almost thirty were published. Few had any considerable circulation outside of their immediate locality. Not one would be rated today as an exclusively religious, scientific, or trade newspaper. Nor was there in the modern sense an illustrated sheet among them. By far the

Newspapers

larger number were party organs, mere bulletins or mouth-pieces, as it were, for the two great social-economic groups who fought so desperately for political supremacy.[1] Systematic, coöperative news gathering machinery did not exist, editors depending in large measure upon their own pens, contributed articles, and material copied from other papers. Statutes, the proceedings of Congress and state legislatures, including important speeches, poetry, advertisements, letters, notices of auctions, long political communications — usually able and often profound — over assumed names such as "Cato," "Junius," or "Camillus" — and, in the port towns, entrances and clearances of vessels, made up the content of most of the papers. Though the majority were principally vehicles of political opinion some were primarily advertising mediums and agencies

[1] Isaiah Thomas in his *History of Printing in America* (vol. ii, pp. 517–522), published in 1810, listed three hundred and fifty newspapers according to their party affiliations. The list follows:

State	Federalist	Republican	Neutral or Unknown	Total
New Hampshire......	8	2	2	12
Massachusetts.......	20	11	1	32
Rhode Island........	4	3	0	7
Connecticut.........	9	1	1	11
Vermont............	8	6	0	14
New York...........	29	28	9	66
New Jersey..........	3	5	0	8
Pennsylvania........	34	29	8	71*
Delaware............	0	2	0	2
Maryland...........	9	11	1	21
District of Columbia..	2	3	1	6
Virginia.............	7	15	1	23
North Carolina.......	5	3	2	10
South Carolina.......	4	4	2	10
Georgia.............	3	7	3	13
Kentucky...........	2	14	1	17
Tennessee..........	1	5	0	6
Ohio...............	3	8	3	14
Louisiana..........	0	0	1	1
Indiana Territory....	0	0	1	1
Mississippi Territory..	1	1	2	4
Orleans Territory.....	5	1	4	10

* Eight of which were printed in German.

for the dissemination of commercial information. Crime was scarcely mentioned, and little attempt was made to print news that would appeal to the poor and uneducated. Moreover, papers were expensive, the dailies costing eight dollars per year and the weeklies from three to five, which meant that the poor could not afford to buy them.

Though paying little attention to news, *The Evening Post* of New York, established by Alexander Hamilton and a group *The Evening* of Federalist associates in 1801, was representative *Post* repre- of the best of the early nineteenth-century news- sentative of papers. Under the editorship of the keen-minded, best news- papers energetic, and courageous William Coleman it soon became the most outstanding of the Federalist papers. Nicknamed the "Field Marshal of the Federal Editors" Coleman, who always wielded a ready pen, stood squarely behind the Hamiltonian program and from him other Federalist sheets took their cue. "The people of America derive their political information chiefly from newspapers," wrote J. T. Callender, one of the leading Democratic editors, in 1802, "Duane upon one side and Coleman upon the other, dictate at this moment the sentiments of perhaps fifty thousand American citizens." William Duane, Philip Freneau, and B. F. Bache, Franklin's grandson, were with Callender the outstanding luminaries among the Democratic editors. The picturesque William Cobbett *alias* Peter Porcupine, founder of *Porcupine's Gazette and United States Advertiser*, while perhaps more able in warring on the Democrats than Coleman, lacked the latter's poise and breadth of vision. That Cobbett's vitriolic pen was particularly effective is evident from the following addressed to him by Mathew Carey, Philadelphia liberal:

Wretch as you are, accursed by God and hated by men, the most tremendous scourge that hell ever vomited forth to curse a people by sowing discord among them, I desire not the honor or credit of being villified by you. . . . To send a challenge to a blasted, posted, loathsome coward . . . would sink me almost to a level with yourself.

The magazines, though less numerous than the newspapers, were nevertheless influential agencies in shaping public opinion.

In character they differed greatly; some were weeklies while others were monthlies; many were devoted to some particular subject, such as religion, for example. The majority, too, were very nationalistic, being extremely sensitive to criticism of the young republic or its institutions.[1] Only a few had an able and dependable staff of contributors, and fortunate indeed was the editor who could count on regular contributions from his friends or from some literary club of which he might be a member. Payment for articles was unknown in America prior to 1819. In that year the *Christian Spectator*, a new magazine, proposed to compensate its contributors at the rate of one dollar per page. At first many contributors refused to accept any payment because of "the principle of the thing." Most of the earlier editors also received no monetary reward. Some of the magazines ran illustrations, notably those published in Philadelphia, where lived David Edwin and James Barton Longacre, the two ablest engravers of the first quarter of the nineteenth century. Magazine advertising was as yet negligible. Finally, we should note that many of the magazines were shortlived and that all had a limited circulation; in fact, a circulation of two thousand copies a year was phenomenal.

Magazines and their character

Undoubtedly the most important magazine in the first two decades of the new century was the Philadelphia *Port Folio*, established in 1801 by Joseph Dennie, Harvard graduate and staunch admirer of English literature, politics, and culture. Personally magnetic and a writer of ability, Dennie attracted such talent as Joseph Hopkinson, Richard Rush, John Quincy Adams, Charles Brockden Brown,

The Port Folio

[1] Both editors and contributors were especially resentful of English criticism. In fact, F. L. Mott in his *History of American Magazines, 1741–1850*, pp. 188–190, goes so far as to refer to the American magazine refutation of English criticism of the United States as "The Paper War." Typical of one of the battles of this "Paper War" was the assertion of an American magazine contributor that the English travelers were "unblushing miscreants — those slanderers by profession, Weld and Volney, Ash and Bülow, Jansen and Moore, with a tribe of others, their associates in infamy, whose very names are offensive to the ear of virtue — wretches whom the troubles of Europe, a state of houseless poverty, restless disposition, the wages of turpitude, or their other crimes and apprehensions of a gibbet, sent forth into our country to repay with defamation the courtesies they experienced, and scatter their poison on the hand that fed them."

and Gouverneur Morris. Strongly Federalist and reactionary, and founded in part "to combat revolutionary doctrines" and to be a torch in "this dark night of Jacobinism," it ran departments of "Literary Intelligence," "Law Intelligence," drama, politics, poetry, music, art, fashion, and occasionally foreign and domestic occurrences and translations of foreign essays. Until the end of Jefferson's second administration, however, politics overshadowed all else, and during these years even the clever editor of *Port Folio* could not find words adequate to express his hatred of democracy. That his hatred was deep-seated is clear from this paragraph which appeared in 1803:

A democracy is scarcely tolerable at any period of national history. Its omens are always sinister, and its powers are unpropitious. With all the lights of experience blazing before our eyes, it is impossible not to discern the futility of this form of government. It was weak and wicked in Athens. It was bad in Sparta, and worse in Rome. It has been tried in France, and has terminated in despotism. It was tried in England, and rejected with the utmost loathing and abhorrence. It is on trial here, and the issue will be civil war, desolation and anarchy. No wise man but discerns its imperfections, no good man but shudders at its miseries, no honest man but proclaims its fraud, and no brave man but draws his sword against its force. The institution of a scheme of polity so radically contemptible and vicious is a memorable example of what the villany of some men can devise, the folly of others receive, and both establish, in despite of reason, reflection and sensation.

This outburst earned for Dennie the title of "Traitor." After 1812 politics were "rigidly" excluded from the *Port Folio*, and more attention was given to literary criticism.

Four other magazines antedating the *Port Folio* gained distinction. These were the *Columbian*, established in Philadelphia in 1786 by a quintuple partnership including Mathew Carey, the *American Museum*, founded by Carey in the same city the following year, the *Massachusetts Magazine or Monthly Museum of Knowledge and Rational Entertainment* started by Isaiah Thomas in 1789, and the *New York Magazine or Literary Repository* begun in 1790 by Thomas and James Swords. Varied in content, all four endeavored to attract as wide an audience as possible. The *Massa-*

Other important magazines

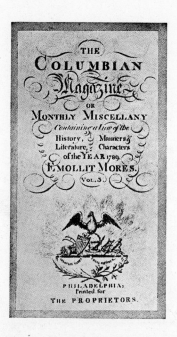

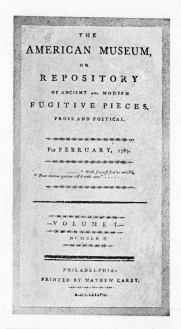

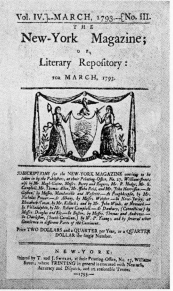

THE FOUR MOST IMPORTANT PRE–REVOLUTIONARY
MAGAZINES

chusetts Magazine, for example, offered its readers "Poetry,
Musick, Biography, History, Physick, Geography, Morality,
Criticism, Philosophy, Mathematicks, Agriculture, Architecture, Chemistry, Novels, Tales, News, Marriages, Deaths,
Meteorological Observations, Etc." The "Etc." covered plays,
essays, proceedings of Congress, and engravings. Of the magazines founded after the *Port Folio* but in the beginning contemporary with it, the *North American Review,* the first number
of which appeared in 1815, was by all odds the most important.
Under the editorship of a coterie of scholarly Bostonians it soon
gained international repute.

6. THE ARTS

The conventional arts — painting, architecture, sculpture,
and music — were, at the turn of the century, still struggling in
an uncongenial environment. Little traveled and Arts handi-
concerned primarily with gaining a livelihood — capped by
with clearing lands, raising crops, building ships, environment
wooing commerce, catching fish, and a dozen other tasks — the
overwhelming majority had little time or inclination for the
finer arts. Unlike the Old World, America in 1800 had no art
tradition of its own aside from that of the Indians, which the
white man ignored. Indeed, what little tradition there was up
to the close of the Revolution was derived almost entirely from
England. Cheap amusements, rather than art treasures, satisfied the rank and file; for them the world of beauty, as expressed
in the arts, was a closed book. Merchant princes and well-to-do
planters, who composed the backbone of American aristocracy,
though patronizing native talent to some extent, were prone to
favor foreign artists and to decorate their homes with foreign
art. With the federal and state governments too immersed in
advancing the material development of the country to be much
interested in promoting art, the artist, unless possessing sufficient means of his own, was often obliged to turn his hand to
other things in order to eke out an existence. Thus the painter
Peale, for example, stuffed birds, practised dentistry, ran a
museum, and mended harnesses and clocks in order to keep
himself alive. Moreover, many of the clergy and laity too con-

tinued to regard the fine arts as inventions of the devil which, like other sinful temptations, ought to be avoided and resisted. In the light of such conditions we can readily appreciate why the artist, no less than the creator of imaginative literature, labored at great disadvantage.

But the fact that the vast majority of the people were too engrossed in material activities to give much heed to canvas or marble, and that an artistic atmosphere was almost entirely wanting, should not lead us to conclude that the arts had no place in the early republic.

Art in the early republic

On the contrary, the foundations of American art were, in a very true sense, laid during these eventful years of tense emotional stress and strain. If painter, architect, sculptor, and musician were perhaps unable to portray the sentiments, ambitions, interests, passions, and conflicts of the period as advantageously as did poet, dramatist, or pamphleteer, it was only because of the media through which they worked and expressed themselves. "The sentiments behind their work and the influences of their environment," to quote from the Beards, "are almost identical. No doubt, the emotions expressed by Barlow's *Columbiad* and by Trumbull's portrayal of Bunker Hill were keyed to the same vibration."

The truth of this statement is at once evident when we turn to the painters. Of the four leading pre-Revolutionary painters — Benjamin West, John Singleton Copley, Charles Wilson Peale, and Gilbert Stuart — Peale alone was an exemplar of republicanism. West (1738–1820), born near Philadelphia of Quaker parents, left America at the age of twenty-two to study abroad.

Noted painters of aristocratic leanings: West, Copley, Stuart

Here he chose to remain, settling in London, where he scored great success as a painter of mythological and historical figures. From 1792 to his death he served as president of the Royal Academy. While he generously befriended American students who found their way to London, his interests were English and aristocratic. Likewise Copley (1737–1815), aristocratic Bostonian and portrait painter of many colonial New England notables and by sympathy a Loyalist, left the New World just before the outbreak of the Revolution. In England, where he spent the rest of his life, he gained an enviable reputation for his historical pictures. His son, Lord Lyndhurst, was three times Lord Chancellor of England. Stuart (1755–1828), a Rhode Islander by birth, also shared the aristocratic leanings of West and Copley. Son of a Tory family, he left for London soon after the first shots at Lexington. A pupil of West, he became famous in fashionable circles as a portrait maker, numbering among his works the portraits of George III and the Prince of Wales. Anxious to make a portrait of Washington, for whom he had great admiration, Stuart, bearing a letter of introduction from John Jay, returned to America in 1792. Between this date and his death he gave to posterity canvas impressions of many great Americans, among them Washington, General Knox, John Adams, Jefferson, Madison, and John Jacob Astor. Easily one of the greatest artists in a remarkable age of portraiture, Stuart had, however, no zeal for republican ideals. By background, training, and experience he was an aristocrat, a fact which his pictures unmistakably betray.

Peale (1741–1827), on the other hand, stands in sharp contrast to his three contemporaries above mentioned. A native of Maryland, he studied under Copley in Boston and later with West in London. Joining the patriot army at the outbreak of the Revolution, he served with distinction during the war and took a lively interest in the struggles which followed. Less versatile than either Copley or Stuart, and lacking their ability to portray elegance of suggestion, his portraits impress because of their simplicity and sincerity. His fourteen intimate portraits of Washington, to say nothing of his portraits of many other famous men, are extremely valuable to both artist and historian. Of all the painters of the period none was so representative of republican tendencies as Peale.

Charles Wilson Peale, republican artist

In addition to his contributions as a painter, Peale was intensely concerned with promoting interest in art and science among his countrymen. In 1784 he founded a Museum of Natural History in Philadelphia, the first of its kind in America. He also arranged for the first exhibition of paintings in the New World and en-

Peale's interest in promoting art

deavored to establish a school of fine arts. Furthermore, he was one of the leading founders of the Pennsylvania Academy of Fine Arts in 1805, and of the Society of Artists of the United States in 1810. An association for promoting the fine arts started in New York in 1801 languished for several years, but was revived in 1816 as the American Academy of Fine Arts, an organization to which Peale was no stranger. The shortlived New York Academy of Fine Arts, incorporated in 1808 under the auspices of John Trumbull, was superseded in 1826 by the National Academy of Design, the first American art society under professional control.

In establishing the Pennsylvania Academy its founders, apparently unbaffled by environmental obstacles and hopeful of the future, quaintly declared that they proposed "to promote the cultivation of the Fine Arts in the United States of America by introducing correct and elegant copies from works of the first masters in sculpture and painting, and by thus facilitating the access to such standards, and also by conferring moderate but honorable premiums, and otherwise assisting studies and exciting the efforts of artists, gradually to unfold, enlighten, and invigorate the talents of our countrymen." Although the new institution encountered many hardships, even in cultured Philadelphia, it managed to survive and to fulfill ultimately, in rich measure, the fondest aspirations of its founders.

The Pennsylvania Academy of Fine Arts

Contemporary with Peale and sharing his affection for republicanism was the painter John Trumbull (1756–1843), son of a colonial governor of Connecticut and a graduate of Harvard. An officer in the Revolutionary Army, he resigned his commission in the midst of the war because of a grievance and went to London where he became a student under West. Quickly winning repute as an historical and portrait painter, he returned to America in 1789, where he started on his long career of picturing on canvas some of the outstanding figures and events in the history of the young republic. "I am fully sensible," he wrote, "that the profession [of painting], as it is generally practiced, is frivolous, little useful to society, and unworthy of a man who has talents for more serious pursuits.

John Trumbull

But to preserve and diffuse the memory of the noblest series of actions which have ever presented themselves in the history of man, is sufficient warrant for it." Trumbull's brilliant pictures of the Revolutionary drama together with his extraordinary gallery of small portraits in oil are extremely valuable historically and constitute his chief claim to fame.

Two other painters of the early republic deserve mention. The first, Washington Allston (1779–1843), a South Carolinian by birth, an idealist, dreamer, and romanticist, studied both in London and Rome. Unlike Peale and Trumbull, the themes for his work were not American but classical and, therefore, reminiscent of the Italian "grand style." The other, John Vanderlyn (1776–1852), native of Kingston, New York, and the first American to matriculate in the Academy of Painting in Paris, was, perhaps, more than any other American of his day, responsible for introducing French influence into American painting.[1] Up to this time American painting had been English both in tradition and taste. Vanderlyn's *Ariadne*, a nude, first exhibited in Paris in 1812, while shocking conventionally-minded Americans, won for him international distinction.

Washington Allston and John Vanderlyn

Nationalism, the existence of opposing social-economic-political groups, as well as Old World influence, were reflected in striking degree in the architecture of the early republic. When building was resumed, after it had been almost completely suspended during the Revolution, a few architectural craftsmen continued work along the old colonial and Georgian lines. The leaders, however, inspired by the same patriotic ideals that motivated poet, painter and dramatist, and feeling that the colonial style, whatever its merits, was provincial and lacking in dignity, sought an architecture worthy of the new sovereign nation. While the introduction of the ornate renaissance Gothic, fostered by king and established church on the other side of the Atlantic, would undoubtedly have been pleasing to some members of New World aristocracy, to the majority it

Architecture of young republic classical

---

[1] For French influence on American art, see Howard Mumford Jones, *America and French Culture, 1750–1848*, chap. ix.

appeared wholly unfitted for a country frontier in character and dedicated in theory at least to republican and humanitarian ideals. Passing over, therefore, the architectural styles then popular in Europe, the young nation turned to the glories of republican Greece and Rome with which it believed it had much in common. The change which took place is well expressed by Lewis Mumford:

> The contrast between the classical and the vernacular, between the architecture of the plantation and the architecture of the village, between the work of the craftsman and the work of the gentleman, became even more marked after the Revolutionary War. As a result of that re-crystallization of American society, the conditions of classical culture and classical civilization were for a short time fused in the activities of the community, even in the town. One may express the transformation in a crude way by saying that the carpenter-architects of the early republic worked upon a classical foundation. It was the Revolution itself, I believe, that twined the classical taste into a myth which had the power to move men and mold their actions.[1]

The leader in this classic movement was none other than Thomas Jefferson. Architect and master builder, he was the

Influence of Thomas Jefferson designer of several structures of which the capitol of Virginia, Monticello (Italian for "little mountain"), his own home, a number of houses for the neighboring gentry — Shadwell, Edgehill, Farrington — and the University of Virginia are the most famous. Indeed, many critics are of the opinion that the University of Virginia, with its long colonnades connecting classical pavilions of varied design which lead up to the central rotunda or library based on the Roman Pantheon, constitutes the finest example of classical architecture in America. Simplicity and beauty, coupled with practicality, were the ideals for which he strove.

> Nowhere else, [writes Fiske Kimball in speaking of Jefferson's architectural drawings,] can the mental processes of an early American architect and the inner development of his designs be followed so closely. . . . In the pervasive classical revival common to Europe

---

[1] Lewis Mumford, *Sticks and Stones: A Study of American Architecture and Civilization*, pp. 56–57.

and America, of which Jefferson's work forms a part, it will be found that his position was not always derivative and secondary, in comparison with European standards, but that in certain respects he anticipated corresponding buildings in other countries, and in some other directions gave to American architecture an original direction.[1]

The classical style thus introduced by Jefferson gained quick popularity, private mansions and public buildings designed along classical lines being built in all parts of the country, particularly in the South. The George Washington Parke Custis home at Arlington, Virginia, and Andalusia, the country seat of Nicholas Biddle on the Delaware, with their great porticos supported by columns covering the entire façade and extending above the second story, are typical of the private dwellings modeled after those of the ancients. Of the public buildings of the period employing classical architectural lines, the White House at Washington, the capitol at Columbia, South Carolina, both designed by James Hoban, the Philadelphia Library by William Thornton, the Bank of the United States (Girard's Bank) by Samuel Blodget, the Bank of Pennsylvania by Henry Latrobe, and the Washington Monument in Baltimore by Robert Mills, a pupil of Latrobe, are outstanding examples. The church edifices erected during the early years of the republic were not very different from those built before the Revolution. Latrobe's Catholic cathedral in Baltimore — the first cathedral in the United States — was completed in 1821.

Examples of classical influence

In town and city planning Jefferson was also a pioneer. With the exception of Philadelphia and possibly Savannah, Georgia, there was little or no city planning in the modern sense of the term during the colonial period. Towns that were not modeled after those of the Old World developed haphazardly. In 1780 the Frenchman Choteau drew up a very simple plan for St. Louis. But it was not until 1791, with the plan for the city of Washington, designed by Jefferson's friend L'Enfant, French engineer and architect, that city planning may be said to have really made a definite beginning in America.

Town and city planning

[1] Fiske Kimball, *Thomas Jefferson, Architect.*

The early republic had no sculpture of its own. The daily battle for existence, the clerical distrust of sensuous beauty, the backward state of our culture generally, and, above all, the absence of a sculptural heritage, account in no small degree for this fact. Like the English, the Americans simply did not express themselves in plastic or marble forms. William Rush (1756–1833) of Philadelphia, who acquired proficiency in carving wooden figureheads for ships, may perhaps be called our pioneer sculptor, but he stands quite alone, for there was almost no demand for sculpture. Indeed, the artist Trumbull scornfully declared in 1820 that "nothing in sculpture would be wanted in this country for yet a hundred years," and John Adams was wont to boast that he "would not give a sixpence for a bust of Phidias or a painting by Raphael." Not until the third decade of the nineteenth century did American sculpture definitely make its appearance. Meanwhile those Americans interested in the art had to depend on Houdon and other foreign artists. The heroic statue of Washington erected in Richmond, Virginia, during this period was, for example, a Houdon creation. A few of the more cultured well-to-do Southerners possessed beautiful importations of Old World marble reliefs.

Early republic without sculpture of its own

Turning to American music we find that it too was, in its beginnings at least, largely overseas in origin. Indeed, with the exception of psalms and hymns little native music was produced in the English mainland colonies prior to the War of Independence. All other forms of music, including even folk songs, were Old World importations. Colonial New York, Philadelphia, Baltimore, Annapolis, and Charleston enjoyed more or less regular operatic seasons on the eve of the Revolution, but the repertoire consisted mostly of English ballad-operas. The musical material for the colonial song recitals, concerts, and college commencements was likewise English with occasionally a bit of French, German, or Italian flavor. Moreover, those well-to-do colonial families who possessed a German flute, a guitar, or harpsichord — the fashionable instrument of the period — or a pianoforte, violin, or bass-viol were merely imi-

American music foreign in origin

tating their aristocratic brethren on the other side of the Atlantic.

While the Revolution may in some respects have checked progress in American musical art, that struggle and the stirring events of the three decades following its close furnished inspiration to the first important American composers of secular music. These were William Billings (1746–1800) and Francis Hopkinson (1737–1791). The former, a Boston tanner by trade, was a self-taught musician who, although without technical ability, had genius for spirited and animated compositions. An ardent patriot, his songs, of which the following is a sample, undoubtedly contributed to the success of the revolutionary cause: *Early American musical composers*

> Let tyrants shake their iron rod
> And slavery clank her galling chains,
> We'll fear them not; we trust in God,
> New England's God forever reigns.

Billings also wrote psalm music and taught singing. He was one of the leaders in encouraging the formation of the Stoughton Musical Society, one of the earliest musical organizations of importance in Massachusetts. Hopkinson is chiefly remembered for his song "My Days Have Been So Wondrous Free," but his opera *The Temple of Minerva* of 1781, glorifying the alliance between France and the new-born republic, indicates that he too was stirred by patriotic emotions.

Although both Billings and Hopkinson rate as America's pioneer composers, neither of them contributed in considerable degree to our better-known patriotic songs. The earliest patriotic song in America — the "Liberty Song" — was the composition of Mrs. Mercy Warren, to whom reference has already been made in this chapter. This appeared in 1768 during the days of excitement preceding the break with England. The tune of "Yankee Doodle," whose origin is veiled in mystery, antedated the Revolution by many years. A set of appropriate patriotic verses for the melody was published in 1779. "Hail Columbia," one of our principal national songs, was written in 1798 by Joseph Hopkinson, son of Francis *Patriotic songs*

Hopkinson, as a glorification of Federalism. "The song," said the Democratic *Aurora*, "is the most ridiculous bombast and the vilest adulation to the Anglo-monarchical party." It was only after a lapse of years and considerable revision that it became a national anthem. The music for "The Star Spangled Banner," the words of which were penned by Francis Scott Key during the War of 1812, was, like the majority of our early patriotic melodies, borrowed. "America," or "My Country, 'Tis of Thee," composed by Reverend Doctor Samuel F. Smith, an Andover, Massachusetts, theological student, was not written until 1832.

At the turn of the century oratorios and concerts, both vocal and instrumental, were becoming more numerous. In the Concerts increase in number larger towns those who were interested and financially able to do so could listen to Haydn, Pleyel, Davaux, Corelli, Stamitz, Handel, and other composers of note. In 1815 the more cultured people of Boston at a great music festival in honor of the anniversary of Washington's birthday established the Handel and Haydn Society, one of the most remarkable organizations of its kind ever founded in America. Henceforth Boston became known as one of the great musical centers of the new republic. The turn of the century also saw the beginning of musical instrument manufacture in America. Jonas Chickering, one of the pioneer manufacturers of pianos on this side of the Atlantic, came to Boston in 1798, where he first found employment as an apprentice to a cabinet maker.

Paralleling the fine arts in development and, like them, borrowing much in the way of technique and inspiration from the The graphic arts: etching Old World, were the graphic arts, etching and engraving. The story of etching in the young republic is little more than a record of attempts by amateurs to achieve success. Instructions, mostly English in origin, for such would-be artists began to appear before the close of the eighteenth century. In 1794, for example, a Philadelphia firm published an edition of an English work entitled *The Artist's Assistant in Drawing, Perspective, Etching, Engraving, Mezzotinto-scraping*, &c. Apparently little effort was made to use etching as a reproductive art in America until near the close of the first quarter of the nineteenth century. Up to that time etching was mostly applied to portraiture or was used as an aid to engraving.

The need for paper money, maps, bookplates, business cards, billheads, and certificates of various kinds, together with the desire of the well-to-do to have their ornaments and family plate marked, served during the colo- *Engraving* nial period to encourage the art of engraving. With the advent of the Revolution the engraver no less than the poet or painter expressed his sentiments in his work. The *Boston Massacre*, a hand-colored engraving by the patriot and silversmith Paul Revere, and the *Surrender of Cornwallis at Yorktown*, by J. F. Renault, are typical. The spirit of patriotism and nationalism to which the Revolution gave rise found expression at the turn of the century in a number of portrait engravings of prominent Americans, particularly Washington, Franklin, Jefferson, and Lafayette. James Barton Longacre's contributions to *Delaplaine's Repository of the Lives and Portraits of Distinguished American Characters* are in this connection the most important. The struggle between the Federalists and the anti-Federalists with its use of caricature, the increased demand for book and magazine illustrations, the desire that the leading events of the War of 1812 be pictured, and the growing need for well executed banknotes and other business forms helped greatly to stimulate the engraver's art.

In concluding this section brief mention should be made of the industrial arts. By 1800 certain American products, notably glassware, silverware, pewter, brassware, furniture, *The industrial* needlework, and pottery, showed unmistakable *arts* evidence that their makers were beginning to find pleasure in self-expression and were striving to turn out articles that were beautiful as well as useful. Steigel glass, famed for its rich coloring, and named for Henry William Steigel, the most noted of our early glass manufacturers, was for many years the best glass produced in America. Paul Revere, skilled in so many accomplishments that he became known as "Boston's general handy man," John Coburn another Bostonian, Thomas Hamersly of New York, and John Bailey of Philadelphia turned out dozens of beautiful pieces of silver. Pewter, an alloy of tin, lead, and copper, while not appearing in as large quantities as in colonial days, was still manufactured. Its popularity declined rapidly after 1820. Most of the brassware used in the colonies was imported from the Old World. By the turn of the century, however, an abundance of knockers, doorknobs, candlesticks, warming pans, and other articles were produced in the young republic. Duncan Phyfe, peer of our early cabinet makers, not only made beautiful furniture for rich New Yorkers who were acquiring fortunes in mercantile pursuits but, perhaps, did more than any other person of his time to educate American taste for the delicate classic style. Phyfe's name, originally spelled "Fife," was changed to "Phyfe" at the suggestion of one of his wealthy women patrons, who told him that "such a name was too ordinary to attract the attention of the giddy rich people." Needlework was no less popular than in colonial days. Indeed, it was one of the chief studies, as we shall presently see, in many young ladies' seminaries. Samplers, patchwork, quilting, and embroidery were made in all parts of the country. Several American potteries were in existence by 1800, but their product was, with very few exceptions, inferior to that of their European competitors.

7. EDUCATION

Frontier conditions, the existence of fairly definite social-economic classes, the traditional notion that only an aristocracy of breeding and wealth should monopolize and receive the benefits of education, the prevalence of state sovereignty and sectional animosity, the desire to strengthen nationalistic ideals, and above all, eighteenth-century liberalism with its emphasis on democracy and human perfectability, were the principal and often conflicting forces which shaped educational ideas in the young republic. The Revolution was scarcely over before a flood of proposals concerning the place and function of education in the new social order began to appear. Anxious to aid

Forces shaping education in young republic

in the solution of what it saw to be both a vital and perplexing problem, the American Philosophical Society offered a prize for "the best system of liberal education and literary instruction adapted to the genius of the Government of the United States; comprehending also a plan for instituting and conducting public schools in this country, on principles of the most extensive utility." Space forbids more than a brief summary of some of the plans and suggestions made by such personages as Washington, Jefferson, Benjamin Rush, Noah Webster, James Sullivan, Robert Coram, Nathaniel Chipman, Samuel Knox, Samuel Harrison Smith, and other less well-known figures.[1]

Unsympathetic, as we have seen, with democracy and its leveling tendencies, the Hamiltonians, with few exceptions, were concerned with educating leaders for democracy rather than in educating the democracy. Ardent champions of a highly centralized national system *Interest of Hamiltonians in education* and of the constitutional framework they had devised for its governance, they were primarily interested in establishing an educational scheme which would train competent administrators, legislators, and judges. It was for this reason, in large measure, that Washington with statesmanlike vision warmly advocated the establishment under federal auspices of a national university at the seat of the general government. Such an institution, he urged, would enable young men from all parts of the country to secure training not only in the arts and sciences but in practical politics. Nor did he lose sight of the nationalizing influences of such an institution. "It is of the highest importance, in my opinion," said he, "that during the juvenile period of life, when friendships are formed and habits established that stick by one, the youth or young men from different parts of the United States would be assembled together, and would by degrees discover that there was not that cause for those jealousies and prejudices which one part of the Union had imbibed against another part — of course sentiments of more liberality would result from it." So close to his heart

[1] For a detailed account of these plans consult A. O. Hansen's *Liberalism and American Education in the Eighteenth Century.*

was the idea of a national institution of higher learning that in his will he made a bequest for its endowment.

Unfortunately, Washington's proposal for a national university, although it had the cordial support of many outstanding leaders, including Charles Pinckney, Thomas Jefferson, and James Madison, and was subsequently renewed from time to time, did not win sufficient public favor to induce Congress to take concrete action. Ignorance, opposition of existing collegiate institutions, state's rights, and distrust of the Hamiltonian group of which Washington was a member account in all probability for the indifference and, in some quarters, disrespect with which the recommendation was received. The Military Academy founded at West Point in 1802 and the Naval Academy established at Annapolis some fifty years later were the only educational institutions at the middle of the nineteenth century supported directly by federal funds that performed in a small way the nationalizing functions which the first president of the Union had in mind.

Congress fails to establish national university

Practically all of the proposals emanating from those who shared Jefferson's philosophy and outlook on life were, as might be expected, heavily laden with eighteenth-century liberalistic concepts. While differing somewhat in details, all more or less agreed that men and institutions were capable of indefinite improvement, that education was the chief means whereby this improvement could be accelerated and guided, that institutions instead of remaining fixed and unchanging should be flexible and evolutionary, that the primary purpose of the state was to further human progress, and that this could best be accomplished through a national system of education which would not only provide uniformity of instruction, texts, control, and supervision, but would be conducted on a scientific, experimental, open-minded basis. The youth of the land were to be taught not merely to obey laws imposed from above, but responsibility for the nation's policies and welfare. Even women, long circumscribed educationally and politically, were to be educated in the principles of democracy and the laws of

Proposals of Jeffersonians embodied eighteenth-century liberalistic concepts

national citizenship in order that they might the better contribute to societal welfare.

Ranking high among those who believed that the safety and welfare of the new-born republic depended upon a proper form of state-supported education based on liberalistic lines was Dr. Benjamin Rush. In his *Thoughts upon the Mode of Education Proper in a Republic*, published in 1786, he outlined his educational creed. Starting with the double premise that American should always be preferred to foreign education, and that any system of education adopted should inculcate a "supreme regard for country," he proposed a series of schools for both sexes culminating in a post-graduate university. All of these schools from lowest to highest would inspire the youth of the land "with republican principles." Every student was to be taught to cultivate a spirit of inquiry and to realize that institutions of every description are subject to change or modification. Teachers were to be carefully trained and adequately paid. So convinced was he that the young republic should not copy European institutions that he facetiously suggested the establishment of special schools to develop skill in forgetting: *Benjamin Rush's plan for national system of education*

> We suffer so much from traditional error of various kinds, in education, morals and government, that I have been led to wish that it were possible for us to have schools established in the United States for teaching *the art of forgetting*. I think three-fourths of our schoolmasters, divines, and legislators would profit very much by spending two or three years in such useful institutions.

Rush's desire that America divorce Old World institutions is evident from an examination of the curriculum for his federal university. Chief among the subjects of instruction were ancient and modern history so that the youth of the country might gain an appreciation of "the progress of liberty and tyranny in the different states of Europe"; the principles and forms of democratic government and international relations; the history and principles of agriculture, commerce, and manufactures; applied mathematics, especially those parts which were useful in business and war — *Rush's emphasis on utilitarianism* "for there is too much reason to fear that war will continue, for some time to come, to be the unchristian mode of deciding disputes between Christian nations"; natural philosophy and chemistry in so far as they served utilitarian ends; natural history, including the history of animals, vegetables, and fossils; philology, rhetoric, criticism, and lectures upon the construction and pronunciation of the English language; German and French — which he maintained should be acquired only through the ear; and athletics and manly exercises which "are calculated to impart health, strength, and elegance to the human body." Greek and Latin were ruled out as wholly unsuited to American needs.

To assist the work of the university Rush proposed that four trained specialists be sent abroad at public expense in quest of "the improvements that are daily made in agriculture, manufactures, and commerce, and in the art of war and practical government." Two others should be similarly employed "in exploring the vegetable, mineral, and animal productions of our country [and] in procuring histories and samples of each of them." The professors of the university were to be liberally compensated and were to be the cream of the intellectual talent of the nation. The chief business of the head of the institution, who was to be a man "of extensive education, liberal manners, and dignified deportment," was to inspire the students "by his conversation and by occasional public discourses, with federal and patriotic sentiments." The degrees conferred by the university were to indicate that its principal purpose was to educate youth for "civil and public life." In fact, Rush suggested that after a lapse of thirty years no person should be permitted by law to hold public office unless he was the holder of a degree from the federal university:

University to be training ground for public service

We require certain qualifications in lawyers, physicians and clergy-men, before we commit our property, our lives or our souls to their care. We even refuse to commit the charge of a ship to a pilot who cannot produce a certificate of his education and knowledge in his business, why then should we commit our country, which includes liberty, property, life, wives and children, to men who cannot produce vouchers of their qualifications for the important work? We are restrained from injuring ourselves, by employing quacks in law; why should we not be restrained in like manner by law, from employing quacks in government?

Rush felt certain that if his educational scheme, including his plan for a federal university, were adopted it would mark the beginning of a golden age in the United States by removing ignorance and prejudice and disseminating enlightenment to every corner of the country. "While the business of education in Europe," said he, "consists in lectures upon the ruins of Palmyra, and the antiquities of Herculaneum, or in disputes about Hebrew points, Greek particles, or the accent and quantity of the Roman language, the youth of America will be employed in acquiring those branches of knowledge which will improve our country, promote population, exalt the human understanding, and establish domestic, social and political happiness." Without such a system of education he was confident that ignorance and disunion, both enemies of progress and happiness, would long prevail.

Importance of adopting a liberal scheme of education

But neither Rush's plan nor the similar plans of James Sullivan, Samuel Knox, Noah Webster, and others for a national system of education gained acceptance. All were doomed to failure by the same forces that negatived Washington's project for a national university. Not only was each state left in control of its own education, but for a generation or more there was lacking anything which might be described as a carefully integrated educational system, national, state or municipal. Indeed, until the time of Horace Mann, education in America was almost wholly a class affair. Out of Jacksonian rather than Jeffersonian democracy, as we shall see, came the American public school system.

Efforts to establish a national system of education fail

During the first decades of the republic, therefore, the college continued to be the outstanding educational institution. Between 1783 and 1800 twenty-one institutions of college grade came into existence, and by 1820 this number had approximately doubled. Among these were a few state universities, but they were relatively unimportant during the first quarter of the new century.   Despite exposure to liberalizing influences,

Character of higher institutions of learning in 1800

the vast majority of the collegiate institutions, both old and new, were strongholds of tradition and conservatism modeled after Cambridge University, England.   While patriotism and nationalism were not neglected, moral and religious motives were overwhelmingly powerful.   In fact, nearly all the newer institutions, like the older ones, were founded and managed by the churches, the trustees, president, and faculty of each college often being of the denomination responsible for its birth or continuance. Nine out of ten of the college executives and many of the faculty were drawn from the ranks of the clergy.[1]   Student bodies were, in proportion to population, very small.   In 1815, to cite a single year, only twenty-three students graduated from Williams, sixty-six from Harvard, sixty-nine from Yale, forty from Princeton, fifteen from the University of Pennsylvania, and thirty-seven from the University of South Carolina.

Instead of the broad liberal program suggested by Rush, the college student of 1800 was dieted for four years with Latin,

The typical college curriculum

Greek, rhetoric, mathematics, logic, moral philosophy, and sometimes with a little history, geography, economics, and natural science, and occasionally with a smattering of political science.   Every student wrestled with Greek and Latin for three years; rhetoric and mathematics were given in the first two years, natural philosophy in the third, and the philosophical studies — logic, metaphysics, ethics, and lectures on the evidences of Christianity — in the fourth.   The classics were regarded by those in control as the very backbone of the entire course.   "With the study or neglect of the Greek and Latin languages," declared the Reverend John Mason, provost of Columbia, "sound learning flourishes or declines. It is now too late for ignorance, indolence, eccentricity, or infidelity to dispute what has been ratified by the seal of ages." Advancing the familiar argument that the classics were molders

---

[1] For an admirable account of the college executive consult G. P. Schmidt, *The Old Time College President.*

of mental discipline, their supporters looked upon scientific and social studies as trivial time wasters. Theology still held the center of the stage.

In a few institutions, however, there was unmistakable evidence at the turn of the century that eighteenth-century liberalism had gained root. The first of these in order of time was the College of William and Mary. Unhampered by sectarian bias, imbued with liberalistic ideals, and firm believer that in education the republic enjoyed its greatest security, Jefferson, while the Revolution was still in progress, set to work to transform his alma mater from a narrow Anglican institution into one where there would be the widest possible range of courses and right of individual choice under a free elective system. As a result the course of study was revolutionized by the introduction of law, history, political economy, and modern languages. Highly encouraged by this success, Jefferson planned to make William and Mary the capstone of a comprehensive educational edifice for Virginia, but when sectarian and other obstacles arose he turned to the thought of a new state-controlled university where he hoped his ideas could be fully expressed. The University of Virginia, founded in 1825, with its wide scope of subjects, lack of uniform entrance requirements, great freedom of choice, and insistence on achievement rather than on form and method, was not only a challenge to the old order but a noble and enduring monument to its founder.

Jefferson's educational scheme

In a few other institutions there were also indications that scientific and social studies were making headway. Physics, chemistry, agriculture, astronomy, history, government, law, commerce, and the modern languages continued to be taught in Franklin's college of Philadelphia. Both Williams College, chartered in 1793, and Union College, chartered the following year, departed from the old standards by permitting the substitution of French for Greek and by introducing other liberalizing courses. Dickinson and Hampden-Sidney, both chartered in 1783, and Bowdoin, established in 1802, also showed distinct leanings in the direction of liberalism. Even the course of study pre-

Other colleges where liberalism gained foothold

pared by President Johnson, of Columbia, foreshadowed a departure from the traditional curriculum:

The chief thing that is aimed at in this college [wrote Johnson] is to teach and engage the children to know God in Jesus Christ . . . and to train them up in all virtuous Habits, and all such useful Knowledge as may render them creditable to their Families and Friends, Ornaments to their Country and useful to the public Weal in their Generations. . . .

[The design of this college is] to instruct and perfect the Youth in the Learned Languages, and in the Arts of reasoning exactly, of writing correctly, and speaking eloquently; and in the Arts of numbering and measuring; of Surveying and Navigation, of Geography and History, of Husbandry, Commerce and Government, and in the Knowledge of all Nature in the Heavens above us, and various kinds of Meteors, Stones, Mines, and Minerals, Plants and Animals, and of everything useful for the Comfort, the Convenience and Elegance of Life, in the chief Manufactures relating to any of these Things; And, finally, to lead them from the Study of Nature to the Knowledge of themselves, and of the God of Nature, and their Duty to him, themselves and one another, and everything that can contribute to their true Happiness, both here and hereafter.

Nearly all the colleges were distressingly poor in equipment and endowment. The students were for the most part young men of competence and serious purpose, and, in sharp contrast with today, were free from distractions. Amusements were few and simple, and athletics did not exist. Clubs and fraternities, other than honorary, had not yet begun. Dancing, theatres, and games of chance and, in the South and West, horse racing, duelling, and the carrying of weapons were taboo. Attendance upon prayers, chapel, and classes was compulsory. Discipline was usually severe, and the person, whether student or faculty member, who failed to conform to the established *mores* was in danger of being ostracized or dropped. Living costs varied greatly from year to year and from institution to institution. The smallness of enrollment and the character of instruction enabled student and faculty to come into close personal contact. Except in a few institutions academic freedom did not prevail; dogma and authority rather

Undergraduate life

than the spirit of scientific inquiry pervaded most college halls.

If higher education in the young republic was shaped largely by Old World influences, so also was secondary and elementary education. Apprenticeship, the dame, parochial, and pauper schools, and the Latin grammar schools of colonial times were in every case, as we have seen, importations from England. Even the colonial textbooks were English. Nor did the patriotic reaction against English ideas, customs, and institutions growing out of the movement for independence greatly modify the situation, for the new nation, despite its pride and complacency, still continued to draw many of its educational notions directly from the former mother country. But borrowings were not confined to England. From the Continent, where the philosophy of Rousseau and the teachings of Pestalozzi had given rise to a rich and varied literature on the training of the young and their relation to society, came new concepts emphasizing the importance of non-formalism, experimentation, and the cultivation of social sympathies.

Secondary and elementary education shaped partly by Old World influences

At the turn of the century only the children of those well up the social-economic ladder could afford more than an elementary schooling. For the middle class, especially, the old Latin grammar school with its limited curriculum and its emphasis on preparation for college seemed wholly inadequate. Socially and economically ambitious and yet anxious to maintain certain standards of respectability, it wanted an institution more utilitarian in character.[1] The private academy, an Old World importation and the forerunner of the present-day high school, with its broad

The typical school of the middle class: the academy

[1] That business was no less an absorbing interest a century ago than it is today, and that it had its critics then as now is evident from the following written from Baltimore in 1824 by Betsy Patterson Bonaparte to Lady Morgan: "[You have] no idea of the mode of existence inflicted on us. The men are all merchants; and commerce, although it may fill the purse, clogs the brain. Beyond their counting-houses they possess not a single idea; they never visit except when they wish to marry. The women are all occupied in *les détails de ménage* and nursing children; these are useful occupations, but do not render people agreeable to their neighbors." E. L. Didier, *The Life and Letters of Madame Bonaparte*, p. 159.

course of study and its freedom from the domination of narrow-minded theologians, filled the need. By the turn of the century academies were to be found in every state; Massachusetts alone had seventeen, New York nineteen, and North Carolina thirty. Fifty years later the number had increased to over six thousand. Attended by the sons and daughters of merchants, lawyers, doctors, and well-to-do farmers, the academies were the chief agencies of secondary education in America until the middle of the nineteenth century. Though an occasional boy or girl from the lower strata of society managed to gain admittance, the academy was primarily a middle class institution which tended in some cases to be somewhat snobbish and undemocratic.

For the children of the lower classes — the artisans, mechanics, fishermen, and poorer farmers — who in all probability would never see the inside of an academy, much less a college, the opportunities in the young republic for even elementary schooling left much to be desired. Though Jefferson, Rush, and other radical leaders who believed that the ideals and interests of the republic would be best served by a literate and well-informed citizenry, worked unceasingly for universal, state-supported education, little headway was made, as we have already noted, until the republic was almost a half century old. Even the high sounding declarations made in constitutional conventions and in legislative halls favoring tax-supported schools, open to the children of all citizens, failed for the time being to accomplish the ends which Jefferson and his fellow philosophers had in mind. The prevalence of agriculture, the relative isolation and independence of urban communities, the unwillingness of property owners to bear additional taxation that better educational facilities might be provided for the masses, the traditional notion that education for the rank and file was a matter of benevolence, the lack of full manhood suffrage in a number of states, and the want of an economic demand for education coupled with indifference and inertia on the part of the populace, were the principal factors that postponed for a generation or more common school education for all children at public expense.

Lack of universal elementary education

Elementary education in the centers of population, therefore, remained in considerable measure in the hands of the parochial and pauper schools until an awakened educational consciousness led to the establishment of state-wide school systems.

Supplementing the sectarian and charity schools were three semi-private philanthropic educational agencies, all imported from England. These were (1) the Sunday school, The Sunday (2) the monitorial or Lancastrian school, and school (3) the infant school. Founded primarily for the purpose of giving working children opportunity for instruction "in reading and the Church catechism" the Sunday school idea gained ground so rapidly that in 1785 The Society for Promoting Sunday Schools throughout the British Dominions was organized. The work of this interdenominational society in helping to educate the poor children of England can scarcely be overestimated. The idea soon spread to the United States. In 1791 The First Day or Sunday School Society was organized at Philadelphia for the purpose of giving instruction to the poor. Sunday schools also sprang up in other centers. Less needed on this side of the Atlantic because of the absence of a submerged mass of paupers, the Sunday schools soon came under sectarian control. Objecting to secular instruction on Sundays, the churches quickly transformed the Sunday schools into out and out social-religious organizations.

The monitorial system of instruction, the essential feature of which was the transmission by the more clever or competent pupils to the other pupils of knowledge which they The monitorial school themselves had learned by rote from a teacher, appears to have antedated the discovery of America. Popularized in England at the turn of the century by Joseph Lancaster, an English Quaker philanthropist, this method of instruction quickly gained a place in the United States. In 1818 Lancaster himself came to America where he spent the remaining twenty years of his life organizing and directing schools and expounding the merits of his system. Its cheapness together with its emphasis on discipline and uniformity appealed to those interested in mass education at a time when money was scarce and when private schools had a reputation for idleness, inattention, and disorder. Lancastrian schools for training teachers — precursors of the modern normal schools — were established in 1818. Without doubt the monitorial schools hastened the adoption of the free school system.

The infant school idea originating with Robert Owen, the New Lanark, Scotland, manufacturer, was, like the Sunday school, **The infant** designed for poor children. Reaching the United **school** States soon after the War of 1812, it was adopted by some of the larger cities where children were denied admittance to the monitorial schools unless they could read and write. In reality the infant school was the predecessor of the primary school.

Country boys and girls received their elementary education in the ungraded district school. Originating in New England **The district** shortly after the Revolutionary War as an out-**school** growth of the old parish school, the district system in time spread over nearly all of the United States. Each district, which was merely a subdivision of a town or county, elected school trustees, levied district school taxes, and selected a teacher and sometimes the textbooks. In many districts, too, the trustees determined the length of the school term and designated the subjects to be taught. Instruction in these schools was confined largely to the three R's — reading, writing, and arithmetic — and good manners. Bible reading was an every day occurrence. Discipline was severe, and rough and tumble fights between teacher and older pupils sometimes occurred. The terms were short, the majority of districts having only one. In those where there were two terms — winter and summer — the latter was usually kept by women, for the men were engaged in farm work. The men teachers received from six to twenty dollars a month and the women from four to ten. Both were "boarded round" by the families of the district. Teachers were held in high respect, although there was often difference of opinion regarding their character and fitness, and a great deal of petty politics was involved in their selection. In every case the voice of the property-owner counted heavily in the affairs of the district.

THE

New-England

PRIMER

Improved.

For the more eafy attaining the true
Reading of Englifh.

To which is added,

The Affembly of Divines,

and Mr. COTTON's

Catechifm.

BOSTON: Printed and Sold by
S. ADAMS, in *Queen-ftreet.* 1762.

In *Adam's* Fall
We Sinned all.

Thy Life to Mend
This *Book* Attend.

The *Cat* doth play
And after flay.

A *Dog* will bite
A Thief at night.

An *Eagles* flight
Is out of fight.

The Idle *Fool*
Is whipt at School.

A
B
C
D
E
F

TITLE PAGE OF ONE OF THE
MANY EDITIONS OF THE
"NEW ENGLAND PRIMER"

SPECIMEN PAGE FROM THE
"NEW ENGLAND PRIMER"

For many years *The New Primer, or an Easy and Pleasant Guide to the Art of Reading to which is added the Catechism —*
Textbooks   the catechism being a score or more selections from the Westminster Assembly Shorter Catechism —
was the principal textbook. Indeed, it continued to be used extensively in rural districts until near the end of the first quarter of the nineteenth century. In the cities and larger towns, however, its grip was broken by texts which placed less emphasis on religious and more on secular material. Among these mention should be made of Dilworth's *A New Guide to the English Tongue,* an English importation; the *Columbian Primer* (1802), a modernized and secularized imitation of the *New England Primer;* the *Franklin Primer* (1802) "containing a new and useful selection of Moral Lessons adorned with a great variety of elegant cuts calculated to strike a lasting impression on the Tender Minds of Children"; Caleb Bingham's *American Preceptor* (1794) which soon displaced the Bible as an advanced reading book; and the *Columbian Orator* (1806) containing selections from poetry and prose for reading and declamation. Like poetry and drama, the American textbook reflected the spirit of the times. The readers, for example, contained numerous patriotic orations of revolutionary leaders; such speeches as Patrick Henry's "Give me Liberty or give me Death" were declaimed in schoolhouses all over the land.

Standing at the head of the textbook list in influence and popularity was Noah Webster's "blue-backed" *American Spell-*
Webster's   *ing Book* (1783), a combined speller and reader, the
Speller   first distinctly American textbook. So great was its popularity that fifty million copies were published. During the twenty years (1807–1827) when Webster was devoting practically his entire time to his *Dictionary of the English Language* he and his family lived entirely upon the royalties from the speller. Ranking with Webster's speller was Warren Colburn's *First Lessons in Arithmetic on the Plan of Pestalozzi* (1821). The Reverend Jedidiah Morse's *Geography* (1784) and his *Elements of Geography* (1795) were also popular, as was Lindley Murray's *Grammar* (1795). The first booklet on United States history did not appear until 1821, although the readers and

THE

Young Chemist's Pocket Companion;

CONNECTED WITH

A Portable Laboratory;

CONTAINING

A PHILOSOPHICAL APPARATUS,

AND A GREAT NUMBER OF

CHEMICAL AGENTS;

BY WHICH ANY PERSON MAY PERFORM AN ENDLESS
VARIETY OF AMUSING AND INSTRUCTING
EXPERIMENTS;

A INTENDED TO PROMOTE THE CULTIVATION
OF THE SCIENCE OF CHEMISTRY.

BY JAMES WOODHOUSE, M.D.

Professor of Chemistry in the University of Pennsylvania, &c.

*At present every thing that is not denominated Chemistry, is but
a small part of a system of natural knowledge.*

PRIESTLEY *on Air.*

Philadelphia:

PRINTED BY *J. H. OSWALD,* NO. 179, SOUTH
SECOND-STREET.

1797.

The *Young Chemist's Pocket Companion* was in all probability the first guide for chemical students published in
America.

earlier geographies contained some historical material. Most of the scientific texts used in the colleges were translations or adaptations of French textbooks.

Education for girls and young women, which up to the close of the Revolution was, as we have seen, rudimentary in character, began to improve at the turn of the century. Especially was this true of higher education. Largely as a result of the splendid efforts of Benjamin Rush, DeWitt Clinton, Emma Willard, and many other equally enthusiastic advocates of more liberal and substantial education for women, a number of female academies and seminaries were founded.[1] While the post-revolutionary years witnessed the beginning of these institutions, it was not until the early nineteenth century that they began to exert a most profound influence. Among the more important were The Female Academy opened by the Moravians at Salem, North Carolina, in 1802; the Catherine Fiske School established at Keene, New Hampshire, in 1814; Joseph Emerson's Ladies' Seminary at Byfield, Massachusetts, begun in 1818, and later removed to Wethersfield, Connecticut; and the Troy (New York) Seminary, started by Emma Willard in 1821. English grammar, arithmetic, geography, some history, and a modern language, particularly French, formed the backbone of the curriculum. Religious and domestic training were also stressed, and occasionally drawing and music.

New concept of women's education

Libraries, both public and private, not only increased in number but reflected the influence of the changing era. In 1816 it was estimated that six hundred tons of paper were used annually in America for books. Four years later it was officially reported that the country had fourteen college, nine public, and five semi-public libraries. Many of the well-to-do, although primarily interested in making money, possessed libraries of considerable size. The library of John Quincy Adams contained no less than five thousand volumes in 1809, and Jefferson's an even larger number, but these two were

Libraries

---

[1] For the rise of female academies and seminaries consult Thomas Woody, *A History of Women's Education in the United States*, vol. i, chap. viii.

exceptional. While books of almost every description were to be found, those concerned with the classics and religion were the most numerous. By 1820 biography, history, poetry, science, fiction, and travel books were increasing at the expense of books of a religious nature. Although the leisured class with time for reading was increasing, the overwhelming majority of the population was still primarily interested in things material. The labor of the hand, as Henry Adams well says, enjoyed precedence over that of the mind. Especially was this true of those hardy pioneers who were laying the foundations of empire in the great valley beyond the Alleghenies. To them we shall now turn our attention.

SUGGESTED READINGS

Henry Adams, *History of the United States of America*, vol. i, chaps. i–vi.

J. T. Adams, *New England in the Republic, 1776–1850*, chap. xii.

Herbert Asbury, *A Methodist Saint. The Life of Bishop Asbury.*

Charles and Mary Beard, *The Rise of American Civilization*, vol. i, chap. x.

M. A. Best, *Thomas Paine, Prophet and Martyr of Democracy*, chap. xiv.

P. W. Bidwell, *Rural Economy in New England at the Beginning of the Nineteenth Century.*

C. H. Caffin, *The Story of American Painting; the Evolution of Painting in America from Colonial Times to the Present.*

A. W. Calhoun, *A Social History of the American Family from Colonial Times to the Present*, vol. ii, chaps. i–ii.

Edward Channing, *A History of the United States*, vol. iv, chap. i.

E. H. Clarke and others, *A Century of American Medicine, 1776–1876.*

O. S. Coad, *William Dunlap, A Study of His Life and Works.*

G. W. Cooke, *Unitarianism in America: A History of Its Origin and Development.*

E. P. Cubberley, *Public Education in the United States*, chaps. iii–iv.

E. S. Dana and others, *A Century of Science in America.*

L. C. Elson, *The History of American Music*, chaps. i–vii.

G. P. Fisher, *Life of Benjamin Silliman*, vol. i.

H. G. Good, *Benjamin Rush and His Services to American Education.*

Peter Guilday, *The Life and Times of John Carroll, Archbishop of Baltimore (1735–1815).*

T. F. Hamlin, *The American Spirit in Architecture* (vol. 13 of *The Pageant of America*), chaps. i–xi.

A. O. Hansen, *Liberalism and American Education in the Eighteenth Century.*

A. B. Hart (Editor), *Commonwealth History of Massachusetts*, vol. ii, chaps. ix–xiii.

F. H. Herrick, *Audubon the Naturalist*, 2 vols.

F. W. Hirst, *Life and Letters of Thomas Jefferson*, book vii.

Arthur Hornblow, *A History of the Theater in America from its beginnings to the present time*, vol. i.

E. F. Humphrey, *Nationalism and Religion in America, 1774–1789.*

Gaillard Hunt, *Life in America One Hundred Years Ago.*

H. M. Jones, *America and French Culture, 1750–1848;* especially chaps. vii–xii.

Fiske Kimball, *Domestic Architecture of the American Colonies and of the Early Republic.*

Fiske Kimball, and G. H. Edgell, *A History of Architecture*, chap. xiii.

Fiske Kimball, *Thomas Jefferson; Architect.*

J. A. Krout, *The Origins of Prohibition*, chaps. i–v.

J. M. Lee, *History of American Journalism*, chaps. viii–x.

O. F. Lewis, *The Development of American Prisons and Prisons Customs, 1776–1845, with Special Reference to Early Institutions in the State of New York.*

J. B. McMaster, *A History of the People of the United States from the Revolution to the Civil War*, vol. iii, chap. xxii.

G. P. Merrill, *The First One Hundred Years of American Geology*, chap. i.

J. L. Mesick, *The English Traveller in America, 1785–1835.*

Lewis Mumford, *Sticks and Stones: A Study of American Architecture and Civilization.*

Allan Nevins, *American Social History as recorded by British Travellers*, chaps. i–viii.

Allan Nevins, *The Evening Post, A Century of Journalism*, chaps. i–vi.

G. C. D. Odell, *Annals of the New York Stage*, vols. i, ii.

V. L. Parrington, *Main Currents in American Thought*, vol. i; (*The Colonial Mind, 1620–1800*, book iii, part ii, chap. iii); vol. ii (*The Romantic Revolution in America, 1800–1860*, book iii, part ii, chap. ii).

John Pell, *Ethan Allen.*

C. A. Peverelly, *American Pastimes.*

F. L. Mott, *A History of American Magazines, 1741–1850*, chaps. iii–iv, supplement to part ii.

A. H. Quinn, *A History of the American Drama from the Beginning to the Civil War*, chaps. ii–vii.

J. H. Randall, Jr., *The Making of the Modern Mind*, chaps. x–xii.

Woodbridge Riley, *American Thought from Puritanism to Pragmatism and Beyond*, chaps. i–iv.

J. M. Robertson, *A History of Free Thought in the Nineteenth Century*, part i, chaps. i–iii.

H. K. Rowe, *The History of Religion in the United States*.

G. P. Schmidt, *The Old Time College President*.

James Schouler, *History of the United States of America under the Constitution*, vols. i–v.

E. F. Smith, *Chemistry in America*, chaps. i–ix.

O. G. Sonneck, *Early Opera in America*.

Vernon Stauffer, *New England and the Bavarian Illuminati*, chaps. i–ii.

Lorado Taft, *The History of American Sculpture*, Introduction and chap. i.

Isaiah Thomas, *The History of Printing in America*, vol. ii.

W. P. Trent (Editor), *Cambridge History of American Literature*, vol. i.

Williston Walker, *A History of the Congregational Churches in the United States*.

Charles Warren, *History of the Harvard Law School and of Early Legal Conditions in America*.

L. A. Weigle, *American Idealism* (vol. 10 of *The Pageant of America*).

F. Weitenkampf, *American Graphic Art*, chaps. i, xii, xiv, xv.

A. H. Wharton, *Social Life in the Early Republic*.

S. T. Williams, *The American Spirit in Letters* (vol. 11 of *The Pageant of America*), chaps. i–iv.

Thomas Woody, *A History of Women's Education in the United States*, vol. i.

R. T. Young, *Biology in America*, chap. i.

CHAPTER VIII

TWO GENERATIONS OF WESTERN FRONTIERSMEN

PROBABLY no other single factor has so profoundly affected American development and shaped American ideals as the West and its frontier. Its influence upon our politics, industry, education, literature — in fact, upon every phase of institutional life — can scarcely be overestimated.

At the close of the Revolution more than ninety per cent of the people of the United States were scattered along the Atlantic *Distribution* seaboard from Maine to Georgia. Stretching three *of people of* thousand miles to the westward and embracing *United States* *at close of* the very heart of the North American continent *Revolution* lay a vast wilderness empire, rich in natural resources and teeming with potential opportunities. Part of this broad expanse comprised the alluvial valley of the Mississippi, flanked on the east by the Appalachians and on the west by the Rocky Mountains. Beyond this great central valley lay the jagged Rocky Mountain plateau and the Pacific coast region. Of this area only that part east of the Mississippi, exclusive of the Floridas, had been nominally secured by the United States in 1783. Covering the western slopes of the Appalachians a densely wooded belt extended almost from the Great Lakes to the Gulf, separating the seaboard states from the timberless prairies of the Mississippi basin. On either side of the Ohio millions of acres of virgin soil seemingly awaited only the hand of the settler to produce luxuriant crops of corn and wheat, and to the southward were immense tracts of land unsurpassed in fertility and peculiarly well adapted to the growth of cotton.

It was in part for possession of this territory that France and Great Britain waged their eighteenth-century struggle for colonial *The advance* supremacy and world mastery. Only a few years *of the frontier* elapsed after the concluding battles of that memorable conflict before the ring of the axe and the crack of the rifle of the American frontiersman resounded along the eastern fringe of this same region. Indeed, long before the outbreak of the Revolution the mighty movement destined to carry the white man over the slopes of the Alleghenies, out across the plains, and ultimately to the waters of the Pacific, was already under way. So rapid was it after 1780 that within two generations the frontier of civilization had advanced beyond the Mississippi.

The reasons for this phenomenal march westward were strikingly similar to those which motivated the seventeenth-century European to seek the New World. Some settlers Motives for went for mere love of adventure, lured on, as it westward expansion were, by the unknown wilderness and the exaggerated tales of daring which found their way back to the seaboard states. Others, not unlike the sixteenth-century European fortune-hunters, went in quest of easy wealth. Still others went to escape the social, political, and religious restrictions and injustices of a crystalized and conforming eastern or Old World society, and a few went with the hope of achieving political fame. But most numerous of all were those who turned to the West with its abundance of practically free land in search of economic opportunity. To the struggling eastern farmer, dissatisfied tradesman, religious dissenter, oppressed mechanic, or ambitious young lawyer, the West was a sort of "promised land" the gates of which were ever open. Hither many repaired, and here, free from the restraints and prejudices of the older communities, they developed new traits, new ideals, and new institutions.

1. THE SETTLEMENT OF THE "OLD WEST" AND THE CONQUEST OF THE NEW

During the colonial period the "Old West," as Professor Frederick Jackson Turner has so aptly called the untenanted lands between the Atlantic settlements and the The coming of Alleghenies, served as a sort of reservoir for those the Germans who faced toward the setting sun. Into this region, for example, poured the Germans and the Scotch-Irish. It is conservatively estimated that by 1775 no less than 225,000 Germans and

385,000 Scotch-Irish had found their way to the New World. While they settled in considerable numbers along the hilly New England frontier and in the fertile Hudson, Mohawk, and Schoharie valleys of New York, it was to Pennsylvania, widely advertised haven of the dissenter and the oppressed, that they flocked. The Germans located in the great valley still renowned as the home of the "Pennsylvania Dutch," but the first quarter of the eighteenth century had hardly passed before many of them, attracted by cheap land, began to move slowly southward. By 1750 they were not only occupying the Virginia Piedmont in increasing numbers, but were streaming into the valley of the Shenandoah and out through the water gaps to the uplands of the Carolinas. At the opening of the Revolution they had a line of thrifty settlements extending from the Mohawk to the Savannah.

Paralleling this line were the settlements of the real frontiersmen — the Scotch-Irish. Like the peace-loving Germans, the The Scotch-Irish majority of these aggressive, individualistic emigrants took up their abode in Pennsylvania. Settling along the old Indian route from Lancaster to Bedford, they soon made their way into the valley of the Juniata and the Redstone country, and by 1775 had established a powerful community around Pittsburg. Like the Germans, they also filtered southward into the up-country of Virginia and along the western bank of the Shenandoah and, finally, into the southern uplands. Frequently their zone of settlement overlapped that of the Germans, but in general the bulk of the Scotch-Irish lived farther to the west. From Maryland southward both Germans and Scotch-Irish were in large measure separated from the tidewater planters by the Blue Ridge Mountains and the pine barrens of the Carolinas and Georgia.

While the Germans and Scotch-Irish were moving southward, other pioneers, having made their way across Virginia by Peopling the way of the James River, were swarming through Shenandoah the Blue Ridge gap into the Shenandoah valley. valley Frederick county, Virginia, with Winchester as its seat, was organized in 1743. Two years later Staunton, the seat of Augusta county, held its first court, and by the middle of the century Virginia and North Carolina had found it desirable to extend their common boundary to the Laurel Fork of the Holston River. Incidentally no love was lost between these men of the back country and those who resided in the coastal plain region. The Easterners who controlled the fluid capital and dominated the legislature and the courts of their respective states were accused of forcing the frontiersmen to pay excessive taxes and exorbitant fees. During 1765–1767 the back-countrymen of North Carolina organized what were known as the Regulators for the purpose of administering their own affairs. Open rebellion soon broke out and did not subside until 1771, when the Regulators were defeated by Governor Tryon's troops in the battle of the Alamance. In reality the disturbance was merely an expression of the contest between the propertied-business men of the older settled communities and the radical small or non-propertied element of the frontier which, as we saw in an earlier chapter, was being waged in every one of the continental English colonies. In 1769 Virginia frontiersmen, led by James Robertson and John Sevier, planted a settlement on the Watauga River, which joins the Holston just below the southern boundary of Virginia. This settlement, situated in one of the most important Appalachian gateways, in reality marked the vanguard of the migration into the Tennessee country.

The transallegheny region had, as we have observed, long attracted the attention of the fortune-hunting land speculator. As early as 1748 the Ohio Land Company, it will be remembered, secured a grant of 200,000 acres in the vicinity of upper Ohio. In 1766 the Vandalia or Walpole Company headed by Benjamin Franklin and Thomas Walpole, a London banker, petitioned for 2,500,000 acres. Three years later the Mississippi Company, the concern in which the Washingtons and the Lees were the guiding spirits, asked for an equal area. At the same time Judge Richard Henderson of North Carolina in association with James Robertson and the intrepid Daniel Boone organized the Transylvania Company and negotiated a private treaty with the Indians which gave the company title to all of the present

Speculative
interest in
the trans-
allegheny

state of Kentucky and to much of middle Tennessee.[1] Lesser companies, as well as several persons not company members, were also interested in securing western domain for speculative purposes.

But these speculative enterprises, as well as actual settlement, were seriously impeded while the transallegheny territory re-

The Revolution and the trans-allegheny country

mained a part of the British Empire. The Proclamation of 1763 was, as we have observed, offensive to both speculator and pioneer, and their hard feeling toward Great Britain reached the point of anger when on the eve of the Revolution the province of Quebec was enlarged to include a large slice of the transallegheny region. When the war itself broke out the British officers at Detroit at once planned to weaken the Americans by sending the Indians against the scattered frontier settlements. To this end the Indians in the Ohio valley were warned that victory by the Americans would mean an extension of white settlement that would in all probability embrace the entire valley. Judge Henderson's claim to Kentucky and part of Tennessee was held up as an omen of what would happen if the Americans won. This warning, sufficient in itself, was reinforced by Sir Henry Hamilton, the British officer in command at Detroit, in his proclamation to the Indians in June, 1777. From this moment the fate of the transallegheny country was at stake, and it was apparent that the Revolution was not to be confined entirely to the Atlantic seaboard.

It is not our purpose to recount the exploits of that redoubtable Virginian, George Rogers Clark, who in 1778–79 in the

George Rogers Clark and the conquest of the Northwest

face of great obstacles raised a small force of frontier volunteers and with it captured the extremely important British Northwest posts of Kaskaskia, Cahokia, and Vincennes. His brilliant and daring feat gave the Americans undisputed possession of the transallegheny country with the exception of Detroit. No less

[1] Because of the inability of the Transylvania Company to secure legal recognition of Henderson's treaty with the Indians (Treaty of Sycamore Shoals) it was unable to retain its territory. Henderson, however, was compensated for his loss by grants in the Cumberland valley. Cf. Archibald Henderson, *Conquest of the Old Southwest.*

NEWLY CLEARED LAND IN AMERICA

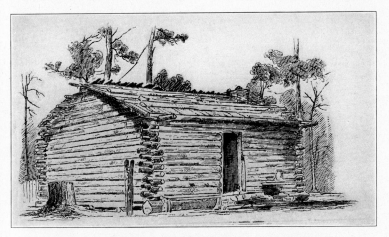

LOG HOUSE IN THE FORESTS OF GEORGIA

important, it enabled the settlement of the region beyond the Alleghenies to continue during the war. Clark's achievement was clinched when by the treaty of peace the Mississippi River was made the western boundary of the United States.

2. The Migration to the Transallegheny

Migration to the transallegheny was very uneven, being accelerated or retarded in large measure by social and economic conditions. When the Atlantic states experienced hard times, the movement was rapid; on the other hand, when times were prosperous, it was slow. The West, too, frequently suffered from economic depression, financial distress, and Indian troubles, which were not conducive to emigration. In other words, migration was most rapid when relatively hard times prevailed in the East and fairly prosperous times in the West. In accordance with this condition four great waves of people poured into the western country between 1780 and 1840.

Migration westward governed by economic conditions

The first of these occurred during the years immediately following the Revolution. The last years of that conflict afforded, as we have observed, another illustration of that age-old paradox that war times are prosperous times, for they were years featured by prosperity, speculation, easy and even extravagant living, and buoyant expectations. Farmers readily disposed of their produce to the belligerent armies; Yankee shippers, notwithstanding British vigilance, sailed the high seas reaping enormous profits in trade with European and West Indian ports; and hustling merchants rapidly sold their goods at fabulous prices to artisans and others who bought with reckless abandon. On every hand prosperity reigned, and everybody optimistically expected it to continue. But dreams and expectations proved most illusory. Scarcely had the treaty of peace been ratified before the new republic found itself in the midst of industrial depression. Business fell off rapidly; ships lay idle at their wharves; farmers, many of them in debt, were unable to market their crops. Everywhere hard times prevailed, and thousands in distress and

Four great waves of migration westward before 1840

1. Post-Revolutionary years

desperation turned to the West for relief. By 1790 the trans-
allegheny population totaled over 221,000, and many leaders
in the Atlantic states, filled with alarm, seriously believed that
the seaboard commonwealths were threatened with depopula-
tion.

With renewed activity on the part of the propertied-business
class, culminating in the establishment of the Federal Constitu-

**Depression
gives way to
prosperity
during last
decade of
eighteenth
century**
tion and the adoption of the Hamiltonian fiscal system, depression gave way to prosperity. Farmers
once more found a ready market for their produce,
shippers again unfurled their sails, and merchants
replenished their stocks. In the course of a few
years depression, unemployment, and hard times
had in large measure disappeared. In consequence the rush
westward, especially from New England and the Middle states,
was gradually arrested. Connecticut and Massachusetts
farmers, it is true, stimulated by the increasing foreign demand
for grain and other agricultural products and attracted by the
cheap and fertile lands of New York, swarmed into the Mohawk
and Genesee valleys between 1794 and 1800. In general, however, only from those regions unaffected by Federalist prosperity, like the back country of the South, did migration to the
West continue unchecked. It was from the latter section that
Kentucky and Tennessee were sufficiently peopled to come into
the Union, the former in 1792 and the latter in 1796.

By the close of the eighteenth century the population of
the young republic was approximately 5,300,000, and of this

**The frontier
of 1800**
number nearly a million were beyond the line of
settlement established by the British government
in 1763. Practically all on both sides of the Alleghenies were
American born. The frontier line of over six inhabitants to
the square mile extended unbroken from southern Maine
across northern Vermont and New Hampshire to Lake Champlain, and thence in winding fashion southward to just below
the mouth of the Savannah River. Three marked bulges or
protuberances westward are noticeable: one in New York along
the Mohawk, another around Pittsburg, and the third in the
upland country of Georgia. West of the unbroken line were

three great island populations: namely, the settlements in the
Blue Grass country of Kentucky, in the valleys of east Tennessee, and in the Cumberland district of central Tennessee.
A few other isolated settlements of trifling density were indications of the westward migration and the beginnings of civilized
life.   Transallegheny towns were as yet lightly populated and
few in number; Lexington had 1797 inhabitants; Frankfort,
628; Nashville, 355; Cincinnati, 500; and Pittsburg, 1565.

The opening years of the nineteenth century witnessed the
second great migration to the western country. With the conclusion of temporary peace between Napoleon and **2. Opening
years of nine-
teenth
century** England early in 1802, business declined sharply.
Once more our farmers were without markets,
once more shipping slackened, and once more
people felt the pinch of hard times. As before, thousands bade
farewell to their old homes and joined the "backwoods democracy" beyond the Alleghenies. Ohio was the destination of
the majority, and their coming enabled it to be admitted as a
state in 1803. Almost before these emigrants had reached their
new homes European hostilities were renewed. As a result
business increased with astonishing rapidity; eastern farmers,
mechanics, and shippers seemed unable to satisfy the growing
demand for American products. Never before had the seaboard
states been so prosperous and, naturally therefore, the movement westward diminished.

But again prosperity was shortlived. In 1807 came the
Embargo followed by the War of 1812 and the Panic of 1819 —
a hectic period in our national development. With **3. War of
1812 and
Panic of 1819** the exception of the opening months of the War of
1812, dull times prevailed for more than a decade
and a half. Taxes mounted higher, farmers became increasingly
unable to make ends meet, traders in many instances were
reduced to beggary, and artisans and mechanics deprived of
employment feared imprisonment for debt. Easterners, therefore, turned to the West in unprecedented numbers. With
them went hundreds of those who at the close of the Napoleonic
Wars left the Old World for the New. No less than 16,000
people were reported to have passed over a Pennsylvania turn-

pike between March and December, 1817. "Old America," wrote Morris Birkbeck, the traveler, "seems to be breaking up and moving westward." So enormous was the movement that wilderness areas were quickly transformed into democratic commonwealths.

The western population of over a million in 1810 increased to 2,217,474 in 1820 and to nearly 3,700,000 in 1830. In less than Rapid growth ten years six new western states were admitted to of trans-allegheny and the Union: Louisiana (1812), Indiana (1816), new common-Mississippi (1817), Illinois (1818), Alabama (1819), wealths and Missouri (1821). Even more significant was the percentage of increase in population in the transappalachian states between 1820 and 1830. Of the four older common-wealths, Kentucky gained 22 per cent, Louisiana 41, and Tennessee and Ohio 61 each. But the rate of increase in the younger states was truly phenomenal: Mississippi gained 81 per cent, Missouri 109, Indiana 133, Alabama 142, and Illinois 185. Between 1810 and 1830 this never-ending stream to the westward had carried over two million souls out of the seaboard states. By 1830 Ohio boasted a population larger than the combined populations of Massachusetts and Connecticut. Along the western water courses villages and infant cities were springing up like mushrooms. New Orleans had a population of approximately 50,000, Cincinnati nearly 25,000, and St. Louis 6,000. Buffalo, Detroit, Chicago, Milwaukee, and Cleveland, which only a few years before had been mere hamlets or fur-trading posts, were growing by leaps and bounds. In comparison with the older section of the country the population of the West was increasing beyond all expectations.

Nor did the march westward cease after 1830. Quite to the contrary, the ranks of the emigrant armies continued to grow. 4. Years But it was not until the Panic of 1837 and the following years of financial depression immediately thereafter Panic of 1837 that the fourth great wave of people streamed into the broad valley of the Mississippi. Not all of them were foreigners just landed on our shores, nor were they composed entirely of that restless eastern element characterized by President Timothy Dwight of Yale as "impatient of the

restraints of law, religion, and morality." The vast majority
were vigorous, industrious, and resourceful people from New
England, New York, and Pennsylvania who turned away from
an economically paralyzed East to begin life anew. Their
number was augmented by an ever increasing host of Germans
and others from Europe. This deluge of newcomers swelled
the population of the West to 6,376,972 by 1840. Areas like
northern Indiana and Illinois, which ten years before had been
practically unpeopled, were now dotted with the cabins of hardy
settlers. During the decade the population of Michigan rose
from 31,639 to 212,267, and in 1837 she was admitted as a state.
At the same time venturous pioneers pushed into lower Wisconsin and across the Mississippi into eastern Iowa. To the
southward Arkansas, Missouri, and Louisiana were gradually
filling up.

Geographically, people moved westward in parallel lines.
Tennessee and Kentucky, for instance, were settled by the
German and Scotch-Irish element of the Piedmont   Source of
or upland regions of Virginia and the Carolinas.   population of
For fifty years after the adoption of the Constitu- Kentucky and
                                                    Tennessee
tion the exodus continued. With the invention
of the cotton gin and the tremendous demand for cotton, the
coast planters, as we have seen, pushed into the interior counties
of the old southern states. Unable to compete, the free farmers
were practically forced either to buy slaves and adopt the
plantation system or sell their land and migrate. The majority,
who were without capital, accepted the latter alternative and
moved on to the West. The supply of cheap land in Kentucky
and Tennessee, however, was quickly exhausted, and the
younger generation together with the new arrivals from the
eastern communities poured into southern Ohio, Indiana, Illinois, Missouri and the Gulf states. Interestingly enough, in
this overflow were two west Kentucky families. In 1816 Abra-
ham Lincoln's father, a poor carpenter, took his family across
the Ohio on a raft and along with other Kentuckians hewed his
way into the forest-covered lands of southern Indiana. Less
than half a dozen years earlier the father of Jefferson Davis had
joined the stream of emigrants which flowed southward to the

rich alluvial plains of the lower Mississippi. Lincoln's ancestors came to Massachusetts in 1637, and the family then migrated slowly through New Jersey, Pennsylvania, and Virginia to Kentucky. The grandfather of the president of the Confederacy migrated from the Old World to Pennsylvania and thence to Georgia; from there his son went into Kentucky.

Southern migration to the middle West was not confined entirely to the descendants of the Germans and Scotch-Irish. **Southern migration to middle West** To Ohio came thousands of industrious and scrupulous Quakers from Virginia, the Carolinas, and Georgia. Likewise many well-to-do Southerners, attracted by the political and economic opportunities of the new country, journeyed west, bringing with them their slaves and southern ideals. Of this latter class relatively few who continued agricultural pursuits crossed the Ohio; they either bought lands in the older communities or found their way to northern Alabama or to the planter state of Missouri.

The population of the Gulf states came almost entirely from the Old South. To this section went many of the independent **Gulf state settlers** up-country yeomanry to renew the struggle for existence. But the region was even more alluring to the planters of Virginia, the Carolinas, and Georgia. Years before the close of the eighteenth century Virginia planters complained of hard times. Excessive cultivation of tobacco and failure to employ scientific methods of rotation and fertilization had exhausted the soil. The competition of Kentucky-grown tobacco, the Embargo and the War of 1812, droughts, ravages of insect pests, and the burden of old debts only added to their distress. The Southwest with its abundance of virgin land seemed to afford their only salvation, and to it they went in great numbers. Into this new El Dorado also went thousands of enterprising Carolina and Georgia planters in search of additional cotton lands. Before 1840 cotton culture had spread from Georgia to Texas, and a new South had been created. Socially and economically it resembled the old patriarchal South, yet fundamentally, as we shall see, it never reproduced the aristocratic system of the older section. Like the farmers of the Northwest, the Gulf-state planters with few exceptions were ultra-nationalists and expansionists, and, as aggressive exploiters, they reduced slavery to a purely commercial basis.

While southern planters and back-countrymen were occupying the lower Mississippi valley, Middle staters and New Englanders, supplemented by German immigrants, were streaming westward. Central Ohio, Indiana, and Illinois were in large measure colonized by people from New York, Pennsylvania, and New Jersey. From Massachusetts and Connecticut an almost endless procession of shrewd Yankees moved northward into Maine, New Hampshire, and Vermont, and then westward. By 1812 they had occupied the western shore of Lake Champlain, the St. Lawrence valley, the greater part of central, western, and southern New York, northeastern and northwestern Pennsylvania, and northeastern Ohio. In addition they had planted flourishing colonies in New Jersey, eastern Pennsylvania, and southern Ohio. After the second War of Independence most of the New Englanders swarmed into northern Indiana and Illinois or into southern Michigan and Wisconsin. Mid-western towns like Kirkland, Granville, Oberlin, Vermontville, Rockford, Beloit, and a score of others were veritable strongholds of New Englandism. Even today they are in many respects more truly representative of Puritan character and notions than the majority of the older New England towns. Between 1830 and 1840 thousands of thrifty, democratically-minded immigrants from southwestern Germany occupied the more sparsely populated sections of the states north of the Ohio. Among them were a large number of able, intelligent men who exerted a powerful influence upon the intellectual life of the Northwest. Thus Ohio, Indiana, and Illinois were settled in the main by Southerners, Northerners, and Germans. In Indiana and Illinois the southern element predominated; in Ohio, the northern. Clashes between the three factions were not infrequent, but under the influence of an environment more or less common to all, there developed a similarity of purpose and of ideals.

Central Ohio, Indiana, and Illinois colonized by Northerners

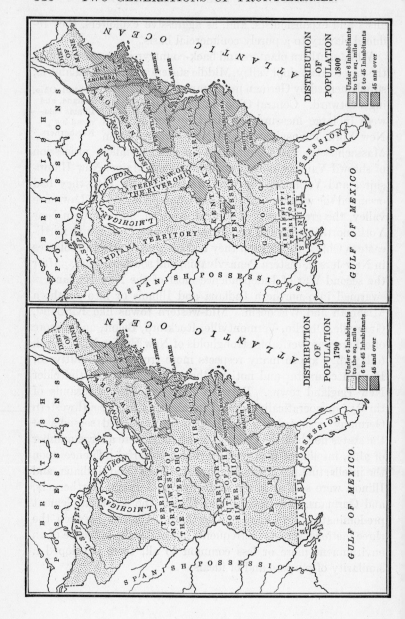

THE PIONEER MOTHER

B. Baker

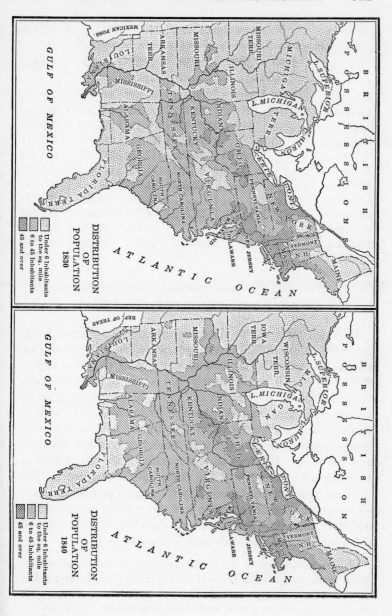

WESTERN POPULATION, 1790–1840

	1790	1800	1810	1820	1830	1840
Kentucky..	73,677	220,955	406,511	564,317	687,917	779,828
Tennessee..	35,691	105,602	261,727	422,823	681,904	829,210
Ohio......	.....	45,365	230,760	581,434	937,903	1,519,467
Louisiana..	.....	......	76,556	153,407	215,739	352,411
Indiana....	.....	5,641	24,520	147,178	343,031	685,866
Mississippi.	.....	8,850	40,352	75,448	136,621	375,651
Illinois	.....	......	12,282	55,211	157,445	476,183
Alabama...	.....	......	......	127,901	309,527	590,756
Missouri...	.....	......	20,845	66,586	140,455	383,702
Michigan...	.....	......	4,762	8,896	31,639	212,267
Arkansas...	.....	......	......	14,273	30,388	97,574
Florida.....	.....	......	......	......	34,730	54,477
Wisconsin..	.....	......	......	......	......	30,945

This table is based on United States Census Reports.

From whatever section the emigrant came, his journey West, especially before 1840, was not an easy one. In striking contrast **Methods of** with the traveler of the present day, who enjoys **getting West** rapid and relatively safe means of transportation, he made his way over rough and often dangerous roads or by slow-moving canal- and river-boats. Railroading prior to 1840 was still in the experimental stage, and up to that time was inconsequential as an agency of transport between the East and the West. Previous to the opening of the Erie Canal in 1825 the vast majority of the rising tide of western settlers went overland. Some traveled by stagecoach or wagon, others on horseback, and not a few on foot. It was the picture of this overland migration that Birkbeck depicted as he journeyed along the National Road through Pennsylvania in 1817.

We are seldom out of sight, (he observed), as we travel on this grand track, towards the Ohio, of family groups, behind and before us . . . A small waggon (so light that you might almost carry it, yet strong enough to bear a good load of bedding, utensils and provisions, and a swarm of young citizens, — and to sustain marvellous shocks in its passage over these rocky heights) with two small horses, sometimes a cow or two, comprises their all; excepting a little store of hard-earned cash for the land office of the district; where they may obtain a title for as many acres as they possess half-dollars, being one-fourth of the purchase money. The waggon has a tilt, or cover, made of a sheet, or perhaps a blanket. The family are seen before, behind, or within the vehicle, according to the road or the weather, or perhaps the spirits of the party. . . . A cart and single horse frequently affords the means of transfer, sometimes a horse and a pack-saddle. Often the back of the poor pilgrim bears all his effects, and his wife follows, naked-footed, bending under the hopes of the family.

Rarely during the first half of the nineteenth century did the emigrant go West alone; not only was he usually accompanied by his immediate family or a part thereof, but also by some neighboring household. It was even common in New England for colonies of eager home-seekers to move West together and there to lay the foundations of the pioneer towns which so closely resembled those of Massachusetts and Connecticut. As typical of this form of migration may be cited the twenty-odd wagons and 116 persons, all from a single New England town, that passed through Hamilton, New York, in 1817, on the way to Indiana. Southerners, too, journeyed to the transappalachian country in groups. The roads leading from Virginia, the Carolinas, and Georgia to Kentucky and Tennessee were, with few exceptions, always crowded with long trains of heavy, lumbering, canvas-covered Conestoga wagons, each drawn by four or six horses, laden with a precious cargo of humanity and household goods. Like the poorer classes of the North, Southerners without means trudged along on foot, carrying their scanty belongings on their back or in carts drawn by themselves. Planters and the well-to-do usually took with them their slaves and herds of cattle and sheep.

Fortunately for the emigrant, several natural highways led to the western country. Before the opening of the Erie Canal the majority of New Englanders either pushed over the Berkshires to Albany and thence along the valley of the Mohawk and the Genesee Turnpike to Lake Erie, or crossed the Hudson farther to the south and moved slowly over the Catskill Turnpike through southern New York to the upper waters of the Allegheny. From this point many leisurely floated down to Pittsburg on lumber rafts constructed from the pine forests of southwestern New York. A considerable number also made their way overland or by boat to New York, Philadelphia, and Baltimore, whence they went by a more southerly route. Most of the emigrants from the Middle states went by way of the old Philadelphia-Lancaster-Bedford-Pittsburg road, built by General Forbes during the French and Indian War. By 1830 the greater portion of this 350 miles of highway had been turnpiked. In many respects the most important route of all extended from Baltimore and Washington up the valley of the Potomac to Cumberland and thence over the National Road to Wheeling on the Ohio. This route, following in part Braddock's line of march to Redstone on the Monongahela, also connected with Pittsburg; over it passed great numbers of Virginians from the uplands and the Shenandoah valley to the Ohio country. Emigrants from southern Virginia and North Carolina generally followed up the Roanoke to the Great Divide, where they either turned to the northwest into the valley of the Kanawha River or to the southwest along the Holston and thence through the famous Cumberland Gap and along the wilderness road into Kentucky or into the valley of the Tennessee. From South Carolina the principal route extended through the Saluda Gap into eastern Tennessee. Two main routes converging at Fort Mitchell stretched from central Georgia into southern Alabama and Mississippi.

Before 1820, and even after that date, portions of these overland routes, especially west of the mountains, were only slightly improved. Swamps and unbridged streams were frequently encountered, breakdowns and delays were common, and the emigrant who averaged twenty miles a day was considered fortunate. As late as 1837 the unfavorable conditions of travel were noted by David Stevenson, a Scotch engineer, on a journey from Pittsburg to Erie:

Travel to West hazardous

Sometimes our road lay for miles through extensive marshes, which we crossed by corduroy roads, formed of trees . . . cut in lengths of

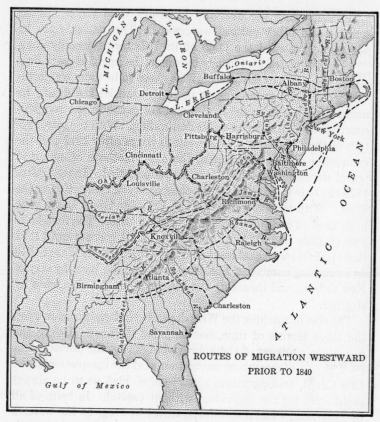

ROUTES OF MIGRATION WESTWARD
PRIOR TO 1840

about ten or twelve feet and laid close to each other across the road to prevent the vehicles from sinking; at others the coach stuck fast in the mud, from which it could be extricated only by the combined efforts of the coachman and the passengers; and at one place we traveled for upward of a quarter of a mile through a forest flooded with water which stood to the height of several feet on many of the trees, and occasionally covered the naves of the coach wheels. The distance of the route from Pittsburg to Erie is one hundred and twenty-eight miles, which was accomplished in forty-six hours, being at the very slow rate of two miles and three-quarters an hour, although the conveyance by which I traveled carried the mail and stopped only for breakfast, dinner and tea, but there was considerable delay caused by the coach being once upset and several times mired.

Supplementing the overland highways were the numerous streams and other natural waterways. The settler, once he reached the Ohio or its tributaries, usually completed his journey by water; he might embark on a raft or flatboat or, if he chose to be more comfortable, on an ark or more substantial keel-boat; he might even resort to the frail birchbark canoe or the roughly-constructed dugout to reach his destination. With the introduction of the steamboat on the western rivers after 1812 and the completion of the Erie Canal, the older methods of emigrant travel were to a considerable extent superseded. Indeed, after 1825 the Erie Canal became the chief artery of emigration to the West. With the exception of Lake Erie, the Great Lakes were little used as emigrant highways prior to 1840. The first Lake Erie steamer was not built until 1818, and it was not until 1832 that the first steamboat reached Chicago. After the War of 1812 an increasing number of Easterners reached the West by way of New Orleans and thence up the Mississippi and its branches by steamer.

Overland routes supplemented by natural waterways

The cost of reaching the West depended in large measure upon the three factors of time, method, and distance. Before the advent of the improved highway, the development of steamboat navigation, and the completion of the Erie Canal, transportation rates were so high as to be almost prohibitive for the individual without capital. In spite of all its annoyances and discomforts, travel by stage to the western country was counted a luxury. Passenger rates were arbitrarily determined on a freight basis, the traveler being considered to weigh 100 pounds; if he was so unfortunate as to tip the scales at 200 pounds he was compelled to pay double fare. Stage rates from Philadelphia or Baltimore to Pittsburg before the Erie Canal came into use were approximately five or six dollars per hundredweight; over other routes the rates were even higher. With the competition of the great New York waterway and the steamboat, however, stage lines were forced to reduce their charges. In 1830 it was possible to travel by stage and steamboat from Philadelphia to St. Louis for about fifty-five dollars, but if the homeseeker chose to patronize two

Cost of reaching West

other conveniences of travel — the taverns and the ferries — his expenses were considerably increased.

Travel by water was, of course, very much cheaper. On the canals expenses averaged about fifty cents a day. Horace Greeley in his *Recollections* tells us that he jour- Relative neyed from Albany to Buffalo by way of the Erie cheapness of Canal at the rate of "a cent and a half a mile, mile water travel and a half an hour," or thirty-six miles for fifty-four cents. In *A New Guide for Emigrants to the West*, published in 1836, rates from Philadelphia to points west by way of the Pennsylvania Canal and the Ohio River were listed as follows:

		Miles	Days	Cost
Fare to	Pittsburg	400	6½	$6.00
" "	Cincinnati......	900	8½	8.50
" "	Louisville	1050	9½	9.00
" "	Nashville	1650	13½	13.00
" "	St. Louis.......	1750	14	13.00

Emigrants and travelers were warned, however, to be somewhat skeptical relative to statements made by stage, steam- and canal-boat agents, to make allowance for delays, additional expense, and other difficulties and, above all, "to feel perfectly patient and in good humor with themselves, the officers, company, and the world," if they should not make as rapid progress or fare as well as they might desire. On the river steamers before 1840 one could secure a cabin passage from New Orleans to Pittsburg for from thirty-five to forty-five dollars; for deck or steerage passengers who furnished their own food and lodging the cost was only one-fifth as great.

But the western journey was least expensive for those emigrants who furnished their own conveyances and camped by the wayside at night. From farmers along the route Cheapest they easily purchased the necessary forage and grain method of for their horses and food for themselves at prices reaching West ridiculously low. Hay and grain for a four-horse team cost from fifty cents to a dollar a day; beef, mutton, and pork could be had for from two to three cents a pound; fresh fowls sold for four to ten cents a pound; and flour often for less than it cost to transport it. For those families with little capital it was imperative that they should make the trip as cheaply as possible in order to save as much as they could toward the purchase of their western home.

Generally speaking, the West was occupied by three classes of frontiersmen. Following in the wake of the fur trader came the genuine pioneer — "the blazer of the westward march of civilization." Pushing into the forest wilderness with his family and sometimes a horse, a cow, and one or two breeders of swine, he proceeded by means of his trusty axe to clear a small patch of ground, to build a rude log cabin, and perhaps a stable and a crib for corn. In this stumpy clearing he managed by means of rough, home-made implements to grow cabbage, beans, sweet corn, cucumbers, potatoes, and sometimes grain for his stock. Forest and stream furnished him with an abundance of game and fish, and by hunting and trapping he secured a little ready cash. If ambitious, he cleared additional land by girdling and burning the forest, fenced his fields, and improved his dwelling. If shiftless and indolent, or a victim of malarial fever, as he often was, he merely eked out an existence in a miserable and unkempt abode. When neighbors began to crowd around, or game became scarce, or his soil grew less productive, he became more and more restive — he craved the wilderness solitude; without formal education and unfamiliar with the refinements of life, civilized society annoyed him. In its presence he felt cramped, out of place, and unhappy, and was ever ready, therefore, to dispose of his cabin and clearing and to push forward to a new frontier beyond the immediate call of civilization. To sell out and remove five or six times in a generation was not an uncommon occurrence.

Three classes of frontiersmen

1. The genuine pioneer

Closely trailing the wilderness invader, came the pioneer farmer. With his hard-earned savings he purchased the clearing of the backwoodsman and, by dint of many sacrifices and careful planning, cleared his land of stumps, added new fields, planted orchards, constructed barns and outbuildings, and eventually erected a frame house that had glass windows and a chimney of brick or stone.

2. The pioneer farmer

In coöperation with his neighbors he improved the roads, built bridges, school houses, churches, and court houses. His finely pulverized land soon produced not only abundant crops for his family and livestock, but gave him a surplus for export. His life was that of a plain, frugal farmer. But as the years rolled by and population increased, he readily took advantage of the rise in property values to sell his farm at a handsome profit to men of capital and enterprise who came from the East. Having disposed of his land, he either pushed on into the interior to purchase another clearing or became a speculator or townsman. Sometimes, however, the pioneer farmer, as well as the backwoodsman, remained on his original tract, improved his property, and shared in the benefits of the steadily advancing civilization. Particularly was this true if he were prosperous and desired to rise in the scale of society.

Long before 1840 the fringe of settlement extended beyond the wooded country to the open prairies. Meanwhile a third type of emigrant was advancing west of the Alleghenies. He was neither roving frontiersman nor pioneer farmer — but a permanent settler. He came not for love of adventure, but to improve his economic and social position. Compared with tax-ridden Europe, or the rocky hills of New England, or the sandy plains of the Atlantic seaboard, the West, with its virgin soil, was to him nothing short of a real paradise. He enjoyed settled conditions and the routine of everyday life, and, therefore, became either a homesteader or the citizen of a rising western town. Largely because of his influence, the countryside underwent another transformation, and small villages rapidly developed into spacious towns and cities with their churches, colleges, and substantial edifices of brick and stone.

3. The permanent settler

Thus wave after wave rolled westward. Had the aeroplane been in use in 1840, a keen observer could have gained a panoramic view of western society. West of the Mississippi his eyes might have followed restless bands of savage Indians; along the frontier he would have discerned hunters and woodsmen blazing the way for civilization; shifting his gaze toward the east he

Various stages of civilization in West of 1840

would have observed a wave of pioneer farmers, followed in turn by a wave of permanent settlers whose institutional life closely resembled that of the coast states. Year after year these successive waves rolled onward, transforming and being transformed.

3. FRONTIER PROBLEMS

Indian relations, title to his land, ready money, a system of credit, and an adequate market for his produce were among the more important problems which the western settler faced. At the close of the Revolution ownership of the vast region west of the Alleghenies was claimed by the Indians and, by a series of acts, Congress attempted to safeguard their rights, at the same time endeavoring to meet the needs of the emigrant by negotiating a number of Indian treaties providing for the cession of considerable tracts of territory. Despite these pacific efforts the Northwest was soon engulfed in Indian warfare, which finally terminated with the overwhelming defeat of the redmen in 1794 at the battle of Fallen Timbers by an army under the command of Anthony Wayne. As a result the Treaty of Greenville, negotiated in 1795, completely crowded the Indians out of southern and eastern Ohio.

Chief problems

1. Indian relations

But the frontiersman was no respecter of Indian treaties, and less than a dozen years elapsed before he was violating treaty agreements by overrunning Indian lands as he pushed his way through northwestern Ohio and Indiana territory into the Wabash country. Wholly in sympathy with the pioneer in his policy of excluding the Indians by any means whatsoever from what they staunchly maintained to be their rightful property was William Henry Harrison, who had been named by President Jefferson as governor of Indiana territory. By treating with certain irresponsible local chieftains he succeeded in 1804 and 1805 in despoiling whole tribes of some of their most valuable hunting grounds. Naturally this action was bitterly resented by more intelligent and foresighted Indian leaders like Tecumseh and his brother, the Prophet, sons of a Shawnee warrior. To fore-

Indians of Northwest crowded back by advancing frontier

stall its repetition they proposed the formation of a confederacy of all the frontier tribes from the Great Lakes to the Gulf, which would confer upon a congress of warriors sole authority to dispose of Indian lands. Scarcely had Prophets Town, the capital of this Indian confederacy, been founded in 1808 before Governor Harrison, again dealing with the same irresponsible sachems, secured title to the rich valley of the Wabash. Three years later the plans of Tecumseh and the Prophet were shattered when Harrison, invading unceded Indian lands, defeated the Indians in the hotly contested battle of Tippecanoe and destroyed the seat of their confederacy.

In the Gulf region Andrew Jackson, who believed the only good Indian to be a dead Indian, at the head of a column of Tennessee frontiersmen, completely defeated the western Creeks, who had been incited to hostilities by the agents of Tecumseh at the battle of Horseshoe Bend in 1814. In consequence the Creek chieftains were compelled to sign a treaty ceding all their territory, with the exception of two isolated tracts, one in western Georgia and eastern Alabama and the other in northern and central Alabama. These conquered provinces, both North and South, opened up vast territories for settlement and relieved the emigrant from danger of Indian attack. *Defeat of western Creeks by Andrew Jackson*

Between the close of the War of 1812 and 1840 Indian title in practically all the territory east of the Mississippi was extinguished. For a time the ancient practice of driving the tribesmen from pillar to post, but always toward the west, prevailed. Finally, in 1825, John C. Calhoun, President Monroe's Secretary of War, worked out a different, if not entirely satisfactory, policy. "One of the greatest evils to which they are subject," said he, "is the incessant pressure of our population which forces them from seat to seat." As a remedy Calhoun urged that the Indians be given permanent homes in the great plain area beyond Missouri. Here were limitless tracts abounding in game where, according to the best scientific opinion of the time, the white man could not live. Calhoun's recommendations were accepted, and during the next fifteen *Change in Indian policy* years the process of transferring the tribes to their new home, west of the new frontier, was carried out.

In the Northwest in 1832 an attempt by the Sac and Fox tribes, under their chief Black Hawk, to regain ceded land in **Difficulties of** western Illinois and southwestern Wisconsin led to **removal** a devastating frontier war in which the Indians suffered defeat. In the Southwest, however, the Indians, who were protected by constitutional guarantees, were dislodged only after a strenuous contest. Here the semi-civilized Creeks, Cherokees, Choctaws, and Chickasaws had ceded large tracts of territory between 1814 and 1830, but they still retained control of 33,571,176 acres in Georgia, Alabama, Tennessee, and Mississippi. That fifty thousand "inferior" people should monopolize such extensive territory seemed preposterous to the hungry landseeker; the individual states affected, particularly Georgia, entertained a similar opinion. Indeed, for forty years the presence of these independent Indian nations within her boundaries had been considered by Georgia as a menace and an obstacle to her development. She, therefore, repeatedly urged that the Federal government acquire title to these lands so that they might be opened up for settlement.

To this end a treaty ceding all Creek lands in Georgia had been negotiated with a few Creek chiefs in 1825 only to be sub- **Reluctance of** sequently repudiated by the majority as fraudulent **Creeks and** and unrepresentative of the will of the Creek nation. **Cherokees to** After careful investigation President John Quincy **leave old** Adams concluded that the Creeks were right and **homes** directed that a new treaty be negotiated. Meanwhile, Georgia, in spite of the threats and remonstrances of the Federal government, insisted upon its right to survey the lands ceded under the original treaty. This unfortunate controversy, in the course of which Georgia threatened to resist the authority of the national government, was satisfactorily adjusted when in 1826 and 1827 the Creeks signed treaties extinguishing their claims to their Georgian territory. The contest between Georgia and the Cherokees was in many respects no less acute. By a revision of their tribal constitution in 1827 the Cherokees, the most highly civilized of the southwestern Indians, indicated their

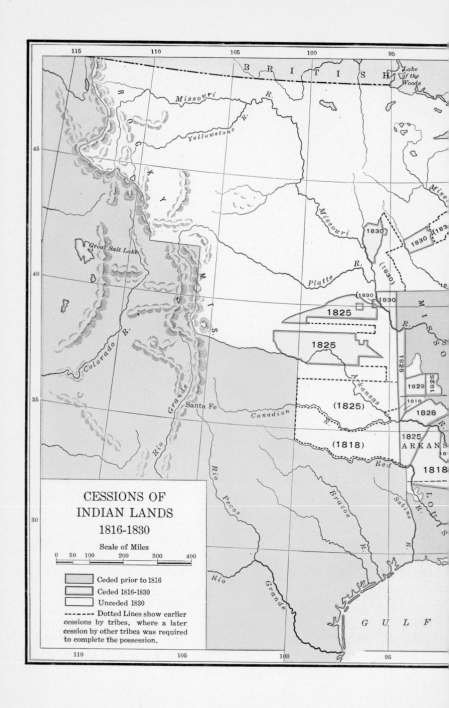

CESSIONS OF
INDIAN LANDS
1816-1830

Scale of Miles

0   50 100   200   300   400

Ceded prior to 1816

Ceded 1816-1830

Unceded 1830

- - - - - Dotted Lines show earlier
cessions by tribes, where a later
cession by other tribes was required
to complete the possession.

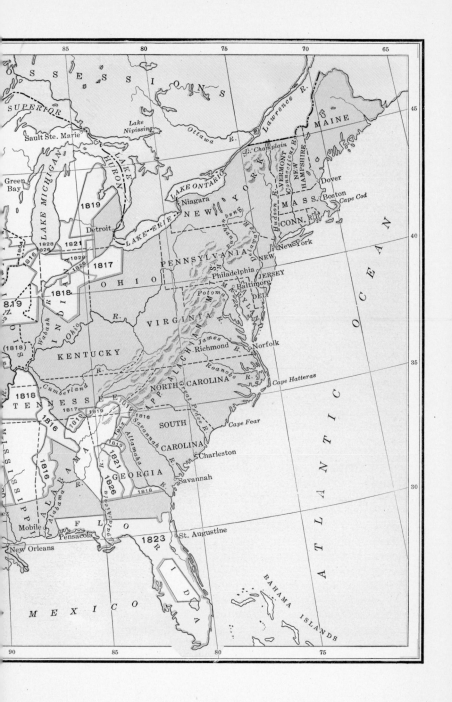

intention of remaining indefinitely as a sovereign community within the boundaries of Georgia. Late in 1828 the legislature of that state, without treaty action or consent of the Federal government, extended her authority over the Cherokee lands by annexing them to five adjacent counties. The statute further directed that after June 1, 1830, all laws of the Cherokee nation should be null and void and its citizens subject to the jurisdiction of the state. The tribal leaders at once protested to Washington, but President Adams, seemingly helpless, took no action.

When President Jackson assumed office, however, he at once took steps to settle the difficulty. Through Secretary of War Eaton the Cherokee representatives were informed that they must either "yield to the operation of those laws which Georgia claims, and has a right to extend throughout her own limits," or else remove beyond the Mississippi. This policy was substantially reiterated by Jackson in his annual messages of 1829, 1830, and 1833. Justice and humanity, he said, required that the southwestern tribes be saved from destruction, a fate which surely awaited them if they remained islands in a white population or continued to be driven "from river to river and mountain to mountain" by a superior race. He therefore proposed that they remove west of the Mississippi where ample territory would be set apart for their occupancy. If they chose to remain, however, they must submit to the laws of the state in which they lived and surrender such lands as they could not profitably use. Although they would not be violently deprived of their treaty rights, every effort would be made, he declared, to induce them to surrender such rights for the benefit of all concerned.

Federal pressure on Creeks and Cherokees

For a time the Indians remained obdurate, the Cherokees seeking to restrain the actions of the irate Georgians. In Worcester *vs.* Georgia, a test case before the United States Supreme Court, Justice Marshall in an elaborate opinion held that the Cherokees were still a nation within whose territory "the laws of Georgia can have no force, and which the citizens of Georgia have no right to

Worcester vs. Georgia

enter but with the assent of the Cherokees themselves or in conformity with treaties and with the Acts of Congress." But Georgia refused to accept the ruling of the Court, and even Jackson, whose sympathy for the pioneer and whose hatred of the Chief Justice were well known, is reputed to have said "John Marshall has made his decision; now let him enforce it." Finally, in 1835, the Cherokees yielded, the majority moving westward to join their fellow-tribesmen who were already settling in the territory set apart for them by Congress. In the ten-year period from 1827 to 1837 over a hundred Indian treaties, most of them treaties of cession, were concluded.

Of no less concern to the western settler than the Indian question was the problem of valid title to his land. By the **2. Land title** close of the Revolution pioneers, as we have seen, had settled the western counties of Pennsylvania and what today constitutes the eastern portions of the present states of West Virginia, Kentucky, and Tennessee. Indeed, until after 1790 the westward movement was confined almost entirely to these regions and to Maine, Vermont, New Hampshire, **Western lands source of jealousy** western New York, and central Georgia. In other words, the territories settled were under the jurisdiction of the states instead of the national government. In 1780 Massachusetts, Connecticut, Virginia, North and South Carolina, and Georgia, by virtue of their old colonial charters, and New York, by treaty with the Iroquois, claimed jurisdiction over the greater portion of the extensive domain between the Applachians and the Mississippi. Many of these claims overlapped and consequently were a subject of bitter dispute. Quite naturally, too, the six states without western territory were jealous of their more fortunate neighbors, who regarded their western lands as a source of future wealth. Thanks to the insistence of Maryland and to the influence of men like Thomas Paine, these western lands, with the exception of West Virginia and Kentucky, were ceded to the United States with the tacit understanding that they should be sold and the money applied on the public debt. By 1786 the territory north of the Ohio had been surrendered; south of that river, however, the claims proved more difficult of adjustment, and it was not until after 1802 that Georgia consented to accept her present boundaries.

The first cessions had scarcely been made when the Congress of the Confederation took steps to organize this immense colonial domain. Accordingly in 1784 it adopted, with two exceptions, a general ordinance drafted by Thomas Jefferson providing that the territory should (1) forever remain a part of the United States; (2) that it should be subject to the Congress and the Articles of Confederation; (3) that it should be divided into ten states; (4) that the constitution of each state be modeled after those of the original states; (5) that a permanent government be formed and the election of a delegate to Congress be provided for when the population numbered 20,000; (6) that each state be admitted to the Union when the number of inhabitants equaled "the least numerous of the thirteen original states," and (7) that each state pay its share of the Revolutionary debts. The article forbidding slavery in any of the territories after 1800 was rejected by a single vote, and the Congress sensibly refused to accept such grotesque names as Assenisippia, Pelisipia, Cherronesus, Metropotamia, and Polypotamia, as proposed by Jefferson for several of the new states.

But the Ordinance of 1784 was only the forerunner of the better known and more important Ordinance of 1787 under which the region north of the Ohio, or the Northwest Territory, was finally organized. Shaped largely by the guiding hand of the Reverend Manasseh Cutler of Salem, Massachusetts, an agent of the Ohio Associates, a New England speculative organization interested in the settlement of the Ohio country, the ordinance provided for (1) the division of the territory into not less than three nor more than five states, instead of ten as planned by Jefferson; (2) the appointment by Congress of a governor, three judges, and a secretary to administer the territory until it attained an adult population of 5,000, when it should have a representative assembly with power to make laws subject to the governor's veto, an appointive council, and a non-voting delegate in Congress; (3) the creation of six "articles of compact" providing for personal liberty, religious freedom, the introduction of a system of free, public education, the exclusion of slavery, and federal supremacy. Before the end of the year the first territorial government had been established and the Ordinance put into operation.

Meanwhile in the so-called Land Ordinance of 1785 the foundations of our national land system had been laid. Applying, Land Ordinance of 1785 as it did, to the region northwest of the Ohio, it provided that as soon as the Indian title thereto had been acquired by the government the territory should be surveyed into a series of townships six miles square, and each township into thirty-six lots or "sections" of 640 acres each. After reserving to the national government one-seventh of every township to satisfy the claims of the soldiers of the Continental Army, and one-third of any mineral ore which might be found, the measure directed that the remainder be distributed among the states, to be auctioned off alternately by townships or by lots at a minimum cash price of one dollar per acre plus thirty-six dollars per township to cover the cost of survey. The Ordinance further provided that the sixteenth section of each township be set aside for the support of education, and that each purchaser receive with his deed a definite description of his holding. Although subsequent amendments to the Ordinance enabled the prospective settler to pay one-third in cash and the balance at the end of three months, only about 73,000 acres had been disposed of to individuals by 1788. Indian menace, sparseness of population, competition of state domains, the size of the lots, and the opportunity for the poorer pioneer to become a squatter, together with the major interest of the government in securing revenues from these western lands instead of putting them into the hands of actual settlers as speedily as possible, account in large measure for the relatively slight amount of land sold.

During these early days Congress also made land grants to a number of private speculative companies. Of these the Ohio Land grants to private companies Company perhaps deserves first mention. Organized by General Rufus Putnam primarily for the purpose of enabling the officers of the Revolutionary Army to retrieve their fortunes, this company through the efforts of the Reverend M. Cutler, to whom we have already alluded, secured 5,000,000 acres in the present state of Ohio. Cutler tells us that only a million and a half acres of this grant went to the Ohio Company, the remainder "for a private speculation in which many of the principal characters of America" were concerned. John Cleve Symmes, a wealthy resident of New Jersey, inspired by the Ohio Company, also organized a company to speculate in western lands and petitioned for 2,000,000 acres in the Ohio country. Incidentally, these sales aided neither the government nor the settler in any considerable degree, but rather speculators and speculative interests.

While the average settler welcomed accurate surveys and desired clear title, he was not always willing to wait for Indian claims to be extinguished. Nor was he satisfied with the method of sale and payment inaugurated by the Ordinance of 1785. Accordingly in 1796 Congress directed that the surveyed lands be sold at auction at Cincinnati and Pittsburg in 640-acre lots on a year's credit and at a minimum price of two dollars per acre. But the sales were disappointing, only 50,000 acres being disposed of in the course of four years. By the Act of 1800 — the Harrison Land Act — the system was further modified and the credit scheme extended. Henceforth the settler could purchase his land in quantities of not less than half-sections of 320 acres at land offices near the frontier; for it he paid two dollars an acre, fifty cents per acre at the time of purchase and the balance in instalments extending over a period of four years. In 1804 the minimum acreage that could be sold was reduced to a quarter-section or 160 acres. By 1820 the government had deeded under the Act of 1800 no less than 18,117,860 acres to purchasers, receiving therefor approximately $46,639,478. In some instances the better lands sold for more than the minimum price.

But the system was still far from satisfactory to either the settler or the government. Taking advantage of the deferred payment plan, thousands of *bona fide* settlers purchased large holdings, expecting to sell part to incoming emigrants at a profit and to keep the remainder for themselves. Speculators in search of easy wealth bought on credit immense tracts which they in turn disposed of on a credit basis to newcomers at vastly higher rates. But the War of 1812, together with the restrictive Acts preceding it, retarded our overseas trade. Hard times ensued, and many soon found themselves unable to make their land payments. To make matters worse, the federal government in 1817 ruled that it would accept payment in specie only. By 1820 more than $21,000,000 was due the government for unpaid instalments. Even before the Panic of 1819 many settlers and speculators alike found themselves unable to pay, and in desperation they appealed to the government for relief. For a time Congress heeded their importunities by simply arranging time extensions, but in 1821 it passed a general Act enabling those who had not completed their payments within the prescribed time to surrender their unpaid-for land and apply any payments already made thereon toward the cost of the land which they retained. The government also, much to the disgust of eastern taxpayers, remitted all interest arrears on unpaid accounts.

While Congress was thus engaged in relieving the overburdened land debtor it proceeded to abolish the credit system. **Land Act of** By the Act of 1820 the public domain was hence- **1820** forth to be sold in 80-acre tracts, for cash, and at a minimum price of one dollar and a quarter per acre. Many eastern business men, particularly the rising manufacturers and the enterprising builders of canals, turnpikes, and railways, roundly denounced the Act. Only higher land values in the West, they maintained, would keep taxes low, check the drain of population westward, and prevent higher wages in the industrial states of the East. Speculators, too, against whom the change of policy was largely directed, were not over-enthusiastic about the new system. For the real settler, however, the act was a godsend, for no longer was he tempted by a credit system to purchase beyond his actual available capital. For a thousand dollars in 1820 he could easily acquire a 320-acre farm on the edge of the Illinois prairie. His land, one-half tillable and one-half pasture and timber, would cost him four hundred dollars; fencing 160 acres of it, one hundred and sixty dollars; the preparation of one-half of it for planting, three hundred and twenty dollars; and cabin, stables, and other farm buildings, one hundred and twenty dollars. If too poor for such an outlay, he might purchase and equip an 80-acre farm for approximately four hundred dollars.

Many a pioneer at first bought no land at all, but simply became an unauthorized dweller or squatter on government domain, hoping that Congress would at some future time legalize his action and allow him to pay for his tract at the minimum price. In the latter respect he was not disappointed, for in spite of the opposition and angry protests of eastern Congressmen, no less than seventeen special Preemption Acts were passed before 1840. The following year Congress enacted a general Preëmption Law, long urged by Thomas Hart Benton, ardent champion of the western pioneer. By its terms the head of a family, a man over twenty-one years of age, or a widow gained the right to settle on a piece of land 160 acres in extent, and to purchase the same at a subsequent date free from competitive bids, at the minimum government price. While the "Log Cabin Bill," as Benton shrewdly dubbed the preëmption measure, was under consideration Easterners, particularly business men, advanced all the arguments at their command against it.

The squatter

Between the date of its passage and the Civil War repeated attempts were made both in and out of Congress to modify the Act of 1820; but, with the exception of liberal grants of territory to several states for internal improvements and to transportation companies, no important change of policy was adopted until 1862, when President Lincoln signed the Homestead Act. Under the law of 1820 large sums poured into the national treasury from land sales. Indeed, the receipts from this source for the single decade 1830 to 1840 totaled almost $82,000,000.

Act of 1820 not modified until 1862

Like his colonial ancestor, the western pioneer was always face to face with the problem of currency and credit. He needed money to cover the cost of his migration, to make the payments on his land, and to provide for himself and his family until his farm should become self-supporting. Having little or no money except what they had borrowed from well-to-do individuals in the East or

3. The problem of currency and credit

from some eastern bank to make the initial payment on their land, the first Westerners to go into the wilderness used barter or else resorted to rude mediums of exchange, such as a given weight of furs, grain, or tobacco. As population increased and trade developed with the Spanish at New Orleans, a small amount of Spanish silver seeped into the western country and, until the War of 1812, remained the principal currency of the region. With the opening of that conflict, however, trade relations with Europe, as we shall see, were interrupted, and the West as well as the South was forced to depend upon the East for manufactured goods. Cotton, tobacco, hemp, flour, grain, whisky, and livestock were sent to New England and the Middle states in exchange for hardware, crockery, boots and shoes, cloth, and other commodities. The resulting balance of trade in favor of the East drained the West of its hard money. The specie in Boston banks, totaling less than $800,000 in 1812, amounted to over $7,000,000 in 1814. Western banks then in existence were forced to suspend specie payments and began to issue unsecured paper currency to meet the demand for money.

When peace came in 1815 an unprecedented wave of prosperity swept over the country and particularly the West. Speculation became epidemic. Farmers, in their enthusiasm

Multiplication of state banks and paper money

for more land, mortgaged their property; newly organized companies projected improvements of every kind; prices rose steadily, and manufactured goods were imported in ever increasing quantities. To satisfy the demand of the speculative populace for ready money, banks — both state and private — multiplied to 307 by 1820, and the country was rapidly flooded with paper currency unprotected by specie reserves. Scarcely a western state legislature met that did not charter a crop of new banks; by 1818 Kentucky had fifty-nine such institutions and Ohio twenty-eight. In Janesville, Ohio, no less than thirty kinds of paper money were circulated in 1817, not to mention the "shinplasters," ranging in face value from three cents to two dollars, issued by city and village authorities, internal improvement and manufacturing companies, merchants, tavern-keepers, and even shoeblacks. "Silver could hardly have been more plentiful at Jerusalem in

the days of Solomon," remarked an observer, "than paper
money was in Ohio, Kentucky, and adjoining regions."

But in spite of the fact that the loaners of this fiat money had
secured mortgages covering most of the property of the borrow-
ers, the paper currency rapidly depreciated. "The
money in circulation," said the traveler Flint, "is
puzzling to traders and more particularly to
strangers; for besides the multiplicity of banks and
the diversity in supposed value, fluctuations are so frequent,
and so great, that no man who holds it in his possession can be
safe for a day. The merchant when asked the price of an article,
instead of making a direct answer, usually puts the question:
'What sort of money have you got?'"

Depreciation of paper currency and its ill effects

Such was the situation when in 1818 the directors of the
second United States Bank, an institution chartered by the
federal government in 1816 and in control of most
of the specie of the country, alarmed by the rapid
expansion of credit, issued instructions virtually
compelling state banks to redeem their notes in specie or close
their doors. The western banks, although unable to meet this
requirement before 1822, brought pressure to bear on their
debtors, and mortgage foreclosures became the order of the day.
Produce prices tumbled, and land values sharply declined.
Western farmers and merchants especially were in desperate
straits, for they were deeply in debt not only to local banks but
to eastern commercial houses and to each other. On every hand
financial ruin and universal distress were evident.

Contraction of currency and distress

For their unhappy condition the western people blamed the
National Bank. "All the flourishing cities of the West," said
Thomas Hart Benton, "are mortgaged to this
money power. They may be devoured by it at any
moment. They are in the jaws of the monster!"
From its inception the "monster" had been regarded by Westerners as an undemocratic, monopolistic institution, the creature of the moneyed East. In 1816 Indiana by
constitutional provision attempted to prevent the establishment within its limits of any bank not chartered by the state;
two years later her example was followed by Illinois.

Western states show resentment to National Bank

Between 1816 and 1819 Ohio, Kentucky, and Tennessee, as well as the agrarian states of Maryland, North Carolina, and Georgia followed the example of Indiana and Illinois by imposing by statute heavy taxes upon branches of the National Bank. Ohio and Tennessee, for example, imposed a tax of $50,000, and Kentucky $60,000. In 1819, however, Chief Justice Marshall in the famous cases of McCulloch *vs.* Maryland and Osborn *vs.* United States Bank held that the act chartering the Bank was constitutional and emphatically asserted that the states had no constitutional power to tax the branches thereof. This ruling was bitterly resented in the West, and in 1821 the legislature of Ohio, after reaffirming the Virginia and Kentucky Resolutions by way of protest, passed an act practically outlawing the United States Bank. Kentucky was equally hostile in attitude toward the institution of the "moneyed aristocrats." But neither she nor her sister states west of the Alleghenies contented themselves with measures of opposition toward the National Bank. Practically every western state took steps to relieve its debtor class; Kentucky, Tennessee, Illinois, and Missouri, for instance, enacted replevin and stay laws granting the debtor an extension of time in satisfying executions of foreclosure. "People's Banks" were chartered, and the sale of land under execution to pay debts was forbidden unless it brought three-fourths of the value set upon it by a board of appraisers, who were usually neighbors and themselves debtors.

These and similar measures led to a bitter struggle, especially in Kentucky, between the "hard money" and "easy money" factions, terminating finally in a victory for the former. Fundamentally the contest was barren of result in so far as it solved the problem either of an adequate currency or a satisfactory credit system. If anything, it left the easy money men more determined than before in their opposition to banks in general and to the National Bank in particular. Most significant of all, it made them enthusiastic and devoted followers of Andrew Jackson, son of the West, who was later to declare uncompromising warfare on the "money monopoly" at whose hands they firmly believed they had suffered.

More vexatious to the western settler than either Indian hostility or the question of land titles or even the matter of money and credit, was the problem of an adequate market for his surplus products. As late as 1825 **4. Adequate markets** western population was over ninety-five per cent agricultural and widely scattered. Western cities, as we have noted, were as yet small and few in number and consequently consumed only a small portion of the surplus grain and livestock of the western farm. Lack of cheap transportation facilities over the Appalachians, before the opening of the Erie Canal and the era of railroading, in large measure cut the Westerner off from the valuable markets of the eastern seaboard. Although many turnpikes were built before the first quarter of the nineteenth century had passed, most of them, as we shall see, being located in the East were not of particular service to the pioneer farmer. Freight charges over the Cumberland Road and other improved eastern highways were prohibitive for bulky and heavy commodities like flour and grain. The maximum price for western wheat before 1825 appears to have been seventy-five cents per bushel, while the cost of transporting it overland from Pittsburg to Philadelphia was three dollars per hundredweight, or approximately one dollar and fifty cents per bushel. Even Virginia farmers residing less than a hundred miles from the tidewater in 1818 complained that it took "one bushel of wheat to pay the expense of carrying two to a seaport town." What was true of wheat was equally true of corn and other agricultural commodities. On his fertile soil the transappalachian farmer could easily produce corn in abundance, but a selling price ranging from twelve and a half to seventy-five cents per bushel amounted to only a fraction of the cost of transporting it overland.

In an effort to overcome this serious handicap the farmers of western New York and northern Ohio sent their produce by water to Quebec and Montreal. Others not so fortunately located turned their crops into whisky or raised livestock, both of which were less expensive to market. Until about 1820 the main highways leading from the West to the East were crowded with droves of cattle and hogs on the way to market **Methods employed by Westerners to lessen transportation costs** from the Ohio valley. Kentucky, it was estimated, transported to the East annually over 100,000 hogs in this manner; other thousands were driven from the same state to the plantations of Virginia and the Carolinas. From the valley of the Ohio too came droves of mules and horses for the southern planter. In the decade from 1820 to 1830 livestock to the value of over two million dollars per year passed through the Saluda and Cumberland gaps to the Old South.

Under such circumstances the western farmer early became a staunch advocate of internal improvements. He welcomed and defended every proposal for better means of communication and transportation. Through his spokesmen, both in and out of Congress, he never lost an opportunity to urge the federal government to link up the West with the East by means of turnpikes, canals, and railroads. Henry Clay spoke for the Westerner when in 1824 he complained that Congress had done "everything on the margin of the ocean but nothing for domestic trade; nothing for the great interior of the country," that "new world" which had come into being after the adoption of the Constitution.

Westerner an advocate of internal improvements

Prior to 1825 the bulk of the surplus products of the West reached the markets of the East and of Europe by way of the Mississippi. Down it and its tributaries floated all kinds of craft loaded with furs, hay, flour, grain, hemp, livestock, tobacco, whisky, and lumber. In 1822, three years before the opening of the Erie Canal, it was estimated that more than three million dollars worth of agricultural produce reached New Orleans from the Ohio valley alone. Even in 1830, after the great New York waterway was open to traffic, approximately $28,000,000 worth of produce from the Mississippi basin was reshipped from New Orleans to the marts of the East and the Old World.

Importance of Mississippi and its tributaries as highways of transportation

The conviction on the part of every pioneer, whether trapper, farmer, land speculator, or trader, that his existence depended on keeping the Mississippi open from its source to its mouth was one of the major reasons for the acquisition by the United States of the vast Louisiana tract. Unfortunately for the Westerner's peace of

Problem of markets intimately related to acquisition of Louisiana

THE MISSISSIPPI AT NEW ORLEANS IN 1828

mind, the mouth of the Mississippi passed into the hands of Spain in 1763 with the French cession of Louisiana. Rivalry and hard feeling soon cropped out between the free and easy western boatmen and the Spanish authorities, with the result that in 1788 the Spaniards attempted to close the river to American commerce.

Angered beyond words, the exasperated Americans simultaneously proposed a filibustering expedition against New Orleans and issued an ultimatum threatening secession should the weak government of the Confederation accede to the Spanish demand that the United States surrender for twenty-five years all claims to navigate the Mississippi. Finally, after prolonged and vexatious parleying, Thomas Pinckney succeeded in negotiating the Treaty of San Lorenzo in 1795, by the terms of which Spain agreed to give citizens of the United States free navigation of the Mississippi and the right to land their goods in New Orleans free of duty or other payment while awaiting transshipment. These privileges, granted for a term of three years only, were withdrawn in 1798. Again the transappalachian people were threatened with ruin, again they memorialized Congress, and again they proposed an expedition against New Orleans. Although the difficulty was once more temporarily adjusted, it was more evident than ever that the peace and prosperity of the West depended upon American ownership of New Orleans and the mouth of the Mississippi. Fortunately for the Westerner a succession of events soon occurred to bring this about.

Foreign control of mouth of Mississippi angers West

The first of these events centered around the irresistible Napoleon in whose hands thrones and nations were already being shifted like so many pawns upon the European chessboard. In his search for new fields of conquest the wily Corsican, together with that crafty diplomat Talleyrand, planned to reëstablish in the heart of the North American continent that vast colonial empire which France had lost a generation before. When, therefore, Spain was called upon to restore Louisiana to France in 1801 she had no alternative other than to comply. Owing to political complications every effort was made to keep the cession strictly secret. De-

France regains Louisiana

spite this fact rumors that Louisiana was once more in the hands of France soon began to circulate, and these rumors threw the West into a fever of excitement. Even many of those whose homes and interests were along the Atlantic seaboard were aroused. "Every eye in the United States," wrote President Jefferson, "is now fixed on this affair of Louisiana. Perhaps nothing since the Revolutionary War has produced more uneasy sensations through the body of the nation. . . . There is on the globe one single spot, the possessor of which is our natural and habitual enemy. It is New Orleans through which the produce of three-eighths of our territory must pass to market. . . . France, placing herself in that door, assumes to us an attitude of defiance. Spain might have retained it quietly for years. Her pacific dispositions, her feeble state would induce her to increase our facilities there. . . . Not so can it ever be in the hands of France. . . . The day that France takes possession of New Orleans fixes the sentence which is to restrain her forever within her low water mark. . . . It seals the union of the two nations who in conjunction can maintain exclusive possession of the ocean. From that moment we must marry ourselves to the British fleet and nation."

In July, 1802, Morales, the Spanish intendant at New Orleans, arbitrarily withdrew the right of deposit. This action, the news **Anxiety of** of which spread rapidly, was interpreted by the **West** angry Westerners as a forerunner of what they might expect from France, for it was now known that the rumors of cession were true. Ablaze with excitement the outraged people of the whole transmontane country clamored for war. Expeditions were organized for the immediate seizure of the coveted territory. Jefferson was flooded with protests and memorials demanding aid. Even the New England Federalists, anxious for any move that would embarrass or discredit Jefferson and his party, did all they could to plunge the country into war with France.

The President, though greatly worried over the situation, wisely refused to be stampeded, and instead of yielding to the call for war set himself to the task of settling the whole question by peaceful negotiation if possible. To this end he induced

Congress to vote an appropriation of two million dollars "to defray any expenses in relation to intercourse between the United States and foreign nations." At the same time he sent James Monroe, his trusted friend, to France and Spain to aid our regular ministers, Livingston and Pinckney, in "enlarging and more effectually securing our rights and interests in the river Mississippi and in the territories eastward thereof." Already Livingston had been instructed to sound Napoleon on the possibility of selling these coveted domains to the United States.

United States moves to acquire New Orleans and mouth of Mississippi

Fortunately for the American negotiators a number of rapidly transpiring events played into their hands. Unexpected opposition in Spain had delayed the transfer of Louisiana; the French armies sent to conquer Santo Domingo preliminary to their transfer to Louisiana had been decimated by incessant warfare against the negroes and by yellow fever; European hostilities, temporarily stopped by the peace of Amiens in 1802, had again been resumed, and Napoleon was therefore in no position for either the conquest or defense of overseas possessions. He knew that in case of war he could not hold Louisiana if the United States should undertake its seizure either alone or in conjunction with the British fleet. Would not the immediate sale of this particular territory, which might perhaps net him fifty million francs at a time when he was short of money, be a wise move?

Factors which induced Napoleon to sell

Apparently he thought so, for on April 11, 1803, he instructed his minister of foreign affairs to open negotiations for the disposal not merely of New Orleans and West Florida, which Livingston for weeks had sought to buy, but all of the vast Louisiana tract. Bewildered momentarily by the Napoleonic decision and by his lack of instruction to acquire an empire, Livingston nevertheless accepted the proposal. To this Monroe gave hearty assent, and for two weeks the negotiators haggled over the terms. Finally on May 2, 1803, the treaty transferring the entire province to the United States was signed, Livingston and Monroe agreeing to pay $11,250,000 in six per cent bonds, and to assume claims held by American citizens against France estimated at $3,750,000. Well might

Louisiana acquired by the United States

Livingston proclaim it "the noblest work of our lives," for not only did the United States obtain control of the great waterway but title to an enormous territory whose limits and resources were as yet unknown.

The news of the purchase delighted the people of the West; henceforth no foreign power could by means of tolls and tariffs **Federalist** interfere with the transit of their produce to the **opposition to** seaboard. But in the older settled East the event **acquisition** was not so well received. Staunch Republicans of the Middle and Southern states, to be sure, shared with the West in its rejoicing. But the Federalists representing the financial and commercial strongholds bitterly condemned it as unconstitutional and prejudicial to the best interests of the Union. New England shippers and Middle states manufacturers, for example, saw no reason for supporting a policy of westward expansion. Why should they be shackled, they asked, with a heavy debt that a distant wilderness might be acquired. They had no desire, they said, to see the East depopulated and business paralyzed for the sake of strengthening the party of Thomas Jefferson, a party which had so rabidly opposed the Hamiltonian program of assumption, the United States Bank, and the tariff. Their interests centered on the Atlantic seaboard; trade and association tied them to Europe rather than to the West, whose growing power was to them a constant nightmare. In the addition of Louisiana many professed to see the inevitable disruption of the Republic, for between men who trapped bears and fought Indians and those who built ships and imported European goods, there seemingly could be no common interests. Above all, men of property and social standing would never submit to the domination of a "hotch-potch of wild men from the Far West."

Of these numerous objections, Jefferson, staunch advocate of strict construction, was concerned with only one, that of con-**Jefferson's** stitutionality. The administration, he frankly ad-**constitutional** mitted, had exceeded its constitutional powers, and **embarrass-** he therefore proposed an amendment to the Con-**ment** stitution confirming the purchase and providing for its government. The President's friends, however, less con-

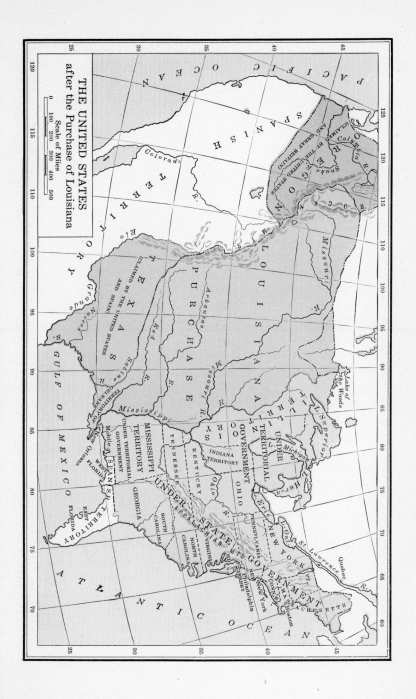

THE UNITED STATES
after the Purchase of Louisiana

Scale of Miles

0   100   200   300   400   500

cerned with the constitutional question than with the acquisition of the territory, unblushingly adopted the Federalist interpretation of "implied powers." The right to acquire foreign territory, they argued, existed as a result of (1) the right to make treaties, and (2) the power to make war and peace. In the midst of the debate came the rumor that Napoleon might change his mind, and accordingly Jefferson pressed the Senate for ratification. The Constitution, he still maintained, did not authorize the purchase but, said he, "If our friends shall think differently I shall certainly acquiesce with satisfaction, confident that the good sense of our country will correct the evil of construction when it shall produce ill effects." Thus circumstances and expediency forced Jefferson to modify his interpretation of the fundamental law of the land. And on October 17, 1803, the treaty was ratified 24 to 7, the die-hards wailing that the Republic was doomed. In December of the same year the Stars and Stripes, to the delight of the western population, were raised over the government buildings at New Orleans, signalizing that Louisiana had passed forever to the United States.

4. FRONTIER IMPERIALISM

An unrestricted highway to the sea was not the only motive back of the Westerner's desire for the acquisition of Louisiana. An enthusiastic expansionist and an ardent believer in the doctrine of Manifest Destiny, he dreamed of the day when not only Louisiana but East and West Florida, Mexico, Cuba, and even Canada should be part of the United States. "Where is it written in the book of fate," queried the editor of the Nashville *Clarion*, "that the American republic shall not stretch her limits from the Capes of the Chesapeake to Nootka Sound, from the Isthmus of Panama to Hudson Bay?" To the Westerner the boundaries of the continent were our "natural frontiers."

Frontiersman an expansionist and a believer in Manifest Destiny

No sooner had the treaty for the purchase of Louisiana been signed than the question arose as to whether the cession included West Florida. Southern planters in quest of new lands longed to add the two Floridas to their ever expanding domain. As long as these tracts remained in alien

The Floridas

hands their swamps and marshlands would afford a refuge for runaway slaves and their Indian population could be used in all sorts of ways detrimental to the United States. Most important of all, perhaps, the people of eastern Tennessee and of the neighboring territory of Mississippi were dependent on the rivers which passed through the Floridas for access to the sea. Finally, there was always the danger that the Floridas might be used as a base by some hostile power, particularly England.

Both Livingston and Monroe asserted that the Louisiana Purchase included West Florida, as the strip of Gulf coast be-

West Florida claimed by United States as part of Louisiana Purchase

tween the Iberville or eastern branch of the Mississippi and the Appalachicola was known, but Spain just as stoutly insisted that it did not. Prior to 1763 the territory in dispute unquestionably had been part of Louisiana, the eastern boundary coinciding roughly with the Perdido River which now forms part of the eastern boundary of Alabama. When in 1763 France relinquished possession of her North American colonies England came into possession of both East and West Florida. In 1783, however, when West Florida again passed into the hands of Spain it was not reunited with Louisiana but maintained as a separate province. Nor did Spain include it in the recession of Louisiana to France in 1800. The American claim was, therefore, dubious, resting upon the boundaries of the Louisiana of 1762.

During the years immediately following the acquisition of Louisiana, when the United States unsuccessfully endeavored to

The United States takes possession of the Floridas

induce Spain to accept its view respecting West Florida, that territory gradually filled up with Americans. In 1810 they revolted against the Spanish authorities, and with the connivance of the American government declared their independence of Spain and asked to be annexed to the United States. They had not long to wait, for in October, 1810, President Madison, heeding the wishes of the frontier expansionists, issued a proclamation declaring that by the Louisiana Purchase the United States extended as far east as the Perdido, and that West Florida was therefore American soil. The fact that Spain was heavily indebted to American citizens for damages done to their trade afforded sufficient excuse to lay claim to East Florida, and early in 1811 Congress authorized the seizure pending negotiations.

The acquisition of Louisiana and the Floridas by no means satisfied the restless frontiersman's appetite for new lands. Indeed, long before these territories were added to **Dreams of** the United States adventurers with grand ideas of **acquiring** empire building — James O'Fallon, William Blount **Mexico** and others — were dreaming of Mexico as a field where they might win power and glory. "The Kentuckyans," wrote the frontier soldier, John Adair, to the notorious General Wilkinson in 1804, "are full of enterprise and although not poor, as greedy after plunder as ever the old Romans were; Mexico glitters in our eyes — the word is all we wait for." Two years later Aaron Burr launched his ill-fated expedition in the probable hope of accomplishing what the whole Southwest dreamed of, namely, the conquest of Mexico His failure did not dampen the imperialistic ardor of the frontiersman. "Citizens of the West," wrote "Americus" of Nashville in 1812, "a destiny still more splendid is reserved for you. Behold the empire of Mexico, a celestial region, whose valiant sons are now struggling for their liberties as we struggled for ours thirty years ago. . . . Here it is that the statesman shall see an accession of territory sufficient to double the extent of the Republic; where the merchant shall see commercial resources unrivalled in other countries; the farmer, a luxuriant soil and delicious climate, where the financier shall be dazzled with gold and silver mines." Less than a generation elapsed after these prophetic words were written before a goodly portion of the coveted Mexico, as we shall see, was added to the United States.

But the lust for expansion was not confined to the Southwest alone. Ever since pre-Revolutionary days frontiersmen from New Hampshire to Kentucky had been intermit- **Frontier** tently outspoken in their demand that the Indian **imperialism** tribes of the Northwest be ousted and that Canada **in the North** be acquired by the United States. Quest for additional land, the desire to obtain control of the flourishing British fur trade, and the wish to destroy forever the alliance between the British and the Indians which had grown up largely as a result of American penetration westward were the principal factors back of this double demand. Considerable progress in excluding the Indian from the Northwest was made before the War of 1812, but it was that conflict — often called our "second war of independence" — that afforded the Westerner opportunity to press his imperialist views.

The War of 1812 was in many respects the direct outgrowth of the Napoleonic wars during which England and France clashed

War of 1812 outgrowth of Napoleonic wars

in a life and death struggle for world supremacy. The contest between the ancient rivals was not many months old before three outstanding facts became evident. First, that the drainage of men from agriculture for their armies would compel both belligerents to rely upon the United States for large exports of food. Secondly, that for the time being they would have to abandon their cherished mercantilistic notions, throw open their colonies to trade, and depend in great measure on the merchant marine of the United States to bring them needed supplies. And, thirdly, that the rights of neutrals would be ignored and that the United States like every other non-combatant nation would be subjected to all sorts of indignity and inconvenience. In this connection three things in particular roiled America and strengthened the hand of those who clamored for war: (1) Interference with our commerce; (2) seizure of seamen from American vessels; and (3) shabby diplomatic treatment.

The very nature of the Old World struggle made interference with our commerce inevitable. Having made himself master of

British Orders in Council and French retaliatory decrees

France, Napoleon resolved to break the backbone of Britain by wresting from her commercial leadership and despoiling her of part of her colonial empire. Frightened by the audacity of the haughty Corsican and by his success in bringing the greater part of the Continent of Europe to his feet, Great Britain fought desperately to thwart him. Failing to crush him on land, she determined to starve him into submission. Accordingly in May, 1806, less than a year after Nelson had annihilated the French fleet at Trafalgar, Great Britain declared a blockade of the coast of the

Continent from the river Elbe to Brest. Napoleon's answer to this policy of strangulation came in November of the same year, when he issued his famous Berlin decree proclaiming a blockade of the British Isles, even though he had no navy to enforce it, and announcing that any vessel stopping at an English port would not be admitted to a French port. Angered by the boldness of this action the British government struck back with a series of retaliatory Orders in Council extending the continental blockade, closing the whole French coasting trade to neutrals, and requiring all neutral vessels bound for the barred zone to clear from a British port, secure a license, and pay certain "transit duties." Not to be outdone, Napoleon in December, 1807, issued his Milan decree in which he declared he would seize and confiscate any ship submitting to search by British officers, paying any tax or duty to the British government, or even coming from or bound to a British port.

While these orders and decrees were not inspired by special hostility to the United States, they nevertheless worked great hardship on our commerce. If a ship sailed directly Effect of for the Continent it was liable to seizure by the strangulation policies on British; if on the other hand it put in at a British American port it might be captured and confiscated by the commerce French. Every American merchantman was thus faced with conflicting rules not of his making. His risks were enormous, but so were the rewards of those who escaped the meshwork of retaliatory measures. Between 1803 and 1812 approximately fifteen hundred American ships were seized by the European belligerents and the greater part condemned for violating restrictions imposed upon them. Yet for the first four years of this period — 1803–1807 — our commerce more than held its own, as shown in the table on page 544.

Of the two combatants France was undoubtedly more harsh and unjust in administering her decrees. Her failure to seize more ships than her rival was due not to any gener- Both belliger- osity on her part but to lack of an adequate weapon ents offensive — a navy. The fact that the French flag had been practically driven from the sea made it impossible for France seriously to interrupt commerce between the United States and England.

EXPORTS OF THE UNITED STATES

(In millions of dollars, round numbers. Fiscal year ending
September 30)

YEAR	DOMESTIC	FOREIGN	TOTAL	YEAR	DOMESTIC	FOREIGN	TOTAL
1790	...	...	20.4	1804	41.4	36.2	77.6
1791	...	...	19.0	1805	42.3	53.1	95.4
1792	...	...	20.7	1806	41.2	60.2	101.4
1793	...	...	26.1	1807	48.6	59.6	108.2
1794	...	...	33.0	1808	9.4	12.9	22.3
1795	...	...	47.9	1809	31.4	20.7	52.1
1796	40.7	26.3	67.0	1810	42.3	24.3	66.6
1797	29.8	27.0	56.8	1811	45.2	16.0	61.2
1798	28.5	33.0	61.5	1812	30.0	8.4	38.4
1799	33.1	45.5	78.6	1813	25.0	2.8	27.8
1800	31.8	39.1	70.9	1814	6.7	0.1	6.8
1801	47.4	46.6	94.0	1815	45.9	6.5	52.4
1802	36.7	35.7	72.4	1816	64.7	17.1	81.8
1803	42.2	13.5	55.7	1817	68.3	19.3	87.6

From Clive Day, *A History of Commerce*, p. 502.

It was our trade with France that suffered most; to nip this
trade at its source Britain virtually blockaded our eastern coast,
and fortunate indeed was the American vessel bound for a
French port that escaped the vigilance of the British navy.

If England's interference with their trade roused the ire of the
Americans, the British practice of impressing seamen fanned
The British that ire to fever heat. England realized that her
practice of one outstanding hope of conquering her mighty
impressment antagonist depended on her navy; without it she
would be powerless. Yet its efficiency was always threatened by
wholesale desertions. Long hours, low wages, filthy and ofttimes
insufficient food, wretched sleeping quarters, severe punishment
for trivial offenses, and the opportunity to escape the European
turmoil caused thousands of British seamen to flee to American
merchantmen. Not being able to spare these men, the British
government, applying the rule "once an Englishman, always an
Englishman," not only refused them the right of expatriation
but directed its naval officers to stop American vessels, search

them, and remove therefrom, by force if necessary, any man whose service might be lawfully claimed. In carrying out their instructions, the searching parties, as the Beards well say, "did not always observe the amenities of the drawing room." More often than not they did their work in high-handed fashion and were not always careful to distinguish between Britishers and Yankees; in fact, many a sailor born under the American flag was dragged away in chains. Even if justified by the doctrine of necessity, such practice was bound to rouse anger and hostility.

All effort — diplomatic and otherwise — on the part of the United States to induce the belligerents to respect the rights of neutrals came to naught. Our notes of protest to England were either ignored or answered in sarcastic and insolent vein. Napoleon's attitude was no better and in some respects more unbearable. He accused Jefferson of being a tool of Great Britain, issued false statements to lure American merchantmen to French waters where he knew they would be seized and confiscated, and made promises which he had no intention of ever fulfilling. *Diplomatic insolence*

Hostile feeling against both belligerents was already running high when in the summer of 1807 the British warship *Leopard* halted the American frigate *Chesapeake* off the Virginia capes for the purpose of searching her for deserters. When the commander of the American ship denied that he had deserters on board and refused to permit the search, the British ship immediately opened fire, killing three and wounding eighteen. Being unprepared for action, the *Chesapeake* was forced to yield, and four men, three of whom were *bona fide* Americans, were taken as alleged deserters. This seemingly inexcusable act so thoroughly aroused American public opinion that the demand for war against Great Britain resounded throughout the length and breadth of the land. *The Chesapeake-Leopard affair*

But Jefferson did not want war. He loved peace and was absolutely convinced that for the United States to go to war against either England or France or to become in any way a party to the European struggle would be a mistake of the first magnitude. Yet he knew that some governmental action was necessary to allay popular passion and *Peaceable coercion* to bring the belligerents to their senses. Failing to accomplish these ends either by warnings and threats or by negotiation, he determined to employ the weapon used so effectively by the colonists before the Revolution, namely, commercial restriction. Once the belligerents were cut off from American exports of food and other supplies, he reasoned, they would right-about-face and sue for terms.

This policy of peaceable coercion or economic pressure had already been instituted in a small way in 1806, when a non-The Embargo importation act closing American ports to certain Act of 1807 British goods was passed in retaliation for Great Britain's blockade of the Continent. But this measure proved wholly inadequate, and accordingly in December, 1807, a more drastic piece of machinery — the Embargo — was instituted. Unhappily for Jefferson and his supporters, the Embargo, which forbade all American vessels to sail from any American port to European ports and required every coasting vessel to give bonds double the value of the vessel and cargo, that it would land its cargo only in an American port, failed to accomplish its purpose. Instead of protecting American overseas trade it tended to destroy this trade. The value of our exports fell from $108,000,-000 in 1807 to $22,000,000 the following year, an enormous decline for a country so dependent on foreign markets. Soon every port was crowded with idle ships. Warehouses were filled with decaying goods. The shipbuilding industry languished, throwing carpenters, sailmakers, sailors, and other workmen out of employment. Merchants, unable to make ends meet, were driven to bankruptcy. Farmers, north, south, and west, found themselves without markets. Prices of manufactured goods doubled, and the national revenue decreased approximately fifty per cent. Even those less conscientious shippers who dared to evade the law by slipping out of port or by smuggling goods across the Canadian and Florida borders were always in danger of being apprehended by federal agents. Massachusetts, the principal shipowning commonwealth in America, was especially hard hit, for the Embargo not only suspended at least half her commerce but greatly curtailed her fishing and whaling industries.

Before the end of 1808 the temper of the country, particularly the commercial Northeast, was worse than prior to the passage of the embargo measure. Federalist politicians joined hands with the economically distressed in accusing Jefferson of bringing the nation to the verge of ruin.

Embargo gives way to non-intercourse

> Our ships all in motion once whitened the ocean,
>   They sailed and returned with a cargo;
> Now doomed to decay, they have fallen a prey
>   To Jefferson — worms — and Embargo.

This rhyme of a Newburyport, Massachusetts, newspaper poet was mild in comparison with the angry protests and savage jibes leveled at the pacific Jefferson. Finally, in March, 1809, the Embargo was lifted and a non-intercourse arrangement substituted for it. The new law, permitting American shippers to trade with any part of the world except England and France, brought some relief to our shipping interests and indirectly to the country at large. It was in turn superseded in 1810 by another measure, known as Macon's Bill No. 2, allowing trade with all the world, but with the provision that in case either Great Britain or France should revoke or modify its obnoxious decrees and the other should not do so, the President should revive the Non-Intercourse Act against the offending nation. But this measure, like its predecessors, failed to put an end to the humiliating conditions under which our shippers were forced to carry on their business. All effort to procure decent treatment by pacific means was apparently futile. War was approaching.

The demand for war came not from northeast shippers, but from nationally-minded frontier expansionists and land-hungry southern planters. Despite affronts and all sorts of inconveniences, the shipping interests were making money and therefore did not want war. But the frontier West, with an eye on Canada, and the planting South, with its heart set on having Florida, were insistent on war. While both sections resented the injustices heaped upon the United States by England and France, it

Frontier West and planting South demand war

was on the former that they focused their hostility. Great Britain, in their opinion, had been the more insulting; moreover, she and her ally, Spain, held the domains which those who clamored for armed intervention wanted the United States to possess. "No man in the nation wants peace more than I," exclaimed Henry Clay in the United States Senate in 1810, "but I prefer the troubled ocean of war, demanded by the honor and independence of this country, with all its calamities and desolation, to the tranquil and putrescent pool of ignominious peace. If we can accommodate our differences with one of the belligerents only, I should prefer that one to be Britain; but if with neither, and we are forced into a selection of our enemy, then I am for war with Britain, because I believe her prior in aggression, and her injuries and insults to us more atrocious in character. . . . It is said, however, that no object is obtainable by war with Great Britain. In its fortunes we are to estimate not only the benefit to be derived to ourselves, but the injury to be done the enemy. The conquest of Canada is in your power. I trust I shall not be deemed presumptuous when I state that I verily believe that the militia of Kentucky are alone competent to place Montreal and Upper Canada at your feet."

That Clay voiced the opinion of both the frontier and the South was evident when the question of our relation with England came up for debate in the Twelfth Congress the following year. In that body those who were outspoken for war and annexation were in control; they came for the most part from western and southern constituencies which if connected would form a great crescent stretching from New Hampshire to Savannah, Georgia. "From end to end," as Professor Pratt points out in his *Expansionists of 1812*, "the crescent traversed frontier territory, bordering foreign soil, British or Spanish, or confronting dangerous Indian tribes among whom foreign influence was suspected and feared. . . . Nothing could better demonstrate the frontier character of the war spirit than to observe its progressive decline as we pass from the rim of the crescent to its center at the national capital. Expansionist enthusiasm declined even more rapidly."

[side note: War party controlling Twelfth Congress a frontier party]

VOTE IN HOUSE OF REPRESENTATIVES ON
DECLARATION OF WAR, JUNE 12, 1812

For War

Against War

Unsettled

The men who came to Washington from these frontier districts were typical of the frontier. "They had," to quote Professor Pratt again, "national patriotism to the point sometimes of chauvinism, resenting with a new bitterness their country's wrongs and scorning the pacific measures hitherto used to repel them. They had unlimited faith in their country's future, believing its destined limits to be no less than the Eastern and Western oceans, the Gulf of Mexico, and the 'regions of eternal frost.' Hence they were for a war which should at the same time defend the country's rights and expand its boundaries; they would punish British insults with the sword, wresting Canada from Great Britain, and the residue of the Floridas from her weak ally, Spain." Clay and Johnson of Kentucky, Grundy and Campbell of Tennessee, Harper of New Hampshire, Calhoun of South Carolina, and Crawford and Troup of Georgia were "manifest destiny" men, "warhawks," and leaders of the war party. "I shall never die contented," said Johnson, "until I see her [Great Britain's] expulsion from North America and her territories incorporated with the United States. . . . The waters of the St. Lawrence and the Mississippi interlock in a number of places, and the Great Disposer of Human Events intended those two rivers should belong to the same people." Calhoun was of the opinion that in four weeks from the time a declaration of war was heard on the frontier, the whole of Upper Canada and a part of Lower Canada would be under the control of the United States.

Speeches and forecasts such as these stirred the rank and file, and during the early months of 1812 the demand for war became more insistent than ever. Finally, on June 12 of that year, the House of Representatives by a vote of seventy-nine to forty-nine and the Senate by nineteen to thirteen, adopted a resolution for war against Great Britain. From an economic as well as from every other point of view the vote to take arms against England for a second time was a sectional one, the commercial Northeast lining up against the agrarian West and South. The attitude of the former is admirably summed up by Pratt: "The Federalist party, grounded chiefly in the mercantile and financial interests of the

Reasons why frontier wanted war

War against Great Britain declared

coast towns, the college-bred professional men, the more solid and 'respectable' elements in society, was fairly homogeneous in its creeds of both foreign and domestic politics. Abroad, it looked upon Napoleon as Anti-Christ and endorsed Pickering's famous toast, 'The world's last hope — Britain's fast-anchored isle.' In home affairs it was convinced, not without cause, . . . that the Republican administration had deliberately resolved to ruin its commerce and dissipate its prosperity. Holding these views it could see no worse national crime than a war against England which would render indirect aid to Napoleon, and no worse disaster to its own interests than a form of expansion which would mean new states to increase the Republican strength in Congress."

Though a unit in demanding war, the "warhawks" and their followers were, as the Beards point out, sharply divided over aims and methods and, as a consequence, failed miserably to accomplish their objectives. The southern wing of the party, primarily interested, as we have seen, in obtaining possession of the Floridas, was far from enthusiastic about annexing Canada for fear it would strengthen the North. The frontiersmen of the Northwest, on the other hand, wanted Canada and frowned upon the possibility of adding territory to the planting South. This sectional feeling, which had shown itself on more than one occasion prior to 1812, gathered momentum with the approach of war. John Randolph, scion of the South and spokesman for its interests, repeatedly warned his brethren that the conquest and annexation of Canada would make the North preponderant. "If you go to war," he exclaimed, "it will not be for the protection of or defense of your maritime rights. Gentlemen from the North have been taken up into some high mountain and shown all the kingdoms of the earth; and Canada seems tempting in their sight. That rich vein of Genesee land, which is said to be even better on the other side of the lake than on this. Agrarian cupidity, not maritime right, urges the war. . . . It is to acquire a preponderating northern influence that you are to launch into war." Northerners were equally outspoken in opposing the addition of the Floridas.

War party divided as to aims and methods

Efforts of the expansionists, North and South, to patch up
their differences and agree to an annexation program satisfactory to both failed to allay sectional animosity.
In fact it was manifest at every turn — in cabinet
meetings, in the making of plans for financing the
war, in the raising and equipping of troops, and in their conduct on the field of battle. Merchants and shippers of the
Northeast stubbornly refused to support a conflict which, as
they boasted, was not of their making. Their spokesmen in
Congress condemned the invasion of Canada, fought conscription, and tried by every means to defeat the administration's
loan bills and tax projects. Outside the halls of Congress they
were no less vehement in their opposition. Individuals, the
press, and official bodies from town meetings to state legislatures
contemptuously labeled it "Mr. Madison's War" — an "unjust," "ruinous," and "unconstitutional" war. Federalist
bankers even went so far as to try to prevent the sale of government bonds. "Probably New England," to quote Henry
Adams, "lent to the British government during the war more
money than she lent to her own." Of the $17,000,000 in specie
in the entire country in 1814 New England banks held ten
million, yet the loans from that section to the United States
during the war were less than three millions as compared with
thirty-five for the Middle states. And to cap the climax, New
England merchants were furnishing the British fleet operating
off the coast and the British armies in Canada with large
quantities of food stuffs and other supplies.

Opposition of the commercial North to the war reached its
climax in the famous Hartford Convention of 1814. In September of that year Massachusetts, under plea of the
necessity for local defense, withdrew her militia
from federal service. Connecticut did likewise.
To make even plainer the opposition of the trading and shipping
interests, the General Court of Massachusetts, responding
to public demand, issued an invitation to her neighboring
commonwealths in October to send delegates to a convention
"for the purpose of devising proper measures to procure the
united efforts of the commercial states, to secure such amend-

Sectional opposition to war

The Hartford Convention, 1814

ments and explanations of the Constitution as will secure them from further evils." Five states, Massachusetts, Connecticut, Rhode Island, New Hampshire, and Vermont responded, and the delegates assembled at Hartford, December 15, 1814.

What action the convention would take was problematical. For ten years and more states' rights and secession had been freely discussed in New England. Indeed, less than The states' a week before the Hartford Convention assembled rights-secession atmosnone other than Daniel Webster, speaking in the phere of New House of Representatives against a proposed England federal conscription law, elaborated in admirable fashion the whole doctrine of states' rights. "No law professedly passed for the purpose of compelling a service in the regular army, not for the emergencies mentioned in the Constitution, but for long periods, and for the general objects of war," said he, "can be carried into effect. The principles of the bill," he continued, "are not warranted by any provision of the Constitution, . . . not connected with any power which the Constitution has conferred on Congress. . . . The Constitution is libelled, foully libelled. . . . Where is it written in the Constitution, in what article or section is it contained, that you may take children from their parents and parents from their children and compel them to fight the battles of any war in which the folly or the wickedness of government may engage it? . . . An attempt to maintain this doctrine upon the provisions of the Constitution is an exercise of perverse ingenuity to extract slavery from the substance of a free government." The highest obligations of state governments, he concluded, bound them to preserve their own rights and the liberties of their people.

Webster's exposition, voicing as it did the same views expounded in the Virginia and Kentucky Resolutions, reflected the spirit of commercial New England. In the Work of Hartford Convention the more radical members Hartford were eager for secession. They were outnumbered, Convention however, by the more moderate faction, whose opinion prevailed. After scolding the administration and threatening nullification if conscription were applied, the Convention recommended seven amendments to the Constitution. Collectively these amendments if adopted would have excluded the slaves from the count in determining state membership in the House of Representatives, made the admission of new states impossible without a two-thirds majority of Congress, prohibited all embargoes of longer than sixty days, prevented a declaration of war without a two-thirds majority, except in case of invasion, and put an end to the monopoly of the presidency by Virginians.

Fortunately the news of peace early in 1815 made it unnecessary for the disgruntled Northeast to resort to more drastic action as it threatened to do if the war continued and steps were not taken to amend the Constitution. Its defiant attitude toward the war, however, and its more or less veiled threats to secede brought down on its head the wrath of the West and South. In both sections press and platform roundly denouncing the Hartford Convention and its work, indignantly urged the federal government to awake to the exigencies of the situation. "No man, no association of men, no state or set of states," said the *Richmond Enquirer*, "has a right to withdraw itself from this Union of its own accord. . . . The majority of the states which form the Union must consent to the withdrawal of any one branch of it. Until that consent has been obtained any attempt to dissolve the Union or to obstruct the efficacy of its constitutional laws is Treason — Treason to all intents and purposes." Apparently the *Enquirer* had, for the time being at least, forgotten the Kentucky and Virginia Resolutions. Moreover, it did not foresee certain events whose occurrence less than a generation later virtually compelled it to stand forth once more as the champion of states' rights.

We need not here record the economic, military, and diplomatic happenings which finally led to peace. Suffice that the United States, unprepared for the struggle precipitated by the expansionists, made one blunder after another and therefore failed to accomplish any of the main objectives for which the war was fought. The invasion of Canada, for example, came to naught. Our port towns were bottled up by the British navy and our commerce all but paralyzed. Washington was occupied temporarily

Hartford Convention and its work condemned by West and South

War of 1812 a disappointment to expansionists

by the British, who destroyed the federal buildings. Worst of all, the government, divided in counsel and without the whole-hearted support of the country, drifted during the course of the war to the verge of economic collapse. The work of the navy and the privateers and the triumph of Jackson at New Orleans were the only outstanding bright spots in a war from which the expansionists hoped for so much.

Instead, therefore, of providing for the annexation of Canada and the Floridas to the United States, the Treaty of Ghent merely made provision for the cessation of hostili- The Treaty of ties, the release of prisoners, the restoration of con- Ghent quests by both sides, and the termination of Indian hostilities. No clause — indeed not even an allusion — was made to neutral rights, to the impressment of American seamen, or to the paralyzation of our commerce by blockade, seizure, and confiscation. Nor was mention made as to the control of the Great Lakes, Indian territories, the fisheries, or the navigation of the Mississippi. From the point of view of the expansionists the document was, as Clay labelled it, "a damned bad treaty," but news of its negotiation was joyously received by an exhausted administration and by the people of the nation.

The hopes of the expansionists for the immediate acquisition of Canada vanished with the close of the War of 1812 and the gradual disappearance of the grievances against The acquisi-Great Britain. For those who had long urged the tion of Florida addition of the Floridas to our widening domain the second struggle with Great Britain did not spell ultimate defeat. Between 1814 and 1819 the old sources of irritation — Indian raids, smuggling, and the escape of negro slaves — increased tremendously. The American demand that these nuisances cease became more insistent, but Spain, rocked by disturbances at home and open rebellion in South America, was unable to suppress them. Matters came to a head late in 1817 when, as a result of fresh Indian raids, a punitive expedition under General Andrew Jackson invaded Florida. St. Marks and Pensacola were captured, two British subjects, Arbuthnot and Ambrister, charged with complicity in the Indian attacks, were hanged, and American sovereignty virtually established over the entire

northern part of the Spanish province. Diplomatic controversy followed, but in 1819 Spain yielded to the inevitable,
the Spanish minister at Washington signing a treaty ceding the
Floridas to the United States in exchange for $5,000,000, the
sum due American citizens for damages to their commerce by
Spanish authorities during the Napoleonic wars. At the same
time the two powers agreed that a line extending from the
mouth of the Sabine River to the 32d parallel, thence north to
the Red River and along it to the 100th meridian, then north to
the Arkansas River, then to the 42d parallel, and from there
westward to the Pacific, should constitute the western boundary
of the Louisiana Purchase. While the acquisition of Florida
was a source of satisfaction to the southern expansionists, it
greatly intensified the sectional jealousy which, as we observed
above, was partly responsible for the failure of the United States
to gain Canada in the conflict of 1812.

We should not conclude this section without briefly noting the
attitude of the Westerner toward the famous declaration of
December 2, 1823, which has come to be known as
the Monroe Doctrine. Originating in part as a
protest against the advance of Russia along the
northwest coast of America and in part as a warning
to those European states contemplating intervention in South America for the purpose of restoring to Spain her
revolted colonies, this doctrine declared that "the American
continents, by the free and independent condition which they
have assumed and maintain, are henceforth not to be considered
as subjects for further colonization by any European powers."
Referring to the new-born Spanish-American republics, the
doctrine further declared that any attempt by any European
power to oppress them, or control in any other manner their
destiny, could not be viewed in any other light "than as the
manifestation of an unfriendly disposition toward the United
States." To these bold statements announcing to the rest of the
world that the American continents, especially North America,
were henceforth to be regarded as a special preserve of the
United States, the Westerner gave hearty assent. Hater of
autocracy, confirmed advocate of democracy and republicanism,

*Westerner
supports
principles
laid down
in Monroe
Doctrine*

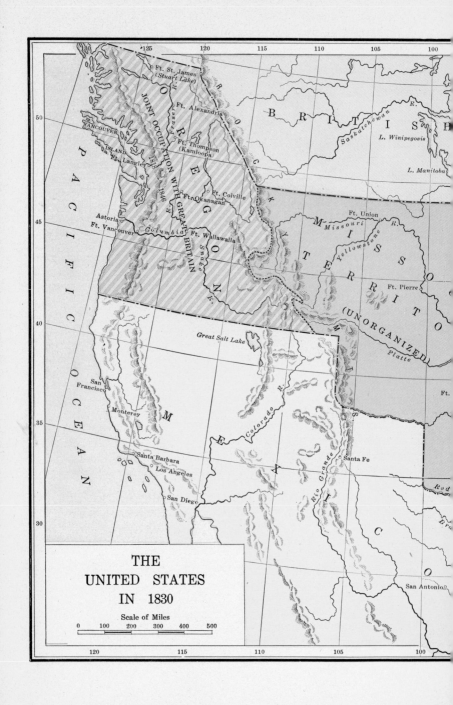

THE
UNITED STATES
IN 1830

Scale of Miles

0   100   200   300   400   500

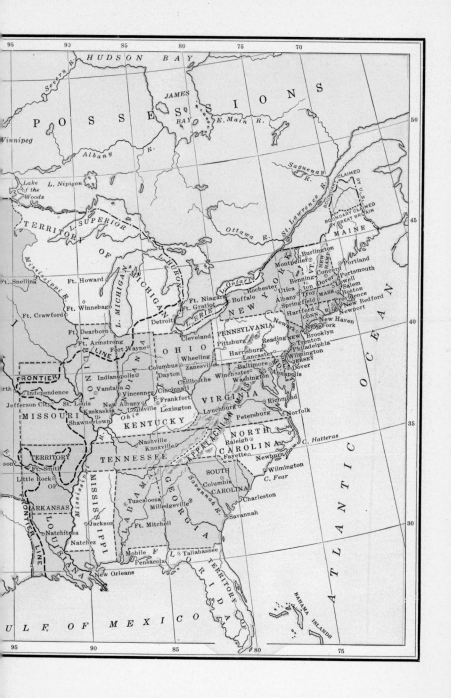

nationally-minded and imperialistically ambitious, he naturally would frown upon any design of Russian aggrandizement in the Northwest or upon any scheme that would give any European state added political or economic advantage in the New World. The Westerner's attitude in this respect was admirably expressed both in and out of Congress by Henry Clay.

5. WESTERN IDEALS AND WESTERN CULTURE

This attitude of the Westerner toward the Monroe Doctrine was typical of western temperament and ideals. In the course of his conquest of forest, beast, and savage, the Western pioneer developed a society vastly different from temperament that of the aristocratic East. The habits and and ideals institutions which he brought with him into the wilderness underwent modification. Thrown upon his own resources he became masterful, resolute, individualistic, and aggressively bold. In his quest for personal aggrandizement he resented governmental restraint; he rebelled against the conventional and, on the basis of eastern standards, was much of a nonconformist. Real or fancied insult provoked temper and speech that would not be found in an eastern drawing room. With him democracy was a passion, although he seems to have had little conception that it was largely the result of an abundance of free land rather than of any peculiar merit of our political institutions. He believed himself to be the equal of anybody and had unbounded faith in the ability of the common people; he loved his family, held woman in high respect, and believed in straightforward dealing with his neighbor. He hated aristocracy, monopoly, and special privilege, and distrusted "trained statesmen and official classes."

That the western pioneer should develop such traits and ideals was most natural. The very vastness of the region into which he had come lent itself to an atmosphere of liberty Effect of and equality. Here he faced no aristocracy, no environment caste system, no monopolization of opportunity. on Westerner Freedom was the essence of the air he breathed. His successful subjugation of the rude forces of nature made him more versatile and more confident. His single-room cabin home with its clay-

chinked walls and split-log floor was a very different type of
abode from the more sumptuous dwellings of the older communities. Even its furnishings were simple; of bureaus and
sideboards there were none; a home-made bedstead with trundle-
bed beneath it, a few splint-bottom chairs for the grown-ups and
three-legged stools or blocks for the children, a movable bench
or rough square table for meals, a shelf or two, a spinning-wheel,
and perhaps a loom were the standard articles of furniture.
From pegs driven into the bare walls hung the family ward-
robe — the dresses, bedgowns, Sunday bonnets and frocks of the
women, the hunting-shirts, pantaloons, and leggings of the men.
Cooking utensils and tableware consisted of a few iron pots,
pewter plates and dishes, spoons, knives, and forks. The food
while wholesome was coarse, and meals were prepared out-of-
doors or over the blazing fire of the cabin hearth. Simplicity
featured every pioneer household.

Hard work, long hours of labor, privation, and frequent misfortune were likewise powerful factors in shaping western notions and western ideals. The pioneer, toiling from
**Factors shap-
ing western
character and
ideals** sunrise to sunset and sometimes longer, was extremely suspicious of merchants and bankers who,
in his opinion, amassed wealth, led easy lives, and
labored not. Of social comforts he enjoyed very few, and during
the long severe winters his family frequently suffered from cold
and want. In the hot summer months fever epidemics often
left their trail of sorrow in many a frontier home. Ignorance of
sanitation, inadequate knowledge of simple curatives, lack of
money, and the impossibility of securing medical aid resulted
yearly in a heavy toll of life, especially among children. But
such afflictions and sorrows were usually regarded as an expression of the will of a divine Creator and were accepted accordingly. Consciously or unconsciously they instilled in the bosom
of the pioneer a spirit of courage, fortitude, and humility.

Yet notwithstanding misfortune and hardship, the Westerner
was optimistic, boastful, ardently nationalistic, and a believer as
**Western
social life** we have seen in the "manifest destiny" of his country. He found time to mix pleasure with his work,
and every community had its dances, weddings, barn raisings,

and corn huskings, at which strong liquor added zest to the occasion. In the older settled regions like Kentucky and Tennessee horse racing, rooster fighting, and gambling were common pastimes and sports. Every western town had its barroom with its assemblage of politicians, land speculators, and hangers-on, where corn and rye whisky were freely dispensed. Fist fights and duels were common occurrences, and no man dared give the lie unless prepared to defend himself. Not unlike their sisters of the East, the women of the older frontier communities had their gossipy parties, quilting bees, church suppers, and other social gatherings. The real pioneer woman, however, usually the mother of a large family, burdened with domestic cares and worries, and with the help she was expected to render out-of-doors, found little time for either levity or tale bearing; her joy was her family, for whom she as a rule labored unselfishly and uncomplainingly.

Perhaps nowhere are the characteristics of western society more strikingly depicted than in the realm of American political philosophy and practical politics. The Westerner, Western political ideals as we have heretofore noted, was at once individualistic, liberty-loving, and confident. His ideal was the self-made man. He entertained a deep-rooted contempt for the expert and the specially trained. Impatient of restraint and "outside" direction, he desired to create his own agencies of government. He condemned property and religious qualifications for voting, rebelled against nominations by congressional caucus, and was outspoken in his opposition to "presidential dynasties." With him political experience did not count. "He knew how to preserve order," Professor Turner writes, "even in the absence of legal authority. If there were cattle thieves, lynch law was sudden and effective; the regulators of the Carolinas were the predecessors of the claims associations of Iowa and the vigilance committees of California. But the individual was not ready to submit to complex regulations. Population was sparse, there was no multitude of jostling interests, as in the older settlements, demanding an elaborate system of personal restraints. Society became atomic. There was a reproduction of the primitive idea of the personality of the

law, a crime was more an offense against the victim than a violation of the law of the land. Substantial justice, secured in the
most direct way, was the ideal of the backwoodsman. He had
little patience with finely drawn distinctions or scruples of
method. If the thing was one proper to be done, then the most
immediate rough and ready effective way was the best way."
Ideals like these, one can readily see, were vastly different from
those of the seaboard communities.

The West, although not without educational facilities, was in
comparison with the East culturally backward for a generation
Western   or more. The majority of the western people tradi-
education   tionally had little or no interest in formal education
of any sort; nor did the dire poverty and hardships of frontier
life contribute to the creation of such an interest. Yet there were
numerous individuals, particularly among the New England
element north of the Ohio, who saw clearly the advantages of a
public school system. Unfortunately the funds from the liberal
federal and state land grants for educational purposes were for
years mismanaged and squandered, and the only efficient common schools worthy of the name were those located in enterprising centers of considerable population. That the western
commonwealths, however, had a definite conception of state-
wide democratic education is evidenced by a study of their basic
laws. Ohio in her first constitution in 1802 forbade the passage
of any law depriving the poor of equal rights in any educational
institution endowed in whole or in part by funds derived from
government land grants; but it was not until 1824 that the state
established a common school system supported by taxation.
Similarly Indiana in her first constitution required the legislature to provide for "a general system of education, ascending
in a regular gradation from township schools to a state university, where tuition shall be gratis and equally open to all." Governors and legislatures made it a matter of good form to mention
the subject of popular education, but for a long time they did
not have the courage to raise the necessary funds for such a
project. In Illinois, Kentucky, and Tennessee bitter struggles
extending over a quarter of a century were waged between the
advocates and opponents of tax-supported common schools.

Meanwhile here and there frontier communities established local schools. The mud-daubed cabin schoolhouse with its clapboard roof, greased-paper window, wooden benches, latch-string door, and large box stove was the first humble forerunner of the magnificent educational plants of the Middle West today. The school term usually covered ten or fifteen weeks of six days each, and the daily sessions often extended over eight or ten hours. The teachers, many of them Irish, Scotch, or English who had met with misfortune in the Old World, and now playing the triple rôle of farmer, parson, and schoolmaster, were both by training and temperament frequently unfitted for their task. Only the fundamentals — reading, writing, and arithmetic, with occasionally a smattering of surveying, geography, and English grammar — were taught. Strict discipline, even to the point of cruelty, was rigidly maintained. In the older sections of the West, south of the Ohio, the children of the more prosperous were instructed by private tutors. According to the census of 1840 the number of persons attending "primary and common" schools in the West was only slightly more than one-eleventh of the whole population as compared with one-sixth for New York, Massachusetts, and Pennsylvania. During the decade of the thirties the grade of teachers showed marked improvement. In 1831 the first General Convention of the Teachers of the Western Country met at Cincinnati, which in reality marked a new era in the history of elementary education in the West.

The West by 1825 could also boast of numerous academies, seminaries, colleges, and embryonic universities. Of the sixty-odd institutions of higher learning in the entire country in 1830, twenty-eight were west of the Alleghenies, with a total student enrollment of approximately fourteen hundred. Many were planted by denominational effort, and nearly all were handicapped by lack of adequate funds and proper equipment. Transylvania University at Lexington, Kentucky, was extremely influential in shaping the culture of the frontier. Founded as a seminary in 1783 and becoming nominally a university in 1798–1799, it was not much more than a grammar school until 1818. In that year

Horace Holley, a Boston Unitarian clergyman and a graduate of Yale, came to Kentucky for the purpose of making Transylvania a real university and the leading center of higher education in the West. Holley's ambition in this respect was fully realized, and when he resigned in 1827 the university had a college of liberal arts and schools of law and medicine, a student body of over four hundred, and numbered among its staff some of the most eminent teachers and scholars of America. Miami University at Oxford, Ohio, was probably the second most influential institution of higher learning west of the Alleghenies prior to 1840.

For many years few books found their way into the West, and libraries were mostly confined to the colleges. By 1830 Transylvania had over two thousand volumes, the majority having come from Europe; ten years later the number had more than doubled. The Miami library had about the same number of volumes as that of Transylvania, while Ohio University had about half as many. A number of the older towns had subscription libraries, but these grew slowly; the Lexington library, the largest of these, had about six thousand volumes in 1837. All told there were probably not more than forty thousand volumes in the college and semi-public libraries of the entire Mississippi valley in 1830, and of these a large number were concerned with religious and theological subjects.

Libraries

Although the West trailed the East from a literary standpoint, it was by no means without its printing presses. By 1840 no less than 385 printing establishments were in operation west of the Alleghenies. Ohio alone had 159. Many of the presses turned out pamphlets and books as well as newspapers. By 1840 probably half a million bound volumes had been printed. Almanacs, of which *The Kentucky Almanack* was the first to appear (1788), and codes of laws were also published. Most of the reading matter except the books was controversial, being either political or religious in nature. With the exception of newspapers, however, schoolbooks outnumbered all other western publications. For a time the West depended upon the East for its texts, but by 1825 it was

Printing establishments

supplying a large part of its own spellers, primers, geographies, and grammars. Among the more important of these were *A Comprehensive Grammar of the English Language* by Leonard Bliss, *The Western Reader* by James Hall, and an *Introduction to Geography and Astronomy* by John Kilbourn.

The first western newspaper, *The Kentucky Gazette*, founded in 1787, was like many of the other pioneer papers a very meager sheet. By the end of the first quarter of the nine- <small>The</small> teenth century, however, the transallegheny news- <small>newspaper</small> papers had both multiplied in number and improved in quality. Of the 598 newspapers published in the United States in 1824 the Postmaster-General credited Ohio with 48, Kentucky with 18, Tennessee with 15, Indiana with 12, and Illinois with 5. In content the eighteenth and early nineteenth century newspapers of the West were very much alike. Foreign news, usually two or three months late, and dispatches from the East, often more than a month old, generally took up from half to two-thirds of the space; government proclamations and laws sometimes encroached upon foreign news or crowded it out entirely. Commercial advertising, except in the larger commercial centers, did not occupy much space, and revenue from this source was negligible. Considerable space was devoted to political controversy, and the editorials were frequently very partisan. A few pioneer papers printed essays and poems and occasionally ran serial stories.

Western periodicals and magazines, though numerous, were frequently short-lived. Nearly all were religious or purely literary in character, although a few journals of <small>Periodicals</small> law, medicine, and agriculture were printed in <small>and</small> limited numbers. Of the literary periodicals which <small>magazines</small> endeavored to be as nearly western in character as possible, *The Western Monthly Magazine* was in many respects the most notable. In the religious field *The Western Messenger,* "Devoted to Religion and Literature," enjoyed a remarkable career under the successive editorship of a group of New England men — Ephraim Peabody, James Freeman Clarke, W. H. Chaning, and James H. Perkins. Practically every religious denomination had its quarterly, monthly, or semi-monthly publication. Of the technical periodicals *The Transylvania Journal of Medicine and the Associate Sciences*, founded in 1828, *The Western Academician and Journal of Education and Science*, established in 1837, and *The Western Farmer*, first published in 1839, were the most important.

Of fiction, verse, and song the West had an abundance. One of the outstanding western writers of short narratives was James

Western fiction

Hall. In his *Legends of the West* and *Tales of the Border*, he perhaps more than any other western author gave an excellent portrayal of western life and civilization. Timothy Flint, famous for his contributions to the literature of travel and observation, was perhaps the leading novelist of the West prior to 1830. Neither his *Francis Berrian* nor his later novels, however, compare in value with his *Recollections* or his *Geography* as sources of information concerning western life. John M'Clung and F. W. Thomas were novelists of somewhat lesser importance. These works of fiction, though now mostly forgotten, give us many vivid glances of western society — of elections, duelling, tar-and-feather justice, and social customs in general.

The western country literally teemed with songs and ballads. The mountains echoed the rough songs of weather-beaten wag-

Songs and verse

oners as their lumbering stages rolled through the Alleghenies. Rough and ready crews of the river boats, always fond of music and dancing, not only sang the praise of Monongahela whisky but chanted love songs and negro melodies. Every frontier village had its troubadour and every backwoods newspaper lacked adequate space for the contributions of aspiring western poets and "poetasters." William Ross Wallace, William Davis Gallagher, Richard Emmons, and Thomas Peirce were undoubtedly the most notable of the western verse-makers. The themes for their verse, which was often pedantic and painfully labored, were drawn from scenes and incidents of frontier life. As literary masterpieces few merit attention, but as historical sources they are of first-rate importance, for they record the hopes and ambitions, the trials and sorrows of those whose energy of body and mind were absorbed in transforming a wilderness into a civilized land.

Even the drama was not neglected by the West. Before the end of the eighteenth century amateur theatricals were being presented in Kentucky. Cincinnati opened its first theatre in 1801, and the frontier towns of Louisville, St. Louis, and Detroit soon followed suit. Before 1830 professional companies were touring the western towns, and while most of the actors who appeared in the western companies were obscure, there were many prominent professionals from the East and from England who visited the West; among these were William and Sophie Turner, Thomas A. Cooper, J. B. Booth, James H. Hackett, and Clara Fisher. As might be expected, most of the western playhouses were primitive; in fact it was not until 1820, when the Cincinnati theatre was erected, that the West began to have anything at all that compared favorably with the theatres of the East. All sorts of plays from Shakespeare down to slapstick comedy were presented, and the performances were as a rule well attended. Plays based on western life awakened but little interest. Frequently the theatre was the scene of continual uproar, and as late as 1840 we find most of the managers posting regulations to the effect that the public should not smoke in the theatre, that men should remove their hats, and that no auditor should disturb the audience by loud talking, stamping of feet, and the like. Those of strong religious inclination waged unrelenting war on the theatres on the ground that they were morally degrading. Among the arguments advanced by those who defended the theatre was the claim that in so far as music, elocution, and painting were concerned, the theatre was by all odds a very important cultural asset.

The drama

Any summary of the cultural life of the West should include brief note at least of those societies organized to promote interest in scholarly things. One of the earliest of these was the Vincennes Historical and Antiquarian Society, established in 1808. In 1827 the first of the western state societies of this kind came into being when the Antiquarian and Historical Society of Illinois was founded. Other western states soon followed Illinois' example, and by 1840 they had performed a very useful service to their several communities

Historical and antiquarian societies

by collecting hundreds of important documents. Among the less important organizations which were influential in promoting western scholarship were the Western Methodist Historical Society, the Historical and Philosophical Society of Ashtabula County, Ohio, and the Western Academy of Natural Sciences.

These societies not only fostered the collection of source materials but encouraged scholarly production. Even before

Scholarly writings

their organization several Westerners were turning out scholarly writings. Of these, Henry Rowe Schoolcraft's books, *A View of the Lead Mines of Missouri, Travels in the Central Portions of the Mississippi Valley,* and *Algic Researches* deserve special mention. A score or more of biographical sketches, political and otherwise, were published before 1830 as well as many historical works. A number of pamphlets and a few books dealing with various aspects of the natural sciences also made their appearance. Few attempts were made to discuss philosophical questions.

Religion played a very pervasive rôle in western society. Indeed, long before the voice of the political spellbinder was

Religion an important factor in western life

heard beyond the mountains, zealous pioneer preachers had penetrated into the wilderness where in rude log church, camp-meeting, or revival they moved souls to new endeavor by their warnings of that eternal damnation and everlasting hell fire which surely awaited the ungodly. Travelers journeying to the West during the first quarter of the nineteenth century were impressed with the number of religious sects with which they came in contact. Timothy Flint, for example, observed in 1814 that "a circulating phalanx of Methodists, Baptists, and Cumberland Presbyterians, of Atlantic missionaries, and of young élèves of the Catholic theological seminaries, from the redundant mass of unoccupied ministers, both in the Protestant and Catholic countries, pervades this great valley." And so it was. Representatives of every creed, whether old or new, journeyed to every corner of the West earnestly exhorting men to lead better lives and to avoid infidelity and sin. Pious eastern folk who regarded the West as a land of wickedness organized Bible and home missionary societies for its conversion.

Of the various religious groups the Roman Catholics were the
first to send their representatives into the western country.
Catholic missionaries carried on their labors in all   Roman
the more important trading posts, yet progress in   Catholicism
the conversion of the natives was very slow. At   in West
Detroit, for example, the Church of St. Anne was founded about
1700, but as late as 1820 the town had only two priests, and the
diocese of Detroit was not established until the decade of the
thirties. Dioceses were also established about the same time at
Cincinnati, St. Louis, and Vincennes. In numbers, however,
the Catholics were exceeded by the stronger Protestant denominations. In 1840 Kentucky had a Catholic population of
approximately thirty thousand, Illinois between five and six
thousand, and Indiana about two thousand. Catholicism in
the West made its first great strides with the coming of the
German and Irish immigrants.

Of all the religious organizations in the West the Methodists,
Baptists, and to some extent the Disciples of Christ and the
Presbyterians — denominations most prevalent in   Protestant
the democratic sections of the East — were most   sects most
active. The simplicity and democracy of the   active in West
Methodist and Baptist creeds especially appealed to the pioneer.
Scores of Methodist circuit riders heroically faced death as they
journeyed along lonely forest trails from settlement to settlement. Like their Puritan ancestors, these pioneer preachers
were God-fearing men who shrank not from toil, dangers, priva-
tions, and worldly hardships. Many of them, like Peter Cartwright and James McCreary, were illustrious pulpit orators who
had an almost incalculable influence over their listeners. Frontiersmen flocked from far and near, on foot, on horseback, and in
wagons, to hear them. Emotions were stirred to their depths,
even to the point of hysteria. Thousands "got religion" or professed conversion; subsequently, of course, hundreds slid back,
but the work of the revivalist in shaping individual conduct
was not in vain. True, he was not always careful to distinguish
between essentials and non-essentials in his bitter denunciations
of certain prevailing social customs such as billiards, card-play-
ing, dancing, profanity, and drunkenness, nor did he refrain

from fiery attacks upon other denominations, which he was
wont to cast, along with infidels and agnostics, into "utter
darkness." Sometimes frontier preachers were physically weak,
but as a rule they were as strong in body as in faith, and many
a hardened sinner was converted by a sound thrashing administered, after due provocation, by some minister of the Gospel.

Religious controversies gave rise to all sorts of private and
public debates and discussions. Christian challenged non-
Christian, Protestant assailed Catholic, and Methodist encountered non-Methodist. Sermons and
religious debates were printed and distributed throughout the
land; every leading sect had its "organ" or periodical, and
questions bearing on social, moral, and religious matters were
widely discussed in the secular newspapers and magazines.
For half a century or more "religious worship, scripture reading,
hymn singing, sermon hearing, and the perusal of controversial
periodicals and tracts, attendance at camp meetings, revivals,
and theological discussions" afforded the material for much of
western thought and conversation. Though debate frequently
waxed warm and clashes were numerous, complete religious
freedom prevailed. Many Westerners, of course, never affiliated
with any organized church; but close contact with nature, savage, storm, and flood tended to develop their religious sense and
to influence their general moral attitude.

Such in brief was western society. As the decades rolled by
the older West socially came more and more to resemble the
East; but it was only a resemblance, for every phase of its
institutional life bore deep-seated characteristics of the frontier.

6. INFLUENCE OF WEST ON EAST

Our story would be incomplete if we failed to note the remarkable reaction of the West upon the East. Perhaps most
important of all was its economic influence. For the
East, the West to all intents and purposes was a
vast agrarian-colonial region; there eastern business men sold
their manufactured goods, invested their surplus capital, obtained their food products, and bought their raw materials.
Eastern cities like Boston, New York, Philadelphia, and Balti-

more vied with each other for what Washington wisely called "the extensive and valuable trade of a rising empire." From these eastern marts improved highways, canals, and railways radiated, as we shall subsequently see, into the western country.

The political influence of the West was hardly less important. There peoples from the seaboard states and Old World lands mingled and fused into a composite race that **Political** fostered and developed a real spirit of American **influence** nationalism which, in large measure, ultimately engulfed the particularism and states' rights notions of the East. The political democracy characteristic of western communities from the beginning likewise reacted upon the older states. Unrestricted suffrage as well as free land attracted people westward, and their exodus, plus the agitation of the democratically minded elements that remained behind, virtually compelled the privileged aristocracy of the East to extend the suffrage to the rank and file. Thus Connecticut in 1818, New York in 1821, and Virginia in 1830, by constitutional enactment liberalized the suffrage and provided for the popular election of most state and local officials. In vain did representatives of the ruling oligarchy, like John Randolph of Virginia and Chancellor Kent of New York, attempt to stem the tide of democracy sweeping out of the West. The demand that "the people rule" was not to be denied. Incidentally, too, the West — though feared and despised by conservative leaders of the East — played a conspicuous rôle in shaping national policy and national legislation. Money and banking, tariffs, public lands, and internal improvements, not to mention Indian relations, foreign affairs, and slavery, concerned the West as well as the East, and it was with these problems that public men wrestled for half a century or more.

Socially and intellectually the West, either directly or indirectly, exercised an immeasurable influence upon the Atlantic states. Conservative Easterners, it is true, de- **Eastern con-** risively thought of the West as a sort of dumping **servatives'** ground and its inhabitants as the scum of society. **opinion of** Thus Timothy Dwight declared that those who **West** went West were "not fit to live in regular society. They are too idle; too talkative; too passionate; too prodigal, and too shiftless to acquire either property or character. They are impatient at the restraints of law, religion, or morality; grumble about the taxes by which Rulers, Ministers and School-masters are supported and complain incessantly, as well as bitterly, of the extortions of mechanics, farmers, merchants and physicians, to whom they are always indebted. At the same time they are usually possessed, in their own view, of uncommon wisdom; understand medical science, politics and religion better than those who have studied them through life; and although they managed their own concerns worse than other men, feel perfectly satisfied that they could manage those of the nation far better than the agents to whom they are committed by the public. . . . After censuring the weakness, and wickedness of their superiors, after exposing the injustice of the community in neglecting to invest persons of such merit with public offices; in many an eloquent harangue, uttered by many a kitchen fire, in every blacksmith's shop, and in every corner of the streets; and finding all their efforts in vain; they become at length discouraged; and under the pressure of poverty, the fear of a gaol, and the consciousness of public contempt, leave their native places, and betake themselves to the wilderness."

That the West had its hangers-on and its undesirables is unquestionable, but that all were of this class is a preposterous assertion. "It is true there are gamblers, and gougers, and outlaws," said Timothy Flint, who knew the West and its people, "but there are fewer of them, than from the nature of things and the character of the age and the world, we ought to expect. . . . The backwoodsman of the West, as I have seen him, is generally an amiable and virtuous man. His general motive for coming here is to be a freeholder, to have plenty of rich land, and to be able to settle with his children about him. It is a most virtuous motive. And notwithstanding all that Dr. Dwight and Talleyrand have said to the contrary, I fully believe that nine out of ten of the emigrants have come here with no other motive." Flint rather than Dwight knew the situation. He knew that the West was draining the East not alone of its criminals and ne'er-do-wells but of some of the most desirable elements of its population. It was this knowledge that caused him to fear that New England as well as other sections of the East might suffer disaster from the migratory movement. "Our dwellings, our schoolhouses, and churches will have mouldered to ruins," he exclaimed; "our graveyards will be overrun with scrub oak; and but here and there a wretched hermit, true to his paternal soil, to tell the tale of other times." We should not forget, however, that the migration of Easterners westward created the opportunity for foreigners to secure employment in the East. In fact, prior to the Civil War no other American agency was directly or indirectly more influential in stimulating immigration from Europe than was the West.

Finally, we should not overlook the effects of the finer and nobler traits and characteristics of frontier society upon eastern life. Rude strength, restless energy, fearlessness, *Effect of finer* generosity, frankness, a ready though sometimes *and nobler* brusque humor, inquisitiveness, inventiveness, de- *aspects of* termination to achieve in a material way and, *upon the East* above all, boundless optimism and confidence went always with the Westerner. With the development of better means of communication, the two sections came more in contact with each other and Easterners gradually caught the spirit of the Great Valley region.

SUGGESTED READINGS

Henry Adams, *History of the United States during the Administrations of Jefferson and Madison*, vol. ii, chaps. vi–ix.

J. T. Adams, *New England in the Republic, 1776–1850*, chaps. xi–xii.

C. W. Alvord, *The Illinois Country*.

C. H. Ambler, *Sectionalism in Virginia, 1776–1861*.

K. C. Babcock, *The Rise of American Nationality* (vol. xiii of *The American Nation*).

J. S. Bassett, *The Life of Andrew Jackson*, 2 vols.

Charles and Mary Beard, *The Rise of American Civilization*, vol. i, chaps. ix–xi.

S. F. Bemis, *Pinckney's Treaty: a Study of America's Advantage from Europe's Distress, 1783–1800*.

S. F. Bemis, *Jay's Treaty: a Study in Commerce and Diplomacy.*

E. J. Bogart and C. M. Thompson, *Readings in the Economic History of the United States,* chap. xi.

W. C. Bruce, *John Randolph of Roanoke, 1773–1833,* 2 vols.

G. S. Callender, *Selections from the Economic History of the United States, 1765–1860,* chaps. xii–xiii.

Peter Cartwright, *Autobiography.*

Edward Channing, *A History of the United States,* vol. i, chap. ii; vol. iii, chap. xvii; vol. iv, chaps. xi–xx; vol. v, chaps. ii, xv.

I. J. Cox, *The West Florida Controversy, 1798–1813. Study in American Diplomacy.*

Joseph Doddridge, *Notes on the Settlement and Indian Wars.*

Edward Eggleston, *The Circuit Rider.*

C. R. Fish, *The Rise of the Common Man, 1830–1850* (vol. vi of *A History of American Life*), chap. vi.

Felix Flügel and H. W. Faulkner, *Readings in the Economic and Social History of the United States,* chaps. i, xi.

Hamlin Garland (Editor), *The Autobiography of David Crockett.*

T. M. Green, *The Spanish Conspiracy: a Review of Early Spanish Movements in the Southwest.*

F. W. Halsey, *Old New York Frontier.*

L. L. Hazard, *The Frontier in American Literature.*

Archibald Henderson, *The Conquest of the Old Southwest.*

B. H. Hibbard, *A History of Public Land Policies.*

B. A. Hinsdale, *The Old Northwest. The Beginnings of Our Colonial System.*

J. K. Hosmer, *The Louisiana Purchase.*

A. B. Hurlbert, *Historic Highways of America,* 16 vols.

J. A. James, *The Life of George Rogers Clark.*

J. E. Kirkpatrick, *Timothy Flint, Pioneer, Missionary, Author, Editor.*

Augustus Longstreet, *Georgia Scenes.*

W. F. McCaleb, *The Aaron Burr Conspiracy.*

J. B. McMaster, *A History of the People of the United States from the Revolution to the Civil War,* vol. iv, chap xxxiii.

L. K. Mathews, *The Expansion of New England.*

J. L. Mesick, *The English Traveller in America, 1785–1835,* chaps. i–ii.

P. G. Mode, *The Frontier Spirit in American Christianity.*

S. E. Morison, *The Life and Letters of Harrison Gray Otis, Federalist, 1765–1848,* 2 vols.

F. A. Ogg, *The Opening of the Mississippi.*

F. A. Ogg, *The Old Northwest* (vol. 19 of *The Chronicles of America*).

V. L. Parrington, *Main Currents in American Thought*, vol. ii (*The Romantic Revolution in America, 1800–1860*), Book i, part iii.

F. L. Paxson, *History of the American Frontier, 1763–1893*, chaps. i–xxxii.

J. M. Peck, *Guide for Emigrants to the West.*

Dexter Perkins, *The Monroe Doctrine*, chaps. i–ii, iv.

J. W. Pratt, *Expansionists of 1812.*

Theodore Roosevelt, *The Winning of the West*, 4 vols.

R. L. Rusk, *The Literature of the Middle Western Frontier*, 2 vols.

J. D. Schoepf, *Travels in the Confederacy*, 2 vols.

L. M. Sears, *Jefferson and the Embargo.*

E. C. Semple, *American History and Its Geographic Conditions*, chaps. iv–vi, ix.

C. L. Skinner, *Pioneers of the Old Southwest* (vol. 18 of *The Chronicles of America*).

G. M. Stephenson, *A History of American Immigration*, chaps. x–xi.

W. E. Stevens, *The Northwest Fur Trade, 1763–1800.*

P. J. Treat, *The National Land System, 1785–1820.*

F. J. Turner, *The Frontier in American History.*

F. J. Turner, *The Rise of the New West* (vol. xiv of *The American Nation*).

F. J. Turner and F. Merk, *List of References on the History of the West* (rev. ed.).

Margaret Van Horn, *A Journey to Ohio in 1810.*

W. H. Venable, *Beginnings of Literary Culture in the Ohio Valley.*

A. T. Volwiler, *George Croghan and the Westward Movement.*

R. G. Wellington, *The Political and Sectional Influence of the Public Lands, 1828–1842.*

A. P. Whitaker, *The Spanish-American Frontier.*

S. C. Williams, *History of the Lost State of Franklin.*

Justin Winsor, *The Westward Movement: The Colonies and the Republic West of the Alleghanies, 1763–1798.*

INDEX

Brown, medical schools, 433; law professorships, 438

Brown, Charles Brockden, life and writings, 454–456

Brown, David, Sedition Acts, 394

Brown, James B., magazine contributor, 465

Brown, John, *Gaspée* affair, 250

Browne, Robert, Separatist leader, 51

Brudzewski, Albertus, sphericity of earth, 8

Bruges, wool manufacture, 24

Brunswick, Duke of, French Revolution, 379

Bryant, William Cullen, democracy of, 462

Buchat, scientific influence, 424

Buffalo, N. Y., growth of, 506

Buffon, scientific influence, 424

Bunker Hill, Daniel Shays, 340

Burgoyne, effect of surrender, 302

Burk, John D., writings, 449

Burke, Edmund, whaling, 139; Old Whig leader, 227; tea episode, 255; Intolerable Acts, 271–272; advocates termination of American Revolution, 305; French Revolution, 379; Thomas Paine, 380; on legal profession, 434–435

Burke, William, quoted, 226

Burr, Aaron, duel with Hamilton, 411; acquisition of Mexico, 541

Bute, Earl of, leader of court faction, 229

Byrd, Colonel William, on slavery, 94; home of, 97; dress, 101; interest in science, 179

Cabot, John, reaches North America, 18; voyages, 25–26

Cabots, trade, 332

Cabral, discovers Brazil, 18

Cadamosto, African discovery, 10

Cahokia, American capture of, 502

Cairo, intellectual center, 3; medieval trade, 13

Calhoun, John C., Indian policy, 521; War of 1812, 550

Callender, J. T., agrarianism, 376;

Sedition Act, 393; democratic editor, 464

Calvert, Sir George, founds Maryland, 44

Calverts, colonization, 45

Calvinism, Scotland, 48; Holland, 48

Camden, Lord, leader Pitt faction, 228; Walpole Company, 283

"Camillus," Jay Treaty, 387

Campbell, War of 1812, 550

Canada, ceded to England, 1763, 127; annexed by Britain, 1763, 224

Canaries, identified, 9; rediscovered, 9

Candles, colonial manufacture, 150

Cape Bayador, discovered, 10

Cape Blanco, discovered, 10

Cape Breton Island, Treaty of Utrecht, 136; colonized, 137

Cape of Good Hope, discovered, 17

Cape Verde, discovered, 10

Capital, colonial manufactures, 153

Capitalism, influence on medieval Europe, 11; new route to Indies, 17; Jefferson unable to uproot, 399

Capitalism *vs.* Agrarianism, 327

Capitol, location of national, 370

Caps, colonial manufacture, 145

Cardplaying, in colonies, 108

Carey, Mathew, prison reform, 420–421; reply to Cobbett, 464; founds magazines, 466

Carleill, Christopher, colonization, 37

Carolinas, founded, 44; English migration, 55; Scotch-Irish settlers, 56; German settlers, 57; Welsh settlers, 58; rice production, 63; colonial land system, 65; land systems, 68; hogs, 80; horses, 80; sheep, 80; slavery, 94; colonial government, 114–115; schools, 117; fur trade, 125; timber, 128; lumber industry, 130; naval store production, 131; tanneries, 144; trade, 160, 162, 163; western lands, 214; paper money, 293; religious situation,